Advertising

Advertising

strategy, creativity and media

Chris Fill
Graham Hughes
Scott De Francesco

PEARSON

Harlow, England • London • New York • Boston • San Francisco • Toronto • Sydney • Auckland • Singapore • Hong Kong
Tokyo • Seoul • Taipei • New Delhi • Cape Town • São Paulo • Mexico City • Madrid • Amsterdam • Munich • Paris • Milan

Pearson Education Limited
Edinburgh Gate
Harlow
Essex CM20 2JE
England

and Associated Companies throughout the world

Visit us on the World Wide Web at:
www.pearson.com/uk

First published 2013

ISBN 978-0-273-76089-4

British Library Cataloguing-in-Publication Data
A catalogue record for this book is available from the British Library

Library of Congress Cataloging-in-Publication Data
A catalog record for this book is available from the Library of Congress

10 9 8 7 6 5 4 3 2 1
17 16 15 14 13

Typeset in 10/12pt Minion by 73
Printed and bound by Rotolito Lombarda, in Italy

Brief contents

To my students, past and present.

Scott De Francesco

To Sue, Alex and Michael.

Graham Hughes

This book is dedicated to my wife Karen, not only for her moral support whilst this book was being written, but also for venturing with me into our new life in the Cotswolds.

Chris Fill

Contents

Companion Website

For open-access **student resources** specifically written to complement this textbook and support your learning, please visit **www.pearsoned.co.uk/fillhughesdefrancesco**

Lecturer resources

For password-protected online resources tailored to support the use of this textbook in teaching, please visit **www.pearsoned.co.uk/fillhughesdefrancesco**

Guided tour

16 CHAPTER 1 AN INTRODUCTION TO ADVERTISING

ViewPoint 1.2 Stroking the public good

For many people advertising is about persuading people to buy products and services. However, advertising can play other roles in society, as demonstrated by the UK Department of Health's campaign to improve the nation's awareness of strokes, and reduce the number of lives lost each year. A stroke is a brain attack caused by an interruption to the flow of blood, and accounts for 45,000 deaths each year. The cost for society in terms of hospital care, rehabilitation schemes, carers and drugs is enormous.

By treating stroke victims quickly, within three hours, the outcomes for people can be drastically improved. However, research showed that the public did not know what the symptoms of a stroke were, and that victims required the same speed of response as those who experience heart attacks.

To convey the symptoms of a stroke the acronym FAST was developed. This stands for Face, Arms, Speech and Time. This enabled the symptoms to be seen, recognised and remembered by the target audience.

Face = Has their face fallen on one side? Can they smile?

Arms = Can they raise both arms and keep them there?

Speech = Is their speech slurred?

Time = Call 999 if you see any single one of these signs.

The visuals also included a picture of a person with 'fire in the brain' to represent the potential damage in a vivid way and so aid flashbulb memory.

The use of television and print media was critical in order to convey the core message and to provide the space to convey all of the information.

The results indicate that awareness and understanding of the FAST acronym, symptoms and the need to act quickly rose significantly not only among the target audience but also among health professionals. The campaign also affected behaviour. For example, the 999 telephone emergency service received 55% more stroke-related calls in the first four months of the campaign, compared to the previous year. Analysis indicates that for every £1 spent on the campaign, £3.50 was generated as a value for society in the first year.

Source: Snow (2010); www.stroke.org.uk/; www.nhs.uk/actfast/

Question

To what extent should health-related campaigns provide information or provoke action?

Task

Find an ad campaign designed to support another illness or disease. Make notes about the probable objectives the campaign attempted to achieve.

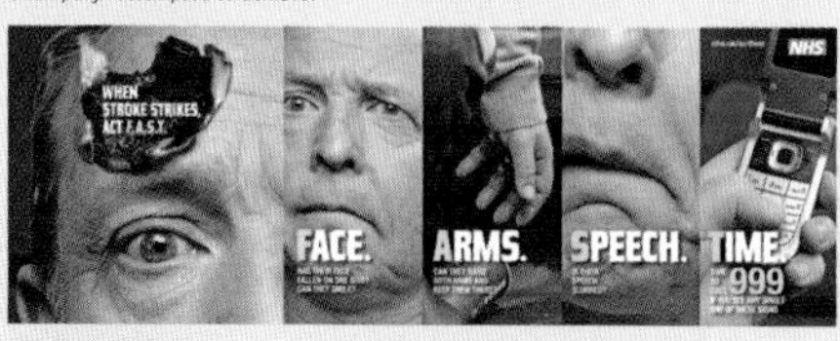

Exhibit 1.5 A shot of the ActFast campaign
Source: NHS

ViewPoint features give a practitioners perspective of the world of Advertising, then poses a question and a task to help you analyse.

Minicases provide a wealth of current examples from around the world.

2 CHAPTER 1 AN INTRODUCTION TO ADVERTISING

Minicase Painting through insight

The premium paint segment in New Zealand has two preference drivers: colour and quality. Of the many brands in the market, two stand out: Resene and Dulux. Resene is perceived to be the best for colour, whilst Dulux is generally regarded as the best-quality paint. However, consumer paint sales in New Zealand were declining and there was no sign of any change to the downward trend. This was because home-decorating projects were being frozen, new projects were being put on hold, all due to the recession taking a grip on disposable income and household expenditure.

Such market stagnation leads many brands to slow down or even stop all of their advertising activities. However, Dulux New Zealand knew that they had to invest in brand communications if they were to protect their market share and engineer a position that could be developed once the recession had been overcome.

Dulux is a well-established brand, not just in New Zealand but in many other countries. The name attracts high recall scores and the brand has a strong reputation. Over the years Dulux had worked hard to earn a strong reputation for paint quality. However, after discussion both internally and externally with significant stakeholders, including employees, customers and retailers, Dulux realised that to maintain market share they needed to change the way people perceived the Dulux colour range. They not only had to own the quality attribute, they also had to dislodge Resene and become the number-one brand for colour as well. In essence, the goal was to become the number-one choice on both preference drivers.

The target audience is typically couples and young families in their early 30s to late 40s. Their home is important to them and they have a strong emotional connection with it. Indeed, research found that Kiwis are incredibly proud not just of their homes but of the unique New Zealand landscape as well. Many New Zealanders want to redecorate but they have limited decorating creativity or confidence when it comes to colour selection. As a result, painting and decorating projects are often postponed as long as possible. When they do start, New Zealanders prefer to use colours that will not date, which in turn can rule out colour experimentation and adventure.

Exhibit 1.1 Dulux Paints campaign (New Zealand)
Source: Dulux

Exhibit 1.4 Andy Warhol *Hamburger* print which mimics commercial work.
Source: Artists Rights Society.

Scholars' paper 1.3 What is the good of marketing?

Wilkie, W.L. and Moore, E.S. (1999) Marketing's contributions to society, *Journal of Marketing*, 63 (special issue), 198-216

The authors were set a considerable challenge when invited to write about the contribution that marketing makes to society at the end of the last millennium. Readers may not agree with the perspectives taken but the ideas and focus enable consideration about the positive and negative ways the marketing system contributes to society.

Zhu and Meyers-Levy (2005) refer to two types of meanings that music can convey. The first is an embodied meaning, which is about hedonism and stimulation and is independent of context. The second is referential meaning, which is context dependent and 'reflects networks of semantic-laden, external world concepts' (p. 333). Both have been found to influence the perceptions people have of advertised products in particular ways. However, through referential meaning it is the interaction of music and society that advertising draws on in order to influence product perceptions.

Scholars' papers point students in the direction of some of the leading academic papers about advertising, providing an immediate link to other ideas and influential thinking.

REVIEW QUESTIONS 325

Chapter summary

In order to help consolidate your understanding of measuring advertising media effectiveness and efficiency, here are the key points summarised against each of the learning objectives.

Review the standard measurement methods used to determine media efficiency

Media strategy decisions are based in part on measurable factors that help determine media efficiency (delivering the intended target audience at the best price). Measurements can differ from television to print to outdoor, but also from traditional to digital, as measurement techniques have become elaborate and complex in recent years, with performance metrics and analytics that promise to quantify effectiveness in new ways.

Utilise measurement techniques and methods in media plan preparation

Numerical calculations are often the first steps taken to parse the good from the bad choices in selecting the appropriate media. CPM (cost per thousand) analysis and ratings are two of the basic units of measurement for selecting the potential of print and broadcast, whilst analytics, multiple platforms and non-standard techniques of information gathering are used to measure digital and emerging media.

Describe the changes and challenges in traditional versus digital measurement

Media accountability has been and remains a contentious issue with traditional media and digital media measurement. Media auditing companies have grown of late and serve as one independent verification tool of audience delivery, but the relationship of actual versus potential consumer engagement and actionable motivation by the consumer is difficult to determine.

Survey new opportunities and challenges for planning and buying media

Once the media plan is approved, the space and time requirements as specified for the scheduled media plan have now to be negotiated and purchased through media outlets. The advertiser not only expects increased sales or an actionable measure from the approved plan, but also scrutinises the plan's overall effectiveness in sending the message to the target audience. Media buy post analysis is vital to the planning cycle, for it ensures accountability and may generate further adjustments in the future.

Review questions

1. How would you respond to the challenges facing the research team at SAS as set out at the start of this chapter?
2. List some of the tools a media planner might use as a starting point to planning media.
3. Describe what is meant by gross impressions. How are gross impressions different from CPM?
4. What are GRPs and what function do they serve?
5. Articulate some of the complex core measurement principles found in measuring mobile media.
6. List several reasons why it is important for an advertiser to monitor the performance of its social media site.

Chapter summaries, Review questions and References conclude each chapter and help the student to reinforce the key learning outcomes from the chapter.

Preface

Thank you for choosing to read our book, *Advertising: strategy, creativity and media.*

Our book is intended to support students, advertising and marketing professionals, and teachers, indeed everyone involved in learning about advertising, media, marketing communications and branding. People studying for university and college degrees and diplomas, and those pursuing professional qualifications in advertising, marketing and communications, such as those offered by the Chartered Institute of Marketing, the CAM Foundation, the Chartered Institute of Public Relations and the Institute of Practitioners in Advertising, should benefit from reading this book. This book and its associated resources are also intended to provide a framework for tutors, lecturers and teaching fellows when developing learning programmes. Whichever user category you might belong to, we hope you will enjoy the contents and find them helpful.

We hope you find this book interesting, engaging, accessible, and a suitable means of disentangling the complexities associated with the evolving advertising and communications industry. We have attempted to cover the major issues and hope that readers understand if they find that some topics have not been included. This is because we wanted the book to address the core advertising topics, yet remain relatively compact and approachable.

Although grounded primarily in English-speaking countries, we have attempted to strike a balance between the need to report local issues and concerns and to celebrate some of the truly great global advertising campaigns. Emerging and key technologies, combined with new consumer behaviours, are an integral part of contemporary advertising, whether that be on a global, national, regional or local basis. We feel that it is important for all readers to be aware of this perspective.

Many advertising textbooks focus just on the historical and/or theoretical aspects of advertising. We accept that there is a role for these two perspectives and we have also included them. However, the focus of our book is on blending theory with practice, to show the practicalities of advertising. To do this we explore both the academic and practical issues of advertising and brand communications. In addition, we incorporate real examples of advertising practice in each chapter and provide tasks and exercises for readers to develop their understanding.

Overview of the book

Advertising: strategy, creativity and media provides a contemporary, consistent yet concise appraisal of the radically evolving world of advertising. We designed this book so that it could be a core learning resource for a one-semester or one-term advertising or brand communications programme. The book embraces a number of key topics, including, but not limited to, account planning, creative strategy and planning, branding, image, organisation, consumer-centrism and issues in social and interactive media. We have made special note of the broader changes occurring in the media industry, both traditional and interactive, which continue to have a dramatic impact on advertising practitioners and consumers. We present these issues and build discussion and insight around these and other salient topics.

This text is one of the few to address the changing nature of advertising, and the challenge of understanding advertising's developing role and deployment in a rapidly changing media environment. Many texts focus on a traditional view of advertising and its association principally with television and print media formats. Media proliferation, changing consumer and other stakeholder perspectives, new approaches to creative execution and a wider recognition of the need to adopt socially responsible advertising platforms are among some of the issues that we include in order to provide a wider perspective of this exciting, stimulating and important subject.

Each chapter considers the main characteristics, the key issues and the prevailing perspective and practice that relate to the topic. Each of the 13 chapters are interlinked and cross-referenced where necessary. Readers are encouraged to consider some of the ideas and challenges faced by those who manage communications. This is facilitated by a questioning style of writing, one in which we ask readers to pause and consider a particular issue before we elaborate and explore possible responses. For example, each ViewPoint or practical example contains a question and a task for readers to complete.

Advertising: strategy, creativity and media contains 13 chapters.

Chapter 1 An introduction to advertising
Chapter 2 OK, so is this the right meaning?
Chapter 3 Advertising: theories, concepts and frameworks
Chapter 4 Advertising: strategies, planning and positioning
Chapter 5 Creativity, content and appeals
Chapter 6 Brand communications: the role of advertising
Chapter 7 The advertising industry
Chapter 8 Traditional media
Chapter 9 Digital media and emerging technologies
Chapter 10 Media planning
Chapter 11 Measuring advertising efficiency and effectiveness
Chapter 12 Standards and responsibilities
Chapter 13 Contemporary issues in advertising

In order to establish a basis for considering contemporary advertising practice, the book begins with a look at the ***scope and significance*** of advertising within business and society. This helps understanding that advertising is not just a marketing tool but an activity that has a much wider societal and cultural role and impact. We examine how advertising and the advertising industry have developed and how advertising interacts with art, music, politics and health.

The book explores what advertising is thought to be and it is therefore important to view ***how communications might work*** and the factors that are thought to influence the communication process. Questions regarding source credibility and attractiveness are addressed in addition to the principles of cognitive processing and how advertising is used to influence attitudes.

We continue to develop our theoretical understanding with an examination of the principal ***theories, concepts and frameworks*** associated with the ways advertising is believed to work and to engage audiences. Here we consider the research of both academics and practitioners who have made significant contributions that help explain complex ideas and processes.

Having established the theoretical basis for advertising, we then review the ***strategies and planning*** associated with managing and implementing the advertising process. This has particular resonance for those businesses wishing to reach global audiences yet also accommodate cultural and regional variances.

Advertising outputs, ads, can be the result of lengthy development processes and need to account for the broader communications, marketing and business objectives that have to be achieved. By accounting for the strategic intentions of a business and by understanding the communication needs of the target audiences, the platform for advertising's ***creative development*** can be shaped more effectively.

In a rapidly changing media environment driven by technological enhancements, creativity and content issues are now of paramount importance in achieving competitive differentiation. Most marketing textbooks studiously avoid addressing issues to do with creativity and associated processes. Although 'creativity' might be considered by some to be too subjective for analysis, we disagree and consider it too important to be overlooked. As a result we explore the topic through the creativity literature in order to provide an objective perspective. We examine those aspects of creativity that contribute toward the successful development and execution of advertising messages.

Brands and branding are increasingly seen as significant topics from both a consumer and a business perspective. The advertising contexts explored in the first chapter provide us with an understanding of the relevance of brands in a modern consumerist society. Brands are considered by many to be an integral part of society, enabling relationships not only with end-user customers but also with an array of other stakeholders. The images, associations and experiences that customers have with brands can be initiated, even shaped, through advertising. It is important therefore to understand the role of advertising within a branding context.

The ***advertising industry***, made up of agencies, consultants and other parties who assist client businesses with the development of their advertising, is significant and one which all those reading about or studying this topic should understand. Much of our focus is on the UK and North American advertising industries, although we encourage readers from other countries to find out about their local advertising industry. The changing role and nature of the industry have put pressure on the structure, systems and operations of the advertising industry. This has impacted on the format, structure and the nature of the agencies involved in working with client businesses. It has also had a significant effect on the relationships between the agency and client and the ways in which such relationships are managed.

Another distinguishing aspect of our book is the range of issues we consider relating to the use of ***media*** and its important role in the delivery of advertising messages. Whilst there is a significant focus on what are popularly referred to as 'new' media and the impact of new technologies, ***traditional media,*** such as TV, newspapers, magazines, billboards, radio and cinema, continue to play a significant role for advertisers and account for large parts of advertising budgets.

Digital media, including online, mobile and social media and in-game advertising, plus a host of other media, are being used in new and innovative ways to target audiences. No doubt by the time some readers engage with this book, developments will have taken place which have again changed the way advertising is used. These changes are inevitable and can transform the very basis of advertising and its contribution to market economies. Innovative media formats, digital and emerging technologies, are now seen to enhance traditional media under the guise of integrated communications.

Against a background of emerging and changing approaches to media use, ***media planning*** has a much greater and more complex role today in the advertising industry than it had previously in the late 20th century. The growing number of media options now requires media planners to be involved at an earlier stage in the strategic planning of an advertising campaign than before. Media planning not only involves making the appropriate traditional and digital media selections it also provides detailed background research on the nature of the market and the consumer.

Once again this book provides an insight into a topic overlooked by many textbooks: media measurement. This concerns recommendations about the use of specific media, which are based on a number of measurable factors (metrics and analytics), budgetary considerations and overall suitability to the strategy. This requires an ***evaluation of media efficiency and advertising effectiveness*** in the planning stages, not as an add-on when a campaign has been implemented. The dynamic and expanding nature of advertising media has created new challenges and new ways of looking at media placement and buying and the evaluation of the decisions made. All of these are considered in this book.

There is a growing recognition that advertisers ensure that they give due consideration to the appropriate ethical, moral, social and legal standards when communicating with customers and other stakeholders. This involves the setting of and adherence to a range of ***standards and responsibilities***. These cover the production of individual product advertisements and the procedures to manage corporate governance effectively. Many individual organisations now use advertising to explain how they are complying with demands from legislators and consumers to adopt socially acceptable and responsible business practices.

Given the nature of advertising and the advertising industry that we have identified throughout this text, there are issues and pressures arising that will continue to lead to change from both academic and practitioner perspectives. The final chapter therefore attempts to identify and explore some of these '***contemporary issues***'. This chapter is not intended to provide a definitive view, but to provoke thought and discussion about some, not all, of the prevailing issues.

Advertising: strategy, creativity and media brings together different ideas relating to advertising, unlike other books that focus on a single perspective or particular topic, such as integrated communications or branding, without considering the whole. This means the approach taken here invites readers to consider advertising as a core business activity, not a peripheral or optional add-on.

To help stimulate thought and consideration about a wide range of interrelated issues, a number of theories and models are advanced. Some of these theories reflect management practice, while others are offered as suggestions for creativity and the innovative use of media. Many of the theories are abstractions of actual practice, some are based on empirical research and others are pure conceptualisation. All seek to enrich the subject, but not all need carry the same weight of contribution. Readers should form their own opinions based upon their reading, experience and judgement.

Design features and presentation

There are a number of features that are intended to enhance each reader's experience. Throughout the text there are numerous colour and black-and-white exhibits, figures (diagrams) and tables of information. These serve to highlight, illustrate and bring life to the written word.

Cases

Each chapter opens with a short, real-life case study. Readers should read these cases and ponder the challenge that emerges at the end of each one, before reading the rest of the chapter. These cases provide a context within which the body of material should be considered.

At the end of each chapter there is a formal question challenging readers to consider how they would respond to the issue presented in the case study, having now read the relevant material. To see how the company proceeded and to view an outline answer, readers are directed online to the website supporting this book.

Chapter objectives

Each chapter opens with a brief commentary on the broad issues that should be addressed and is followed by both the aims of what is to be covered and a list of learning objectives. This helps to signal the primary topics that are covered in the chapter and so guide the learning experience.

ViewPoints

In each chapter there are at least four stand-alone examples. These are referred to as ViewPoints and are used either to illustrate particular points by demonstrating theory in practice, or to complement individual examples explained in the chapter. These examples are easily distinguishable through the colour contrasts and serve to demonstrate how a particular aspect of advertising has been used in a particular context. We hope readers enjoy these ViewPoints and that they attempt some of the questions or tasks that follow each ViewPoint.

Scholars' papers and exhibits

The book draws on a variety of academic materials and applies these to practice. Academic material is explained and evaluated throughout the text, but in addition each chapter includes four Scholars' papers. These refer to particular journal papers that have made significant contributions to our knowledge. These papers may be old or new, but their content is relevant and pertinent to our understanding and knowledge of advertising.

In addition, each chapter contains several exhibits. These are illustrations, pictures of ads, or visuals of people in the industry and are often self-contained examples or vignettes. Some exhibits are attached to ViewPoints, which are case histories or examples of a particular advertising practice.

Summaries and questions

At the end of each chapter there is a summary and a series of review or discussion questions. Readers are encouraged to test their own understanding of the content of each chapter by considering some or all of these discussion questions. In this sense the questions support self-study but tutors might wish to use some of these as part of a seminar or workshop programme.

Support materials

Students and lecturers who adopt this text have a range of support materials and facilities to enhance their reading experience.

Readers are invited to visit the companion website for the book at **www.pearsoned.co.uk/fillhughesdefrancesco**. Here students have access to further materials including a bank of multiple-choice questions, an online glossary and annotated weblinks. For lecturers and tutors not only is there an instructor's manual containing a range of teaching schemes, PowerPoint slides and exercises in downloadable format, but there is also a password-protected section of the companion website for their use.

Acknowledgements

This book could not have been written without the support of a wide range of brilliant people. Contributions range from those who provided information and permissions, those who wrote minicases, answered questions and those who tolerated our length of time to complete the manuscript, to those who sent through photographs, answered phone calls and emails and those who simply liaised with others.

Scott De Francesco

I'd like to thank Jytte Jensen for her careful reading of and suggestions on the text, Dr Peter Rojcewicz for his continued intellectual support, my daughter Ariane who reminded me to 'keep the text real for students', and Svetlana whose often tepid response to my initial topical examples pushed me to seek new, more enthusiastic ones.

Graham Hughes

I would like to acknowledge the contribution of all those colleagues and friends, too numerous to mention, who have over the years contributed towards my knowledge, understanding and interest in the field of marketing communications. My fellow authors who have supported and cajoled throughout the writing process! My wife Sue – the book's finished! All at Pearson for their encouragement and technical expertise.

Chris Fill

There are many people who should be acknowledged for their help and guidance during the development of this book. Among these are the various students I have had the pleasure to teach in the UK, Europe and beyond. There are colleagues I have worked with at the University of Portsmouth and elsewhere, and of course all those who have made suggestions, provided materials and who have enabled me to write.

We also wish to thank several people at Pearson and their associates, who have taken our manuscript, managed it and published it in this form. In particular we wish to acknowledge the various editors who have been involved in this book's creation. First is David Cox, who researched the market, convinced people of the need to write this book, and got the project off the ground. Second, Rachel Gear for enabling the processes through which the book evolved through Pearson, and finally Amanda McPartlin, for seeing the book through production and onto the shelves. We also wish to thank Emma Violet who supported the book and found the resources whenever they were required. In addition we should like to thank Alison Prior for finding the pictures and images in order to bring the book to life, and to Beth Wright and her team for transforming the manuscript into the final product. Thank you all.

For further insight and information please see the Pearson Companion Web site that supports this book, www.pearsoned.co.uk/fillhughesdefrancesco, and also www.fillassociates.co.uk.

Publisher's acknowledgements

We are grateful to the following for permission to reproduce copyright material:

Figures

Figure 3.3 from How advertising works: a planning model, *Journal of Advertising Research*, October (Vaughn, R. 1980), Copyright World Advertising Research Centre (WARC), reproduced with permission, www.journalofadvertisingresearch.com; Figure 3.4 adapted from *Advertising Communications & Promotion Management*, 2nd ed., McGraw-Hill (Rossiter, J.R. and Percy, L. 1997) John R. Rossiter, used with permission of John R. Rossiter; Figure 4.5 from *Marketing Communications: interactivity, communities and content*, 5th ed., Pearson Education Ltd. (Fill, C. 2009) p. 309, © Pearson Education Ltd. 2006, 2009; Figure 4.6 from *Marketing Communications*, Thomson Learning (Egan, J. 2007), used with permission of John Egan; Figure 4.7 from Marketing Communications: The Official CIM Coursebook, Butterworth-Heinemann (Hughes, G. and Fill, C. 2008) p. 46, Figure 2.1; Figure 4.8 from ISBA/Engine Report, p.17, Copyright ISBA/Engine 2012; Figure 4.10 from *The Marketer's Handbook*, John Wiley & Sons (Young, L. 2011) p. 454, Figure V.2, reproduced with permission of John Wiley & Sons Ltd.; Figure 4.11 from The planning and implementation of integrated marketing communications, *Marketing Intelligence & Planning*, vol. 27 (4), pp. 524–38 (Caemmerer, B. 2009), © Emerald Group Publishing Limited, all rights reserved; Figure 7.1 from *The Future of Agency Relationships*, Forrester Research, Inc. (Corcoran, S., Frankland, D. and Drego, V.) p. 3, 29 March 2010; Figure 7.6 from *The Future of Agency Relationships*, Forrester Research, Inc. (Corcoran, S., Frankland, D. and Drego, V.) p. 6, 29 March 2010; Figures 7.7 and 7.8 from Ad spending: growing market share, *Harvard Business Review*, January/February, pp. 44–8 (Schroer, J. 1990), Copyright © 1990 Harvard Business School Publishing Corporation, all rights reserved, reprinted by permission of Harvard Business Review; Figure 7.9 from Ad spending: maintaining market share, *Harvard Business Review*, January/February, pp. 38–42 (Jones, J.P. 1990), Copyright © 1990 Harvard Business School Publishing Corporation, all rights reserved, reprinted by permission of Harvard Business Review; Figure 8.1 from Top magazine markets (no. of titles 2008), extracted from Adstats: Magazines In Focus, FIPP World Magazine Trends, http://www.fipp.com; Figure 8.2 from Top 10 paid-for dallies 2009, extracted from Adstats: Global press trends, WAN-IFRA World Press Trends 2010, http://www.wan-ifra.org/, WAN-IFRA; Figure 9.1 from Growth trends in media usage over last 5 years % change, UK Adults, 2005–2010, The Magazine Handbook 2010/2011, The Association of Magazine Media, http://www.magazine.org, MPA; Figure 9.3 from Global youth mobile phone usage advanced data users, 15–24 H1 2010, News Release (January 2011), http://www.nielsen.com, Nielsen; Figure 10.1 from Share of Total Adspend by Country, 2011, WARC, International Ad Forecast 2011/12 (July), www.warc.com, reproduced with permission; Figure 10.2 from http://www.censusscope.org/us/chart_ancestry.html, Census Scope; Figure 10.3 from Millennials: Confident. Connected. Open to Change, http://www.pewsocialtrends.org/2010/02/24/millennials-confident-connected-open-to-change/, © 2010 Pew Research Center, Social & Demographic Trends Project; Figure 11.1 from US Advertising CPM by Media, 2008, www.emarketer.com, eMarketer Inc.; Figure 11.2 from *Social Media Marketing Industry Report*, Social Media Examiner (Stelzner, M. 2011) http://www.socialmediaexaminer.com; Figure 11.3 from *Quarterly Digital Intelligence Briefing*, Econsultancy/Adobe (Charlton, G. 2011); Figure 12.1 from *Advertising: What the UK really thinks*, Credos (2011)

Tables

Table 1.1 from *Advertising Statistics Yearbook*, Advertising Association (2007), reproduced with permission, www.warc.com; Table 2.2 from Dialogue and its role in the development of relationship specific knowledge, *Journal of Business and Industrial Marketing*, Vol. 19 (2), pp. 114–23 (Ballantyne, D. 2004), © Emerald Group

Publishing Ltd., all rights reserved; Table 4.3 from *Marketing Communications: interactivity, communities and content*, 5th ed., Pearson Education Ltd. (Fill, C. 2009) p. 311, © Pearson Education Ltd. 2006, 2009; Table 5.2 from Factors framing strategy for brand communication, *Journal of Advertising Research*, Vol. 47 (3) (September), pp. 364–77 (Tsai, S-P. 2007), Figure 1, p. 365, World Advertising Research Center (WARC), used with permission, www.journalofadvertisingresearch.com; Tables 6.3 and 6.4 from The relative importance of brands in modified rebuy purchase situations, *International Journal of Research in Marketing*, Vol. 27 (3), pp. 248–60 (Zablah, A.R., Brown, B.P. and Donthu, N. 2010), with permission from Elsevier; Table 7.1 from *Marketing Communications: interactivity, communities and content*, 5th ed., Pearson Education Ltd. (Fill, C. 2009) p. 91, © Pearson Education Ltd. 2006, 2009; Table 7.3 from Top UK advertisers 2010, http://www.nielsen.com, Nielsen; Table 13.4 from Measuring the hidden power of emotive advertising, *International Journal of Market Research*, Vol. 47 (5), pp. 467–86 (Heath, R. and Hyder, P. 2005), World Advertising Research Center (WARC), reproduced with permission; Table 13.6 from Integrated marketing communications: From media channels to digital connectivity, *Journal of Marketing Communications* Vol. 15 (2-3) April–July, pp. 85–101 (Mulhern, F. 2009), reprinted by permission of the publisher (Taylor & Francis Ltd., http://www.tandf.co.uk/journals)

Text

Extract on page 103 from 'Live well for less', www.jsainsburys.co.uk, reproduced with kind permission of Sainsbury's Supermarkets Ltd.

In some instances we have been unable to trace the owners of copyright material, and we would appreciate any information that would enable us to do so.

Photographs

The publisher would like to thank the following for their kind permission to reproduce their photographs:

(Key: b-bottom; c-centre; l-left; r-right; t-top)

2 Dulux . **3 Image courtesy of The Advertising Archives. 6 Mary Evans Picture Library. 14 Artists Rights Society:** Warhol Foundation. **16 NHS** . **29 Alamy Images:** M40S Photos. **38 Qvest. 41 Volkswagen Group. 45 Image courtesy of The Advertising Archives. 55 LG-one. 56 Image courtesy of The Advertising Archives. 63 Alamy Images:** Chloe Johnson. **64 Image courtesy of The Advertising Archives. 65 Image courtesy of The Advertising Archives. 67 The History of Advertising Trust. 84 Rex Features. 90 Ulster Bank. 97 Whitbread. 100 Pictures courtesy of BP plc. 115 Ruby Agency. 122 Getty Images:** Bloomberg. **138 Buckshee Productions. 140 Image courtesy of The Advertising Archives. 141 © Damien Hirst. 143 Image courtesy of The Advertising Archives. 154 Image courtesy of The Advertising Archives. 163 Stobart Group. 168 Rex Features:** Sipa Press. **173 Image courtesy of The Advertising Archives. 175 Getty Images:** AFP. **177 Alamy Images:** Artostock.com. **187 Rex Features:** Jim Holden. **191 Image courtesy of The Advertising Archives. 193 DDB. 195 Press Association Images:** Chris Rodburn. **215 Rex Features:** Lehtikuva Oy. **220 Kerrang!. 229 Getty Images:** Corey Sipkin / NY Daily News Archive. **235 Alamy Images:** Kasia Nowak. **239 Abe's Penny:** Peter Killeen & Eric Ledgin. **245 Getty Images:** Barry Brecheisen / Film Magic. **247 Dreamstime.com:** Youssouf Cader. **248 Alamy Images:** Jim West. **262 Getty Images:** AFP. **265 Press Association Images:** Glen Argov / Landov. **267 E M Clements Photography. 277 Alamy Images:** David Pearson. **281 Alamy Images:** Aerial Archives. **288 Getty Images:** Jordan Strauss / Wire Image. **295 Waves Magazine. 297 Shutterstock.com:** Dave H 900. **303 KD Paine & Partners LLC. 311 Alamy Images:** Net Photos. **312 Alamy Images:** Chris Jobs. **322 Iloveqatar.net. 329 Shutterstock.com:** ®. **339 Image courtesy of The Advertising Archives. 343 Diageo plc. 345 Image courtesy of The Advertising Archives. 352 Kraft Foods UK:** JWT advertising. **357 Radiotjanst. 366 Getty Images. 369 Alamy Images:** London Photos / Homer Sykes. **379 Rex Features:** KPA / Zuma

All other images © Pearson Education

Every effort has been made to trace the copyright holders and we apologise in advance for any unintentional omissions. We would be pleased to insert the appropriate acknowledgement in any subsequent edition of this publication.

apter 1
ntroduction to advertising

Understanding a little of the background, scope and significance of advertising's role within business and society is important if we are to appreciate the dynamics of contemporary advertising practice. Indeed, an appreciation of the reach and interplay between advertising and society can open our eyes to the potency of advertising that is far beyond its marketing brief.

There are different types of advertising, and the various interpretations of what advertising is and how it is defined need to be clarified if ideas and thoughts are to be developed coherently.

Aims and learning objectives

The main aims of this chapter are to explore the scope, background and types of advertising and to then consider its role as a marketing instrument.

As a result of reading this chapter readers should be able to:

1. understand the general background and development of advertising
2. discuss the significance and scope of the advertising industry
3. explain the nature and role of advertising in society
4. write several definitions about advertising
5. appraise the different types of advertising
6. examine advertising as a form of communication
7. assess the role of advertising as a form of engagement.

Minicase Painting through insight

The premium paint segment in New Zealand has two preference drivers: colour and quality. Of the many brands in the market, two stand out: Resene and Dulux. Resene is perceived to be the best for colour, whilst Dulux is generally regarded as the best-quality paint. However, consumer paint sales in New Zealand were declining and there was no sign of any change to the downward trend. This was because home-decorating projects were being frozen, new projects were being put on hold, all due to the recession taking a grip on disposable income and household expenditure.

Such market stagnation leads many brands to slow down or even stop all of their advertising activities. However, Dulux New Zealand knew that they had to invest in brand communications if they were to protect their market share and engineer a position that could be developed once the recession had been overcome.

Dulux is a well-established brand, not just in New Zealand but in many other countries. The name attracts high recall scores and the brand has a strong reputation. Over the years Dulux had worked hard to earn a strong reputation for paint quality. However, after discussion both internally and externally with significant stakeholders, including employees, customers and retailers, Dulux realised that to maintain market share they needed to change the way people perceived the Dulux colour range. They not only had to own the quality attribute, they also had to dislodge Resene and become the number-one brand for colour as well. In essence, the goal was to become the number-one choice on both preference drivers.

The target audience is typically couples and young families in their early 30s to late 40s. Their home is important to them and they have a strong emotional connection with it. Indeed, research found that Kiwis are incredibly proud not just of their homes but of the unique New Zealand landscape as well. Many New Zealanders want to redecorate but they have limited decorating creativity or confidence when it comes to colour selection. As a result, painting and decorating projects are often postponed as long as possible. When they do start, New Zealanders prefer to use colours that will not date, which in turn can rule out colour experimentation and adventure.

Exhibit 1.1 Dulux Paints campaign (New Zealand)
Source: Dulux

To overcome these obstacles Dulux knew they had to use advertising as their central form of communication. Advertising could not only help demonstrate their colour range and depth, but it would also enable an opportunity to create an emotional connection with their target audience. By bonding closely, customers experience higher levels of brand trust and are therefore more disposed to new approaches and techniques. However, if the goal was to become the strongest for colour, it was realised that care had to be taken not to lose quality perceptions.

So one of the goals for the advertising campaign was to create a powerful emotional connection with consumers, so that a distinctive colour positioning for Dulux could be established. If this was achieved then this would provide a more compelling reason for consumers to want to purchase Dulux, even to ask for Dulux as their preferred brand of paint. From this point, the marketing team at Dulux New Zealand had to decide what the nature of the creative platform for their advertising should be. In addition they had to establish which types of message and media should be used to reach their audiences and influence their perceptions.

Source: Clemenger BBDO (2009); www.dulux.co.nz/

Introduction

The spectacular Guinness ad, 'Surfer', tells a story through the metaphor of galloping sea horses and surfers. The 1999 ad used state-of-the-art technology to tell us that it takes time to pour a glass of Guinness, just as it takes time to wait for the ultimate surf wave. The ad was filmed in Hawaii using four local surfers, helicopters and jetskis, plus, back in the UK, Lipizzaner stallions and computers; and it cost over £1 million. Just as Guinness drinkers should wait 119.5 seconds for their pint of Guinness to be poured and settled, the theme of 'All good things come to those who wait' was re-enacted as surfers waiting for the definitive wave.

Exhibit 1.2 *Guinness 'Surfers'* - All good things come to those who wait.
Source: Image courtesy of The Advertising Archives

The amount of money invested in this ad tells us something about the importance of advertising to Guinness. The ad says something about the power of advertising and the emotions it can evoke. The imagery and storytelling reflect the creativity often embedded in successful advertising and it makes a statement about the need to communicate with and engage audiences, not just those who might be beer drinkers.

'Advertisements are unique composites of words and pictures, sounds and movement, and symbols and slogans.' These words, written by Unwin in 1974 (p. 24), are in many ways still true today. The nature, form and presentation of these advertising attributes may have changed but this characterisation of what constitutes advertising still prevails in the modern, digital era.

Our individual daily involvement with advertising can stimulate a range of responses that can shape many facets of our lives. O'Neill (2005) cites Lasn who states that we encounter around 3,000 commercial messages each day, the vast majority of which pass us by without a glimmer of perceptual acknowledgement.

To those ads that we do sense, our responses can vary considerably. Some are grounded in the satisfaction of information received or reinforced, feelings of pleasure, comfort or motivation and overall sense of enrichment that some advertising can provide. Some ads leave us irritated, disgusted or bewildered, whilst the majority skirt over us, seemingly unnoticed, yet still decorating our worlds. Advertising, as we will see in this book, is big business. It helps to drive economies, provide employment, circulate cash and enable growth. It can also support society in other ways, through its culture, health and education programmes. Advertising can also be seen to be misleading, offensive, false, or even socially irresponsible, which means that there need to be some controlling mechanisms, either as formal legal regulation, or informal self-imposed voluntary measures (Harker 2008).

In this book we explore the nature of advertising, often from a managerial perspective. We consider the theories and concepts, and the practices and behaviours of those who collaborate to make the ads. We achieve this through the provision of examples of advertising practice, drawn from around the world, although inevitably there is a UK and European focus.

This chapter starts with a consideration of the background and development of advertising before examining the scope of the advertising industry. This is followed by a view of the significance of advertising in society. This is a huge topic and so, due to the limitations of this book, we can only introduce and touch upon some of the relevant topics. From here we look at some definitions and types of advertising before concluding the chapter with an assessment of the role of advertising as a form of engagement.

Brief background and development of advertising

The origins of advertising can be traced back to early civilisations. For example, wall painting can be considered an expression of an ancient form of advertising. This practice has been traced back to 4000 BC in ancient Egypt and as Indian rock-art paintings. We also know that the Egyptians developed wall posters and sales messages using papyrus. Both the Greek and Roman societies developed advertising materials, principally for lost and found, and political as well as commercial purposes, with the Romans using posters to promote gladiator fights and circuses.

As literacy levels remained poor among the general population of most societies, the use of signs, symbols and images was an important form of communication. For example, a loaf of bread, a shoe or a tankard of ale was used to depict a baker, a cobbler or an inn respectively. Street barkers were placed outside shops whilst town criers were paid by shopkeepers and merchants to announce developments, offers and the location of their establishments.

However, the commercial practice of advertising became increasingly sophisticated and prevalent as a result of two main developments. The first concerned the improvement in

Scholars' paper 1.1 **Well, what has happened so far?**

Pollay, R.W. (1978) Wanted: A history of advertising, *Journal of Advertising Research*, 18, 5 (October), 63-8

Pollay, a distinguished academic, uses this short paper to reflect on the reasons why so little has been written about the history of advertising. It is useful because it provides snippets of advertising literature and suggests that the 'history of advertising . . . is perhaps one of the keys to our understanding of the evolution of our complex urban society' (p. 63).

education which enabled a considerable increase in the number of people who could read and write. The second concerned developments in technology. Two of the more significant developments have been the printing press and the internet. These transformed communication by considerably increasing both the speed of production and the distribution of promotional materials, and also enabled improved targeting and reach of advertising messages.

The educational improvements and the development of printing techniques saw the widespread use of handbills. Newspapers became affordable, and ads to promote books, and medicines in particular, became familiar features. However, there were some instances of misleading or dubious claims which inevitably led to the first regulations aimed at controlling advertising.

With the Industrial Revolution, advertising became more affordable and helped to propel the growth of economies. Manufacturers used advertising to drive demand as both production and competition increased.

The first advertising agencies appeared in the 19th century. These were essentially space brokers, individuals who purchased large amounts of space in newspapers at discounted rates, and who then resold smaller blocks to client advertisers at higher rates. At this stage clients still prepared their own copy, artwork and layout, or creative element. However, this changed as individuals started to offer specialised advertising skills and soon full-service agencies appeared, offering space buying, planning and creative activities.

The advent of radio saw the emergence of individual programme sponsorship. A business would provide financial support for a programme in return for frequent mentions, especially at the start and finish. Some of the prominent sponsors of radio dramas were soap manufacturers, which gave rise to the contemporary term, 'soap opera'. This practice developed into selling small amounts of radio time to many different businesses throughout a broadcast, a model that was to be adopted by commercial television companies.

The first television programmes were sponsored in the same way as radio programmes. The television programmes were produced by an advertising agency yet paid for by a single sponsor. The *Colgate Comedy Hour* and *Kraft Television Theater* typified the approach. This period is referred to as the 'single-sponsor' era. Not surprisingly, these sponsors had considerable power over a show's content, to the extent of even using their advertising agencies to write the show.

Television's powerful combination of visual and audio elements led to a recognition that brand recall through television was more effective than radio. This led to an unprecedented growth and investment in this form of communication. However, production costs started to rise to the extent that a single sponsor struggled to support a programme. According to Weinstein (2004), the DuMont Television Network was the first television company to sell advertising time, multiple spots, to several sponsors, at a time when the established practice was to use a single sponsor for each show. Some say NBC were the first, but whoever it was, the move towards involving several advertisers, each buying time within a single programme, signalled the era of 'participation advertising'. The move away from sponsorship effectively shifted control over the content of programmes from single sponsors to media owners. Gibbs SR Toothpaste was the first UK television ad, a one-minute advert broadcast in 1955.

Exhibit 1.3 The General Electric All-Steel Refrigerator.

This historic 1930 print advertisement extols the functional attributes of the General Electric refrigerator. As well as the photograph of the product, a wealth of information is conveyed in the text. This focuses on quality, durability and low cost of ownership. The overall message is that any family can (and should) now own a GE refrigerator.

Source: Mary Evans Picture Library

The arrival of cable and satellite television saw the development of a variety of new channels such as QVC and the Home Shopping Network. These channels, not programmes, were based on a new business model, that of just advertising products and services. Experiments with interactive advertising were undertaken, although these have not been entirely successful.

ViewPoint 1.1 A glass and a half of chocolate advertising

When John Cadbury placed his first ad in the *Birmingham Gazette* on 1 March 1824 his copy read as follows:

> John Cadbury is desirous of introducing to particular notice 'Cocoa Nibs', prepared by himself, an article affording a most nutritious beverage for breakfast.

At the time this was considered to be very concise.

Cocoa Essence was first advertised in 1866 and the largely informational message stressed three attributes: its strength, lack of starch and lower fat content. However, food products were subject to adulteration in order to drive better profits. Cadbury's seized the opportunity to develop a unique selling proposition and its advertising stressed the product purity and reinforced this with medical testimonials:

> *We have carefully examined the samples brought under our notice and find that they are genuine, and that the Essence of cocoa is just what it is declared to be by Messrs. CADBURY Brothers. - Lancet*

> *Cocoa treated thus will, we expect, prove to be one of the most nutritious, digestible and restorative of drinks - British Medical Journal*

From this the slogan 'Absolutely Pure, therefore Best' became the anchor for a 30-year advertising campaign.

From the turn of the century Cadbury became synonymous with exemplary ads in both the press and posters. Cecil Aldin, a local artist, was hired to illustrate them. From 1928 Cadbury stressed the high milk content in its products and invested heavily in advertising. Poster campaigns using the iconic 'glass and a half' measure of milk helped establish Cadbury Dairy Milk as one of the first truly recognisable high-street brands.

Cadbury's Drinking Chocolate was one of the very first adverts to appear on commercial television when broadcasting began on 22 September 1955. Cadbury's concentrated on a more generic message, and used a cut-down version of a 1951 film, 'The Bourneville Story'.

In 1957 the first of 13 one-minute films appeared. Each of these was a travelogue which described the harvesting of an ingredient used at Cadbury. The 1970s was a golden age of television advertising, with hugely popular campaigns for Flake, Cadbury's Dairy Milk, Fruit & Nut and Whole Nut, Fry's Turkish Delight, Fudge and Milk Tray.

Source: www.cadbury.co.uk/cadburyandchocolate/ourstory/Pages/

Question

Why do you think the image of a 'glass and a half' measure of milk proved to be so successful?

Task

Find three different Cadbury's ads from different decades. What are the similarities and what differences or changes do you notice?

The development of the internet led to an initial flurry of dot.com companies. The only source of income for many of these companies was advertising revenue. The crash at the end of the 20th century led to several revised models, one of which was driven by Google. Their approach to online advertising was based on text-search facilities and small sponsored-link ads. This method is designed to assist users and enable them to search interactively for relevant information, rather than interrupt or annoy them with ads informing them about unrelated products. More recent advances with real-time bidding apps and mobile advertising seek to develop efficiency, speed, ubiquity and location- and proximity-based advertising.

The significance and scope of the advertising industry

The advertising industry is an integral element of the broader communications industry in which there are four principal actors. These are the media, the clients, the agencies and finally the thousands of support organisations, such as production companies and fulfilment houses, who enable the whole process to function. It is the operations and relationships between these organisations that not only drive the industry but also form an important context within which the advertising industry functions. Contextually the industry operates within a set of rules, both formal and informal, that society deems necessary in order to control and regulate the actions of advertisers and agencies. Detail about the advertising industry and its operations and processes can be found in Chapter 7. In addition, a discussion concerning the ethical issues and the way the advertising industry is regulated can be found in Chapter 12. The purpose of this section is to set out the scope and significance of the advertising industry. Figure 1.1 sets out the core stakeholders and context within which the advertising industry in most countries operates.

Dimensions of the advertising industry

Levy (2010) reports that global adspend increased by 12.8% during the first six months of 2010, compared to the same period in 2009. She reports that Nielsen's Global AdView Pulse report shows that adspend increased in 35 of the 37 countries covered in the research. 2010 was a significant year as some confidence returned to the global economy, with just a few exceptions. In the first half of 2010, both Latin America and the Middle East and Africa recorded year-on-year increases, of 44.5% and 23.8% respectively. Europe experienced an 8% adspend increase for the first six months of 2010 (Levy 2010).

However, in order to appreciate the significance of any industry it is helpful to first examine its size and value. In this case we use the UK advertising industry but the principles drawn apply to most developed economies.

The total spend for UK advertising, as can be seen from Table 1.1, was £16.2 billion in 2011. The figure for 2006 was £19 billion. What happened to cause the reduction? The answer of course is the recession. Indeed the figures for 2008 and 2009 are considerably lower. The 2010

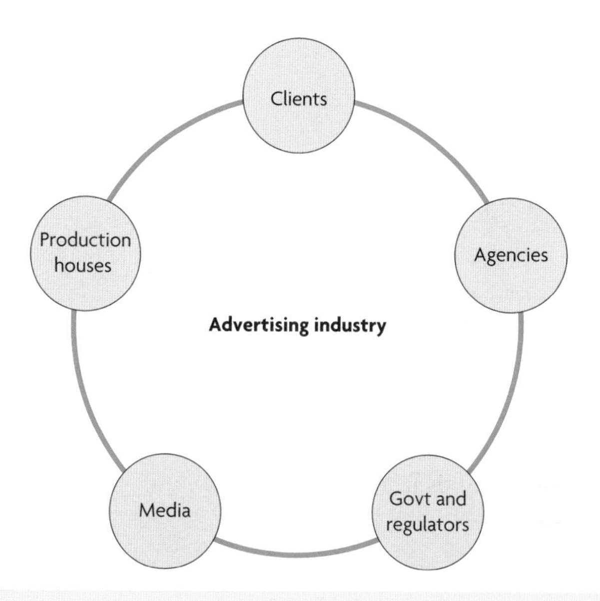

Figure 1.1 Core stakeholders in the advertising industry

Table 1.1 Total UK advertising expenditure (including direct mail)

	2011 (£m)	2006 (£m)	2000 (£m)
Press	3,945	8,346	8,604
Television (excl. sponsorship)	4,159	4,594	4,646
Direct mail	1,729	2,322	2,049
Outdoor and transit	886	1,084	810
Radio	427	534	595
Cinema	182	188	128
Internet	4,784	2,016	155
Total	**16,182**	**19,084**	**16,988**

Source: http://expenditurereport.warc.com/.

figures show that the advertising industry was recovering slowly, with television, radio and newspaper adspend growing by 15.8%, 11% and 9.5% respectively, and the 2011 figures show further growth, but still a long way from the highs of 2006.

More significantly, these figures show that the overall value of advertising investment can be used as a barometer of an economy's health. As an economy begins to stall there is a tendency for businesses to cut back their advertising spend. At the first signs of recovery, investment in advertising, note not spend, begins again, as businesses seek to capture the rise in confidence and the upturn in production and output.

This notion of advertising as an investment, or, as many refer to it, as spend, reflects two very different perspectives. As a generalisation, those who regard advertising as an investment are primarily marketers at heart. However, the term expenditure, or spend as it is popularly referred to, is often adopted by financiers, accountants and industry commentators and journalists.

Industry structure

The shape and size of the advertising industry have evolved through time. Some argue that the industry has not changed enough or as quickly as necessary, but it has altered. Over the last few decades the number of organisations populating the industry has increased in response to changes in technology, the growth in the number of activities and with it the real value of advertising practice.

The configuration of the agency services industry partly reflects the moves made by the larger agencies to consolidate their positions. They have attempted to buy smaller, often medium-sized, competitors in an attempt to protect their market shares or provide an improved range of services for their clients. This has led to an industry characterised by a large number of very large agencies and an even larger number of very small agencies. These smaller agencies have formed as the result of people formerly employed in large agencies becoming frustrated with having to work within tight margins and increased administration leaving and setting up their own fledgling businesses. This pattern was observed previously when media planning houses developed. Some were entirely independent and others, such as Zenith, were dependent upon a parent organisation.

As a broad interpretation, the industry consists of some very large agencies, a large number of very small agencies and relatively few medium-sized agencies. Although ownership has been an important factor driving industry development, the current preference for loose,

Scholars' paper 1.2 **Windmills, canals and advertising**

Röling, R.W. (2010) Small Town, Big Campaigns. The Rise and Growth of an International Advertising Industry in Amsterdam, *Regional Studies*, 44, 7 (August), 829-43

A rare marketing-oriented paper that considers advertising historically by describing four waves of international advertising development, from the early twentieth century.

From this the author identifies an emerging group of smaller independent agencies that have used Amsterdam as a hub to create advertisements for the international market. Differences between the various types of advertising agency and their positioning is examined, all of which helps to explain Amsterdam's importance as a centre for advertising since the early 1990s.

independent networks has enabled some large organisations to offer clients an improved range of services (integrated marketing communications, or IMC) and the small agencies a chance to work with some of the bigger accounts. The recession has led to some of the smaller agencies disappearing and most of the others restructuring and slimming down to match the lower levels of business.

Single-stop shopping

As with most industries, the structure of the communications industry has evolved in response to changes in the environment. However, if there is a holy grail of communications it is an agency's ability to offer clients a single point from which all of their integrated communication needs can be met. In search of this goal, WPP and Saatchi & Saatchi set about building the largest marketing communications empires in the world, Green (1991). The strategy adopted in the early 1980s was to acquire companies outside its current area of core competence, media advertising. Organisations in direct marketing, market research, sales promotion and public relations were brought under the Saatchi banner.

By offering a range of services under a single roof, rather like a 'supermarket', the one-stop shopping approach made intrinsic sense. Clients could put a package together, rather like eating from a buffet table, and solve a number of their marketing requirements – without the expense and effort of searching through each sector to find a company with which to work.

Green also refers to the WPP experience in the late 1980s. J. Walter Thompson and Ogilvy and Mather were grouped together under the umbrella of WPP and it was felt that synergies were to be achieved by bringing together their various services. Six areas were identified: strategic marketing services, media advertising, public relations, market research, non-media advertising and specialist communications. A one-stop shopping approach was advocated once again.

The recession of the early 1990s brought problems to both of these organisations, as well as others. The growth had been built on acquisition, which was partly funded from debt. This required considerable interest payments, but the recession brought a sharp decline in the revenues of the operating companies, and cash-flow problems forced WPP and Saatchi & Saatchi to restructure their debt and their respective organisations. As Phillips (1991) points out, the financial strain and the complex task of managing operations on such a scale began to tell.

However, underpinning the strategy was the mistaken idea that clients actually wanted a one-stop shopping facility. It was unlikely that the best value for money was going to be achieved through this, so it came as no surprise when clients began to question the quality of the services for which they were paying. There was no guarantee that they could obtain from one large organisation the best creative, production, media and marketing solutions to their problems. Many began to shop around and engage specialists in different organisations (à la carte) in an attempt to receive not only the best quality of service but also the best value for money. Evidence for this might be seen in the resurgence of the media specialists whose very existence depends on their success in media planning and buying. By 1990 it was estimated that in Britain 30 per cent of market share in media buying was handled by specialist media companies.

It is no wonder then that clients, and indeed many media people working in agencies who felt constrained, decided to leave and set up on their own account. The feeling was that full-service agencies were asking too much of their staff, not only in terms of providing a wide range of integrated marketing services generally, but also in giving full attention and bringing sufficient expertise to bear in each of the specific services they had to offer (account management, creative, production, media research, etc.).

The debate about whether or not to use a full-service agency becomes even more crucial, perhaps, for those in specialist areas. For example, a large number of business-to-business communication agencies have been set up by people leaving full-service agencies. They spotted opportunities to provide specialist services in a market area that at the time was under-resourced, often marginalised or even ignored. In many ways it comes back to the quality of relationships. Arguments for the specialist agency were based on the point that, while there may be some convergence of approaches between consumer goods marketing and business-to-business advertising, it can be easier for a business-to-business advertising agency to do consumer advertising than it is to do the reverse.

There is a spectrum of approaches for clients. They can find an agency that can provide all of the required marketing communication services under one roof, or find a different agency for each of the services, or mix and match. Clearly the first solution can only be used if the budget holder is convinced that the best level of service is being provided in *all* areas, and the second only if there are sufficient gains in efficiency (and savings in expenditure) to warrant the amount of additional time they would need to devote to the task of managing marketing communications.

One area that has experienced significant change has been media. Industry concentration and the development of global networks have shifted the structure and composition of the industry. Clients have responded by centralising their business into a single media network agency in search of higher discounts and improved efficiency. An organisation needs to determine a competitive approach that will allow it to influence the industry's competitive rules, protect it from competitive forces as much as possible and give it a strong position from which to compete. At the turn of this century media networks had yet to find a competitive form of differentiation although some were beginning to offer additional services as a way of trying to enhance brand identities (Griffiths 2000). At the time the power of the media agencies, the low switching costs of buyers and the large threat of substitute products made this a relatively unattractive industry. Media are now perceived to be much more important and much more significant than they used to be and as a result have developed increased market value.

The nature and role of advertising in society

Much of advertising mirrors social standards, lifestyles, values and aspirations, very often represented in an idealised form. This is designed to promote recognition, understanding and involvement by the target audience (Unwin 1974) and to help form the bonds that constitute a relationship between the advertiser and audience.

Indeed, the cultural values of a society can be seen to be represented within the advertising that the society deems to be acceptable. As Unwin suggests, the creative style used to communicate brand ideas and associations constitutes a 'language of advertising'. The prevailing cultural norms envelop this advertising dialect, and in doing so communicate a society's overall values and overshadow the actual stereotypical content.

As if to emphasise Unwin's view, Varey (2002: 269) refers to advertising as 'an institutional model of communication that is deeply rooted in daily interests and has continued to contribute to the reproduction of the social conditions and values of a mode of living and a social system'. Advertising is an integral part of society.

Advertising and culture

Perhaps the most visible articulation of the interchange between advertising and society can be seen in the use of advertising and related communications within the cultural dynamics that frame the actions and beliefs of different societies.

The values, beliefs, ideas, customs, actions and symbols that are learned by members of particular societies are referred to as culture. The importance of culture is that it provides individuals with identity and the direction of what is considered to be acceptable behaviour. Culture is acquired through learning. If it were innate or instinctive, then everyone would behave in the same way. Human beings across the world do not behave uniformly or predictably. Therefore different cultures exist, and from this it is possible to visualise that there must be boundaries within which certain cultures, and hence behaviours and lifestyles, are permissible or even expected. These boundaries are not fixed rigidly, as this would suggest that cultures are static. They evolve and change as members of a society adjust to new technologies, government policies, developments in language, changing values and demographic changes, to mention but a few dynamic variables. From an advertising perspective, the prevailing culture in a country, region or society must be respected, otherwise it is likely that a brand or an organisation will be rejected. For example, the Dove ads in which happy women of all shapes and sizes pose in their underwear have had to be shown in different ways to meet the needs of different cultures. In Brazil the women are depicted hugging each other, yet in the United States they stand slightly apart from each other, as body contact in the United States is not part of the culture (Laurance 2007).

Culture has multiple facets, and those that are of direct relevance to advertising are the values and beliefs associated with *symbols*, such as language and aesthetics, *institutions* and *groups*, such as those embracing the family, work, education, media and religion, and finally *values*, which according to Hofstede et al. (1990) represent the core of culture.

One of the most important international, culturally oriented research exercises was undertaken by Hofstede (1980, 1991). Using data gathered from IBM across 53 countries, Hofstede's research has had an important impact on our understanding of culture (Hickson and Pugh 1995). From this research, several dimensions of culture have been discerned. The first of these concerns the individualist/collectivist dimension. It is suggested that individualistic cultures emphasise individual goals and the need to empower, to progress and to be a good leader. Collectivist cultures emphasise good group membership and participation. Consequently, difficulties can arise when advertising and communications between these two types of culture have meanings ascribed to them that are derived from different contexts.

In addition to these challenges, comprehension (ascribed meaning) is further complicated by the language context. In high-context languages, information is conveyed through who is speaking and their deportment and mannerisms. Content is inferred on the basis that it is implicit: it is known and does not need to be set out. This is unlike low-context languages, where information has to be detailed and 'spelled out' to avoid misunderstanding. For example, advertising creative strategy, according to Okazaki and Alonso (2003), asserts that the Japanese prefer a more subtle, soft approach. In contrast, North Americans prefer a more direct, hard-sell strategy with direct, explicit messages.

People in different cultures can exhibit characteristics that suggest they feel threatened or destabilised by ambiguous situations or uncertainty. Those cultures that are more reliant on formal rules are said to have high levels of uncertainty avoidance. They need expert advice, so advertising messages that reflect these characteristics, are logical and clear, and provide information directly and unambiguously (in order to reduce uncertainty) are likely to be more successful.

Zandpour and Harich (1996) used these cultural dimensions, together with an assessment of the advertising industry environment in each target country. The results of their research suggest that different countries are more receptive to messages that have high or low levels of logical, rational and information-based appeals (think). Other countries might be more receptive to psychological and dramatically based appeals (feel).

Research concerning the effectiveness of advertising strategies in the United States and Australia (Frazer and Sheehan 2002) found that safety appeals were more frequently used in Australia than in the United States. This may well reflect varying cultural values regarding concern for safety-related issues, concern for the environment and varying regulatory requirements.

Advertising and art

We can see how advertising mirrors culture by considering the way in which the interaction is reflected in particular parts of society. For example, advertising can be reflected in art, just as art is reflected in advertising. Andy Warhol used product advertising in his *Coca-Cola, Listerine* and 1980s *Hamburger* works, as a commentary on the society's values.

His work is considered to have a simplicity and scale that replicated typical 1980s billboard advertisements. In *Hamburger*, the symbolic representation of a hamburger is matched with the name of the product. His use of red and yellow imitates the corporate colours of McDonald's, and suggests a Pavlovian relationship between the symbolism of the colours and the subconscious feelings of hunger. See Exhibit 1.4.

Another of Warhol's prominent works depicted the entire range of 32 soups made by Campbell. It was first exhibited in 1962, with each of the 32 canvases resting on a shelf mounted on the wall, like groceries in a store. Here art is used to comment on society, this time its use of marketing and business.

The interaction between art and advertising can be observed in the way different forms or schools of art have been represented. For example, Impressionism, Art Deco, Symbolism and Futurism can all be observed in billboards and posters at different points through the 20th century. Surrealism is reflected in photography with Bernstein (2010) signalling the Benson and Hedges work as classic examples of avoiding the cigarette advertising regulations that were in force at the time.

Advertising and music

Advertising can also be seen to reflect the prevailing style of music that society enjoys and accepts. Music is a frequently used advertising executional cue, and has been since the early days of broadcast communications (Allan 2008). From radio jingles to the use of a range of musical styles for television and more recently video advertising, music has become an integral part of advertising. The first acknowledged use of a pop song in an ad happened in 1985 when Burger King used Aretha Franklin's 'Freeway of Love', to sell fast food (Oughton 2011).

Exhibit 1.4 Andy Warhol *Hamburger* print which mimics commercial work.
Source: Artists Rights Society.

Scholars' paper 1.3 **What is the good of marketing?**

Wilkie, W.L. and Moore, E.S. (1999) Marketing's contributions to society, *Journal of Marketing*, 63 (special issue), 198–216

The authors were set a considerable challenge when invited to write about the contribution that marketing makes to society at the end of the last millennium. Readers may not agree with the perspectives taken but the ideas and focus enable consideration about the positive and negative ways the marketing system contributes to society.

Zhu and Meyers-Levy (2005) refer to two types of meanings that music can convey. The first is an embodied meaning, which is about hedonism and stimulation and is independent of context. The second is referential meaning, which is context dependent and 'reflects networks of semantic-laden, external world concepts' (p. 333). Both have been found to influence the perceptions people have of advertised products in particular ways. However, through referential meaning it is the interaction of music and society that advertising draws on in order to influence product perceptions.

Advertising and politics

The use of political advertising is well documented. For example, early in the 20th century advertising was used to support and enforce government policies and to enlist soldiers for the First World War. These posters were essentially propaganda and used fear appeals to assert the government's power. Here the advertiser assumed superiority and that their communications were in the audience's best interests. Such patronisation is not always so readily observable in contemporary political advertising.

The power of advertising can also be observed when the increasing loss of scientists and engineers to the United States in the 1960s led the British government to consider banning foreign recruitment advertising (Loder 2000).

Advertising and health

One of the first claims that advertising should be used to promote public health was made by Schevitz (1915). Referring to the use of posters, streetcar displays and newspaper advertising, Schevitz advocated the increased use of advertising in order to improve the health of the public, and reduce the incidence of tuberculosis in particular.

Advertising has been used extensively by different societies in order to control the health of the public. Even though the role of advertising in public health is controversial, advertising has been used to promote health checks, vaccinations, good eating, lifestyle- and health-related behaviours that extend life. Campaigns directed at particular diseases, addictions or health issues such as smoking and obesity have received wide coverage.

There is general agreement that advertising that uses emotional appeals, such as fear, rather than rational, information-based messages, is better at motivating a change in behaviour (Hassard 1999). However, there is little agreement about how health advertising should be used. For example, Veer et al. (2008) cite Pechmann and Reibling (2000) who found that advertising campaigns that emphasise how smoking harms families are effective, yet Hill et al. (1998) argue for advertising messages that demonstrate the negative consequences of smoking to the smokers themselves.

Whatever the correct approach, the point to be made is that advertising is used as a means of influencing the health of society. Whether this is achieved by providing information or encouraging behaviours deemed to be important, advertising is regarded as an instrument to be used for the public good. See ViewPoint 1.2.

Advertising and film

At the beginning of this chapter reference is made to the Guinness ad, 'Surfer'. This ad features a juxtaposition of galloping white horses and surfers waiting to ride a huge wave. That ad was made in 1999 and received a string of major awards. In 2001 the first of a trilogy of *Lord of the Rings* fantasy films, *The Fellowship of the Ring*, was released. In the film there is a sequence referred to as 'Riders at the River Bruinen'. Here horses are seen to rise out of the spray in a similar splash of 'hooves, manes and surf' (BBC 2002), evoking memories of Guinness and the ad. This interplay between advertising and film, whether deliberate or not, demonstrates a way in which advertising permeates different aspects of our lives, in this case film.

A comprehensive analysis of the role of advertising in society is not possible in this text. However, it appears that advertising, not publicity, is an integral element within society. Apart from its anchor role in business and marketing, it also impacts culture, art, music, theatre, politics, education, law and health among other elements.

ViewPoint 1.2 Stroking the public good

For many people advertising is about persuading people to buy products and services. However, advertising can play other roles in society, as demonstrated by the UK Department of Health's campaign to improve the nation's awareness of strokes, and reduce the number of lives lost each year. A stroke is a brain attack caused by an interruption to the flow of blood, and accounts for 45,000 deaths each year. The cost for society in terms of hospital care, rehabilitation schemes, carers and drugs is enormous.

By treating stroke victims quickly, within three hours, the outcomes for people can be drastically improved. However, research showed that the public did not know what the symptoms of a stroke were, and that victims required the same speed of response as those who experience heart attacks.

To convey the symptoms of a stroke the acronym FAST was developed. This stands for Face, Arms, Speech and Time. This enabled the symptoms to be seen, recognised and remembered by the target audience.

Face = Has their face fallen on one side? Can they smile?

Arms = Can they raise both arms and keep them there?

Speech = Is their speech slurred?

Time = Call 999 if you see any single one of these signs.

The visuals also included a picture of a person with 'fire in the brain' to represent the potential damage in a vivid way and so aid flashbulb memory.

The use of television and print media was critical in order to convey the core message and to provide the space to convey all of the information.

The results indicate that awareness and understanding of the FAST acronym, symptoms and the need to act quickly rose significantly not only among the target audience but also among health professionals. The campaign also affected behaviour. For example, the 999 telephone emergency service received 55% more stroke-related calls in the first four months of the campaign, compared to the previous year. Analysis indicates that for every £1 spent on the campaign, £3.50 was generated as a value for society in the first year.

Source: Snow (2010); www.stroke.org.uk/; www.nhs.uk/actfast/

Question

To what extent should health-related campaigns provide information or provoke action?

Task

Find an ad campaign designed to support another illness or disease. Make notes about the probable objectives the campaign attempted to achieve.

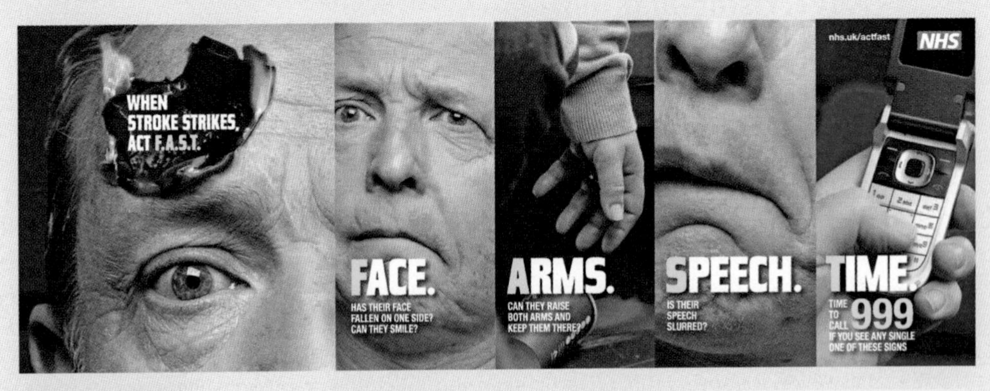

Exhibit 1.5 A shot of the ActFast campaign
Source: NHS

Definitions - what is advertising?

Our consideration of the significance, scope, and role of advertising within society and business enabled us to highlight some of the ethical and cultural issues that surround, pervade and attract advertising. However, it seems appropriate that we now attempt to clarify what advertising is and, of course, what it is not.

For many consumers everything they see, hear or log on to that attempts to influence them to consider products and services constitutes a form of advertising. For them any of the various promotional methods and techniques such as public relations, sponsorship credits, promotions or direct mail is advertising. This blurred vision of the commercial communication landscape is of no consequence to the public. For those practising marketing or the communication disciplines these differences are important as there are important, significant differences between the elements that configure the marketing communications mix. One of these elements, and some might argue the most significant, is advertising.

The Institute of Practitioners of Advertising present a variety of definitions some of which have their roots in the pre-digital era. The two that follow are not so much definitions but perspectives held by two of the great advertising men of the 20th century.

> Advertising says to people, 'Here's what we've got. Here's what it will do for you. Here's how to get it'. (Leo Burnett)
>
> I do not regard advertising as entertainment or an art form, but as a medium of information. (David Ogilvy)

Both assume a utilitarian orientation, that advertising has a functional rather than frivolous or peripheral role to play in either marketing or society as a whole.

Academics Richards and Curran (2002) found variances in the way advertising was defined by authors of various textbooks. They also noted that many of the definitions used the same or similar words. These core words were *paid*, *non-personal*, *identified sponsor*, *mass media*, and *persuade* or *influence*. This enabled them to propose a definition that encapsulated a general consensus around the essence of these words. They referred to this as a *current* definition.

> Advertising is a paid, non-personal communication from an identified sponsor, using mass media to persuade or influence an audience.

This interpretation, however, is debatable. The development of digital technology and the internet in particular has led to a plethora of new communication techniques and approaches that raise questions about the validity of some of the words in the *current* definition. Is 'paid' still viable: can some forms of advertising be unpaid? Surely the use of commercial text messaging indicates that advertising can be 'personal' and the 'mass media' label must therefore be an invalid restriction.

Using a Delphi research approach, Richards and Curran (2002) sought to develop a more contemporary definition of advertising. After much discussion and re-evaluation of the issues and wording, a consensus formed around the following *proposed* definition:

> Advertising is a paid, mediated form of communication from an identifiable source, designed to persuade the receiver to take some action, now or in the future.

These changes might be subtle but they represent an important and methodical attempt to review and update the meaning of advertising. The word 'mediated' replaces the restrictiveness of *mass media*. 'Source' replaces *identified sponsor*, and 'persuasion' replaces the duplication apparent in *persuade* and *influence*. Whether this proposed definition has infiltrated the textbooks and dictionaries published since 2002 should be the subject of further research. However, marketing practitioners and students are encouraged to use the proposed definition and to ignore the cry of consumers who will no doubt continue to lump promotional activities under the advertising banner.

Types of advertising

There are many ways of categorising advertising, but for our purposes five perspectives encapsulate the variety of types available. These are the source, the message, the recipient, the media and place. See Figure 1.2.

The source or sender of a message results in different forms of advertising. Using the value chain as a frame, we can identify manufacturers, who in turn will use *manufacturing advertising* to promote their brands to end users, and retailers who use advertising to attract consumers, *retail advertising*. On some occasions manufacturers collaborate with retailers and use *cooperative advertising*.

Outside the commercial arena, governments use *collective advertising* to communicate with nations, regions and districts, whilst many not-for-profit organisations use *ideas-based advertising*.

The message can provide a further way of categorising advertising. *Informational advertising* uses messages that predominantly provide information about product and service attributes and features. *Transformational advertising* uses messages that are essentially emotional and which have the capacity to transform the way an individual feels about a product or service.

Institutional or *corporate advertising* is undertaken by organisations to express values, intentions, position, or other organisational-based issues. It can also be withdrawn, as Ford announced when hearing about the phone hacking revelations and the *News of the World*.

Theme advertising is most easily represented by recruitment ads. The origins of recruitment advertising are of course rooted in hiring help and employees in order to develop an organisation. However, more recently some employers have started to use this type of advertising as a form of reputational instrument. Whether it is through broadcast, print, or online and social network media, advertising is used to influence corporate image and reputation in order to

Figure 1.2 Types of advertising
Source: Based on Pelsmaker et al. (2010)

ViewPoint 1.3 Bricking it with the BDA

Keeping a brand at the front of an audience's mind is one thing but making a whole product category the centre of attention requires a different approach. The Brick Development Association (BDA) attempted this in 2011 when it launched a campaign ('Naturally') to re-establish bricks as the real building blocks in the 21st century. The BDA represents the paver and clay brick industries in the UK and Ireland. These include a range of people from planners, architects, developers and specifiers to engineers builders, landscapers and property owners. The association felt it important to show why brick is best and why it is the best natural building material.

The main goal of the association's generic advertising campaign was to reach key decision makers in the UK's construction industry. The communication goal was to create awareness of the natural benefits of choosing brick for a variety of building projects, and to position brick as a superior building material to other competitive external materials, such as timber, PVC and other rendered blockwork. All of these are more expensive and costly to the environment. The key messages were related to the various misunderstandings about the attributes of brick as a building material. These included durability, cost and environmental issues.

- **Durability:** Brick represents a 'built to last' quality as it is proven to last centuries and requires little maintenance.
- **Cost effective:** A recent survey by the Royal Institute of Chartered Surveyors (RICS) stated that brick is more cost effective than any other cladding material.
- **Environment friendly:** Brick is made from a natural material and manufactured locally for local markets, therefore minimising the impact on the environment.

The advertising creative featured a brick in line drawings to represent various attributes. For example, a single brick was depicted as the load on a lorry, to symbolise transportability. A brick was shown in a piggy bank, to enable associations with savings and cost effectiveness. Ads were placed offline and online, all supported by public relations direct mail and promotional merchandise activities. The BDA's website was used to enable the industry and the media to find out more about campaign activity, linked to each key message.

Source: Paley (2011); www.brick.org.uk/

Question

How else might the BDA have attempted to change perceptions of brick as a building material? Is advertising the right tool to use?

Task

Choose another building material, see if there is an association or supporting body and make notes about how effective its communications appear to be.

create perceptions that the organisation is a desirable place to work. This might be to sow the seeds and build relationships, in order to recruit at some point in the future, rather than now.

Generic advertising is used to promote a category of products such as dog food, New Zealand lamb, or South African wine. For example, Kolsarici and Vakratsas (2010) cite Ono (1994) and Campbell's generic campaign 'Never Underestimate the Power of Soup'. This was used to promote the general qualities of soup as a meal, and the result was increased sales for the brand. See ViewPoint 1.3 for an example of a generic ad campaign for the promotion of bricks as a superior building material.

Reputational or corporate advertising seeks to build goodwill and relationships, at either a product/service or corporate level.

Scholars' paper 1.4 Go on then, shock me!

Dahl, D.W., Frankenberger, K.D. and Manchanda, R.V. (2003) Does it pay to shock? Reactions to shocking and non-shocking advertising content among university students, *Journal of Advertising Research*, 43, 3 (September), 268-81.

Although the use of shock tactics within advertising is relatively well known, the number of research papers that have been published on the topic are limited. This type of advertising is not well understood from an academic perspective, so this paper is very useful. Not only does it address the topic and find some interesting results, it also provides good background material and literature review.

Finally in this section, *direct response advertising* is used to provoke action. Sometimes referred to as call-to-action advertising, this approach is often used to support sales promotion programmes.

The recipient of advertising messages may be *consumers* or *businesses*. The latter can be broken down to *industrial* and *trade* advertising. The former represents advertising for products that are used within production and manufacturing processes, whereas the latter concerns products that are resold down the supply chain.

The media category refers to the type of media used to carry advertising messages. For example, *broadcast advertising* refers to the use of television and radio, *print advertising* to newspapers and magazines, *out-of-home* to billboards, posters, transport and terminal buildings, *digital* to internet, mobile and online advertising. In addition there is *ambient advertising* (petrol-pump nozzles, golf holes, washrooms) and *cinema advertising*. Each of these media is explored in greater detail later in the book. Related to this are display ads that are placed in media for recipients to view, consider, process and form views. These might be magazine or newspaper ads, or banners and pop-ups. Digital media enable interactivity and here both search and social media advertising have become prominent types of advertising.

Place advertising is most commonly represented by *international advertising*. Reference is normally made to *standardised advertising*, where a single message is used in all countries and regions, and to *adapted advertising* where messages and media are altered and amended to reflect local needs and customs.

Advertising and communication

Traditionally advertising has been used to develop brand identities by stimulating awareness and perception. Advertising had evolved to a point in the 1980s where the focus on developing brand identities and brand values alone was commercially insufficient for clients. The subsequent growth of direct marketing approaches and one-to-one, preferably interactive, communications has become paramount. Marketing budgets have swung in sympathy, and are now very often allocated towards communications that drive a call to action, and in particular online communications have been taking a progressively larger share of advertising budgets since 2004. So the imperative today is about generating a behaviourial rather than an attitudinal response to advertising and other marketing communications campaigns.

So, in this context, what is the role for advertising and what strategies should be used in the contemporary media landscape? One approach would be to maintain current advertising strategies on the grounds that awareness and perception are always going to be key factors. Another approach would be to call for advertising to be used solely for direct response work. Neither of these two options seems appropriate or viable in the 21st century.

In an age where values and response are both necessary ingredients for effective overall communication, advertising strategy in the future will probably need to be based on emotional engagement and an increased level of integration with a range of other forms of communication. Customers will want to engage with the values offered by a brand that are significant to them individually. However, clients will also need to engage with them at a behavioural level and to encourage individuals to want to respond to advertising. Advertising strategy should therefore reflect a brand's context and be adjusted according to the required level of engagement regarding identity development and the required level of behavioural response. Advertising will no longer be able to rightly assume the lead role in a campaign and should be used according to the engagement needs of the audience first, the brand second, and the communication industry third. One of the more integrative approaches concerns the need to use advertising to drive web traffic. This offline–online bridge is a critical aspect of many communication strategies.

Advertising, whether it is on an international, national, local or direct basis, has the potential to engage audiences. Engagement is enabled either by changing perceptions and building brand values or by encouraging a change in behaviour, often delivered through a call to action.

Advertising in the business-to-business market is geared, primarily, to providing relevant factual information upon which 'rational' decisions can be made. Regardless of the target audience, all advertising requires a message and a carrier to deliver the message to the receiver. This text concentrates on these two main issues, while acknowledging the wider role that advertising plays in society.

Engagement and the role of advertising

Engagement is a term that is used regularly and inconsistently by commentators, journalists and academics. Originally engagement was used in the context of media and media usage. Subsequently it has been used as means of explaining the relationship people have with brands (Rappaport 2007). These are both object-oriented interpretations and we know that engagement can be a transient, as well as a long-term, experience and has a contextual element, which is why we use the term engagement as a form of communication.

For engagement to occur there must first be some attention or awareness, be that overt or at a low level of processing. Engagement can be considered to consist of two main components, an intellectual and an emotional element (Thomson and Hecker 2000). The intellectual element is concerned with audiences engaging with a brand on the basis of processing rational, functional information. The emotional element is concerned with audiences engaging and aligning themselves with a brand's values on the basis of emotional and expressive information.

It follows that communication strategies should be based on the information-processing styles and needs of audiences and their access to preferred media. Communications should reflect a suitable balance between the need for rational information to meet intellectual needs and expressive types of communication to meet emotional needs in an organisation's different audiences. These ideas are important foundations and will be returned to later.

Organisations communicate with a variety of audiences in order to pursue their marketing and business objectives. Advertising can be used to engage with a variety of audiences and in such a way as to meet the needs of the audience. In this case it is not just the choice of media that is influential, but also the content. Messages should encourage individual members of target audiences to respond to the focus organisation (or product/brand). This response can be immediate through, for example, purchase behaviour or use of customer care lines, or it can be deferred as information is assimilated and considered for future use. Even if the information is discarded at a later date, the communication will have attracted attention and consideration of the message.

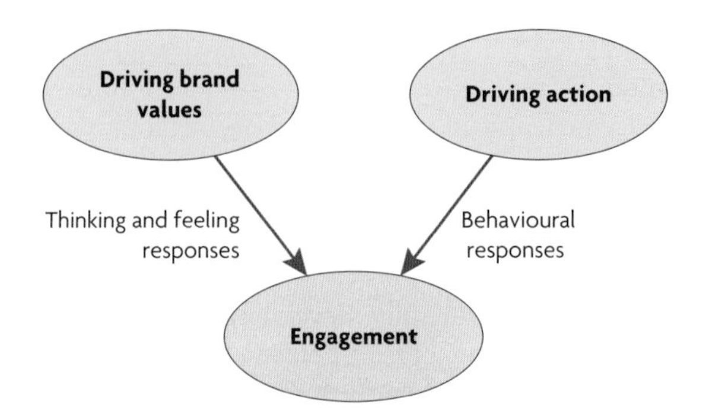

Figure 1.3 Factors that drive engagement opportunities

The reason to use advertising will vary according to the prevailing situation or context but the essential goal is to provoke an audience response. This response might be geared to developing brand values and the positive thoughts an individual might have about a brand. This is grounded in a 'thinking and feeling orientation', a combination of both cognitive thoughts and emotional feelings about a brand.

Another type of response might be one that stimulates the audience to act in particular ways. Referred to as a behavioural or sometimes brand response, the goal is to 'encourage a particular behaviour'. For example, this might involve sampling a piece of cheese in a supermarket, encouraging visits to a website, placing orders and paying for goods and services, sharing information with a friend, registering on a network, opening letters, signing a petition or telephoning a number. Figure 1.3 presents the factors that can drive engagement opportunities.

Apart from generating cash flows, the underlying purpose of these responses can be considered to be a strategic function of developing relationships with particular audiences and/or (re) positioning brands. For example, the marketing communications used to support Comfort Fabric Conditioner in Southeast Asia up until 2006 was based largely on a behavioural strategy. This used direct response advertising and sales promotions to compete in a price-based market. However, sales were declining steadily, so Unilever turned to a strategy that was designed to develop the perceived value of the brand by provoking a brand-value response. The 'Andy and Lily in Clothworld' campaign transformed the brand in three years, with 40% growth in year one and incremental sales worth $157 million across three years (Wiesser et al. 2010).

Engagement therefore can be considered to be a function of two forms of response: a brand-values or a behavioural response. The quality of engagement cannot be determined but it can be argued that advertising should be based on driving a particular type of response that captivates an individual. For example, the UK supermarket Waitrose has positioned itself for many years as an upmarket food store providing high-quality food. The recession in 2008 threatened their performance targets as people started to shop at alternative, value-oriented stores. The strategy was to introduce a new brand, 'Essential Waitrose'. In 2009 Waitrose experienced the fastest growth of all the supermarkets, with the essential range contributing 16% of total revenue, up from 5% in 2008 (Nairn and Wyatt 2010). This move from a brand-value (ad response) to a behavioural (brand response) use of advertising reflects the growing preference of many advertisers, especially post recession, to drive people into action rather than use advertising just to manage perception, attitudes and brand values.

From this it can be concluded that the primary role of advertising is to engage audiences in order to develop awareness, build brand associations, cultivate brand values and help position brands in markets or in the minds of target audiences.

When engagement occurs, an individual might be said to have been positively captivated, and as a result opportunities for further communication activity should increase. Engagement

ViewPoint 1.4 Attracting new teachers through behavioural engagement

The path to becoming a teacher can be fraught, involving many stages and numerous high-risk decisions. Two main markets for teachers can be identified. First there are final-year undergraduates about to enter the job market, and second there are career switchers. These are graduates aged 25–45, looking for a change in their career.

Responsibility for the recruitment of up to 40,000 new schoolteachers every year, in England and Wales, rests with the Training and Development Agency for Schools (TDA). For the period 1998 to 2005 advertising had been used to help recruit record numbers of additional teachers, mainly through the use of advertising to counteract the negative perceptions of the profession.

However, by 2007 the number of eligible enquiries and applications was starting to decline and the percentage of people applying in the same year as they first enquired had dropped from 50% to 37%. In other words, the campaign was still generating the right positive attitudes, but it was failing to generate the right behaviour. Research indicated that the cause of the decline rested with career switchers. They regarded this career change as a huge life decision, with some equating it to emigrating, and others to leaping out of a plane. They saw risks associated with paying mortgages and supporting families, earning lower salaries and having to start their careers all over again. They also wondered if they would be any good at it, so there was the fear of failure. The result was decision paralysis, as career switchers felt they could not move forward, let alone complete the long application process.

The realisation that an individual's progress towards becoming a teacher was far from linear and consisted of various steps forward, sideways and then even some backward, all laced with a lack of decisiveness and uncertainty, indicated that advertising needed to be present at all times in this process. By helping to keep people moving towards another positive TDA experience, and ultimately to application, the use of advertising, and media in particular, was equated to that of a pinball machine helping to keep potential teachers 'in play'. This meant cutting the big bursts of media usage and spreading activity. Now media was to be used to prompt people into action and to be present at all parts of the journey to making an application.

Reaching people when they are more likely to feel glum became an important media-planning approach. So ads were placed in newspapers popular with commuters, on Monday mornings. Poster sites on the underground and rail platforms were used as this is where people stand in the same place every day. Press was used to highlight priority subjects such as ICT and physics, and digital posters were used to inspire readers. This material even appeared on Facebook.

Media activity was integrated with the other disciplines involved with the campaign, such as public relations, event management, direct marketing and telemarketing. The PR strategy used real-life stories in national and local media to bring to life how switching careers to teaching could be rewarding. Articles about how teaching is really fulfilling were available on the TDA website. Train to Teach events were held across the country, and advertising, email and outbound telemarketing was used to encourage people to pre-register.

Most of the ad content featured real teachers. Their role was to reassure career switchers that 'people like them' had made the switch, survived and were happy. Real teachers were also used at events, on social-networking profiles, and in films and articles made for press and online publishers.

These behavioural triggers helped to 'nudge' people along the application process by reframing a big decision into a series of small steps. The campaign achieved a minimum payback of £101 for every £1 spent, and increased the number of enquiries and applications to become teachers to record-breaking levels.

Source: Boyd et al. (2010)

Question

Consider the ways advertising is used to attract people to other professions. How might these be used to recruit teachers?

Task

Make a list of the qualities you look for in a teacher, select the top three and consider how these might be incorporated into a recruitment advertising campaign.

involves attention getting and awareness but it also encompasses the decoding and processing of information so that meaning can be attributed to an incoming message.

Successful engagement suggests that understanding and meaning have been conveyed effectively. At one level, engagement through one-way communication enables a target audience to understand product and service offers, to the extent that the audience is sufficiently engaged to want further communication activity. This is what advertising does well. At another level, engagement through two-way or interactive advertising enables information that is relationship specific (Ballantyne 2004) to be exchanged. Advertising is not always able to generate or sustain this frequency or type of information exchange so other communication tools are often used to support these relationship needs.

The communication mix has expanded and become more complex managerially, but essentially it is now capable of delivering two main solutions. On the one hand it can be used to develop and maintain brand values, and on the other it can be used to change behaviour through the delivery of calls to action. From a strategic perspective, the former is oriented to the long term and the latter to the short term. It is also apparent that the significant rise of below-the-line tools within the mix is partly a reflection of the demise of the USP, but it is also a reflection of the increasing financial pressures experienced by organisations to improve performance and improve returns on investment.

Chapter summary

In order to help consolidate your general understanding of advertising, here are the key points summarised against each of the learning objectives.

Understand the general background and development of advertising

Despite many signs of the use of advertising in earlier civilisations, advertising only became a commercial force when the Industrial Revolution accelerated the need to stimulate demand in order to satisfy the increased production capacity. Developments in education and technology assisted the growth and the increasing sophistication that typifies contemporary advertising practice.

Discuss the significance and scope of the advertising industry

The advertising industry is an integral element of the broader communications industry in which there are four principal actors. These are the media, the clients, the agencies and finally the thousands of support organisations, such as production companies and fulfilment houses, who enable the whole process to function. It is the operations and relationships between these organisations that not only drive the industry but also form an important context within which the advertising industry functions.

The shape and size of the advertising industry have evolved through time. Over the last few decades the number of organisations populating the industry has increased in response to changes in technology, the growth in the number of activities and with it the real value of advertising practice.

Explain the nature and role of advertising in society

Much of advertising mirrors social standards, lifestyles, values and aspirations, very often represented in an idealised form. This is designed to promote recognition, understanding and involvement by the target audience (Unwin 1974) and to help form the bonds that constitute a relationship between the advertiser and audience.

Advertising, not publicity, is an integral element within society. Apart from its anchor role in business and marketing, it influences and is influenced by culture, art, music, theatre, politics, education, law and health, to cite a few elements.

Write several definitions about advertising

For many people everything they see, hear or log on to that attempts to influence them to consider products and services constitutes a form of advertising. For them any differences between the various promotional methods and techniques such as public relations, sponsorship credits, promotions or direct mail do not exist. This, of course, is incorrect and one of the more recent views of advertising is that:

> Advertising is a paid, mediated form of communication from an identifiable source, designed to persuade the receiver to take some action, now or in the future.

Appraise the different types of advertising

There are many ways of categorising advertising, but we considered five different perspectives in order to encapsulate the variety of types available. These are the source, the message, the recipient, the media and place.

Examine advertising as a form of communication

In an age where values and response are both necessary ingredients for effective overall communication, advertising strategy will probably need to be based on emotional engagement and an increased level of integration with a range of other forms of communication.

Assess the role of advertising as a form of engagement

Advertising can be used to drive one of two forms of response: a brand-values or a behavioural response. As the primary role of advertising is to drive audience engagement a brand-values response might be considered to be about developing awareness, building brand associations, cultivating brand values and helping to position brands in markets. A behavioural response, on the other hand, is about provoking action in the form of using advertising to encourage a visit to a website, make a call, download a video, redeem a coupon or share a viral or other piece of information.

Review questions

1. With regard to the challenges presented in the Dulux minicase at the start of the chapter, what would you propose the new creative strategy be, and in broad terms, what messages and media would you suggest the company use?
2. Draw a timeline and on it place as many significant advertising developments and events as you can recall. Once this is completed supplement your knowledge by first referring back to this chapter and then to other external sources.
3. Why is the financial element associated with advertising sometimes referred to as 'spend' and sometimes as an 'investment'? Does it matter?
4. Write notes characterising the structure of the advertising industry in a country of your choice.
5. What does single-stop shopping mean in an advertising context?
6. To what extent is advertising an integral part of society? Find three examples to support your view.

7. Write two definitions of advertising. How are these different and which do you prefer?
8. Identify four different types of advertising and offer two examples to illustrate each of them.
9. Prepare a short presentation in which you explain the role of advertising.
10. Engagement can be considered to be a function of two forms of response. What are they?

Chapter references

Allan, D. (2008) A content analysis of music placement in prime-time television advertising, *Journal of Advertising Research* (September), 404–17

Ballantyne, D. (2004) Dialogue and its role in the development of relationship-specific knowledge, *Journal of Business and Industrial Marketing*, 19, 2, 114–23

BBC (2002) *'Surfer' – The Guinness TV Advert*, retrieved 18 July 2011 from www.bbc.co.uk/dna/h2g2/A767207

Bernstein, D. (2010) Examining advertising's 'artistic' credentials, *Campaign*, 15 October, 19

Boyd, D., Vaas, A., Smith, A. and Caig, J. (2010) TDA teacher recruitment: best in class, *IPA Effectiveness Awards*, London: IPA

Clemenger BBDO (2009) Dulux Colours of New Zealand, The Communication Agencies Association of New Zealand, Silver, New Zealand Effies Awards, retrieved 23 May 2011 from www.warc.com/

Dahl, D.W., Frankenberger, K.D. and Manchanda, R.V. (2003) Does it pay to shock? Reactions to shocking and non-shocking advertising content among university students, *Journal of Advertising Research*, 43, 3 (September), 268–81

Frazer, C.F. and Sheehan, K.B. (2002) Advertising strategy and effective advertising: comparing the USA and Australia, *Journal of Marketing Communications*, 8, 149–64

Green, A. (1991) Death of the full-service ad agency? *Admap* (January), 21–4

Griffiths, A. (2000) More than a media network, *Campaign Report*, 20 October, 3–4

Harker, D. (2008) Regulating online advertising: the benefit of qualitative insights, *Qualitative Market Research: An International Journal*, 11, 3, 295–315

Hassard, K. (1999) *Australia's National Tobacco Campaign: Evaluation Report Volume One*. Canberra: Commonwealth Department of Health and Aged Care

Hickson, D.J. and Pugh, D.S. (1995) *Management Worldwide*. London: Penguin

Hill, D.J., Chapman, S. and Donovan, R.J. (1998) The return of scare tactics, *Tobacco Control*, 7 (Spring), 5–8

Hofstede, G. (1980) *Culture's Consequences: International Differences in Work-Related Values*. Thousand Oaks, CA: Sage

Hofstede, G. (1991) *Cultures and Organisations*. London: McGraw-Hill

Hofstede, G., Neuijen, B., Ohayv, D.D. and Sanders, G. (1990) Measuring organisational cultures: a qualitative and quantitative study across twenty cases. *Administrative Science Quarterly*, 35, 2, 286–316

Kolsarici, C. and Vakratsas, D. (2010) Category- versus brand-level advertising messages in a highly regulated environment, *Journal of Marketing Research*, XLVII (December), 1078–89

Laurance, B. (2007) Unilever learns to join the dots. *Sunday Times*, 18 March, 11

Levy, K. (2010) UK adspend returns to double-digit growth, *campaignlive.co.uk*, 12 October 2010, retrieved 12 July 2011 from www.brandrepublic.com/news/1034276/UK-adspend-returns-double-digit-growth

Loder, N. (2000) UK discussed ban on foreign job ads in 1960s, *Nature*, 403, 121 (13 January), retrieved 15 July 2011 from www.nature.com/nature/journal/v403/n6766/full/403121a0.html

Nairn, A. and Wyatt, M. (2010) Essential Waitrose, *IPA Effectiveness Awards*, 2010, London: IPA

Okazaki, S. and Alonso, J. (2003) Right messages for the right site: online creative strategies by Japanese multinational corporations, *Journal of Marketing Communications*, 9, 221–39

O'Neill, B. (2005) Could you feel sorry for an ad man? *BBC News Channel*, Monday 21 November, retrieved 13 October 2011 from http://news.bbc.co.uk/1/hi/magazine/4456176.stm

Ono, Y. (1994) Campell's new ads heat up soup sales, *The Wall Street Journal* (17 March), B3.

Oughton, J. (2011) Being modern: advertising music, *The Independent*, May, retrieved 14 July 2011 from www.independent.co.uk/news/media/advertising/being-modern-advertising-music-2285843.html

Paley, V. (2011) Built to last, *B2B Marketing Magazine*, 10

Pechmann, C., and Reibling, R.T. (2000) Anti-smoking advertising campaigns targeting youth: case studies from USA and Canada. *Tobacco Control*, 9 (Sup II), 18–31.

Pelsmaker, P. de et al. (2010) *Marketing Communications: a European Perspective*, 4th edn. Harlow: Pearson Education

Phillips, W. (1991) From bubble to rubble, *Admap* (April), 14–19.

Pollay, R.W. (1978) Wanted: a history of advertising, *Journal of Advertising Research*, 18, 5 (October), 63–8

Rappaport, S. (2007) Lessons from online practice: new advertising models, *Journal of Advertising Research* (June), 135–141

Richards, J.I. and Curran, C.M. (2002) Oracles on 'advertising': searching for a definition, *Journal of Advertising*, XXXI, 2 (Summer), 63–77

Schevitz, J. (1915) Advertising as a force in public health education, *American Journal of Public Health*, 8, 12, 916–21. Reproduced in *American Journal of Public Health*, July 2010, 100, 7

Snow, C. (2010) Stroke awareness – how the Department of Health's stroke awareness campaign acted fast, *IPA Effectiveness Awards*, London: IPA

Thomson, K. and Hecker, L.A. (2000) The business value of buy-in. In *Internal Marketing: Directions for Management* (eds R.J. Varey and B.R. Lewis), 160–72. London: Routledge

Unwin, S.J.F. (1974) How culture affects advertising expression and communication style, *Journal of Advertising*, 3, 2, 24–7

Varey, R.J. (2002) *Marketing Communication: Principles and Practice*. London: Routledge

Veer, E., Tutty, M. and Willemse, J. (2008) It's time to quit: using advertising to encourage smoking cessation, *Journal of Strategic Marketing*, 16, 4 (September), 315–25

Weinstein, D. (2004) *The Forgotten Network: DuMont and the Birth of American Television*. Philadelphia: Temple University Press

Wiesser, B., Soliman, A., Brenikov, D. and Chee, Y.Y. (2010) Comfort challenges the 'rules' and wins big in South-East Asia – IPA Effectiveness Awards Case Study, *IPA*, retrieved 12 January 2012 from www.ipa.co.uk/

Wilkie, W.L. and Moore, E.S. (1999) Marketing's contributions to society, *Journal of Marketing*, 63 (Special Issue), 198–216

Zandpour, F. and Harich, K. (1996) Think and feel country clusters: a new approach to international advertising standardization, *International Journal of Advertising*, 15, 325–44

Zhu, R. and Meyers-Levy, J. (2005) Distinguishing between the meanings of music: when background music affects product perceptions, *Journal of Marketing Research*, XLII (August), 333–45

apter 2

so is this the right meaning?

Increasingly advertising is about directed communication. For it to be effective, audiences need to derive meaning from such messages and be able to respond in a way that is both anticipated and desired by the sender of the message. To achieve this it is necessary to understand how communication works and to appreciate the way people process and use information.

Aims and learning objectives

There are two main aims of this chapter. The first is to explore different ideas about the way communication works. The second is to consider source credibility and how cognitive processing contributes to our understanding about how we process and assign meaning to advertising messages.

As a result of reading this chapter readers should be able to:

1. evaluate ideas about how communication is thought to work
2. appraise the key influences on the communication process
3. explain source credibility and source attractiveness
4. explore the principles of cognitive processing
5. describe the elements of the attitude construct
6. discuss ways in which advertising can be used to influence attitudes
7. use examples to illustrate how the elaboration likelihood model works.

Minicase Finding a match.com

Although perceptions of online dating have changed considerably in recent years, there are certain segments that remain unconvinced that this activity is socially acceptable and represents appropriate behaviour. Nevertheless the online dating market has grown considerably and has attracted many players. Competition has intensified with a variety of sites appealing to different market segmernts. Free sites often focus on niche markets and attract display advertising as their main revenue stream (e.g. www.PlentyofFish.com). Paid-for subscription sites appeal to a wide cross-section of society, and are sustained by members paying a subscription fee (e.g. eHarmony.co.uk).

Dating sites often target specific markets as this helps to focus communications on people with similar interests. This is because potential members are more likely to register if they know that the existing members have the same or similar interests and views. This boosts networking activity among members, improves efficiency and member satisfaction and reduces wastage.

Owners of dating websites nearly always join up with social networks. This helps to spread the net of connections and attract friends and contacts of current members. Dating forums enable members to meet many other people who are already interested in dating. Link exchanges with reciprical advertising arrangements are commonplace among free-to-use sites whilst the use of affliate marketing with commission payments for each new member registered provides a new commercial focus. The larger subscription sites often engage in offline advertising, with the market leaders using television to reach their target audiences to establish awareness, build credibility and encourage registrations.

Generating the right content is also a critical element for dating websites. For example, writing articles about dating issues and offering free advice or dating information can boost search rankings as well as provide credibility and improve a site's reputation. By submitting these types of articles to dating directories, these brands can also promote their website through a link at the bottom of the article. However, one of the strongest attributes is the testimony of members who successfully find partners and develop lasting relationships. Here storytelling plays a key role in attracting and renewing the membership database. These stories,

Exhibit 2.1 Match.com
Source: Alamy Images

submitted by happy customers, constitute user-generated content and are used prominently on websites to create trust and confidence.

The largest paid-for competitor in the UK is match.com, which is owned by Meetic, an international dating organisation listed on the European stock exchange 'Euronext'. Match.com can attract around 700,000 unique visitors in a single month. Their advertising campaigns are used to either inform and generate awareness or focus on educating potential users about the site's focus on finding love, compatibility and forming long-term relationships. Many of match.com's previous campaigns have been about customer acquisition and the recruitment of new clients to swell the database. One such campaign featured two luckless and lazy middle-aged men, *Cupid* and *Fate*, who were too sluggish to bring about romance. Although the campaign achieved many of its goals, the characters were dropped from subsequent advertising work.

At all times it is important for the market leader, match.com, to reinforce its brand, maintain market leadership and penetrate the market to attract members. To achieve these objectives positioning is important and for match.com this involves reinforcing trust and reaffirming the success that their members have had in finding partners.

Match.com knew that to grow they had to change the attitudes of people yet to use an online dating website. In addition they had to establish the important point that match.com was different from other sites. To assist this two new products were developed. The first was match.com's unique 'Love guarantee' promotion. If a subscriber fails to meet someone special after six months' use of the website, they are offered an extension to the subscription, free of charge. This served to emphasise and reinforce its impressive record of successful matchmaking. The second goal was to highlight a new product, a scientifically based personality test, formulated by anthropologist Dr Helen Fisher. This personality test (based on the Myers-Briggs test) brings people closer to finding their perfect match, because they understand their character types.

The issue then was how to develop an advertising campaign that conveyed these new products and in a way that had meaning for potential members of match.com.

Source: Based on Barda (2009); www.match.com

Introduction

Communication is a complex activity and various ideas have evolved to explain this fundamental human activity. At the root of the subject, however, is the simple concept that communication is the process by which individuals share meaning. Therefore, it is important to understand the complexity associated with information processing, in order to appreciate the meaning people give to the messages they receive and share with others. Knowing this can help shape the way we communicate and, of course, influence the way advertising is used.

This chapter starts with an evaluation of the different models and theories about how communication works. We then consider ideas about the credibility we bestow on ads and the various messengers used to deliver brand messages. The chapter closes with a review of the principles of cognitive processing. This is the foundation upon which most of advertising, theory and practice, is founded. Sometimes referred to as information processing, this long-established approach is now challenged by some, for example Heath and Feldwick (2008). Their ideas are explored at the end of this chapter and in Chapter 13.

The core model of communication

The first core model developed to explain how communication works was developed by Wilbur Schramm (1955). He determined that communication consisted of a series of core, essentially sequential activities. These are: encoding or designing a message, transmitting the message through a medium, and a receiver decoding the message and attributing a meaning to what has been decoded. Feedback to the source of the message may occur in some communication contexts. These elements are explained breifly in Table 2.1.

Table 2.1 Elements of the communication process

Element of communication	Explanation
Source	an individual or organisation sending the message
Encoding	transposing the intended meaning of the message into a symbolic style that can be transmitted and understood by the receiver
Signal	the transmission of the message using particular media
Decoding	unravelling the symbols to interpret what is being communicated
Receiver	individuals attribute meaning to the message they have received
Feedback	the receiver provides information on receipt of the original message to its source
Noise	distortion of the communication process, which makes it difficult for the receiver to receive, interpret or assign meaning to a message as it was intended by the source

The term 'linear model' was given to this early interpretation because the elements are considered to work in a sequential manner. This approach is also referred to as the 'one-way model'. This linearity emphasises the 'transmission of information, ideas, attitudes, or emotion from one person or group to another (or others), primarily through symbols' (Theodorson and Theodorson 1969). There are several issues associated with this approach as we will explore later, but the core model and its components are easy to understand and to interpret at a simple level. However, it is the quality of the linkages between the various elements in the process that determine whether a communication event will be successful. Each element is now considered in turn. The model is depicted in Figure 2.1.

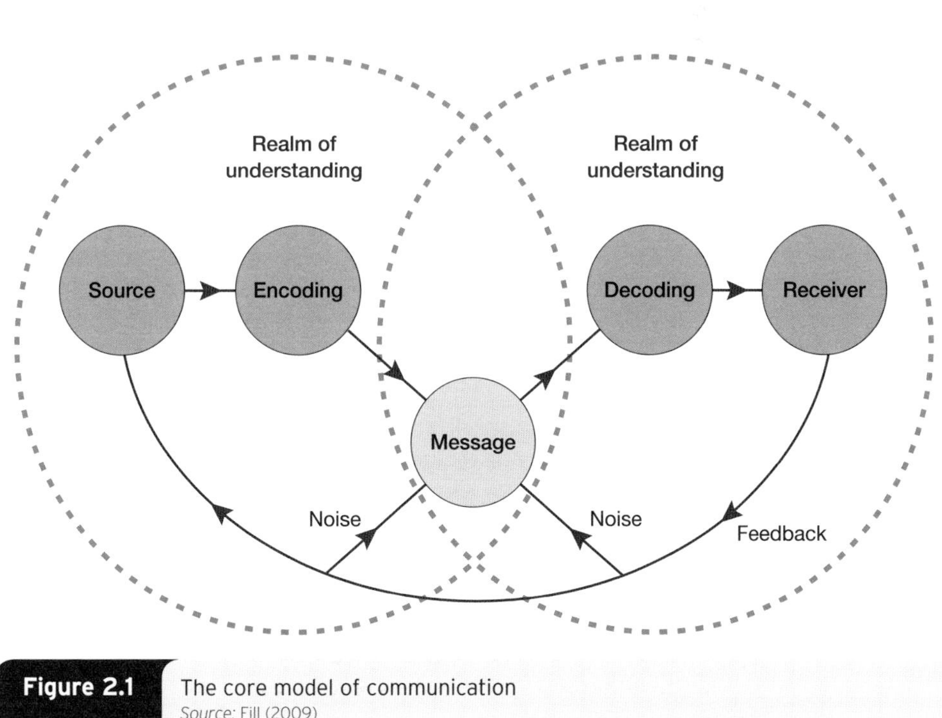

Figure 2.1 The core model of communication
Source: Fill (2009)

The source/encoding link

It is the source, an individual or organisation, that identifies a need to transmit a message and which then selects a combination of appropriate stimuli (text, pictures, symbols or music) to represent the message to be transmitted. This is called encoding. The purpose is to create a message that is capable of being understood by the receiver.

There are a number of reasons why the source/encoding link might break down. For example, the source may fail to diagnose a particular situation accurately. If a problem that customers experience is not fully understood, or the customer purchase journey or level of knowledge is not correctly gauged, inappropriate information may be included in the message. If transmitted, this may lead to misunderstanding, misinterpretation or even confusion by the receiver. For example, if the level of education of the target receiver is not appreciated, a message might be encoded in words and symbols that are beyond the comprehension of the receiver.

Some organisations spend a great deal of time and expense on marketing research, trying to develop their understanding of their target audience. The source of a message is an important factor in the communication process. A receiver who perceives a source lacking conviction, authority, trust or expertise is likely to discount any advertising message received from that source, until such time as credibility is established.

ViewPoint 2.1 Understanding Chinese office coffee drinkers

The per capita consumption of coffee in China is just three cups per year. The market is dominated by higher-income, white-collar workers, the majority of whom are based in urban areas. In addition to being frequent coffee users they are also characterised by their heavy usage of digital media.

Within this small but potentially large market, Nescafé is by far the leading coffee brand. With 98% awareness in tier-one Chinese cities, and 75% market share across the country, Nescafé are in a strong position to exploit the growth opportunities.

Understanding the nature and disposition of the target market, Nescafé developed an online office comedy. This was an adaptation of the internationally recognised French comedy, Camera Café, where a camera hidden in a coffee machine records events around it. The aim was to entertain office coffee drinkers by reflecting their working environment and provide some amusement and refreshment, analogous to a cup of coffee.

Using rewritten scripts, some new characters and Chinese-oriented jokes, 60 episodes, each of five minutes' length, a coffee break, were created. Many of the scenes in the comedy featured a coffee station full of Nescafé products.

The video was launched on YouKu.com, a leading Chinese video-sharing site, and strategic media placements were used to drive traffic. An interactive facility was provided through a fan page on a social networking site.

This approach had not been attempted previously but the show was a resounding success. The statisitcs reveal that there are over 115,000 social network fans, 12 million video views and nearly 250,000 page views. Brand favourability rose 12% and purchase intention 8%. The success is attributable partly to the innovative strategy but the real factor rests with the understanding of and insight into the target market, and then using these to develop a message that could be easily understood and enjoyed. The Camera Café approach has been used in other countries, such as the Philippines, Poland and the USA.

Source: Based on Warc (2010); www.gmanews.tv/story/139656; www.showbizcafe.com/en/news/

Question

In your opinion, why has video advertising become so popular?

Task

Find three video ads that you like, and write a few notes explaining why you like them.

The source is an integral part of the communication process, not just the generator of detached messages. Patzer (1983) determined that the physical attractiveness of the communicator, particularly if it is the source, contributes significantly to the effectiveness of persuasive communications.

This observation can be related to the use by organisations of spokespersons and celebrities to endorse products. Spokespersons can be better facilitators of the communication process if they are able to convey conviction, if they are easily associated with the object of the message, if they have credible expertise and if they are attractive to the receiver, in the wider sense of the word.

This legitimate authority is developed in many television advertisements by the use of the 'white coat', or product-specific clothing, as a symbol of expertise. By dressing the spokesperson in a white coat, they are immediately perceived as a credible source of information ('they know what they are talking about'), and so are much more likely to be believed.

The use of chefs to support food-related brands is a well-established practice. Jamie Oliver was used to support Sainsbury's for over 10 years. He appeared in over 100 different Sainsbury's ads, offering endorsements that often resulted in huge short-term sales bursts for the products featured. He once suggested grating nutmeg over spaghetti bolognese, and that led to the supermarket selling nine tonnes, or two years' worth, of the spice immediately following the ad.

Signal

Once encoded, the message must be put into a form that is capable of transmission. It may be oral or written, verbal or non-verbal, in a symbolic form or as a sign. Whatever the format chosen, the source must be sure that what is being put into the message is capable of transmission and being decoded by the receiver.

The channel is the means by which the message is transmitted from the source to the receiver. The channel may be personal or non-personal. The former involves face-to-face contact and word-of-mouth communications, which can be extremely influential. Non-personal channels are characterised by mass-media advertising, which can reach large audiences.

Decoding/receiver

Decoding is the process of transforming and interpreting a message into thought. This process is influenced by the receiver's realm of understanding, which encompasses the experiences, perceptions, attitudes and values of both the source and the receiver. The more the receiver understands about the source and the greater their experience in decoding the source's messages, the more able the receiver will be to decode the message successfully.

Feedback/response

The set of reactions a receiver has after seeing, hearing or reading the message is known as the response. These reactions may vary from the extreme of clicking a button, dialling an enquiry telephone number, returning a coupon or even buying the product, to storing information in long-term memory for future use. Feedback is that part of the response that is sent back to the sender, and it is essential for successful communication. The need to understand not just whether the message has been received but also which message has been received is vital. For example, the receiver may have decoded the message incorrectly and a completely different set of responses may have been elicited. If a suitable feedback system is not in place then the source will be unaware that the communication has been unsuccessful and is liable to continue wasting resources. This represents inefficient and ineffective marketing communications.

The evaluation of feedback is vital if sound communications are to be developed. Only through evaluation can the success of any communication be judged. Feedback through personal selling can be instantaneous, through overt means such as questioning, raising objections or signing an order form. Other means, such as the use of gestures and body language, are less overt, and the decoding of the feedback needs to be accurate if an appropriate response is to be given. For the advertiser, the process is much more vague and prone to misinterpretation and error.

Feedback through mass-media channels is generally much more difficult to obtain, mainly because of the inherent time delay involved in the feedback process. There are some exceptions, such as the overnight ratings provided by the Broadcasters' Audience Research Board to the television contractors, but as a rule feedback is normally delayed and not as fast.

Noise

A complicating factor, which may influence the quality of the reception and the feedback, is noise. According to Mallen (1977), noise is 'the omission and distortion of information', and there will always be some noise present in all communications. Management's role is to ensure that levels of noise are minimised, wherever it is able to exert influence.

Noise occurs when a receiver is prevented from receiving all or part of a message in full. This may be because of either cognitive or physical factors. For example, a cognitive factor may be that the encoding of the message was inappropriate, thereby making it difficult for the receiver to decode the message. In this circumstance it is said that the realms of understanding of the source and the receiver were not matched. Another reason noise may enter the system is that the receiver may have been physically prevented from decoding the message accurately because the receiver was distracted. Examples of distraction are that the telephone rang, or someone in the room asked a question or coughed. A further reason could be that competing messages screened out the targeted message.

Realms of understanding

The concept of the 'realm of understanding' is an important element in the communication process. This is because successful communications are more likely to be achieved if the source and the receiver understand each other. This understanding concerns attitudes, perceptions, behaviour and experience: the values of both parties to the communication process. Therefore, effective communication is more likely when there is some common ground, a realm of understanding between the source and receiver.

Scholars' paper 2.1 **Innovation diffusion through communication**

Peres, R., Muller, E., and Mahajan, V. (2010) Innovation diffusion and new product growth models: a critical review and research directions, *International Journal of Research in Marketing*, 27, 91–106

Rather than direct you to the seminal papers by Rogers (1962, 1983) on adoption and diffusion, this paper provides a more contemporary perspective on the ideas about diffusion in an age of social networks. Here the authors provide an interesting review of the literature and propose a new definition of the diffusion of innovations. They see it as 'the process of the market penetration of new products and services that is driven by social influences, which include all interdependencies among consumers that affect various market players with or without their explicit knowledge'.

Some organisations, especially those in the private sector, spend a huge amount of money researching their target markets and testing their advertisements to ensure that their messages can be decoded and understood by the target audience. The more that organisations understand their receivers, the more confident they become in constructing and transmitting messages to them. Repetition and learning, as we shall see later, are important elements in advertising. Learning is a function of knowledge and the more we know, the more likely we are to understand.

Factors that influence the communication process

The linear, sequential interpretation of the communication process fails to represent all forms of communication accurately. It was developed at a time when broadcast media dominated commercial communication and can be argued to no longer provide an accurate representation of contemporary communication processes. Issues concerning media and audience fragmentation, the need to consider social and relational dimensions of communication and the impact of interactive communication have reduced the overall applicability of the linear model.

However, there are two particular influences on the communication process that need to be considered. First, the media used to convey information, and second, the influence of people on the communication process. These are considered in turn.

The influence of the media

The dialogue that advertising seeks to generate with audiences is partially constrained by an inherent time delay based on the speed at which responses are generated by the participants in the communication process. Technological advances now allow participants to conduct marketing communication-based 'conversations' at electronic speeds. The essence of this speed attribute is that it allows for real-time interactively based communications, where enquiries are responded to more or less instantly.

Digital-based technologies and the internet in particular provide an opportunity for interaction and dialogue with customers. With traditional media the tendency is for monologue or at best delayed and inferred dialogue. One of the first points to be made about these new, media-based communications is that the context within which marketing communications occur is redefined. Traditionally, dialogue occurs in a (relatively) familiar context, which is driven by providers who deliberately present their messages through a variety of communication devices into the environments that they expect their audiences may well pass or recognise. Providers implant their messages into the various environments of their targets. Yuan et al. (1998) refer to advertising messages being 'unbundled', such as direct marketing, which has no other content, or 'bundled' and embedded with other news content such as television, radio and web pages with banner ads. Perhaps more pertinently, they refer to direct and indirect online advertising. Direct advertising is concerned with advertising messages delivered to the customer (email) while indirect advertising is concerned with messages that are made available for a customer to access at their leisure (websites).

Digital media-based communications tend to make providers relatively passive. Their messages are presented in an environment that requires targets to use specific equipment to actively search them out. The roles are reversed, so that the drivers in the new context are active information seekers, represented by a target audience (members of the public and other information providers such as organisations), not just the information-providing organisations.

The influence of people

The traditional view of communication holds that the process consists essentially of one step. Information is directed and shot at prospective audiences, rather like a bullet is propelled from a gun. The decision of each member of the audience to act on the message or not is the result of a passive role or participation in the process. Organisations can communicate with different target audiences simply by varying the message and the type and frequency of channels used.

The core model has been criticised for its oversimplification, and it certainly ignores the effect of personal influences on the communication process and potential for information deviance. To accommodate these influences two further models are introduced, the influencer model and the interactional model of communication.

The influencer model of communication

The influencer model depicts information flowing via media channels to particular types of people (opinion leaders and opinion formers) to whom other members of the audience refer for information and guidance. Through interpersonal networks, **opinion leaders** not only reach members of the target audience who may not have been exposed to the message, but may reinforce the impact of the message for those members who did receive the message (see Figure 2.2). For example, feedback and comments from travellers on Tripadvisor.com assist others when making travel plans, and constitute opinion leadership. However, editors of travel sections in the Sunday press and television presenters of travel programmes fulfil the role of opinion formers and can influence the decision of prospective travellers through their formalised knowledge.

Sometimes referred to as the two-step model, this approach indicates that the mass media do not have a direct and all-powerful effect over their audiences. If the primary function of the mass media is to provide information, then personal influences are necessary to be persuasive and to exert direct influence on members of the target audience.

The influencer approach can be developed whereby communication involves interaction among all parties to the communication process (see Figure 2.3). This interpretation closely resembles the network of participants who are often involved in the communication process.

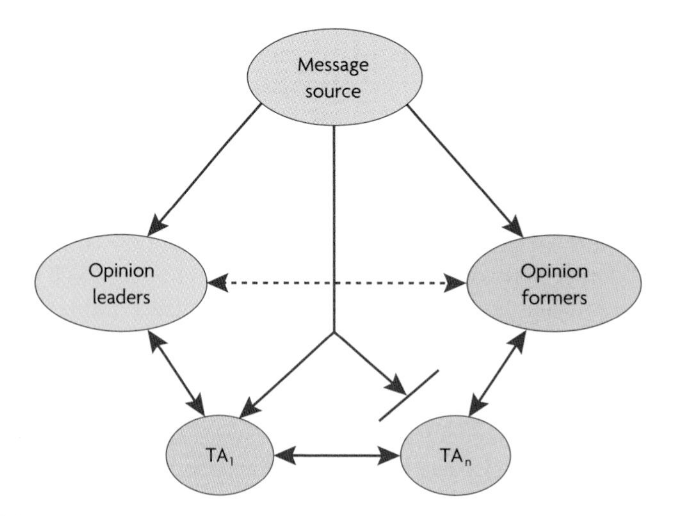

Figure 2.2 The influencer model of communication
Source: Fill (2009)

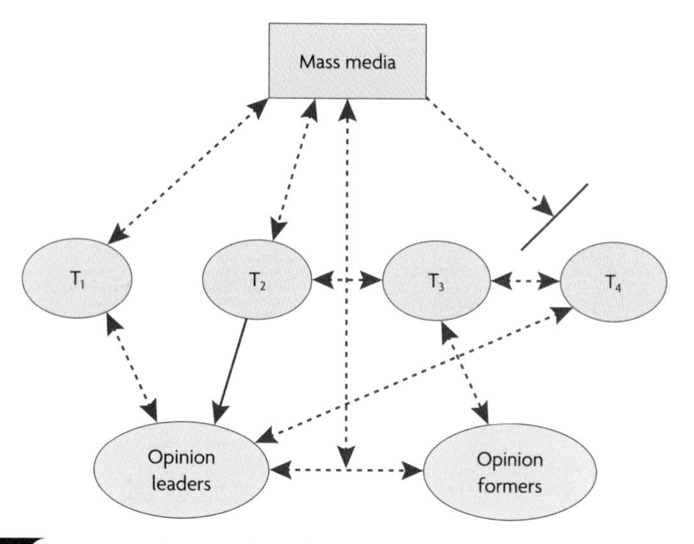

Figure 2.3 Multi-step variation of the Influencer model of communication
Source: Fill (2009)

ViewPoint 2.2 Opinion leadership in action

Understanding the power of communication through opinion leaders and formers is one thing; reaching them is another.

The recent launch and growth of Crabbie' s Alcoholic Ginger Beer involved a campaign designed to build links with food. The campaign featured a three-week national TV advertising programme, supported by trade press advertising, video on demand, and a digital programme. This link was assisted by the appointment of Michelin-starred celebrity chef Atul Kochhar. As ginger is an Asian as well as a West Indian spice, Atul Kochhar created four exclusive Indian recipes that use ginger to give a British twist to authentic Indian cuisine. Using Atul Kochhar gave the campaign message credibility and enabled the product to reach a wide audience, including exposure through the BBC Good Food Show in Birmingham and London.

QVEST is an international fashion magazine, published in Germany every three months. The magazine content is focused around fashion, design, interior, beauty, automotive, jewellery, accessories, art and culture. It collaborates with authors, photographers, stylists and artists in key cities around the world. The goal is to seek out bold, innovative people, to present new, unseen images and fresh, relevant ideas.

What is critical about QVEST is their readership. The company claim that advertising in QVEST, whether offline or online, enables clients to reach people that traditional fashion magazines don't: for example, creatives, lifestylists and opinion leaders, all of whom prefer to associate themselves with unusual and special people, material, products and objects. What characterises readers is that they set trends: they are role models and communicators who have a strong influence on others.

Effective opinion leadership is partly based on credibility, and to help substantiate this with its clients, QVEST lists the awards it has won as part of its advertising rate card.

Source: Based on www.qvest.de/wpcontent/uploads/mediadaten/20110527_QVEST_Mediadaten-ENG.pdf

Question

Which one of these two examples demonstrates the use of opinion formers?

Task

Consider who you might choose to be an opinion former for a brand of running shoe, cosmetics and tablet, and give reasons for your choice.

PHOTOS BY BRUNO BISANG, HENRIK BÜLOW, SIMON PROCTER, RANKIN, UTE BEHREND, RYAN MICHAEL KELLY, IMMO KLINK, MISCHA KUBALL, PER ZENNSTRÖM, RALPH BAIKER, KOURTNEY ROY, JACQUELINE HASSINK, MARINA KLOESS, JÜRGEN ALTMANN

QVEST

ART & FASHION EDITION

RANKIN JUST SHOT HIS WIFE
MEL RAMOS - STILL ALIVE
FASHION MONEY FOR ART
TODAY YOU GET FRIENDS
OOOPS ART
MISCHA KUBALL'S MIGRANT MODELS
WHAT JULIAN SCHNABEL IS INTERESTED IN
AND FOR SURE A LOT OF FASHION

POLAROIDS

OF THE LAST 30 YEARS WORK WITH NAOMI CAMPBELL, CARLA BRUNI, CLAUDIA SCHIFFER, MONICA BELLUCCI, TYRA BANKS FROM THE PRIVATE ARCHIVE OF

BRUNO BISANG

Exhibit 2.2 Cover of QVEST
Source: Qvest

The interactional model of communication

The models and frameworks used to explain the communication process so far should be considered as a simplification of reality and not a true reflection of communication in practice. The linear model is unidirectional, and it suggests that the receiver plays a passive role in the process. The influencer model attempts to account for an individual's participation in the communication process. These models emphasise individual behaviour but exclude any social behaviour implicit in the process.

The interactional model of communication attempts to assimilate the variety of influences acting upon the communication process. These include the responses people give to communications received from other people and machines. Increasingly communication is characterised by attributing meaning to messages that are shared, updated and a response to other messages. These 'conversations' can be termed interactional and are an integral part of society. Figure 2.4 depicts the complexity associated with this form of communication.

Interaction is about actions that lead to a response. The development of direct marketing helped make significant inroads in the transition from what is essentially one-way to two-way and then interactive-based communication. Digital technology has further enabled this interaction process. However, interaction alone is not a sufficient goal simply because the content of the interaction could be about a radical disagreement of views, an exchange of opinion or a social encounter.

Ballantyne (2004) refers to two-way communication with audiences in two ways. First, as a 'with' experience, as manifest in face-to-face encounters and contact centres. He also distinguishes a higher order of two-way communication based on communication 'between' parties. It is this latter stage that embodies true dialogue where trust, listening and adaptive behaviour are typical. These are represented in Table 2.2.

A key question emerges: what is interaction and what are its key characteristics? If we can understand the dynamics and dimensions of interactivity then it should be possible to develop more effective marketing communications. In the context of advertising, interactivity can be

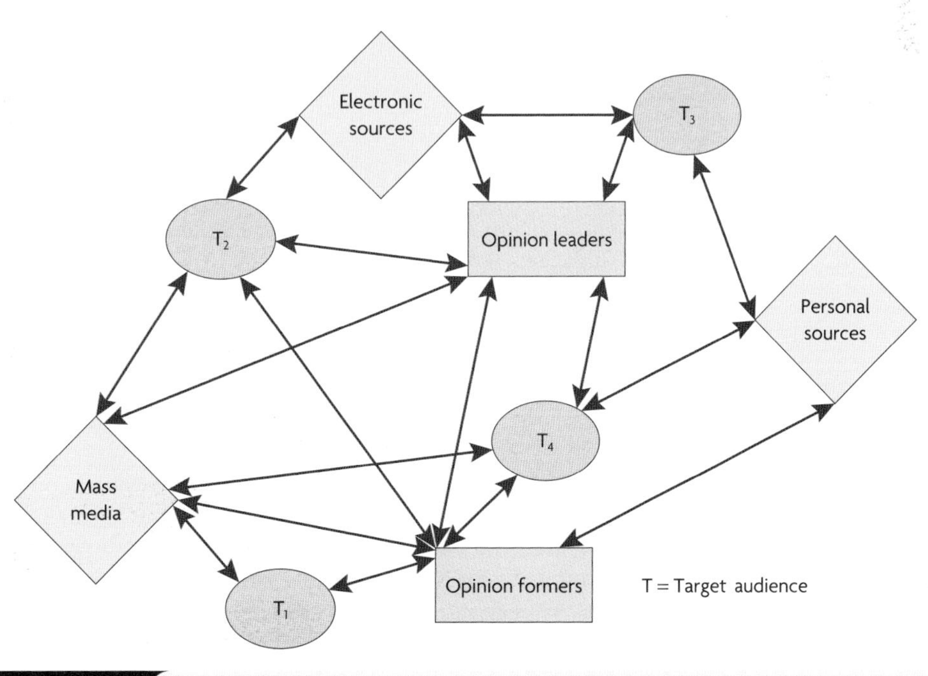

Figure 2.4 The interactional model of communication
Source: Fill (2009)

Table 2.2 Communication matrix

Direction	Mass markets	Portfolio/mass-customised	Networks
One-way planned communications designed to inform and persuade Medium to high wastage	Communication 'to' Planned persuasive messages aimed at securing brand awareness and loyalty; e.g. communication of USPs and ESPs	Communication 'for' Planned persuasive messages with augmented offerings for target markets; e.g. communicating targeted life cycle products, guarantees, loyalty programmes	
Two-way formal and informal with a view to listening and learning Minimal wastage		Communication 'with' Integrated mix of planned and interactively shared knowledge; e.g. face to face, direct (database), contact centres, interactive B2B internet portals	Communication 'between' Dialogue between participants based on trust, learning and adaptation with co-created outcomes; e.g. key account liaison, expansion of communities, staff teamwork

Source: Ballantyne (2004)

considered from one of two perspectives. One is the technology, tools and features (e.g. multimedia, www, online gaming) that provide for interaction. The second, according to Johnson et al. (2006), is the added value that interactivity is perceived to bring to the communication process.

Arising out of interaction is dialogue. This occurs through mutual understanding and a reasoning approach to interactions, one based on listening and adaptive behaviour. Dialogue is concerned with the development of knowledge that is specific to the relationship of the parties involved. Ballantyne refers to this as 'learning together' (Ballantyne 2004: 119).

The adoption of dialogue as the basis for communication changes an organisation's perspective of its audiences. Being willing and able to enter into a dialogue indicates that there is a new emphasis on the relationships organisations hold with their stakeholders.

Dialogue requires interaction as a precursor. In other words, for dialogue to occur there must first be interaction and it is the development and depth of the interaction that lead to meaningful dialogue.

The influencer model is important because it demonstrates the importance of people in the communication process. However, successful communication is often determined by the level of interactivity the message encourages. Until the development of digital technologies, advertising messages can be considered to be essentially one-way communication. Messages are communicated either directly to end-user audiences or indirectly, through various influencers. However, advertising's capacity to interact with audiences increased considerably with digital technology, and with it an emphasis on direct and personalised communication. Cheng et al. (2009) identify four forms of interactive digital advertising: website, email, SMS, and MMS-type advertising. Each form appeals to different audiences but they each offer a measure of consumer control in that individuals can determine what they see on their screens and when they see it. They also suggest that attitudes towards interactive digital advertising can be considered as 'informative', 'entertaining' and 'irritating'. This study and others, such as Chung and Ahn (2007), indicate that individuals display different attitudinal and behavioural responses to different types of interactive advertising, based partly on their personality.

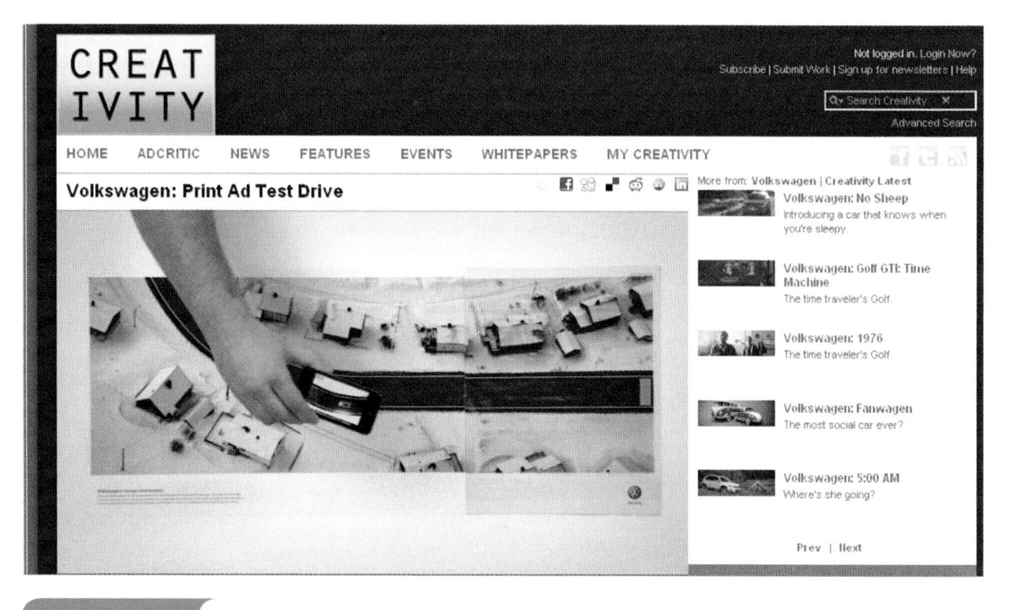

Exhibit 2.3 Volkswagen use interactive advertising

This is a prototype of a mobile ad which uses augmented reality technology. Following a brief description of the Volkswagen car, users place their smartphone over the printed ad and then manoeuvre the car and test its different functions.

Source: Volkswagen Group

Other types of communication

Each of the communication models, theories and concepts presented so far can be used to interpret how advertising might communicate. In addition to these there are other richer models of communication, which consider not only social behaviour but also the context within which behaviour occurs. Communication events, just as advertising, always occur within a context (Littlejohn 1992) or particular set of circumstances, which not only influence the form of the communication but also the nature and the way the communication is received, interpreted and acted upon. There are a huge number of variables that can influence the context, including the disposition of the people involved, the physical environment, the nature of the issue, the history and associated culture, the goals of the participants and the expected repercussions of the dialogue itself. Littlejohn identifies four main contextual levels: interpersonal, group, organisational and mass communication. These levels form part of a hierarchy whereby higher levels incorporate the lower levels but 'add something new of their own'.

The relational approach means that communication events are linked together in an organised manner, one where the events are 'punctuated' by interventions from one or more of the participants. These interventions occur whenever the participants attempt cooperation or if conflict arises.

In addition to the relational dimension, communication can also be understood in terms of formal and informal networks. The regular use of these patterned flows leads to the development of communication networks which have been categorised as prescribed and emergent (Weick 1987). Prescribed networks are formalised patterns of communication, very often established by senior management within an organisation or by organisational representatives when interorganisational communications are considered. It follows that emergent networks are informal and emerge as a response to the social and task-oriented needs of the participants.

The relational and network approaches to communication are both interesting and relevant and provide greater insight than the linear and influencer models. Indeed, it can be said very confidently that the linear or one-way model of communication fails to accommodate the various complexities associated with communication. As discussed earlier, the model is too simplistic and fails to represent many aspects of communication events. Although the linear model is essentially sequential rather than interactional, it is still used and practised by many organisations. Varey (2002) refers to this as the 'informational' model of communication and as both Grunig (1992) and Ballantyne (2004) suggest it is just one of a number of ways in which communication can work. Communication in a collaborative context, where interaction and dialogue are essential factors, has been referred to by Varey as 'transformational' communication.

Range of communication forms

From this it is possible to determine that there are a number of models and interpretations about the way communication works. In some ways they all have a role to play, simply because there is no single form of communication that applies to all situations. The range of communication forms is depicted in Figure 2.5.

No single model of communication can be used to interpret how advertising works simply because advertising is used at a number of different levels and in different contexts. The highly interactive and personalised nature of digital interactive advertising contrasts vividly with the way a static Sachin Tendulkar billboard in Mumbai or a print ad in the *Asia Times* communicates with passers-by and readers respectively. We have introduced these different forms of communications at this stage as reference will be made to them in the rest of the book.

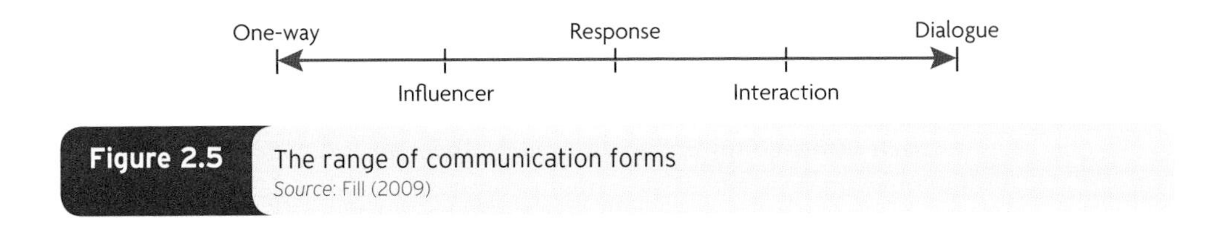

Figure 2.5 The range of communication forms
Source: Fill (2009)

Source characteristics

Advertising messages, regardless of the medium used to deliver them, are perceived in many different ways and they are influenced by a variety of factors. However, a critical determinant concerns the characteristics that are attributed to the source of an ad. Now although McCracken (1989: 311) states that he sees 'mysteries everywhere' in the source-effect literature, indicating a lack of agreement about what constitutes a key source attribute, he, along with Hovland and Weiss (1951) and Kelman (1961) among others, have all found that source characteristics can influence attitudes and that source credibility and attractiveness are two key characteristics.

Credibility consists of three core elements: expertise, motivation and trustworthiness. Credibility theory (Hovland and Weiss, 1951) holds that if a messenger is perceived to be an expert or to be trustworthy, the message conveyed by the messenger is more likely to be perceived as credible. Kyung et al. (2011) cite the work of Hovland, Janis and Kelley (1953) who refer to 'the extent to which a communicator is perceived to be a source of valid assertions and the degree of confidence in the communicator's intent to communicate the assertions he or she considers most valid'. Source credibility is an important concept in advertising (Dholakia and Sternthal 1977; Sternthal, Dholakia and Leavitt 1978), witnessed by the array of different spokespersons used to communicate messages about a wide range of products and services.

Scholars' paper 2.2 **Making sure the source is credible**

Kelman, H. C. (1961) Process of opinion change, *Public Opinion Quarterly*, 25 (Spring), 57-78

Kelman suggested that successful communications emanate from sources that are credible, attractive and powerful. Subsequently, there has been much research into the impact and effect of source credibility in different situations and on different subjects. The prevailing view remains that people think more about messages from sources that they consider to be highly credible than they do about those from low-credibility sources.

The physical attractiveness of a messenger is also an important source characteristic. The source-attractiveness model holds that the effectiveness of a message is influenced by the receiver's perception of the similarity, likeability, attractiveness and familiarity of the source (McGuire 1985). Messengers perceived to be physically attractive lead to two main outcomes. The first is that more attention is given to such advertisements than to advertisements where source attractiveness is low. Second, these advertisements are evaluated more positively (Baker and Churchill 1977). It is not surprising therefore that if advertising needs the attention of the target audience and to build positive attitudes, then agencies and clients should give a great deal of care and consideration to the selection of the messenger.

However, as Kang and Herr (2006) report, there is great diversity in the literature on source effects, partly due to the diversity of source cues. This might be due to the many other dimensions and also because sources vary in expertise, trustworthiness and attractiveness.

Establishing credibility

Credibility can be established in a number of ways. One simple approach is to list or display the key attributes of the organisation or the product and then signal trustworthiness through the use of third-party endorsements and the comments of satisfied users.

A more complex approach is to use referrals, suggestions and association. Trustworthiness and expertise are the two principal elements of source credibility. One way of developing trust is to use spokespersons to speak on behalf of the sponsor of an advertisement and in effect provide a testimonial for the product in question. Credibility, therefore, can be established by the initiator of the advertisement or by a spokesperson used by the initiator to convey the message.

Effectively, consumers trade off the validity of claims made by brands against the perceived trustworthiness (and expertise) of the individuals or organisations who deliver the message. The result is that a claim may have reduced impact if either of these two components is doubtful or not capable of verification but, if repeated enough times, will enable audiences to accept that the products are very effective and of sufficiently high performance for them to try.

Credibility established by the initiator

The credibility of the organisation initiating the communication process is important. An organisation should seek to enhance its reputation with its various stakeholders at every opportunity. However, organisational credibility is derived from the image, which in turn is a composite of many perceptions. Past decisions, current strategy and performance indicators, the level of perceived service and the type of performance network members (e.g. high-quality retail outlets) all influence the perception of an organisation and the level of credibility that follows.

One very important factor that influences credibility is branding. Private and family brands in particular allow initiators to develop and launch new products more easily than those who do not have such brand strength. Brand extensions have been launched with the credibility of the product firmly grounded in the strength of the parent brand name. For example, Kalashnikov, manufacturers of the well-known AK-47 rifle, extended into the alcohol market using the brand Kalashnikov Vodka. Consumers recognise the name and advertising helps them make associations that reduce their perceived risk and in doing so provide a platform to try the new product.

The need to establish high levels of credibility also allows organisations to divert advertising spend away from a focus on brands to one that focuses on the organisation. Corporate advertising seeks to adjust organisation image and to build reputation.

Credibility established by a spokesperson

People who deliver the message are often regarded as the source, when in reality they are only the messenger. These people carry the message and represent the true source or initiator of the message (e.g. manufacturer or retailer). Consequently, the testimonial they transmit must be credible. There are four main types of spokesperson: the expert, the celebrity, the chief executive officer and the consumer.

The expert has been used many times and was particularly popular when television advertising first established itself in the 1950s and 1960s. Experts can be recognised quickly because they either wear white coats and round glasses or dress and act like 'mad professors'. Through the use of symbolism, stereotypes and identification, these characters (and indeed others) can be established very quickly in the minds of receivers and a frame of reference generated that does not question the authenticity of the message being transmitted by such a person. Experts can also be users of products, for example professional photographers endorsing cameras, secretaries endorsing word processors and professional golfers endorsing golf equipment.

ViewPoint 2.3 Smoking seeks credibility

The notion that, to be effective, advertising, should be considered credible is not new or surprising. However, it is interesting to consider the different ways in which trust and expertise have been conveyed by advertisers over the years.

The tobacco industry has been reliant on establishing credibility through advertising for a long time, until it was banned. It did this through images ranging from the depiction of lonely men trusting a cigarette to bring comfort (Strand) and cowboys demonstrating ruggedness and their expert choice of cigarette (Marlboro) to the use of sport star Joe DiMaggio's implied trust, and, incredibly, doctors!

During the period 1920 to 1950 tobacco companies used the medical profession to provide the credibility that the industry lacked. There are numerous examples of tobacco companies using advertising campaigns that co-opted medical authorities into endorsing smoking. For example, Camel claimed that 'More doctors smoke Camels than any other cigarette.' Whether this statistic was true is not the point. It is the depiction of medical professionals, experts symbolised through their white coats, to suggest that smoking was socially acceptable, and even good for you, that is deemed to be shocking today.

Cugelman writes: 'Through visual and written arguments, the [Camel] ad makes a number of appeals directly to audiences' trust and credibility judgements. Visually, the background is built from a collage of images portraying the truth-seeking and independent nationwide survey that proves their claim, that more doctors smoke Camels. Secondly, the primary image shows a healthy-looking older doctor who's enjoying a puff of smoke while the body copy informs readers that he is just one of many doctors across the country who enjoy smoking, implying that the medical community endorses smoking.'

Other co-opted sources included smoking scientists, spacemen, dentists, nurses, celebrities, clergy, and even Santa Claus.

Source: Cugelman (2011); http://www.cugelman.com/research/reflections-on-source-credibility-and-online-campaigns.htm; http://lane.stanford.edu/tobacco/index.html

Question

How else might expertise be conveyed through advertising?

Task

You have been asked to launch a new electrical product for the consumer market. How would you use advertising to convey credibility?

Exhibit 2.4 Strand ad
Source: Image courtesy of The Advertising Archives

Entertainment and sporting celebrities are being used increasingly (Dix et al. 2010) to provide credibility for a range of high-involvement products (e.g. Nicole Kidman for Omega watches and the fragrance Chanel No 5) and low-involvement product decisions (e.g. Indian cricket captain Mahendra Singh Dhoni whose endorsements include Reebok, Aircel, Godrej and TVS). They also serve to grab the attention of people in markets where motivation to decide between competitive products may be low. Agrawal and Kamakura (1995) found that the use of celebrities can help consumers remember the message of the advertisement and the brand name the celebrity is endorsing and help create the brand's personality. The celebrity enables the message to stand out among the clutter and noise that typify many markets. It is also hoped that the celebrity and/or the voice-over will become a peripheral cue in the decision-making process: Sienna Miller for Boss Orange, and Alesha Dixon for Weight Watchers.

There are some potential problems that advertisers need to be aware of when considering the use of celebrities. First, does the celebrity fit the image of the brand and will the celebrity be acceptable to the target audience? Consideration also needs to be given to the longer-term relationship between the celebrity and the brand. Should the lifestyle of the celebrity change, what impact will this change have on the target audience and their attitude towards the brand?

The second problem concerns the impact that the celebrity makes relative to the brand. There is a danger that those receiving the message remember the celebrity but not the brand that is the focus of the advertising spend. The *celebrity* becomes the hero, rather than the product being advertised. Loveless (2007) reports on the financial services company First Plus who used celebrity mathematician Carol Vorderman to endorse their loan products. Some saw a discontinuity with this celebrity's values, and the possibility that the company she was endorsing might make some people worse off was highlighted. In these situations the endorser can overshadow the product to the extent that consumers might have trouble recalling the brand.

Finally, White et al. (2009) used meaning transfer theory to investigate consumer perceptions when a celebrity endorser attracts negative information or news comment. Their research found that negative messages about a celebrity endorser can impact on a brand. However, negative comments about a brand tend not to be transferred to an endorser.

Some *CEOs* have relished the chance to sell their own products and there have been some notable business people who have 'fronted' their organisation. Steve Jobs was a high-profile endorser of Apple to the extent that share value fell when he took time off for illness. Here, the CEO openly promotes his company. This form of testimonial is popular when the image of the CEO is positive and the photogenic and on-screen characteristics provide for enhanced credibility.

When using *consumers* as the spokespersons to endorse products, the audience is being asked to identify with a 'typical consumer'. The identification of similar lifestyles, interests and opinions allows for better reception and understanding of the message. Consumers are often depicted testing similar products, such as margarine and butter. The Pepsi Challenge required consumers to choose Pepsi over Coca-Cola through blind taste tests. By showing someone using the product, someone who is similar to the receiver, the source is perceived as credible and the potential for successful influence is considerably enhanced.

The use of spokespersons can be an important factor when establishing source credibility. Kyung et al. (2011) found that spokespersons perceived to be sincere, competent, sophisticated and rugged tend to have a positive influence on the level of source expertise. To assist source attractiveness, excitement, competence, sophistication and ruggedness were considered influential and competence was closely associated with perceived source trustworthiness.

Whatever the right personality traits, advertising practitioners know intuitively and through experience that selecting the right spokesperson can be a critical factor when developing a campaign.

Cognitive processing

For a long time research, theories and measurement techniques concerning advertising have all been largely based on information or cognitive processing. Indeed, information processing is considered by many to be the paramount framework through which it is possible to interpret how people make sense of and give meaning to ads.

The information-processing school believe that the cognitive interpretation is a valid approach to understanding how information is used. Cognitive processing tries to determine 'how external information is transformed into meanings or patterns of thought and how these meanings are combined to form judgements' (Olsen and Peter 1987).

By assessing the thoughts, that is the cognitive processes, that occur to people as they read, view or hear an ad message, an understanding of their interpretation can be useful in campaign development and evaluation (Greenwald 1968; Wright 1973). These thoughts are usually measured by asking people to write down or verbally report the thoughts they have in response to such a message. Thoughts are believed to be a reflection of the cognitive processes or responses that receivers experience and they help shape or reject a communication.

Understanding what people think and feel about ads can help shape not just content but also placement. For example, information processing can be considered as either 'item-specific' processing or 'relational' processing. Sar et al. (2010) cite Hunt and Einstein (1981) when explaining what these mean. Item-specific processing concentrates on either the distinctiveness or the specific attributes of an object/ad. Relational processing refers to the elaboration of information regarding the categories to which an object/ad might be associated. Sar and colleagues consider how mood might influence advertising messages, and find that negative moods tend to generate item-specific processing, whereas positive moods support relational processing. Their research suggests that the placement of ads, the media-planning activity, should be influenced by the type of mood the programme induces and the level of associated competitive ad clutter. So, if the mood of the programme in which an ad is to be placed is negative and the level of competitive ad clutter is high, or if the programme induces a positive mood and is paired with a low level of competitive ad clutter, both ad recall and evaluation will be high.

At a general level researchers have identified three broad types of cognitive response and have determined how these relate to attitudes and intentions. Figure 2.6 shows these three types of response, but readers should appreciate that these types are not discrete; they overlap each other and blend together, often invisibly.

Product message thoughts

These are thoughts that are directed to the product or the ad itself. Much attention has been focused on the thoughts that are related to the message content. Two particular types of response have been considered: counterarguments and support arguments.

A counterargument occurs when the message receiver disagrees with the content of a message. So an ad for a bathroom cleaner that claims to remove all known germs may get the reaction 'I don't believe it, nothing is that good', a counterargument. A support argument occurs when the receiver agrees with the message and says 'That looks useful, I will get some and try it', a support argument.

In most situations, ads should encourage the generation of support arguments.

Source-oriented thoughts

A further set of cognitive responses is aimed at the source of the ad. This concept is closely allied to that of source credibility, where, if the source of the message is seen as annoying or

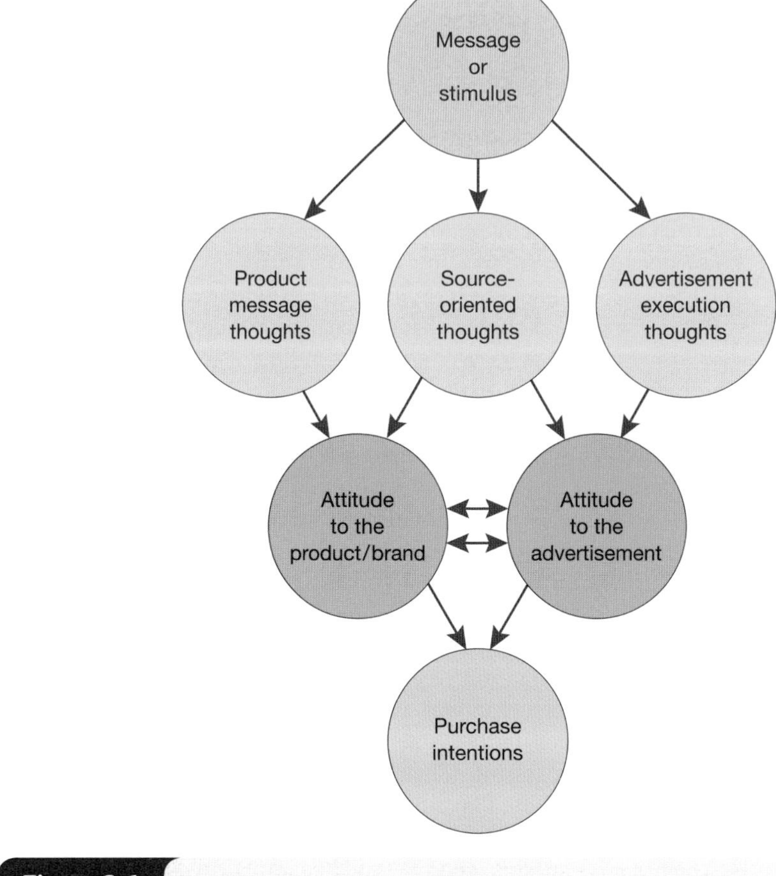

Figure 2.6 Cognitive processing model
Source: Fill (2009)

distrustful, there is a lower probability of message acceptance. Such a situation is referred to as source derogation; the converse is a source bolster. Those responsible for communications should ensure, during the planning stage, that receivers experience bolster effects to improve the likelihood of message acceptance.

Ad execution thoughts

This relates to the thoughts an individual may have about the overall design and impact of the ad. Many of the thoughts that receivers have are not always product related but are emotionally related towards the ad itself. Understanding these feelings and emotions is important because of their impact upon attitudes towards the message, most often an advertisement, and the offering.

Attitudes towards the message

It is clear that people make judgements about the quality of advertisements and the creativity, tone and style in which an ad (or website, promotion or direct-mail piece) has been executed. As a result of their experiences, perception and degree to which they like an advertisement, they form an attitude towards the ad (message) itself. From this base an important stream of thought has developed about cognitive processing. Lutz's work led to the attitude-toward-the-ad concept which has become an important foundation for much of the related marketing

Scholars' paper 2.3 So, why do I need your attention?

Heath, R. and Feldwick, P. (2008) 50 years using the wrong model of TV advertising, *International Journal of Market Research*, 50, 1, 29-59

For several years Heath and Feldwick have challenged the dominance and pervasiveness of the information-processing approach and believe that attention is not necessary for ads to be effective. Students will find this paper helpful because it sets out the arguments and history associated with information processing. The authors argue that people can be influenced by advertising, even when they cannot recall ads. Decision making is founded on emotions triggered through associations made at subconscious levels.

communications literature. As Goldsmith and Lafferty (2002: 319) argue, there is a substantial amount of research that clearly indicates that advertising that promotes a 'positive emotional response of liking an ad is positively related to subsequent brand-related cognitions (knowledge), brand attitudes and purchase intentions'. Chen and Wells (1999) also show that the attitude-toward-the-ad concept applies equally well with digital media and online communications. They refer to an attitude-toward-the-site concept and similar ideas developed by Bruner and Kumar (2000), and conclude that the more a website is liked, the more attitudes improve to the brand and purchase intentions.

It seems highly reasonable, therefore, to conclude that attitudes-toward-the-message (and delivery technique) impact on brand attitudes, which in turn influence consumers' propensity to purchase. It is also known that an increasing proportion of advertisements attempt to appeal to feelings and emotions. Not only are these types of ad more effective (Binet and Field 2007), but also many researchers believe that attitudes towards both the advertisement and the brand should be encouraged. This is because they are positively correlated with purchase intention and can accelerate word-of-mouth communication.

Similarly, time and effort are allocated to the design of sales promotion instruments, and increasing attention is given to the design of packaging in terms of a pack's communication effectiveness. Similar care is given to the wording of advertorials and press releases. Perhaps above all else, more and more effort is being made to research and develop websites with the goal of designing them so that they are strategically compatible, user friendly and functional, or to put it another way, liked. However, although there are arguments that any model developed to explain how advertising works should be based around the attitude-toward-the-ad concept, a more recent emphasis indicates that it is the development of the attitude-toward-the-brand that is key to effective communication.

Attitudes

Attitudes are predispositions, shaped through experience, to respond in an anticipated way to an object or situation. Attitudes are learned through past experiences and serve as a link between thoughts and behaviour. These experiences may relate to a product, to the messages transmitted by different members of a channel network (normally mass-media communications) and to the information supplied by opinion leaders, formers and followers.

Attitudes tend to be consistent within each individual: they are clustered and very often interrelated. This categorisation leads to the formation of stereotypes, which is extremely useful for advertisers and the design of messages. Stereotyping allows for the transmission of a lot of information in a short time period (30 seconds) without impeding learning or the focal part of the message.

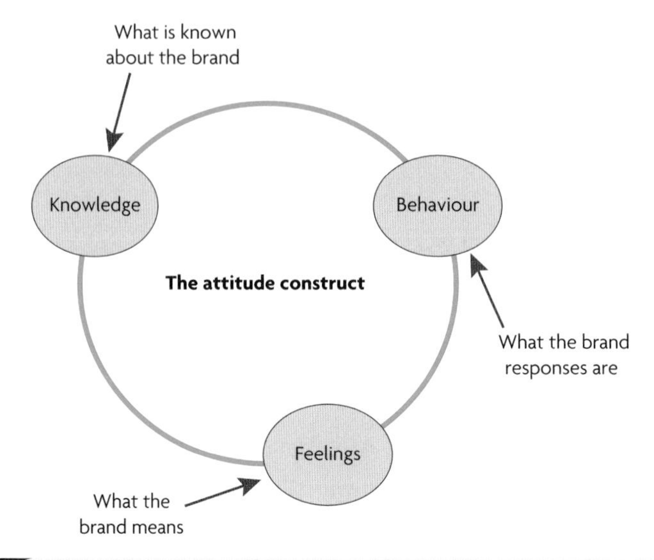

Figure 2.7 The three elements of the attitude construct
Source: Fill (2009)

Attitude components

Attitudes are hypothetical constructs, and classical psychological theory considers attitudes to consist of three components. These are cognitive, affective and conative, as set out in Figure 2.7.

Cognitive component (learn)

This component refers to the level of knowledge and beliefs held by individuals about a product and/or the beliefs about specific attributes of the offering. This represents the learning aspect of attitude formation. Advertising is used a great deal to create attention and awareness, to provide information, to educate audiences about how to use the product or behave, and to help audiences learn and understand the features and benefits a particular product/service offers.

Affective component (feel)

By referring to the feelings held about a product, good, bad, pleasant or unpleasant, an evaluation is made of the object. This is the component that is concerned with feelings, sentiments, moods and emotions about an object. Advertising is used to influence emotions and induce feelings, by making associations, about a brand. It is thought that brand preference is partly driven by the associations advertising helps people to make.

Conative component (do)

This is the action component of the attitude construct and refers to the individual's disposition or intention to behave in a certain way. Some researchers go so far as to suggest that this component refers to observable behaviour. Advertising, therefore, should be used to encourage audiences to do something – for example, visit a website, phone a telephone number, take a coupon, book a visit, or press red (on a remote control unit) for interactivity though digital television.

This three-component approach to attitudes is based upon attitudes towards an object, person or organisation. The sequence of attitude formation is generally considered to be learn, feel and do. However, this approach to attitude formation is limited in that the components are seen to be of equal strength. Observation of human behaviour suggests that there are occasions when learning develops as a result of behaviour, or feelings themselves drive the whole process. A single-component model has been developed where the attitude only consists of the individual's overall feeling towards an object. In other words, the affective component is the only significant component.

Using advertising to influence attitudes

Advertising can be an effective influence on the attitudes held by a target audience. When developing advertising-led campaigns, consideration needs to be given to the current attitudes of the target audience and those that might be desirable. The focus of a campaign can be on whether the audience requires new information (learning), the type of emotional disposition (feeling) or whether the audience needs to be encouraged to behave in a particular way (doing).

In today's competitive environment in which product life cycles have shortened, innovation is increasingly critical and organisations require marketing staff to be accountable for their investments, there is greater urgency to encourage potential customers to test, use or behave towards a brand in particular ways. Marketing communications can induce behavioural change by encouraging people to buy a brand and this might require the use of direct marketing, sales promotions and personal selling. When the emphasis of a campaign is on driving behaviour and action, direct response advertising can be effective. It is said that 40% of television ads have a telephone number or website address.

In some circumstances change might be in the form of motivating customers to visit a website, to fill in an application form, call for a brochure or download a document, or just encouraging them to visit a shop and sample the brand, free of money and any other risks. This 'doing' component of the attitude construct is commonly referred to as a 'call to action'.

Changing attitudes

Advertising can be used to either maintain or change attitudes held by stakeholders. Attitudes can be changed in other ways, for example through changes to product and service elements, pricing and channel decisions. However, advertising has a pivotal role in conveying each of these aspects to the target audience. Branding is a means by which attitudes can be established and maintained in a consistent way and it is through the advertising that brand equity can be sustained. The final point that needs to be made is that there is a common thread between attributes, attitudes and positioning. Attributes provide a means through which brands can be differentiated from competitors' products. Advertising is used to convey information about these attributes. People form attitudes as a result of their interpretation of the advertising messages they perceive, and from that they position brands in their minds.

There are certain environmental influences which impact on the attitudes people hold towards particular products and services. These are partly a reflection of the way they interpret the communications surrounding them, partly a result of their direct experience of using them and partly a result of the informal messages received from family, friends and other highly credible sources of information. These all contribute to the way people position products and services and the way they understand them relative to competing products.

Cognitive component

When an audience lacks information, misunderstands a brand's attributes or has an inappropriate perception of a brand, the essential task of advertising is to provide audiences with the right, or up-to-date, information. This enables perception, learning and attitude development based on clear truths. This is a rational, informational approach, one that appeals to a person's ability to rationalise and process information in a logical manner. It is therefore important that the level and quality of the information provided are appropriate to the intellectual capabilities of the target audience. Other tasks include showing the target audience how a brand differs from those of competitors, establishing what the added value is and suggesting who the target audience is by depicting them in the message.

Television, print and the internet are key media used to deliver information and influence the way people perceive a brand. Rather than provide information about a central or popular attribute or aspect of an offering, it is possible to direct the attention of an audience to different aspects of the object and so shape their beliefs about the brand in different ways to competitors. So, some crisp and snack-food manufacturers used to communicate the importance of taste. Now, in an age of chronic social obesity, many of these manufacturers have changed the salt and fat content and now appeal to audiences on the basis of nutrition and health. They have changed the focus of attention from one attribute to another.

Although emotion can be used to provide information, the dominant approach is informational.

Affective component

Having established that a brand might be useful, it is important that the audience develop positive attitudes towards a brand based on an emotional attachment or set of values. Advertising is often used to convey a set of emotional values that will appeal to and hopefully engage a target audience.

When attitudes to a brand or product category are discovered to be either neutral or negative, it is common for brands to use an emotional rather than rational or information-based approach. This can be achieved by using messages that are unusual in style, colour and tone, and because they stand out and get noticed they can change the way people feel and their desire to be associated with that object, brand or product category. There is great use of visual images and the appeal is often to an individual's senses, feelings and emotional disposition. The goal is help people feel 'I (we) like, I (we) desire (aspire to), I (we) want or I (we) belong to' whatever is being communicated. Establishing and maintaining positive feelings towards a brand can be achieved through reinforcement and to do this it is necessary to repeat the message.

Creating positive attitudes used to be the sole preserve of advertising but today a range of tools and media can be used. For example, product placement within films and videos helps to show how a brand fits in with a desirable set of values and lifestyles. The use of suitable music, characters that reflect the values of either the current target audience or an aspirational group, a tone of voice, colours and images all help to create a particular emotional disposition and understanding about what the brand represents or stands for.

Perhaps above all else the use of celebrity endorsers to create desire through association is one of the main ways attitudes are developed, based on an emotional disposition. This approach focuses on changing attitudes to the communication (attitudes-to-the-ad) rather than the offering. Fashion brands are often presented using a celebrity model and little or no text. The impact is visual, inviting the reader to make positive attitudes and associations with the brand and the endorser. See the successful ads for Marks & Spencer and Top Shop.

Marmite use an emotional approach based on challenging audiences to decide whether they love or hate the unique taste. The government have used a variety of approaches to change people's attitude to drink/driving, smoking, vaccinations, tax, pensions and the use of rear seat belts to name but a few of their activities. They will often use an information approach, but in some cases use an affective approach based on dramatising the consequences of a particular behaviour to encourage the audience to change their attitudes and behaviour. The overriding strategy is therefore emotional.

Exhibit 2.5 LG
Source: LG-one

Conative component

In some product categories people are said to be inert because they are comfortable with a current brand, have little reason to buy into a category, do not buy any brand or are just reluctant to change their brand. In this situation attitude change should be based on provoking behaviour. The growth and development of direct marketing and web-based communications are based on the desire to encourage people to do something rather than undertake passive attitude change that does not necessarily result in a sale. So a conative approach stimulates people to try, test, trial, visit (via a showroom or website) a brand, usually free and often without overt commitment.

Sales promotion, personal selling and direct marketing are the key tools used to drive behavioural change. For example, sales promotions are geared to driving behaviour by getting people to try a brand, direct marketing seeks to encourage a response and hence engage in interaction, and salespeople will try to close a customer to get a sale. Advertising can be used to raise awareness and direct people to a store or website.

In addition to these approaches, experiential marketing has become very popular as it is believed that direct experience of touching, feeling or using a product helps establish positive values and develop commitment. So, many car manufacturers offer opportunities to test drive a car for not only a few hours but several days. They have test circuits where drivers can spend time driving several different cars in the range across different terrain. Thetrainline.com used sheep in several ads in an attempt to change people's attitudes towards e-commerce by persuading them to break away from established behaviour and to buy tickets online and in advance. Some ads were banned by the Advertising Association on the grounds of exaggeration and misleading viewers.

The elaboration likelihood model

As we will see in Chapter 3, ads are thought to work in many ways. However, underlying most of them are the founding ideas that ads should generate either a cognitive or an emotional response in order to bring about a change in attitude towards a brand.

One approach that harnesses both the cognitive and emotional approaches has been developed by Petty and Cacioppo (1984). Referred to as the elaboration likelihood model (ELM), this approach helps to explain how cognitive processing, persuasion and attitude change occur when different levels of message elaboration are present. Elaboration refers to the extent to which an individual needs to develop and refine information necessary for decision making to occur. If an individual has a high level of motivation or ability to process information, elaboration is said to be high. If an individual's motivation or ability to process information is poor, then their level of elaboration is said to be low. The ELM distinguishes two main processes, as depicted in Figure 2.8.

Under the central route the receiver is viewed as very active and involved. As the level of cognitive response is high, the ability of the message (advertisement) to persuade will depend on the quality of the argument rather than executional factors. For example, the purchase of a consumer durable such as a car or washing machine normally requires a high level of involvement. Consequently, potential customers would be expected to be highly involved and willing to read brochures and information about the proposed car or washing machine prior to demonstration or purchase. Their decision to act would depend on the arguments used to justify the model as suitable for the individual. For the car purchase these might include the quiet and environmentally friendly engine, the excellent fuel consumption and other safety and performance indicators, together with the comfort of the interior and the effortless driving experience. Whether the car is shown as part of a business executive's essential 'kit' or the commercial is flamboyant and rich will be immaterial for those in the central route.

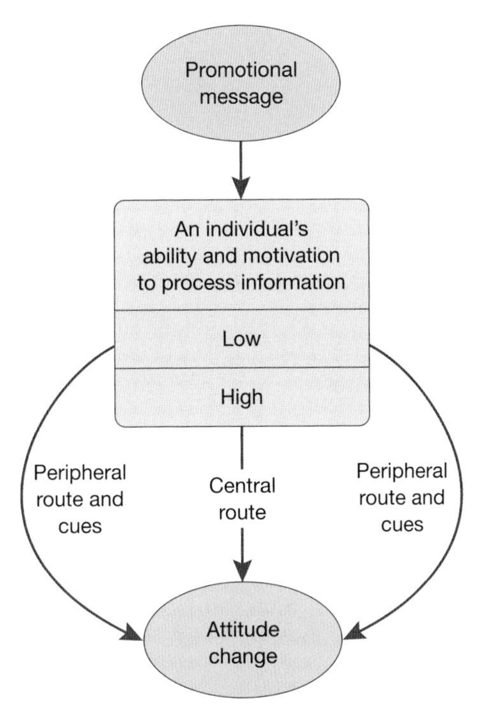

Figure 2.8 The elaboration likelihood model
Source: Based on Petty and Cacioppo (1984)

Under the peripheral route, the receiver is seen to lack the ability to process information and is not likely to engage cognitive processing. Rather than thinking about and evaluating the message content, the receiver tends to rely on what have been referred to as 'peripheral cues', which may be incidental to the message content. Comparethemarket.com uses peripheral cues to attract attention to their brand. See ViewPoint 2.4 and Exhibit 2.6 for an example of this approach.

ViewPoint 2.4 Meerkats go peripheral

Most price-comparison websites offer great functionality but they tend to use similar messages focused on savings and convenience. Achieving any real advantage can be difficult as although people remember the various compare brands, they find great difficulty attributing the right attributes to the right brand. Advertising, especially offline, is important to establish name recognition, recall and search to drive market share. Having the financial resources to fund a major campaign is normally an opportunity only open to the large operators.

At one time comparethemarket.com was ranked fourth in the market where their name was unmemorable, their name and identity were very similar to their nearest competitor, gocompare.com, they had been last into the market and they had no point of differentiation or reason why audiences would give them any attention.

In order to create competitive advantage and to get people interested in their brand a strong point of differentiation was required. People do not process advertising messages about price comparison sites with avid interest and attention, nor do they think through the various reasons why they should go to a site, or even remember each one correctly, if at all.

Comparethemarket.com needed to break away from the rational-attribute-based positioning offered by their competitors. They needed to become more of an entertainment brand and to be perceived as interesting, fun, and liked.

This was achieved by trying to reduce the search costs associated with the word 'market'. Each time someone clicks 'market' a £5 charge was incurred by comparethemarket.com. By changing peoples' perception to another M word, which would be cheaper when clicked, overall search costs could be reduced. Google charge more if users search for something generic (e.g. car insurance), less if the search is by brand name.

The result was Aleksandr Orlov, a puppet Russian meerkat and founder of www.comparethemeerkat.com, a site for comparing meerkats. The core message is that Orlov is frustrated by the confusion between Comparethemarket.com and Comparethemeerkat.com. Not only did the search cost reduce to 5p per click, but a whole new brand concept emerged as the public enthusiastically embraced the meerkat and family joke. Soon after launch the comparethemeerkat.com campaign site was used to encourage users to actually compare meerkats, and even select their own particular meerkat.

The TV campaign was a huge success and spawned a raft of marketing activities. The campaign achieved all of its 12-month objectives in just nine weeks. It also propelled the brand to number 1 position in terms of spontaneous awareness and consideration, slashed the cost per visit by 73% and increased quote volumes by over 83%. The issue here, however, is: why was it so successful?

There are many ways of interpreting the campaign, including the use of subtle humour, storytelling and novelty in a dry sector. However, key to enable this to work was the use of peripheral cues to deliver entertainment. People are not interested in ads about insurance but do connect with characters that are entertaining and novel. Orlov is a peripheral cue, a character that people can recognise, and with the help of advertising, build associations with the comparethemarket.com brand.

Source: Ramsay (2009); Jukes (2009); VCCP (2009)

Question

How realistic is the ELM as an interpretation of the way advertising works?

Task

Gocompare.com is a competitor to comparethemarket.com. Find out how they responded to the success of the meerkat campaign.

Exhibit 2.6 Aleksandr Orlov; the lead meerkat

Source: Image courtesy of The Advertising Archives

Scholars' paper 2.4 Let's look at this another way

Petty, R.E. and Cacioppo, J.T. (1984) Source factors and the elaboration likelihood model of persuasion, *Advances in Consumer Research*, 11, 1, 668-72

This is an important paper because it introduces the elaboration likelihood model. This is based on ideas about how people process ads, relative to how motivated they are to process the information. When people lack motivation and are unable to process a message, they prefer to rely on simple cues in the persuasion context, such as the expertise or attractiveness of the message source. When people are highly motivated and able to process the arguments in a message, they are interested in reviewing all the available information.

In low-involvement situations, a celebrity may serve to influence attitudes positively. This is based upon the creation of favourable attitudes towards the source rather than engaging the viewer in the processing of the message content. For example, Gary Lineker was the celebrity spokesperson used to endorse Walkers crisps for many years. Gary Lineker, former Tottenham and England football hero and now BBC sports presenter, was an important peripheral cue for Walkers crisps (more so than the nature of the product), in eventually persuading consumers to try the brand or retaining current users. Think crisps, think Gary Lineker, think Walkers. Where high involvement is present, any celebrity endorsement is of minor significance to the quality of the message claims.

Communication strategy should be based upon the level of cognitive processing that the target audience is expected to engage in and the route taken to effect attitudinal change. If the processing level is low (low motivation and involvement), the peripheral route should dominate and emphasis needs to be placed on the way the messages are executed and on the emotions of the target audience (Heath 2000). If the central route is expected, the content of the messages should be dominant and the executional aspects need only be adequate.

Chapter summary

In order to help consolidate your understanding of communication theory and the way in which people assign meaning to ads, here are the key points summarised against each of the learning objectives.

Evaluate ideas about how communication is thought to work

There are a number of models and interpretations about the way communication works. These range from the core linear model to the influencer, interactional, relational and network interpretations. They all have a role to play, simply because there is no single form of communication that applies to all situations.

Appraise the key influences on the communication process

There are two particular influences on the communication process that need to be considered. The first concerns the media and the technology that is used to convey information. The second concerns the influence of people on the communication process. This involves people assuming the roles of opinion leaders and formers, both propelling brand and advertising messages to others.

Explain source credibility and source attractiveness

The source of a message is understood to influence attitudes and the source has two main characteristics credibility and attractiveness. Credibility consists of three core elements: perceived expertise, motivation and trustworthiness. The physical attractiveness of a messenger is also an important source characteristic. The source-attractiveness model holds that the effectiveness of a message is influenced by the receiver's perception of the similarity, likeability, attractiveness and familiarity of the source.

Explore the principles of cognitive processing

The cognitive or information-processing approach assumes that people process messages (ads) in an attentive, rational and logical manner. Information is stored in memory and is refreshed by incoming information and a decision is made consciously and logically. Both informational and emotional content are processed rationally.

Describe the elements of the attitude construct

Attitudes are hypothetical constructs, derived from classical psychological theory. Attitudes are considered to consist of three components. These are the cognitive or learning element, the affective or feeling and emotional element, and finally the conative or behavioural element when people are motivated and take action as a result of an ad.

Discuss ways in which advertising can be used to influence attitudes

Through consumer insight it is possible to understand an audience's relative attitudinal strengths. So, if a brand is new or has been reformulated, then the audience will need to be informed and an emphasis on the cognitive, knowledge, element will be important. However, if an audience prefers a competitor brand, advertising will need to either stimulate action (conative) or develop new brand values (affective).

Use examples to illustrate how the elaboration likelihood model works

The ELM helps to explain how cognitive processing, persuasion and attitude change occur when different levels of message elaboration are present. Elaboration refers to the extent to which an individual needs to develop and refine information necessary for decision making to occur. If an individual has a high level of motivation or ability to process information, elaboration is said to be high. Here the the ad should influence audiences based on the quality of the argument provided. If an individual's motivation or ability to process information is poor, then their level of elaboration is said to be low. In this situation advertising and influence should emphasise the use of 'peripheral cues', elements that are incidental to the message content.

Review questions

1. With regard to the challenges presented in the match.com minicase at the start of the chapter, what would be the core aspects of an advertising campaign that conveyed their new products?
2. List the elements that configure the core (linear) model of communication.
3. Write brief notes explaining how media influence communication.
4. Without referring to the text, draw the influencer model of communication.
5. Cheng et al. (2009) identified four forms of interactive digital advertising. What are they?
6. Develop a presentation in which you explain the range of communication forms.
7. Describe each of the three core elements that constitute source credibility.

8. Select three CEOs of your choice and consider the extent to which they 'front' their organisations.
9. Evaluate cognitive processing, using the model by Lutz et al. (1983) to shape your response.
10. Write a short series of notes explaining how advertising can be used to influence attitudes, and how the ELM can explain attitude change.

Chapter references

Agrawal, J. and Kamakura, W.A. (1995) The economic worth of celebrity endorsers: an event study analysis, *Journal of Marketing*, 59, (3), 56–62

Baker, M.J. and Churchill, G. A., Jr. (1977) The impact of physically attractive models on advertising evaluations, *Journal of Marketing Research*, 14, (4), 538–55

Ballantyne, D. (2004) Dialogue and its role in the development of relationship-specific knowledge, *Journal of Business and Industrial Marketing*, 19, 2, 114–23

Barda, T. (2009) Case study: match makers, *The Marketer*, May, 20–23

Binet, L. and Field, P. (2007) *Marketing in the Era of Accountability*. Institute of Practitioners in Advertising, Henley-on-Thames: WARC

Bruner, G.C. and Kumar, A. (2000) Web commercials and advertising hierarchy of effects, *Journal of Advertising Research,* January/April, 35–42

Chen, Q. and Wells, W.D. (1999) Attitude toward the site, *Journal of Advertising Research*, September/October, 27–37

Cheng, J.M-S., Blankson, C., Wang, E.S-T. and Chen, L.S-L. (2009) Consumer attitudes and interactive digital advertising, *International Journal of Advertising*, 28, (3), 501–25

Chung, H. and Ahn, E. (2007) The effects of web site structure: the role of personal difference, *Cyberpsychology & Behavior,*10, (6), 749–55

Cugelman (2011) Reflections on source credibility and online campaigns, retrieved 10 Spetember 2011 from www.cugelman.com/research/reflections-on-source-credibility-and-online-campaigns.htm

Dholakia, R. and Sternthal, B. (1977) Highly credible sources: persuasive facilitators or persuasive liabilities? *Journal of Consumer Research*, 3(4), 223–32

Dix, S., Phau, I. and Pougnet, S. (2010) 'Bend it like Beckham': the influence of sports celebrities on young adult consumers, *Young Consumers*, 11, (1), 36–46

Fawkes, D. (2011) Observed: Volkswagen's interactive ad, 21 March 2011, retrieved 13 October 2011 from http://johnnyholland.org/2011/03/22/observed-volkswagens-interactive-ad/

Fill, C. (2009) *Marketing Communications: Strategies*, Harlow: F/T: Prentice Hall.

Goldsmith, R.E. and Lafferty, B.A. (2002) Consumer response to web sites and their influence on advertising effectiveness, *Internet Research: Electronic Networking Applications and Policy*, 12(4), 318–28

Greenwald, A. (1968) Cognitive learning, cognitive response to Persuasion and attitude change. In *Psychological Foundations of Attitudes* (eds A. Greenwald, T.C. Brook and T.W. Ostrom), 197–215. New York: Academic Press

Grunig, J. (1992) Models of public relations and communication. In *Excellence in Public Relations and Communications Management*(eds J.E. Grunig, D.M. Dozier, P. Ehling, L.A. Grunig, F.C. Repper and J. Whits), 285–325. Hillsdale, NJ: Lawrence Erlbaum

Heath, R. (2000) Low-involvement processing, *Admap* (April), 34–6

Heath, R. and Feldwick, P. (2008) 50 years using the wrong model of TV advertising, *International Journal of Market Research*, 50, (1), 29–59

Hovland, Carl I. and Walter Weiss (1951) The influence of source credibility on communication effectiveness, *Public Opinion Quarterly*, 15 (Winter), 635–50

Hovland, C.I., Janis, I.L. and Kelley, H.H. (1953) *Communication and persuasion: Psychological studies of opinion change*. New Haven, CT: Yale University Press

Hunt, R. R. and. Einstein, G.O. (1981) Relational and item-specific information in memory, *Journal of Verbal Learning and Verbal Behavior*, 20 (October), 497–514

Johnson, G.J., Bruner II, G.C. and Kumar, A. (2006) Interactivity and its facets revisited, *Journal of Advertising*, 35(4) (Winter), 35–52

Jukes, M. (2009) Creative review: Comparethemarket.com, 26 February retrieved 20 September from www.brandrepublic.com/InDepth/Features/930643/APG-Creative-Strategy-Awards---Comparethemarketcom-meerkat-campaign-VCCP

Kang, Y-S. and Herr, P.M. (2006) Beauty and the beholder: toward an integrative model of communication source effects, *Journal of Consumer Research*, 33 (June) 123–30

Kelman, H.C. (1961) Process of opinion change, *Public Opinion Quarterly*, 25 (Spring), 57–78

Kyung, H., Kwon O. and Sung Y. (2011) The effects of spokes-characters' personalities of food products on source credibility, *Journal of Food Products Marketing*, 17, 65–78

Littlejohn, S.W. (1992) *Theories of Human Communication*, 4th edn. Belmont, CA: Wadsworth

Loveless, H. (2007) Our Carol Vorderman loan nightmare, *Mail on Sunday*, 28 October. Retrieved 26 March 2008 from www.thisismoney.co.uk/campaigns/loansinsu/article

Lutz, J., Mackenzie, S.B. and Belch, G.E. (1983) Attitude toward the ad as a mediator of advertising effectiveness, *Advances in Consumer Research*, X. Ann Arbor, MI: Association for Consumer Research

McCracken, G. (1989) Who is the celebrity endorser? Cultural foundations of the endorsement process, *Journal of Consumer Research*, 16 (December), 310–21

McGuire, W.J. (1985) Attitudes and attitude change. In *Handbook of Social Psychology* (eds G. Lindzey and E. Aronson), Vol. 2: 233–346, New York, NY: Random House

Mallen, B. (1977) *Principles of Marketing Channel Management*. Lexington, MA: Lexington Books

Olsen, J.C. and Peter, J.P. (1987) *Consumer Behavior*. Homewood, IL: Irwin.

Patzer, G.L. (1983) Source credibility as a function of communicator physical attractiveness, *Journal of Business Research*, 11, 229–41

Peres, R., Muller, E. and Mahajan, V. (2010) Innovation diffusion and new product growth models: a critical review and research directions, *International Journal of Research in Marketing*, 27, 91–106

Petty, R.E. and Cacioppo, J.T. (1984) Source factors and the elaboration likelihood model of persuasion, *Advances in Consumer Research*, 11, (1), 668–72

Ramsay, F. (2009) Building on animal magic, *Marketing*, 19 August, 20–21

Rogers, E.M. (1962) *Diffusion of Innovations*, 1st edn, New York: Free Press

Rogers, E.M. (1983) *Diffusion of Innovations*, 3rd edn, New York: Free Press

Sar, S., Nan, X. and Myers, J.R. (2010) The effects of mood and advertising context on ad memory and evaluations: the case of a competitive and a non-competitive ad context, *Journal of Current Issues and Research in Advertising*, 32, 2 (Fall)

Schramm, W. (1955) How communication works. In *The Process and Effects of Mass Communications* (ed. W. Schramm), 3–26. Urbana, IL: University of Illinois Press

Shannon, C. and Weaver, W. (1962) *The Mathematical Theory of Communication*. Urbana, IL: University of Illinois Press.

Sternthal, B., Dholakia, R.R. and Leavitt, C. (1978) The persuasive effect of source credibility: tests of cognitive response, *Journal of Consumer Research*, 4(4), 252–60

Theodorson, S.A. and Theodorson, G.R. (1969) *A Modern Dictionary of Sociology*. New York: Cromwell

Varey, R. (2002) Requisite communication for positive involvement and participation: a critical communication theory perspective, *International Journal of Applied Human Resource Management*, 3(2), 20–35

VCCP (2009) Comparethemarket.com 'meerkat campaign', *campaignlive.co.uk* retrieved 17 September 2009 from http://www.brandrepublic.com/InDepth/Features/930643/APG-Creative-Strategy-Awards---Comparethemarketcom-meerkat-campaign-VCCP

Warc (2010) Nestlé: Nescafé Camera Café, Warc Prize Entrant, retrieved 26 October 2010 from www.warc.com/articlecentre

Weick, K. (1987) Prescribed and emergent networks. In *Handbook of Organisational Communication* (ed. F. Jablin). London: Sage

White, D.W., Goddard, L. and Wilbur, N. (2009) The effects of negative information transference in the celebrity endorsement relationship, *International Journal of Retail & Distribution Management*, 37, (4), 322–35

Wright, P.L. (1973) The cognitive processes mediating the acceptance of advertising, *Journal of Marketing Research*, 10 (February), 53–62

Yuan, Y., Caulkins, J.P. and Roehrig, S. (1998) The relationship between advertising and content provision on the internet, *European Journal of Marketing*, 32(7/8), 667–87

Chapter 3

Advertising: theories, concepts and frameworks

Our understanding about advertising can only be enhanced by exposure to the research undertaken by both academics and practitioners. Advertising is a complex topic and any attempt to oversimplify it can be misleading and may be ill advised. However, many have attempted the simplification approach and it is important to report their work and their contributions to our knowledge.

Aims and learning objectives

The main aim of this chapter is to examine the principal theories, concepts and frameworks about how advertising works.

As a result of reading this chapter readers should be able to:

1. examine ideas about the role of information processing and emotion in advertising
2. review the nature and role of awareness and perception in advertising
3. appraise the principal sequential frameworks by which advertising is thought to influence individuals
4. review the eclectic models of advertising
5. appraise the strong and weak theories of advertising
6. consider ways in which advertising can be used strategically
7. examine ideas concerning the use of advertising to engage audiences
8. describe the different ways advertising might work as determined by the IPA.

Minicase Johnnie Walker keeps striding

Johnnie Walker is a premier whisky brand, whose roots in Kilmarnock, Scotland were laid in the early 1800s. Since then successive generations of the Walkers have developed the brand, preserving the quality blend, introducing square bottles to get more in a box and to protect them in transit, using ships' captains to act as brand ambassadors, and using a unique diagonal label in order to use bigger print for the name to stand out. The Johnnie Walker brand became recognised internationally and in the early 1900s the Johnnie Walker® Red Label and Johnnie Walker® Black Label were registered. These have been preserved and added to with the Green, Gold and premier Blue Labels.

In 1908 whilst at lunch with the Walker brothers, Tom Browne, a renowned cartoonist, made a sketch on the back of a menu of a striding man. This was later adopted as the iconic signifier for the Johnnie Walker brand and was used in its advertising for many years before being replaced.

In the 1990s the brand experienced declining sales during difficult trading conditions, mainly due to the market entry of cheaper brands. A campaign was developed to re-establish the brand's credentials and to reverse the commercial performance of the Johnnie Walker whisky brand. Research undertaken by the agency found that people viewed masculine success as best demonstrated not through material wealth, but through a person's desire for self-improvement. So, when the striding man image was resurrected from the brand's history, an association with progress, forward thinking and development was established. The campaign idea, 'Keep walking', emerged naturally with the striding man representing the association with the human need for progress. The emotional tie to the brand appealed at a deep level to consumers and represented a means by which people could both recognise and become involved with the brand and its communications. Technically the 'Keep walking' principle represented a unique creative platform from which a raft of advertising and brand communications could be developed with an inherent consistency, coherence and integration potential.

The ad campaign used TV and print with the TV campaign based on individual 'walks'. These are stories of personal progress experienced by celebrities and notable people whilst the print work used inspiring quotes about journeys of progress.

Once the personal walks campaign had become established and understood, the campaign evolved to accommodate various expressions of progress, as this enabled the needs of different Johnnie Walker brands to be addressed. It was at this point that the brand was placed in a wider range of media channels including websites, sports sponsorship via Formula 1, internal and consumer awards and a charitable fund.

The 'Keep walking' global campaign ran in more than 120 markets, using over 50 TV ads and more than 150 print ads. In eight years the campaign generated incremental sales of $2.21 billion (£1.4 billion), or a sales growth of 48%. The brand was also recognised professionally, picking up numerous awards, including the Grand Prix, a gold award and a special prize of best international multimarket campaign.

Since then a more recent campaign extended the walking theme. Called 'Walk with giants', the campaign shared the stories of some of the world's most inspirational men, including Sir Richard Branson, Sir Ranulph Fiennes, Lewis Hamilton, Jenson Button and Ozwald Boateng.

The question now was how the Johnnie Walker brand should be developed. How should the 'Keep walking' platform evolve or, even, should the 'Keep walking' theme be jettisoned and replaced with a new approach?

Source: IPA (2011); Brook (2008); www.diageo.com

Exhibit 3.1 The Johnnie Walker striding man
Source: Alamy Images

Introduction

Understanding how advertising might work, with its rich mosaic of perceptions, emotions, attitudes, information and patterns of behaviour, has been a challenge for many eminent researchers, authors and marketing professionals. Any attempt to understand the various theories and frameworks that have been developed to explain advertising must be cautioned by an appreciation of the complexity of and some of the contradictions associated with this fascinating subject.

This chapter has three main sections. The first considers the use of information and emotion in advertising. The second considers some of the underpinning concepts and theories associated with advertising, whilst the third section considers some of the main models and frameworks that have been developed to explain how advertising works.

In what might be loosely termed the modern era, the broad task of advertising for many has been to communicate a product's unique selling proposition (USP). These USPs were based on product features and related to particular attributes that differentiated one product from another. If this uniqueness was of value to a consumer then the USP alone was thought sufficient to persuade consumers to purchase. Washes whiter (Persil), cleans faster (Flash), and lasts longer (Duracell) are typical USP claims that are still visible today.

However, the reign of the USP was short-lived when technology enabled me-too and own label brands to be brought to market very quickly, sometimes in hypercompetitive conditions, and product life cycles became increasingly shorter. The power of the USP was eroded and with it the basis of product differentiation as it was known then. In addition, the power and purpose of advertising's role to differentiate brands were challenged. Many brands today claim to have a USP. This is incorrect and tardy, as what is claimed to be unique is nothing other than a distinctive element of the offering, something that is or can be easily replicated and claimed by other brands.

Exhibit 3.2 Pain relief, a universal USP!

Many pharmaceutical companies such as Johnson and Johnson, GlaxoSmithKline and Aventis have pain-relief products. Advertising is often focused on a USP about the speed at which the pain is relieved. J&J's Tylenol brand, for example, claimed that Tylenol helped customers 'get back to normal'.

Source: Image courtesy of The Advertising Archives

What emerged are emotional selling propositions or ESPs. Advertising's role therefore became more focused on developing brand values that were based on emotion and imagery. This approach to communication builds brand awareness, desire and aspirational involvement. Emotional claims and responses are far more difficult to copy, and represent a more authoritative, and indeed customer-oriented, basis on which to base advertising appeals. 'As good as it's always been' (Hovis), 'Love it or hate it' (Marmite), and 'The world's favourite airline' (British Airways) are just three of the thousands of emotional hooks dangled in front of increasingly aware and discerning audiences. However, ESPs often fail to provide customers with a rationale or explicit reason to purchase, what is often referred to as a 'call to action'.

At the time, the other tools of the communication mix were required to provide customers with an impetus to act. For example, sales promotions, event marketing, roadshows and, later, direct marketing evolved to fulfil this need. These tools are known collectively as below-the-line communication tools and their common characteristic is that they are all capable of driving action or creating behavioural change. For example, sales promotions can be used to accelerate customer behaviour by bringing forward sales that might otherwise have been made at some point in the future. Methods such as price deals, premiums and bonus packs are all designed to change behaviour by calling customers to action. This may be in the form of converting or switching users of competitive products, creating trial use of newly introduced products or encouraging existing customers to increase their usage of the product.

So, the advent of ESPs was good in the sense that it provided exciting new ways to communicate with consumers and build brand values. However, the market was beginning to require more than brand values, and other tools and approaches were being used to induce behaviour.

Exhibit 3.3 'Take a Benylin day'

When we get a cold and feel low we would like to take a day off to recuperate. Benylin's advertising built on this consumer insight and emotionally connected with consumers when its advertising gave permission to take a 'Take a Benylin day'. The ad featured a woman waking up and feeling sick, struggling to get out of bed. A voice-over asks: 'What if today you just worked at feeling better? Benylin can handle your cold and flu symptoms. The rest is up to you. Take a Benylin day.' Apart from increasing market share, the ESP became their own as no competitor could make the same claim. It also attracted a lot of complaints.

Source: Image courtesy of The Advertising Archives

The use of information and emotion in advertising

Early views of advertising suggested that advertising only works by people responding to advertising in a logical, rational and cognitive manner. They also suggested that people only take out the utilitarian or functional aspects of advertising messages (cleans better, smells fresher). This cognitive issue was considered in Chapter 2. This is obviously not true and there is plenty of evidence to show that ads that have substantial emotional content are more effective than informational ads (Cox et al. 2011) and lead to stronger levels of engagement.

Most advertised brands are not normally new to consumers as they have some experience of the brand, or the category, whether that be through use or just through communications. This experience affects their interpretation of advertising as memories have already been formed.

Consumers view advertising in the context of their experience of the category and memories of the brand. Aligned with this approach is the concept of likeability, where the feelings evoked by advertising trigger and shape attitudes to the brand and attitudes to the advertisement (Vakratsas and Ambler 1999). Feelings and emotions play an important role in

ViewPoint 3.1 An emotional recovery for Hovis

Hovis is a long-established and well-known brand of bread but by 2006 the brand was under attack from a regional challenger brand, Warburtons. Not only was the brand losing substantial sales volume, but it was also losing share value of nearly £360 million of sales and had a 20% gap with the fast-rising Warburtons brand. The declining performance affected staff morale, retailers who were becoming unsettled and investors in Premier Foods, who owned the brand. Something had to be done.

Research showed that consumers perceived bread to be a boring category and that they increasingly discriminated between good bread (natural, healthy, tasty, from real bakers) and bad bread (processed, unhealthy, no taste). Although Hovis was now placed in the bad bread category, the recovery strategy was predicated on the goal of becoming perceived as a good bread.

In 1974 Hovis had used an ad called 'Boy on bike' with the lad on a journey to get back home with the loaf. The strapline 'As good for you today as it's always been' emphasised values, health, nostalgia and emotion. Supported with memorable music, the sepia-tinted film portrayed old-fashioned values, yet it won numerous awards and became a classic. It was this ad that was revived but this time the lad was seen clutching a loaf of Hovis and running through some of the major events of the last century. This time the words 'for you' were dropped to remove the focus on health, and the good-bread strategy was ready.

The 'As good today as it's always been' campaign was developed into an epic 122-second ad. The ad was made with some Hovis staff and journalists as extras, to boost staff morale and coverage respectively. The ad was placed in appropriate emotive programmes, such as *Coronation Street* and the Pride of Britain Awards. In addition, cinema, newspapers, outdoor and online media were also used. These were supported by a range of public relations plus door-drop and insert activities.

Apart from the numerous awards which the campaign won, 'Go on, lad' delivered on a number of important criteria. Perceptions of Hovis shifted radically to one of a modern brand with differentiated products; it became perceived as a 'good bread'. Sales rose 14% year on year, making it the fastest-growing FMCG brand in the UK in 2009, the market share gap with Warburtons was reduced to just 6 percentage points, an estimated £90 million worth of profit was generated, and Premier's share price outperformed other UK food producers.

Source: Nairn (2010); Turner (2008)

Question

How else might Hovis have used emotion to differentiate itself?

Task

Select another food product and make notes about the extent to which its advertising reflects information and emotional content.

Exhibit 3.4 Grab from Hovis TV Campaign
Source: The History of Advertising Trust

advertising especially when advertising is used to build awareness levels and brand strength. The Institute of Practitioners in Advertising (IPA) provides substantial evidence of the effectiveness of emotion in advertising, some of which is considered later in this chapter.

However, as Hollis (2010) points out, there is a danger that rational and emotional responses are seen as two separate events. This is not the case, as there is an element of emotion and information in all communications. The real question is what should be the balance between these two desirable responses in a particular campaign. Hollis refers to the 'Dirt is good' campaign run by the washing brand Persil. This highly successful campaign did not use demonstration, nor did it make any explicit claim that Persil would get clothes clean, no matter what kids did. The claim was implicit, that you can let your children get grubby and you can trust Persil to be effective. In order for this approach to work, it was important that people understood and believed that Persil had the functional capability. This had been established previously through the 'Persil washes whiter' campaigns, so now the functional element could be expressed implicitly. What this says is that emotional and informational messages should and do work together, not independently.

Most of the models presented below have been developed on the principle that individuals are cognitive information processors and that ads are understood as a result of information processing. The best examples of these are the hierarchy of effects or sequential models where information is processed step by step. This view is not universally accepted. Researchers such as Krugman (1971), Ehrenberg (1974), Corke and Heath (2004) and Heath and Feldwick (2008) dispute the importance of information processing, some denying that attention is necessary for people to understand ads and believing that the creativity within an ad is more important in many circumstances than the rational message many ads purport to deliver. These points are considered later in this chapter.

Awareness

Conventional wisdom indicates that awareness of the existence and availability of a product/service, or an organisation, is necessary before information can be processed and purchase behaviour expected. Much of advertising activity is directed towards getting the attention of the target audience, simply because of the vast number of competing messages and 'noise' in the marketplace. The goal is to get the undivided attention of the audience, to create awareness of the key messages and induce engagement opportunities. Awareness precedes engagement, and therefore needs to be created, developed, refined or sustained, according to the characteristics of the market and the particular situation facing an organisation at any one point in time. See Figure 3.1.

In situations where an audience experiences high involvement and is fully aware of a product's existence, attention and awareness levels need only be sustained, and efforts need to be applied to other communication tasks, which may be best left to the other elements of the communications mix. For example, sales promotion and personal selling are more effective at informing, persuading and provoking purchase of a new car once advertising has created the necessary levels of awareness.

Where low levels of awareness are found, getting attention needs to be a prime objective so that awareness and engagement opportunities can be developed. Where low involvement exists, the decision-making process is relatively straightforward. With levels of risk minimised, buyers with sufficient levels of awareness may be prompted into purchase with little assistance of the other elements of the mix. Recognition and recall of brand names and corporate images are felt by some (Rossiter and Percy 1991) to be sufficient triggers to stimulate a behavioural response. The requirement in this situation would be to refine and strengthen the level of awareness in order that it provokes interest and stimulates a higher level of involvement during recall or recognition.

Where low levels of awareness are matched by low involvement, the prime objective has to be to create awareness of the product in association with the product class. It is not

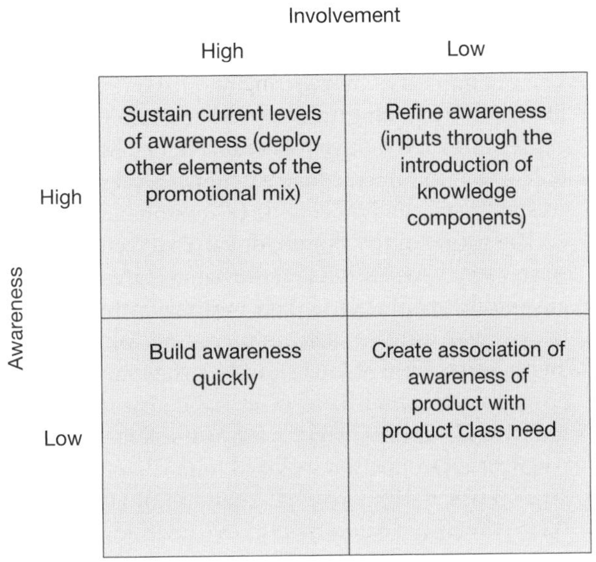

Awareness / Involvement	High	Low
High	Sustain current levels of awareness (deploy other elements of the promotional mix)	Refine awareness (inputs through the introduction of knowledge components)
Low	Build awareness quickly	Create association of awareness of product with product class need

Figure 3.1 An awareness grid

surprising that organisations use awareness campaigns and invest a large amount of their resources in establishing their brand's presence. Many brands seek to establish 'top of mind awareness' as one of their primary objectives for their advertising spend. For example, Comparethemarket.com, a price-comparison car insurance website, decided to differentiate themselves in an intensely competitive market. They decided to change the way their name was perceived because name familiarity is key (and their name was unmemorable), and their identity and name were very similar to their nearest competitor (Gocompare.com). By adopting the name 'meerkat' and developing an association with Comparethemeerkat.com, brand name awareness rose considerably (Jukes 2009). See ViewPoint 2.4 for more information about this campaign.

Once awareness has been created in the target audience, it should not be neglected. If there is neglect, the audience may become distracted by competing messages and the level of awareness of the focus product or organisation may decline.

Perception

Perception is concerned with how individuals see and make sense of their view of the world. It is about how people select, organise and interpret stimuli so that they can understand the world. In our case the way individuals perceive advertising stimuli shapes the meaning they attribute to the message. Of course, it also shapes the way advertising materials are created, designed and presented.

Each day, individuals are exposed to a tremendous number of stimuli. De Chernatony (1993) suggests that each consumer is exposed to over 550 advertisements per day while Lasn (1999) estimated that this should be 3,000 advertisements per day (cited by Dahl et al. 2003). In addition, there are thousands of other non-commercial stimuli that each individual encounters. To cope with this bombardment, our sensory organs select those stimuli to which attention is given. These selected stimuli are organised in order to make them comprehensible and are then given meaning. In other words, there is an interpretation of the stimuli that is influenced by attitudes, values, motives and past experiences as well as the character of the stimuli themselves. Stimuli, therefore, are selected, organised and interpreted, and each is looked at in turn.

Perceptual selection

The vast number of messages mentioned earlier need to be filtered, as individuals cannot process them all. The stimuli that are selected result from the interaction with the stimulus and the expectations and motives of the individual. Attention is an important factor in determining the outcome of this interaction: 'Attention occurs when the stimulus activates one or more sensory receptor nerves and the resulting sensations go to the brain for processing' (Hawkins et al. 1989).

The nature of the stimuli, or external factors, such as the intensity and size, position, contrast, novelty, repetition and movement, are features that have been developed and refined by advertisers to attract attention. Animation is used to attract attention when the product class is perceived as bland and uninteresting, such as margarine or teabags. Unexpected camera angles and the use of music can be strong methods of gaining the attention of the target audience, or reminding them of a brand. For example, music in the style of Frankie Goes to Hollywood was an integral part of the hugely successful Virgin Atlantic 'Still red hot' campaign. Sexual attraction, referred to in Chapter 2 as a part of source credibility, can be a powerful means of capturing the attention of audiences. When associated with a brand's values these stimuli can be a very effective method of getting attention. See ViewPoint 6.4 for more information about the 'still redhot' campaign.

The expectations, needs and motives of an individual, or internal factors, are equally important. Individuals see what they expect to see, and their expectations are normally based on past experience and preconditioning. From a communications perspective the presentation of stimuli that conflict with an individual's expectations will invariably receive more attention. The attention-getting power of erotic and sexually driven advertising messages is understood and exploited. For example, jeans manufacturers such as Levi's, Wranglers and Diesel often use this type of stimulus to promote their brands. However, advertising research based on recall testing often reveals that the attention-getting stimulus, for example, the male or female, generates high recall scores but the product or brand is very often forgotten. Looked at in terms of Schramm's model of communication, the process of encoding was inaccurate, leading to inappropriate decoding.

Of particular interest is the tendency of individuals to select certain information from the environment. This process is referred to as selective attention. Through attention, individuals avoid contact with information that is felt to be disagreeable in that it opposes strongly held beliefs and attitudes.

Individuals see what they want or need to see. If they are considering the purchase of new furniture, there will be heightened awareness of furniture advertisements and a correspondingly lower level of awareness of unrelated stimuli. Selective attention allows individuals to expose themselves to messages that are comforting and rewarding. For example, reassurance is often required for people who have bought new cars or expensive technical equipment and who have spent a great deal of time debating and considering the purchase and its associated risk.

Perceptual organisation

For perception to be effective and meaningful, the vast array of selected stimuli needs to be organised. The four main ways in which sensory stimuli can be organised are figure–ground, grouping, closure and contour. These are explained in Table 3.1.

These methods are used by individuals in an attempt to organise stimuli and simplify their meanings. They combine in an attempt to determine a pattern to the stimuli, so that they are perceived as part of a whole or larger unit. This is referred to as gestalt psychology.

Perceptual interpretation

Interpretation is the process by which individuals give meaning to the stimuli once they have been organised. As Cohen and Basu (1987) state, by using existing categories, meanings can be

Table 3.1 Four ways to organise perceptual stimuli

Method of organisation	Explanation
Figure-ground	Individuals tend to perceive objects when they stand proud of a general background: for example, trees standing out against a sky and words on a page. This has obvious implications for advertisers and the design of advertisements, to draw attention to important parts of the message, most noticeably the price, logo or company/brand name.
Grouping	Objects that are close to one another tend to be grouped together and a pattern develops. Grouping can be used to encourage associations between a product and specific attributes. For example, food products that are positioned for a health market are often displayed with pictures that represent fitness and exercise, the association being that consumption of the food will lead to a lifestyle that incorporates fitness and exercise, as these are important to the target market.
Closure	When information is incomplete individuals make sense by filling in the gaps. This is often used to involve consumers in the message and so enhance selective attention. Advertisements for American Express charge cards or GM credit cards ('if invited to apply'), for example, suggest that ownership denotes membership, which represents exclusiveness and privilege.
Contour	Contours give objects shape and are normally formed when there is a marked change in colour or brightness. This is an important element in package design and, as the battle for shelf space in retail outlets becomes more intense, so package design has become an increasingly important aspect of attracting attention. The Coca-Cola bottle and the packaging of the Toblerone bar are two classic examples of packaging that convey the brand.

given to stimuli. These categories are determined from the individual's past experiences and they shape what the individual expects to see. These expectations, when combined with the strength and clarity of the stimulus and the motives at the time perception occurs, mould the pattern of the perceived stimuli.

The degree to which each individual ascribes meaning, resulting from the interpretation process, is dependent upon the levels of distortion that may be present. Distortion may occur because of stereotyping: the predetermined set of images which we use to guide our expectations of events, people and situations. Another distortion factor is the halo effect that occurs when a stimulus with many attributes or dimensions is evaluated on just a single attribute or dimension. Brand extensions and family branding strategies are based on the understanding that if previous experiences with a different offering are satisfactory, then risk is reduced and an individual is more likely to buy a new offering from the same 'family'.

Advertising and perception

Individuals, therefore, select and interpret particular stimuli in the context of the expectations arising from the way they classify a particular situation. The way in which individuals perceive, organise and interpret stimuli is a reflection of their past experiences and the classifications used to understand the different situations each individual frames every day. Individuals seek to frame or provide a context within which their role becomes clearer. Shoppers expect to find products in particular situations, such as rows, shelves or display bins of similar goods. They also develop meanings and associations with some grocery products because of the utility and trust/emotional satisfaction certain pack types evoke. The likelihood that a sale will be made is improved if the context in which a purchase transaction is undertaken does not contradict a shopper's expectations.

Advertising should attempt to present objects (products and services) in a frame or 'mental presence' (Moran 1990) that is recognised by a buyer, such as a consumption or purchase situation. A product has a much greater chance of entering an evoked set if the situation in which it is presented is one that is expected and relevant. However, a new pack design can provide differentiation and provoke people into reassessing their expectations of what constitutes appropriate packaging in a product category.

Javalgi et al. (1992) point out that perception is important to product evaluation and product selection. Consumers try to evaluate a product's attributes using the physical cues of taste, smell, size and shape. Sometimes no difference can be distinguished, so the consumer has to make a judgement on factors other than the physical characteristics of the product. This is the basis of branding activity, where a personality is developed for the product which enables it to be perceived differently from its competitors. The individual may also set up a separate category or evoked set in order to make sense of new stimuli or satisfactory experiences.

Finally, individuals carry a set of enduring perceptions or images. These relate to themselves, to products and to organisations. For example, many consumers perceive the financial services industry negatively. Apart from the recent recession and economic turmoil, this is because of the inherent complexity associated with the product offerings and the rumble of negative publicity caused by the debate over bankers' bonuses.

The concept of positioning a product in the mind of a consumer is fundamental to advertising. The image an individual has of an organisation is becoming recognised as increasingly important, judging by the proportion of communication budgets being given over to corporate reputation, branding and communications activities.

Advertising models and concepts

For a message to be communicated successfully, it has to be meaningful to the recipient. Messages need to be targeted at the right audience, be capable of gaining attention, be understandable, relevant and acceptable. For effective communication to occur, messages should be designed that not only fit the cognitive capability of the target audience but also engage them emotionally and follow the 'model' of how advertising works.

Unfortunately, there is no such single model, despite years of research and speculation by a great many people. However, from all the work undertaken in this area, a number of views have been expressed, and the following sections attempt to present some of the more influential perspectives.

Sequential models

Various models have been developed to assist our understanding of how these activities are segregated and organised effectively. Table 3.2 shows some of the better-known models developed to explain how advertising works.

AIDA

Developed by Strong (1925), the AIDA model was designed to represent the stages that a salesperson must take a prospect through in the personal-selling process. This model shows the prospect passing through successive stages of attention, interest, desire and action. This expression of the process was later adopted, very loosely, as the basic framework to explain how persuasive communication, and then advertising in particular, was thought to work.

Hierarchy of effects models

An extension of the progressive, staged approach advocated by Strong emerged in the early 1960s. Developed most notably by Lavidge and Steiner (1961), the hierarchy of effects models

Table 3.2 Sequential models of advertising

Processing	AIDA sequence[a]	Hierarchy of effects sequence[b]	Information sequence[c]
		Awareness	Presentation
			↓
Cognitive			Attention
		↓	↓
	Attention	Knowledge	Comprehension
	↓	↓	↓
	Interest	Liking	Yielding
		↓	
Affective		Preference	
	↓	↓	↓
	Desire	Conviction	Retention
Conative	↓	↓	↓
	Action	Purchase	Behaviour

Source: [a] Strong (1925); [b] Lavidge and Steiner (1961); [c] McGuire (1978)

represent the process by which advertising was thought to work and assume that there is a series of steps a prospect must pass through, in succession, from unawareness to actual purchase. Advertising, it is assumed, cannot induce immediate behavioural responses; rather, a series of mental effects must occur with fulfilment at each stage necessary before progress to the next stage is possible.

The information-processing model

McGuire (1978) contends that the appropriate view of the receiver of persuasive advertising is as an information processor or cognitive problem solver. This cognitive perspective becomes subsumed as the stages presented reflect similarities with the other hierarchical models, except that McGuire includes a retention stage. This refers to the ability of the receiver to retain and understand information that is valid and relevant. This is important, because it recognises that

Scholars' paper 3.1 Linking advertising with purchasing

Lavidge, R.J. and Steiner, G.A. (1961) A model for predictive measurements of advertising effectiveness, *Journal of Marketing*, 25, 6 (October), 59–62

Published in the *Journal of Marketing* in 1961, this paper was pivotal in changing the way we considered advertising. Up until then advertising research and measurement was very much oriented to techniques and methods. This paper asked the question: what is advertising supposed to do and what function should it have?

The answer was broadly that advertising should help consumers move through the various steps in the purchasing process. Lavidge and Steiner then made the link to the attitude construct, upon which so much work and so many ideas have subsequently emerged.

advertising messages are designed to provide information for use by a prospective buyer when a purchase decision is to be made, at some time in the future, not immediately.

Issues with the sequential approach

For a long time the sequential approach was accepted as the model upon which advertising should be developed. However, questions arose about what constitute adequate levels of awareness, comprehension and conviction and how to determine which stage the majority of the target audience has reached at any one point in time.

The model is based on the logical sequential movement of consumers towards a purchase via specified stages. The major criticism is that it assumes that the consumer moves through the stages in a logical, rational manner: learn, then feel and then do. This is obviously not the case, as there any number of purchases where a feeling and emotion drive a purchase: fashion, for example. There has been a lot of research that attempts to offer an empirical validation for some of the hierarchy propositions, the results of which are inconclusive and at times ambiguous (Barry and Howard 1990). Among these researchers is Palda (1966), who found that the learn–feel–do sequence cannot be upheld as a reflection of general buying behaviour and provided empirical data to reject the notion of sequential models as an interpretation of the way advertising works.

The sequential approach sees attitude towards the product as a prerequisite to purchase, but there is evidence that a positive attitude is not necessarily a good predictor of purchase behaviour. What is important, or more relevant, is the relationship between attitude change and an individual's intention to act in a particular way (Ajzen and Fishbein 1980). Therefore, it seems reasonable to suggest that what is of potentially greater benefit is a specific measure of attitude *towards* purchasing or *intentions* to buy a specific product. Despite measurement difficulties, attitude change is considered a valid objective, particularly in high-involvement purchasing situations.

All of these models share the similar view that the purchase-decision process is one in which individuals move through a series of sequential stages. Each of the stages from the different models can be grouped in such a way that they are a representation of the three attitude components, these being cognitive (learn), affective (feel) and conative (do) orientations. This could be seen to represent the various phases in the buying process, especially those where there is high involvement in the decision process. However, they do not adequately reflect the reality of low-involvement decisions.

These models, essentially hierarchy of effects frameworks, were the first attempts to explain how advertising works. The sequential nature of these early interpretations was attractive because they were easy to comprehend, neatly mirrored the purchase decision process and provided a base upon which campaign goals were later assigned (DAGMAR: defining advertising goals for measured advertising results). However, as our knowledge of buyer behaviour increased and as the significance of the USP declined, so the popularity of these explanations about how advertising works also waned. Now they are insignificant and are no longer used as appropriate interpretations of how advertising works.

Eclectic models of advertising

A number of new frameworks and explanations have arisen, all of which claim to reflect practice. In other words, these new ideas about how advertising works are partly a practitioner reflection of the way advertising is considered to work, or at least used by advertising agencies.

The term eclectic is used (Fill 2011) because these models are essentially an assortment of diverse ideas but have central cohesion about modelling advertising practice. The first to be considered here are four main advertising frameworks developed by O'Malley (1991) and Hall

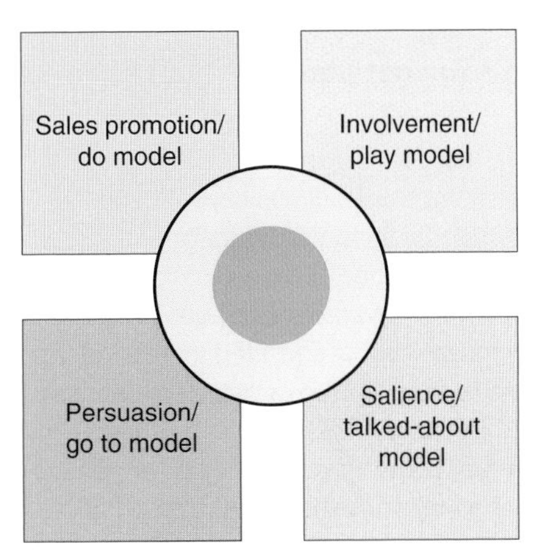

Figure 3.2 The eclectic model of advertising
Source: Based on Hall (1992), O'Malley (1991) and Willie (2007)

(1992). These reflect the idea that there are four key ways in which advertising works, depending on context and goals. This also says that different advertising works in different ways; there is no one all-embracing model. These ideas were updated by Willie (2007) to incorporate the impact of digital media and interactivity. Figure 3.2 depicts the essence of these ideas.

The persuasion/go to model

Analogue – This framework assumes advertising works rationally, and that a 'brand works harder for you'. This is based on messages that are persuasive, because they offer a rational difference, grounded in the old idea of unique selling propositions (USPs). Persuasion is affected by gradually moving buyers through a number of sequential steps, as depicted through hierarchy of effects models such as AIDA.

Digital – Digitisation enables persuasion to be extended into opportunities for exploration, as individuals can now be encouraged to search, find out more, and 'go to'. Willie points out that this is still persuasion, but it is occurs through guided exploration, rather than just telling.

The involvement/play model

Analogue – Involvement-based advertisements work by drawing the audience into the advertisement and eliciting a largely emotional form of engagement. Involvement with the brand develops because the messages convey that the 'brand means more to you'. As Willie indicates, involvement can be developed through shared values (Dove), aspirational values (American Express) or by personifying a brand, perhaps by using celebrities (Adidas).

Digital – Today, digitisation develops the notion of involvement by encouraging people to play. This is about content creation and consumers controlling brands. User-generated content can be seen through ads (crowd sourcing), blogs, wikis, videos and social networking, for example.

The salience/talked-about model

Analogue – The salience interpretation is based upon the premise that advertising works by standing out, by being different from all other advertisements in the product class. The ads used by brands such as Cillit Bang, Gocompare.com, Injurylawyers4u and Sheila's Wheels were deemed by UK consumers to be irritating, partly because the messages make people think about the brand more frequently than they would prefer.

ViewPoint 3.2 Crown get people talking about paint

Research by Crown Paints had found that consumers regarded the brand as approachable, personal and similar to being a family member. Their research also uncovered six consumer segments. These were named as Adventurous Confidents, Involved Mainstreamers, Fashion Followers, Experienced Mainstreamers, Proud Conventionalists and Only When I Have To groups. However, although awareness levels were found to be nearly 100%, Crown is very much a challenger brand to Dulux.

A repositioning campaign was launched called 'It's not just paint, it's personal' and was designed to build on the research insight and to develop the personal element of the brand association. This was achieved by encouraging consumers to become involved with the brand and to contribute to its development.

Two competitions were held. The first was to find a new musician to provide a soundtrack for the new ad. This was overseen by a panel of music experts and leading music blog www.anewbandaday.com.

The goal of the second competition was to get homeowners to disclose what inspires them. For this a dedicated micro-site, www.whatispersonaltoyou.com, was used for consumers to upload photos and stories. From this Crown developed a 'What's personal to you' map of inspiration. Shortlisted inspirations were reviewed by a panel of experts including Crown Paints' own Trends Panel.

The campaign was first launched internally with new signage, merchandise, refurbishment and a newsletter, all designed to communicate relevant messages to staff. From there the campaign went external with television, newspapers, Sunday supplements and home-interest magazines, either inviting people to the competitions or establishing what the Crown brand stands for.

All of this advertising work is supported by colour cards, a Crown paint app, social media and of course the Crown Paints website.

Source: Gray (2011); www.bjl.co.uk/; www.thedrum.co.uk/news/

Question

Which of the eclectic models can best be used to interpret the Crown campaign?

Task

Find three ads which are designed to stimulate consumer conversations. Do they work?

Digital – Contemporary interpretations of salience incorporate ideas about sharing messages about the brand either directly or virally, and getting the brand discussed, mentioned and talked about.

The sales promotion/do model

Analogue – This view holds that advertising activities are aimed ultimately at shifting product, that is, generating sales. Messages are invitations to participate in promotions, sales and various forms of price deals. This framework, oriented mainly to direct-response work, is based on the premise that the level of sales is the only factor that is worth considering when measuring the effectiveness of an advertising campaign.

Digital – Digitisation has not affected this framework, simply because sales promotion was always a 'do' or behavioural model.

The analogue-based frameworks represent communications that induce audiences into thinking and value-based responses. The digital-based frameworks represent a behavioural response that is related to the brand, not the communications. These two fundamentally different types of response can be seen in Table 3.3. Furthermore, the models bring to attention two important points about people and advertising. Advertisements are capable of generating two very clear types of response: a response to the advertisement itself and a response to the featured brand. Both have clear roles to play in advertising strategy.

Table 3.3 Digital and analogue advertising messages

Analogue delivered messages say		Digitally delivered messages encourage
This is the reason why this brand is different	Persuasion	People to explore a brand, for example, through search
Imagine you are associated with the brand	Involvement	People to play and create content
Please think about this brand	Salience	People to talk and share information about a brand
Act now because you will be rewarded	Promotion	People to act now because they will be rewarded

Scholars' paper 3.2 **Pairing analogue with digital models**

Willie, T. (2007) New models of communication for the digital age, *Admap*, 487 (October), 48-50

This paper, published in 2007, helped our knowledge of the way in which advertising might work in the digital age. Using a paper written in the early 1990s in which four models of advertising were identified, Willie develops an interesting view of how the original models might be interpreted today. He makes suggestions based on pairing each of the original models with digital activity. So persuasion is paired with exploration, involvement with play, salience with sharing and promotion with transaction. Easy to read, and very illuminating.

The essential point is that unlike the sequential models, these more recent interpretations recognise that advertising cannot be explained by a single framework or model. The conclusion should be that advertising works in different ways to reflect different media channels, and to suit different contexts.

The strong and weak theories of advertising

The explanations offered to date are all based on the premise that advertising is a potent marketing force, one that is persuasive and one which is 'done' to people. More recent views of advertising theory question this fundamental perspective. Prominent among the theorists are Jones, McDonald and Ehrenberg, some of whose views will now be presented. Jones (1991) considers the new views as the strong theory of advertising and Ehrenberg (1974) as the weak theory of advertising. Each is now considered in turn.

The strong theory of advertising

All the models presented so far are assumed to work on the basis that they are capable of affecting a degree of change in the knowledge, attitudes, beliefs or behaviour of target audiences. Jones refers to this as the strong theory of advertising, and it appears to have been universally adopted as a foundation for commercial activity.

According to Jones, exponents of this theory hold that advertising can persuade someone to buy a product that they have never previously purchased. Furthermore, continual long-run purchase behaviour can also be generated. Under the strong theory, advertising is believed to be capable of increasing sales at the brand and class levels. These upward shifts are achieved through the use of manipulative and psychological techniques, which are deployed against consumers who are passive, possibly because of apathy, and are generally incapable of processing information intelligently. The most appropriate theory would appear to be the hierarchy of effects model, where sequential steps move buyers forward to a purchase, stimulated by timely and suitable promotional messages.

The weak theory of advertising

Increasing numbers of European writers argue that the strong theory does not reflect practice. Most notable of these writers is Ehrenberg (1988, 1997), who believes that a consumer's pattern of brand purchases is driven more by habit than by exposure to promotional messages.

The framework proposed by Ehrenberg is the awareness–trial–reinforcement (ATR) framework. Awareness is required before any purchase can be made, although the elapsed time between awareness and action may be very short or very long. For the few people intrigued enough to want to try a product, a trial purchase constitutes the next phase. This may be stimulated by retail availability as much as by advertising, word of mouth or personal-selling stimuli. Reinforcement follows to maintain awareness and provide reassurance to help the customer repeat the pattern of thinking and behaviour and to cement the brand in the repertoire for occasional purchase activity. Advertising's role is to breed brand familiarity and identification (Ehrenberg 1997).

Following on from the original ATR model (Ehrenberg 1974), various enhancements have been suggested. However, Ehrenberg added a further stage in 1997, referred to as the nudge. He argues that some consumers can 'be nudged into buying the brand more frequently (still as part of their split-loyalty repertoires) or to favour it more than the other brands in their consideration sets' (p. 22). Advertising need not be any different from before; it just provides more reinforcement that stimulates particular habitual buyers into more frequent selections of the brand from their repertoire.

According to the weak theory, advertising is capable of improving people's knowledge, and so is in agreement with the strong theory. In contrast, however, consumers are regarded as selective in determining which advertisements they observe and only perceive those that promote products that they either use or have some prior knowledge of. This means that they already have some awareness of the characteristics of the advertised product. It follows that the amount of information actually communicated is limited. Advertising, Jones continues, is not potent enough to convert people who hold reasonably strong beliefs that are counter to those portrayed in an advertisement. The time available (30 seconds in television advertising) is not enough to bring about conversion and, when combined with people's ability to switch off their cognitive involvement, there may be no effective communication. Advertising is employed as a defence, to retain customers and to increase product or brand usage. Advertising is used to reinforce existing attitudes, not necessarily to drastically change them.

Unlike the strong theory, this perspective accepts that when people say that they are not influenced by advertising they are in the main correct. It also assumes that people are not apathetic or even stupid, but capable of high levels of cognitive processing.

In summary, the strong theory suggests that advertising can be persuasive, can generate long-run purchasing behaviour, can increase sales, and regards consumers as passive. The weak theory suggests that purchase behaviour is based on habit and that advertising can improve knowledge and reinforce existing attitudes. It views consumers as active problem solvers.

These two perspectives serve to illustrate the dichotomy of views that has emerged about this subject. They are important because they are both right and they are both wrong. The answer to the question 'How does advertising work?' lies somewhere between the two views and is dependent upon the particular situation facing each advertiser. Where elaboration is likely to be high if advertising is to work, then it is most likely to work under the strong theory.

Scholars' paper 3.3 The ATR model

Ehrenberg, A.S.C. (1974) Repetitive advertising and the consumer, *Journal of Advertising Research*, 14, 2 (April), 25-34

This paper set out many of Ehrenberg's ideas and beliefs about how advertising works. He regards advertising as a weak force and introduces the ATR model (awareness, trial and reinforcement). Advertising can work at each of these stages but its main role is to reinforce and support repeat buying behaviour, rather than actively change behaviours and create new sales.

This paper laid the foundation for a new stream of research and enabled researchers to break away from the 'Advertising only works by persuasion' school of thought.

For example, consumer durables and financial products require that advertising urges prospective customers into some form of trial behaviour. This may be a call for more information from a sales representative or perhaps a visit to a showroom. The vast majority of product purchases, however, involve low levels of elaboration, where involvement is low and where people select, often unconsciously, brands from an evoked set.

New products require people to convert or change their purchasing patterns. It is evident that the strong theory must prevail in these circumstances. Where products become established their markets generally mature, so that real growth is non-existent. Under these circumstances, advertising works by protecting the consumer franchise and by allowing users to have their product choices confirmed and reinforced. The other objective of this form of advertising is to increase the rate at which customers reselect and consume products. If the strong theory were the only acceptable approach, then theoretically advertising would be capable of continually increasing the size of each market, until everyone had been converted. There would be no 'stationary' markets.

Considering the vast sums that are allocated to advertising budgets, not only to launch new products but also to pursue market-share targets aggressively, the popularity and continued implicit acceptance of the power of advertising suggest that a large proportion of resources are wasted in the pursuit of advertising-driven brand performance. Indeed, it is noticeable that organisations have been switching resources out of advertising into sales promotion activities. There are many reasons for this but one of them concerns the failure of advertising to produce the expected levels of performance: to produce market share. The strong theory fails to deliver the expected results, and the weak theory does not apply to all circumstances. Reality is probably a mixture of the two.

Using advertising strategically

There are many varied and conflicting ideas about the strategic use of advertising. For a long time the management of the tools of the communication mix was considered strategic. Indeed, many practitioners still believe in this approach. However, ideas concerning integrated marketing communications and corporate identity have helped provide a fresh perspective on what constitutes advertising strategy. Furthermore, issues concerning differentiation, brand values and the development of brand equity have helped establish both a strategic and a tactical or operational aspect associated with advertising.

One of the first significant attempts to formalise advertising's strategic role was developed by Vaughn when working for the advertising agency Foote, Cone and Belding (FCB). These ideas (see below) were subsequently debated and an alternative model emerged from Rossiter and Percy. Both frameworks have been used extensively by advertising agencies, and although their influence has now subsided, the underlying variables and approach remain central to strategic advertising thought.

The FCB grid

Vaughn (1980) developed a matrix utilising involvement and brain specialisation theories. Brain specialisation theory suggests that the left-hand side of the brain is best for handling rational, linear and cognitive thinking, whereas the right-hand side is better able to manage spatial, visual and emotional issues (the affective or feeling functions).

Vaughn proposed that by combining involvement with elements of thinking and feeling, four primary advertising planning strategies can be distinguished. These are: informative, affective, habitual and self-satisfaction. See Figure 3.3 – the FCB grid.

According to Vaughn, the grid is intended to be a thought provoker rather than a formula or model from which prescriptive solutions are to be identified. The FCB grid is a useful guide to help analyse and appreciate consumer–product relationships and to develop appropriate communication strategies. The four quadrants of the grid identify particular types of decision making and each requires different advertising approaches. Vaughn suggests that different orderings from the learn–feel–do sequence can be observed. By perceiving the different ways in which the process can be ordered, he proposed that the learn–feel–do sequence should be visualised as a continuum, a circular concept. Communication strategy would, therefore, be based on the point of entry that consumers make to the cycle.

Some offerings, generally regarded as 'habitual', may be moved to another quadrant, such as 'responsive', to develop differentiation and establish a new position for the product in the

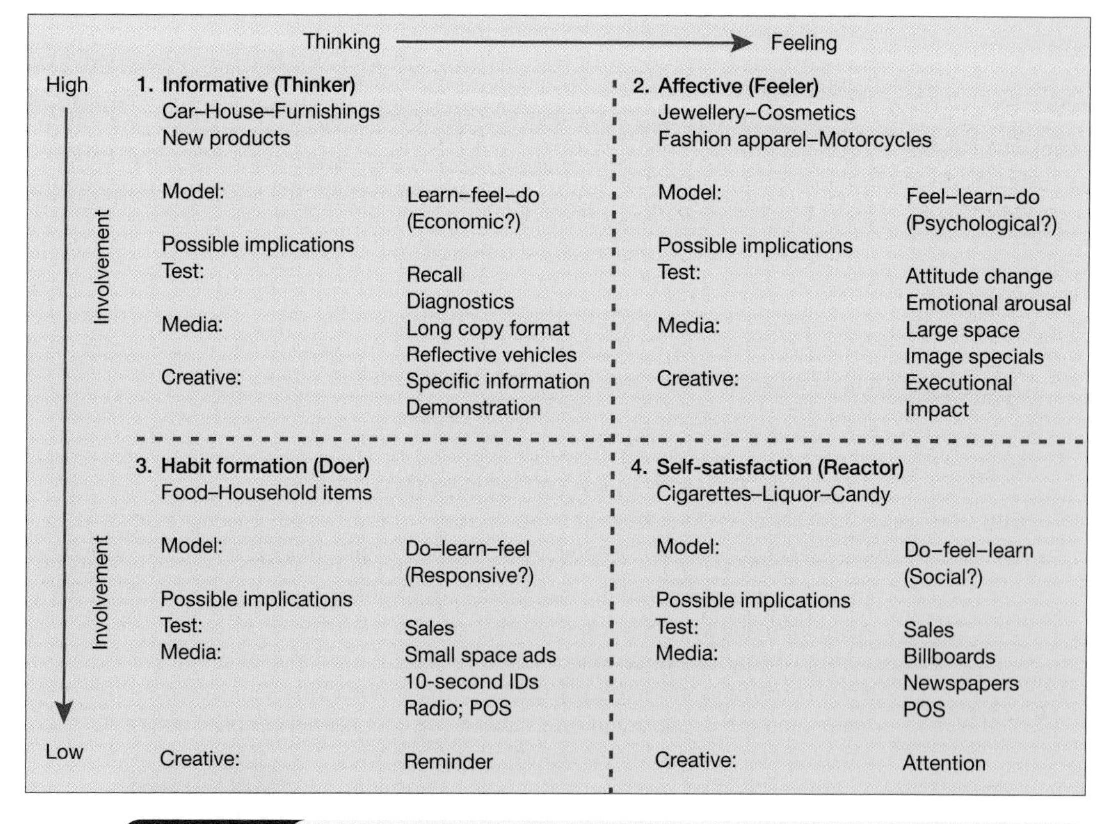

Figure 3.3 The FCB grid
Source: Vaughn (1980)

minds of consumers relative to the competition. This could be achieved by the selection of suitable media vehicles and visual images in the composition of the messages associated with an advertisement. There is little doubt that this model, or interpretation of the advertising process, has made a significant contribution to our understanding of the advertising process and has been used by a large number of advertising agencies (Joyce 1991).

ViewPoint 3.3 Sleeping with wolves . . . well, nearly

Each of the 57 Shangri-La Hotels and Resorts epitomises the very essence of Asian hospitality, and the group has grown steadily over the past 40 years. However, as part of its global expansion strategy it set itself the business goal of increasing its revenue by US$90 million. This equated to selling 10 more rooms per hotel each night.

Rather than use promotional pricing it decided to develop a stronger Shangri-La brand, to drive more visitors and secure longer-term growth. The target audiences were the 66,000 employees and the aged 35+, upmarket, premium business travellers who account for around 70% of Shangri-La's business. These travellers spend a lot of time away from home, preferring to stay at familiar five-star hotels. However, research showed that the luxury could never compensate them for the loneliness and alienation of yet another foreign trip.

The Shangri-La delivers Asian luxury service with a smiling face and a respectful bow and treats each guest as if they are royalty. Yet at the Shangri-La the culture expresses a deeper sense of humanity, with staff referring to and treating guests as if they were visitors to their own homes. Even the training materials emphasised 'everything should come from the heart'. Loyal guests called Shangri-La 'a part of the family' (http://www.warc.com/Content/ContentViewer.aspx?MasterContentRef=eb33cafb-d6aa-4f7d-a29a-9379d5c07663&q=salience-94019fn07). From this the engagement strategy started to emerge, namely that at Shangri-La the guest was not a King - but Kin, a human being.

In order to convey this proposition communications needed to be very distinctive, unorthodox for the sector yet emotionally engaging. Using visual and aural language to express pure luxury, stories were told, using metaphors about the benevolence of animals who embraced humans as their own. This was expressed through a striking film and three print executions. These depicted a traveller lost in the snow, who to his surprise was rescued by wolves. These were supported by the line 'There is no greater act of hospitality than to embrace a stranger as one's own. Shangri-La. It's in our nature.'

Ahead of the campaign launch, all staff were presented with a brand manifesto which was also printed in a pocket book. This contained Shangri-La's proposition translated into principles of behaviour. All staff training was redesigned and all 66,000 employees attended launch events at every hotel to see the creative before anyone else. With huge jigsaw puzzles to illustrate the print executions, and postcards inviting staff to feed back their views of the proposition, the goal was to convey the importance of each member of staff as an integral part of the brand promise.

The media strategy included the usual high-reach media of in-flight TV and magazines and lifestyle and business press. However, it also included BBC News24, CNN and Starworld, and similar media, as this reflected the frequency with which business travellers attempt to reconnect with home when they visit their home news portals, business sites, TV channels and magazines.

In 2010, revenue increased by US$302.7 million year on year. The campaign generated an extra 937,980 room sales, which is equivalent to 45 more rooms per hotel per night. This exceeded the objective by more than four times. The media spend amounted to US$7.5 million, which meant that the campaign paid back US$40 for each US$1 media spend.

Source: Moustou and Tam (2011); www.shangri-la.com; Walters (2010)

Question

Which of the quadrants in the FCB grid might this campaign best fit?

Task

Find another luxury hotel brand and evaluate their brand promise.

The Rossiter-Percy grid

Rossiter et al. (1991), however, disagree with some of the underpinnings of the FCB grid and offer a new one in response (revised 1997). The fundamental ideas are reproduced as Figure 3.4. They suggest that involvement is not a continuum because it is virtually impossible to decide when a person graduates from high to low involvement. They claim that the FCB grid fails to account for situations where a person moves from high to low involvement and then back to high, perhaps on a temporary basis, when a new variant is introduced to the market. Rossiter et al. regard involvement as the level of perceived risk present at the time of purchase. Consequently, it is the degree of familiarity buyers have at the time of purchase that is an important component.

A further criticism is that the FCB grid is an attitude-only model. Rossiter et al. quite rightly identify the need for brand awareness to be built into such grids as a prerequisite for attitude development. However, they cite the need to differentiate different purchase situations. Some brands require awareness recall because the purchase decision is made prior to the act of purchasing. Other brands require awareness recognition at the point of purchase, where the buyer needs to be prompted into brand-choice decisions.

The other major difference between the two grids concerns the 'think–feel' dimension. Rossiter et al. believe that a wider spectrum of motives must be incorporated, as the FCB 'think–feel' interpretation fails to accommodate differences between product category and brand purchase motivations. For example, the decision to use a product category may be based on a strictly functional and utilitarian need. The need to travel to another country often designates the necessity of air transport. The choice of carrier, however, particularly over the North Atlantic, is a brand-choice decision, motivated by a variety of sensory and ego-related inputs and anticipated outputs.

Rossiter et al. disaggregate motives into what they refer to as informational and transformational motives. By detailing motives into these classifications, a more precise approach to advertising tactics can be developed. Furthermore, the confusion inherent in the FCB grid, between the think and involvement elements, is overcome.

It should be understood that these 'grids' are purely hypothetical, and there is no proof or evidence to suggest that they are accurate reflections of advertising. It is true that both models have been used as the basis for advertising strategy in many agencies, but that does not mean that they are totally reliable or, more importantly, that they have been tested empirically so that they can be used in total confidence. They are interpretations of commercial and psychological activity and have been instrumental in advancing our level of knowledge. It is in this spirit of development that these models are presented in this text.

There are parts in both of these frameworks that have a number of strong elements of truth attached to them. However, for products that are purchased on a regular basis, pull strategies should be geared to defending the rationale that current buyers use to select the brand. Heavy buyers select a particular brand more often than light users do from their repertoire. By

Scholars' paper 3.4 **The Rossiter-Percy grid**

Rossiter, J.R. and Percy, L. (1997) *Advertising Communications & Promotion Management,* 2nd edn. New York: McGraw-Hill.

Following the AIDA and ATR models, plus the popularity of the FCB grid, took managerial understanding of advertising to a new level. Rossiter and Percy published their grid to overcome the perceived shortcomings in the FCB grid, yet retaining the simplicity of the grid approach which they believe makes these models easy to understand and more likely to be of practical assistance to managers.

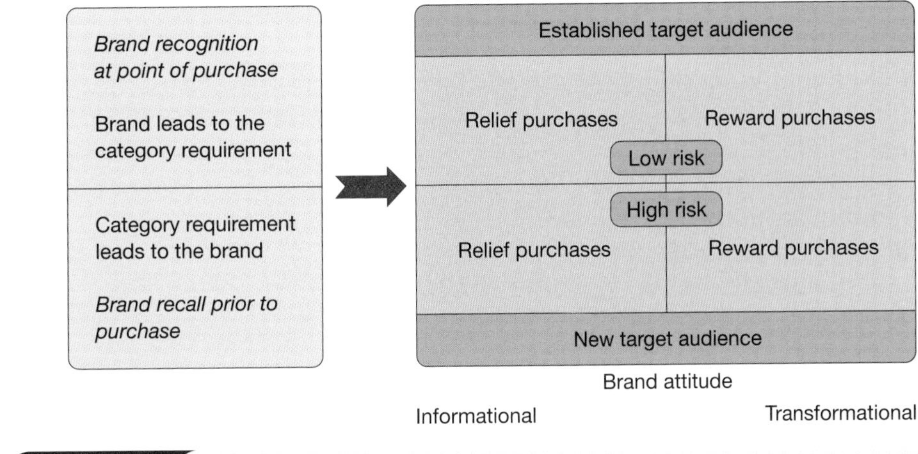

Figure 3.4 The Rossiter–Percy grid
Source: Adapted from Rossiter and Percy (1997)

providing a variety of consistent stimuli, and by keeping the brand alive, fresh buyers are more likely to prefer and purchase a particular brand than those that allow their brands to lose purchase currency and the triggers necessary to evoke memory impressions.

For products purchased on an irregular basis, marketing communications need only touch the target audience on a relatively low number of occasions. Strategies need to be developed that inform and contextualise the purchase rationale for consumers. This means providing lasting impressions that enable consumers to understand the circumstances in which purchase of a particular product/brand should be made once a decision has been made to purchase from the product category. Here the priority is to communicate messages that will encourage consumers to trust and bestow expertise on the product/brand that is offered.

The Institute of Practitioners in Advertising

The Institute of Practitioners in Advertising (IPA) has examined hundreds of successful advertising campaigns as part of its long-running Advertising Effectiveness Awards programme. From these the IPA has identified particular campaigns, and their characteristics, that are effective in terms of influencing consumers and achieving their campaign goals. These are:

- **Emotional involvement:** these campaigns work by generating consumer emotions or feelings which are then transferred to a brand. This helps to build consumer/brand empathy. Sometimes information is included in these campaigns, but the informational element plays a minor role.
- **Fame:** by getting talked about and making waves, these campaigns become famous. The brand stands out because of the strong emotional responses the campaign generates.
- **Information:** these campaigns work by providing brand-related information. This might be about the user, the brand, the category or the user's world. These are purely informational campaigns and do not have any emotional content. Sometimes referred to as 'reason-why' ad campaigns, the communication is about the functional benefit and advantage a brand has over other brands.
- **Persuasion:** is generated by first using information or news to get the audience's attention. This is a rational approach based on challenging existing beliefs or knowledge. Then an emotional component is introduced to make the message memorable.
- **Reinforcement:** as the name suggests, the aim of these campaigns is to reinforce existing behaviour rather than change it. Particular usage occasions and events are often used to strengthen the bonding.

ViewPoint 3.4 Ring me for fame

A classic fame campaign was the '118 118' launched in 2003 by The Number. This featured two runners each with droopy moustaches, with 118 118 emblazoned across their running vests, to represent the brand. The goal was to create awareness of the new directory enquiries number, following deregulation of the industry.

The target market was 25–44-year-olds who live in urban areas and have busy lifestyles. They account for 89% of all directory enquiry calls. Each of the 20 competitors would feature the number 118 followed by three other digits. So although price was going to be important it was critical to create a clear brand.

The campaign launched with a website called www.mysteryrunners.com. This had photos, videos and interviews. In March a campaign was rolled out that used TV, outdoor and radio, with cinema and press added later in the year. However, TV was important for building the brand, and it took over 50% of the £11.5 million budget. By August the 118 runners had become a national icon, with press coverage of the deregulation showing the runners in more than 80% of the articles about the switch.

It is estimated that the 118 118 advertising generated 53.4 million calls after the switch-off and the campaign generated £45.4 million in income.

The 118 118 service has now expanded into new areas beyond directory enquiries. However, the two runners have reappeared in different guises. For example in 2006 they were used in ads which parodied the television show *The A-Team*. In other formats they appeared as 'mad professors', the show *Lost* was hijacked, whilst ITV1 Movies were sponsored, before the runners were animated.

Source: Binet and Field (2007); www.thinkbox.tv/server/show/ConCaseStudy.3

Question

To what extent are fame campaigns a risky approach to advertising?

Task

Identify two major competitors to 118 118 and assess their advertising.

Exhibit 3.5 118 118 runners
Source: Rex Features

More complex: these types of campaign reflect a combination of the other types. The majority comprise emotional involvement with either an information or rational persuasion approach.

The IPA data (Binet and Field 2007) reveal that the use of emotional or transformational appeals (emotional involvement, fame and more complex) are more likely to generate strong business results than rational-based informational campaigns (information and persuasion). This is because emotional messages are memorable and are able to build attitudes much more powerfully than rational-based informational messages. Indeed, each of the three elements of an attitude, cognitive, affective and conative, respond strongly to emotional messages.

Chapter summary

In order to help consolidate your understanding of advertising theories and concepts, here are the key points summarised against each of the learning objectives.

Examine ideas about the role of information processing and emotion in advertising

Most advertising contains an element of emotion and information, but finding the balance between these two responses for a particular campaign can be difficult. Whatever is decided, there is agreement that emotional and informational content should work together, not independently.

Review the nature and role of awareness and perception in advertising

Awareness precedes engagement, and therefore needs to be created, developed, refined or sustained, according to the characteristics of the market and the particular situation facing an organisation at any one point in time.

Perception is concerned with how individuals see and make sense of their view of the world. Here it is about how people select, organise and interpret advertising stimuli as this shapes the meaning they attribute to the message. Of course, it also shapes the way advertising materials are created, designed and presented.

Appraise the principal sequential frameworks by which advertising is thought to influence individuals

The sequential frameworks (e.g. AIDA) represent the first attempts to explain how advertising works. The sequential nature of these early interpretations was attractive because they were easy to comprehend, neatly mirrored the purchase-decision process and provided a base upon which campaign goals were later assigned (DAGMAR). However, as our knowledge of buyer behaviour increased and as the significance of the USP declined so these sequential models also declined in terms of our understanding about advertising. Now they are insignificant and are no longer used as appropriate interpretations of how advertising works.

Review the eclectic models of advertising

A number of new frameworks and explanations have arisen, all of which claim to reflect advertising practice. In other words, these new theories about how advertising works are a reflection of practice, of the way advertising is considered to work, or at least used by advertising agencies and interpreted by marketing research agencies. The first of these information-processing models were developed by O'Malley (1991) and Hall (1992) and then updated by Willie (2007) to incorporate digital facilities. Referred to as eclectic models, they suggest that there are four main advertising frameworks: persuasion, sales, salience and involvement.

Appraise the strong and weak theories of advertising

The strong theory of advertising reflects the persuasion concept, and has high credibility when used with new brands. However, the contrasting view is that advertising should be regarded as a means of defending customers' purchase decisions and for protecting markets, not building them. Reality suggests that the majority of advertising cannot claim to be of significant value to most people and that the strong and the weak theories are equally applicable, although not at the same time nor in the same context.

Consider ways in which advertising can be used strategically

Advertising, once considered the prime form of mass persuasion, is now subject to many different views. Those who are sceptical of advertising's power to persuade consumers to change their purchasing habits now explore ideas concerning advertising's strategic role in reinforcing brand messages and repositioning brands.

The FCB and Rossiter–Percy grids represent formalised attempts to interpret the strategic use of advertising. Intended to provide agencies with a method that might ensure consistency, meaning and value with respect to their clients' brands, these are no longer considered by agencies to be sufficiently flexible, rigorous or representative of how contemporary advertising performs.

Examine ideas concerning the use of advertising to engage audiences

A more current perspective of advertising strategy suggests that advertising should become more engaged with the customer's experience of the brand and not be rooted just in the development of brand values.

Advertising strategy should therefore reflect a brand's context and be adjusted according to the required level of engagement regarding identity development and the required level of behavioural response. The IPA show that emotionally driven ads are better at driving favourable commercial outcomes than ads that focus on the provision of rational information.

Describe the different ways advertising might work as determined by the IPA

The IPA has identified effective campaigns, and categorised them according to their characteristics. Advertising therefore can work through driving emotional involvement, generating fame, providing information, persuasion, reinforcing perceptions, attitudes and behaviours, or through a more complex route which combines the other types. The majority comprise emotional involvement with either an information or rational persuasion approach.

Review questions

1. With regard to the challenges presented in the Johnnie Walker minicase at the beginning of the chapter, should the 'Keep walking' platform be developed and if so how? If not, what would you replace it with?
2. Which of the models and frameworks presented in this chapter best represents the 'Keep walking' campaign?
3. Find two advertisements and write notes explaining how they depict the role of advertising.
4. Why is the use of emotion such an important part of advertising?
5. What are the essential differences between the involvement/play and salience/do frameworks of advertising? Find advertisements that are examples of these two approaches.
6. Write a short presentation explaining the differences between the strong and weak theories of advertising.

7. Select an organisation of your choice and find three ads it has used recently. Are the ads predominantly trying to persuade audiences or are they designed to reinforce brand values?
8. Draw the FCB grid and place on it the following product categories: shampoo, life assurance, sports cars, kitchen towels, box of chocolates.
9. Prepare a report explaining the differences between the Rossiter–Percy and FCB grids.
10. Write brief notes explaining the three most effective advertising strategies as determined by the IPA.

Chapter references

Ajzen, I. and Fishbein, M. (1980) *Understanding Attitudes and Predicting Social Behavior*. Englewood Cliffs, NJ: Prentice-Hall

Barry, T. and Howard, D.J. (1990) A review and critique of the hierarchy of effects in advertising, *International Journal of Advertising*, (9), 121–35

Binet, L. and Field, P. (2007) *Marketing in the Era of Accountability*. Institute of Practitioners in Advertising, Henley-on-Thames: WARC

Brook, S. (2008) Johnnie Walker strolls off with three IPA awards, *Guardian*, 4 November 2008, retrieved 18 January 2012 from http://www.guardian.co.uk/media/2008/nov/04/advertising-marketingandpr1

Cohen, J. and Basu, K. (1987) Alternative models of categorisation, *Journal of Consumer Research* (March), 455–72

Corke, S. and Heath, R.G. (2004) The hidden power of newspaper advertising, *Media Research Group Conference*, Madrid (November)

Cox, K., Crowther, J., Hubbard, T. and Turner, D. (2011) *IPA – New Models of Marketing Effectiveness: From Integration to Orchestration*. Henley: WARC

Dahl, D.W., Frankenberger, K.D. and Manchanda, R.V. (2003) Does it pay to shock? Reactions to shocking and nonshocking advertising content among university students, *Journal of Advertising Research*, 43, (3) (September), 268–81

De Chernatony, L. (1993) The seven building blocks of brands, *Management Today* (March), 66–7

Ehrenberg, A.S.C. (1974) Repetitive advertising and the consumer, *Journal of Advertising Research*, 14, 2 (April), 25–34

Ehrenberg, A.S.C. (1988) *Repeat Buying*, 2nd edn. London: Charles Griffin

Ehrenberg, A.S.C. (1997) How do consumers come to buy a new brand? *Admap* (March), 20–4

Fill, C. (2011) *Essentials of Marketing Communications*. Harlow: Financial Times/Prentice Hall

Gray, R. (2011) Pots of personality, *themarketer*, May, 24–7

Hall, M. (1992) Using advertising frameworks, *Admap* (March), 17–21

Hawkins, D., Best, R. and Coney, K. (1989) *Consumer Behavior*. Homewood, IL: Richard D. Irwin

Heath, R. and Feldwick, P. (2008) 50 years using the wrong model of TV advertising, *International Journal of Market Research*, 50, (1), 29–59

Hollis, N. (2010) Emotion in advertising: pervasive, yet misunderstood. Millward Brown: Point of View

IPA (2011) *New Models of Marketing Effectiveness: From Integration to Orchestration*. WARC

Javalgi, R., Thomas, E. and Rao, S. (1992) US travellers' perception of selected European destinations, *European Journal of Marketing*, 26, (7), 45–64

Jones, J.P. (1991) Over-promise and under-delivery, *Marketing and Research Today* (November), 195–203

Joyce, T. (1991) Models of the advertising process, *Marketing and Research Today* (November), 205–12

Jukes, M. (2009) Creative review: Comparethemarket.com, 26 February retrieved 20 September from www.brandrepublic.com/InDepth/Features/930643/APG-Creative-Strategy-Awards-– Comparethemarketcom-meerkat-campaign-VCCP

Krugman, H.E. (1971) Brain wave measurement of media involvement, *Journal of Advertising*, 11, (1), 3–9

Lasn, K. (1999) *Culture Jam: The Uncooling of America*. New York: Eagle Brook

Lavidge, R.J. and Steiner, G.A. (1961) A model for predictive measurements of advertising effectiveness, *Journal of Marketing*, 25, 6 (October), 59–62.

McGuire, W.J. (1978) An information-processing model of advertising effectiveness. In *Behavioral and Management Science in Marketing* (eds H.L. Davis and A.J. Silk), 156–80. New York: Ronald/Wiley

Moran, W. (1990) Brand preference and the perceptual frame, *Journal of Advertising Research* (October/November), 9–16

Moustou, C. and Tam, C. (2011) Shangri-La Hotels & Resorts: turning a human touch into business advantage, WARC Asia Prize Contender, retrieved 24 May from www.warc.com/Content/ContentViewer.aspx?MasterContentRef=eb33cafb-d6aa-4f7d-a29a-9379d5c0 7663&q=Shangri-La

Nairn, A. (2010) Hovis – As good today as it's ever been, *Grand Prix, Gold, IPA Effectiveness Awards*, London: IPA

O'Malley, D. (1991) Sales without salience? *Admap* (September), 36–9

Palda, K.S. (1966) The hypothesis of a hierarchy of effects: a partial evaluation, *Journal of Marketing Research*, (3), 13–24

Rossiter, J.R. and Percy, L. (1997) *Advertising Communications & Promotion Management*, 2nd edn. New York: McGraw-Hill

Rossiter, J.R., Percy, L. and Donovan, R.J. (1991) A better advertising planning grid, *Journal of Advertising Research*, (October/November), 11–21

Strong, E.K. (1925) *The Psychology of Selling*. New York: McGraw-Hill

Turner, C. (2008) Hovis revives its wholesome heritage in 15m relaunch, *Marketing Week*, Thursday 7 August, retrieved 22 May 2011 from www.marketingweek.co.uk/analysis/hovis-revives-its-wholesome-heritage-in-15m-relaunch/2061897.article

Vakratsas, D. and Ambler, T. (1999) How advertising works: what do we really know? *Journal of Marketing*, 63 (January), 26–43

Vaughn, R. (1980) How advertising works: a planning model, *Journal of Advertising Research* (October), 27–33

Walters, R. (2010) Shangri-la Hotel & Resorts embrace strangers in new global campaign created by O&M Hong Kong, Monday, 31 May, retrieved 24 May 2011 from www.campaignbriefasia.com/2010/05/shangri-la-hotel-resorts-embra.html

Willie, T. (2007) New models of communication for the digital age, *Admap*, 487 (October), retrieved 23 July 2010 from www.warc.com

Chapter 4
Advertising: strategies, planning and positioning

When we see an ad on TV or in a magazine, its appearance has not 'just happened'. It is the result of significant levels of activity between the client and their advertising agencies, often over long periods of time. This activity is not just a question of 'creating' the ad itself but involves a detailed consideration of the overarching strategy and the thorough planning necessary to implement any management activity. As you can imagine, using advertising to reach global audiences, with their cultural and regional variations and preferences, becomes an even more complex and challenging endeavour.

Aims and learning objectives

The aims of this chapter are to explore the issues associated with advertising strategy, the planning of advertising campaigns, and the positioning of brands effectively.

The learning objectives of this chapter are to:

1. introduce the concept of strategy
2. evaluate the generic approach to marketing communications strategy
3. explain the role of objectives in the advertising planning process
4. consider various frameworks and processes used for planning communications and advertising campaigns
5. explore the principles of positioning
6. assess the merits of different positioning strategies.

Minicase Ulster Bank . . . ing on students

Ulster Bank is one of the 'Big Four' banks in Northern Ireland and the Republic of Ireland. They are a banking brand with a rich heritage and history. As a brand, they are proud to have been there for their customers throughout Ireland's colourful and troubled past, including the passing of Home Rule, the Easter Rising and the Battle of the Somme, stating that 'we were there, through it all'. However, despite this legacy and strong sense of nostalgia among their customers, Ulster Bank has not been immune to the effects of the financial crisis, and the other influences on the banking sector.

One important sector that they wanted to penetrate was the student market. Students represent future profitability and allow for a host of other cross-selling opportunities, such as car loans, mortgages, pensions and investments. In 2002 the average student debt in the UK was £10,000 (Tank and Tyler 2005) and this has continued to increase year on year. This in turn increases the demand by students for banking services. In addition, consumers are reluctant to switch bank accounts, citing fear of confusion about the complex administration and bureaucracy, plus possible fees and issues with credit ratings. Therefore, if students can be successfully recruited, they are likely to become lifelong and profitable customers. However, students are difficult to sign up, as their primary reason for choosing a bank is the convenience of a particular location. Therefore, any bank that does not have a local branch must be creative with their advertising strategy.

When Ulster Bank decided to market a better student bank offering, they had to think carefully about the marketing communications. According to a Mintel report, the banking market had remained stagnant for a number of years. More important than this, however, was the fact that students represent the most inaccessible market segment, other than the elderly. The end of university grants, and steadily increasing fees, ensured that students would have to rely on banks more than ever. In response to this increased demand, many banks began to offer special packages with benefits tailored specifically for students. However, with many banks offering virtually identical packages to students, including fee-free banking, overdrafts and student credit cards, students can be left with a difficult decision to make. These tailored packages typically come at a loss to the banks who work on the principle that graduates will purchase and use more financial products throughout their life than non-graduates.

This heightened competition to attract customers from a traditionally inaccessible market segment epitomises the need for an effective advertising campaign in order to differentiate from competitors' offerings. Tank and Tyler (2005) describe retail bank advertising campaigns for the student market as lacking imagination.

Exhibit 4.1 Still from the Ulster Bank campaign
Source: Ulster Bank

Smith and Summers (1996) highlighted that most banks and larger banking institutions have a flawed idea of students and, importantly, have very little idea of how to communicate with them effectively. Most bank student offerings are largely undifferentiated, reflected in poor advertising campaigns.

Unfortunately, most of the banks put little or no effort into developing advertising campaigns aimed specifically at students, and for those who do, the ads are often unattractive to students as they have been badly thought out, are indistinguishable from the advertising campaigns aimed at different segments of the market (e.g. homeowners), or simply reflect the bank's lack of knowledge about positioning and the student market. These inaccurate or ill-thought-through campaigns simply serve to leave students feeling patronised and less likely to opt for any particular bank offerings.

The problems, therefore, were first how to position the bank effectively in this target market, and second, how to develop an advertising campaign that would reach students and engage them sufficiently to want to sign up with the Ulster Bank.

Source: Written by Matthew Kearney (Ulster University) and Kevin Heavern (Ulster Bank)

Introduction

Ideas about what strategy might be, what it is and how it works have occupied the minds of philosophers, historians, politicians, management academics and of course advertising practitioners for a considerable period of time. To say that a consensus of thought has been reached would be stretching the imagination. However, some core ideas appear to be agreed. These concern the point that strategy is concerned with the long term, that strategy can take different forms and styles, as we shall see, and that strategy is concerned with the 'big picture', and is not concerned with tactics or operational issues.

In the light of these core points we start this chapter with a consideration of some of the central ideas about what strategy might be, from a general perspective. From here we develop ideas about how these might transform into marketing, and advertising strategy in particular. We embrace the views of academics and practitioners and then consider ways in which advertising might be developed from a marketing route.

From here we look at issues concerning the way advertising might be planned and the issues associated with developing coherent and integrated campaigns designed to build brands. The chapter closes with a review of positioning and an insight into the different brand strategies that can be used to develop competitive advantage. Indeed, as we shall see, positioning is an integral part of advertising strategy and is therefore considered throughout the chapter.

There are two forms of positioning and care must be taken to avoid confusion. **Strategic or market positioning** refers to the competitive market standing of a firm against its competitors. Here the task is for an organisation to use its particular resources to build positional advantages in product markets (Day and Wensley 1988) So, if a hotel group intends to become the best hotel group for leisure breaks, it needs to develop the necessary facilities and to allocate resources to enable this position to be realised.

Brand positioning refers to the process of creating and altering perceptions held by consumers about a firm's products or brands (Crawford 1985). As Fuchs and Diamantopoulos (2010) state, strategic positioning is concerned with setting the basic direction on which the development of the brand positioning can take place.

What is strategy?

Hambrick (1983) suggested that the disparity of views about strategy is due to the multidimensional nature of the strategy concept, that strategy is situational and that it varies according to industry and the environment in which it operates. In other words, contextual issues determine the nature of strategy. In many ways this may be true, especially if one adopts the configurational approach advocated by Mintzberg and Ghoshal (2003). However, this does not help us understand what strategy is.

The one main area wherein most authors find agreement concerns the hierarchical nature of strategy within organisations (Kay 1993; Johnson et al. 2008; Mintzberg and Ghoshal 2003). This refers to the notion that there are three main levels of organisational strategy: corporate, competitive and functional. Corporate strategy is considered to be directional and sets out the broad, overarching parameters and means through which the organisation operates in order to realise its objectives. Strategies at the functional level, for example marketing, finance and production, should be integrated in such a way that they contribute to the satisfaction of the higher-level competitive strategies, which in turn should satisfy the overall corporate goals. Competitive-level strategies are important because not only do they set out the way in which the organisation will compete and use resources, but they should also provide clear messages about the way in which the organisation seeks to manage its environment.

Two main strategy schools of thought can be identified, namely the planning and the emergent approaches. The planning school is the pre-eminent paradigm and is based on strategy development and implementation, which is explicit, rational and planned as a sequence of logical steps. Andrews (1987) comments that strategy is concerned with a company's objectives, purpose and policies and its plans to satisfy the goals using particular resources with respect to a range of internal and external stakeholders. The organisation interacts with and attempts to shape its environment in pursuit of its goals. This perspective of strategy was first formulated in the 1950s and 1960s when the operating environments of most organisations were simple, stable and thus predictable. However, these conditions rarely exist in the 21st century and the validity of the rational model of strategy has been questioned.

The emergent school of thought considers strategy to develop incrementally, step by step, as organisations learn, sometimes through simple actions of trial and error. The core belief is that strategy is comprised of a stream of organisational activities that are continuously being formulated, implemented, tested, evaluated and updated. Chaffee (1985) suggests that strategy should be considered in terms of a linear, adaptive or interpretive approach, each one reflecting a progressively sophisticated perspective. While the linear approach reflects the more traditional and deliberate approach to strategy (Ansoff 1965; Andrews 1987), the adaptive strategy is important because it reflects the view that organisations flex and adjust to changing environments while the interpretive or higher-order point of view considers strategy to be a reflection of the influence of social order on strategic decision making.

Views on strategy have evolved as our understanding has developed. Strategy is not just about a deliberate, planned approach to business development, although it can be at the functional and competitive levels. Strategy is about the means, speed and methods by which organisations adapt to and influence their environments in order to achieve their goals. What is also clear is that the demarcation between an organisation and its environment is less clear than it used to be. An imaginary line was once used to refer to a border between an organisation and its environment. This line has gone as organisations are now viewed as boundary free. The implications of this borderless concept for advertising are potentially enormous. Not only do contemporary views of strategy amplify the significance of the interaction between strategy and an organisation's environment but they also stress the importance for strategy, at whatever level, to be contextually oriented and determined.

Strategy can be applied at a number of different levels. Corporate or business strategy should determine the purpose and direction of an organisation as a whole. Marketing strategy sets out the role this discipline will play in contributing to the achievement of the corporate goals. Communications are part of the marketing mix and appropriate strategies are set accordingly. As one element of the communications mix, advertising strategy identifies the input that this form of communication can make. In this sense strategies are hierarchical but there should be a clear relationship between each level and an awareness that strategies need to be integrated. Advertising strategy needs to reflect and be consistent with the strategies at other levels as well as the strategies in other communication-based disciplines. Figure 4.1 illustrates these strategic relationships.

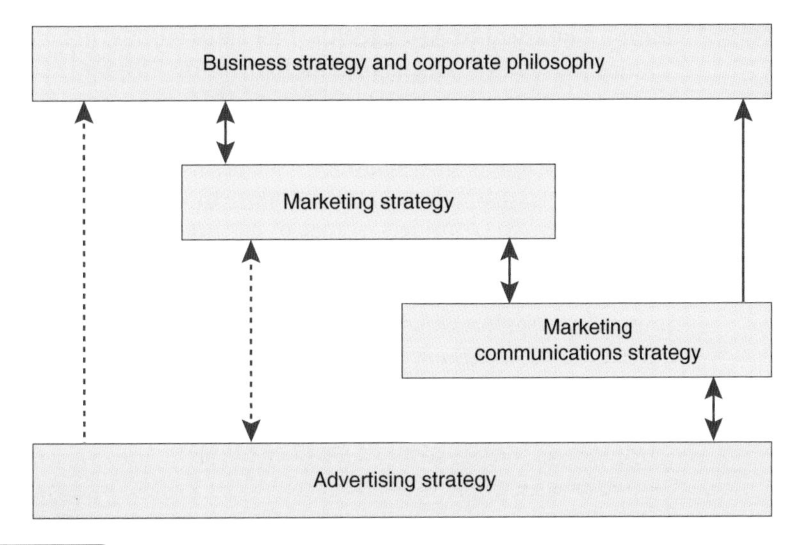

Figure 4.1 Strategic relationship of advertising to business strategy

Integration

Throughout this book we refer to the concept of integration from a number of perspectives. It features significantly when exploring different strategic approaches to communications and advertising planning. Schultz et al. (1993) were among the first academics to give integration serious attention. Despite the considerable interest it has received since, there is no universally accepted definition, either commercially or theoretically.

Smith et al. (1997) examined integrated marketing communications (IMC) from a strategic as well as a tactical perspective. They proposed definitions of IMC which considered common characteristics:

- those that refer to *all* marketing communications
- a strategic management process based on economy, efficiency and effectiveness
- the ability to be applied within any type of organisation.

Various interpretations of the term integrated have been used as alternative ways of exploring the roles and applications of marketing communications. These include 'coordinated' (Hughes and Fill 2008) and 'holistic' (IPA et al. 2007). Whatever terminology is used, success is measured in terms of how effective the resulting communications have been in achieving the objectives set. A significant aspect in the development of IMC has been the change in the nature of the ways communications are thought to work. Hughes (1998) highlighted the shift in emphasis from *promoting to* a target audience to *communicating with* the audience. Two-way, response-driven communication is now prevalent, even for fast-moving consumer goods brands operating on a global scale. There is an increasing emphasis on ensuring that communications are effective at every touchpoint where customers engage a brand.

Schultz and Kitchen (2000: 65) define IMC as 'a strategic business process used to plan, develop, execute and evaluate coordinated measurable, persuasive brand communication programmes over time with consumers, customers, prospects and other targeted, relevant external and internal audiences'. This definition recognises the need for organisations to communicate with a range of target audiences, not only the buyer or end user.

In 2004 Schultz reflected that IMC had been concentrated too much on tactical implementation, particularly from a creative perspective. He believes firms need to examine horizontal integrating processes and develop systems for internal marketing communications and create strategic planning frameworks 'that work across disciplines, not just across communications forms'. Lancaster (2004) suggests two methods for IMC to break through the communications 'clutter' barrier. The first is the requirement for creative executions to extend beyond traditional communications message formats, and into product and service innovation in order to achieve added value. This would emphasise the impact of creativity on the whole marketing mix and not simply the promotional element. The second is that brands should *collude* with customers in terms of how brand engagement should match customer lifestyles and attitudes.

Fill (2009: 256) considers a range of perspectives of IMC and proposes that they 'are more likely to occur when organisations attempt to interact with their various internal and external audiences. The communication mix used in any interaction should be audience-centred and internally consistent with the organisation's objectives and strategies. Target audiences should perceive these communications and associated cues as relevant, likeable, timely and of value.'

Communications strategies

Many organisations do not develop and implement a communications strategy. They may develop brand strategies, advertising strategies and indeed some form of integrated marketing communications strategies but there is little evidence that organisations develop corporate-led communications strategies. Steyn (2003) believes that this might be because practitioners do not fully understand the word *strategy*, while Moss and Warnaby (1998) suggest that academics have neglected the role of corporate communications in the strategy process. Undoubtedly ideas concerning communication and strategy have not always been well articulated and there is certainly little agreement on what constitutes corporate communications and marketing communications strategies.

Marketing communications strategy is concerned with two key dynamics. The first is concerned with who, in broad terms, is the target audience. End-user customers need to derive particular benefits based on perceived value from the exchange process. These benefits are very different from those that intermediaries expect to derive, or indeed any other stakeholder who does not consume the product or service. The second dynamic concerns the way in which an audience understands the offering they are experiencing either through use or through communications. The way in which people interpret messages and frame objects in their mind is concerned with positioning.

Advertising strategy, therefore, is concerned with audiences and positioning.

Audiences

The prevailing approach to marketing communications (advertising) strategy has traditionally been founded upon the configuration of the 'promotional' mix. Strategy was an interpretation of the mix and hence the resources an organisation deployed. This represents a production rather than market orientation to marketing communications and is misplaced. This inside-out form of strategy is essentially resource-driven. However, a market orientation to strategy requires a consideration of the needs of the audience first and then a determination of the various messages, media and disciplines to accomplish the strategy: an outside-in approach.

Consumer purchase decisions are characterised by a single-person buying centre whereas organisational buying decisions can involve a large number of different people, fulfilling different roles and all requiring different marketing communication messages. It follows from this that the approach to communicating with these two very different target sectors should be radically different, especially in terms of what, where, when and how a message is communicated. Once communication objectives have been established, it is necessary to formulate appropriate strategies.

Communication objectives that are focused on consumer markets require a different strategy from those formulated to satisfy the objectives that are focused on organisational customers. In addition, there are circumstances and reasons to focus communications on the development of the organisation with a corporate brand and range of other stakeholders. Often, these corporate brands need to work closely with the development of product brands.

Positioning

As noted earlier, positioning is an integral concept, and for some is the essence of strategy. Wind (1990) stated quite clearly that positioning is the key strategic framework for an organisation's brand-based communications, as cited by Jewell (2007). All products and all organisations have a position in the minds of audiences. The task, therefore, is to actively manage the way in which audiences perceive brands. This means that advertising strategy should be concerned with achieving effective and viable positions so that the target audience understands what the brand does and what it means (to them) and can ascribe value to it. This is particularly important in markets that are very competitive and where mobility barriers (ease of entry into and exit from a market, e.g. plant and production costs) are relatively low.

Positioning is about visibility and recognition of what a product/service/organisation represents to a buyer. In markets where the intensity of rivalry and competition is increasing and buyers have greater choice, identification and understanding of a product's intrinsic values become critical. Channel members have limited capacities, whether this is the level or range of stock they can carry or, for retailers, the amount of available shelf space that can be allocated. An offering with a clear identity and orientation to a particular target segment's needs will not only be stocked and purchased, but can warrant a larger margin through increased added value.

It is generally accepted that positioning is the natural conclusion to the sequence of activities that constitute a core part of the marketing strategy. Market segmentation and target marketing are prerequisites to successful positioning. It has also been established that marketing communications should be an audience-centred rather than product-centred activity. From this it can be concluded that advertising and indeed marketing communications strategies are essentially about positioning. For new products and services, advertising needs to engage target audiences so that they can understand what the brand means and how it differs from similar offerings and as a result position it in their minds. For the vast majority of products and services that are already established, advertising strategy should be concerned with either maintaining a strong position or repositioning it in the minds of the target audiences. Further issues on positioning are considered later in the chapter.

The three Ps of marketing communications strategy

As a result of understanding the broad nature of the target audience and the way we want them to position the offering in their minds, it is possible to identify three generic marketing communications strategies:

Pull positioning strategies – these are intended to influence end-user customers (consumers and B2B);

Push positioning strategies – these are intended to influence marketing (trade) channel buyers;

Profile positioning strategies – these are intended to influence a wide range of stakeholders, not just customers and intermediaries.

These are referred to as the three Ps of marketing communications strategy and as advertising is a part of marketing communications, these strategic initiatives can in principle be legitimately applied to advertising. Push and pull relate to the direction of the communication in the marketing channel: pushing communications down through the marketing channel or pulling consumers/buyers into the channel via retailers, as a result of receiving a communication. They do not relate to the intensity of communication and only refer to the overall approach. Profile refers to the reputation of the organisation as a whole and therefore the identity is said to be 'profiled' to various other target stakeholder audiences, which may well include consumers, trade buyers, business-to-business customers and a range of other influential stakeholders.

Normally, profile strategies do not contain or make reference to specific products or services that the organisation offers. See Table 4.1. This may be blurred where the name of a company is the name of its primary (only) product, as is often the case with many retail brands.

Table 4.1 Generic marketing communications strategies

Strategy	Target audience	Message focus	Communication goal
Pull	Consumers	Product/service	Purchase
	End-user B2B customers	Product/service	Purchase
Push	Channel intermediaries	Product/service	Developing relationships and distribution network
Profile	All relevant stakeholders	The organisation	Building reputation

Profile strategies work to build the reputation of a brand and are often focused on the organisation, not its product offering.

All three of these strategies are intended to position the offering or organisation in particular ways, in the minds of the target audience.

Marketing communications strategy is about the way an organisation positions its products and services in the minds of its customers and stakeholders, and advertising strategy contributes and reinforces the chosen positioning. It must do this in the light of its business and marketing strategies and the prevailing contextual conditions, in order to encourage a degree of interaction and dialogue with selected stakeholders.

A pull positioning strategy

If messages designed to position a brand are to be conveyed to a targeted, end-user audience, then the intention is invariably to generate increased levels of awareness, change and/or reinforce attitudes, reduce risk, encourage involvement and ultimately provoke a behavioural response. This motivation is to stimulate action so that the target audience expects the offering to be available to them when they decide to enquire, experiment or make a repeat purchase. This approach is a *pull (positioning)* strategy and is aimed at encouraging customers to 'pull' products through the channel network. See Figure 4.2 for visual interpretation of this process.

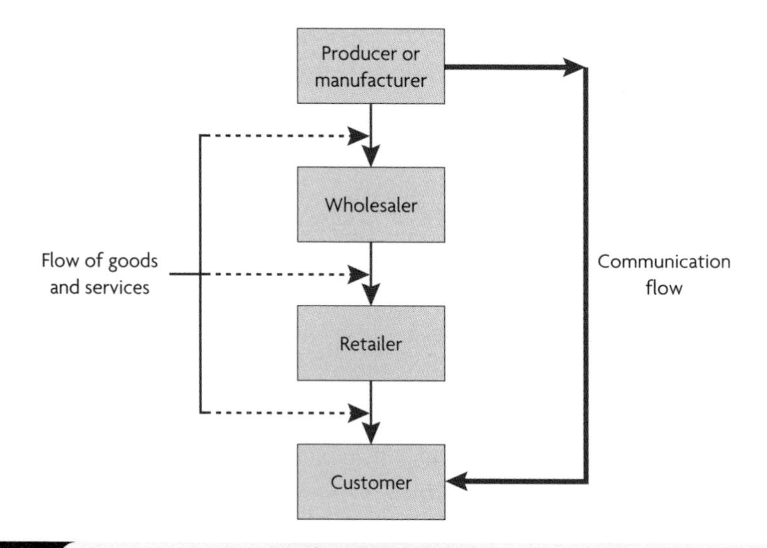

Figure 4.2 Direction of pull positioning strategy

Exhibit 4.2 Costa targets coffee lovers

In this ad, Costa has a clear message that their brand has been voted the nation's favourite. It is aimed directly at all coffee-shop customers. The ad provides information, namely the results of a market research survey, which are detailed in small print at the end of the ad. It also delivers an emotional appeal, through the heart-shaped image on the coffee, and the words 'For coffee lovers'.

Source: Whitbread

To accomplish and deliver a pull positioning strategy, the traditional approach has been to deliver mass-media advertising supported by below-the-line communications, most notably sales promotions. There has been greater use of direct marketing in non-fast-moving consumer goods sectors and use of the web and digital media presents opportunities to reach audiences in new ways, thereby reducing any reliance on the old formulaic approach to pull-based strategies. Exhibit 4.2 gives an example of a print advertisement to illustrate the use of a pull strategy.

A pull positioning strategy, therefore, refers to advertising, including media and messages, that is designed to position an offering in the minds of particular end-user customer audience(s).

A push positioning strategy

A second group or type of target audience can be identified, based first on their contribution to the marketing channel, and second because these organisations do not consume the products and services they buy, but add value before selling the product on to others in the demand chain. The previous strategy was targeted at customers who make purchase decisions related largely to their personal (or organisational) consumption of products and services. This second group buys products and services, performs some added-value activity and moves the product through the marketing channel network. This group is a part of the B2B sector, and the characteristics and issues are those associated with trade channel marketing communications.

Trade channel organisations, and indeed all B2B organisations, are actively involved in the development and maintenance of interorganisational relationships. The degree of cooperation between organisations will vary and part of the role of marketing communications is to develop and support the relationships that exist.

A *push positioning* communications strategy involves the presentation of information in order to influence other trade channel organisations and, as a result, encourage them to take stock and to allocate resources (e.g. shelf space), and to help them to become fully aware of the key attributes and benefits associated with each product with a view to adding value prior to further channel transactions. This strategy is designed to encourage resale to other members of the network and contribute to the achievement of their own objectives. This approach is known as a *push* strategy, as it is aimed at pushing the product down through the channel towards the end users for consumption. See Figure 4.3 for a visual interpretation of this process.

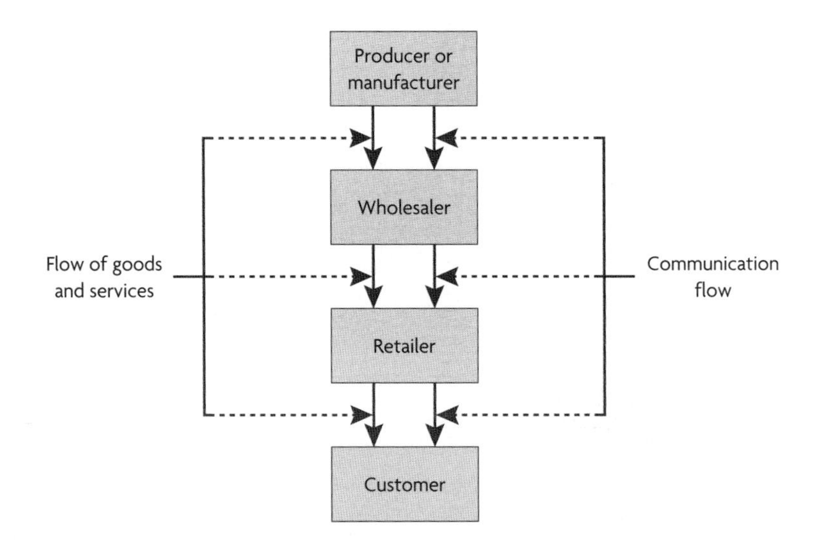

Figure 4.3 Direction of push positioning strategy

A profile positioning strategy

The strategies considered so far concern the need for dialogue with customers (pull) and trade channel intermediaries (push). However, there is a whole range of other stakeholders, many

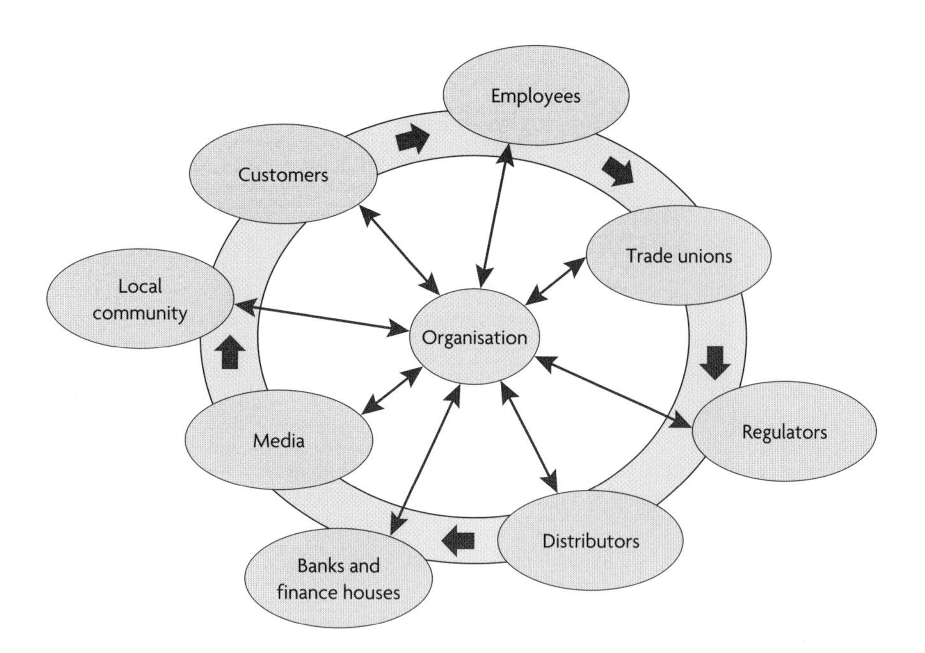

Figure 4.4 Direction of profile positioning strategy

of whom need to know about and understand the organisation rather than actually purchase its products and services. See Figure 4.4 for a visual interpretation of this process. This group of stakeholders may include financial analysts, trade unions, government bodies, employees or the local community. It should be easy to understand that these different stakeholder groups can influence the organisation in different ways and, in doing so, need to receive (and respond to) different types of messages.

Communications used to satisfy this array of stakeholder needs and the organisation's corporate promotional goals are developed through what is referred to as a profile strategy, a major element of which is corporate branding.

The awareness, perception and attitudes held by stakeholders towards an organisation need to be understood, shaped and acted upon. This can be accomplished though continual dialogue, which will normally lead to the development of trust and commitment and enable relationships to grow. This is necessary in order that stakeholders act favourably towards an organisation and enable strategies to flourish and objectives to be achieved.

To build corporate brands, organisations must develop modern integrated communication programmes with all of their key stakeholder groups. Audiences demand transparency and accountability, and instant online access to news, developments, research and networks means that inconsistent or misleading information must be avoided. As if to reinforce this, a survey reported by Gray (2000) found that CEOs rated the reputation of their organisations as more important than that of their products. However, the leading contributor to the strength of the corporate brand is seen to be their products and services, followed by a strong management team, internal communications, PR, social accountability, change management and the personal reputation of the CEO.

Stakeholder analysis is used in the development of strategic plans, so if an organisation wants its communications to support the overall plan, it makes sense to communicate effectively with the appropriate stakeholders. Rowe et al. (1994) point out that, because of the mutual interdependence of stakeholders and the focus organisation, 'each stakeholder is in effect an advocate of any strategy that furthers its goals'. It follows, therefore, that it is important to provide all stakeholders with information that enables them to perceive and position

Helping to move the Games smoothly.

At BP, we're dedicated to fuelling the success of London 2012. We're using our latest technology to help over 5000 Games vehicles run smoothly with our advanced fuels, lower carbon biofuels and engine oils. We're also supporting British athletes like Lizzie Armitstead as she prepares for the Games.

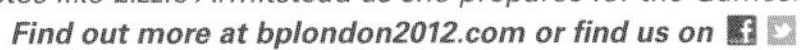

London 2012. Fuelling the Future.

Exhibit 4.3 BP fuelling London 2012

This is one of a number of print advertisements BP developed in support of their sponsorship of the London Olympics in 2012. By associating BP with a major global event they are seeking to favourably influence a range of stakeholders including investors, government, suppliers and pressure groups, as well as customers. As the official oil and gas partner for the games, BP will fuel vehicles used during the Olympics. The association also includes support for the Cultural Olympiad, which includes arts and education projects.

Source: Picture courtesy of BP plc

the organisation, so as to generate the desired corporate image. This requires a communications strategy that addresses these particular requirements, even though there may not be any immediately recognisable shift in performance.

A *profile positioning* strategy focuses an organisation's communications upon the development of stakeholder relationships, corporate image and reputation, whether that be just internally, just externally or both. To accomplish and deliver a profile strategy, advertising's contribution is to provide support, credibility and trust to enable product and service behaviour.

The Institute of Practitioners in Advertising (IPA) describe the achievement of a successful communications strategy as a 'holy grail' in marketing. This view is based on the complex issues that might affect such development. Challenges include media fragmentation, pressures on consumer time, new technologies, agency–client relationships and evaluation. They argue for a 'holistic approach to planning how a brand engages its audience' as a platform for developing effective communications strategy. How firms might go about this process is published in the form of joint industry guidelines: 'Communications strategy – a best-practice guide to developing communications campaigns'.

Advertising strategies

Whilst the pull, push and profile strategies might be described as generic and require the use of all elements of the communications mix, advertising strategies are often described in more specific terms. It is here perhaps that the definitions and meanings of strategy become more complex or even blurred. Strategies can be developed and applied to branding, creative, positioning, media and other contexts. We explore some of the strategic issues associated with these areas in other parts of the book.

Advertising strategies are often described in terms of the kinds of appeals the content of the advertising uses. Essentially these are emotional or informational. However, this demarcation is too broad and there is always a blend of emotional and informational content in all ads. The IPA refer to influence strategies and identify six types of influence used by clients.

Generally, emotional influence strategies are more successful than information strategies, especially when markets are buoyant (Binet and Field 2007). The IPA found that fame campaigns were the most successful of these strategies but the success of these different strategies is dependent on context (see Table 4.2).

Table 4.2 Influence strategies

Influence strategy	Explanation
Emotional involvement	Touches feelings or emotions so that there is empathy between a consumer and the brand, a relationship develops and choice is influenced.
Fame	Seeks to get a brand talked about and to make it famous, so that it is perceived as bigger and more important than before.
Information	Uses a logical, rational argument about a brand (user or category). 'Works fastest' or 'No other brand works faster' are typical approaches.
Persuasion	Seeks to get the audience's interest through information and news, and then adds an emotional element in order to make the message memorable.
Reinforcement	By maintaining existing behaviour through encouraging increased frequency or weight of brand usage, the aim is to build loyalty.
More complex	These combine two or more of the above influence strategies.

Source: Based on Binet and Field (2007)

Scholars' paper 4.1 **Some brands need a touch of advertising**

Dens, N. and De Pelsmacker, P. (2010) Consumer response to different advertising appeals for new products: the moderating influence of branding strategy and product category involvement, *Journal of Brand Management*, 18, 50-65

The authors examine the relationship between branding strategy, advertising execution strategies and product category involvement. Among the principal outcomes of their research the authors suggest that consumers prefer extensions of existing brands rather than new brands. Advertising execution strategies can have significant impact on product and brand attitudes and purchase intention for new brands. Informational appeals are most successful in high-involvement circumstances.

Conceptually, advertising strategy should be based around a core theme, or platform. Such thematic thinking should encapsulate the essence of the brand, often referred to as a brand proposition or promise. This is used to shape all aspects of a campaign, including the other disciplines, and is shared among all participating agencies. The proposition influences the planning, the creative idea, the media mix, and campaign implementation and evaluation. As a result, levels of integration can improve, conflicts are avoided, or at least minimised, and, above all else, the brand is perceived to have a clear and consistent position in the market.

Objectives and strategic development

Effective strategic development at all levels needs to be based on the setting of clear and detailed objectives.

Understanding the firm's current and past situation and the audience's perspective through the context analysis (see below) should provide a base for thinking about what it is that needs to be achieved through advertising, and how it is to be accomplished. We cannot realistically set objectives for advertising and other communication activities without considering how these relate to what we are trying to achieve from a business and marketing perspective. Business objectives are often set out in company mission statements and relate to being leaders in specific fields of operation. However, these are too broad and are not quantified. This makes them impractical for use in campaign activity. Binet and Field (2007) identify the use of profitability, market-share gains and return on investment as appropriate business (or marketing) goals. In addition, communication objectives, such as improving awareness levels, changing an audience's perception or attitude toward a brand or even influencing beliefs, should be set.

As with all objectives they should be SMART – specific, measurable, achievable, realistic and timed. In terms of being *specific* it is important to identify the variable or element to which the objective relates. This could be an increase in brand awareness levels amongst the designated target audience. Having identified what is being measured, what *measurement* criteria will be used? So having identified that we want to increase brand awareness, we need to know what current levels are. This would normally be expressed as a percentage of the target audience determined from market research. The measurement criteria would then be by how many percentage points we are seeking to increase. The objectives quite clearly need to be

ViewPoint 4.1 Retailer aims to make customers' lives easier

In September 2011, Sainsbury's supermarkets announced significant changes to their corporate aims and objectives. Their revised business goal is to 'make all our customers' lives easier every day by offering great quality and service at fair prices'. Alongside this they have set a vision 'to be the most trusted retailer where people love to work and shop'.

Under the central theme of 'Live well for less', Sainsbury's corporate objectives are stated as:

> The company's strategy centres around five areas of focus. These areas are underpinned by Sainsbury's strong heritage and brand which consistently sets it apart from major competitors.

- Great food at fair prices
- Accelerating the growth of complementary non-food ranges and services
- Reaching more customers through additional channels
- Growing supermarket space
- Active property management.

Mike Coupe, Sainsbury's group commercial director, said: 'Sainsbury's *Live well for less* marks a huge step forward in how we deliver to our customers. We know that budgets are under more and more pressure but people still want to have the quality products and goods that they can trust. *Live well for less* will drive everything we do. We are not resting on our laurels, we are ensuring that we will help customers to enjoy competitive prices, without compromising on quality or values.'

To support the new corporate theme, Sainsbury's launched a major marketing communications campaign across broadcast, print and online. A new TV advert highlighted Sainsbury's pledge to help its customers to live well for less by showing the satisfaction viewers can gain from enjoying the small things in life.

These revised objectives recognise the importance of marketing factors such as product range development, pricing, store location planning and promotional activities when setting targets for market-share gains. The communications identified the role that advertising plays in relation to the business and marketing goals. Communications and subsequent advertising objectives can be set to achieve targets with specific outcomes. These might include creating or raising awareness levels, changing or reinforcing attitudes and perceptions and affecting consumer behaviour.

Earlier Sainsbury's campaigns have featured celebrity chef Jamie Oliver as their focal point for promoting food lines. They have also become the first-ever sole sponsor of the London 2012 Paralympic Games. Activities related to this sponsorship will take place at all the company's stores, including family fun days. This is consistent with the vision identified earlier to be a trusted retailer and a good example of a profile-related positioning strategy.

Source: Based on www.jsainsburys.co.uk, accessed 3 October 2011

Question

How effective do you think it is to use celebrities to advertise brands such as Sainsbury's?

Task

Compare and contrast the corporate objectives of Sainsbury's with those of their major competitors.

achievable and *realistic* in the context of the resources available and the timescales set. The *timing* of campaign activities needs to be clearly scheduled and understood by all parties involved. Further issues concerning the role and nature of advertising goals are explored in Chapter 13.

Scholars' paper 4.2 Setting advertising goals for the first time

Colley, R. (1961) *Defining Advertising Goals for Measured Advertising Results*. New York: Association of National Advertisers

Colley is credited with introducing the idea that good advertising practice required setting precise advertising goals. Defining Advertising Goals for Measured Advertising Results, or DAGMAR as it inevitably became, was first published in this book. In tune with the then current practice, Colley recommended a hierarchical model of communications, one which paralleled the purchase-decision process. Colley's model is significant in its focus on the setting and measurement of objectives and is not purely an examination of the communications process itself. It has also been used widely in the context of setting advertising budgets, which are examined in Chapter 7.

Advertising planning and frameworks

The development of a carefully structured marketing communications plan is a critical facet of the communications process. If there is any lack of clarity in the planning phase, this will have significant consequences for the activity which follows.

In the same way that advertising strategy is a subset of an overarching communications strategy, so, when planning, advertising needs to be considered relative to the other communication tools being used. In developing a marketing communications plan, adopting a systematic process is important in order to ensure that all parts of the plan are given detailed attention. Planning needs some degree of flexibility in adapting to the individual needs of the business. A planning framework can assist in making sure all facets are given due consideration in developing effective marketing communications. Fill (2009) proposes a marketing communications planning framework (MCPF) as a suitable model for thorough consideration of all of those factors. This is illustrated in Figure 4.5.

This serves a number of purposes. One is to identify specific aspects of such a plan and the general order in which they occur and to suggest that all the parts are integrated as part of an overall plan. The MCPF recognises the linkages between the parts of the plan as well as links

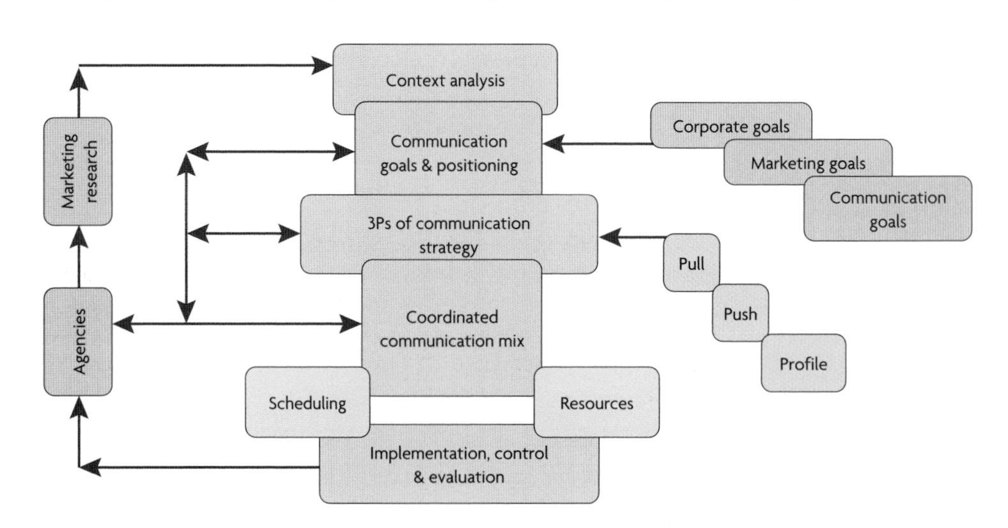

Figure 4.5 The marketing communications planning framework (MCPF)
Source: Fill (2009)

Table 4.3 Elements of a context analysis

Contexts	Explanation
Business	Corporate and marketing strategy and plans Brand/organisation analysis Competitor analysis
Customer	Segment characteristics Levels of awareness, perception and attitudes towards the brand/organisation Level of involvement Types of perceived risk Decision-making unit (DMU) characteristics and issues
External	Who are the key stakeholders and why are they important? What are their communication needs? Social, political, economic and technological restraints and opportunities
Internal	Financial constraints Organisation identity Culture, values and beliefs Marketing expertise Agency availability and suitability

with other elements of the business. For example, communications objectives need to be tied in with what the business as a whole is trying to achieve and what role communications play as part of a wider marketing mix (see Table 4.3).

In line with many other planning frameworks and processes, the MCPF begins with developing an understanding of the current business and marketing situation. Fill suggests that this might be best achieved via a series of context analyses examining different elements of the organisation's situation.

Putting the car market in context

The global car market is well developed and highly competitive. A number of the world's largest companies are involved in automotive manufacturing – Ford, General Motors, Nissan, Honda and Toyota – and have production facilities in many different countries and market cars on a global scale. Advertising has long played a significant role for all manufacturers and accounts for a significant level of expenditure. Here we explore the range of issues that would need to be considered in a context analysis as a platform for the development of effective communications and advertising.

Business context

Automotive markets consist of large global players competing aggressively across a range of different sectors. As an industry it has been the subject of widescale merger and acquisition activity, as competitors battle for market share and profitability resulting from manufacturing and distribution economies of scale. Ford acquired Jaguar and Volvo brands in attempting to establish themselves in the sports and prestige sectors of the market. Jaguar and Land Rover are now owned by the Indian Tata group. Nissan and Renault have joint-venture operations in the European market. Where such activity takes place, in most cases original brand names are maintained.

Customer context

Variations in product designs and specifications meet the needs of a wide range of different market segments. Producers such as Ford and Peugot compete in the high-volume sectors where price levels would be in the region £10,000 to £25,000. Brands including BMW and Mercedes produce and market in lower volumes but at significantly higher prices with premium specifications. Market trends have seen increasing popularity and demand for SUV/people carriers and four wheel drive models in response to changing lifestyles of customers. Consumer attitudes and perceptions related to car purchase are commonly based on emotive and other personal feelings. This provides significant scope for positioning and creative advertising development.

Internal context

Car manufacturers employ significant numbers of people across the globe. The level of merger, acquistion and joint-venture activity identified in the business context has led to manufacturing plant closures and associated job losses. This has had significant impact on communities in those geographic areas. Internal communication plays a key role in providing employees with information on company actions and developments. Market demand has been constrained in most markets as a result of the economic recession, resulting in pressure on profitability, and indeed many producers continue to report heavy financial losses. Despite this, significant budgets are allocated toward advertising expenditure as manufacturers attempt to defend and grow market share.

External context

Given the scale and scope of manufacturing and marketing on a global basis, there can be significant variance in political, economic, social, technological, legislative and environmental circumstances. This can impact on a number of aspects of a manufacturer's business, not least influencing consumer demand as economic conditions worsen. Environmental concerns surrounding oil consumption and pollution put pressure on manufacturers to find alternative power sources including electrically powered vehicles.

Objectives

We identified earlier how objectives might be set and what they should be related to. They should be based on the outcomes of the context analysis.

Strategies

We discussed the three principal communications strategies above – pull, push and profile. In planning terms, each strategy will be considered as to how it might best be deployed to achieve the objectives set within the boundaries identified in the context analysis. For most firms all three strategic approaches might be relevant. We therefore also need to consider the relationship between the strategies. Fill (2009) describes this as 'strategic balance'.

Communications mixes

Advertising is one element of the communications mix. For consumer brand companies it is usually the major element, but it does not operate in isolation from other parts of the mix. This was discussed when considering issues of integration. In planning the use of different parts of the mix there is a need to evaluate how effective each part will be in achieving set objectives and the appropriate strategic context. Each strategy requires its own communications mix.

Resources

The internal context analysis will have provided details of the financial resources available and the level of managerial expertise within the organisation that can be allocated to communications development. Within the MCPF, it is necessary to consider in more detail the specifics of allocation to different activities. In terms of advertising, how much will a new campaign cost and who will manage it? The methods identified in Chapter 7 to set budgets will be used to consider how much finance is available overall. The plan will determine how it will be spent. This is achieved utilising project-planning techniques such as Gantt charts and spreadsheet analysis.

Scheduling and implementation

Determining the most effective timing of activities including media planning would again involve detailed project planning. This could be done internally but for major companies it would be the responsibility of advertising and/or media agencies.

Control and evaluation

We shall examine how advertising can and should be evaluated in more detail, in Chapter 11. In Chapter 7 we discuss the change in the ways advertising agencies are remunerated with shifts from paying media commissions to performance-based methods. It is therefore of increasing significance to measure the effectiveness of different activities including media to allow performance to be assessed against the objectives set. This might involve the use of market research to measure advertising awareness through recall and recognition tests, sales or market-share movements or responses to sales promotion activity. Increasingly, econometrics are being utilised to measure returns on investment linked to sales. Econometrics allows all factors, including the communications, to be taken into account in measuring performance. What would have happened anyway if an advertising campaign had not taken place? In the joint industry guidelines on evaluation published by the IPA et al. (2005), Waitrose's head of marketing, Amanda Bindon, states: 'Evaluating marketing communications should be a core part of our discipline. A culture of testing new ideas, then amending strategy in the light of the findings, is a critical part of the evaluation of a communications strategy. But what is really vital is the effect on the business because that's what generates the budget. If you can work in partnership with the finance team to agree measurement procedures and criteria, you have a much more robust argument to support your budget.'

Egan (2007) recommends basing communications planning on a SOSTCE (situation, objectives, strategies, tactics, control and evaluation) framework. This is illustrated in Figure 4.6.

Although this is similar to many planning models including the MCPF, Egan highlights the need for plans to be continually revised based on continuing assessment of the current situation and evaluation of the plans, effectiveness and efficiency. As in the MCPF, the SOSTCE model recognises the need for the communications plan to relate to corporate and marketing objectives.

Scholars' paper 4.3 **Linked up in the sky**

Elms, S. (2011) Integrated planning – cloud thinking, *Admap*, April, 10-12.

This article considers issues related to the difficulties in planning in the context of consumer decision making. Consumers are influenced by their own 'cloud of noise' at different times and in different ways. Within this cloud are stored an individual's emotions, knowledge and experiences concerning the brands they have associations with. Relationships with brands might be planned or unplanned. The paper argues that brand communications are not linear and that planners need to accept this in order to better understand how they might influence behaviour.

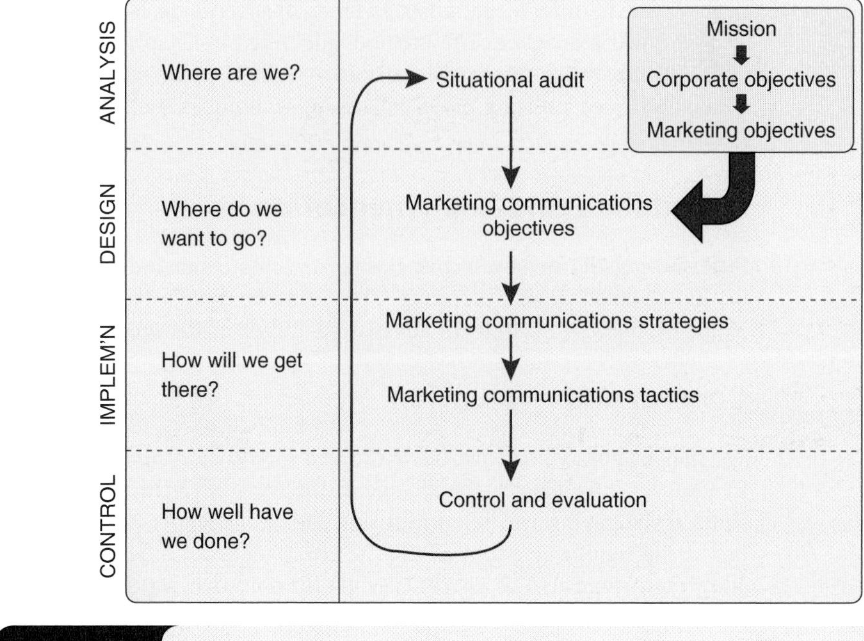

Figure 4.6 SOSTCE marketing communications plan
Source: Egan (2007)

For advertising purposes, Hughes and Fill (2007) suggest a campaign planning model. This is, of course, part of a secondary process identifying the need for detailed planning at a tactical level. This model is shown in Figure 4.7.

See ViewPoint 4.2, which examines the campaign plan for the Pringles snack brand development in the Chinese market.

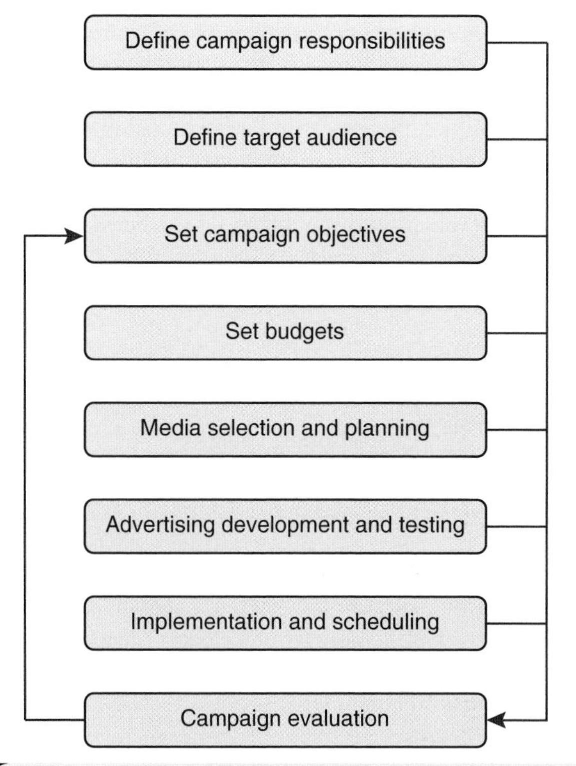

Figure 4.7 The advertising campaign planning process
Source: Hughes and Fill (2008)

ViewPoint 4.2 Pringles crunch into China

The snack brand Pringles had only a small share of the highly competitive market in China. Additionally, their 50% price premium made life even more challenging. In 2009, the product was made 'crunchier' than earlier offerings. An integrated campaign was launched aimed at promoting the functional product benefit - 'crunchiness' - fun and engaging. Following the Hughes and Fill model, the campaign consisted of the following stages:

Campaign responsibilities

Agency, Grey Advertising in Hong Kong, was appointed to develop the campaign for Pringles.

Target audience

This was termed Generation (Gen) Y - single males and females 18-24 years old. In most other markets, the target audience is primarily mothers with children.

Campaign objectives

- Engage target audience.
- Strengthen brand equity attributes (crunchiness).
- Drive sales and profit.

Budget

Media budget was less than $1 million.

Media selection and planning

- Online videos
- Application game and social-networking site
- Bulletin Board System (BBS) programme - internet forum
- Flash mobbing video in Beijing - used on video-sharing sites
- Online press releases
- In-store activity

Advertising development and testing

Consumer insights were gained via visits to Gen Y homes, accompanied store visits and social interaction. This identified that Gen Y spend little time watching TV compared to online sources of entertainment. Other information was gathered from published market research, magazines, blogs and websites. Qualitative product research was carried out on the crunchiness - 'KaCha' - concept. Positive results were followed up using quantitative techniques.

Implementation and scheduling

Three branded online videos were launched at the end of July 2009. Two weeks later, three unbranded videos with twisted endings were released.

- Game and brand zone was live in mid August 2009.
- End of August - BBS programme launched.
- Flash mobbing, one month after online videos.
- August-September - in-store activities, point of sale and tastings.

Campaign evaluation

- Sales outperformed category average annualised growth.
- Online videos achieved excellent impact on brand metrics and significantly increased all Pringles brand equity attributes (Millward Brown). Over 10 million hits in eight weeks.
- Brand zone and application game performed much better than most site campaigns (Millward Brown).
- Flash mobbing video generated over 1.1 million views (Hill and Knowlton).

Source: Based on www.warc.com/prize

Question

Why were the media chosen by Pringles effective in this case?

Task

Prepare an outline advertising campaign plan for a consumer brand in a market of your choice.

This process highlights the need to align specific and meaningful ***objectives*** with the realistic costs that would be required to achieve them. Individual agencies involved in developing campaigns need to set objectives associated with their communications disciplines – advertising, PR, sales promotion, etc. – in the light of the overall campaign objectives. It should be clear at the outset how the achievement of objectives will be evaluated during the course of the campaign. Options recommended for ***customer targeting*** are based on criteria including user behaviour, lifestyles and attitudes, geo-demographics and database segmentation. See ViewPoint 4.3. The ***customer journey*** recognises the purchase-decision-making processes involved in acquiring products and services. Further, it is important to identify the roles for different media usage at different stages of the process. The development of ***communications ideas*** might take a number of different forms. ISBA have developed a set of guidelines for developing integrated communications plans, see Figure 4.8. The idea could suggest some kind of 'higher purpose'. The Dove soap brand challenged stereotypical images for the sector by promoting Dove as the soap for real women, with women in the advertising, not retouched images of models. Ideas might be '*platform*'-based involving an event, a competition or a promotion. Examples include Nike's Human Race London or the Red Bull Air Race. Government campaigns such as quitting smoking are highlighted as examples where the communications idea is related to '*behavioural change*'. '*Brand icons/devices*' have become popular forms of expressing communications ideas (see Figure 4.8).

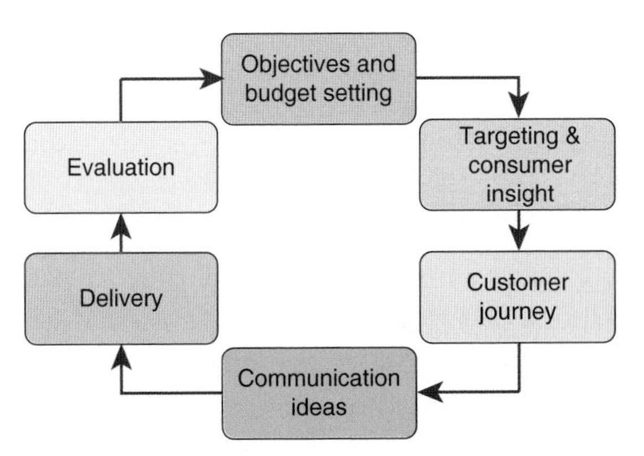

Figure 4.8 ISBA integrated communications planning process
Source: ISBA

ViewPoint 4.3 It's how they behave and what they look like

Detailed knowledge of customers is significant for accurate segmentation and targeting. Who they are and what they do are key questions to understand. What they do with the products they buy is increasingly a key area for market research attention. The French cosmetic company L'Oréal has identified that women in Korea apply a wider range of cosmetic-related products to their faces than women in other markets, more than 25 types at any one time. This compares to 20–25 in Japan and is more than double that of US and European females. Japanese women apply up to 50 coatings of mascara compared to 5–10 applications by European users. Observation-based research in homes and 'evaluation centres' is used for such assessments. Brazilian females will change the colour of their nail varnish daily to match the colour of their clothing. This level of customer knowledge aids product development, segmentation and targeting, packaging design and positioning via creative advertising.

After launching the Axe deodorant brand in Japan, Unilever identified that the product was being used on some half the number of occasions it was in other markets. In Japan deodorant spraying by males is not a routine daily grooming process. It is, however, done as part of grooming for socialising and special events. In order to persuade users to make spraying more of a daily routine, a campaign was developed to send messages via a mobile phone wake-up service, with a sexy voice reminding participants to spray when they got up. The campaign created huge market buzz and Axe repeat purchase rose significantly resulting from the change in male behaviour.

A number of brands in the United States including Kraft and Adidas have been testing new ways of identifying customers and making product recommendations. New technology developed by Intel scans faces of customers in-store to determine gender and age profiles. Adidas is testing 'digital walls' to display products for individual customers based on facial recognition. Kraft is considering the trial of kiosks in supermarkets where consumers can interact with suggested brands based on recognition. Universal Studios in Japan use facial recognition of annual pass holders to facilitate speedy entry to their theme park. Google have developed similar technology but have been reluctant to go to full launch. Facebook's use of facial recognition to aid photo tagging has come under threat in some markets for violation of privacy and data protection laws.

Source: Based on Lucas (2010); WARC (2011); Li and Sarno (2011)

Question

What other bases can a firm use to segment their target audiences? How would these inform marketing communications?

Task

Identify what kinds of information related to product usage would assist producers of the following: a) beer; b) shampoo; c) instant coffee.

Comparethemarket's creation of the meerkat character has produced significantly enhanced results. The icon could be a real person used in celebrity endorsement. '*Tone of voice or visual style*' can be an effective way of establishing a brand's communication idea. The Lloyds/TSB 'For the journey' campaign utilises a distinctive animated visual style. Communications ideas should be '*integratable*'– capable of working across media channels, easy to pass on via word of mouth, generate involvement and engagement, be relevant and meaningful to the target audience. Effective ***delivery*** involves an integrated approach to campaign project management of budgets and time schedules. As identified earlier, ***evaluation*** needs to be considered when setting objectives identifying both what needs to be measured and what forms of evaluation will be appropriate. Differences between outputs, out-takes and outcomes are suggested as bases for measurement. Outputs can include column inches resulting from PR activities, attendances at a promoted event or visits to websites. Out-takes relate to changes in (customer) awareness, (product/service) consideration and (customer) attitudes. Outcomes might be 'interim'– obtaining quotations, for example – or 'business' specific – achievement of sales or profit targets.

Baskin (2011) considers a range of issues associated with developing and planning integrated campaigns. She suggests there is some industry confusion regarding the terminology used to describe different approaches to planning. These include media neutral planning (MNP), communications planning (CP) and integrated planning (IP).

Baskin proposes three interpretations for successful integrated campaigns. Firstly, '*matching shoes and handbag*' requires that creative executions correspond with each other, and are presented consistently in strategically relevant environments. The O2 mobile phone network launch using blue bubbles is highlighted as an example of this approach. Secondly, communications should be led by a '*core objective and strategic vision*' and not be guided by media choice. This is beneficial when considering campaigns that seek to effect behavioural change such as the UK government's anti-smoking promotions. The final interpretation is a '*platform idea*'. Here an event, promotion or competition is used to unite operations and communications. The Nike Grid, a real-life gaming platform for young runners in London, is considered an effective example of a platform which builds on the brand's strengths. It ran for two weeks and was developed by multiple agencies.

A similar perspective on communications planning is taken by McKenzie and Royne (2009). They suggest a customer-centric approach to CP aimed at making 'every consumer touchpoint a unique one so that messages are carefully and specifically targeted'. They describe the development of CP by Procter and Gamble involving detailed consumer research to maximise consumer engagement. Customer understanding will aid the integration of the communications planning agencies involved in the account. They propose that although CP has yet to be fully developed, there is some concensus within the communications industry that one of the key planning principles is the need for detailed customer information.

Positioning

Having made decisions on segmenting their markets and identifying target audiences, companies then need to design marketing mixes, *products and services*, which meet the needs of customers more effectively than those of their competitors. This is part of the positioning process. Figure 4.9 identifies the main criteria that need to be evaluated at this stage.

Using positioning examples related to the car market, the following are regarded by Fuchs and Diamantopoulos (2010) to be the most common positioning platforms:

- **Features or concrete attributes:** e.g. horsepower; price; air conditioning.
- **Abstract attributes:** e.g. quality; style; sporty; fast acceleration; innovativeness.

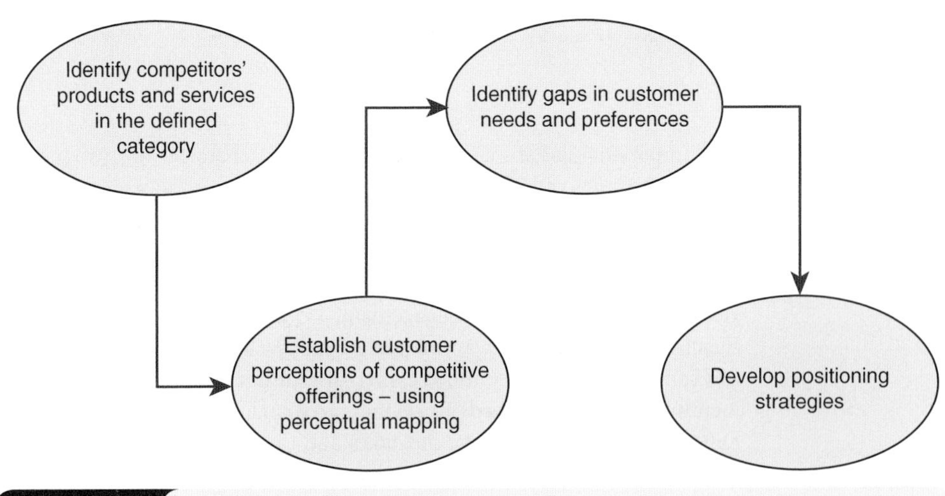

Figure 4.9 Key stages in developing positioning platforms

Scholars' paper 4.4 Position and succeed

Ries, A. and Trout, J. (1972) The positioning era cometh, *Advertising Age*, 24 April, 35–8

This is a classic paper that should be read by everyone associated with this subject. It was the first paper to outline the positioning concept. Ries and Trout argue that what matters is not what a marketer does to a product itself, but how they influence the mind of a prospective customer. As the level of competition has extended so much, there is often little to choose between the actual products themselves. It should therefore be the role of marketing to differentiate based on what customers think about them. Such differences might be real or just perception.

- **Direct functional benefits;** e.g. cost reduction; park in smallest slots; comfort; convenience; durability; superior service; ease of use.
- **Indirect or symbolic benefits;** e.g. draws people's looks; makes driver feel younger; gives you respect; driving experience; driving fun.
- **Surrogate or user-based positioning;** e.g. user type 'for people who never grow up'; making associations with Formula 1 or great writers; highlighting the pioneer status; product category disassociations; 'the bestselling car'.

Whilst it is usually clear what a product is, a car for example, what makes one car different, or *appear* different, from another can be achieved via effective positioning. It is the development of effective positioning platforms that provides the basis for advertising strategies to be created. Young (2011) considers that 'positioning should be distinctive, appealing and relevant. It should have rational and emotional components and the emotional part may well be dominant.'

Positioning involves the development of all elements of the marketing mix. In terms of creating advertising themes and messages, these might be based on individual parts of this mix. Price, for example, is commonly used by consumer brand manufacturers to differentiate their products from competitors'. This does not always mean the brand is the lowest price in the category as there are brands that set out to position themselves at the high (price) end of the market. A feature of Stella Artois advertising for a period of time was that the beer was 'reassuringly expensive'. Table 4.4 provides a list of some of the most common ways in which brands set out their brand positioning.

Whilst these examples emphasise individual positioning strategies, brands can achieve competitive advantage by using advertising to promote a number of positioning ideas. Brands are increasingly perceived by consumers in terms of providing a range of brand values and not just for the recognisable product or service benefit that they deliver. Cadbury's use of gorillas playing drums, toy trucks driving around a virtual airfield or a boy and girl raising their eyebrows in time with the music soundtrack and a squeaky balloon has little if any direct relationship to the chocolate as a brand of confectionery. This does not stop the ads being highly effective in lifting the brand's market share and winning creative awards. The advertisements are attempting to demonstrate the additional brand values associated with Dairy Milk, and resulted in a 10% increase in sales of the brand. Tyler (2010) reports on the eyebrows advert being voted ad of the year by website www.tellyads.com. She quotes a spokesman from Cadbury as saying that their 'aim was to create commercials that replicated the '*feel good*' moment of opening a chocolate bar and taking that first bite'.

Cramer and Koene (2011) reflect on research which indentifies 24 human drivers that might influence consumer perceptions and how brands can be positioned. These drivers focus on what individuals consider to be of value to them and include sexuality, materialism, freedom and creativity. Drivers stimulate differing emotional responses to brands. In the watch market, Rolex creates associations to status and ambition whilst Swatch relates to fun and creativity.

Table 4.4 Positioning strategies

Platform	Example	Platform	Example
Price	DFS - UK - furniture - £300 off every sofa	**Performance**	Toyota NZ Hilux - Australia/New Zealand - car - tougher than you can imagine
Quality	Tesco - UK - foods - quality and freshness every day	**Security**	Barclays - UK - banking - growth with security
Benefits	Garnier Fructis - Australia - Shampoo - eco-friendly	**Guarantee**	Nestlé - UK - breakfast cereals - whole grain guarantee
Functions/ features	Audi A8 - UK - cars - no detail is too small	**Distribution/ logistics**	Royal Mail - UK - postal services - handle with care
Lifestyles	McDonald's - China - fast food - let's meet up	**Overcoming perceived risks**	Ronseal - UK - varnishes - it does exactly what it says on the tin
Experience	Schweppes - UK - tonic water - experience counts	**Product usage**	Café Viet - Vietnam - coffee - are you strong enough to try?
Tradition	Warburtons - UK - bread - family bakers - born and bred	**Segmentation variables**	Burger King - UK - fast foods - I am man
Nationality	Rekorderlig - Australia - cider - beautifully Swedish	**Abstract**	Cadbury's Dairy Milk - UK - chocolate - raising eyebrows

Fuchs and Diamantopoulos (2010) consider positioning platforms using three key dimensions. The first is differentiation. Here the brand must be perceived as unique or different from competing brands. The second, favourability, is about the brand being liked by consumers. The third dimension is credibility, the believability of the brand promise and the willingness and ability of the organisation to deliver what they promise. Jointly these three dimensions, differentiation, favourability and credibility, determine the success of the overall brand positioning.

Using the five different types of positioning platforms identified earlier, their research found that benefit and second, surrogate (user) positioning platforms are more effective than feature positioning platforms, across all three of the effectiveness dimensions. This, they suggest, implies that marketers should be cautious about using feature positioning. For marketers, therefore, surrogate positioning is a viable alternative to traditional (feature and benefit) forms of positioning. They also found that the majority of brands are positioned along one dominant positioning base.

Successful and effective positioning should be based on consistent and long-term application. Making frequent changes to the way brands are promoted can lead to confusion amongst customers. If a position lacks clarity why should a customer spend time in making judgements as part of their decision-making processes? Most of the positioning platforms identified in Table 4.4 can usually be articulated clearly and creatively in words and pictures to produce effective advertisements. Abstract themes often based on emotional message appeals are more challenging both in terms of creativity and also from a consumer-understanding perspective.

Competitive positioning can often be best evaluated by using positioning or perceptual mapping. An example of a positioning map is illustrated in ViewPoint 4.4. This shows how Renault attempted to reposition their brand in the German car market to be more closely associated with market-leader brands whose customer perception of safety attributes were most positive.

Young (2011) outlines how perceptual maps should be developed. Conjoint consumer research is recommended in order to identify buyer values, such as attitudes, response to

Exhibit 4.4 Positioning every little spud carefully

The Quality and Freshness Every Day logo provides a clear indicator of Tesco's positional stance. In this product category freshness is an implied indicator of quality. This is supported by the tempting and appealing visual image of the cooked potatoes ready to eat. The copy also provides reassurance from stating that they are harvested daily.

Source: Rudy Agency

brand imagery and brand experiences. These values can then be plotted on a scatter diagram, as illustrated in Figure 4.10. In this illustration brand values are based on price–quality associations. Other physical or emotional attributes could be used where they are identified as significant in the consumer decision-making process.

As will be apparent from the above discussion, positioning issues play a central role in underpinning advertising strategy and tactics. This discussion is continued in Chapter 5 where we examine the development of creativity and content to reflect a brand's positioning requirements.

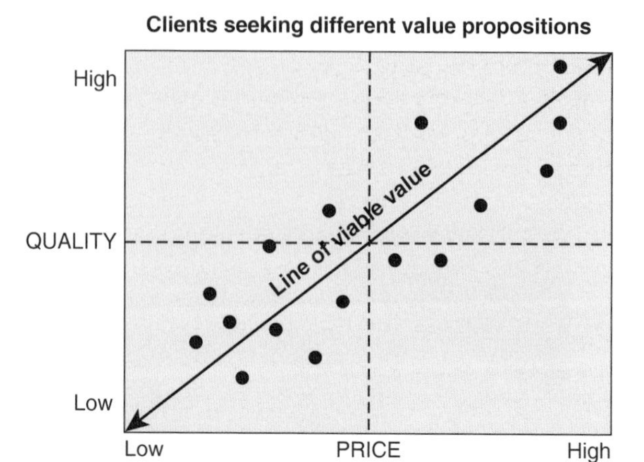

Figure 4.10 A scatter diagram
Source: Reproduced with permission of John Wiley & Sons, 2011

ViewPoint 4.4 Adopting a safe position in Germany

Renault sought to reposition themselves in the highly competitive German market. The French car manufacturer was seeking to expand their market share in the German market, the largest car market in the EU. This was no easy task with 10 of the top-selling models being produced by Volkswagen, Mercedes and DaimlerChrysler. Indeed, country of origin (COO) has been a major feature of advertising campaigns by a number of car producers. In Germany such campaigns were focused on German engineering skills resulting in high-quality and reliable cars. Renault's market research identified that there were other important attributes that influenced German car buyers. Safety was a most significant factor influencing purchase but again German manufacturers were perceived as highly rated on this criterion. Although some other imported models were rated favourably, Renault lagged behind other producers. Renault's director of marketing communications decided therefore to adopt safety as the focal attribute for their planned advertising campaigns. Renault had the advantage of technical evidence that would support their claims regarding the safety as eight of their models had won the European New Car Assessment Programme, making Renault the official manufacturer of the safest cars in Europe.

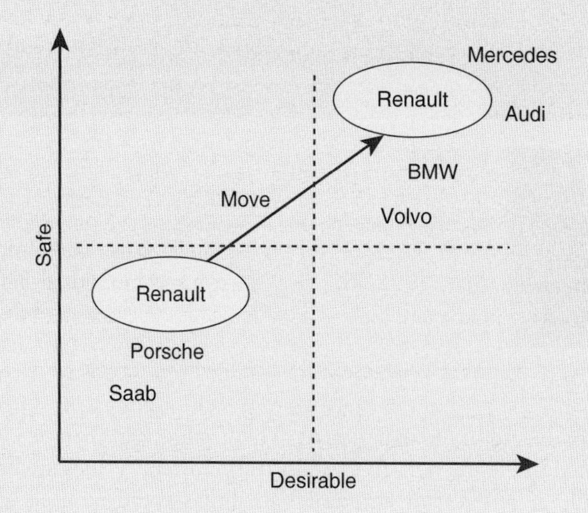

Figure 4.11 Renault positioning map
Source: Caemmerer (2009)

The campaign was targeted at potential new car buyers, male aged between 30 and 49 years. This had been identified by market research as the most profitable segment of the German market. The principal objective of the campaign was to create desire for the Renault brand amongst the target audience by increasing awareness of the brand's unique safety features. It was decided to combine the safety position with the COO angle, resulting in the core message: 'Die sichersten Autos kommen aus Frankreich' ('The safest cars come from France'). Advertising media selected included cinema, TV and viral video via the internet. The safety awards for the Renault models were based on crash tests using dummies. This seemed like a good theme for the advertising but rather than simple replication of the technical tests the creative execution involved slow-motion filming of typical food products associated with other car-producing countries - German sausage, Japanese sushi rolls and Swedish crispbreads. Giant versions of the products were all seen crashing into barriers and splitting into thousands of pieces. A French baguette, on the other hand, is seen absorbing the impact and remaining in one piece. The films were supported with stirring musical accompaniment with French vocal. The film can be accessed via the YouTube link below.

Campaign evaluation demonstrated significant increase in the levels of awareness amongst the target audience relating to Renault's safety. Higher levels of purchase intention were also recorded following the campaign. It was also noted that competitor brands either stayed the same or suffered reduced customer perceptions associated with safety.

Source: Based on Caemmerer (2009); www.youtube.com/watch?v=Vk-bF40ENHO

Question

How might Renault's competitors respond to a campaign of this kind?

Task

Review the advertising of at least five car manufacturers and identify the ways in which they position their brands.

Chapter summary

In order to help consolidate your understanding of advertising strategy and planning from a general perspective here are the key points summarised against each of the learning objectives.

Introduce the concept of strategy

The term strategy is widely used in business and in a variety of contexts. The two broad approaches are the planning and emergent schools of strategy. Strategy has a long-term perspective and is about the means, speed and methods by which organisations adapt to and influence their environments in order to achieve their goals. Three main levels of organisational strategy can be identified: corporate, competitive and functional. This hierarchical nature identifies the need for links and relationships between corporate and discipline-based strategies.

Evaluate the generic approach to marketing communications strategy

Advertising strategy can be considered to be a derivative of the generic three Ps of marketing communications strategy. This refers to strategy as a function of two elements, audiences and positioning. Pull positioning strategies focus on communicating with end users/consumers. Push positioning strategies relate to communication with members of marketing/distribution channels. Profile positioning strategies recognise the need for communications with a wide range of organisational stakeholder groups.

Advertising strategies are often linked with different kinds of appeal, principally emotional or informational.

Explain the role of objectives in the advertising planning process

The setting of advertising campaign objectives is a necessity and is considered to be good practice. These should be a mix of business and communication-related goals. All should be set using the SMART format, enabling them to be measured for effective strategic development.

Consider various frameworks and processes used for planning communications and advertising campaigns

In the light of the complexity and variety of elements involved in planning advertising activities, the use of frameworks and schematics can structure and bring order to this marketing management activity. The MCPF presents the core elements and activities that need to occur in the planning phase. Agencies and their clients normally create their own frameworks and processes but they will have similar characteristics.

Explore the principles of positioning

Positioning is an integral and significant part of advertising strategy. It is concerned with how a target audience perceives a brand, not what the brand actually is. Following detailed assessment of their target audiences, organisations seek a base for differentiating their product or service from their competitors', so that it has high perceived value. This will include establishing customer perceptions and attitudes towards a firm and their competitors' offerings. Perceptual mapping and positioning statements offer an effective way of identifying relative competitive positions in given market sectors.

Assess the merits of different positioning strategies

There are a number of platforms on which a position can be established. These include price, benefits, features, lifestyle, experience, performance and tradition.

Review questions

1. With regard to the challenges presented in the Ulster Bank minicase at the beginning of the chapter, what positioning strategies would you use and which media should be selected to support the positioning strategy?
2. What are the key differences between the planning and emergent schools of strategy?
3. Why is integration considered to be important in the development of strategic communications plans?
4. Explain the significance of distinguishing between business and communications objectives. Provide examples of each.
5. Prepare notes for developing a context analysis for an organisation of your choice.
6. How do pull, push and profile positioning strategies differ in terms of their target audiences? Provide examples.
7. Using secondary research, prepare a presentation showing the key stages of a plan for advertising the launch of a new consumer product in a country of your choice.
8. Why are customer perceptions important in developing effective positioning?
9. Create a perceptual map for the main competitors in one of the following market sectors: beer, airlines, banks.
10. Using www.nmauk.co.uk or www.tellyads.com or by reviewing media in a country of your choice, provide a list of examples to illustrate the positioning platforms suggested in Table 4.4.

Chapter references

Andrews, K. (1987) *The Concept of Corporate Strategy*. Homewood, IL: Richard D. Irwin

Ansoff, H.I. (1965) *Corporate Strategy*. New York: McGraw-Hill

Baskin, M. (2011) Integrated marketing, WARC Best Practice. February. Retrieved 16 August 2011 from www.warc.com

Binet, L. and Field, P. (2007) *Marketing in the Era of Accountability*. Institute of Practitioners in Advertising, Henley-on-Thames: WARC

Caemmerer, B. (2009) The planning and implementation of integrated marketing communications, *Marketing Intelligence and Planning*, 27, 4, 524–38

Chaffee, E. (1985) 'Three models of strategy', *Academy of Management Review*, **10**(1), 89–98

Colley, R. (1961) *Defining Advertising Goals for Measured Advertising Results*. New York: Association of National Advertisers

Cramer, K. and Koene, A. (2011) Brand positioning: create brand appeal, *Admap*, January, 16–18

Crawford, M.C. (1985) A new positioning typology, *Journal of Product Innovation Management*, 2, December, 243–53

Day, G.S. and Wensley, R. (1988) Assessing advantage: a framework for diagnosing competitive superiority, *Journal of Marketing*, 52, 2, 1–20

Dens, N. and De Pelsmacker, P. (2010) Consumer response to different advertising appeals for new products: the moderating influence of branding strategy and product category involvement, *Journal of Brand Management*, 18, 50–65

Egan, J. (2007) *Marketing Communications*. London: Thomson Learning

Elms, S. (2011) Integrated planning – cloud thinking, *Admap*, April, 10–12

Fill, C. (2009) *Marketing Communications; Interactivity, Communities and Content*, 5th edn. Harlow: FT Prentice Hall

Fuchs, C. and Diamantopoulos, A. (2010) Evaluating the effectiveness of brand-positioning strategies from a consumer perspective, *European Journal of Marketing*, 44, 11/12, 1763–86

Gray, R. (2000) The chief encounter, *PR Week*, 8 September, 13–16

Hambrick, D.C. (1983) High-profit strategies in mature capital goods industries: a contingency approach, *Academy of Management Journal*, 26, 687–707

Hughes, G. (1998) Marketing communications activities. In Kitchen, P. (1998) *Marketing Communications: Principles and Practice*. London: Thomson Business Press

Hughes, G. and Fill, C. (2007) Redefining the nature and format of the marketing communications mix, *The Marketing Review*, 7, 1 (Spring) 45–57

Hughes, G. and Fill, C. (2008) *Marketing Communications*. Oxford: Butterworth-Heinemann

IPA et al. (2005) *Evaluation – Best Practice Guidelines*, August. London: IPA

IPA et al. (2007) *Communication Strategy – Best Practice Guide*, February. London: IPA

Jewell, R.D. (2007) Establishing effective repositioning communications in a competitive marketplace, *Journal of Marketing Communications*, 13(4), 231–41

Johnson, G., Scholes, K. and Whittingham, R. (2008) *Exploring Corporate Strategy*, 8th edn. Harlow: Pearson Education

Kay, J. (1993) The structure of strategy, *Business Strategy Review*, 4(2) (Summer), 17–37

Lancaster, G. (2004) Integrated future, *Marketing Business*, January, 20

Li, S. and Sarno, D. (2011) Advertisers start using facial recognition to tailor pitches. *Los Angeles Times*, 21 August, www.latimes.com, accessed 26 August 2011

Lucas, L. (2010) Up-close and personal brands, *Financial Times*, 14 October, 15

McKenzie, K.E. and Royne, M.B (2009) Defining and understanding communications planning: a current assessment and an exploratory study, *Journal of Promotion Management*, 15, 341–56

Mintzberg, H. and Ghoshal, S. (2003) *Strategy Process: Concepts, Context and Cases*. Global edn. Englewood Cliffs, NJ: Financial Times/Prentice-Hall

Moss, D. and Warnaby, G. (1998) Communications strategy? Strategy communication? Integrating different perspectives, *Journal of Marketing Communications*, 4(3), 131–40

Ries, A. and Trout, J. (1972) The positioning era cometh, *Advertising Age*, 24 April, 35–8

Rowe, A.J., Mason, R.O., Dickel, K.E., Mann, R.B. and Mockler, R.J. (1994) *Strategic Management: A Methodological Approach*, 4th edn. Reading, MA: Addision-Wesley

Schultz, D. (2004) Integrated future, *Marketing Business*, January, 21

Schultz, D. and Kitchen, P. (2000) *Communicating Globally: An Integrated Marketing Approach*. Basingstoke: Macmillan Press

Schultz, D.E., Tannenbaum, S.I. and Lauterborn, R.F. (1993) *The New Marketing Paradigm: Integrated Marketing Communications*. Lincolnwood, IL: NTC Business Books

Smith, P., Berry, C. and Pulford, A. (1997) *Strategic Marketing Communications*. London: Kogan Page

Smith, A. and Summers, D. (1996), Get 'em young – The youth market is presenting banks with a seriouschallenge, *Financial Times*, UK, p. 11, 22nd February

Steyn, B. (2003) From strategy to corporate communication strategy: a conceptualisation, *Journal of Communication Management*, 8(2), 168–83

Tank, J. and Tyler, K. (2005) 'UK student banking revisited: Influences and the decision-making process', *Journal Of Financial Services Marketing*, 10, 2, pp. 152–164

Tyler, J. (2010) Cadbury's eyebrows TV ad wins top award, www.birminghammail.net, accessed 26 August 2011

Wind, Y.J. (1990) Positioning analysis and strategy. In *The Interface of Marketing and Strategy* (eds G. Day, B. Weitz and R. Wensley), 387–412. Greenwich, CT: JAI Press

WARC (2011) Axe, Wake Up Service, www.warc.co./prize accessed 17/08/2011

Young, L. (2011) How to use brand positioning, *WARC Best Practice*, July

Chapter 5

Creativity, content and appeals

Developing ads that are understood, have meaning and are relevant to the target audience is a critical part of the advertising process. Advertising messages need to work within specific cultures, regions, and different contexts where there are varying levels of advertising literacy, media accessibility, education and opportunities for involvement. Therefore, understanding the market and having the right creative approach for the development of effective messages are critical to advertising.

Only recently have creativity and content issues received primary attention. Determining what it is that is communicated has become recognised as a key element in brand communications. It is a key part of advertising, and for some it is advertising strategy itself.

Aims and learning objectives

The main aim of this chapter is to explore issues concerning the nature, characteristics and approaches to developing creative advertising messages.

As a result of reading this chapter readers should be able to:

1. explain ideas about what creativity might be and how it is used
2. appraise the nature of the creative process including the relationships between agencies and clients
3. consider the roles and skills of those involved in developing creative advertising
4. determine the key elements of creative advertising content
5. discuss the core forms of message appeals
6. examine how creativity in advertising can be evaluated.

Minicase Creative repositioning needed by Volvo

The Swedish car manufacturer Volvo has traditionally positioned its brands on a safety platform. This strategy has been at the expense of design and style which have been effectively implemented by competitors in the luxury car segments such as BMW, Audi and Mercedes. This has meant that Volvo were never likely to be market leaders, but have nevertheless created a loyal customer base for whom safety is a key factor in their purchase-decision making. They are happy to trade off the fact that the car they are driving is not the height of stylish or modern design.

In creative terms, Volvo TV advertisements were unlikely to show cars being driven in exotic locations. Instead they would show cars in test centres with dummies in the seats and crashing into barriers. This clearly demonstrated the brand safety values, that if involved in an accident, the car would be damaged but the passengers would emerge relatively unscathed. One of the classic features of any Volvo car is that the side lights would always be on when the car is in operation, an essential safety characteristic. This became such a well-known symbol that folklore suggests that even after an old Volvo has been through a car 'crusher', each corner of the metal cube that emerges is brightly lit!

In 1999, Volvo car operations were purchased by Ford. They were attempting to increase their presence in the luxury segments by adding the Volvo brand to a stable that already included the British iconic brand Jaguar. This led to new model developments, more attractive in design terms. Volvo needed to ensure that the sleeker design features would not be interpreted by their loyal customers as the car being any less safe. At the same time it was hoped that improved design would attract new customers who had previously thought of the brand as old-fashioned and ugly. The advertising and other marketing communications had to be carefully planned in order not to alienate existing customers but provide sufficient incentive for drivers of competitive products to consider a switch in brands.

Creatively this included a change from an emphasis on cars being deliberately crashed to one that highlights the importance of design from a wider perspective with brand values significantly beyond inherent safety aspects. The Volvo director of brand

Exhibit 5.1 A Volvo car
Source: Getty Images

strategy, Sven de Smet, explained the shift away from overt claims on safety: 'If you step into a BMW, it's all about driving pleasure. Of course they also have air bags and crumple zones just as we do. But why people buy a BMW is not because it's a safe car. So we have to learn from that and evolve: although I will be the first to admit that it's difficult to reinterpret what you are all about. It is our challenge to interpret functionality in an interesting way' (Josephs 2004).

Ford's success in repositioning the Volvo brand has been limited. A lack of significant investment in both production and marketing saw global market share and sales falling. In 2010, the Volvo brand was acquired by a Chinese automotive manufacturer, Geely Holding Group. Geely hope to re-establish the brand in the luxury market and have targeted to achieve global sales of 800,000 units by 2020, a significant increase on the current annual figure of 450,000. In order to achieve these targets, advertising will focus on promoting how great the cars are rather than apologising for how boring they were perceived to be.

Roberts (2011) reports on changes in the use of agencies by Volvo. The current multi-agency 'Team Volvo' has been dismantled and the account switched to Havas Arnold, who previously had responsibility for North America. They will also now control advertising in the UK and China from 2012. The new creative strategy to be developed will be led by Sean Thompson as global executive creative director. It will be interesting to see how Thompson and his team meet this challenge and the kind of appeals that will give Volvo the kind of image they seek.

Source: Josephs (2004); Roberts (2011)

Introduction

Advertising can be interpreted as a signal of a client's belief in their product and of the marketing effort they have made. The more that is spent on advertising the greater the client's risk. From this observation, consumers can experience reduced levels of uncertainty and have more confidence that the advertiser will keep their promise (Kirmani 1997).

Ambler and Hollier (2004) argue that advertising expense may be a signal of wealth, that if an advertiser can afford such wastefully expensive advertising, this is evidence of the brand's ability to serve the market and of its previous success. Indeed, these authors refer to the interesting concept of 'perceived corporate ability'. This concerns consumers' beliefs that an organisation can generate new products and is capable of improving the quality of their existing products. This is a powerful concept because research shows that not only are new products introduced more successfully when 'perceived corporate ability' is high, but the valuation of the company also increases (Luo and Bhattacharya 2006).

From this Dahlen et al. (2008) argue that advertising creativity can also be considered to be a signal of 'brand ability', the equivalent of corporate ability. The generation of creative advertising concepts can be a signal of an ability to work and think in new and different ways relative to the history of the brand and compared to category advertising standards. It might also say something about higher product quality, and how interesting a brand might be. This is because creative advertising says something about a client's perceived effort and confidence to convey the brand's offer, and to say something different from the competition.

Dahlen et al. (2008) find that the level of advertising creativity sends signals similar to those about advertising expense. More rather than less advertising creativity generates signals that the client is making a big(ger) marketing effort.

Lawson (2011) identifies the contribution that advertising makes to the UK economy and the role for creativity. He argues that 'our [the advertising] industry needs to help our clients build their brands by being nimble, integrated and above all, creative. Creativity is what will continue to set brands apart and fortunately, it's what the UK does best.' In this sense, advertising becomes an investment rather than an expense.

What is creativity?

Whatever it is, creativity matters, and is generally agreed to be a central element of effective advertising (Kim et al. 2010; El-Murad and West 2004).

Early holistic ideas about creativity considered it to be about a violation of expectations, often expressed through contradictory ideas (Blasko and Mokwa 1986; Reid and Rotfield 1976). These views have given way to a general agreement that creativity in advertising has two main characteristics. The first is that creative ads are divergent, or unique and novel, the second, that they are relevant or meaningful (Smith and Yang 2004). These authors contest that a creative ad uses a divergent appeal (unexpected and unusual such as fear or humour), to deliver a relevant core message about the brand (such as an attribute or benefit), yet still allows the audience to interpret and assign meaning to the message within the linkage between the fear or humour and the product. Ideas about divergence and relevance have several interpretations and these are represented in Table 5.1, drawn from Smith et al. (2008).

Shimp (2010) proposes that creative advertising shares three common elements: *connectedness, appropriateness* and *novelty,* what he refers to as the 'CAN' model. Connectedness is described as showing empathy with the target audience and creating a bond with the consumer. Appropriateness suggests that the advertising has to be pertinent to the brand and fit the brand's positioning. Novelty includes being unique, fresh and unexpected but still retains the ability to resonate.

Table 5.1 Interpretations of the dimensions of creativity

Dimension	Explanation
Divergence	
Originality	Ads that contain elements that are rare or surprising, or move away from the obvious and commonplace
Flexibility	Ads that contain different ideas or switch from one perspective to another
Elaboration	Ads that contain unexpected details or finish and extend basic ideas so they become more intricate, complicated, or sophisticated
Synthesis	Ads that combine, connect or blend normally unrelated objects or ideas
Artistic value	Ads that contain artistic verbal impressions or attractive colours or shapes
Relevance	
Ad-to-consumer relevance	Refers to situations where the ad contains execution elements that are meaningful to consumers. For example, using Beatles music in an ad could create a meaningful link to Baby Boomers, thereby making the ad relevant to them
Brand-to-consumer relevance	Refers to situations where the advertised brand (or product category) is relevant to potential buyers. For example, the advertisement could show the brand being used in circumstances familiar to the consumer

Source: Smith et al. (2008)

Scholars' paper 5.1 Can we define creativity?

El-Murad, J. and West, D. (2004) The definition and measurement of creativity: what do we know? *Journal of Advertising Research*, 44/2 (June), 188-201

The paper looks at creativity as arguably the most important element in achieving advertising success. It reviews trends in creativity research in order to establish what is known about advertising creativity, how it can be measured and how it can be enhanced and encouraged. Theories underpinning creativity are examined in order to establish a definition. Issues including the marketing environment and management practice are discussed as well as assessing 'myths' surrounding creative enhancement. Identifies a management need to address obstacles including self-doubt, fear of risk taking, opposition and criticism. Provides a good basis for understanding key principles in understanding what creativity is and the barriers to successful development.

Creativity and attention

Creativity in advertising is considered to be important because of the common belief that creativity is an effective way of getting people to attend to an ad (Rossiter and Percy 1998; Yang and Smith 2009).

A great deal of research into creativity in advertising is concerned with what is referred to as 'attention effects'. This is related to the links between increased attention to an ad, heightened motivation to process the message, and the depth of processing that follows (Smith and Yang 2004). Here, as Baack et al. (2008) comment, the amount of attention paid to advertisements is a function of the amount of cognitive capacity allocated to a task. Only when consumers focus more attention on the advertisement itself, rather than divide their attention among multiple tasks, do higher levels of processing occur. So, the more a creative ad displays high originality or divergence and is personally relevant, the greater the attention it attracts, which leads to a greater depth of message processing, leading to higher recall and recognition scores.

However, Yang and Smith (2009) and Heath et al. (2009) question the proposition that creativity works by increasing attention. They all agree that some attention is necessary but it is not about the direction of attention; it is about the level of attention that is important. Yang and Smith had inconclusive results from their research yet Heath (2010) found that creativity does not increase attention; if anything, it decreases it. However, as Binet and Field (2007) found, emotion-based ads are more successful than information-led campaigns. The conclusion therefore is that creative ads enable open-minded message processing, which in turn can increase a willingness to view an ad again. In addition, as Percy and Elliott (2009) indicate, creative advertising should also be capable of being transferable, that is, utilised across media, and be capable of extension as the campaign progresses and develops.

The importance of context

According to Kim et al. (2010), it is crucial that creative advertising has a product, or audience-relevant context, if it is to be effective. This contrasts with fine art where creativity is not bounded by this type of contextual constraint or the setting of objectives by one party, as its goal is to please or stimulate the viewer's senses.

Kim et al. (2010) argue that it is the surrounding culture that influences advertisers, ad creators and consumers when determining what constitutes the contextual component of advertising creativity. They offer the research findings of Koslow, Sasser and Riordan (2003: 94) who found that 'creatives perceive advertisements to be more appropriate if the ads are artistic, whereas account executives perceive advertisements to be more appropriate if the ads are strategic'.

Interpretations of what constitutes advertising creativity therefore vary depending on the viewer's context. This may be relative to their role (a client striving to meet market-share targets), culture (the societal values and norms of behaviour) or perspective (media commentator or blogger).

Culture is a critical component of international advertising effectiveness as it influences how consumers in different countries and regions perceive advertising. In Asian countries, for example, collectivistic values such as sharing, trustworthiness and sincerity are a key aspect of advertising. In contrast, American and European cultures are more individual and the advertising stresses individualistic appeals, such as 'the one for you', and 'you have the right to be you'. This can lead to different interpretations or forms of originality in advertising. For example, in Asian advertising there is an absence of what Westerners refer to as the 'big idea', when referring to creativity, and a much stronger focus on making the brand and the message socially appropriate (Han and Shavitt 1994).

The idea that culture influences creativity can also be seen in terms of what people attend to when viewing ads. People in Asian cultures tend to practise holistic processing and prefer to consider the entire picture or field. Westerners practise analytic processing and attend to the primary object and its categories. To illustrate this, Kim et al. cite the work of Masuda and Nisbett (2001), who showed American and Japanese students images of a fish in the centre of an underwater scene, against a background of rocks and plants. When a new background was introduced the Japanese participants had greater difficulty recognising the target fish than the Americans. So removing an object from its context indicates an Asian preference for context rather than content-focused advertising.

Finally, advertisers in many Asian nations use emotional rather than cognitive or rational appeals. This is because they prefer to help consumers feel happy and relaxed. Mircale (1987: 75) suggests this is why advertisers in these cultures are prone to using 'famous talents, parodies, fantasies, classical music, melancholy, nostalgia, and humor'. He says this leads to advertising in Asian regions that is perceived to be pleasant, friendly and understanding. This compares to American advertising which stresses product benefits, calls to action and reasons to buy.

Creative roles and skills

Before we look at the detail of what might constitute creative advertising in terms of process, content and message appeals, it is necessary to consider the principal creative roles in advertising agencies. Who does the creating? The 'creative partnership' of the copywriter and art director typifies the approach adopted by most advertising agencies for the development of creative ideas on behalf of their clients. These titles might suggest that creativity is largely about words and pictures but this might be an oversimplification. The words and pictures in their early forms are the initial expressions of the creative ideas of those involved. The skills of the creative teams are therefore not just about how good they are at writing words or drawing pictures but how effective they are in developing ideas that can be interpreted in words and pictures to meet the needs of the client's advertising brief. Additionally, there is not necessarily a clearly defined line that says the copywriter just writes the words and the art director just draws the pictures. Working as a team, either of the partners might come up with a good headline or a smart visual. In other words, be creative!

The creative department of an advertising agency will normally be headed by a creative director. More often than not, this person will be a partner or owner of the business. See ViewPoint 5.1 for a profile of Sir John Hegarty, the worldwide creative director and founder

ViewPoint 5.1 Sir John Hegarty, a leading creative light

Sir John Hegarty has been a leading light in the advertising industry for over 45 years. He was fired from Benton and Bowles in 1967 as a junior art director for insubordination. This was not to hinder his career and in 1970 he became a founding partner of Saatchi and Saatchi. In 1973 he co-founded TBWA before forming his current agency BBH with John Bartle and Nigel Bogle in 1982. In 1990 he was voted Advertising Man of the Decade and was awarded a knighthood in 2007 for services to advertising. In 2011 he was given a special award at the Cannes Lions International Festival of Creativity. Not a bad track record for someone insubordinate!

In 2011 he published his views in book form, *Hegarty on Advertising: Turning Intelligence into Magic*. He describes the fundamentals of a successful advertising campaign as being 'exactly what it was 50-100 years ago . . . It's vital to advertise something of value. Understand that value and find a way of expressing it in a way that captures people's imagination. And probably the most effective strategy you can use in advertising is to tell the truth. If you look back at many of the greatest campaigns, that's exactly what they did.'

One of Hegarty's most memorable campaigns was in the mid 1980s for Levi's. This involved the then unknown actor Nick Kamen, who stripped down to his boxer shorts in a laundrette to the soundtrack of Marvin Gaye's 'I Heard It on the Grapevine'. At the time the Levi's brand was declining in popularity but the campaign uplifted sales by some 800%, put Marvin Gaye back in the charts and sent the sales of boxer shorts rocketing.

As BBH's worldwide creative director, Hegarty has certainly been involved in many successful campaigns. He follows the emphasis on creativity laid down by Bill Bernbach of DDB in the late 1960s proposing that 'creativity isn't an occupation, it's a preoccupation'. Amongst BBH's current list of global clients are British Airways, Google, Burberry, Sprite and Baileys.

Hegarty identifies a number of key issues relating to creativity and those who are involved in it within the advertising industry:

- **'Don't chase the money, chase the opportunity.'** It is now much easier for those aspiring to get into the advertising business. Media developments now mean that an ad does not have to wait to get TV exposure, it can be aired quickly and easily via YouTube.
- **'Technology is a tool for creativity.'** Clearly advances in technology are influencing idea generation and creative outputs but this also means that it is getting harder to keep advertising and ads fresh. Technology presents an opportunity to challenge and disrupt the status quo.
- **'Write from your own philosophy and beliefs.'** Telling the truth is a key element of advertising; telling it with wit and intelligence is an important factor in engaging with the target audience.
- **'Creativity is an expression of one's self.'** There is a need for those involved in creative advertising to be inquisitive and seek reference points from as wide a range of sources as possible. Advertising is about storytelling, which requires crafting.
- **'80% idea, 20% execution.'** Given the volume of advertising production, Hegarty argues that a significant percentage of this is poor. Good is not good enough; creatives need to be prepared to throw away ideas that might be good and search for something great.
- **'Never be ordinary.'** Advertising is about making a difference and this requires those involved in producing it to be different.

Source: Based on Hegarty (2011); www.bbh.co.uk, accessed 5 October 2011; www.lcc.arts.ac.uk, accessed 5 October 2011; www.ica.org.uk, accessed 5 October 2011; www.hegartyonadvertising.com, accessed 5 October 2011

Question

Explain what Hegarty means by storytelling in advertising.

Task

Look at some examples of BBH's creative work on their website. Which ads do you like and why?

of the agency Bartle, Bogle and Hegarty. Under the creative director's leadership, most advertising agencies of any size will employ a number of creative partnerships to work on different client accounts. Once established, these types of partnerships may last considerable periods of time and and it is common practice for them to move from agency to agency as creative 'pairs'.

One of the significant issues for creatives is the need to take into account not just what they are advertising, the product or the service, but also how it will be communicated. Which media will be used? The writing and visualisation skills of the creatives will need to adapt to the media format(s) being considered, whether press, TV, digital, billboards, radio, cinema or others. Will the 'creative idea' work across different media and how will the words and pictures vary?

Although usually responsible for generating the initial creative ideas for advertising campaigns and presenting them for client approval, the creative process continues through the production development where additional creative inputs are generated. For example, these might come from finished-art workers, photographers, film directors or digital content producers. This type of work is usually subcontracted out from the agency but overseen by the creatives responsible for the campaign.

Southgate (2009) sees the traditional roles of creatives changing with wider collaboration between account planners, media planners, the client and account managers. As the generator of the creative brief, the account planner now often continues involvement through the whole creative and production phases. Media planners, particularly as a result of the emergence of digital media channels, can now advise on a wider range of opportunities that creatives may have limited knowledge of. It is considered that the client is now much more heavily involved in the creative development, rather than simply being presented with 'finished' ideas in pitches. Account managers and others with account responsibilities are also playing a more active role in creative execution. It is also becoming increasingly common for both clients and agencies to utilise the services of freelance creatives who are independent of a larger agency structure.

The creative process

Hegarty (2011) proposes that the creative process is completely dysfunctional and it is unpredictability that makes advertising exciting. Creativity has to surprise and challenge, it has to be daring and motivating. 'In a creative organisation, if you understand that, then there's a good chance you'll be successful and continue being successful.'

Academic interest and investigation into the processes associated with the development of creative advertising are thin. Na et al. (2009) and others have interpreted the process in terms of a linear sequence of activities. For example, Hill and Johnson (2004) developed a 13-point stage process in which they refer to the advertising problem delineation communication and response process (APDCR). Na and colleagues (2009) offer a less detailed approach, highlighting four stages of decision making.

As with any collaborative service-based project, the level of interaction between client and provider is crucial with regard to the quality and success of creative advertising. Indeed, the relationship that develops or exists between these two parties is an important factor, although little research has been undertaken in this area.

There are many other possible influences on the creative process. One major factor concerns the prevailing regulations and industry standards about what is acceptable behaviour. Closely associated with this are client attitudes towards risk and the extent to which the organisation wants to push the boundaries of advertising outputs.

Perhaps one of the more interesting yet under-researched areas concerns the nature of the relationship between client and agency and the effect that the interaction between these two parties can have on the development of creative advertising. Two main relationship styles have been observed: master–servant and partnership. With the former the agency experiences little involvement by the client and has a relatively free rein to develop work. The collaborative implication of the partnership approach can lead to conflict as well as mutually rewarding outputs. However, some organisations are known to require an excessive number of reviews and approval meetings in the process can dilute creativity (Hotz et al. 1982), just as excessive client involvement can impede and even frustrate the development of creative advertising (LaBahn and Kohli 1997).

Another influential element concerns the propensity for the client and agency not only to share information but also to provide information that that can assist the development of creative advertising. For example, the information contained in the creative and client briefings should be as detailed as possible in order to shape quality creative outcomes (Hackley 2000) but there is substantial anecdotal and some empirical evidence to indicate that as many as 40% of clients fail to give agencies sufficient information (Helegsen 1994) and that some clients do not provide a creative brief at all (Rossiter 2008).

The creative code

We have seen that there are many internal and external influences on the creative process and indeed individual stakeholders can have varying levels of impact on the development of creative advertising. Stuhlfaut (2011) refers to clients, agency managers, media specialists, account planners and market conditions, which have all been shown to have varying levels of influence on the creative process and its outputs.

However, the development of advertising materials and associated processes occurs within organisations and is therefore embedded within the prevailing organisational context and culture. This embraces the organisational climate, leadership style, the available mix of skills/resources, and structure and systems.

Stuhlfaut refers to organisational culture as a learned system of meaning, which is shared among participants. People use an implicit framework of language, behaviour and symbols to communicate these meanings and provide a common bond within their community. Organisations such as advertising agencies, and all those working within creative departments, work within and are constrained by this framework of organisational culture.

We know that individuals tend to identify with their (employer's) organisation and to a greater or lesser extent align themselves with the organisation's values. It is not unrealistic to expect that creatives would choose to use methods, styles, techniques and strategies that fit with the perceived values, and which serve to constrain the range of creative outcomes and outputs. For new creatives, therefore, it is important to learn and understand the values as this influences what they do, how they do it, and how creative success is determined.

Another way of considering these issues is to ask if the creatives have the right skills, if there is an appropriate amount of development time and if the budget is sufficient. Although the larger advertising budgets might attract better agency service, the budget itself does not appear to be a significant factor in shaping creative advertising output (Koslow, Sasser and Riordan 2006).

An alternative approach to a review of creativity is to consider how all of these influences compete and result in considerations of power over a campaign. As Hackley and Kover (2007: 65) observe, this usually means that creatives 'operate in a climate of latent or actual conflict'. With political power resting with clients and account managers, creatives, Hackley and Kover report, have to use cunning strategies to get their work accepted.

It is from this that Stuhlfaut offers an interesting concept, which he refers to as the creative code. Citing Goodenough (1981: 52), the code shapes the development of advertisements, which are regarded as cultural artefacts or 'material manifestations of what is learned'. Through this process a sub-cultural creative code is understood and made available to others. Just as organisation theory suggests that people make mental maps of their experiences in order to help them behave appropriately (Weick 1979), so a creative code serves to direct or limit what internal and external stakeholders believe an acceptable creative approach might be.

However, this raises questions about whether a weak culture and code serve to encourage greater creativity because there are fewer constraints. To what extent does a creative code influence the creative process, and how might an agency or client influence the creative code, in order to achieve particular types of output?

Creative content

So what goes into ads that make them 'creative'? Content varies significantly, partly because of the nature of what is being advertised (e.g. product, service, organisation), and partly because of the creative approach being adopted, the type of message appeal being deployed, information sources and the media being used. In order to be successful it is first necessary to identify the client's needs and communicate them with those responsible for creative development.

Creative briefing

One of the first stages involved in developing creative advertising content is the briefing to agencies of the client's requirements. In Chapter 7 we consider the process through which prospective clients appoint advertising agencies. This includes a briefing process providing the agency with sufficient details about the client, its business, competition, products and services, marketing environment, customers and other stakeholders. From this the agency's account planner can distil key information that will provide the creatives with a basis for beginning the creative process and developing effective creative ideas. This brief will articulate the overarching campaign strategy. Each agency has a different style for their creative briefs although they will often contain similar information. In most cases they will be presented on one sheet of paper. Burtenshaw et al. (2006: 90) suggest that a good creative brief 'should be written in a way that stimulates creativity and promotes original ideas'. They identify five criteria that a creative brief should satisfy:

1. *Opening dialogue* – important background information that stimulates debate.
2. *Point of focus* – 'What do you want to say and who do you want to say it to?'
3. *Contract* – not a legal one but a statement of intent, a common reference point agreed between agency and client.
4. *Checklist* – which clarifies aims, objectives and deliverable outcomes.
5. *Framework* – the brief is a framework from which creativity can emerge. Needs to be flexible and not over-restrictive.

These criteria are evident in the example of a creative brief from agency hhcl/red cell for Iceland's range of frozen foods shown in Figure 5.1.

Message framing

The principle of building a border around an idea or story and then presenting a contained and managed view of an issue is well known and practised regularly by politicians and advertising and public relations professionals. Known as framing, the concept has roots in communication studies, psychology and sociology. As with a number of concepts there is little agreement on framing and, as Tsai (2007) indicates, it is controversial and empirically unproven. However, of the many definitions Dan and Ihlen (2011) cite Entman's (1993: 52) as the one definition that is quoted more often than others. To frame is to 'select some aspects of a perceived reality and make them more salient in a communicating context, in such a way as to promote a particular problem definition, causal interpretation, moral evaluation, and/or treatment recommendation'.

Iceland Range
Creative Brief

What is . . .
Iceland is a predictable frozen food supermarket that appeals to deal-hunting Mums on a budget

What if . . .
We revealed some of Iceland's hidden secrets and told Mum about all the other great reasons to shop there?

Why is advertising needed?
Iceland is more than just deals, but you'd never know it with all the deal advertising it does. There is in fact a huge level of product innovation that Mums never know about because they've never been told. Whenever we have researched ideas around their ranges or new products, Mums have always asked (in a rather frustrated way) 'why don't they tell us about all these brilliant things?' Iceland now wants to communicate three ranges designed for these budget-conscious busy Mums: Kids Crew. Pizzas and the Christmas lines Party Fayre and Christmas Made Easy.

What is the role for advertising?
This advertising is not just about informing Mums about three ranges, but pitching it in a way that tells them there is more to Iceland than they had ever realised

How do we do this?
By creating an idea or territory that pulls these ranges together and surprises Mum with Iceland's hidden secrets. This element of 'surprise' or intrusiveness is important as Mums are used to OTT advertising from Iceland and anything too passive, despite how well branded it is, is not usually recalled as Iceland advertising.

Who are we talking to?
Think of the typical, hard-working, under-appreciated Mum trying to feed a demanding family on a tight budget. Iceland is a godsend to them with its amazing deals and the advertising draws them in on a regular basis. However they either go straight for the deals or look for favourites, rarely taking the time to browse and find all the new things Iceland are introducing.
They are family and house proud, live vicariously through celebrity gossip magazines and soaps, have a wide network of sassy Mum-friends (these Mums are surprisingly switched on and 'street smart') and are always looking for something new to make life just a bit easier. Their family is everything, kids especially and it's the needs of the latter that often inform and dictate their needs

Core thought
There's more to Iceland than anyone ever knew

Tone of voice
Enthusiastic, straight-forward and fun

Mandatories
'Because Mums are heroes' endline

What are the ranges?
Kids Crew:
Women's press (assume full page colour) in September to coincide with the start of the new school term

'Surprising' news: A revamped range of kids' food, the hero products of which conform to or exceed Government guidelines on nutrition
Insight: Making it easier for Mum to give good and tasty food to their kids

Pizza range:
Women's press (assume full page colour) in October

'Surprising' news: Iceland have the largest pizza selection on the high street, offering everything from basic pizzas to a new premium pizza line produced in Italy and hand topped with premium ingredients
Insight: The biggest selection of pizzas on the high street (with specific focus on the new premium range)

Christmas range:
TV and Women's press (assume full page colour) in OctoberlDecember

'Surprising' news: Iceland leads the market when it comes to Christmas food with an extraordinarily wide selection across the Party Fayre line (principally party/buffet food) and the Christmas Made Easy line (everything needed for the Christmas dinner itself)
Insight: Guaranteed to make this Christmas the easiest ever
Note: As this is a Christmas ad we need the requisite level of 'Christmasiness' to give it a festive flavour

Figure 5.1 Example of a creative brief
Source: IPA

By cropping and framing an item, any distracting or contradictory elements are removed and focus can be given to the interpretation intended by the source. Gamson and Modigliani (1989) indicate that those who use framing to influence public opinion often compete with each other to frame the issues of interest. The goal of these *framing contests* (Pan and Kosicki 2001) is to get first the media to adopt that particular frame and then the audience.

The framing principle is used in advertising to present predetermined brand elements. Competitors frame their messages and stories in order that their brands stand out, have clarity and focus and are positioned distinctly and clearly.

Message framing works on the hedonic principles of our motivation to seek happiness and to avoid pain. So messages can be framed to either focus a recipient's attention to positive outcomes (happiness) or take them away from the possible negative outcomes (pain). For example, a positively framed message might be a yoghurt that is presented as 'containing real fruit' or a car as 'a stylish design'. Conversely, messages could be presented as 'contains only 5% fat' and 'low carbon emissions'; these are regarded as negatively framed. According to Buda (2003), negative framing gets more attention and information is processed more intensely than with positively framed messages.

Many practitioners work on the basis that positive messages are better than negative ones, whereas others believe negative framing promotes deeper thinking and consideration. However, there is little empirical evidence to support any of these views. Therefore, in an attempt to understand when it is better to use positive or negative framing Tsai argues that it is necessary to develop a holistic understanding of the target audience. This involves considering three factors: self-construal; consumer involvement; and product knowledge. These are explained in Table 5.2.

Tsai believes that these three factors moderate an individual's response when they are exposed to positively or negatively framed brand messages. In turn these influence the three main dimensions of a brand's communication. These are generally accepted by researchers such as MacKenzie and Lutz (1989) and Lafferty et al. (2002) to be attitude to the ad, attitude to the brand and purchase intention. Tsai develops a conceptual model to demonstrate this through which he argues brand communication persuasiveness is moderated by these three factors.

His research concludes that positive message framing should be used when the following exists:

Independent self-construal × low consumer involvement × low product knowledge

Negative framing should be used when there is:

Interdependent self-construal × high consumer involvement × low product knowledge

Table 5.2 Factors associated with message framing

Factor		Explanation
Self-construal	Independent	Individuals (the self) seek to distinguish themselves from others. These individuals respond best to positive framing.
	Interdependent	Individuals (the self) try not to distinguish themselves from others. These individuals respond best to negative framing.
Consumer involvement	High involvement Low involvement	Refers to the extent to which personal relevance and perceived risk influences decision making within a product category. When high, negative framing is preferred; when low, positive framing is preferred.
Product knowledge	High Low	Product knowledge consists of two elements: behavioural (usage) experience and mental (search, exposure and information). Message framing is more suitable where product knowledge is low.

Source: Based on Tsai (2007)

Scholars' paper 5.2 Rapid response for creative content

Sheehan, K.B. and Morrison, D.K. (2009) The creativity challenge: media confluence and its effects on the evolving advertising industry, *Journal of Interactive Marketing*, 9(2) (Spring), 84–8

This paper is helpful because it considers issues associated with creativity in a changing and challenging media environment. It is becoming increasingly important for brands to communicate 'as live' via new media channels. This represents a very different challenge in creative terms as those responsible no longer have the time to craft message content over time with the luxury of testing to support potential effectiveness. Identifies four major challenges as engagement, consumer-generated media (CGM), social media and training. Provides references to examples of how some brands are facing these challenges and to further academic research in the areas concerned.

While message framing may provide a strategic approach to the way in which messages should be presented, it is also necessary to consider how the detail of a message should be included in order to maximise effectiveness. Consideration is now given to the balance of information and emotion in a message, the structure in terms of how an argument should be presented and the actual appeal, whether it be based on information or emotion.

User-generated content (UGC)

So far in this chapter attention has been given to the issues associated with organisationally driven creativity. However, it is important to consider the increasing numbers of messages that are developed and communicated by ordinary individuals, just like you and me. Not only are these used to communicate with organisations of all types and sizes but they are also shared with peers, family, friends and others in communities such as social networks and specialist-interest online communities (e.g. reunion and family history sites). This is referred to as user-generated content (UGC) and can be seen in action at YouTube, Flickr, Twitter and DIGG.

UGC can be considered to be all of the ways in which people make use of social media (Kaplan and Haenlein 2010) and describes the various forms of media content that are publicly available and created by end users. Christodoulides et al. (2011) state that for something to be regarded as UGC, three core conditions need to be met. First, the content needs to be published either on a publicly accessible website or on a social-networking site accessible to a selected group of people. Second, the material needs to show some creative effort. And finally, it has to have been created outside professional routines and practices.

Email enables viewers to interact with television and radio programmes, with presenters encouraging audiences to write and tell them 'what you think' about a topic. Discussion boards and online forums can only work through consumer participation and user-generated content. One of the more common forms of UGC is blogging. This involves individuals, sometimes in the name of organisations, but more often as independent consumers, posting information about topics of personal interest. Sometimes these people develop opinion-leader status and organisations feed them information about the launch of new brands, so that they pass on the information to opinion followers.

Social networks thrive on the shared views, opinions and beliefs, often brand related, of networked friends. YouTube and Flickr provide opportunities for consumers to share video and photos respectively, with all material posted by users. Users post their content and respond to the work of others, often by rating the quality or entertainment value of content posted by others.

ViewPoint 5.2 Creative ideas and original content key for brands

Major brands are now seeking more original methods for engaging consumers. US food group Kraft is basing its approach on a deeper understanding of how consumers treat information which is changing rapidly due to the emergence of new technologies. They have sought to develop closer working relationships with their advertising agencies by accessing many smaller agencies and building their own in-house account planning team. A promotion which launched an iPhone app for the Jell-O cube achieved nearly 200,000 downloads within two weeks.

General Electric (GE) used a range of digital tools to form a highly tailored campaign, uploading video and competitions to encourage open innovation. GE argue that with good ideas and good content it is possible to break through despite obstacles and high levels of competitive activity using similar approaches.

Coca-Cola utilises a concept of 'liquid and linked content'. The platform for this is combining simple big ideas based on deep consumer insights which transfer easily between different media. Jonathan Mildenhall, Coke's vice president for global advertising strategy and content excellence, states 'when ideas are linked to business objectives, they help us earn disproportionate market share. Branded stories must provoke conversation.'

Coke sees content development as replacing traditional advertising. In addition to tangible product attributes, the ability of the brand to tap into 'cultural touchpoints and passion points,' including the Olympic Games and Soccer World Cup, is seen as a key factor in continuing consumer involvement. In addition to traditional media, Coke are seeking to utilise earned media such as social media, retail cooperation, packaging and transport liveries.

Other brands are looking at new ways of working with agencies to develop innovative creative content. Motor giant Ford has formed a 'Team Detroit' unit consisting of several WPP Group agencies, consolidating creative activity within a major agency network. Ford believe consolidating agency creative inputs aids finding ideas that suit all of their customers. Beer brand Heineken require their agencies to 'draw in customers' in order to develop creative thinking.

Source: Based on www.warc.com, accessed 4 July 2011, 8 September 2011, 11 October 2011; www.forbes.com, accessed 11 October 2011

Question

What form would 'retail cooperation' take in helping Coke generate advertising content?

Task

Provide examples of crowdsourcing and open sourcing to generate advertising content for a consumer brand of your choice.

What is interesting is that although people understand the rules and norms associated with communicating across peer groups and social networks, organisations have yet to master these new environments. Firms are not able to use traditional forms of free communication with as much credibility and authority as individuals regularly do within these contexts. One of the reasons for this is the democratisation of the media and the language codes that have emerged. A simple example is SMS texting. Although used by millions every day to great effect, mobile communications and text messaging are only now becoming commercially prominent, mainly as a result of smartphone technology.

Sourcing content

UGC can be derived through one of three main processes:

- **Crowd source** – Organisations can prompt the public into action, via the web community, to develop specific types of content and materials. Where organisations deliberately invite the entire web community to suggest material that can be used commercially, in return for a reward, the term crowdsourcing is used. In this circumstance the crowd may consist of amateurs or businesses. The difference between crowdsourcing and outsourcing is that the latter is directed at a predetermined, specific organisation.

- **Open source** – The public may take the initiative themselves and communicate with a specific organisation or industry. Where a group of people voluntarily offer ideas and materials, without invitation, prompting or the offer of a reward by an organisation, the term open-source materials is used.
- **Friend source** – the public may exchange information and ideas amongst themselves, without any direct communication with an organisation or brand owner. This occurs when friends and families communicate and share ideas and materials among themselves, for their own enjoyment, bonding and enrichment.

Some marketers are using the increasing occurrence of UGC as an opportunity to listen to and observe consumers and to find out what meanings they attribute to products, brands and company actions. Some companies invite consumers to offer content for ads via crowdsourcing.

Message appeals

The presentation of a message requires that an appeal be made to the target audience. The appeal is important, because unless the execution of the message appeal (the creative) is appropriate or relevant to the target audience's perception and expectations, the chances of successful communication are reduced.

Shimp (2010) identifies that although advertisers aim for their ads to be creative, they also need them to 'stick' in the memory of the receiver. His 'sticky theory' is based around the concept of advertising being remembered, having impact and promoting change in the target audience's behaviour or attitudes. In order to achieve this, Shimp describes six common features of advertising messages that have a lasting impact and stick. These are presented in Figure 5.2.

This is not to say that ads not containing all the sticky features will not be either creative or effective but Shimp's idea provides a good checklist for developing potentially successful advertising messages.

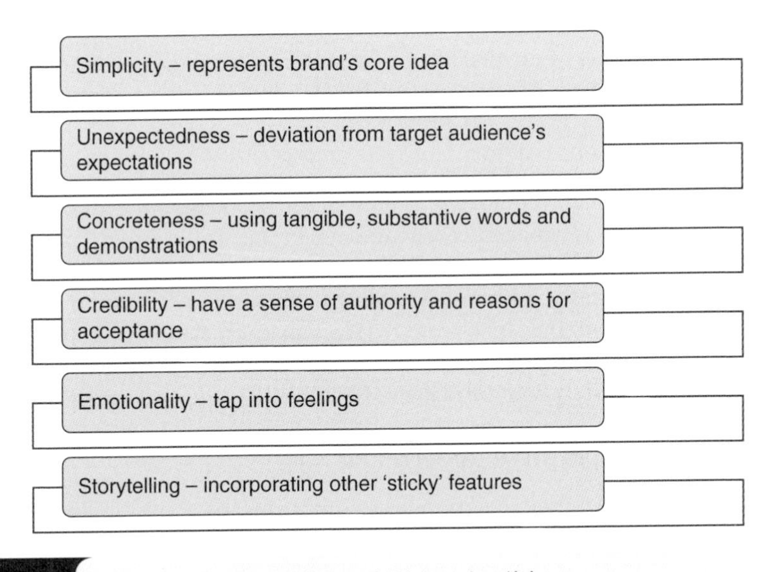

Figure 5.2 Shimp's common features of sticky advertising

There are two main factors associated with the presentation. Is the message to be dominated by the need to transmit product-oriented information or is there a need to transmit a message that appeals predominantly to the emotional senses of the receiver? The main choice of presentation style, therefore, concerns the degree of factual information transmitted in a message against the level of imagery thought necessary to make sufficient impact for the message to command attention and then be processed. There are numerous presentational or executional techniques, but the following are some of the more commonly used appeals.

Information-based appeals

Information or rational appeals can be presented in one of four main ways. These are factual, slice-of-life, demonstration and comparative approaches.

Factual

Sometimes referred to as the 'hard sell', the dominant objective of these appeals is to provide often detailed information. This type of appeal is commonly associated with high-involvement decisions where receivers are sufficiently motivated and able to process information. Persuasion, according to the elaboration likelihood model (ELM), is undertaken through the central processing route. This means that ads should be rational and contain logically reasoned arguments and information so that receivers are able to complete their decision-making processes.

Slice of life

As noted earlier, the establishment of credibility is vital if any message is to be accepted and processed. One of the ways in which this can be achieved is to present the message in such a way that the receiver can identify immediately with the scenario being presented. This process of creating similarity is used a great deal in advertising and is referred to as slice-of-life advertising. For example, many washing powder advertisers use a routine that depicts two ordinary women (assumed to be similar to the target receiver), invariably in a kitchen or garden, discussing the poor results achieved by one of their washing powders. Following the advice of one of the women, the stubborn stains are seen to be overcome by the focus brand.

On successful decoding of this message the overall effect of this appeal is for the receiver to conclude the following: that person is like me; I have had the same problem as that person; they are satisfied by using brand X, therefore I, too, will use brand X. This technique is simple, well tried, well liked and successful, despite its sexist overtones. It is also interesting to note that a number of surveys have found that a majority of women feel that advertisers use inappropriate stereotyping to portray female roles, these being predominantly housewife and mother roles.

Demonstration

A similar technique is to present the problem to the audience as a demonstration. The focus brand is depicted as instrumental in the resolution of a problem. Commercials for headache remedies, floor cleaners and tyres have traditionally demonstrated the pain, the dirt and the danger respectively, and then shown how the focus brand relieves the pain (Panadol), removes the stubborn dirt (Flash or Cillit Bang) or stops in the wet on a coin (or the edge of a rooftop – Continental tyres). Whether the execution is believable is a function of the credibility and the degree of lifelike dialogue or copy that is used.

Comparative advertising

Comparative advertising is a popular means of positioning brands. Messages are based on the comparison of a brand with either a main competitor brand or all competing brands, with the aim of establishing and maintaining superiority. The comparison may centre on one or two key attributes and can be a good way of entering new markets. Entrants keen to establish a presence in a market have little to lose by comparing themselves with market leaders. However, market leaders have a great deal to lose and little to gain by comparing themselves with minor competitors.

Emotions and feelings-based appeals

Appeals based on logic and reason are necessary in particular situations, especially where there is high involvement. However, as products become similar and as consumers become more aware of what is available in the category, so the need to differentiate becomes more important. Increasing numbers of advertisers are using messages that seek to appeal to the target's emotions and feelings, a 'soft sell'. Ads for cars, toothpaste, toilet tissue and mineral water often use emotion-based messages to differentiate their products' position.

There are a number of appeals that can be used to elicit an emotional response from an individual receiver. Of the many techniques available, the main ones are fear, humour, animation, sex, music, and fantasy and surrealism.

Fear

Fear is used in one of two ways. The first type demonstrates the negative aspects or physical dangers associated with a particular behaviour or improper product usage. Drink-driving, life assurance and toothpaste advertising typify this form of appeal. For example, Scottish Widows, a financial services brand belonging to Lloyds TSB, has used a woman dressed in a black cape to symbolise the 'Widow'. The 'Widow' has become synonymous with the brand, even taking on iconic status, especially as research shows that four out of five people can link the image with the company.

The second approach is the threat of social rejection or disapproval if the brand is not used. This type of fear is used frequently in advertisements for such products as anti-dandruff shampoos and deodorants and is used to support consumers' needs for social acceptance and approval.

Fear appeals need to be constrained, if only to avoid being categorised as outrageous and socially unacceptable. There is a great deal of evidence that fear can facilitate attention and interest in a message and even motivate an individual to take a particular course of action: for example to stop smoking. Fear appeals are persuasive, according to Schiffman and Kanuk (1991), when low to moderate levels of fear are induced. Ray and Wilkie (1970), however, show that should the level of fear rise too much, inhibiting effects may prevent the desired action occurring. This inhibition is caused by the individual choosing to screen out, through perceptive selection, messages that conflict with current behaviour. The outcome may be that individuals deny the existence of a problem, claim there is no proof or say that it will not happen to them.

Humour

If receivers are in a positive mood they are more likely to process advertising messages with little cognitive elaboration (Batra and Stayman 1990). The use of humour as an emotional appeal is attractive because it can attract attention, stimulate interest and foster a positive mood. This can occur because there is less effort involved with peripheral rather than central cognitive processing, and this helps to mood protect. In other words, the positive mood state is more likely to be maintained if cognitive effort is avoided. Both Yellow Pages and 118 118 have used humour to help convey the essence of their telephone number service brands and to help differentiate them from the competition.

Zhang and Zinkhan (2006) found that humour is more effective when there is low rather than high involvement. They also consider whether the media used also influence humour. For example, television and radio demand less effort to process messages compared with print work. The choice of media used to deliver humorous content can therefore be critical.

Whilst using humour might be an attractive basis for creative execution, it does represent some challenges. All ads have 'lifespans' in terms of receiver familiarity, boredom, etc. after repeat exposures. When we tell someone a joke they may find it really humorous first time around and still funny after several hearings. But jokes lose their humorous edge on multiple

Exhibit 5.2 John Smith's use of humour
Source: Buckshee Productions

hearing and thus lose their effectiveness. Care therefore needs to be exercised in deploying humour in advertising. One approach to dealing with this is to refresh the humorous message with frequent updates of the themes on which it is based. John Smith's beer did this effectively using comedian Peter Kay in different humorous situations – as a footballer, a diver and other family-based scenarios. Exhibit 5.2 shows one of the images from this campaign.

It is also argued that humour is effective because argument quality is likely to be high. That is, the level of counterargument can be substantially reduced. Arguments against the use of humour concern distraction from the focus brand, so that while attention is drawn, the message itself is lost. With the move to global branding and standardisation of advertising messages, humour does not travel well. While the level and type of humour are difficult to gauge in the context of the processing abilities of a domestic target audience, cultural differences seriously impede the transfer of jokes around the world.

Research by consultants Millward Brown (2007) shows that humour is used more widely in some markets than others. Spain, the Netherlands and Chile are more exposed to funny ads than other markets. Humour is used much less frequently in China. The basis for humour also differs across markets. Sarcasm is not widely appeciated in China, irony is popular in the UK, humour based on sexual themes is taboo in Singapore and more accepted in parts of Europe compared to the UK.

A study by Shabbir and Thwaites (2007) identifies that in a significant number of cases, humour has been used to mask deceptive advertising claims. This raises ethical issues and challenges for advertising standards bodies.

Animation

Animation techniques have advanced considerably in recent years, with children as the prime target audience. However, animation has been successfully used in many adult-targeted advertisements. Animation is a popular creative device in markets such as Japan and China. Exhibit 5.3 shows skateboarding animated cows in a Chinese ad for McDonald's in China. The

Scholars' paper 5.3 Does humour work for global brands?

Laroche, M., Vinhal Nepomuceno, M., Huang, L. and Richard, M-O. (2011) What's so funny? The use of humor in magazine advertising in the United States, China and France, *Journal of Advertising Research*, 51, 2, 404–16

Humour is a common basis for advertising message appeals and this is an interesting paper not least because of the countries included in the study. Does humour work differently across different continents and cultures? The authors use a content-analysis method to examine how widely humour is used and its use in advertising different types of product. Compares use in luxury goods and personal consumer products including automobiles. Humour was found to be used most widely in general in the United States and most commonly used in automobile advertising in China. Identifies similar levels of the use of humour in advertising luxuries in China and France.

main reason for using animation is that potentially boring and low-interest/involvement products can be made visually interesting, with animation providing a means of gaining attention. A further reason for the use of animation is that it is easier to convey complex products in a way that does not patronise the viewer.

Sex

Sexual innuendo and the use of sex as a means of promoting products and services are both common and controversial. Using sex as an appeal in messages is excellent for gaining the attention of buyers. Research shows, however, that it often achieves little else, particularly when the product is unrelated. Therefore, sex appeals normally work well for products such as perfume, clothing and jewellery but provide for poor effectiveness when the product is unrelated, as with cars, photocopiers and furniture.

The use of sex in advertising messages is mainly restricted to getting the attention of the audience and, in some circumstances, sustaining interest. It can be used humorously, as in the Brazilian Bit Copa drink ad in Exhibit 5.4.

Millward Brown (2008a) identify muted responses to the use of sexual imagery particularly in Asian markets. Strong sexual imagery is ineffective in China although sexual imagery itself may

Exhibit 5.3 Animation adds life to Google

Source: Google

Exhibit 5.4 Funny Bit Copa
Source: Image courtesy of The Advertising Archives

work when associated with love, marriage, career and success. Censorship laws are also very restrictive when it comes to the use of sexual images. Understanding how the target audience wil respond to sexual imagery is important. There is a need for its use to be seen as realistic and within moral codes. Conservative cultures such as the Middle East will view advertising containing sexual images with some hostility. Even within European markets, responses to sexual imagery will vary.

Music

Music can provide continuity between a series of advertisements and can also be a good peripheral cue. A jingle, melody or tune, if repeated sufficiently, can become associated with the advertisement. Processing and attitudes towards the advertisement may be directly influenced by the music. Music has the potential to gain attention and assist product differentiation. Braithwaite and Ware (1997) found that music in advertising messages is used primarily either to create a mood or to send a branded message. In addition, music can also be used to signal a lifestyle and so communicate a brand identity through the style of music used.

Many advertisements for cars use music, partly because it is difficult to find a point of differentiation and music is able to draw attention, generate mood and express brand personality (e.g. BMW, Nissan Micra, Peugeot, Renault).

Some luxury and executive cars are advertised using commanding background music to create an aura of power, prestige and affluence, which is combined with strong visual images in order that an association be made between the car and the environment in which it is positioned. There is a contextual juxtaposition between the car and the environment presented. Readers may notice a semblance of classical conditioning, where the music acts as an unconditioned stimulus. Foxall and Goldsmith (1994) suggest that the stimulus elicits the unconditioned emotional responses that may lead to the purchase of the advertised product.

Music has been identified as having a significant effect on the level of interest in an ad. Millward Brown (2008b) report on an ad for a non-alcoholic drink in Australia. This featured a well-known piece of music. The music started six seconds into the ad and built in intensity. It then stopped for a few seconds and continued quietly for the rest of the ad. Interest tracing clearly identified different levels of interest as the music content altered throughout the ad.

Website www.songsofthesalesman.co.uk identifies an interesting mix of the most popular types and composers of music used in advertising. There is a mix of classical and popular music and amongst the most used are compositions by Tchaikovsky, Elgar, Queen, Louis Armstrong, James Brown and Moby.

Fantasy and surrealism

The use of fantasy and surrealism in advertising has grown partly as a result of the increased clutter and legal constraints imposed on some product classes. By using fantasy appeals, associations with certain images and symbols allow the advertiser to focus attention on the product. The receiver can engage in the distraction offered and become involved with the execution of the advertisement. If this is a rewarding experience it may be possible to affect the receiver's attitudes peripherally. Readers may notice that this links to the earlier discussion on 'liking the advertisement'. Exhibit 5.5 provides a surreal approach to promoting car colours.

An interesting contribution to the discussion of message appeals has been made by Lannon (1992). She reports that consumers' expectations of advertisements can be interpreted on the one hand as either literal or stylish and on the other as serious or entertaining, according to

Exhibit 5.5 Audi A1 paintwork by Damien Hirst

Source: © Damier Hirst

the tone of voice. This approach vindicates the view that consumers are active problem solvers and willing and able to decode increasingly complex messages. They can become involved with the execution of the advertisement and the product attributes. The degree of involvement (she argues implicitly) is a function of the motivation each individual has at any one moment when exposed to a particular message.

Advertisers can challenge individuals by presenting questions and visual stimuli that demand attention and cognitive response. Guinness challenged consumers to decode a series of advertisements that were unlike all previous Guinness advertisements and, indeed, all messages in the product class. The celebrity chosen was dressed completely in black, which contrasted with his blond hair, and he was shown in various time periods, past and future, and environments that receivers did not expect. He was intended to represent the personification of the drink and symbolised the individual nature of the product. Audiences were puzzled by the presentation and many rejected the challenge of interpretation. 'Surfer' and 'Bet on black' are more recent Guinness campaigns that seek to convey the importance and necessity to wait (for the drink to be poured properly). To accomplish this, it portrays a variety of situations in which patience results in achievement.

When individuals respond positively to a challenge, the advertiser can either provide closure (an answer) or, through surreal appeals, leave the receivers to answer the questions themselves in the context in which they perceive the message. One way of achieving this challenging position is to use an appeal that cognitively disorients the receiver (Parker and Churchill 1986). If receivers are led to ask the question, 'What is going on here?' their involvement in the message is likely to be very high. Benetton consistently raises questions through its advertising. By presenting a series of messages that are socially disorienting, and for many disconcerting, Benetton continually presents a challenge that moves away from involving individuals into an approach where salience and 'standing out' predominate. This high-risk strategy, with a risk of rejection, has prevailed for a number of years. See ViewPoint 5.3, which looks at Benetton's more recent campaigns.

ViewPoint 5.3 Benetton returns to 'edgy' advertising

The Italian fashion brand Benetton is no stranger to the world of controversial advertising. In the 1990s they employed photographer Oliviero Toscani to produce taboo-challenging campaigns which amongst other themes included a man dying of Aids, a catholic priest and nun embracing, bloodied newborn babies and the bloodstained shirt of a dead soldier. These ads brought regular streams of complaint to the Advertising Standards Authority. None of these images bore any resemblance to the products Benetton were marketing. Using what they described as social themes, the company claimed 'by eliminating the product from its ads, violating the taboo of disagreeable themes, associating its name with the representation of conflict and pain and, above all, abandoning the false, comfortable world of advertising stereotypes, Benetton cracked the foundation that held up the culture, language and specificity of the classic advertising message.' They certainly achieved that aim!

Against a background of difficult retail conditions in some markets, Benetton have more recently returned to a more provocative approach to promoting the brand image. A new creative chief, You Nguyen, was recruited from Levi-Strauss in June 2011, with a brief to grab global attention. In September 2011, the first part of the new strategy was launched. This included in-store installations of tailors' dummies posed in exotic sexual positions and covered in colourful wool. Benetton's head, Alessandro Benetton, dismisses advertising which just shows the product. They are seeking a deeper connection of values with consumers.

In November 2011, Benetton launched the Unhate Foundation, seeking 'to contribute to the creation of a new culture of tolerance, to combat hatred, building on Benetton's underpinning values'. This is aimed at reaching social stakeholders in the international community. Activities include live actions, groups of young people posting manifestos of kissing world leaders on walls in key locations, Tel Aviv, Rome, New York, Milan and Paris. Other activities included a film by French director Laurent Chanez focusing on the balance between love and hate. A website including an Unhate kissing wall was developed and a four-metres-long sculpture, the Unhate dove, was created by Erik Ravelo, using empty bullet shells from different war zones.

Exhibit 5.6 A Benetton ad from the UNHATE campaign
Source: Image courtesy of The Advertising Archives

In addition to these initiatives and events, a global advertising campaign using newspapers, magazines and websites was developed. This included images of world political and religious leaders kissing. Benetton claim the kiss represents the most universal symbol of love. Amongst others the ads featured Barack Obama and Chinese leader Hu Jintao; Pope Benedict XVI and Ahmed Mohamed el-Tayeb, imam of the Al-Azhar mosque in Cairo (the most important and moderate centre for Sunni Islamic studies in the world); the Palestinian president Mahmoud Abbas and the Israeli prime minister Benjamin Netanyahu. These symbolic images of reconciliation - with a touch of ironic hope and constructive provocation - were designed to stimulate reflection on how politics, faith and ideas, even when they are divergent and mutually opposed, must still lead to dialogue and mediation.

Source: Based on Clark (2011); Anon (2010); and www.press.benetton.com, accessed 22 November 2011

Question

How effective do you think Benetton's approach is?

Task

Identify other possible 'kissing partnerships' for Benetton to use.

The surrealist approach does not provide or allow for closure. The conformist approach, by contrast, does require closure in order to avoid any possible counterarguing and message rejection. Parker and Churchill argue that, by leaving questions unanswered, receivers can become involved in both the product and the execution of the advertisement. Indeed, most advertisements contain a measure of rational and emotional elements. A blend of the two elements is necessary and the right mixture is dependent upon the perceived risk and motivation that the target audience has at any one particular moment.

The message appeal should be a balance of the informative and emotional dimensions. Furthermore, message quality is of paramount importance. Buzzell (1964) reported that 'Advertising message quality is more important than the level of advertising expenditure' (30). Adams and Henderson Blair (1992) confirm that the weight of advertising is relatively unimportant, and that the quality of the appeal is the dominant factor. However, the correct blend of informative and emotional elements in any appeal is paramount for persuasive effectiveness.

Evaluating creativity

We have so far looked at what creativity might be, how the process is managed and the approaches that are used when developing advertising messages. One remaining question concerns how we know how effective all this creative activity has been. Can we measure the contribution creativity has played in successful advertising? These are not easy questions to answer directly, as there are a number of issues that need to be considered. Some of these relate to what and when creativity is being evaluated: initial ideas following the creative briefing or the results of campaigns which have been fully developed and executed?

Initial ideas should be considered within the agency before presentation to the client. The client would then have the opportunity to evaluate these concepts against the criteria set out in the brief. This might be part of the agency pitching process or an ongoing activity with the incumbent agency handling the account. Evaluation, including research amongst the target audience, would then take place as the campaign is developed before final implementation. Did the campaign meet the aims and objectives set and, if so, what made it work?

Baskin (2010) identifies some of the challenges faced in evaluating creative work: it 'is a big ask, and despite attempts by agencies to set out clear formulae and rational criteria for evaluating their creative concepts, all too often it is the client's "hidden" criteria that dominate the call, and these can be very subjective and hugely variable'. Baskin further argues that in order to overcome such subjectivity, evaluation criteria should be part of the creative brief. Not all client organisations rely on such 'subjectivity'; some provide those involved in evaluating creative work with training. These include Unilever, Procter & Gamble, Masterfoods and Diageo.

There are of course, many examples of successful advertising. Some of these are apparent by studying the winners of the various industry awards programmes. For example, awards programmes such as the IPA Effectiveness Awards, the APG (Account Planners Group) Creative Strategy Awards, the Jay Chiat Strategic Excellence Awards, the Cannes Lions Creative Effectiveness Awards: each have identified criteria for judging entries. For the Cannes Lions, the criteria are based on the creative idea (25%), strategy (25%) and results and effectiveness (50%) (see ViewPoint 5.4). The international jury is made up of global effectiveness and research specialists, planners, strategists and clients (www.canneslions.com).

The IPA, along with other communications bodies, have developed a set of industry guidelines for judging creative ideas. These guidelines identify the importance of a shared understanding of what is a 'good idea' and its influence on the agency and client relationship. Michael Brockbank, Unilever's former vice president of brand communication, is quoted in this guide: 'Funny phrase, "creative judgement" – as if there's such a thing as "uncreative judgement"! In my experience, people who demonstrate good creative judgement have an intuitive understanding of other people and an ability to step into their shoes; they get under their customer's skin, into their thoughts and emotions and see ideas through their eyes.'

These industry guidelines identify ten considerations for judging creative ideas. These are presented in the form of a jigsaw puzzle – when it's put together you can see what the whole picture looks like. This is shown in Figure 5.3.

ViewPoint 5.4 Winning at Cannes Creative Festival

The Cannes Lions International Festival of Creativity was established in 1954 as the International Advertising Film Festival. The Festival alternated between Venice and Cannes before establishing a permanent base in Cannes in 1984. It represents the major opportunity for global brands and their agencies to present their creative work for peer review. It also provides a platform for advertising industry speakers on topical issues and opportunities for open discussions via themed workshops. Originally founded to review cinema advertising, the Festival now covers a wide spectrum of media advertising, reflected in the awards presented for creative effectiveness.

Each year a Grand Prix, or overall winner, award is made to the submission that most closely matches the awards criteria - creative idea (25%), strategy (25%) and results and effectiveness (50%). A small number of Creative Effectiveness Lions awards are presented to other submissions which were highly rated. In 2011 the Grand Prix winner was the PepsiCo-owned Walkers Crisps brand in the UK. Lions awards went to Gillette Mach 3 shaving products (Procter & Gamble, India), McDonald's (UK), Old Spice men's fragrances (Procter & Gamble, USA), The Pacific TV programme (TVNZ, New Zealand) and Snickers chocolate bar (Mars, UK). Apart from the New Zealand submission, all of the other winners were for global brands taking local, culturally specific approaches.

Walkers had identified that lunching habits had changed. More people were eating sandwiches as part of their lunch and taking less time over eating them. The aim of the campaign was to encourage consumers to eat crisps alongside their sandwich. Research had identified that consumers thought eating crisps with their sandwich was a positive idea but did not actively consider the combination when purchasing. Added to this, crisps and sandwiches were not shelved close to each other. The principal creative idea proposed that Walkers crisps could make any sandwich more exiting. The creative 'twist' was to present this idea suggesting that Walkers could make any sandwich more exciting, including the town of Sandwich in the UK.

The brand had for some years used celebrity endorsement to underpin their advertising. Ex-England footballer Gary Lineker had been the mainstay of these campaigns, depicted in a variety of humorous situations. For the sandwich campaign, Walkers used a number of celebrities involved in a number of surprise community events over a three-day period. Pop group JLS took the sixth form college assembly, Chelsea footballer Frank Lampard coached the college football team, Formula 1 racing driver Jenson Button drove a black taxicab, celebrity chef Marco Pierre White sold gourmet sandwiches from a market stall, actress Pamela Anderson served pints at the local pub and comedian Al Murray hosted the quiz. Gary Lineker acted in the role of compère for this event.

The idea was to capture the genuine surprise and excitement of the locals on film in order to produce television commercials and online video content. Teaser advertisements using this film footage were shown on TV and online. To ensure reactions were genuine, a great deal of effort went into keeping plans secret and the events were filmed unscripted and unrehearsed.

The event-based campaign helped Walkers to influence key audiences, because it allowed them to become involved. They arranged for journalists to be 'embedded' in Sandwich over the course of the three days, and invited members of the sales team and representatives from Walkers' key retail customers.

The inherent PR newsworthiness of the initial idea contributed significantly to its creative effectiveness. This was effectively followed through with the advertising demonstrating the surprise and excitement generated linking directly to show how exciting Walkers (and therefore their crisps) were in association with Sandwich the town and (therefore) with sandwiches bought for lunch.

Source: Based on www.pepsico.co.uk, accessed 5 December 2011; www.canneslions.com, accessed 5 December 2011; www.warc.com, accessed 5 December 2011

Question

Are these kinds of creative awards a good indicator of creative effectiveness?

Task

Use the Cannes Lions website to review other winners of their awards.

Be knowledgeable in advance -
to assess ideas you need to be able to place them in a broader context and compare them against ideas you have seen elsewhere and considered 'good' or 'bad'.

2

Come to the meeting with a smile -
join the creative presentation hoping to enjoy yourself and ready to be inspired. When people are having fun, they listen and contribute.

3

Back to the brief -
reminding yourself of your brief is essential. It provides you with a framework against which to evaluate the idea. Make sure the agency does this too before they present.

4

Empathise -
try to empathise with the people bringing the ideas to you. Creative people are different. It matters less to them that a job is done on time and within budget than that it is done really well.

Figure 5.3 Ten-piece jigsaw - judging creative ideas
Source: IPA et al. (2007)

5

Clarify -
if the idea is not simple and single-minded, then perhaps the brief was not simple and single-minded either. Is it on brief? What exactly is the idea? What sort of an idea is it? What sort of an execution is it? How is the idea going to work?

6

Question yourself -
your first reaction to the work will almost certainly be subjective. Establish what influences may be at work on your opinion before you start to concentrate on it objectively.

7

Question the idea -
the clients who know how to use open questions are those who end up with great work, because they encourage ideas to develop. Start with Who? What? Why? Where? How? When? They involve and stimulate.

8

Reflection -
listen to the agency, make notes, then go away and think. Reflection is when you ask the HOW questions. How can we take the idea on? How can we adapt it? How can we make it better?

9

Refinement and the role of research -
These are the WHY questions. The first is, Why change anything? The less you do to a new and challenging idea, the more you might learn about it in research.

10

Relax -
You've done everything you can to help the idea survive and flourish. There is every reason to believe the idea will be a success.

Scholars' paper 5.4 **Are creative campaigns effective?**

Field, P. (2011) The value of creativity, *Market Leader*, Quarter 2

This paper presents a detailed analysis of award-winning case studies from the IPA Effectiveness Awards and the Gunn Report creative awards database. The IPA case study analysis considers hard business results (*non-creative campaigns*) whereas the Gunn Report cases are judged on creative criteria (*creative campaigns*). The study examines the commercial benefits of creativity in communications, including online. The author identifies that the two groups are quite evenly matched in terms of the criteria that can affect effectiveness such as market share and maturity. The paper discusses the relative merits of funding creative versus non-creative campaigns and the issues concerning funding including extra share of voice (ESOV). The need is highlighted for campaigns to consider both creativity and effectiveness measured in commercial terms.

Chapter summary

In order to help consolidate your understanding of creativity in advertising here are the key points summarised against each of the learning objectives.

Explain ideas about what creativity might be and how it is used

Creative advertising is considered to be divergent and there are a number of bases on which this can be effectively achieved. Determining a specific definition of creativity is challenging although consideration of relevant theoretical underpinning provides scope for reasonable definitions to be arrived at. Advertising objectives often include the need to gain attention and creativity plays a central role in how this is attained. Context including the culture in which advertising is deployed is another significant issue for creative execution.

Consider the roles and skills of those involved in developing creative advertising

The traditional model for creative development within advertising agencies is the formation of a creative team or partnership. This would normally consist of a copywriter and an art director working to a creative brief prepared by an agency's account planner following briefing by the client. Increasingly, this is becoming more of a collaborative exercise including advertising production and media planners.

Appraise the nature of the creative process including the relationships between agencies and clients

The relationship between the client and their creative provider, usually an agency, plays an important role in determining the process used for creative development. Levels of interaction between the two parties and the exchange of relevant information are key factors.

Determine the key elements of creative advertising content

The intitial starting point for determining content is the completion of the creative brief. This will inform the creative team of the client's key requirements including ideas about brand positioning and specific communications objectives. This provides the framework for identifying relevant message framing. Such framing might be positive or negative. Content sources are considered.

Discuss the forms of message appeals

There are numerous bases for creating message appeals. These could be informational based or emotional/feelings based. Product or service attributes might determine which type of appeal would be appropriate. A balance between the two types of appeal could be effective in some cases. Creative devices such as music, humour and animation aid in achieving the correct appeal format.

Examine how creativity in advertising can be evaluated

Given the relatively subjective nature of creativity, specific measurement criteria are difficult to identify. This does not mean that it cannot or should not be evaluated. Advertising effectiveness is now a significant issue within the advertising industry and creativity is a significant factor in how it is achieved. Industry and academic guidelines are presented alongside examples of campaigns which have won awards for creative excellence.

Review questions

1. Given the strength of Volvo's safety positioning, presented in the Volvo minicase at the beginning of the chapter, how do you think Havas Arnold should develop the brand's creative strategy and appeals?
2. How do cultural issues impact on creativity in advertising?
3. Why is context significant in developing creative advertising?
4. Identify five major challenges facing those involved in creative roles in advertising.
5. Do you agree with Hegarty's view of the creative process being 'dysfunctional'? Discuss the relevant issues.
6. Is the creative team (copywriter and art director) approach still a good model for creative advertising development?
7. Use the framework of the creative brief in Figure 5.1 to produce a brief for a consumer brand of your choice.
8. Explain the difference between information- and emotional-based message appeals.
9. Identify the advantages and disadvantages of using humour in advertising.
10. To what extent can creativity be evaluated effectively?

Chapter references

Adams, A.J. and Henderson Blair, M. (1992) Persuasive advertising and sales accountability, *Journal of Advertising Research*, 32(2) (March/April), 20–5

Ambler, T. and Hollier, E.A. (2004) The waste in advertising is the part that works, *Journal of Advertising Research*, 44(4), 375–89

Anon (2010) Edgy marketing, *The Marketer*, November, 6–7

Baack, D.W., Wilson, R.T. and Till, B.D. (2008) Creativity and memory effects: recall, recognition, and an exploration of nontraditional media, *Journal of Advertising*, 37, 4 (Winter), 85–94

Baskin, M. (2010) *Evaluating Creative Work*, WARC Best Practice, December, www.warc.com, accessed 24 November 2011

Batra, R. and Stayman, D.M. (1990) The role of mood in advertising effectiveness, *Journal of Consumer Research*, 17 (September), 203–14

Binet, L. and Field, P. (2007) *Marketing in the Era of Accountability*. Institute of Practitioners in Advertising, Henley-on-Thames: WARC

Blasko, V.J. and Mokwa, M.P. (1986) Creativity in advertising: a janusian perspective, *Journal of Advertising*, 15, 4, 43–50

Braithwaite, A. and Ware, R. (1997) The role of music in advertising, *Admap* (July/August), 44–7

Buda, R. (2003) The interactive effect of message framing, presentation order, and source credibility on recruitment practices, *International Journal of Management*, 20 (2), 156–63

Burtenshaw, K., Mahon, N. and Barfoot, C. (2006). *The Fundamentals of Creative Advertising*. Switzerland: AVA Publishing

Buzzell, R. (1964) Predicting short-term changes in market share as a function of advertising strategy, *Journal of Marketing Research*, 1(3), 27–31

Christodoulides, G., Jevons, C. and Blackshaw, P. (2011) The voice of the consumer speaks forcefully in brand identity: user-generated content forces smart marketers to listen, *Journal of Advertising Research*, Supplement, March, 101–8

Clark, A. (2011) It's back to the edge for Benetton, *The Times*, 10 September, 71

Dahlen, M., Rosengren, S. and Torn, F. (2008) Advertising creativity matters, *Journal of Advertising Research*, September, 392–403

Dan, V. and Ihlen, Ø. (2011) Framing expertise: a cross-cultural analysis of success in framing contests, *Journal of Communication Management*, 15(4), 29

El-Murad, J. and West, D. (2004) The definition and measurement of creativity: what do we know? *Journal of Advertising Research*, 44(2) June, 188–201

Entman, R. M. (1993). Framing: toward clarification of a fractured paradigm, *Journal of Communication*, 43(4), 51–8

Field, P (2011) The value of creativity, *Market Leader*, Quarter 2

Foxall, G.R. and Goldsmith, R.E. (1994) *Consumer Psychology for Marketing*. London: Routledge

Gamson, W. A. and Modigliani, A. (1989) Media discourse and public opinion on nuclear power: a constructionist approach, *American Journal of Sociology*, 95, 1–37.

Goodenough, W.H. (1981) *Culture, Language, and Society*. Menlo Park, CA: Benjamin/Cummings

Hackley, C. (2000) Silent running: tacit discursive and psychological aspects of management in a top UK advertising agency, *British Journal of Management*, 11, 239–54

Hackley, C. and Kover, A.J. (2007) The trouble with creatives: negotiating creative identity in advertising agencies, *International Journal of Advertising*, 26, 1, 63–78

Han, S.P. and Shavitt, S. (1994) Persuasion and culture: advertising appeals in individualistic and collectivistic societies, *Journal of Experimental Social Psychology*, 30, 4, 326–50

Heath, R.G. (2010) Creativity in TV ads does not increase attention, *Admap* (January) retrieved 23 October 2011 from www.warc.com

Heath, R.G., Nairn, A.C. and Bottomley, P.A. (2009) How effective is creativity? Emotive content in TV advertising does not increase attention, *Journal of Advertising Research* (September) 450–63

Hegarty, J. (2011) *Hegarty on Advertising: Turning Intelligence into Magic*. London, Thames and Hudson

Helegsen, T. (1994) Advertising awards and advertising agency performance criteria, *Journal of Advertising Research*, 34 (July/August), 43–53

Hill, R. and Johnson, L.W. (2004) Understanding creative service: a qualitative study of the advertising problem delineation, communication and response (APDCR) process, *International Journal of Advertising*, 23, 3, 285–307

Hotz, M.R., Ryans, J.K. and Shanklin, W.L. (1982) Agency/client relationships as seen by influentials on both sides, *Journal of Advertising*, 11, 1, 37–44

IPA et al. (2007) *Judging Creative Ideas Best Practice Guide*. February, London: IPA

Josephs, J. (2004) Volvo safe? www.brandchannel.com, November 22, accessed 18 November 2012

Kaplan, A.M. and Haenlein, M. (2010) Users of the world, unite! The challenges and opportunities of social media, *Business Horizons*, 53, 1 (January–February) 59–68

Kim, B.H., Han, S. and Yoon, S. (2010) Advertising creativity in Korea: scale development and validation, *Journal of Advertising*, 39, 2 (Summer), 93–108

Kirmani, A. (1997) Advertising repetition as a signal of quality: if it's advertised so much, something must be wrong, *Journal of Advertising* 26(3), 77–86

Koslow, S., Sasser, S.L. and Riordan, E.A. (2003) What Is Creative to Whom and Why? Perceptions in Advertising Agencies, *Journal of Advertising Research*, 43, (March), 96–110

Koslow, S., Sasser, S.L. and Riordan, E.A. (2006) Do marketers get the advertising they need or the advertising they deserve? *Journal of Advertising*, 35, 3, 81–101

LaBahn, D.W. and Kohli, C. (1997) Maintaining client commitment in advertising agency/client relationships, *Industrial Marketing Management*, 26, 6, 497–508

Lafferty, B.A., Goldsmith, R.E. and Newell, S.J. (2002) The dual credibility model: the influence of corporate and endorser credibility on attitudes and purchase intentions, *Journal of Marketing Theory and Practice*, 10(3), 1–12

Lannon, J. (1992) Asking the right questions – what do people do with advertising? *Admap* (March), 11–16

Laroche, M., Vinhal Nepomuceno, M., Huang, L. and Richard, M-O. (2011) What's so funny? The use of humor in magazine advertising in the United States, China and France, *Journal of Advertising Research*, 51, 2, 404–16

Lawson, P. (2011) www.ft.com, accessed 5 November 2011

Luo, X. and Bhattacharya, C.B. (2006) Corporate social responsibility, customer satisfaction, and market value, *Journal of Marketing*, 70 (4), 1–18

MacKenzie, S.B. and Lutz, R.L. (1989) An empirical examination of the structural antecedents of attitude toward the ad in an advertising pretesting context, *Journal of Marketing*, 53, 48–65

Masuda, T. and Nisbett, R.E (2001) *Attending Holistically vs. Analytically: Comparing the Context Sensitivity of Japanese and Americans*. Ann Arbor: University of Michigan Press

Millward Brown (2007) Should I use humour in advertising? January, www.millwardbrown.com, accessed 30 November 2011

Millward Brown (2008a) What are the pitfalls of using sexual imagery in advertising? July, www.millwardbrown.com, accessed 30 November 2011

Millward Brown (2008b) How to make the best use of music in an ad. July, www.millwardbrown.com, accessed 30 November 2011

Mircale, G. E. (1987) Feel–do–learn: an alternative sequence underlying Japanese consumer response to television commercials. In *Proceedings of the 1987 Conference of the American Academy of Advertising*, 73–78. Columbia: University of South Carolina

Na, W., Marshall, R. and Woodside, A.G. (2009) Decision system analysis of advertising agency decisions, *Qualitative Market Research: An International Journal*, 12, 2, 153–70

Pan, Z. and Kosicki, G. (2001) Framing as a strategic action in public deliberation. In *Framing Public Life: Perspectives on Media and Our Understanding of the Social World* (eds S.D. Reese, O.H. Gandy and A.E. Grant), 35–65. Mahwah, NJ: Lawrence Erlbaum

Parker, R. and Churchill, L. (1986) Positioning by opening the consumer's mind, *International Journal of Advertising*, 5, 1–13

Percy, L. and Elliott, R (2009) *Strategic Advertising Management*, 3rd edn. Oxford: Oxford University Press

Ray, M.L. and Wilkie, W.L. (1970) Fear: the potential of an appeal neglected by marketing, *Journal of Marketing*, 34 (January), 54–62

Reid, L.N. and Rotfield, H.J. (1976) Toward an associative model of advertising creativity, *Journal of Advertising*, 5, 4, 24–9

Roberts, G. (2011) Sweden: Volvo Car revamps advertising agencies, www.just-auto.com, 12 December, accessed 18 January 2012

Rossiter, J. and Percy, L. (1998) *Advertising, Communications, and Promotion Management*. Singapore: McGraw Hill, International Editions

Rossiter, J.R. (2008) Envisioning the future of advertising creativity research: alternative perspectives. Defining the necessary components of creative, effective ads, *Journal of Advertising*, 37, 4, 139–44

Schiffman, L.G. and Kanuk, L. (1991) *Consumer Behavior*, 4th edn. Englewood Cliffs, NJ: Prentice-Hall

Shabbir, H. and Thwaites, D. (2007) The use of humour to mask deceptive advertising, *Journal of Advertising*, 36 (2) (Summer), 75–85

Sheehan, K.B. and Morrison, D.K. (2009) The creativity challenge: media confluence and its effects on the evolving advertising industry, *Journal of Interactive Marketing*, 9 (2) (Spring), 84–8

Shimp, T. (2010) *Integrated Marketing Communication in Advertising and Promotion*, 8th edn. South Western: Cengage Learning

Smith, R.E. and Yang, X. (2004) Toward a general theory of creativity in advertising: the role of divergence, *Marketing Theory*, 4 (1/2), 31–58

Smith, R.E., MacKenzie, S.B., Yang, X., Buchholz, L.M. and Darley, W.K. (2007) Modelling the determinants and effects of creativity in advertising, *Marketing Science*, 26, 6, 819–33.

Smith, R.E. Chen, J. and Yang, X. (2008) The impact of advertising creativity on the hierarchy of effects, *Journal of Advertising*, 37, 4 (Winter), 47–61

Southgate, N. (2009) *Warc Best Practice*, Issue 506

Stuhlfaut, M. (2011) The creative code: an organisational influence on the creative process in advertising, *International Journal of Advertising*, 30, 2, 283–304

Tsai, S.-P. (2007) Message framing strategy for brand communication, *Journal of Advertising Research*, 47(3) (September), 364–77

Weick, K.E. (1979) Cognitive processes in organizations, in *Research in Organizational/ Behavior. Vol. 1* (eds B.M. Staw and L.L. Cummings), 41–74. Greenwich, CN: JAI Press

www.songsofthesalesman.co.uk, accessed 5 December 2011

Yang, X. and Smith, R.E. (2009) Beyond attention effects: modelling the persuasive and emotional effects of advertising creativity, *Marketing Science*, 28, 5, 935–49

Zhang, Y. and Zinkhan, G.M. (2006) Responses to humorous ads: does audience involvement matter? *Journal of Advertising*, 35 (4) (Winter), 113–27

napter 6

nd communications: role of advertising

Brands are an integral part of society and they enable relationships not only with end-user customers but also with an array of other stakeholders. Brands have been defined and characterised in many ways, sometimes with little agreement, but recently a wider relationship perspective has emerged.

Communication is a critical element in the development of successful brands. Advertising has for a long time been a significant way in which people recognise, understand and develop meaningful brand relationships. Therefore, as the images, associations and experiences that customers have with brands can be initiated, even shaped, through advertising, it is important to understand how advertising can be used effectively in this context.

Aims and learning objectives

The main aim of this chapter is to explore ways in which communications can be used effectively to develop brands.

As a result of reading this chapter readers should be able to:

1. explain the three brand Ps of advertising (brand promise, positioning, performance)
2. consider a range of brand definitions
3. describe the essence of different types of brands
4. evaluate the characteristics of brands
5. examine how people use advertising to form associations with brands
6. evaluate the role of advertising and communications in developing and sustaining brands
7. explain the issues associated with developing and measuring brand equity.

Minicase Diamonds, because she's worth it

When De Beers was formed in 1888 the company quickly assumed a monopolistic role over the entire production and distribution of diamonds sourced in South Africa. Since then it has consistently controlled over 80% of the world market for diamonds. This grip has been achieved by the company's control over the world's supply of rough diamonds. Whenever challenged, De Beers would simply flood the market with diamonds, eliminating any price advantage the competitor might offer. When diamonds were discovered in Siberia in the 1950s, De Beers bought the entire Russian output.

De Beers also drove demand for diamonds, typified by their entry into the American market in 1938. With

Exhibit 6.1 A diamond is forever ad
Source: Image courtesy of The Advertising Archives

interest in diamonds falling, De Beers teamed up with one of the first US advertising agencies, N.W. Ayer. The brief was to find a slogan to support a new De Beers advertising campaign. The agency's copywriter, Frances Gerety, allegedly scribbled the phrase 'a diamond is forever' when searching for inspiration shortly before leaving the office one day. Since then 'A diamond is forever' has been and still is the official slogan of De Beers. The slogan is regarded as the main reason De Beers was able to influence the American public so successfully, and helped to establish the cultural expectation that a diamond engagement ring is a necessity to fulfil the engagement ritual.

De Beers has used a range of marketing strategies to influence markets. These include writing scenes for Hollywood films that required the use of diamonds as a symbol of true romance. Others involve giving diamonds to film stars as symbols of everlasting love, placing stories and photographs in magazines and newspapers about celebrities, to reinforce the link between diamonds and romance. De Beers use fashion designers and editors to talk about the 'trend towards diamonds' and they even commission artists such as Picasso, Dali and Dufy to paint pictures for advertisements, to suggest that diamonds are unique works of art.

Their strategy to control the supply of rough diamonds has always been under attack, and at the turn of the 21st century, it became unsustainable. De Beers repositioned itself using the new name the 'Diamond Trading Co.' (DTC) for its marketing activities. The De Beers name was maintained and used for the new upmarket diamond stores that it developed, and by 2012 it had 43, with nearly half in Asia. In addition, the Diamond Information Center (DIC) was formed in order to manage the placement of diamond jewellery with celebrities at events such as the Oscars, Fashion Week and the Grand Prix series.

There are several trends in the US market that offer opportunities for diamond usage. First there is the increasing frequency with which people in developed economies are getting married. This increases the number of opportunities to celebrate the occasion with a diamond ring. There are also an increasing number of self-sufficient, affluent women, people who can afford to buy diamonds for themselves.

The DTC responds to these trends with two main forms of advertising. The first is referred to as 'Occasion' campaigns, which seek to reinforce the accepted behaviour that engagements are symbolised with a diamond ring. These campaigns led to an excess of smaller stones, which in turn inspired the hugely successful 'three-stone anniversary ring'. The advertising campaign tag line for this product was 'For your past, present and future'.

In response to the second trend, DTC use campaigns to 'Celebrate women'. The 'Celebrate her' campaign has focused on men buying jewellery to celebrate their partners. Various campaigns, some humorous, many romantic, use print and television as the main media. Luxury magazines are an important medium, not only because of the context in which diamonds can be represented and the detail that photography can draw out, but also because high-worth clients are attracted to the editorial content which is reinforced by matched or complementary ads.

However, the 'Celebrate her' approach can also be reinterpreted as 'Celebrate me'. The challenge facing De Beers was to find ways in which brand advertising could be used to help women make the associations that legitimised a decision to buy diamonds for themselves.

Source: Goldstein (2011); Lamb (2011); Reilly (2004); Stoklosa (2010)

Introduction

Understanding the nature and characteristics of brands is important if the role and versatility of advertising are to be fully appreciated. The purpose of this chapter is to explore the dynamics and range of brands, and from that point examine ways in which advertising and communications are used to develop brand value. The chapter concludes with a brief consideration of the meaning of brand equity, the value that brands represent.

Brands are promises which frame the way a brand is positioned in the minds of stakeholders, and which structure their expectations. Ideally these expectations match the promise, which is realised or experienced through brand performance. Brand performance can be experienced directly, perhaps through consumption, sampling or first-hand interpretation, or indirectly through observations and comments made by other people and the media. Successful brands deliver consistently on their promises, by meeting or exceeding expectations, and in doing so reinforce the positioning and the credibility of the promise.

Therefore, successful brands might be considered to encapsulate three core brand elements; promises, positioning and performance. These are depicted at Figure 6.1, as the three brand Ps.

Central to the interaction of these three brand Ps is communication. Communication is used to make the promise known, to position a brand correctly and to encourage and realise brand performance. Unsurprisingly, advertising has a critical role to play in building and sustaining this interaction of branding elements.

Consistent brand performance, fulfilled brand promises and strong levels of customer satisfaction through time can help consumers to trust a brand. As we know, trust over time leads to commitment (Morgan and Hunt 1994), reflected in customers prioritising a brand within their evoked set for a product category. Accepting that consumers are active problem solvers means that brands can be regarded as a way in which the amount of decision-making time and associated perceived risk can be reduced for buyers. This is because brand names provide information about content, taste, durability, quality, price and performance, without requiring a buyer to undertake time-consuming comparison tests with similar offerings or other risk-reduction approaches to purchase decisions.

In much of the literature, brands assume a myopic perspective, namely one centred just on customers. In reality brands encompass a range of stakeholders (de Lencastre and Côrte-Real 2010) and branding should be considered not only from a managerial but also from service, relational and social perspectives (Brodie and De Chernatony 2009).

This chapter is constructed around these three brand Ps. It commences with a review of the types, nature and characteristics of the brands which together with an understanding of brand associations help frame an appreciation of brand promises. The section on the role of advertising reflects issues concerning positioning, although this topic is addressed in more detail in Chapter 4. The closing section on brand equity explores how brands are measured and valued, effectively a reflection of brand performance.

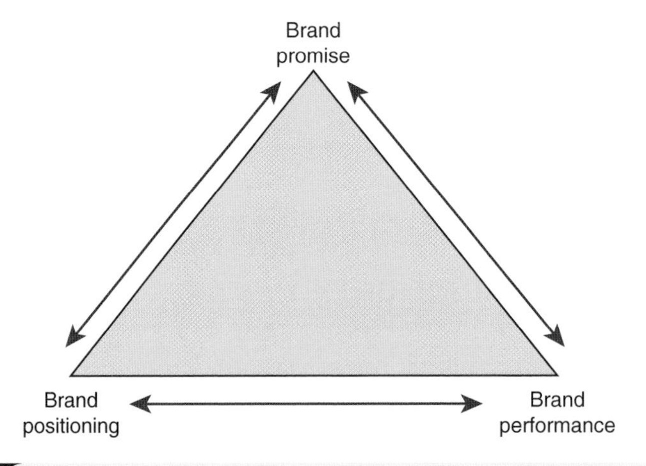

Figure 6.1 The triangulation of the three brand Ps

Brand definitions

Research by De Chernatony and Dall'Olmo Riley (1998a) suggests that there is little close agreement on the definition of a brand. They identified 12 types of definition. Some of the more commonly quoted definitions are presented in Table 6.1.

De Chernatony (2009: 101) suggests that from a managerial perspective, there is a 'plethora of interpretations', which can lead to brand management inefficiencies. To support his argument, he identifies a spectrum of brand interpretations, ranging from differentiation through to added value.

These authors identified that brands are a product of the work of managers who attempt to augment their products with values and associations that are recognised by, and are meaningful to, their customers. In other words, brands are a composite of two main constructs, the first being an identity that managers wish to portray (the promise and expectation) and the second being images, construed by audiences, of the identities they perceive (the image and realisation of the promise). The development of social media including user-generated content in the form of blogs, wikis and social networks have added a new dimension to the managerial-driven perspective of brands. Consumers are assuming a greater role in defining what a brand means to them and are prone to sharing this with their friends, family and contacts rather than with the organisation itself. What this means is that brand managers have reduced levels of influence over the way their brands are perceived and this in turn impacts on the influence they have managing brand reputation.

It is important therefore, to recognise that both managers and stakeholders are involved in the branding process. In the past the emphasis and control of brands rested squarely with brand owners. Today, this influence has shifted to stakeholders, and consumers in particular, as they redefine what brands mean to them and how they differentiate among similar offerings and associate certain attributes or feelings and emotions with particular brands. Indeed, there is discussion suggesting that brands should be considered outside the narrow marketing perspective as they are a construct of a wider realm of influences, including those of culture and society and, for example, the social, service and relational perspectives. For those interested in these issues see Brodie and De Chernatony (2009), and for developments in managerial aspects, see De Chernatony (2009) and de Lencastre and Côrte-Real (2010).

Table 6.1 Brand definitions

Author	Brand definition
Alexander (1960) American Marketing Association	A name, term, sign, symbol, or design, or a combination of them, intended to identify the goods or services of one seller or group of sellers and to differentiate them from those of competitors
Assael (1990)	name, symbol, packaging and service reputation
Schmitt (1999)	a rich source of sensory, affective, and cognitive associations that result in memorable and rewarding brand experiences
Riezebos (2003)	every sign that is capable of distinguishing the goods or services of a company and that can have a certain meaning for consumers both in material and in immaterial terms
Keller (2008)	something that has actually created a certain amount of awareness, reputation, prominence . . . in the marketplace
De Chernatony (2009)	a cluster of values that enables a promise to be made about a unique and welcomed experience

Scholars' paper 6.1 Brand worlds united

Berthon, P., Pitt, L., Chakrabarti, R., Berthon, J-P. and Simon, M. (2011) Brand worlds: from articulation to integration, *Journal of Advertising Research* 51 (March) (Supplement), 182–8

There are many papers on branding but this one looks back over the last 50 years of branding research, and provides an interesting view of how brands have evolved. The authors move from the origins of branding through mimesis, expression and symptom to self-organising phenomena. They use Popper's 'Three worlds' hypothesis (We, I and It) to show how the different streams of branding research can be integrated.

For a long time advertising was regarded as the main tool to build and sustain brands. The emphasis was on building brand values. Increasingly relationship marketing and digital technologies have changed the way consumers interact with brands and with their expectations of what a brand offers. This has led to the use of different tools, media and approaches to build brands. These include creating opportunities for brand experiences and online interactivity to build bonds and brand relationships.

Types of branding

When considering the different types of brand various criteria can be used to categorise them. Brands can be considered in terms of their source, their scope or how they are used, their geographic coverage or the audiences they are intended to serve. These are set out in Table 6.2.

Of these various types a few are referred to in the literature more frequently than others: namely manufacturer's brands, distributor brands, corporate brands, online brands and business-to-business brands. A short review of these follows.

Brand category – source

The source category refers to the origin or root of a brand. These are the most common ways of referring to brands.

Manufacturers' brands help to identify the producer of a brand at the point of purchase. For example, Apple, Samsung, Ford and Coca-Cola are all strong manufacturers' brands. This type of brand usually requires the assistance of channel intermediaries for wide distribution. Brand communications are driven by the manufacturer in an attempt to persuade end users to adopt the brand, which in turn stimulates intermediaries and distributors to stock and distribute the brand. Brand communications, and advertising in particular, are important to develop awareness, brand values and valuable associations.

Table 6.2 A categorisation of brand types

Category of brands	Brand types
Source	manufacturer, distributor, generic, co-brands, online, cause related
Scope	umbrella, multi-brand, personal, celebrity, fashion
Geography	global, international, local, regional, national, place
Audience	consumer, B2B, service, corporate, employer

Distributor brands, often referred to as own-label, store or private-label brands, do not associate the manufacturer with the offering in any way. Distributor brands are owned by channel members, typically a wholesaler, such as Nurdin & Peacock, or retailers, such as Asda (George fashion), the Swedish supermarket Axfood with their Eldorado brand, and Shoppers Stop and Pantaloon in India. This type of brand offers many advantages to both the manufacturer, who can use excess production capacity, and retailers, who can earn a higher margin than they can with manufacturers' branded goods and at the same time develop store loyalty and image. Venture brands are a further attempt by retailers to self-manage their brand portfolios. Whereas store brands tend to offer standardised me-too brand copies, venture brands seek to offer consumers something different in the identified categories, without any store packaging or identification. So, in 2011 Tesco introduced the Parioli Italian range of pasta, sauces and olive oils, ChokaBlok ice cream and the Lathams and Nutricat premium pet food ranges, with a full-page ad in Tesco's magazine, all as part of the venture brand strategy.

ViewPoint 6.1 Coca-Cola means lifestyle . . . today

Coca-Cola is a classic example of a manufacturer's brand. Distributed in over 200 countries, the Coca-Cola brand drives revenue of £4.4 billion (2010), and seeks to achieve three billion servings, each day, by 2020.

To help achieve these impressive performance figures, Coca-Cola has used advertising consistently since its launch in 1886. The goal is invariably brand awareness, to help audiences make brand associations, and to position the brand as an accompaniment or a catalyst for a joyous life. This joyous life has for a long time, in Coca-Cola's terms, been associated with the American way of life and values. This has often been depicted through the 'Coca-Cola girl', to represent images of American beauty.

Early Coca-Cola print ads were derived from their first calendar. Magazines, newspapers and advertising cards were popular before playing cards, posters, serving trays, uniquely shaped bottles, jewellery, sports programmes, bookmarks, sheet music, signage, delivery trucks, Santa icons and even the sides of buildings became legitimate media vehicles.

Coca-Cola ads have reflected prevailing cultural and political contexts. In the 1980s the Watergate scandal and the Vietnam war resulted in Coke trying to protect the world with a hillside of singers wanting 'to teach the world to sing and . . . furnish it with love'.

In the 1980s, the brand worked with the Bobby Brown band, New Edition, in an attempt to align itself with popular culture and to reach the MTV generation. Michael Jackson's huge success with Pepsi may have been a catalyst. The next decade drew ads where Coke was to be a part of a fun-filled life, immortalised as 'Always Coca-Cola'.

Since then ads have drawn associations with happiness, lifestyle and health, the most recent being a gang of insects relieving a man sleeping under a tree of his bottle of Coke, and using it to replenish nature.

The target for these ads has been consumers, pulling them into the brand and touchpoints where the brand is available.

Source: Barda (2010); Parsons (2011); www.topdesignmag.com/vintage-coca-cola-girl-ads/; www.prnewswire.com/news-releases/worlds-largest-private-collection-of-coca-cola-advertising-art-and-memorabilia-to-become-available-to-public-80000-pieces-in-collection-worth-10-million-120769309.html

Question

Other than advertising, how else could brands like Coca-Cola help audiences make brand associations?

Task

Choose another manufacturer's brand and track the way advertising has been used to help consumers make brand associations.

Some manufacturers refuse to make distributor products in an attempt to restrict the availability and number of brands from which consumers can choose. There have been occasions where multiple grocers have launched products that are alleged to be too similar to key manufacturer brands. Often this leads to channel conflict as the name and/or packaging of the distributor brand is alleged to resemble too closely that of the brand leader.

Channel members have the additional cost of promotional initiatives which are necessary in the absence of a manufacturer's support. Advertising is not a major part of the brand communications mix used to support distributor brands. Some retailers use in-store activities, plus signage and out-of-home work such as posters and billboards in the vicinity of stores, plus direct mail and customer magazines.

Generic brands contain the same content and functional nutritional qualities of both manufacturer and distributor brands. This is because generics are required to meet the same standards as set by the local/regional regulators (Cunningham et al. 1982). The key difference is that generics are stripped of all advertising and brand communications, including merchandising and elaborate and persuasive packaging. This enables generics to be sold at very low prices. Once a popular option, generic brands have lost market share as distributors use their store brands, which include packaging and in-store merchandising, with sales promotions and low prices to win share.

Online or *pure digital brands* such as Amazon, Google and lastminute.com are characterised by the absence of an offline retail presence. This context therefore deprives consumers of many of the normal cues used to sense and interpret brands. Opportunities to touch, smell and feel, to try on and physically assess and compare products are largely removed and a new set of criteria has to be used to convey and interpret brand associations.

Without wishing to state the obvious, websites provide one of the main ways in which consumers experience online brands and help shape the way promises are made and met. The website acts as a prime means of differentiating online brands and contributes to the brand experience.

Online advertising fulfils important roles not only of enabling and directing traffic to a brand's website, but of creating and maintaining positive brand associations. Online and mobile users generally exhibit goal-directed behaviour and experiential motivations. Goal-directed behaviour that is satisfied is more likely to make people want to return to a site. Therefore, it can be concluded (broadly) that satisfying experiential motivations makes people stay, and in doing so boosts the potency of an online brand.

Brand category - scope

The scope category of brands refers to what a brand's function is and how brands are organised and used structurally. These are often interpreted as brand strategies.

Umbrella or *family brands* are used to embrace a range of products and services under a single brand identifier. This approach signals consistent quality, and can reduce risk for stakeholders and ease the process of introducing new products. Umbrella branding is a useful approach when the range of product and service offerings is extensive, complex or unknown. High-technology companies and both country and place marketing use advertising to convey a simple identity in order to aid recall, recognition and positioning.

Multi-branding refers to the strategy whereby all brands in a portfolio have a unique form of identification. Unlike family or umbrella branding where all the products in a product line are given the same brand name, and the same potential for both positive and negative halo effects, multi-branding requires each product to have its own unique identity. This uniqueness provides a clear aid to marketing communication, and assists definitive positioning. There are also certain advantages associated with brand management after merger and acquisition. The grocery majors, Procter & Gamble, Kraft and Unilever, both use the multi-brand approach.

Celebrity and *personal brands* are not yet an established part of the academic literature. The research interest with celebrities tends to emphasise their impact as celebrity endorsers and the way they impact on brand awareness and image. The term celebrity brands can refer to A-listers in sports, film, and entertainment, celebrities who attract unusual levels of attention through their activities away from their core activity. This might include their involvement with charities, relationships or scandals (Luo et al. 2010). So while Tom Hanks and David Beckham are endorsers of brands such as Adidas, Brylcreem, Pepsi and Vodafone, Beckham might be considered to be a brand in his own right. Those interested in this topic might wish to read Vincent, Hill and Lee (2009).

Brand category - geographic

The geographic category refers to a brand's intended location or domain.

International and *global brands* have a wide remit but of course there is a long-standing debate about whether brands and their communications should be standardised or adapted to meet local cultures, media and educational contexts. In many circumstances a mid position is established, referred to by some as a 'glocalised' approach. Global brands carry status, gravity and esteem but their success is also attributable to lower unit costs due to economies of scale associated with production, distribution, packaging, advertising and brand communications and access to worldwide media discounts (Johansson and Ronkainen 2005).

Schuiling and Kapferer (2004: 98) cite Wolfe (1991) when defining *local brands* as brands that exist in one country or in a limited geographical area. They might belong to a local, international, or global firm. The authors define *international brands* as brands that 'have globalized elements of the marketing strategy or mix. In a more radical sense, *global brands* are defined as brands that use the same marketing strategy and mix in all target markets' (Levitt 1983).

Country and *place* brands are concerned with the selection of 'a consistent mix of brand values and brand elements with clear connections to a place of origin' (Iversen and Hem 2008: 611). Place branding involves multiple stakeholders and invariably lacks the control of a central authority (Frost 2004). One way to overcome the potential discontinuities inherent in this context is to use umbrella branding. This can provide messages, often delivered through advertising, that explain the core attributes of a place. Local offerings can then communicate their fit with the core values of the place brand and reinforce associations.

Brand category - audience

The audience category refers to the market a brand is designed to operate in.

Consumer brands are the most visible, and for most of us, the most familiar. Brand communications, and advertising in particular, are used extensively.

Business-to-business brands represent a market much bigger than the consumer market. It is interesting that so little research has been published about business-to-business branding. Kotler and Pfoertsch (2006) determined that business-to-business (B2B) branding does influence decision making. However, as Bendixen et al. (2004) suggest, the degree of influence is much weaker than that found in consumer markets. Indeed, they confirm that price, logistics and service are more important to organisational buyers than the brand name.

In an attempt to investigate a deeper appreciation of the way B2B branding might work, Zablah et al. (2010) examined how different aspects of branding correspond with the stages of the organisational buyer decision process. Using Keller and Lehmann's (2006) contention that brand performance is dependent on a prospective buyer's 'mindset', they utilised a brand performance framework, consisting of brand consciousness, brand sensitivity, brand preference and brand importance. These are explained in Table 6.3. Zablah and colleagues argue that constructs can be conceptually organised using a four-stage model. This is a sequential framework of beliefs–attitudes–intentions–behaviours that captures the different expressions of brand influence within organisational buying.

Table 6.3 Dimensions of brand performance

Brand dimension	Explanation
Brand preference (attitude)	the extent to which an organisation perceives one brand to be more desirable than comparable alternatives
Brand consciousness (beliefs)	the belief that well-known brands are superior to lesser-known brands
Brand sensitivity (intentions)	the extent to which the buying centre relies on brand information for decision-making purposes
Brand importance (behaviour)	the extent to which buying centre members rely upon brand information when making a purchase decision

Source: Zablah et al. (2010)

Their results indicate that relatively high levels of brand importance are only likely to occur when brand sensitivity is a main factor in product-choice decision making. They also found that *brand consciousness* is the primary determinant of brand importance, when competitive intensity is low or when marketing maintenance repair and operations supplies. *Brand preference* is the primary determinant of brand importance when there is high competitive intensity or when marketing high-tech products. They also found that brand-conscious buyers do not appear to become 'brand switchers' when faced with highly competitive situations. In addition, buyers within small firms are more likely to form strong brand preferences than buyers in much larger firms.

Apart from the importance of supplying brand information, one of the implications arising from this research is that B2B brand communications should be used contextually. When the environment in which decision-making teams and buyers operate, and how they perceive the world, are understood, communications can be used to impact perceptions of brand importance more effectively. See the Eddie Stobart example of contextual branding activities, shown in ViewPoint 6.2.

Service brands are important because they have the potential to overcome the problems associated with the inherent intangibility of services. Through the use of brands, consumers are enabled with symbolic signals to recognise and form images (Baek and Whitehill King 2011). A service brand can also reduce financial, psychosocial, physical and performance risks.

ViewPoint 6.2 Eddie Stobart delivers strong B2B branding

The Eddie Stobart story has its roots in the 1960s in what was then an agricultural contracting firm, based in a small village in the UK's Lake District. The iconic B2B brand that Eddie Stobart is today emerged when Edward Stobart took over from his father in the 1970s. He expanded the business into road transport and warehousing and today the Stobart Group has a road haulage fleet of over 2,250 trucks and offers integrated sea, rail and road freight transport.

Increasingly the Stobart promise includes sustainability, with the goal of reducing impact on the environment. An example of this is the Eddie Stobart train. This runs five times daily carrying goods for Tesco from Daventry in the Midlands to Livingston in Scotland. This, it is claimed, saves 13,000 lorry journeys a year and its rail services save 4,804.65 tons of carbon dioxide per year compared with road movements.

The success of the expansion and branding can be partly attributed to the branding strategy. In a market characterised by price and commoditisation, Stobart revolutionised road haulage, first by giving each of its lorries a unique female name. The first four were Twiggy, Dolly, Tammy and Suzie, after female stars in the 1970s. Since then all of their trucks have been named in this way.

By naming the lorries, providing uniforms for drivers and requiring them to return waves from passing families, the Stobart brand became one of the first to provide real-time brand interaction, way before the advent of digital media. 'Stobart spotting' became an established family game when travelling, often incorporated into 'I spy' games. Eddie Stobart is a household name, and has a merchandising division and an Eddie Stobart fan club with 25,000+ members, who have submitted over 1,400 names for new lorries.

The Eddie Stobart brand combines both rational and emotional features, with the emotional elements more prominent than in most B2B brands. By utilising a striking livery with the use of transit advertising, and a clearly differentiated brand promise, based on punctuality and consistency, Stobart remains the iconic brand in the multimodal logistics, warehousing and biomass fuel sectors.

Source: Aspinall (2011); Bland and Brodie (2008); Rudduck (2011); www.stobartgroup.co.uk/

Question

Which of the brand dimensions depicted in Table 6.3 applies to the Eddie Stobart branding?

Task

Identify another logistics company and evaluate ways in which it develops its brand.

Exhibit 6.2 An Eddie Stobart truck
Source: Stobart Group

Advertising, together with other forms of communication, have a critical role in establishing service brand credibility and reducing risk.

Corporate brands are becoming increasingly popular. One of the reasons for this is that the costs associated with supporting a corporate single brand are far lower than those necessary to support a range of products and services. Corporate brands are used to differentiate and position an organisation, so that financial markets, suppliers, employees, channel network partners, trade unions, competitors, customers and other stakeholder groups understand what the organisation represents and what the promise is that it makes to them all.

Corporate advertising can be an integral part of an organisation's corporate communication programme. However, advertising's role should be very specific as the development of a corporate brand requires the full use of the corporate identity mix. This mix embraces both planned and unplanned communication, and symbolism; and the behaviour of both managers and employees is a critical element. Indeed, it is becoming increasingly common to read about

Table 6.4 Business vs consumer market differences and their implications for the relative importance of B2B brands

		Implications for the relative importance of brands in business markets		
Market differences	**Description**	**Decreased**	**Increased**	**Rationale**
Decision-making process	Purchase processes are more systematic and objective-driven ('rational') in business than consumer markets; purchase situations impact perceived risk (Bendixen et al. 2004; Kotler and Pfoertsch 2007; Rosenbroijer 2001; Webster and Keller 2004).	√		Systematic decision making, which is subject to supervisor review, is less susceptible to the influence of emotional or attitudinal (e.g., brand) factors.
Group dynamics	Purchase decisions in business markets often involve groups of individuals with distinct roles and agendas while individual decision-making tends to be the norm in consumer markets (Johnston and Bonoma 1981; Kim et al. 1998; Webster and Keller 2004).	√		The likelihood that brand considerations permeate the deliberation process is reduced, given that brand awareness and purchase criteria are likely to differ across buying centre participants.
Nature of demand	Demand for business products is derived from the demand for consumer products (Webster & Keller, 2004).	√		The inherent value of brands as a vehicle for self-expression is generally reduced in business markets.
Branding emphasis	Corporate (as opposed to product) branding is more prevalent in business than consumer markets (De Chernatony and McDonald 1998; Malaval 2001; Michell et al. 2001).		√	Corporate brands can be leveraged across product categories and purchase situations to influence buyer decision processes.
Marketing communications mix	Interpersonal communication (e.g., personal selling) has a heightened role in business markets when compared to consumer markets (Gilliland and Johnston 1997; Minett 2002; Turley and Kelley 1997).	√		Brand considerations are reduced to a supplemental role as interpersonal interactions strongly inform buyer decision processes.

Source: Zablah, Brown and Donthu (2010); used with permission

companies developing their brands from the inside, with employees supporting and even advocating company values and strategies.

Employer brands are a specialist or niche development out of corporate brands. Formerly referred to as employee relations, a part of organisational communication, the focus of the employer brand rests with communication with both current and prospective employees of an organisation. The goal is to develop feelings and behaviours that develop the reputation and that make the organisation a desirable place to work (Moroko and Uncles 2008). An alternative view holds that employer branding is concerned with 'the package of functional, economic and psychological benefits provided by employment and identified with the employing company' (Ambler and Barrow 1996: 186).

To complete this section it is appropriate to compare the consumer and business markets and to consider the impact on B2B brands. Table 6.4 sets out some critical differences.

Brand characteristics

The essence of a strong brand is that it is sufficiently differentiated to the extent that it cannot be easily replicated by its competitors and valued stakeholders. This level of differentiation requires that a brand possess many distinctive characteristics and to achieve this it is important to understand how brands are constructed.

Brands consist of two main types of attributes: intrinsic and extrinsic (Riezebos 2003). Intrinsic attributes refer to the functional characteristics of the product such as its shape, performance and physical capacity. If any of these intrinsic attributes were changed, it would directly alter the product. Extrinsic attributes refer to those elements that are not intrinsic and if changed do not alter the material functioning and performance of the product itself. For example, devices such as the brand name, advertising and marketing communications, packaging, pricing, and increasingly customer brand experiences, all enable consumers to form associations that help give meaning to a brand. Buyers often use the extrinsic attributes to help them distinguish one brand from another because in certain categories it is virtually impossible for them to make decisions based on the intrinsic attributes alone.

All brands consist of a mixture of intrinsic and extrinsic attributes and management's task is to decide on the balance between them. Indeed, this decision lies at the heart of branding in the sense that it is the strategy and positioning that lead to strong brands.

Biel (1997) refers to brands being composed of three elements. The first refers to the functional abilities or its core skill, the second to its brand personality, and the third to brand relationships. These are explored in turn.

Scholars' paper 6.2 Brand relationships for everyone

Fournier, S. (1998) Consumers and their brands: developing relationship theory in consumer research, *Journal of Consumer Research*, 24, 4, 343–73

Fournier argues that it is important to understand people's life experiences as this frames the assortment of brands and the relationships they develop with brands. She argues that meaningful consumer brand relationships are shaped not by symbolism or functional category measures, or by involvement, but through the ego significance a brand offers an individual. This much-cited paper should be read by all involved in both academic and practitioner brand management.

Brand skills

A core function of a brand is its ability to deliver a functional or performance outcome. Biel refers to this as a brand's claim or promise and this must be delivered if the brand is to have long-term credibility. The particular attributes that distinguish a brand are referred to as brand skills. He refers to cold remedies and their skill to relieve cold symptoms for six hours, 12 hours or all day. Other skills include motor oil that protects an engine, lipsticks that do not bleed, hair colorants that provide the right shade, and software that protects computers from viruses and hackers. A failure to deliver on any of these skills will often result in brand rejection. The idea about brand skills can be seen in the Boots product Perfect and Protect. The BBC's science programme *Horizon* featured the search for an anti-ageing product that worked. The programme reported a team of expert dermatologists at Manchester University. They claimed that their independent research scientifically proved that the Boots No. 7 'Protect and Perfect' actually worked.

Boots had prepared by shipping in 21 weeks' supply of the product prior to the *Horizon* programme. Within 24 hours of the programme being aired, sales rose by 2,000 per cent, the shelves in Boots up and down the country were empty, four-figure waiting lists were reported, Boots' web store received 4,000 requests in one evening, and within days the product was being traded on eBay for up to £100. Consumers reacted positively to the brand skill being proven (Sudbury 2009).

Brand personality

The second element identified by Biel is the personality of a brand. This refers to a brand's emotional traits relating to lifestyle and perceived values. For example, some brands might be perceived as exciting, innovative, adventurous, intoxicating or dangerous. Other brands might be regarded as bland, boring, dull or uninteresting.

Brand personification, the idea that a brand can be imagined as a person, and hence have a personality, has been considered for a long time (McCracken 1989; Belk 1988). Aaker (1997) suggests that brand personality should be seen as the set of human characteristics that consumers associate with a brand. Kylie Minogue endorses car brand Lexus, and, in doing so, helps consumers to make associations between the Lexus and its values and the effervescent personality of the singer and celebrity.

As we know, brands are capable of triggering associations in the minds of consumers, and do not need to be based solely on utilitarian or functional features. These associations may sometimes enable consumers to construe a psychosocial meaning associated with a particular brand. Indeed, Belk (1988) discusses the notion that brands offer a means of self-expression, whether this is in terms of who they want to be (desired self), who they attempt to be (ideal self) or who they think they should be (ought self). From this it is possible to interpret brands as a mechanism for individuals to signal their preferred personality.

The functional characteristics of a brand are easily copied by competitors and provide little opportunity for sustainable differentiation. Using emotions and symbolism not only offers consumers additional reasons to engage with a brand (Keller 1998), but also puts up competitive barriers simply because the emotional attachment a brand offers cannot be copied or replicated by competitors.

Aaker (1997) developed the brand personality scale, which consists of five main dimensions of psychosocial meaning. These subsume 42 personality traits. The five dimensions, depicted in Figure 6.2, are sincerity (wholesome, honest, down-to-earth), excitement (exciting, imaginative, daring), competence (intelligent, confident), sophistication (charming, glamorous, smooth), and ruggedness (strong, masculine).

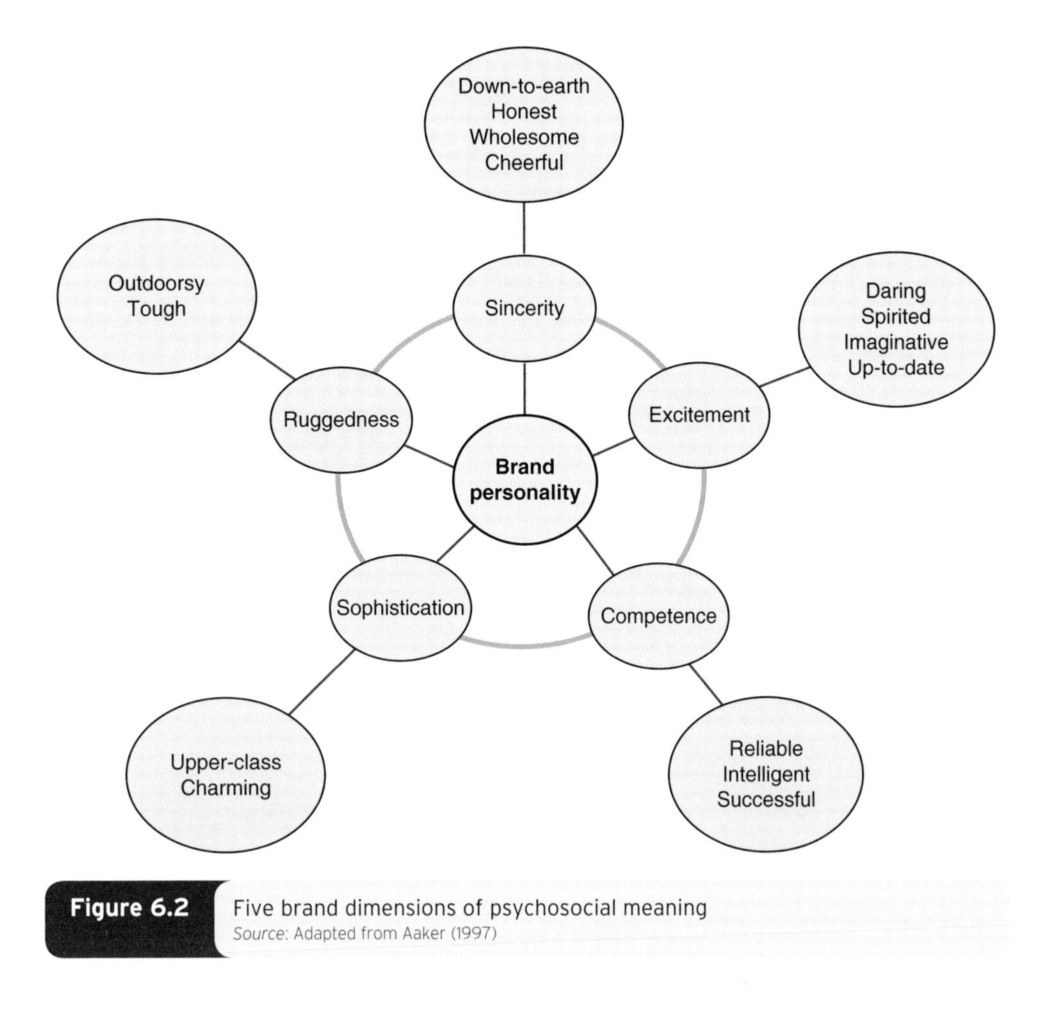

Figure 6.2 Five brand dimensions of psychosocial meaning
Source: Adapted from Aaker (1997)

These dimensions are founded on empirical research in the mid-1990s and revealed that in the USA, MTV was perceived to be best at excitement, CNN at competence, Levi's at ruggedness, Revlon at sophistication and Campbell's at sincerity.

Aaker's work on the psychosocial aspects of branding are recognised as the key dimensions of brand personality. Her framework has been used frequently and cited many times by researchers and authors. Various authors, such as Linville and Carlston (1994) and Phau and Lau (2001), report findings that consumers prefer brands that they feel possess personalities that are similar to their own, as cited by Arora and Stoner (2009). Indeed, people prefer brands that project a personality that is consistent with their self-concepts. As Arora and Stoner (2009: 273) indicate, 'brand personality provides a form of identity for consumers that expresses symbolic meaning for themselves and for others'. Brand personality is a core aspect of brand management and therefore a key task for advertising.

Brand relationship

Recognising that people interact with their preferred brands leads to the third branding element. This is concerned with building an individual buyer–brand relationship. Blackston (1993) argues that successful branding depends on consumers' perceptions of the attitudes held by the brand towards them as individuals. He illustrates the point with research into the credit card market, where different cards share the same demographic profile of users and the same conventional brand images. Some cards provide recognition or visibility of status, which

ViewPoint 6.3 Red Bull's exciting personality

The global leader in the energy drinks market is Red Bull. Packaged in a distinctive, slim blue-silver can, Red Bull is intended for all those occasions when consumers need a boost of energy. Positioned to appeal to a variety of markets such as stressed workers, overworked taxi drivers, exam-anxious students and pressured journalists, it can also appeal to surfers in the summer and snowboarders in the winter. The question is, how does this brand sustain its scope and vibrancy?

Red Bull's brand personality has been carefully shaped and is reflected in its slogan, 'It gives you wings'. Red Bull is edgy, it is about stamina, fun, excitement, danger and adrenalin as it associates itself with extreme activities, such as cliff diving, wakeboarding, urban free-riding, and extreme sailing, plus bike trick contests, mountain biking, and BMX jumping and racing. Red Bull also sponsors many sports: the most prestigious might be Formula 1 racing, but there are also the Red Bull Air Race World Series, street culture and music events.

Red Bull uses advertising to convey its values and to build awareness. To do this they utilise paid-for media such as television, print and cinema as key media channels to reach their target audiences. However, the personality of the brand is conveyed through its associations and sponsorship of dangerous events, with public relations used to communicate the experiences people have of these activities. Perhaps above all else the website provides a hub for its communications, where extensive use of video is made to replay events and activities. The brand's social media activities are used to stimulate word-of-mouth communication which induces a strong sense of credibility.

Source: Deodhar (2010); Turner (2008); www.redbull.com

Question

To what extent is the Red Bull personality a function of positioning?

Task

Identify five events with which Red Bull associate themselves. How do each of these reflect the personality?

Exhibit 6.3 Cliff diving brings thrills for Red Bull devotees
Source: Rex Features

by association are bestowed upon the owner in the form of power and authority. In this sense the card enhances the user. This contrasts with other cards, where the user may feel intimidated and excluded from the card because as a person the attitudes of the card are perceived to be remote, aloof, condescending and hard to approach. For example, respondents felt the cards were saying 'If you don't like the conditions, go and get a different card' and 'I'm so well known and established that I can do as I want.'

The implications for brand development and associated advertising message strategies become clearer. In line with this thinking, Biel cites Fournier (1995), who considers the customer behaviour in consumer markets to gain insights into the brand relationships that consumers develop. She developed a model that characterises the main types of relationships that consumers can have with brands. These are understood in terms of levels of intimacy, partner quality, attachment, interdependence, commitment and love.

Gupta, Melewar and Bourlakis (2010) consider the impact of brand personification in terms of the ability of a representative of the brand to drive the relationship. This occurs most frequently in business-to-business settings. The authors go so far as to propose that the management of business-to-business relationships should be entrusted to brand representatives.

So Biel believes that brands consist of three elements: brand skills, personality and relationships. These combine to form what he regards as 'brand magic', which underpins added or brand value.

Kapferer (2004) refers to a brand identity prism and its six facets, presented in Figure 6.3. The facets to the left represent a brand's outward expression, while Kapferer argues that those to the right are incorporated within the brand, an inner expression or spirit as he refers to it. These facets represent the key dimensions associated with building and maintaining brand identities and are set out in Table 6.5. These are interrelated and define a brand's identity, while also representing the means by which brands can be managed, developed and even extended.

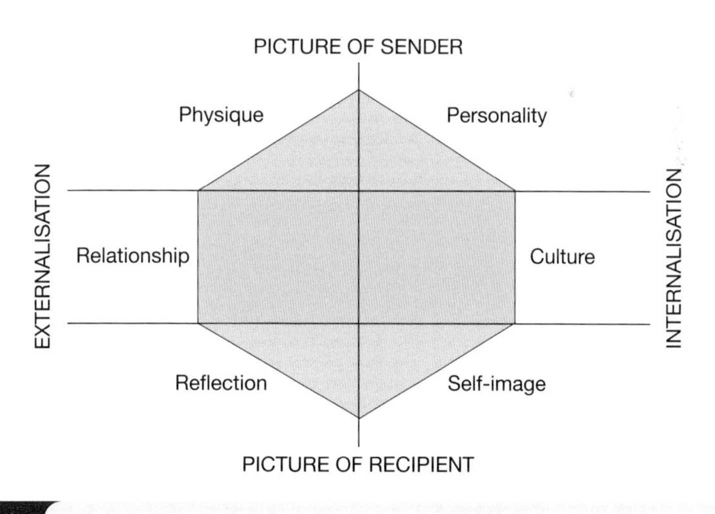

Figure 6.3 Kapferer's brand prism
Source: Kapferer (2004)

Brand value

The final key element is brand value. Brands enable customers to derive extra benefits as one brand can provide different advantages from another. These advantages might be in the form of rational attribute-based advantages (e.g. whiter, stronger or longer) or they may be more emotionally based advantages derived through the augmented aspects of the products (e.g. the

Table 6.5 Brand facets

Brand facet	Explanation
Physique	Refers to the main physical strength of the brand and its core added value. What does the brand do and what does it look like? e.g. the Coca-Cola bottle
Personality	Those human characteristics that best represent the identity, best understood by the use of celebrity spokespersons who provide an instant personality
Culture	A set of values which are central to a brand's aspirational power and essential for communication and differentiation
Relationship	A brand's relationship defines the way it behaves and acts towards others. Apple exudes friendliness, IBM orderliness and Nike provocation. Important in the service sector
Customer reflection	Refers to the way customers see the brand . . . for old people, for sporty people, clever people, people who want to look younger. This is an outward reflection
Self-image	Refers to how an individual feels about themselves, relative to the brand. This is an inner reflection

Source: Based on Kapferer (2004)

Scholars' paper 6.3 All things strategic with brands?

Doyle, P. (1992) Building successful brands: the strategic options, *Journal of Product & Brand Management*, 1, 4, 77-95

Doyle writes clearly and succinctly and in this 1992 paper he sets out how he sees what a brand is. For him successful brands are built upon the principle of seeking to build sustainable differential advantages for the customer. This is achieved through quality, service, innovation and differentiation. Doyle explores a range of brand-related issues and asks what the role of advertising is in building differential advantage.

He answers this and also suggests that brand extension strategies are dependent on the similarity of positioning strategies between existing and new brands.

way you feel about a brand). This is evidenced by the vigour with which Levi Strauss resisted the distribution of its jeans through price-oriented distributors such as Asda. One of the arguments proposed by the company was that the inherent brand value was effectively removed through this form of distribution.

Riezebos (2003) argues that value is added to brands through three main components: perceived performance, psychosocial meaning and the extent of brand-name awareness. These are set out in Table 6.6. Brand value is developed using different combinations of these three components.

Brand communications, and advertising in particular, are required to build these elements so that consumers deduce particular meanings, perceive and value certain performance characteristics and build awareness and name familiarity.

Table 6.6 Brand added value

Added value component	Explanation
Perceived performance	Derived from consumer perceptions of relative quality and perceived associations concerning key attributes
Psychosocial meanings	Refers to the immaterial associations consumers make about brands, from which they deduce meanings about personality and expressions of individuality
Brand-name awareness	The level of name awareness can provoke feelings of familiarity and reduced risk or uncertainty

Source: After Riezebos (2003)

Brand associations

Associations perform a critical role in the way we evaluate products and make choices. We use associations made about brand names and product attributes as cues to retrieve information about product performance. We store information about brands in long-term memory and retrieve it when making purchase decisions (Romaniuk and Gaillard 2007) or when involved in category-related discussions.

Brand associations are concerned with the way people store brand-related information in memory and involve the perceptions and meanings that they attribute to a brand. These associations enable brand recall so that brand information can be updated as fresh information becomes available.

Keller (1993) believes that brand associations constitute the tangible and intangible product attributes and benefits aligned with attitudes which are needed to create a brand image in the mind of a consumer. Keller believes brand associations comprise information about three elements. The first element is the brand's attributes, the product's make-up and performance, plus price and packaging. The second is the benefits the brand offers, that is the value that consumers perceive in the offering. The third element concerns an individual's attitudes towards the brand, in effect their overall assessment.

Understanding the concept of brand associations is important because they should be used to shape communications about a brand. Advertising needs to not only establish favourable brand associations in order to create the conditions for future recall and evaluation, but also to prompt purchase decisions. In addition, most authors agree that positive brand associations also lead to brand equity.

The role of advertising and communications in branding

Advertising plays a vital role in the development of brands and is a major way through which products become brands. The way in which brand communications are used to build brands is determined strategically by the role that the brand is expected to play in achieving an organisation's goals. De Chernatony and Dall'Olmo Riley (1998b) argue that there are several roles that brand communications and advertising can play in relation to brand development. For example, they suggest that during introduction, brand communications need to inform and sometimes educate audiences regarding how or when a brand should be used. The role during brand extensions is to show buyers how the benefits from the established brand have been transferred or extended to the new brand.

Another role, based on the work of Ehrenberg (1974), is to remind buyers and reinforce their perceptions and in doing so defend the market. However, above all of these, brand communications have a primary role, namely to build associations through which consumers identify, recognise, understand, assign affection to, become attached to, and develop relationships with a brand. These associations can be many and varied but they are crucial to brand strength and equity.

The way in which brands develop these associations is partly a function of the size of the financial resources that are made available. As a result, the route to building brand associations can be considered in terms of one of three main ways (Fill 2011).

- ***Above the line***: Should the budget be high, and the audience sufficiently large, advertising will often be the main way through which brand name associations are shaped. The brand name itself will not need to be related to the function or user experience of the brand as the advertising will be used to create and maintain brand associations. Emotional propositions predominate, although information-based approaches are possible.
- ***Below the line***: Where financial resources are restricted and advertising is not an option, the brand name needs to be closely related to the function and user experience of the product. In the fast-moving consumer goods (FMCG) sector, field marketing and packaging also play a significant role in building brand associations. Functional associations tend to predominate.
- ***Around the line***: Whether resources are tight or available, there are circumstances when the use of a formal mix of brand-building tools and traditional media is inappropriate. Here word-of-mouth communication and brand experience are sufficient to propel a brand's visibility. Emotional propositions predominate, although information-based approaches are possible.

Each of these is now considered in turn.

Brand building: above the line

When there are sufficient resources, competitive conditions are intense and margins small, advertising is used to help consumers to make brand associations. Two main approaches can be used: a rational or an emotional approach. When a rational approach is used the functional aspects of a brand are emphasised and the benefit to the consumer is stressed. Very often product performance is the focus of the message and a key attribute is identified and used to position the brand. Typically, unique selling propositions (USPs) were often used to draw attention to a single superior functional advantage that consumers found attractive. For example, a washing powder that washes clothes whiter, drinks that have the highest percentage of fruit juice content and paint that covers more square metres than any other paint.

Many brands now try to present two or even three brand features, as use of the USP has lost ground. For example, when Britvic launched Juice Up into the chilled fruit juice sector to compete with Sunny Delight, it used the higher fruit juice and lower sugar attributes as the main focus of the communications strategy. The rational approach is sometimes referred to as an informative approach (and complements functional positioning).

When an emotional approach is used, advertising should provide emotional selling points (ESPs). These can enable consumers to make positive brand associations based on both psychological and socially acceptable meanings, a psychosocial interpretation. Product performance characteristics are dormant while consumers are encouraged to develop positive feelings and associations with the brand. A further goal can be to create positive attitudes towards the advertising itself, which in turn can be used to make associations with the brand. In other words, the role of likeability becomes paramount when using an emotional advertising approach. Therefore, these types of advertisements should be relevant and meaningful, credible, and be of significant value to the consumer. In essence, therefore, emotional advertising is about people enjoying the advertisement (and complements expressive positioning).

ViewPoint 6.4 Virgin Atlantic do it up there - above the line

The 'Still red hot' campaign to celebrate and reinforce Virgin Atlantic's 25th birthday, is a great example of the advertising-led approach to above-the-line brand development communications.

The £6 million campaign was launched with a 90-second TV commercial that celebrated Virgin's first flight in 1984. The TV work was supported by various outdoor executions.

This was achieved by setting the ad back in 1984, opening with a headline on the front page of the *Sun* about the miners' strike. This was followed by a shot of a yuppie walking into the airport talking on his chunky mobile. The centrepiece was the airline's glamorous hostesses, turning heads as they strode through the airport, each dressed in the airline's red uniform. The supporting music was 'Relax', the classic 1980s track by Frankie Goes to Hollywood. Passengers were shown with jaw-dropping gawps and one remarking that he needs to change his job, while another responds 'I need to change my ticket.'

Since this epic was rolled out and won lots of awards, fresh campaigns to reach specific audiences have been used. Economy advertising was adapted to convey price-led messages, but still under the whole creative idea, and was placed in press, outdoor and digital. Premium Economy used glamorous press, digital and outdoor executions; Upper Class 'Still red hot' executions were placed in business press and outdoor.

A 'Still red hot' website was created to act as the hub for all the activity. The campaign won Silver at the 2010 IPA Effectiveness Awards. What is more, Virgin's bookings rose despite the recession.

Source: IPA (2011); Lovell (2009)

Question

How would you categorise the 'Still red hot' proposition?

Task

Make notes comparing the Virgin Atlantic advertising with that of another airline of your choice. Use material from this chapter to structure your thoughts.

Exhibit 6.4 Shot from the 'Still red hot' campaign
Source: Image courtesy of The Advertising Archives

Brand building: below the line

When the marketing communications budget is limited or where the target audience cannot be reached reasonably or effectively through advertising, then it is necessary to use various other communication tools to develop brand associations.

Direct marketing and public relations are important methods used to build brand values, especially when consumers experience high involvement. The internet offers opportunities to build new dot.com brands, and the financial services sector has tried to harness this method as part of a multichannel distribution policy. What appear to be overridingly important for the development of brands operating with limited resources are the brand name and the merchandising activities, of which packaging, labelling and point-of-purchase activites are crucial.

Apart from clarity, the brand name should describe either the functionality of the brand or who owns it. For example, *dialadogwash.com* describes precisely what the brand does, its functionality, and even how you can contact them. *Snapontools* provides another example while a large number of web addresses convey the same functional information. Here lastminute.com, timesonline and srilankatourism.org are notable examples.

In addition, as differentiation between brands becomes more difficult in terms of content and distinct symbolism, the nature of the service encounter is now recognised to have considerable impact on brand association. The development of loyalty schemes and carelines for FMCG, durable and service-based brands is a testimony to the importance of developing and maintaining positive brand associations. In addition, the packaging and associated labelling can shape the way a brand is perceived.

A large number of consumer brands use below-the-line branding because they lack the resources for a heavyweight advertising programme. However, most B2B brands use this approach not because of a lack of resources, but because of the nature of the product, the audience and the type of decision making. See ViewPoint 6.5 for an example of brand building in business marketing.

ViewPoint 6.5 Building brands of steel with Tata

The steel industry has traditionally been perceived to be essentially a commodity market. Commodity sales are grounded in price and functional attributes. Over the years India's giant Tata Steel concentrated on developing the quality of their steel by investing in state-of-the-art production processes. This has ensured that Tata Steel's key attributes, its formability and flatness, were superior to those offered by competitors. Sales were made to distributors, known as the institutional market, who sold on to end users. However, as the institutional market became saturated, Tata saw the potential to sell into the retail segment for cold rolled steel (CRS), a market previously untouched by steel producers. To do this, however, Tata needed to develop a brand as it was necessary to de-commoditise the perception of steel and create new perceptions of value, based on relationships, not price.

The brand name Tata Steelium was developed but one of the first steps was to enhance the product by making the 'Steelium' coils and sheets available in a wide range of thickness, width and grade combinations to meet end-user needs. Each of these had the Tata Steelium logo embossed on every one-metre length of CRS. The packaging was changed so that not only was the Steelium brand easily identifiable, but it also provided the necessary protection and information about the grade, size, weight, number of pieces/coil length, and bar code. This was unique in the market. Tata Steelium used distributors who only handled Tata products. A fixed price for customers was ensured to avoid channel deals and the inevitable conflicts that had been a feature of distributors selling a range of products from different producers.

The channel strategy is an important part of the Tata brand. Tata Steelium is only available through Tata-appointed distributors. These are created in each major location, based on consumption patterns and strategic business volumes, and they are exclusive to Tata. These distributors appoint dealers who together sell Steelium products within strictly defined territories. Tata help recruit and train the staff of the distributors and dealers. This helps to shape and maintain a high reputation, superior customer service, brand culture and consistency. The development of personal relationships with the distributors is also considered important. Regular visits by account managers are designed to help distributors/dealers to improve their operations.

The Steelium brand promise therefore consists of superior product quality, consistency, variety, availability and delivery. This is augmented by a dedicated exclusive distributor network that provides personalised support within a collaborative framework. This has helped Steelium customers to achieve their own productivity increases, as it meant they could avoid the inefficiencies attached to having to buy odd-sized CRS.

The Tata Steelium brand promise is communicated not through advertising but through customised direct mailings, brochures and information sent to customers, through their distributors. Regular meetings are held for distributors and dealers and customers. This provides support for recruitment and the development of salespersons in line with the Tata brand requirements. The Tata Steel website carries a lot of information about the brand. In addition to providing brochures and product-related specifications, the website encourages people to post enquiries and suggestions directly to Tata. The website is designed to develop a sense of community feeling.

Enquiries from prospective customers are then forwarded to the appropriate distributor. This is supported by a call-free helpdesk and an email service for detailed written enquiries.

Source: Bhattacharya and Datta (2010); Modi and Singh (2010)

Question

To what extent should the below-the-line approach be rephrased as a relationship approach to brand development?

Task

Identify five key characteristics of the Tata Steelium brand.

Exhibit 6.5 Visual identity of the Tata Steel brand
Source: Getty Images

Brand building: around the line

Although not an entirely contemporary strategy, a further approach involves the development of brands without the use of formal communication tools or conventional media. The key to success is to seed the brand through word-of-mouth communication. Two of the most notable examples are Google and Hotmail. Both are global brands and both have been developed without any advertising, sales promotion or direct marketing. They have used some public relations but their market dominance has been developed through word-of-mouth communication (often viral) and experience through usage strategies. Where advertising is used, its role is not to build associations but to direct traffic to a website.

Digital communications, in particular social networks, email, viral marketing, blogging and in some cases Twitter, have enabled people to pass on news and views about brands. When opinion leaders and formers are targeted with relevant and interesting brand-related material they pass on information and views, usually with exponential impact. Brand-based conversations among consumers enable the development of brand associations.

Brand experience has become an important factor in both marketing practice and the marketing literature. These experiences are considered to be the 'internal responses (sensations, feelings and thoughts) and behavioural responses evoked by brand-related stimuli that are part of a brand's design and identity, packaging, communications and environments' (Brakus et al. 2009: 53).

Consumers experience brands in a number of ways, but perhaps the most common experiences occur at one of three distinct points. According to Arnould et al. (2002), cited by Brakus et al. (2009), these are when searching for brands, when they buy brands and when they consume them. Brakus et al. (2009) go on to demonstrate that brand experiences consist of four dimensions, all of which vary according to brand type and category. These are sensory, affective, intellectual and behavioural. Therefore, the sound management of these elements and dimensions can have a positive impact on developing the right brand associations.

Advertising therefore plays different roles in each of these three approaches to brand communications. Advertising is no longer the only approach to brand development; indeed it may not be relevant in some cases. Brand communications embrace a range of activities. These include symbolism, unplanned communications, such as those derived through earned media (consumer-to-consumer conversations and blogs), plus the behaviour exhibited by those either working for the brand or others who support it, such as retailers and service providers. A fourth group of communications includes those associated with the connections formed

ViewPoint 6.6 Around the line with Armenian brandy

The target market for Armenian brandy in Russia and Eastern Europe is 30- to 50-year-olds. Their preferred brand is Ararat, which has a 20% market share and is regarded as the premier brand. For many the Ararat brand is regarded as the key symbol of Armenia and it has strong associations with Armenian culture and tradition.

Since 1989, however, fake Armenian brandies have continued to damage consumer confidence in Ararat. The brand was also beginning to be associated with the Soviet era, and this threatened its premium and contemporary associations.

In order to re-establish the brand's position and provide a clear differentiation with the counterfeiters, a new platform was developed. Called 'Engaging and inspiring legends for today', the campaign sought to stimulate word-of-mouth communication and reposition the Ararat brand. The foundation for the campaign was based on the target market's known enjoyment of films and preference for dramas and stories that feature great mythologies and traditions.

The normal route for this type of campaign would be an above-the-line programme, but this was not possible due to media restrictions. Alcohol advertising is not permitted through broadcast media, although outdoor, print and online advertising are permitted. The solution was the production of a 20-minute feature film about a well-known Armenian legend, called Akhtamar, about unrequited love. It just so happens that this is also the name of one of Ararat's premium products. This story was retold in a contemporary manner yet still served to underline the brand's unique cultural heritage.

The film was accessible through a branded website but offline media, such as billboards, trailers and print, were used to announce the film's availability. The branded website ran a 60-second trailer teasing the audience and creating expectations. When the film was launched both offline and online advertising was used to drive traffic, and sales promotions (e.g. DVD on- and off-pack activity) were used to provoke action.

Thirty of the top bloggers on cinema, photography and advertising were seeded in order to spread information and create interest. There was a press-only film review event plus a red-carpet premiere event for 700 guests, driving more pre-release awareness and media relations opportunities.

The focus of this campaign was a film, only available online, around which other media and marketing communications tools were deployed in a supporting role. The communication outcomes were statistically impressive and the business outcomes resulted in market share in Russia holding to 20% during a recession. Sales of Ararat in Armenia grew by 6%, whilst Akhtamar products grew by 31%.

Source: Based on EACA (2010); Anon (2009)

Question

What might have prevented the Ararat brand being developed with an above-the-line route?

Task

Identify a brand of your choice and consider the way in which social media have been or should be used.

Exhibit 6.6 Advertising shot of Ararat brandy
Source: Alamy Images

through co-branding, the use of ingredient brands, geographical identifiers, support services and award symbols.

Brand communication is the means through which products can evolve into brands. People make associations immediately they become aware of a brand name. It is the brand manager's task to ensure that the associations made are appropriate and provide a means of differentiation and continuity. By communicating the key strengths and differences of a brand, by explaining how a brand enables a customer to create value for themselves, and by reinforcing and providing consistency in the messages transmitted, a level of integration can be brought to the way a brand is perceived by the target market.

The importance of branding as a part of integrated marketing communications should not be forgotten, and to do this internal brand education is crucial. The way individual employees relate to a brand and the way the brand is articulated by senior management are important parts of brand education. Brands are not just external elements, they should form part of the way in which an organisation operates, part of its cultural configuration.

In line with moves towards integrated marketing communications and online and mobile communications, many organisations are moving the balance of their communication mix away from an emphasis on advertising (especially offline) towards a mix that emphasises other tools and media. For example, mobile phone companies have used advertising to develop brand awareness and positioning and have then used the web, sales promotion and direct marketing activities to provide a greater focus on loyalty and reward programmes. These companies operate in a market where customer retention is a challenge. Customer loss (or churn rate) used to exceed 30 per cent and there was a strong need to develop brand communication strategies to reduce this figure and provide for higher customer satisfaction levels and, from that, improved profitability. Online advertising, with search and social media in particular, is an area of current growth and potency.

Brand equity

The concept of brand equity has arisen from the increasing recognition that brands represent a value to both organisations and shareholders. Brands as assets can impact heavily on the financial well-being of a company. Indeed, Pirrie (2006: 40) refers to the evidence that organisations with strong brands 'consistently outperform their markets'.

According to Ehrenberg (1993), market share is the only appropriate measure of a brand's equity or value and, as a result, all other measures taken individually are of less significance, and collectively they come together as market share. However, this view excludes the composition of brands, the values that consumers place in them and the financial opportunities that arise with brand development and strength.

For Eng and Keh (2007) the key role of advertising is to promote ideas, goods or services because this creates brand equity. As Keller (2003) presents it, brand equity represents the added value the product generates from past brand investments. Chaudhuri (2002) suggests that advertising directly or indirectly affects brand equity measured as brand sales, market share and relative price.

Organisations invest large amounts in advertising with a view to developing brand value. As Chauvin and Hirschey (1993) observe, the evidence indicates these advertising investments have a positive influence on future cash flows and the market value of the firm. Barth et al. (1998) believe that estimates of brand value are significantly and positively related to share prices.

However, the return on these investments should not be considered in just the short term. As Eng and Keh (2007) state, there are lagged effects as well, and advertising effects can last up to four years, at least for the top brands. So, although advertising plays a key role in determining firm performance, as Lodish et al. (1995) found, this value is generated as a direct result of many years of advertising campaigns.

Scholars' paper 6.4 **Building brand strength**

Farquhar, P. H. (1990) Managing brand equity, *Journal of Advertising Research*, 30, 4, RC7-RC12

This paper is worth reading, if only because it is the most cited paper in the history of the *Journal of Advertising Research*.

Farquhar considers that brand equity should be managed in three stages (Park, Jaworski and MacInnis, 1986). The introductory stage requires a quality product from which a brand image can be developed based on positive consumer perceptions. The second stage concerns elaboration. This concerns the development of positive attitudes into a brand that can be easily remembered, and brand thoughts that lead to consumer behaviour based on brand experiences. Fortification, the third stage, concerns leveraging the brand through extensions.

Lasser et al. (1995) identify two main perspectives of brand equity, namely a financial and a marketing perspective. The financial view is based on a consideration of a brand's value as a definable asset, based on the net present values of discounted future cash flows (Farquhar 1990). The marketing perspective is grounded in the beliefs, images and core associations consumers have about particular brands. Richards (1997) argues that there are both behavioural and attitudinal elements associated with brands and recognises that these vary between groups and represent fresh segmentation and targeting opportunities. A further component of the marketing view is the degree of loyalty or retention a brand is able to sustain. Measures of market penetration, involvement, attitudes and purchase intervals (frequency) are typical. Feldwick (1996) used a three-part definition to bring these two approaches together. He suggests brand equity is a composite of:

- *brand value*, based on a financial and accounting base
- *brand strength*, measuring the strength of a consumer's attachment to a brand
- *brand description*, represented by the specific attitudes customers have towards a brand.

In addition to these, Cooper and Simmons (1997) offer *brand future* as a further dimension. This is a reflection of a brand's ability to grow and remain unhindered by environmental challenges such as changing retail patterns, alterations in consumer buying methods and developments in technological and regulative fields. As if to reduce the increasing complexity of these measures, Pirrie (2006) argues that brand value needs to be based on the relationship between customer and brand owner and this has to be grounded in the value experienced by the customer, which is subsequently reflected on the company. For consumers the brand value is about 'reduction': reducing search time and costs, reducing perceived quality-assurance risks, and making brand associations by reducing social and ego risks. For brand owners, the benefits are concerned with 'enablement'. She refers to enabling brand extensions, premium pricing and loyalty.

Attempts to measure brand equity have to date been varied and have lacked a high level of consensus, although the spirit and ideals behind the concept are virtually the same. Table 6.7 sets out some of the approaches adopted. As a means of synthesising these approaches the following are considered the principal dimensions through which brand equity should be measured:

- *brand dominance*: a measure of its market strength and financial performance
- *brand associations*: a measure of the beliefs held by buyers about what the brand represents
- *brand prospects*: a measure of its capacity to grow and extend into new areas.

Brand equity is considered important because of the increasing interest in trying to measure the return on promotional investments. This in turn aids the valuation of brands for

Table 6.7 Five approaches to measuring brand equity

Source	Factors measured
David Aaker	Awareness, brand associations, perceived quality and market leadership, loyalty, market performance measures
BrandDynamics, BrandZ (Millward Brown)	Presence, relevance to consumer needs, product performance, competitive advantage, bonding
Brand asset valuator (Young and Rubicam)	Strength (differentiation and relevance), stature (esteem and knowledge)
Interbrand Global Top 100 (Omnicom)	Intangible future earnings, the role of the brand, brand strength

Sources: Adapted from Cooper and Simmons (1997); Haigh (1997); Pirrie (2006); http://www.brandassetvaluator.com.au/, www.millwardbrown.com/Sites/; http://www.interbrand.com/best_brands_2006_FAQ.asp

balance-sheet purposes. A brand with a strong equity is more likely to be able to preserve its customer franchise and so fend off competitor attacks. From the BrandZ Top 100 model, Farr (2006) determined that the top brands are characterised by four factors. They are all strong in terms of innovation, great customer experience, clear values and strong sector leadership.

Developing brand equity is a strategy-related issue, and whether a financial, marketing or twin approach is adopted, the measurement activity can help focus management activity on brand development. However, there is little agreement about what is measured and how and when it is measured. Ambler and Vakratsas (1998) argue that organisations should not seek a single set of measures simply because of the varying circumstances and contextual factors that impinge on brand performance. In reality, the measures used by most firms share many common elements.

Remembering the three brand Ps introduced at the beginning of this chapter, it seems fitting to close with a link back to this triangular notion of brand promise, positioning and performance and their interaction with advertising. Clayton and Heo (2011: 314) report that research to date indicates that price-based ads in the long term appear to weaken brand associations to the extent that they 'denigrate brand equity, and thus erode margins, profits and loyalty'. As one of the marketing goals is to increase brand equity, because this enables premium pricing, it seems sensible to use non-price ads as these have been found to strengthen associations and enhance brand equity.

Chapter summary

In order to help consolidate your understanding of branding and the way in which communications are used to develop brands, here are the key points summarised against each of the learning objectives.

Explain the three brand Ps of advertising (brand promise, positioning, performance)

Successful brands can be considered to encapsulate three core elements, to which advertising contributes. These are brand promise, positioning and performance.

Communication is used to make the promise known, to position a brand correctly and to encourage and realise brand performance. Advertising has a critical role to play in building and sustaining this reinforcing interaction of branding elements.

Consider a range of brand definitions

There are numerous definitions of a brand but in essence they are a composite of the related visual, performance and behavioural elements. Both managers and stakeholders contribute to the branding process.

Describe the essence of different types of brands

Various approaches are taken to categorise brands, but more generally the different types can be considered in terms of their source, how often they are used, their geographic coverage and the audiences they are intended to serve.

Evaluate the characteristics of brands

Strong brands are characterised by their ability to be differentiated clearly from their competitors. Differentiation can be achieved by attending to a brand's three main elements. The first of these are the functional abilities, the brand's core skill at delivering the promise. The second is brand personality, the emotional traits which relate to lifestyle and perceived values. The third element is brand relationships, a recognition that people interact with their preferred brands, which leads to an individual buyer–brand relationship.

Examine how people use advertising to form associations with brands

Brand associations are concerned with the way people store brand-related information in memory and involve the perceptions and meanings that they attribute to a brand. These associations enable brand recall so that brand information can be updated as fresh information becomes available.

Evaluate the role of advertising and communications in developing and sustaining brands

Brand associations are developed in one of three main ways and are a function of the size of the financial resources that are made available. Where the budget is high, an above-the-line approach, using advertising, is the primary approach to developing brand associations. Where resources do not allow the use of advertising, a below-the-line approach is used. Here sales promotion, direct marketing and public relations are the key tools. The brand name needs to be closely related to the function and use experience of the product. An around-the-line approach is based on the use of word-of-mouth communication and brand experience to propel a brand's visibility.

Explain the issues associated with developing and measuring brand equity

There are two main perspectives of brand equity: a financial and a marketing perspective. The financial view is based on a consideration of a brand's value as a definable asset, based on the net present values of discounted future cash flows (Farquhar 1990). The marketing perspective is grounded in the beliefs, images and core associations consumers have about particular brands. By bringing these two elements together, brand equity is a composite of: *brand dominance* (market strength and financial performance); *brand associations* (what buyers believe a brand represents); and *brand prospects* (its growth potential).

Review questions

1. In view of the De Beers minicase set out at the beginning of this chapter, suggest ways in which advertising might be used to build brand associations that 'allow' women to buy diamonds for themselves.

2. What are the three brand Ps and how do they interact?
3. Choose two brand definitions and write some brief notes comparing them.
4. Select two manufacturer brands from two different sectors, visit their websites and consider their characteristics. What similarities can you identify?
5. How might brands be categorised?
6. Prepare a short presentation to explain Biel's ideas about *brand magic*. Use examples to illustrate the different stages.
7. Choose a brand and consider the way it is used strategically. In what ways might the brand owner develop the brand?
8. What are brand associations and why are they important?
9. Critically appraise each of the three ways communications and advertising are used to develop brands.
10. Describe brand equity and explain the three main elements identified by Feldwick.

Chapter references

Aaker, J. (1997) Dimensions of brand personality, *Journal of Marketing Research*, 34 (August), 347–56

Alexander, R.S. (1960) *Marketing Definitions: A Glossary of Marketing Terms*. Chicago, IL: American Marketing Association

Ambler, T. and Barrow, S. (1996) The employer brand, *Journal of Brand Management*, 4, 3, 185–206

Ambler, T. and Vakratsas, D. (1998) Why not let the agency decide the advertising? *Market Leader*, 1 (Spring), 32–7

Anon (2009) Ararat awards brief to Amsterdam Worldwide, *Campaign*, 20 March, retrieved 13 October 2011 from http://www.brandrepublic.com/news/892371/World-Amsterdam—Ararat-awards-brief-Amsterdam-Worldwide/?DCMP=ILC-SEARCH

Arnould, E.J., Price, L.L. and Zinkhan, G.L. (2002) *Consumers*, 2nd edn. New York: McGraw-Hill/Richard D. Irwin

Arora, R. and Stoner, C. (2009) A mixed method approach to understanding brand personality, *Journal of Product & Brand Management*, 18, 4, 272–83

Aspinall, A. (2011) Delivering the goods, *B2B Marketing*, 7, 5 (May), 16–17

Assael, H. (1990) *Marketing: Principles and Strategy*. Orlando, FL: Dryden Press

Baek, T.H. and Whitehill King, K. (2011) Exploring the consequences of brand credibility in services, *Journal of Services Marketing*, 25, 4, 260–72

Barda, T. (2010) Pop culture, *The Marketer* (May), 24–7

Barth, M.E., Clement, M.B., Foster, G. and Kasznik, R. (1998) Brand values and capital market valuation, *Review of Accounting Studies*, 3 (1/2), 41–68

Belk, Russell (1988), Possessions and the extended self, *Journal of Consumer Research*, 15, 2 (September), 139–68

Bendixen, M., Bukasa, K.A. and Abratt, R. (2004) Brand equity in the business-to business market, *Industrial Marketing Management*, 33, 371–80

Bhattacharya, K. and Datta, D. (2010) Tata Steelium – a success story in B2B branding, *Vikalpa*, 35, 2, (April–June), 101–26

Biel, A. (1997) Discovering brand magic: the hardness of the softer side of branding, *International Journal of Advertising*, 16, 199–210

Blackston, M. (1993) A brand with an attitude: a suitable case for treatment, *Journal of Market Research Society*, 34, 3, 231–41

Bland, B. and Brodie, S. (2008) Eddie Stobart trucks along with reverse takeover of Westbury Property, *Telegraph*, retrieved 8 August 2011 from www.telegraph.co.uk/sponsored/business/businesstruth/focus_on/3567503/Eddie-Stobart-trucks-along-with-reverse-takeover-of-Westbury-Property.html

Brakus, J.J., Schmitt, B.H. and Zarantonello, L. (2009) Brand experience: what is it? How is it measured? Does it affect loyalty? *Journal of Marketing*, 73 (May), 52–68

Brodie, R.J. and De Chernatony, L. (2009) Towards new conceptualizations of branding: theories of the middle range, *Marketing Theory*, 9, 1, 95–100

Chaudhuri, A. (2002) How brand reputation affects the advertising–brand equity link, *Journal of Advertising Research*, 42 (May/June), 33–43

Chauvin, K.W. and Hirschey, M. (1993) Advertising, R&D expenditures and the market value of the firm, *Financial Management*, 22 (Winter), 128–40

Clayton, M. and Heo, J. (2011) Effects of promotional-based advertising on brand associations, *Journal of Product & Brand Management*, 20, 4, 309–15

Cooper, A. and Simmons, P. (1997) Brand equity lifestage: an entrepreneurial revolution. TBWA Simmons Palmer. Unpublished working paper

Cunningham, I.C.M., Hardy, A.P. and Imperia, G. (1982) Generic brands versus national brands and store brands, *Journal of Advertising Research*, 22, 5 (October/November), 25–32

De Chernatony, L. (2009) Towards the holy grail of defining 'brand', *Marketing Theory*, 9, 1, 101–5

De Chernatony, L. and Dall'Olmo Riley, F. (1998a) Defining a brand: beyond the literature with experts' interpretations, *Journal of Marketing Management*, 14, 417–43

De Chernatony, L. and Dall'Olmo Riley, F. (1998b) Expert practitioners' views on roles of brands: implications for marketing communications, *Journal of Marketing Communications*, 4, 87–100

De Chernatony, L. and McDonald, M. (1998). Creating powerful brands in consumer, service, and industrial markets, 2d ed. Oxford, England: Butterworth Heinemann.

de Lencastre, P. and Côrte-Real, A. (2010) One, two, three: a practical brand anatomy, *Brand Management*, 17, 6, 399–412

Deodlar, A. (2010) The brands I love: Red Bull, retrieved 12 September 2011 from www.ashishdeodhar.com/the-brands-i-love-red-bull/

EACA (2010) Pernod Ricard Rouss: Akhtamar, *European Association of Communications Agencies*, retrieved 16 September 2010 from www.warc.com/ArticleCenter

Ehrenberg, A.S.C. (1974) Repetitive advertising and the consumer, *Journal of Advertising Research*, 14 (April), 25–34

Ehrenberg, A.S.C. (1993) If you are so strong why aren't you bigger? *Admap*, October, 13–14

Eng, L.L. and Keh H.T. (2007) The effects of advertising and brand value on future operating and market performance, *Journal of Advertising*, 36, 4 (Winter), 91–100

Farquhar, P.H. (1990) Managing brand equity, *Journal of Advertising Research, Marketing Research*, 30(4), 7–11

Farr, A. (2006) Soft measure, hard cash, *Admap*, November, 39–42

Feldwick, P. (1996) What is brand equity anyway, and how do you measure it? *Journal of Market Research*, 38, 2, 85–104

Fill, C. (2011) *Essentials of Marketing Communications*. Harlow: FT/Prentice Hall

Fournier, S. (1995) A consumer–brand relationship perspective on brand equity. Presentation to Marketing Science Conference on Brand Equity and the Marketing Mix, Tucson, Arizona, 2–3 March. Working paper 111, 13–16

Frost, R. (2004) Mapping a country's future, BrandChannel.Com/Interband, UK

Gilliland, D. and Johnston, W. J. (1997). Toward a model of business-to-business marketing communications effects, *Industrial Marketing Management*, 26, 15–29.

Goldschein, E (2011) The incredible story of how De Beers created and lost the most powerful monopoly ever, 19 December, retrieved 19 January 2012 from www.businessinsider.com/history-of-de-beers-2011-12?op=1

Gupta, S., Melewar, T.C. and Bourlakis, M. (2010) A relational insight of brand personification in business-to-business markets, *Journal of General Management*, 35, 4 (Summer) 65–76

Haigh, D. (1997) Brand valuation: the best thing to ever happen to market research, *Admap*, June, 32–5

IPA (2011) *New Models of Marketing Effectiveness From Integration to Orchestration*, WARC.

Iversen, N.M. and Hem, L.E. (2008) Provenance associations as core values of place umbrella brands: a framework of characteristics, *European Journal of Marketing* 42, 5/6, 603–26

Johansson, J.K. and Ronkainen, I.A. (2005) The esteem of global brands, *Brand Management*, 12, 5 (June), 339–54

Johnston, W.J. and Bonoma, T.V. (1981). The buying center: Structure and interaction agents, *Journal of Marketing*, 45, 143–156

Kapferer, J.-N. (2004) *The New Strategic Brand Management*. London: Kogan Page

Keller, K.L. (1993) Conceptualizing, measuring, and managing customer-based brand equity, *Journal of Marketing*, 57, 1, 1–22

Keller, K.L. (1998) *Strategic Brand Management: Building, Measuring and Managing Brand Equity*. Englewood Cliffs, NJ: Prentice Hall

Keller, K.L. (2003) *Strategic Brand Management: Building, Measuring, and Managing Brand Equity*, 2nd edn. Upper Saddle River, NJ: Prentice Hall

Keller, K.L. (2008) *Strategic Brand Management: Building, Measuring and Managing Brand Equity*. Englewood Cliffs, NY: Pearson Education

Keller, K.L. and Lehmann, D.R. (2006) Brands and branding: research findings and future priorities, *Marketing Science*, 25, 6, 740–59

Kim, J., Reid, D.A., Plank, R.E. and Dahlstrom, R. (1998) Examining the role of brand equity in business markets: A model, research propositions, and managerial Implications, *Journal of Business-to-Business Marketing*, 5(3), 65–89

Kotler, P. and Pfoertsch, W. (2006) *B2B Brand Management*. New York, NY: Springer

Kotler, P., & Pfoertsch, W. (2007) Being known or being one of many: The need for brand management for business-to-business (B2B) companies, *Journal of Business-to-Business Marketing*, 22(6), 357–362

Lamb, R. (2011) Chanel, De Beers marry advertising with editorial content in T&C magazine, 7 February, retrieved 19 January 2012 from http://www.luxurydaily.com/chanel-debeers-filter-the-print-pages-of-tc-for-affluent-women/

Lasser, W., Mittal, B. and Sharma, A. (1995) Measuring customer-based brand equity, *Journal of Consumer Marketing*, 12, 4, 11–19

Levitt, T. (1983) The globalisation of markets, *Harvard Business Review*, 83, 3 (May), 92–102

Linville, P. and Carlston, D.E. (1994) Social cognition of the self. In *Social Cognition: Impact on Social Psychology* (eds P.G. Devine, D.L. Hamilton and T.M. Ostrom), 143–93. San Diego: Academic Press

Lodish, L.M., Abraham, M., Kalmenson, S., Livelsberger, J., Lubetkin, B., Richardson, B. and Stevens, M.E. (1995) How TV advertising works: a meta-analysis of 389 real-world split cable TC advertising experiments, *Journal of Marketing Research*, 32, (May), 125–39

Lovell, C. (2009) Virgin Atlantic ad recreates 80s launch, *Campaignlive*, Monday, 5 January 2009, retrieved 13 August 2011 from www.campaignlive.co.uk/news/870984/Virgin-Atlantic-ad-recreates-80s-launch/

Luo, L., Chen, X., Han, J. and Park, C.W. (2010) Dilution and enhancement of celebrity brands through sequential movie releases, *Journal of Marketing Research*, 47 (December), 1114–28

Malaval, P. (2001) *Strategy and management of industrial brands*, Boston: Kluwer Academic Publishers.

McCracken, G. (1989) Who is the celebrity endorser? Cultural foundations of the endorsement process, *Journal of Consumer Research*, 16 (December), 310–21

Michell, P., King, J. and Reast, J. (2001) Brand values related to industrial products, *Industrial Marketing Management*, 30, 415–425

Minett, S. (2002) *B2B marketing: A radically different approach for business-to-business marketers*, Edinburgh Gate, Harlow: Pearson Education

Modi, P. and Singh, R. (2010) Tata Steelium – a success story in B2B branding, *Vikalpa*, 35, 2 (April–June) 127–30

Morgan, R. M. and Hunt, S. D. (1994) The commitment–trust theory of relationship marketing, *Journal of Marketing*, 58 (July), 20–38

Moroko, L. and Uncles, M.D. (2008) Characteristics of successful employer brands, *Journal of Brand Management*, 16, 3, 160–75

Park, C.W., Jaworski, B.J. and MacInnis, D.J. (1986) Strategic brand concept-image management, *Journal of Marketing*, 50, (October) 135–145

Parsons, R. (2011) Coca-Cola: a history in ads, *Marketing Week*, Friday 6 May, retrieved 9 August 2011 from www.marketingweek.co.uk/sectors/food-and-drink/soft-drinks/coca-cola-a-history-in-ads/3026155.article

Phau, I. and Lau, K.C. (2001) Brand personality and consumer self-expression: single or dual carriageway? *Journal of Brand Management*, 8, 6, 428–44

Pirrie, A. (2006) What value brands? *Admap*, October, 40–2

Richards, T. (1997) Measuring the true value of brands, *Admap*, March, 32–6

Reilly, S. (2004) De Beers SA: A diamond is forever, NYU Case Number: MKT04-01, retrieved 19 January 2012 from http://www.scribd.com/doc/41493358/De-Beers-Case

Riezebos, R. (2003) *Brand Management*. Harlow: FT/Prentice Hall

Romaniuk, J. and Gaillard, E. (2007) The relationship between unique brand associations, brand usage and brand performance: analysis across eight categories, *Journal of Marketing Management*, 23, 3/4, 267–84

Rosenbroijer, C.J. (2001). Industrial brand management: A distributor's perspective in the UK fine-paper industry, *Journal of Product & Brand Management*, 10, 7–24

Rudduck, G. (2011) Edward Stobart, haulage king, dies at 56, *Telegraph*, 31 March 2011, retrieved 8 August 2011 from www.telegraph.co.uk/finance/newsbysector/transport/8419961/Edward-Stobart-haulage-king-dies-at-56.html

Schmitt, B.H. (1999) *Experiential Marketing*, New York: Free Press

Schuiling, I. and Kapferer, J-N. (2004) Real differences between local and international brands: strategic implications for international marketers, *Journal of International Marketing*, 12, 4, 97–112

Stoklosa, C. (2010) Best ads: De Beers' right hand ring campaign 10 September, retrieved 19 January 2012 from www.cassandrastoklosa.com/best-ads-de-beers-right-hand-ring-campaign/

Sudbury, L. (2009) Minicase—Because it works. In C. Fill (2009) *Marketing Communications: interactivity, communities and content*, 5e., Harlow : FT/Prentice Hall, p67–68

Turley, L.W. and Kelley, S.W. (1997) A comparison of advertising content: Business-to-business versus consumer services, *Journal of Advertising*, 26(4), 39–48

Turner, C. (2008) How Red Bull invented the 'cool' factor, *UTALK Marketing*. Retrieved 12 February 2008 from www.utalkmarketing.com/pages/article

Vincent, J., Hill, J.S. and Lee, J.W. (2009) The multiple brand personalities of David Beckham: a case study of the Beckham brand, *Sport Marketing Quarterly*, 18, 173–80

Webster, F.E., Jr. and Keller, K.L. (2004). A roadmap for branding in industrial markets, *Brand Management*, 11(5), 388–402

Wolfe, Alan (1991) The single European market: national or euro-brands *International Journal of Advertising*, 10, 1, 49–58

Zablah, A.R., Brown, B.P. and Donthu, N. (2010) The relative importance of brands in modified rebuy purchase situations, *International Journal of Research in Marketing*, 27, 248–60

Chapter 7

The advertising industry

Rapid changes in recent years concerning the way organisations communicate with their various target audiences have led to pressure on the structure and operations of the advertising industry. The changes so far have largely involved the format, structure and nature of the agencies involved in working with client businesses. However, as with most organisations, change is not always readily accepted and the advertising industry still has a number of issues that it needs to overcome in order to develop successful creative advertising.

Aims and learning objectives

The main aim of this chapter is to explore how organisations work with various external agencies to produce effective advertising for their products and services.

The learning objectives of this chapter are to:

1. review the role of advertising in an integrated communications context
2. examine the different types of agency and the roles they play in providing services to their clients
3. understand how agencies operate and the individual roles played by agency personnel
4. appraise the criteria for agency selection and the processes involved in their appointment
5. consider how relationships between agencies and clients are managed
6. examine the ways in which agencies are remunerated for their services
7. appraise the practices that are used to determine advertising budgets.

Minicase Help is at hand: a new agency approach

New advertising agencies emerge on a frequent basis, as spin-offs from existing agencies or new entrants into the field. To establish themselves in an already crowded marketplace it is important for any new agency to consider what they have to offer and how different this might be from the competition. Costa (2010) identifies examples of some smaller agencies that have established themselves to address specific market-sector needs. These include Dubit and Kids Industries, which are focused on youth sectors, and the Bloke division of research agency 2CV, which specialises in information related to 30- to 50-year-old males.

Some client reflections on the future of agency relationships include Kellogg's former UK marketing director Kevin Brennan (now at Premier Foods): 'Brand strategy is where agencies can differentiate themselves and add value. Clients are crying out for more strategic thinking from their agencies. I want agencies to come through our door and not be afraid to challenge us.' Boots UK executive marketing director Elizabeth Fagan: 'You get a feeling early on whether the talent within an agency is right for your brand. For their part, clients must be clear about their own brand strategy and what is important to their customers. When they are clear about this they need agencies that "get" their brand strategy.'

The Help Agency was established in 2010 with the co-founders coming from advertising and marketing backgrounds. Dean Hodgetts began his career with multinational advertising groups before running his own integrated agency for 10 years. Andy Wakefield worked as creative director for a number of small, medium and large agencies, winning a number of prestigious awards. Hugh Dennis was once a Unilever marketer responsible for multi-million-pound brands but is now better known as a comedian on *Mock the Week*, and the actor playing the disgruntled dad in the popular TV show *Outnumbered*. The rationale for the Help Agency is based on the founders' commitment to charity work. Their focus is on working for smaller, lesser-known charities. Hodgetts claims that the larger

Exhibit 7.1 Hugh Dennis: co-founder of The Help Agency
Source: Rex Features

traditional agencies tend to concentrate on 'high-profile, shock-tactic campaigns for big charities just to get noticed', while Help is set up to help the charities that these agencies aren't interested in dedicating resources to.

Help is structured along the lines of a traditional agency and provides the range of services you might expect from a larger outfit. These include advertising, brand development, website design and direct marketing, as well as charity-sector-specific services including affiliation schemes and gift programmes and other donor communications consulting.

One issue that was of significant concern for the agency when they were considering establishing the new business was the question of remuneration. They were keen to help smaller charities but they could not operate on offering clients pro bono services and needed to make a profit. Given the background of the individuals involved, they understood traditional models of agency remuneration relating to commission and fee payments and they studied newer models including payment by results. The need was to develop a payment system that would incentivise potential clients in the charity sector to use Help's services without being perceived as 'just another ad agency'.

Source: Costa (2010); www.thehelpagency.com

Introduction

In Chapter 1 we considered the broad structure of the advertising industry. The shift by many clients towards a single-stop shopping approach, when appointing external agencies, was noted. In this chapter we build on this and explore how agencies are structured to cater for the changing communications needs of their clients, including the use of an extended media mix now apparent in most consumer and business markets.

The so-called 'full-service' advertising agency (see below) has been the traditional business model and basis for agencies seeking to manage all of the advertising needs of a client. As clients' communications needs have changed, however, and the communications context has evolved, these agencies have had to adapt in order to cater for a new advertising climate. This in turn has led to changes in the relationships that exist between agencies and clients in order to provide a sound basis for long-term business development. Many different agency types have emerged to cater for specialist requirements, including the growth of agencies to handle the media planning and buying needs which would originally have been within the scope of a full-service agency. As well as agency structures we shall examine the bases for agency selection and the financial issues associated with agency remuneration and the allocation of resources for advertising.

Organisations choose to use the services of external agencies and consultancies for a variety of reasons. These include the expertise they provide in a particular discipline, their independent advice, or to save the costs and risks associated with employing their own personnel and developing their own advertising materials. The latter is known as an in-house approach. Advertising agencies can provide expertise in creativity, advertising production, research and account planning. They view their clients' products and services without bias and can sidestep any conflict that might exist within a client's business. Although there are quite clearly costs involved in utilising agency services, these do not carry the same level of overheads that would be incurred by employing staff directly.

Corcoran et al. (2010) report on how agencies have evolved over time as a result of technological and social change, marketing strategy change and marketer–agency relationships change. Figure 7.1 shows how agencies have adapted to such changes in a series of 'eras'. Changes are largely based on changes in client needs.

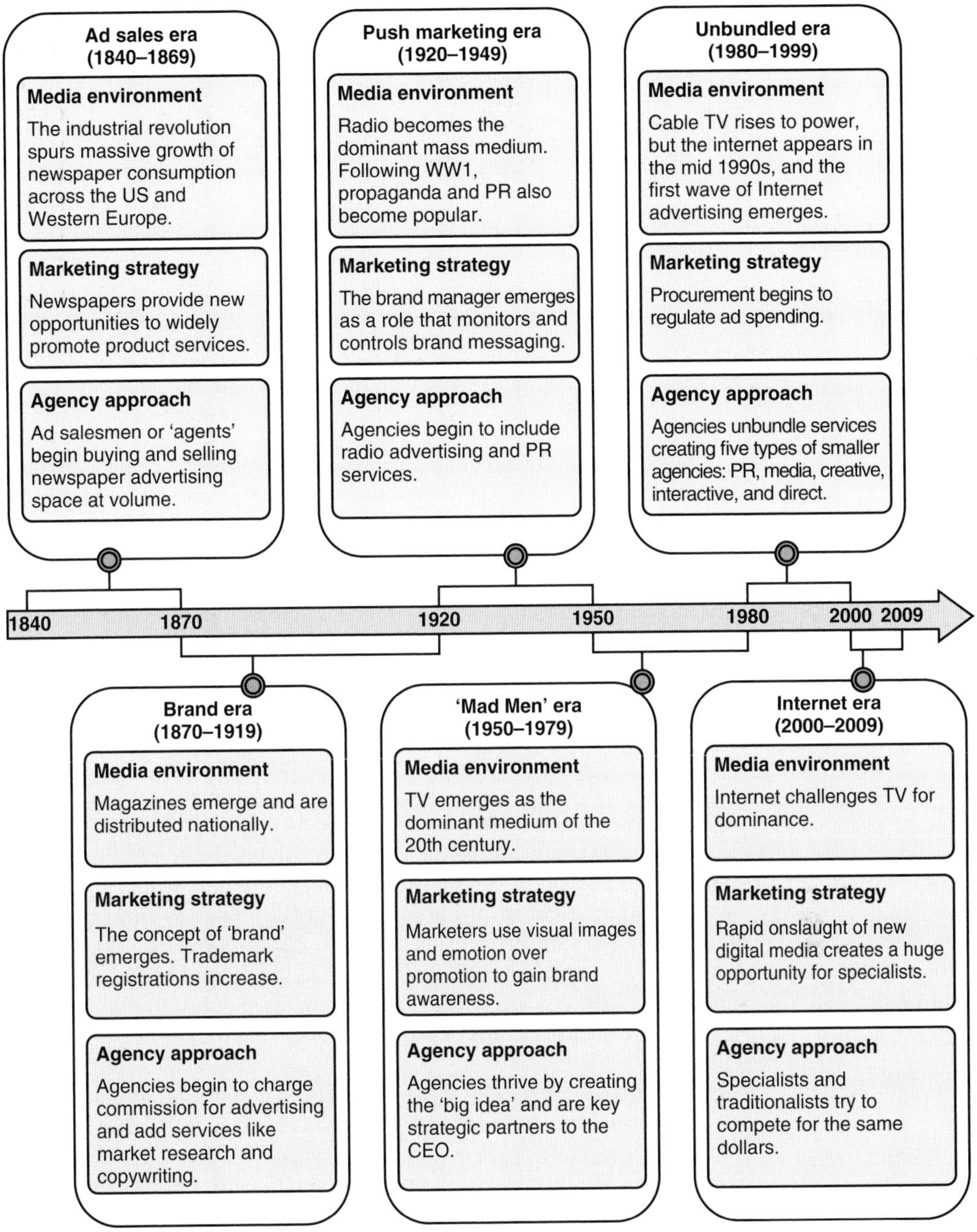

Ad sales era (1840–1869)

Media environment
The industrial revolution spurs massive growth of newspaper consumption across the US and Western Europe.

Marketing strategy
Newspapers provide new opportunities to widely promote product services.

Agency approach
Ad salesmen or 'agents' begin buying and selling newspaper advertising space at volume.

Brand era (1870–1919)

Media environment
Magazines emerge and are distributed nationally.

Marketing strategy
The concept of 'brand' emerges. Trademark registrations increase.

Agency approach
Agencies begin to charge commission for advertising and add services like market research and copywriting.

Push marketing era (1920–1949)

Media environment
Radio becomes the dominant mass medium. Following WW1, propaganda and PR also become popular.

Marketing strategy
The brand manager emerges as a role that monitors and controls brand messaging.

Agency approach
Agencies begin to include radio advertising and PR services.

'Mad Men' era (1950–1979)

Media environment
TV emerges as the dominant medium of the 20th century.

Marketing strategy
Marketers use visual images and emotion over promotion to gain brand awareness.

Agency approach
Agencies thrive by creating the 'big idea' and are key strategic partners to the CEO.

Unbundled era (1980–1999)

Media environment
Cable TV rises to power, but the internet appears in the mid 1990s, and the first wave of Internet advertising emerges.

Marketing strategy
Procurement begins to regulate ad spending.

Agency approach
Agencies unbundle services creating five types of smaller agencies: PR, media, creative, interactive, and direct.

Internet era (2000–2009)

Media environment
Internet challenges TV for dominance.

Marketing strategy
Rapid onslaught of new digital media creates a huge opportunity for specialists.

Agency approach
Specialists and traditionalists try to compete for the same dollars.

1840 1870 1920 1950 1980 2000 2009

Figure 7.1 How agencies have adapted to each major era
Source: Forrester Research Inc, March 29, 2010

Agency structures and integration

The development and interest in integrated marketing communications (IMC) and the concept of media neutrality referred to in Chapter 4 have led agencies to adapt their structures to meet the needs of the changing communications landscape. Although the focus of this text is advertising, we cannot ignore the integration issue as it has had and will continue to have an

Table 7.1 Integrated agency options

Type of agency	Explanation
Integrated agency	A single agency that provides the full range of communication disciplines
Complementary agencies	The client selects a range of different agencies, each from a different discipline, and self-manages them or appoints a lead agency
Networked agencies	A single group agency is appointed (e.g. WPP or Interpublic) who then appoints agencies within their own profit-oriented network
Mini-group agencies	Clusters of small independent specialist agencies who work on a non-competitive basis for a client

Source: Fill (2009)

effect on the way in which the industry develops. Advertising no longer exists, if it ever really did, in isolation from other elements of the marketing communications mix.

For major consumer brands, TV advertising has traditionally dominated the communications mix and to a large extent still does. The larger, full-service agencies discussed below have been structured around the use of TV as the significant media channel. Moves toward a more integrated approach to customer communications have not always been warmly accepted throughout the agency sector. However, client needs will always hold sway over how they outsource their communications activities and agencies have had to learn to adapt.

This adaptation has led to the development of a number of options which agencies might opt for when configuring how they can meet their clients' needs.

Fill (2009) has identified four principal agency structure options, which are set out in Table 7.1.

One significant issue in this overarching debate is that of the degree of control to be maintained by the client and/or the agency in driving the communications strategy using the varying elements of the communications mix. From the agency's perspective this might be based on which element of the mix they seek to push for profitability purposes. The client will ultimately wish to maximise communication effectiveness, which might conflict with the agency's view. We shall explore this in the context of the client–agency relationship later in the chapter. The client might wish to use a mix of agency structures by compiling a 'roster 'of agencies that they can utilise over a period of time to meet their integrated requirements.

For global brands the appointment of agencies often centres around the standardisation/adaptation debate when considering the question of IMC. Standardisation refers to the use of the same campaign materials in each market in which the client operates. The possible advantages of operating in this way are based on cost efficiencies and relative ease of coordination. This route may be effective when there is a requirement to present a consistent brand image in all markets. It is important to consider local market conditions and brand objectives which might make adapting campaigns to suit local conditions more appropriate. One suggestion is that standardisation is the only route via which IMC can be effectively achieved. However, there are difficulties in defining what is a truly global brand and to what extent therefore IMC principles can be applied. If there is to be a more widespread approach to adaptation, this implies the need for strong internal integration within the client's business at business-unit and agency level. It might also be a question of the types of messages that are to be delivered. Fielding (2000) shows that many Japanese and Korean advertising messages emphasise product-related information, whereas many Western brands require an emphasis on the development of brand personality and individual character. These differences suggest the need for consistency in the core message with a degree of local or regional adaptation for IMC objectives to be achieved.

ViewPoint 7.1 Procter & Gamble's BAL agency model

For an organisation with 400 brands, operating in 80 countries and employing 135,000 people, it is important for Procter & Gamble (P&G) to manage its agencies effectively and efficiently. A brand agency leader (BAL) model was introduced in 2006 in an attempt to streamline agency management. P&G's financial director, Rich Delcore, is reported to claim that the BAL programme now accounts for over 40% of new sales and is soon to reach 60% as the programme develops.

BAL is centred around a 'one-agency mentality' very different from what Delcore calls the 'spaghetti chart' of an organisation with internal and external silos across different communications platforms, advertising agencies, PR, digital, strategy, and media management. At brand level, there is now one global creative director and a global planner. For each brand BAL has seven main components:

- A lead P&G person
- A lead agency
- BAL leads an integrated agency team
- Responsibility for managing work of each member agency
- BAL is accountable for team performance
- Members of BAL team agree single global fee
- BAL owns partner-agency compensation over and above fee.

Further benefits of the BAL system include improved integrated communications, increased flexibility and faster executions, and added value derived from stronger agency partnerships and collaborations.

For the Oral-B toothbrush brand available in 180 different markets, adoption of the BAL model led to significant changes in approaches to creative development. P&G used seven agencies in advertising, planning, shopper marketing, digital, PR and design, each with their different ideas as to how the brand should be presented. BAL responsibilities were placed with the Publicis agency in New York. All other agencies involved in the account report through Publicis. The agency created a 'team manifesto' for sharing ownership so that all work would be seamlessly integrated. The BAL programme was supported with the setting up of a creative agency leader (CAL). The CAL has responsibility for breaking down different team briefs into a shared document and sharing knowledge, integrating ideas and engaging appropriate technological expertise.

Source: Based on Williams (2011); Precourt (2010); www.warc.com, accessed 15 March 2011

Exhibit 7.2 Image of the Oral-B brand
Source: Image courtesy of The Advertising Archives

Question

Is the BAL model suitable for either a standardised or adapted approach to advertising?

Task

Assess whether the integrated agency structures in Table 7.1 offer beneficial alternatives to the BAL model.

Advertising agency structures and types

The services provided by advertising agencies have commonly centred around two principal areas: creative development in copywriting and art direction; and media planning and buying. Whilst the nature of these services has changed over time, not least as a result of advances in technology, they still, by and large, provide a platform for agency structure. Here we explore the main agency structures or types which exist to service differing client needs.

Full-service agencies

The most usual type of (advertising) agency is the full-service agency. This type of agency offers the full range of services that a client requires in order to advertise its products and services. Typical full-service agencies, including Bartle Bogle Hegarty (BBH) and Abbott Mead Vickers (AMV BBDO), offer services including strategic planning, research, creative development, production, interactive, and media planning and buying. This does not necessarily mean that such an agency needs to be large, employing thousands of people. A small or mid-size agency can offer a full service which might include the subcontracting of some activities while still maintaining overall responsibility. Further discussion of some of the issues concerning full-service agencies follows later.

There are a number of advantages for a client in utilising a full-service agency (see Figure 7.2). One significant advantage is the provision of additional resources to work and to share ideas and responsibilities. Working with a full-service agency facilitates access to a huge pool of skills, whenever required. Aspects of each of the other communication disciplines can be incorporated into the development of effective advertising solutions. The full-service approach provides a sound platform for working integratively with other agencies from other communications disciplines. Organisations using full-service agencies are usually able to allocate significant budgets to their advertising, but may at the same time retain relatively low levels of resources internally to support the coordination of communications campaigns.

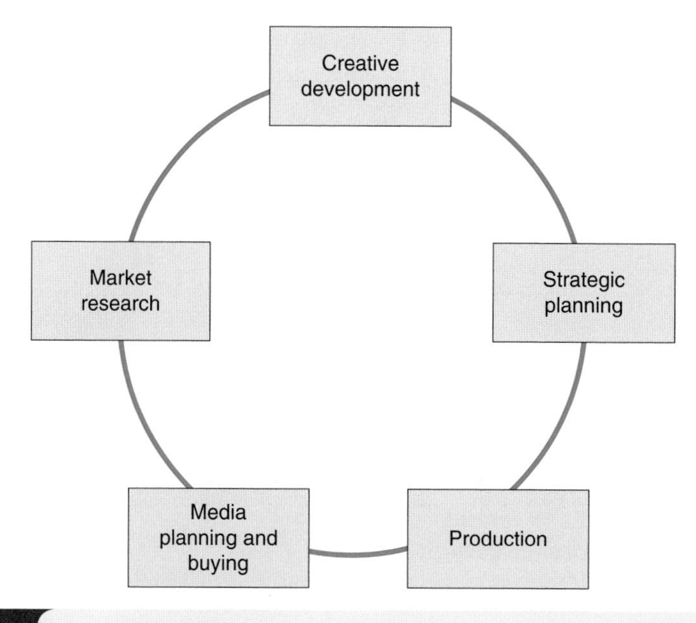

Figure 7.2 Core activities in a full-service agency

ViewPoint 7.2 DDB - some of the original 'Madmen'

The title of the hit TV series *Madmen* based around the New York advertising business of the 1950s is nothing specifically to do with the state of minds of the leading players. Having said that, some of the storylines and actions might make you think it is! The title refers to the geographic location of the offices of many of the advertising businesses of the time, Madison Avenue. In fact, many advertising companies still have their headquarters there.

One such business is DDB Worldwide Communications. As with many advertising companies, the firm's title is based on the initials of the founding partners, in this case Ned Doyle, Maxwell Dane and Bill Bernbach, who started their company located on Madison Avenue in 1949. Today DDB employs over 12,000 staff in 200 offices representing clients in over 90 countries. Significant clients include brands such as McDonald's, Nestlé, Johnson and Johnson, VW and Philips Electronics.

Bill Bernbach has been described as 'the real Madman' and 'the father of modern advertising'. Bernbach's philosophy was that great advertising came from understanding human behaviour and the power of creativity. He was the first adman to initiate the copywriter-art director combination to achieve advertising creativity, still the mainstay approach in most agencies.

Today the company philosophy is still true to the founder's creative principles:

> Before we describe 'how we do it', it might be an idea to tell you what the 'it' is. The 'it' is the creative generation and execution of ideas that change the way people think about brands. Sounds simple, right?
>
> In theory, yes, but in practice, marketing has become much more complex and leads us to 'How we do it'. The simple fact is - there is no one way to do it. How can you template a process when no two brands are alike, no two clients are alike, and no two consumers are alike?
>
> At DDB we are guided by playbooks, not rule books. Rigid methodologies minimize creativity. Paint-by-numbers gets you the same painting every time.
>
> That is not to say we do not have tried-and-true approaches to building and growing world-class brands - we do. But rather than share our methodologies, we rather you spend time on the rest of this site and take a look at examples of our work, peruse some of our thinking, participate in our debates and discussions - basically get to know who we are.
>
> Nine times out of ten, companies like ours are chosen as partners based on chemistry. So we should meet and you can share your challenges and opportunities: we love to solve complex business problems, take away your worries, and have a lot of fun doing it.

DDB regularly publishes downloadable Yellow Paper research reports, surveys and debates on business communication. It also makes available insight and opinions about issues in the advertising world and their opinions. Recent examples include 'Behaviour planning versus channel planning', 'Do you know your audience as well as you think?', 'Introducing social creativity'.

Source: Based on www.ddb.com, accessed 17 October2011; www.mandmglobal.com, accessed 17 October 2011

Question

Is creativity still the crucial element in effective advertising campaigns?

Task

Access the DDB website, download and read the most recent Yellow Paper.

Exhibit 7.3 DDB logo
Source: DDB

Boutiques

In the same way that a small fashion retailer offers a customer a more limited range of products and services than the national high-street chain or department store, the boutique-agency approach focuses on the creative elements of advertising including copyrighting, developing creative content and other artistic services. These agencies provide clients with alternative sources of ideas, new ways of thinking about a problem, issue or product. Clients may choose to use boutiques because they either wish to use particular styles and approaches for their creative work or they want to generate a raft of creative ideas. They may be used in conjunction with full-service operations where it is felt they can add something to a problem-solving situation.

Media specialists

As media decisions play a significant role in determining advertising effectiveness, numbers of large advertisers have over a period of time shifted the media elements of their advertising away from the full-service agency to specialist media agencies. The media specialist delivers media strategy and consulting advice for both client advertisers and agencies. Their core business, however, is focused on the planning, scheduling, buying and monitoring of their client's media. Child (2007) reports that advertisers believe the role of strategic media planning is 50% more important today than it was seven years previously. One of the principal advantages of using media specialists is that they have the capacity to buy media time and space at rates far lower than a client or advertising agency can procure them. This is because of the sheer volume of business that media specialists buy on behalf of a range of clients. Child also believes that there are some indications that clients believe it is more important to have a global media network rather than a global advertising agency.

Two main forms of media specialist have emerged: media independents, where the organisation is owned and run free of the direction and policy requirements of a full-service agency, and media dependents, where the organisation is a subsidiary of a creative or full-service organisation. Major media specialists include ZenithOptimedia, MEC and Carat.

ViewPoint 7.3 Global communications at WPP and Dentsu

WPP is one of the world's leading communications services groups with 2010 revenues of some $15 billion. Formed in 1985 by Sir Martin Sorrell as a small holding company for marketing services companies, the WPP Group now provides services across communications disciplines, media and information. Advertising agencies include J. Walter Thompson, Young & Rubicam and Ogilvy & Mather.

Clients include over 350 companies from the Fortune Global 500, operating in over 100 countries. WPP represent at least three communications disciplines for over 700 clients and for almost 350 clients in six or more countries. Major clients include HSBC, Vodafone, Procter & Gamble, Ford and Shell.

In terms of coordination, over 300 clients work with three or more WPP companies, 150 clients work with four or more and over 100 clients are served in six or more countries. North America accounts for 35% of WPP's revenues and the UK 12%. Latin America is identified as WPP's strongest growth region and accounts for 12% of revenues.

Other major groups competing alongside WPP on a global scale include Omnicom, Interpublic, Publicis, Havas and Dentsu. Dentsu has its origins in Japan, having been formed in 1901 as the Japan Advertising Service and Telegraphic Service Co. The Dentsu Group now operates via a global network, although, unlike WPP, which is a conglomerate of individual agencies acquired over a period of time and retaining their individual identities, Dentsu is a single-branded agency with all parts of the network operating under the Dentsu name. Major clients include Canon, Hitachi, Tetley and Omega.

Exhibit 7.4 WPP
Source: Press Association Images

Sources: Based on Sweney (2011); www.wpp.com, accessed 8 August 2011; www.dentsu.com, accessed 14 October 2011

Question

Why is Latin America considered to be a growth area for WPP?

Task

List the advantages and disadvantages of WPP'S individual approach to agency identity compared to Dentsu's single-brand identity.

Scholars' paper 7.1 Agencies expand into China

Cheung, F.S.L., Mirza, H. and Leung, W. (2008) Client following revisited: a study of transnational advertising agencies in China, *International Journal of Advertising*, 27, 4, 593-628

As many of the globe's top brands seek to develop unfamiliar but potentially huge markets such as China, approaches to agency selection and development need to be given careful consideration. Transnational clients tend to seek the services of agents who have overseas facilities. This paper seeks to identify and evaluate the motives of firms (agencies) to make foreign direct investment in other markets, such as China. A model based on ownership, location and internationalisation is used to explore the issues involved.

Traditional models of agency development are examined in the context of market development in China. The Chinese market is fragmented regionally, which agencies need to consider as they develop. Examples of transnational agency development in other markets are considered as part of the analysis.

Digital advertising agencies

Digital media agencies have developed as a result of the huge and rapid growth of the digital media industry. The recent rapid growth in the number of online brands has transformed the way business is conducted. Also, most significant traditional product and service brands are seeking to reach customers by adding interactive capabilities to their existing marketing channels. To some extent, such agencies could be described as full service as they provide a complete range of advertising services but are focused on digital and interactive networks.

These shifts are reflected in a trend towards a polarisation on either traditional or digital work. There is a general absence of agencies that can work in both arenas (Grosso et al. 2006) and one of the outcomes of this skill shortage is that spending on online ads might slow.

Agency operations and roles

Most communications agencies are generally organised on a functional basis. There are typically departments for planning, creative and media functions, coordinated on behalf of the client by an account manager or executive.

Account managers

The account manager has a very significant role as they are responsible for maintaining the communication flow between a client and its agency. The quality of the communications between the two main parties can be critical to the success of individual campaigns and to the development of the relationship between the two organisations. Acting at the boundary of the agency's operations, the account manager fulfils several roles, from internal coordination and negotiation to presenter (of the agency's work), conflict management and information gatherer. The account manager has to balance the tensions arising from achieving their client's needs alongside those of their employer and colleagues.

The basis for agency and client communication is the client brief. This is often first developed as part of the agency selection process and then maintained by the account manager on behalf of the agency as the business relationship develops.

In order to establish a level playing field in terms of clarity and detail of agency briefs, a joint communications industry initiative seeks to establish common working practices. The outcome has been the development of a 'briefing template' intended to be used by all across the communications agencies in the industry. Eight key headings emerged from the report and these can be seen in Figure 7.3.

The IPA Guide has been endorsed by client organisations such as Volkswagen and Barnardo's. Alan Doyle, VW's communications manager, believes that 'the key to effective briefing is to provide a simple insight that can be dramatised memorably. Ensure that you know exactly what you want. Then tell the agency as clearly as possible.' Andrew Biel, UK director of marketing and communications at Barnardo's, states 'without clear briefs as a sound starting point you have little chance of success'.

Account planners

The role of the account planner has been the subject of much academic and practitioner discussion (Collin 2003; Grant et al. 2003; Zambarino and Goodfellow 2003). The general conclusion of this research is that the role of account planner has evolved as the communications industry has fragmented and a new role has emerged in response to integrated marketing communications and media-neutral planning initiatives.

Project management – Provide basic project details, e.g. timescales, contacts and people, project numbers

Where are we now? – Describe current brand details e.g. background, position, competitors, key issues

Where do we want to be? – What needs to be achieved in terms of goals e.g. sales, market share, ROI, shareholder value, awareness, perception, etc.

What are we doing to get there? – What is the context in terms of the marketing strategy, overall communication strategy and campaign strategy?

Who do we need to talk to? – What is understood about the audiences the communications are intended to influence?

How will we know if we have arrived? – What will be measured, by whom, how and when to determine whether the activity has been successful?

Practicalities – Budgets, timings and schedules, creative and media imperatives

Approvals – Who has the authority to sign off the brief and the agency work?

Figure 7.3 An agency briefing template
Source: The full guide can be found at www.ipa.co.uk

The traditional role of the account planner has been to provide knowledge about the client's target consumers and to develop this into a strategic underpinning for the creative and media disciplines. As the methodologies of clients have changed in respect to dealing with media planning, the role of the account planner has moved to focus on the creative aspects of agency work. With the further development of integrated communications it is expected that the account planning role will become more strategically focused.

Creative roles

In a full-service agency, creative teams normally consist of a copywriter and an art director, supported by a service team. The copywriter is responsible for the 'words' and the art director for the 'pictures'. Whilst these terms are still widely used within the advertising industry to describe individual roles, how individuals go about performing their duties has changed significantly, resulting from advances in technology and so-called shifts toward new media. The creative team is responsible for transforming the communications need identified in the client brief into effective advertising solutions. These solutions would need to reflect how the client wishes to deploy appropriate media.

Multi-taskers

Many of the newer, younger agencies that emerge from shifts toward digitally based advertising are managed without the control and structures evident in large, centralised agencies.

Scholars' paper 7.2 Account planning perspectives

Collin, W. (2003) The interface between account planning and media planning - a practitioner perspective, *Marketing Intelligence and Planning*, 21(7), 440-5

This is one of a number of articles on account planning in a special issue of this journal. It examines the way in which the role has developed and the challenges faced as a result of the changing nature of the ways in which marketing communications are organised. The author has agency experience of both account and media planning and uses this when presenting an insider's guide from both perspectives. Collin suggests that clients are increasingly seeking strategic advice on communications from media specialists rather than agency planners.

Project teams comprise expert individuals working on a number of projects. As a result many individuals are now multi-tasking, assuming a range of roles with new titles. In some agencies the title 'head of content' has arisen to reflect the significance of content issues in the new media market. Project managers assume responsibility for the implementation phase and the coordination of all aspects of a client's technological facilities. In terms of overall organisation, the result is flatter structures, with more flexible working practices.

Advertising agency selection

An organisation's need to appoint an advertising agency might result from a number of different situations. It could be a new business start-up with no previous advertising history or an established business wishing to change their agency due to poor performance, a breakdown in their relationship, new needs, or a drive for a fresh approach. Around these basic scenarios could be a range of more specific communications needs.

The formal process of selecting an agency, as set out in Figure 7.4, reflects how it 'should be', or an idealised approach. However, the reality is more often than not influenced by

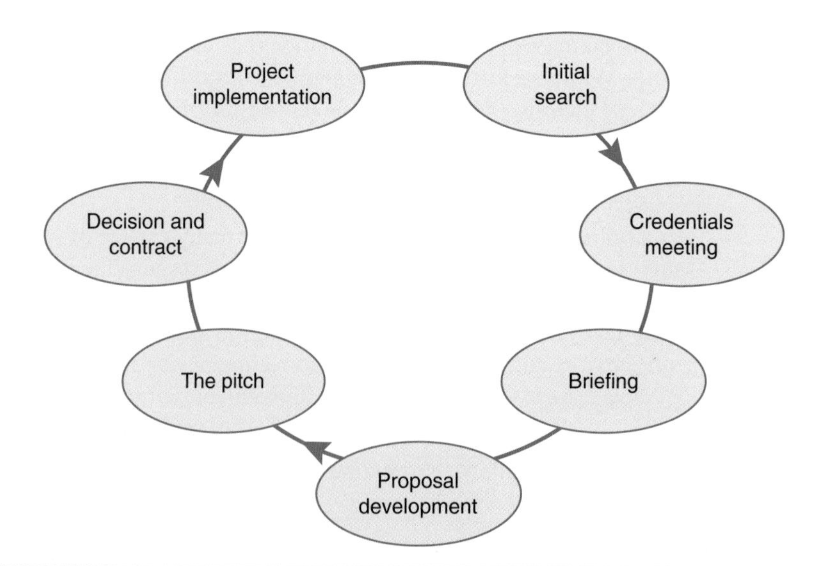

Figure 7.4 Agency selection process

political and personal issues, some of which might appear on the surface to be contradictory. Almost more than anything, the advertising industry is a 'people' business and therefore significantly influenced through human behaviours, personalities and attitudes. What might appear to make sound business sense could be ignored based on the nature of personal relationships between individuals involved in the process.

Logically the process commences with a *search*, undertaken in order to identify a list of potential agency candidates. The client might begin with reference to agency information supplied by the Institute of Practitioners in Advertising (IPA) and/or by utilising the services provided by such companies as the AAR Group. AAR provide advertisers with information about agencies that might suit their needs and on an ongoing basis provide agency–client relationship management advice. More informally, scanning magazines such as *Campaign* or *Marketing Week* might provide information on the kind of work agencies are producing for other businesses, and personal recommendations obtained from contacting the satisfied clients of an agency are also a valuable basis for identifying agencies with effective track records. The search process would ideally produce a shortlist of six to ten potential agencies for further review.

Next, the client will visit each of the shortlisted candidates in what is referred to as a *credentials presentation* or *chemistry meeting*. This is a crucial stage in the process, as it is now that the agency is evaluated for its degree of fit with the client's expectations and requirements. Information derived from an agency's website could fulfil this role, which would save time and costs. Although the agency's track record, resources, areas of expertise and experience can all be made available via the internet, this does not replace personal interaction which, as indicated above, is often a key factor in the decision-making-process. Therefore face-to-face meetings are arranged to establish possible relationship chemistry.

Following this exercise, it should be possible to shortlist three or possibly four agencies for the next stage in the process: the pitch. Where a client is seeking to change their existing agency, it is normal practice for them to include this agency in the pitching process. The shortlisted agencies are now provided with a more detailed outline or *brief* of the client's communications situation. What is contained in this brief may vary but the list in Table 7.2 gives some indication of the kinds of information that could be provided. As indicated, the brief could include information relating to both specific advertising needs and the general nature of the client's business.

Following receipt of the brief, the agencies are normally given around six to eight weeks for *proposal development*. The timescale may be less depending on the urgency of the client's needs. In developing their ideas, it is common practice for the agencies involved to invest in further research into the client's market including competition, distribution and consumer behaviour. This research and the time spent by individuals within the agency working on the proposal are costs which are normally borne by the agencies themselves. They are seen as necessary investments in developing their client base and therefore the size of their overall businesses.

The *pitch* is a presentation by each of the agencies, outlining how they would approach and resolve the strategic and creative issues, derived from the client's briefing and their own research. Logically, the account would be awarded to whichever agency produces the most suitable proposal. However, suitability is a relative term, and a range of issues can affect the final decision as to which agency might best meet the needs of a client. The selection process is aimed at bringing together two organisations whose structures and cultures may be different but whose future cooperation is essential for successful advertising effectiveness. Agencies need to have access to comprehensive and often commercially confidential information about their client's products and markets if they are to operate efficiently. In addition to the establishment of a business relationship, the appointment is about bringing together the individuals from each party. This will have been considered at the chemistry meeting outlined above. The pitch provides a further opportunity for assessing how well these relationships might work. In some instances the relative importance of the personal relationship potential might outweigh the actual advertising ideas.

Table 7.2 Some of the contents of a typical agency briefing

Topic	Explanation
Current situation	The history of the brand, previous campaign successes (or failures) and the reasons for mounting the new campaign
Promotional objectives	Having set your marketing objectives (often expressed in terms of sales volume), you then have to address the promotional objectives. These will vary according to your overall plans, but could include: • To encourage product trial • To raise awareness levels • To encourage direct sales • To increase distribution outlets
Target markets	A good definition of the target market will include not only socio-economic details (e.g. age, class, sex), but also psychographic information on users. This will have a bearing on the nature and tone of the promotional activity, its overall focus and content
Product/service	In providing your agency with a detailed brief, this section is very important. It should include any original research results or focus group research to establish what the perceived benefits are, so that these can be promoted strongly, both visually and in words
Budget	The budget should be carefully planned with consideration given to your total budget as it often includes funds not only for the cost of the media, but also for the production of promotional material
Competitors	You should know your competitors and their products as well as you know your own. Make it your business to find out and include the results of your findings in your brief
Timescales	This should include the start date of the campaign and the period over which it is to run. Media scheduling will play a vitally important role at this stage, with the need to establish the consistency of the campaign in terms of the 'drip-drip' approach or indeed the necessity for a 'burst'-style campaign

Agency appointments might not always result from pitches and as Jones (2004) reports, nearly one-third of clients move their accounts without involving pitches. One of the reasons for this is the increasing cost involved in running the whole process, as much as £50,000 according to Jones. Indeed, Wethey (2006) questions the whole validity and efficacy of the pitching process. He argues that many pitches are a waste of resources (time and money), that too many agencies devote too much of their resources chasing new business, that pitches do not solve client problems and that the whole process is often unrealistic.

The agency selection process is finalised when terms and conditions are specified in a mutually agreed *contract*. Examination of trade journals such as *Campaign*, *Marketing* and *Marketing Week* will provide regular announcements of agency appointments.

Developing and managing agency relationships

Once an agency relationship has been established, the client and the agency will establish operational teams, systems, contracts and reporting lines. The key roles played by agency staff have already been outlined above.

A successful relationship is built on trust and commitment. As indicated earlier, agencies are often selected on the basis of personal compatibility between individuals in the respective teams. This requires mutual trust and commitment for the relationship to flourish. It is often the strong relationships that exist between individuals that lead to agency changes when client managers leave one organisation and move to another and transfer their agency alliances.

Spanier (2010) reports on examples of agencies that have retained clients over long periods of time. These include Abbott Mead Vickers, which has worked for retail supermarket chain Sainsbury's for over 30 years; and DDB, which has held the Volkswagen car account for more than 25 years. On a much longer scale, JWT has had Shell as a client for approaching 50 years, Rolex for over 60 and Unilever for over 100.

The changing nature of the advertising and media landscape seems to have driven many clients into seeking changes in their agency relationships, including the frequency with which they make changes. To some extent this results from a change in the way firms relate to and communicate with their customers, often in a more personal and direct fashion, which alters the basis for communication away from a mass context to an individual one.

As we have already indentified, many agency–client relationships are based on the establishment of global networks requiring sophisticated communications between client and agency personnel. Advances in technology now enable such communications to take place rapidly and with significant levels of complexity. Time spent in arranging face-to-face meetings to discuss plans and creative work can now be undertaken using file transfer protocol (FTP) sites which allow for significant volumes of data to be accessed and worked on by a number of parties. Microsoft's SharePoint provides secure platforms with collaboration tools for sharing ideas and business information.

Agency Assessments International (AAI), a consultancy operating in the advertising industry, have developed what they call an agency relationship optimiser (ARO). This service is offered to clients wishing to identify potential problems with their agencies. It can be applied in a number of different ways: as a diagnostic tool, as a best practice measurement device or for campaign management and control purposes. The ARO system provides regular and mutual evaluation, monitoring and feedback. It is an online process that can be tailored to match individual client needs. Figure 7.5 identifies the key elements that the ARO system includes.

The client–agency relationship may be seen in the context of the network of organisations and structures, as well as the exchanges or interactions that occur within that network. These interactions relate to the activities that are undertaken with the resources available, against the agreed strategic, marketing and communications goals. The quality of the agency–client relationship is a function of trust, developed within this organisational network based on mutual confidence. Commitment is derived from a belief that a relationship is worth continuing and that maximum effort is warranted to maintain the relationship (Morgan and Hunt 1994). The changes in remuneration systems discussed below have also resulted in a new focus for the client–agency relationship, most notably the shift toward payment based on results.

- Skills set approach
- 360-degree review
- Identification of priority issues

- 'Share of vote' allocation to reflect most significant opinions
- Web enablement for comparisons across brands, markets and agencies

- Automatic collation of qualitative commentaries
- Aggregation of quantitative scores
- Online action plans

Figure 7.5 The agency relationship optimiser (ARO)

The creation of global marketing services groups such as WPP, discussed previously, has led to some fundamental shifts in the nature of client–agency relationships with sophisticated and complex structures required in order for advertising and other communications to be developed effectively.

The US-based research consultancy Forrester published a report on the future of agency relationships in 2010. The research included interviews with major businesses, agencies and media groups. One of the principal outcomes of this was the creation of what Forrester term an 'adaptive marketing' era. This idea is based around the ways in which agencies are having to 'reinvent themselves' in adapting to changes in marketing strategy, media, technology and society. In seeking to assess potential agency partners, clients are recommended to use a 3i system: ideas, interaction and intelligence. The report describes a number of client–agency eras dating back to the Industrial Revolution in the context of the media environment, predominant marketing strategy and agency approach. See Figure 7.1. The current adaptive era suggests a shift in focus with consumers able to opt out of communications they find irrelevant. The report highlights the need to adopt a mindset of providing consumer experiences, not campaigns, based on individual customer participation rather than being part of a segmented target audience.

A framework is presented in Figure 7.6 which details the proposed 3i system highlighting the importance of each element and what needs to be considered in assessing implementation.

Some practical steps are recommended:

- *Redefining agency roles* – removing differences between above- and below-the-line agencies
- *Test partners from non-agency world* – looking beyond the traditionally defined agency format to companies such as Google and Sapient

Why is it still important?	What do you need to consider?
Ideas	
• Ideas are fundamental to engaging with customers, but they need to be vetted.	• How should we manage, filter, and prioritise ideas that come from diverse sources?
• Ideas need to span touchpoints and be appropriate in those touchpoints.	• How do we find and disseminate ideas that encourage social participation?
• Experiences become more prominent than campaigns.	• How do we create ideas that work in harmony but are appropriate to specific channels?
Interaction	
• Understanding interactions will drive future marketing success.	• Which agencies can successfully work across different types of media (paid, owned, and earned)?
• Paid media shifts from the foundation of campaigns to the catalyst of experiences.	• What new metrics exist beyond impressions, reach, and frequency?
• Earned and owned media help deliver experiences to consumers who are initiated in paid media.	• Who do I trust to engage or talk back to consumers?
Intelligence	
• Greater emphasis on accountability and more opportunity to measure.	• How do we integrate online and offline data? How de we manage structured and unstructured data?
• Enables brands to optimise products and experiences.	• Do I have the resources and technical skills to manage my own data?
• Provides insights to treat consumers as individuals.	• Can we analyse data quickly enough to respond and optimise experiences?

Figure 7.6 The 3is of agency selection and why they matter
Source: Forrester Research Inc, 29 March 2010

Scholars' paper 7.3 Outcomes of advertiser-agency relationships

Duhan, D.F. and Sandvik, K. (2009) Outcomes of advertiser-agency relationships: the form and the role of cooperation, *International Journal of Advertising*, 28, 5, 881-919

Duhan and Sandvik examine the theoretical basis for developing and comparing two models of the role of cooperation between agencies and their clients. The first is a shared-influence model and the second a sole-mediator model. The two models have the same form of advertiser-agency relationship, including trust, commitment, cooperation, agency performance and advertisers' willingness to pay more, but differ in the nature of the influence of the relationship and outcome components. They discuss why some relationships are more successful than others. The paper provides a comprehensive review of the academic literature underpinning relationships and the models developed give both parties a basis for performance assessment.

- *Creating productive relationships via procurement* – treating agencies as vendors in the same way as other office suppliers
- *Testing incentive-based compensation* – quantifying agency performance; Procter & Gamble moving from media commission to sales-based commission
- *Start process in more advanced markets* – adapting agency structures and relationships for growth markets including China, India and Brazil.

Among a number of predicted outcomes of the adaptive era is one that sees consumers becoming an integral part of the 'connected agency' structure. Also, a new marketing language will arise with terms such as 'GRPs' and 'above the line' becoming less important against 'influence, lifetime value and sentiment'. Marketers will need to manage media holistically across digital, broadcast and branded entertainment in all formats, earned, owned and paid. For more information readers should access www.forrester.com.

Agency remuneration

One factor that has a significant impact on the quality of the relationship between the parties is the remuneration or reward for the effort and added value that the agency makes in attempting to meet and satisfy the needs of its client. One long-standing and major cause for concern and complaint among marketing and brand managers is the uncertainty over how much their advertising programmes will finally cost and the complexity surrounding the remuneration system itself. Often the uncertainty arises as a result of 'translating' creative ideas into fully blown campaigns, including the costs of media.

There are three main ways in which agencies are paid. These are *commission*, *fees* and *payment by results*. Very often a mix of remuneration systems is utilised to reflect the nature of the client's advertising needs.

Commission

Traditionally, advertising agencies would be paid on a commission basis by media owners. A figure of 15% emerged as the norm and seemed a fair reward for the efforts of the agency. Media-related commissions, however, led to conflict within the client–agency relationship. Clients began to believe that agencies might be working in the interests of the media owner rather than theirs. Questions were raised about whether the agency was being rewarded for the actual work it did in terms of creativity and production or the amount of media expenditure involved.

Client discontent is not the only reason why agency remuneration by commission has been called into question. Recessionary pressures have had significant impact on advertising budgets, meaning less revenue and profit for agencies and their clients. Increasing competition means accepting lower profit margins in order to retain business. Snowden stated as long ago as 1993: 'Clients are demanding more for less.' She went on to say: 'It is clear to me that the agency business needs to address a number of issues; most important amongst them, how agencies get paid. It is the key to the industry's survival.' Since that time, of course, the advertising and media landscape has gone through dramatic change.

Fees and bonuses

Budgetary constraints, among other issues, have seen agency remuneration directed towards non-commission payment systems. Fees, supplemented by bonuses for effective performance, have become increasingly popular. The payment of bonuses has become more widespread than it once was. However, although the intention is to reward excellent work, some agencies

ViewPoint 7.4 Coca-Cola's recipe for agency compensation

In 2008, Coca-Cola spent some $3 billion on global advertising. At that time they rolled out a three-year programme for changing the compensation model for all local and global marketing initiatives. In previous years, agency remuneration had been based on media commissions before moving into fixed fee structures in the mid 1990s. Sarah Armstrong, the brand's director for worldwide media and communication operations, reported that the value-based system would focus on outputs and outcomes.

Campaigns are allocated priority levels and each agency's ability to deliver results is assessed as part of the process for determining the level of remuneration. Agencies can earn up to 30% margin if agreed targets are achieved. At a minimum level, agencies would be compensated for expenses incurred. Agencies are no longer asked what a campaign will cost but are given expected deliverables by Coca-Cola and the fee levels based on value summaries.

Whilst the Coca-Cola model represents a shift away from cost-based remuneration, the UK government's Central Office of Information (COI) maintains a procurement framework that, although still considering cost elements, also includes other service factors. It maintains a roster of agencies and selects from this on the basis of a tendering system for specific campaigns. The framework's award selection criteria seek the most economically advantageous response in terms of:

- value for money
- quality
- relevant experience
- flexibility
- innovation
- customer service
- technical excellence
- capacity.

Sources: Precourt (2009); www.warc.com, accessed 15 March 2011; www.coi.gov.uk/suppliers.php, accessed 21 October 2011

Question

Is payment by results just an attempt to reduce costs by the client?

Task

Identify two other actual examples of agency remuneration practice.

perceive bonuses as a route used by clients to reduce payments, and client refusal to pay bonuses has a strongly negative impact on business relationships (Child 2007).

It is likely that there will continue to be a move away from a reliance on the payment of commission as the only form of remuneration to the agency. Fees in a variety of forms, such as retainers or for individual projects, have been in operation for some time. Indeed, many agencies charge a fee for services over and above any commission earned from media owners. The concerns for agencies surround the basis on which fees are calculated, and this extends to all areas of marketing communications, not just advertising. Protracted and complicated negotiations can damage client–agency relationships.

Payment by results

Payment by results (PBR) might be seen as an acceptable form of transition from commission and fees to a system based on performance effectiveness. For the agency, however, there are some potential problems largely relating to the fact that the agency does not have total control over its own performance, with final decisions about how much is spent on media and which creative ideas are used being taken by the client. The agency has no control over the other marketing activities of the client, which might also impact on the success of the campaign. Indeed, this raises the whole question of what 'success' is and how it might be measured. Despite these considerations, it appears that PBR is starting to become an established form of remuneration.

Advertising budgets

Having examined earlier possible remuneration systems through which advertising agencies are paid for work undertaken for their clients, in this section we explore some of the methods deployed for the actual setting of advertising budgets. This is a key task within advertising and the broader framework of marketing communications.

The determination of the correct level of expenditure should be based on a thorough analysis of the contextual situation, rather than the use of norms, rule of thumb, or 'gut feel'. According to Broadbent, 'the amount to be spent is determined by a process, not a formula'. Hence, there is no simple solution. Various methods of budget determination have been suggested and the issue is one of deciding which approach is right for the situation.

Some of the principal approaches that have been used over time are now briefly examined.

Percentage of sales

One of the most widely used methods of budget determination is the setting of a ratio based on past/current advertising expenditure and sales. Previous year's expenditures are calculated as a percentage of total sales, and the resultant figure is used to calculate the budget for the coming year. So, if £25 million sales were achieved with an advertising budget of £500,000 the percentage would be 2%. The assumption would then be that a similar percentage might achieve a higher level of sales in the forthcoming year.

Whilst this might seem on the surface to be a clear and straightforward mechanism, there are potential difficulties. Data used may be considerably out of date by the time that it is utilised. The full extent of the current year's sales may not be known, thus there would be reliance on figures that could at worst be 12 months old. Use of this model would only see an increase in budget if forecast sales were to increase. There could of course be situations where sales are anticipated to reduce. If sales are expected to decline, then the future advertising budget would be reduced to bring it into line with the defined ratio. In order to halt such sales declines it may be more appropriate to actually increase budgets. The approach assumes that advertising is the sole driver of sales, which of course it is not.

ViewPoint 7.5 Who spends the most?

The budgets spent on advertising differ widely among companies, even within the same industry. UK industry spend on advertising totalled £15.5 billion in 2010. Table 7.3 presents the amounts spent by the leading advertisers. Here we can compare the differences between competitors Procter & Gamble (P&G) and Unilever and supermarket retail groups Tesco and Asda. There is significant difference between the two fast-moving consumer goods brands but little difference between the retailers. P&G and Unilever are, of course, advertising individual brands within their respective portfolios. This includes supporting new brand launches as well as promoting existing brands. In any one period differences in marketing activity could have a significant effect on the amount of budget required.

Although Tesco has a larger market share than Asda in the UK, these figures identify similar levels of advertising expenditure. As market leader, it could be argued that there is a need for Tesco to outspend their rivals. As the second largest supermarket group in the UK, Asda are clearly targeting the use of advertising to challenge their rivals, with other competitors in this sector spending considerably less.

The government's communications body, the Central Office of Information, reduced its advertising expenditure in 2010 by almost a half. Budget pressures resulting from the UK's economic situation led to dramatic reductions in spending.

Source: Based on O'Reilly (2011); www.adassoc.org.uk, accessed 22 December 2011, Nielsen Media Research, www.rankingthebrands.com, accessed 24 October 2011

Question

Does spending more than competitors guarantee advertising success?

Task

Use information from trade magazines such as *Marketing*, *Marketing Week* and *Campaign* and compile a list of recent advertising campaigns and how much they cost.

Table 7.3 Top UK advertisers 2010

Advertiser	2010 UK expenditure (£million)
Procter & Gamble	203.9
British Sky Broadcasting	145.1
Unilever	125.5
Tesco	114.6
Asda	113.3
Central Office of Information (COI)	105.4
DFS Furniture	94.3
Reckitt Benckiser	80.9
BT	79.4
Kellogg's	76.9

Percentage of gross margin

Here gross margin levels replace sales as the basis for calculating the future level of expenditure. Gross margin is normally defined as net sales less the cost of goods.

Affordability

The premise here is to take into account the overarching business situation and recognition of all business costs involved in achieving financial objectives. In some instances, advertising and other promotional costs may be perceived as being 'optional' against other 'essentials' such as manufacturing and distribution costs. This might be particularly significant in more difficult economic climates. This would then raise a question about whether a business can afford not to advertise in order to maintain customer awareness levels. For small and medium-size businesses, realistic business pressures need to be accounted for but in order to retain customer loyalty, decisions to reduce levels of communication need to be considered with care.

Competitive parity

Another common approach to budget setting is to base budgets on an assessment of a competitor's expenditure. Parity with a nominated competitor or competitors may be achieved just by setting similar levels of expenditure to theirs.

This method has the benefit of ensuring that brand expenditure levels are maintained in line with those of the competition. However, there can be difficulty in being able to make an accurate assessment of the level of each competitor's spend. It is possible to obtain a reasonable fix on advertising spend from published information such as Nielsen Media Research. Using published figures, however, does not take into account each individual firm's business situations, strategies, levels of media discounting, sales and profit levels, and new product launch programmes.

Share of voice

Share of voice (SOV) is about the percentage any one brand contributes to the overall volume of advertising undertaken in a category or market. Should one advertiser spend more than any other, its SOV is the greater, and the argument is that it will be these messages that are received and which stand a better chance of being heard and acted upon. It is assumed that all other elements that impact sales are self-cancelling, so that the only determining factor is share of voice.

This concept can be taken further and combined with another: share of market (SOM). When a brand's market share is equal to its share of advertising spend, equilibrium is said to have been reached (SOV = SOM).

The concepts SOV and SOM frame an interesting perspective of competitive strategy based upon the relative weight of advertising expenditure. Schroer (1990) reports that, following extensive research on the US packaged goods market (FMCG), it is noticeable that organisations can use advertising spend to maintain equilibrium and to create disequilibrium in a market. The former is established by major brand players maintaining their market shares with little annual change to their advertising budgets. Unless a competitor is prepared to inject a considerable increase in advertising spend and so create disequilibrium, the relatively stable high spend deters new entrants and preserves the status quo. Schroer claims that if the two market leaders maintain SOV within 10% of each other then competitive equilibrium will exist. This situation is depicted in Figure 7.7. If a market challenger launches an aggressive assault upon the leader by raising advertising spend to a point where SOV is 20–30% higher than the current leader, market share will shift in favour of the challenger.

In Figure 7.7, brands 1, 3, 4 and 6 have an SOM that is greater than their SOV. This suggests that their advertising is working well for them and that the larger organisations have some economies of scale in their advertising. Brands 2 and 5, however, have an SOM that is less than their SOV. This is because brand 2 is challenging for the larger market (with brand 1) and is likely to be less profitable than brand 1 because of the increased costs. Brand 5 is competing in a niche market, and, as a new brand, may be spending heavily (relative to its market share) to gain acceptance in the new market environment.

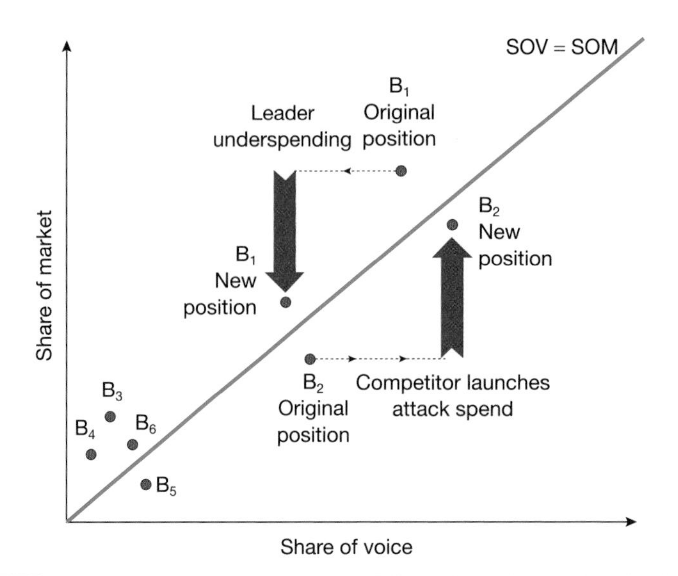

Figure 7.7 Strategy to gain market share by an increase in adspend
Source: Schroer (1990); used with permission of Harvard Business School Press

This perspective brings implications for advertising spend at a strategic level. This is shown in the matrix, Figure 7.8, which shows that advertising spend should be varied according to the spend of the company's competitors in different markets. The implications are that advertising budget decisions should be geared to the level of adspend undertaken by competitors in particular markets at particular times. Decisions to attack or to defend are also set out. For example, promotional investments should be placed in markets where competitors are underspending. Furthermore, if information is available about competitors' costs, then decisions to launch and sustain an advertising spend attack can be made in the knowledge that a prolonged period of premium spending can be carried through with or without a counter-attack.

This traditional perspective of static markets being led by the top two brands using heavy above-the-line strategies and the rest basing their competitive thrusts on price-based promotions has been challenged by Buck (1995) by reference to a study of Superpanel data by Hamilton. It was found that the brand leaders in many FMCG markets spent nearly 50% more than the industry average on advertising, while the number 2 brands spent about 8% less than

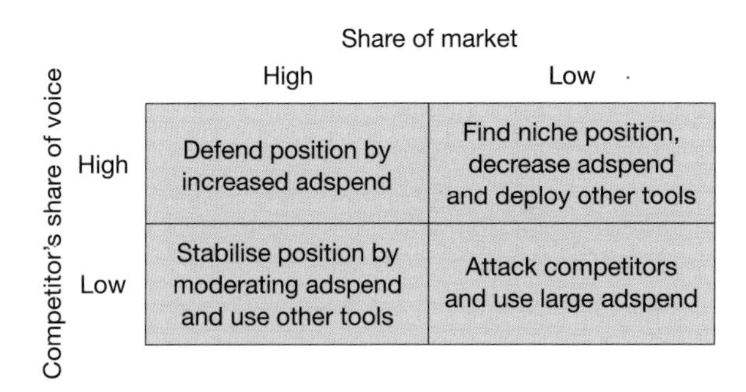

Figure 7.8 Strategies for advertising spend
Source: Reprinted by permission of Harvard Business School Press, from Ad spending: growing market share, *Harvard Business Review* (January/February), by J. Schroer, Boston, MA 1990, pp. 44-8, copyright © 1990 by Harvard Business School Publishing Corporation, all rights reserved.

the industry average. In addition, the gap with the other actors was not as significant as Schroer reported. This is, of course, a comparison of European and US markets, and there is no reason why they should be identical or even very similar. However, the data are interesting in that the challenge of brand 2, postulated by Schroer, is virtually impossible in many of the UK, if not also in European, markets.

The concepts of SOV and SOM have also been used by Jones (1990) to develop a new method of budget setting. He suggests that those brands that have an SOV greater than their SOM are 'investment brands', and those that have an SOV less than or equal to their SOM are 'profit-taking brands'.

There are three points to notice. First, the high advertising spend of new brands is an established strategy and represents a trade-off between the need for profit and the need to become established through advertising spend. The result, invariably, is that smaller brands have lower profitability because they have to invest a disproportionate amount in advertising. Second, large brands are often 'milked' to produce increased earnings, especially in environments which emphasise short-termism. The third point is that advertising economies of scale allow large brands to develop with an SOV consistently below SOM.

Using data collected from an extensive survey of 1,096 brands across 23 different countries, Jones 'calculated the difference between share of voice and share of market and averaged these differences within each family of brands'. By representing the data diagrammatically (Figure 7.9), Jones shows how it becomes a relatively simple task to work out the spend required to achieve a particular share of market. The first task is to plot the expected (desired) market share from the horizontal axis; then move vertically to the intersect with the curve and read off the SOV figure from the vertical axis.

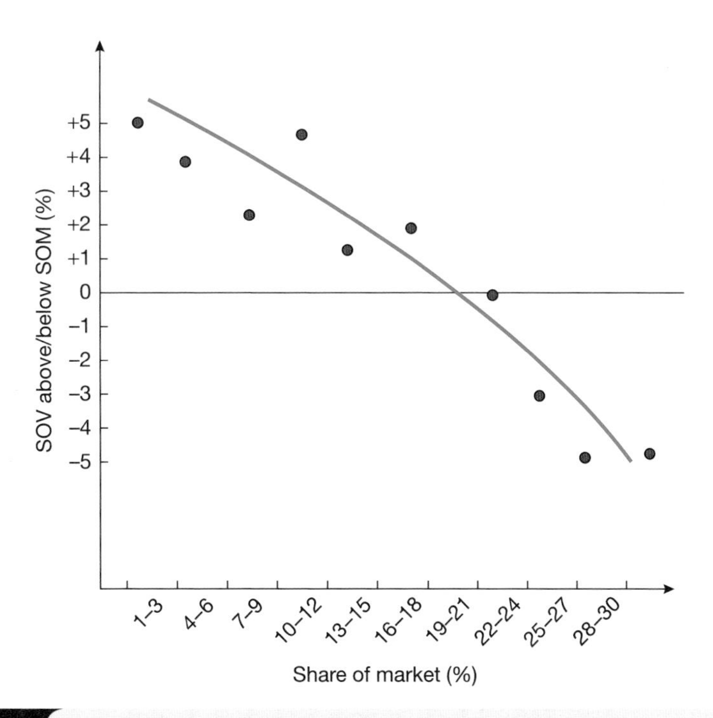

Figure 7.9 Curve comparing SOV with SOM

Source: Reprinted by permission of Harvard Business School Press, from Ad spending: maintaining market share, *Harvard Business Review* (January/February), by J.P. Jones, Boston, MA 1990, pp. 38–42, copyright © 1990 by Harvard Business School Publishing Corporation, all rights reserved.

Scholars' paper 7.4 **Shouting louder than the rest**

Schroer, J. (1990) Ad spending: growing market share, *Harvard Business Review*, January/February, 44-8

This article is based on research amongst US FMCG firms that shows how varying ad spends can be used to maintain equilibrium or create disequilibrium in a market. Schroer identifies that if two market leaders maintain SOV within 10% of each other, competitive equilibrium in terms of share of market (SOM) will be maintained. Further, if a challenger raises SOV by 20-30% more than the current market leader, they will increase SOM.

Field, P. (2009) Account planners need to care more about share of voice, *Admap*, September, 28-30

This study utilises data from the IPA databank of effectiveness case studies for the past 20 years. This shows evidence of the relationship between SOV and SOM. The author encourages account planners to engage with the principle alongside media planners, in the context of shifts in agency remuneration based on payment by results.

Assessing brands in the context of the advertising resources they attract is a slightly different way of reflecting their power and importance to their owners. If the SOV approach is limited by its applicability to stable, mature market conditions then at least it enables the promotional spend to be seen and used as a competitive weapon.

Media multiplier

As media costs are a major element of the overall cost of advertising, it is not unreasonable to base ongoing budgets on forecasts of increases in this area. This approach should ensure that the real level of advertising expenditure is maintained. However, using this as the sole measure fails to acknowledge any of the other variables which could have an impact on the achievement of advertising objectives.

Objective and task

This method relates to the specific objectives which the advertising seeks to achieve, and what needs to be done in specific advertising terms. It was established by Colley (1961) as an attempt to apply a more scientific approach to budget determination. He set out the principles of 'defining advertising goals for measured advertising results' (DAGMAR), proposing that advertising should be specifically budgeted to accomplish defined goals or objectives. We looked at DAGMAR in Chapter 4.

A derivative of DAGMAR is the objective-and-task method which requires that specific objectives for the campaign are defined at the outset. These may be expressed in terms of increasing brand awareness, changing consumer attitudes or perceptions, encouraging product trial or encouraging comprehension. Numerical targets are set and the costs of achieving these targets calculated. The budget is therefore based on a series of goals rather than on past or future results and is considered to be more realistic in marketing terms.

Adoption of this approach is highly dependent on access to sufficiently detailed information to ensure that all relevant variables are considered.

Experimentation

Whilst it may be appropriate to establish some kind of 'centralised' approach to setting advertising budgets, the pace of change within the industry, not least rapid advances in media availability, suggests scope for a level of experimentation in resource allocation. This is different from just establishing contingencies for unexpected events, as it provides a basis for innovation and variation from traditional practice. It would be most often deployed alongside a more formalised budget allocation method.

To conclude this chapter and budgeting, it is worth considering which of these various techniques are used in practice. West and Prendergast (2009) researched the various levels of sophistication used by organisations to set their advertising and promotions budgets. They found that on average organisations use two methods to determine their communications budgets. Of these, judgemental methods such as 'the affordable' and the 'objective-and-task' methods account for over 50% of the methods used. What they also found was that the prevailing organisational culture, as manifest through the 'personalities, organisation, timing, planning, and the nature of the market and access to data' underpinned the responses of those interviewed. In other words, culture shapes the nature of risk taking and the size and shape of the budgets, the frame in which financial decisions are made.

Chapter summary

In order to help consolidate your understanding of advertising from a general perspective here are the key points summarised against each of the learning objectives.

Review the role of advertising in an integrated communications context

In today's complex communications environment it is important to consider the different elements of the communications mix from an integrated perspective. Consumers are engaging with communications in very different ways than in the past, given the advent of new, often personalised, media platforms. As a result advertising may now be considered to work in different ways. The advertising industry therefore has to look at adopting an integrated approach to deliver relevant messages to target audiences. For those agencies operating for clients on a global basis, this entails change in the way they are structured and managed.

Examine the different types of agency and the roles they play in providing services to their clients

In addition to the traditional full-service agency format there is now a range of specialist providers, most notably in the areas related to media planning and buying. To handle the needs of global brands this has led to the creation of various 'mega' agency groups such as WPP and Omnicom, which handle all the communications of their clients' businesses.

Understand how agencies operate and the individual roles played by agency personnel

The major functions or disciplines within a typical agency involve research, planning, creating ads, media planning and buying. Key personnel include account managers, account planners, creatives, multi-taskers, and media planners and buyers. It is important to remember that effective advertising involves a coordinated or team approach. Individuals can play significant parts but the ability to work together is an essential criterion. For example, the role of the account manager is crucial in ensuring all elements are working to the same, agreed objectives.

Appraise the criteria for agency selection and the processes involved in their appointment

The key stages include searching for a suitable range of agencies, credential meetings, initial briefings and development of proposals, the pitch and finally awarding a contract to the winning agency. The industry bodies, including the IPA, have set out criteria in the form of guidelines that should be followed for agency selection that ensures fairness for the agencies involved in pitching for new business.

Consider how relationships between agencies and clients are managed

Long term client–agency relationships are founded on trust and commitment. This often centres around the personal relationships that might exist between particular client and agency personnel. The use of systems and technologies is also instrumental in developing relationships.

Examine the ways in which agencies are remunerated for their services

Clients are becoming increasingly demanding in terms of what they expect agencies to do and most particularly how much they pay for their services. Models of agency compensation are shifting from a commission based on media expenditure toward payment based on performance and the achievement of agreed targets. This puts pressure on agencies to perform, which includes examining their structures and operating platforms.

Appraise the models that are used for determining advertising budgets

Budgets can be set using a number of methods. These include percentage of sales, percentage of gross margin, media multiplier, affordability, competitive parity, share of voice, and objective and task. The choice of method depends on the client's communications needs and the scope and scale of their operations. It may be necessary to utilise more than the 'standard' approach for different parts of the communications mix.

Review questions

1. Advise how The Help Agency, described in the minicase at the start of this chapter, might develop an effective remuneration system that would be attractive to potential small charity-sector clients.
2. Explain the advantages and disadvantages of the standardised and adapted approaches when appointing an advertising agency.
3. Make notes outlining ways in which advertising agencies can differentiate themselves.
4. What factors need to be considered in appointing an advertising agency by a major supplier of personal care products in China?
5. Explain how the role of the account planner has changed as a result of the growth of an integrated approach to marketing communications.
6. What is the purpose of holding a chemistry meeting when searching for an advertising agency?
7. Discuss the main factors that might lead to conflict between a client and their advertising agency.
8. Write a short profile of a leading individual in advertising.
9. Why has payment by results become a more common basis for agency remuneration?
10. Compare the benefits of share of voice and objective and task methods of setting advertising budgets.

Chapter references

Broadbent, S. (1989) *The Advertising Budget*, London: IPA/NTC Business Books
Buck, S. (1995) The decline and fall of the premium brand, *Admap*, March, 14–17

Cheung, F.S.L., Mirza, H. and Leung, W. (2008) Client following revisited: a study of transnational advertising agencies in China, *International Journal of Advertising*, 27, 4, 593–628

Child, L. (2007) How to manage your relationship, *Marketing Agency* (December), 4–7

Colley, R. (1961) *Defining Advertising Goals for Measured Advertising Results.* New York: Association of National Advertisers

Collin, W. (2003) The interface between account planning and media planning – a practitioner perspective, *Marketing Intelligence and Planning*, 21(7), 440–5

Corcoran, S., Frankland, D. and Drego, V. (2010) *The Future of Agency Relationships.* Cambridge, MA: Forrester Research

Costa, M. (2010) Remodelling the agency relationship for the 3.0 age, *Marketing Week*, 5 August, accessed 20 January 2012 at www.marketingweek.co.uk

Duhan, D.F. and Sandvik, K. (2009) Outcomes of advertiser–agency relationships: the form and the role of cooperation, *International Journal of Advertising*, 28, 5, 881–919

Fielding, S. (2000) Developing global brands in Asia, *Admap*, June 26–9

Fill, C. (2009) *Marketing Communications: Interactivity, Communities and Content*, 5th edn. Harlow: FT/Prentice Hall

Grant, I., Gilmore, C. and Crosier, K. (2003) Account planning: whose role is it anyway? *Marketing Intelligence and Planning*, 21, 7, 462–72

Grosso, C., Guggenheim Shenkan, A. and Sichel, H.P. (2006) A reality check for online advertising, *McKinsey Quarterly*, 3

Jones, J.P. (1990) Ad spending: maintaining market share, *Harvard Business Review*, January/February, 38–42

Jones, M. (2004) 10 things agencies need to know about clients, *Admap*, May, 21–3

Morgan, R.M. and Hunt, S.D. (1994) The commitment–trust theory of relationship marketing, *Journal of Marketing*, 58 (July), 20–38

O'Reilly, L. (2011) P&G biggest spending advertiser in 2010, www.marketingweek.com, accessed 24 October 2011

Precourt, G. (2009) Coca-Cola and ANA members rethink agency evaluation. WARC (October), retrieved 10 May 2011 from www.warc.com

Precourt, G. (2010) Procter & Gamble's BAL compensation moves beyond experimentation. WARC (March), retrieved 15 March 2011 from www.warc.com

Schroer, J. (1990) Ad spending: growing market share, *Harvard Business Review*, January/February, 44–8

Snowden, S. (1993) The remuneration squeeze, *Admap*, January, 26–8

Spanier, G. (2010) What's the secret of a long-term relationship in advertising? *London Evening Standard*, 19 July, retrieved 8 August 2011 from www.thisislondon.co.uk

Sweney, M. (2011) Sir Martin Sorrell's WPP increases profits by 37%, retrieved 24 August 2011 from www.guardian.co.uk

West, D. and Prendergast, G.P. (2009) Advertising and promotions budgeting and the role of risk, *European Journal of Marketing*, 43, 11/12, 1457–76

Wethey, D. (2006) The shocking truth about the pitch, *The Marketer*, September, 7–8

Williams, T. (2011) Why most 'full agency' agencies are actually specialist agencies, *Ignition*, 5 December 2011, retrieved 22 December 2011 from www.ignitiongroup.com/propulsion/entry/why-most-full-service-agencies-are-actually-now-specialist-agencies/

www.forrester.com accessed 10/08/2011

www.ipa.co.uk accessed 15/09/2011

Zambarino, A. and Goodfellow, J. (2003) Account planning in the new marketing and communications environment (has the Stephen King challenge been met?), *Marketing Intelligence and Planning*, 21(7), 424–34

Chapter 8
Traditional media

Among the many changes that have impacted on the advertising industry in recent years have been the rapid developments in digital technologies. As a result considerable focus has been given to online, mobile and social media marketing, with increasing proportions of marketing budgets being allocated to these new forms of communications. However, traditional media continue to fulfil important roles for many advertisers, to the extent that television advertising is considered to be more effective today than it was 20 years ago.

Aims and learning objectives

The aim of this chapter is to explore the nature and characteristics of traditional media.

The learning objectives of this chapter are to:

1. list and classify the traditional advertising media
2. explain the basic concepts used in advertising media
3. outline the structure of print and electronic media
4. describe the uses of out-of-home media, direct mail and alternative media
5. consider the relative weaknesses and strengths in using traditional media.

Minicase Flying in Finnair to Asia

In 2011, Finnair, Finland's flagship airline carrier, launched one of its largest branding campaigns to up its game as an airline that offers a 'fresh and high-quality way to travel' between Europe and Asia. Even though Finnair had in fact been flying to Asia for many years, it decided to reposition itself as a major player in traffic in both directions between Asia and Europe, offering another option for business and leisure travellers via Helsinki.

The first Finnair flight was made to Bangkok in 1976. Non-stop flights from Helsinki to Tokyo were introduced in 1983. Five years later, Finnair operated direct flights from Helsinki to Beijing, the first direct connection between Europe and China by a Western European airline. Finnair continued to expand its Asian operations by adding a flight to a second major Japanese city (Osaka) in 1995.

In the new millennium, Finnair continued to add new routes to Asia. Its first flight to Hong Kong occurred on 7 February 2002, then flights to Shanghai, and Nagoya, Finnair's third Japanese destination, became operational in 2006. That same year, Finnair began full operations to its first Indian destination, Delhi; and later a direct service to Seoul, South Korea, starting in the summer of 2008, further strengthened the company's Asian network. Finnair also began flying to Singapore in May 2011, and increased its flight frequency to Hong Kong in June 2011. In May 2012, it became the first European company to fly to the Chinese city of Chongqing.

Finnair also scheduled flights from Manchester (UK) and Dusseldorf (Germany) to Asia, via Helsinki, yet the brand remained relatively unknown in Europe as an option to Asia. It therefore wanted to raise awareness and build credibility of its brand with 30- to 59-year-old high-level business executives in Europe, who were predominately male and frequently travelled on business to Asia.

The airline company also wanted to promote its new daily direct *return* route from Singapore, showcasing Helsinki as a gateway to the rest of Europe – the only airline to offer a daily connection between Singapore and Northern Europe with a timetable tailored to the needs of business passengers.

Exhibit 8.1 Finnair
Source: Rex Features

Finnair believed that it could leverage its position on the global map. The flight over the north and Finnish airspace cuts the flying time considerably (compared to flights from east to west). But in addition, research demonstrated that the route via Helsinki to much of Asia from both Europe and North America resulted in a reduction in carbon emissions by as much as 10%. Finnair's research also claimed that by using Helsinki as a stop-off point to Asia, airlines could further cut emissions. When a long-haul flight takes off, most of the payload is not passengers or cargo but fuel. Breaking the journey into smaller hops cuts the use of fuel.

Jonne Lehtioksa, Finnair's sales director for Hong Kong and Macau, admitted that the brand had been quiet in advertising in Asia and communications had to start from the basics. While the Asian market is extremely competitive, Lehtioksa was confident that Finnair would find its niche among corporate and business travellers with a campaign that would be the first major step towards expanded market share.

There were several challenges faced by Finnair. These included how to convince travellers to fly to Asia with Finnair when most direct routes to China, India and southeast Asia already flew over Finland; to convince travellers who fly to Europe to use Helsinki as a gateway and quick connection to the rest of Europe; to convince the business traveller that breaking the journey into smaller hops (via Helsinki) cuts the fuel load and is good for the environment; to promote Finnair travel as a fresh, quality, and an overall superior travel experience from flight to the airport. Above all else, which media should be used to carry these messages?

Sources: Littbarski (2011); Low (2011); Ng (2010); Pearce (2009)

Introduction

Advertisers use a variety of media so that they can deliver their planned messages and, in many cases, listen to and interact with target audiences. This chapter considers the characteristics of traditional media and how they enable brand communications. It commences with a discussion of the central role of the media in the marketing communications process. It then examines in turn each of the traditional media, specifically print, broadcast (or electronic), out-of-home, direct mail and alternative media. This includes a consideration of the trends and developments in each class of media plus an examination of their individual strengths and weaknesses and how they can contribute to a media plan.

The advertising media are a marketing communications umbrella concept that covers the media vehicles or channels that carry advertising messages to the prospective consumer audience. It is part of the promotional aspect of the four elements typically used to describe the marketing mix, first put forth in the 1960s (McCarthy 1960) to explain the process of using marketing communications strategically to target the consumer.

Media strategy and media planning are the processes by which one determines the best use of advertising media – television, a consumer magazine, a giant poster, banner ads or Facebook – in which to place those messages and thereby meet the marketing communications objectives that have been decided upon in advance.

The vehicle, as we use it (other terms, such as channel, are used), carries the message. Look around you at the moment: something within your grasp is a potential advertising vehicle. It may be the notation on a pen, or a logo emblazoned on a T-shirt, a sweet wrapper or an icon on your iPad screen. Handwriting or fonts on the printed page are also media. How you utilise a font in Word, or how you use your handwriting utensil to create letters is a message of sorts. Advertisers attempt to select and choose the most efficient media in which to carry their evocative messages to the intended audience. A formal layout of these choices is called a media plan and is organised by a media planner.

Strategic media planning and placement for the media are a complex challenge. This is because media planners must make use of their knowledge of consumer demographic, psychographic, behavioural and other characteristics. They must in addition have a sound grasp of the essence of the medium that might best appeal to the prospective consumer.

Media planners must not only possess up-to-date knowledge of the marketplace, but they must also establish and maintain professional relationships with media, companies and clients with expertise in the field. As media planners, they are obliged to negotiate with media vendors, work with agency colleagues and clients to develop strategic recommendations that will satisfy marketing objectives and manage the day-to-day activities of the media schedule.

Media planners often define the marketing communications goals of a media plan using the two related concepts of reach and frequency. *Reach* is the total number of people exposed (note that exposure is defined as the measure of the opportunity of a reader to be exposed – see Chapter 10) to the media vehicle, whether an ad in a magazine or a commercial on TV. *Frequency* is a measure of repetition. Essentially, these terms in combination represent the total number of people exposed to a message, the number of times. The objective is to achieve the highest reach possible within media schedules to ensure that more people have the potential to be exposed to the brand, which in turn, ideally, results in building brand awareness, customer loyalty, purchases and the like. Higher frequency is desirable because research suggests (Krugman 1975) that consumers need multiple exposures (repetition) to a particular advertising message before they remember it. We will discuss these concepts further in the chapters to follow.

In general, media for advertising can be broken down into two distinct areas: *addressable media* are used generally to deliver customised marketing messages to target clearly identifiable prospects or current customers; *interactive media* are two-way or multiple-generated media that allow companies and consumers to send and receive messages to and from each other. The benefit of interactive media (especially with SMS text, telephony and even personal selling) is that they allow the advertiser or the consumer to transfer instantly information from one end of the consumer–marketer spectrum to the other. These 'marketing conversations' enable consumers to connect with a company, for companies to review responses, and then make any necessary adjustments in order to maximise customer service. Marketing conversations fine-tune, verify or confirm the integrative quality of a message, and may create an emotional bond between the two parties.

Media strategy is making media decisions based on an understanding of customers' wants and needs and the ability to evaluate the available media options to reach them. Grasping the significance of reach, frequency, addressable and interactive media, among other concepts, is paramount to developing a media strategy for marketing communications and to enable advertisers to achieve their marketing and advertising objectives.

Print media

Print media include all printed advertisements on some kind of paper, and which are found in newspapers, magazines, direct mail inserts, catalogues or other portable printed material. Print advertising (sometimes called press advertising) is featured within the news, editorial and entertainment content of these print vehicles. The yellow-page and other business directories are also considered a part of print advertising. The choices among available print vehicles are vast and complex, and vary in terms of cost and in the discernible advantages and disadvantages in their use and placement. The print media are particularly subject to clutter (subject to an overload of commercial messages), so that all aspects of print must be fully considered before choosing the most effective delivery vehicle for the product, service or event message.

Some consumers still prefer receiving news or entertainment in a physically flexible form, such as a newspaper or a magazine. The consensus among them is that reading physical print is more rewarding and engaging. The print vehicle in their grasp commands their attention. Dahlén (2005) and Bronner and Neijens (2006), among others, suggest that this degree of engagement directly affects advertising effectiveness, while Malthouse and Calder (2010) agree that more engaging (higher level of engagement) magazines or even simple units of

Scholars' paper 8.1 **The impact of advertising**

Appel, V. (1987) Editorial environment and advertising effectiveness, *Journal of Advertising Research*, 27(4), 11-16

Appel's classic article on understanding the way a medium impacts the advertising placed within it is a precursor to the discussion on editorial environment as an important component of audience involvement and effectiveness. In his essay, Appel re-examined previous research and surmised that editorial environment as a mediator of advertising effectiveness is much more complex than would at first appear. Numerous investigators have attempted to demonstrate the validity of the concept but none has done so to the point where it is generally accepted. Researchers who wish to study the problem must be careful to separate out the effects of differences in audience composition from differences in editorial environment.

direct mail – with a greater level of detail or more intense imagery, perhaps – will have a higher overall level of advertising effectiveness. Even though the print medium continues to lose advertising revenue to the digital media *du jour*, print-loyal advertisers and clients insist that print works best for delivering messages to local and finely targeted audiences.

Using print brings its own set of advantages and disadvantages in reaching a particular audience. Print can offer high-impact executions (fashion magazines), appeal to educated customers (newspapers of record) or provide good editorial environment (popular dialogue publications) in delivering its message. Print is available in a range of versatile formats: newspapers and magazines, coupons, direct mail flyers, inserts, one-off speciality brochures, collateral, handouts, to mention a few. All of these in their unique ways may benefit the advertiser to deliver the marketing communications message.

Magazines

Magazines are the most specialised of all print advertising media and have proliferated to serve a wide range of segmented readers in both the consumer and the business environments. There are now literally thousands of consumer magazines worldwide, satisfying many specific needs (see Figure 8.1). Early magazine production was limited to general mass appeal (such as the former American news and picture magazines *Life* and *Look*) and indeed, some mass-appeal magazines still exist, but, generally, most magazines today address specific target audiences that match consumers' demographics, lifestyle psychographics, or leisure and professional interests.

Consumer magazines are classified by frequency of publication – weekly, monthly, bimonthly, for example – and are divided into general-interest magazines (the French *Le Nouvel Observateur*) and specialised consumer variations (*Le Cycle*, for cycling enthusiasts, also from France). Consumer magazines are also categorised as either *paid-circulation* or *controlled-circulation publications*. Paid-circulation publications sell subscriptions or single-copy purchases and have certain advantages, some suggest, even in the face of a waning subscription base. The paid-circulation model assures advertisers that the audience is likely to read the magazine. If advertisers want to know that readers actually read a publication (as evidenced from a subscription or purchase) a beneficial relationship between consumer and publication may evolve.

Controlled-circulation publications (commonly newsletters and smaller magazines) are generally distributed free of charge to those working in a given area or affiliated with a given organisation. *NY Press*, serving the medical staff and community of New York Presbyterian Hospital of Columbia and Cornell Universities, is fairly typical of the controlled-circulation vehicles found in trade, industrial or organisational environments. It serves as an in-house mechanism to promote products, services and sponsorships to various stakeholders within the

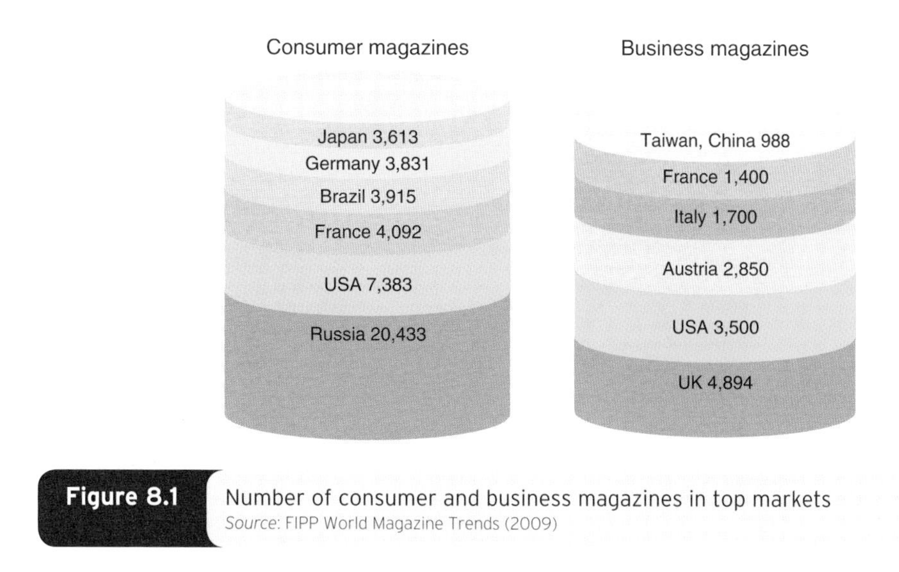

Figure 8.1 Number of consumer and business magazines in top markets
Source: FIPP World Magazine Trends (2009)

hospital. Controlled-circulation publications contain a high proportion of direct response advertising, and provide no guarantees that the intended audience will read the publication. However, publishers tend to prefer the controlled-circulation model because the advertising rate base generally does not fluctuate, as might be the case with paid-circulation publications either from news-stand purchases or from subscriptions. Thus, publishers can build stable, longer-term relationships with advertisers to the benefit of both.

Business or trade magazines are also classified in unique ways: a *vertical publication* presents editorial content and information across an entire industry, an example being the international *Retail Digital* magazine, which gives an in-depth look at specific industry issues such as multichannel marketing, supply chain, property and retail technology for retailers, whilst a horizontal publication, such as *CIO Magazine* in the UK, in its online or printed version, offers a business function (senior executorial) or editorial content (IT issues) that appeals to people of similar interests or responsibilities – or horizontal interests – in a particular industry or discipline. *CIO Magazine* (2011) defines its content as 'must-have information for senior IT managers and directors to help them drive the business, technology and leadership issues facing their business today' (para. 1).

Despite these challenging times for print media, the magazine industry has evolved into a medium with a capacity to target specific consumer and niche markets. Literally thousands of special-interest consumer and business-related titles around the world continue to appeal to a variety of lifestyles and interests. In North America alone, media companies such as Standard Rate and Data Service (SRDS), Audit Bureau of Circulations (ABC) and Business Publications Audit Worldwide (BPA) track circulation figures for thousands of magazines.

Magazine performance has remained relatively successful over the past 20 years due to its ability to tailor-make formats to address segmented audiences and concerns. Opportunities are enhanced because of the variety of magazine formats and ad sizes, multi-page combinations, colour reproduction and quality. Not only can magazines address the various degrees of skill sets of those who sail and sailing enthusiasts, but they can also feature the various skills of sailing types. A cursory look at the segmented sailing magazine market reveals print vehicles that cover leisure sailing (*Sailing*, *Yachting World*), the kinds of sailing vessels (*Catamaran Sailor Magazine*, *Traditional Boats and Tall Ships*), the type of sailor, such as recreationalists and weekenders (*Yachting*), regatta and offshore sailboat racers (*Sail Racing* and *Seahorse* magazines) and exploratory sailors (*International Journal of Nautical Archaeology*). Add to this

Exhibit 8.2 Kerrang! Rock magazine turned 30 in June 2011

Kerrang! (Bauer Media) is the world's biggest selling weekly rock magazine. Its special interest is heavy metal rock (hence, the onomatopoetic word that lends itself to the title) and skews to a male audience interested in iconic male metal bands and trends in heavy metal music. It's multi-platformed by having K!TV, Kerrang!Radio and offers editions in Australia and Spain.

Source: Kerrang! Press Gazette 2011

any number of international magazines devoted to sailing outside the English-speaking world (*Lescasle Nautique* [French-Canadian], *Rejs* [Poland] and *Yelken Dünyasi* [Turkey]), and we are dealing with a fairly formidable and inclusive audience to which we could address a specific message related to sailing.

Some strengths in using magazines in the media plan

Magazines offer quality reproduction and attractability

Magazines are high-production, quality vehicles that often enjoy loyal readership. The environment in which an ad appears may have a dramatic effect on the perception of the product or service advertised. *Vogue* magazine in its many international manifestations is sometimes criticised for its wall-to-wall advertising clutter, but the high-gloss, heavy stock paper on which *Vogue* images are printed appeals to a consistent readership and lends a certain respectability and professionalism that makes it a lead user in fashion trends and trending (Ives 2011). The elegant and beautiful photographs in *Art & Antiques*, too, enhance the surrounding environment with brand-relevant imagery and associations that often transfer to other brands that appear in the same publication. In this way, high-quality magazines boost brand favourability by association (Appel 1987).

Magazines are highly selective

Magazines offer a high degree of audience selectivity, and can reach a specific targeted audience efficiently. They are often subject-specific or niche publications and can pinpoint audiences that range from pet owners to dental cosmetologists seeking the latest technology for improving and beautifying their customers' teeth. *The Australian Women's Weekly*, whose editorial content includes kitchen, fashion, health and celebrity stories targeted to female audiences, is not unlike other female-targeted publications, save that its content is unique to female audiences in Australia and New Zealand. There is a magazine for virtually everyone.

Magazines last longer than other media

Imagine that you are in a supermarket, examining the various expiry dates on products on the shelves. Some products' usability, or the shelf life of the product, expires next week, some next month, some next year. Compared to other media, magazines enjoy a longer shelf life because their 'expiry date' is extended by their presence in the beauty salon, the doctor's surgery or the travel agent bureau. Magazines tend to be kept for longer periods of time; they are passed along and viewed by multiple audiences, thereby extending their usefulness to the advertiser, and unlike with other media (digital, print and broadcast in particular), consumers cut out and save magazine articles, ensuring an even longer-lasting message. These behaviours prolong the potential for consumer exposure.

Magazines have inherent design flexibility and can be customised

Unlike some print media, magazines are especially good for being able to highlight the product in detail. This holds true for both consumer and business publications. The unique colour reproduction available in the magazine process enables great benefit to the product. In addition to general quality reproduction capabilities, magazines also offer a great deal of flexibility in the type, size, colour combinations and positioning of the product within their pages. Customisation techniques may vary in name from country to country, but the essential characteristics of customisation are similar across the print media.

Magazines can also provide many creative technical or mechanical possibilities that give them a unique appeal. *Gatefolds* make possible a third page that folds out and can be used for rollouts of new brands or special occasions. *Bleed pages* contain no margin of white space around the advertisements, enabling products to appear larger than they are (without the aid of a white spaced margin). *Inserts*, scent strips, pop-ups and 3D stickers, and DVDs or CDs are some of the inserts that magazines employ to break through the clutter of ads and to attract the readers' attention by using an advanced, robust content-management solution. An increasing number of design firms specialise in custom-tailored magazine inserts to add sound, lights, scent, touch and taste to maximise magazine impact for the reader.

Split runs are two or more versions of an ad printed in alternate copies of a particular issue, thereby allowing the marketing professional to judge which of the ads generates more responses, and perhaps also providing some clues as to the relative effectiveness and usability of each of the ads. A premium *cover position* may be desirable for a company that seeks a highly visible position within the context of the magazine.

A less costly way to benefit from the use of magazine space is to work with specialised size formats, such as a *junior unit* (generally up to 60% of the ad page, surrounded by editorial context) and *island halves* (half-page positioned on two or more sides by editorial matter). Half-pages, quarter-pages and column-thirds are some other common sizes available to the discretion of the advertiser.

Magazines easily cross platforms

Magazines fit easily into cross-media or multi-platform campaigns that use online and offline advertising. Combined with the physical print vehicle, magazines aligned to media websites can offer the same content and in this way build on their audience base. Web-based magazines can also adapt to the various reading devices that are available through smartphone or pad technology to enhance their use of digital advertising.

Some weaknesses in using magazines in the media plan

Magazines need long lead times and tolerate little deadline flexibility

Often to place an advertisement in a magazine, the advertiser must adhere to inflexible, long lead times, meaning that the magazine publication will need galleys sometimes two to three (or more) months in advance to meet its printing schedule deadlines. Factors may change during this time, the message may become irrelevant or the market may change. It is difficult for magazines' lack of immediacy to compete with the timeliness, for instance, of online media.

Clutter

As is the case with several media, the consumer is exposed to a large number of advertising or marketing messages in the magazine format. This forces the advertiser's promotional message to compete with many other messages for the reader's attention and may minimise the impact of any single message.

Not appropriate as a mass medium

The magazine is not a good vehicle for delivering a mass audience at a reasonable price. Firstly, the nature of the medium is suitable for highly selective segments and finely tuned targets, so its ability to reach mass audiences is limited. Secondly, as we will see in subsequent chapters, a magazine's ability to reach a targeted audience is relatively high, but the cost to reach a mass audience would be prohibitive.

ViewPoint 8.1 Arla seek to Integrate with a loyalty campaign

Arla Foods wanted to develop a 'We care' support campaign to enhance consumer preference and loyalty towards Arla Foods' organic brand Harmonie® and its dairy products throughout Scandinavia.

Harmonie® is an organic brand owned by the Danish-Swedish cooperative, Arla Foods. The dairy division is the world's largest supplier of organic dairy products. Arla Foods believed that Harmonie® would work well in establishing a preference-building campaign, which included answering questions about organics, nature and the role of Generation K in the environment.

Kunde & Co (Copenhagen, Denmark), one of the largest agencies in Scandinavia specialising in developing what the company calls a brand's 'value position', took the approach of enhancing preference and building loyalty for Harmonie® through an integrated campaign and communication concept using traditional print ads, music, a website, carton panels and POS material. All played pivotal parts towards encouraging consumer involvement in the organic dairy brand.

The primary target group for the campaign was families with children, and a subset target of children themselves. The campaign used the print media in the form of women's magazines and the Danish children's magazine *Donald Duck* as part of its media strategy. These vehicles allowed the 'Klimaspire' ('climate sprouts' or 'little climate buds') story to be unfolded in detail, while a shorter advertised version of the story featured on milk and yoghurt cartons. Advertisements on milk cartons invited children aged 8 to 14 to visit the accompanying website and sing or write something on behalf of the climate. The ads helped create awareness and drove traffic to Harmonie®'s campaign site.

The campaign also included web banners and POS material in supermarkets to draw attention to the Harmonie® campaign and was centred around Klimaspiren.dk, focusing on the voice of youth in the environmental and climate debate in support of the Danish national association, Nature.

The website received almost 100,000 unique visitors and 890,213 clicks over the course of the campaign. Many of the visitors were children and young people who wanted to sing their version of the Klimaspire song that was written especially for the campaign and recorded by Danish Eurosong stars Amalie and Mathias.

The unique strengths of printed media integrated with other media spread the campaign messages about organics, nature and the environment to the consumers, increasing awareness of the brand's organic products.

Source: www.kunde-co.dk; J. Albris (personal communication, 5 June 2011)

Question

Why did Harmonie® choose to include the print medium in its campaign targeted to children?

Task

Choose a national ad from a country of your choice. State the reasons why you believe this ad works especially well for the country in question.

Newspapers

Newspaper readership, once the stalwart foundation of the print medium, has been on the wane in many developed countries for some time (Tillinghast 1981; Patterson 2007; Franklin 2008; Fortunati and Sarrica 2011). Newspapers have even become irrelevant for some population segments, particularly younger consumers. An impromptu survey of our students over the past few years indicates that perhaps a scant two or three read a newspaper on a regular basis, if at all. Some of the world's leading newspapers have gone into administration; others are inevitably about to do so. Readership is down, and advertising expenditure (adspend) continues to decrease despite the efforts newspapers take to rejuvenate or maintain the medium.

The World Press Trends 2010 reports that 1.7 billion people read a newspaper every day, representing over 25% of the world's adult population. When non-daily newspapers are added, newspapers' global reach extends to 37% (World Press Trends 2010), and stable or increased circulation figures are reported by a majority of countries. However, consumers are changing the way they receive their news ration in the morning, noon or night and global newspaper advertising revenue has fallen year on year in recent years (Layton 2008). Daily newspapers in some countries (USA, UK, Germany), heavily dependent on advertising revenue, must clamour for consumers' attention as one among many sources. Increasing patterns of consuming online and unimpressiveness or lack of attention-grabbing qualities make it difficult for newspapers to counter their downward trend (Chappuis, Gaffey and Parvizi 2011).

As newspaper readership and paid-for subscriptions begin to dwindle, there are few statistics that point in a positive direction for the future of the integrated print subscription model. Some newspapers are attempting to reinvent their purpose by switching to web-only editions; some have adjusted their target audience to a younger, urbane and well-educated set; others (Schwartz 2005) have made perceptual and integral links for the advertiser between the hard copy edition and internet access to the paper's website.

To compete for the advertising dollar or pound or euro, many newspapers are not only investing in revamping their websites, but also in a multi-pronged approach, aggressively attempting to drive traffic from the print publication to the website. Others have continued to segment the newspaper itself into various speciality sections. Pad and smartphone editions provide easy access through the use of personalised application technology (apps). iMonitor™ (McPheters & Company 2011) even provides print media with an efficiency mechanism for worldwide media-related iPad apps, designed to track print media and to judge app performance on delivery, download speeds, readability and navigability.

Newspapers are also looking to social networks for their survival as social media are being put to use as an integral part of a 'new' newspaper or news organisation. By clearly defining the social media the newspaper should be using and then aligning it with a connection between readership and the proper social network arena, some newspaper organisations believe that one can create and build brand loyalty with local (and various national) online audiences. How this can be done is still not clear, though one organisation speaks of creating a social media 'map' that will allow one to evaluate properly the networks for possible associations, including blog posts, live chats, wikis and photo gallery sites. One such example, the *Newspaper Map* (Watling 2011), combines the traditional print medium in a seamless way with application technology and online versions.

This trend in Western countries does not yet seem to apply in such proportions to Asia. As Figure 8.2 indicates, newspapers see their greatest strength in Asia. The irony in this is that regions of Asia are perhaps the most digitally connected areas on the planet, yet they still harbour affection for the printed press.

Metro International, a Swedish company based in Luxembourg, meets the challenge of dwindling newspaper readership in other ways. It publishes successfully a *Metro* alternative to the traditional paid-for daily. As of 2011, variations of *Metro* serve over 100 municipalities around the world. Primarily a local advertising venue with cursory reporting, Metro International's advertising sales have grown dramatically since launch of the first edition in 1995 (Metro International SA 2007). The basic format of the free publication is similar throughout major urban areas, with some countries, such as Chile and Mexico, altering the name to *Publimetro*. Distribution is free and revenues are generated entirely through advertising. *Metro* is primarily intended for commuters on public transport, although several countries support national editions. The editorial content is unique in *Metro* because it delivers summarised local content and many pages of local advertising targeted directly to audiences within its respective municipalities.

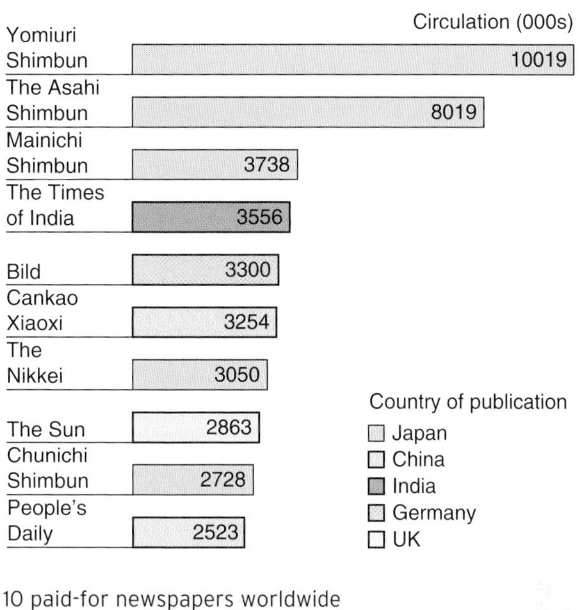

Figure 8.2 Top 10 paid-for newspapers worldwide
Source: *WAN-IFRA* World Press Trends 2010

Newspaper advertising

Essentially, there are three major types of advertising found in newspapers: display, classified and special inserts.

Display is generally akin to print advertisements found in magazines. It uses headlines and subheads, illustrations and images, white space and other visual design characteristics coupled with copy in the same way as do magazines. Many newspapers have added colour to their display ads over the last 15–20 years.

Classified ads provide newspapers with a substantial amount of revenue, are local for the most part and represent categories such as employment, real estate, automotive and the all-pervasive 'personal' columns. Most of these ads appear in smaller typeface and are sold by line or by word.

Special advertisements in the form of special inserts may market a local business, a new or existing business (often with a call-to-action discount coupon), a local candidate for political office or a cause such as the Animal Welfare Society. *Pre-printed inserts* are published offsite and inserted into the newspaper before distribution. Many retailers utilise special inserts for sales in special postal code or zip code circulation zones to reach shoppers in areas serving their local stores or retail shops.

Some strengths in using newspapers in the media plan

Extensive local penetration and coverage

Newspapers are still relatively popular for retailers as advertising media vehicles due to their high penetration in local areas (Nyilsy, Whitehall King and Reid 2011). In Western countries and in particular English-speaking countries, newspapers in the service of *local* communities are still thriving. Information on weekend events, local sports items and features, and corporate outings, though decreasingly so, can best be reached through the local newspaper.

In some countries such as the UK and Italy, major newspapers cover and are available in an entire geoeconomic area, whereas in larger countries such as Canada, Australia and Russia, stronger regional newspapers dominate the newspaper scene and affect the placement of local advertising.

Flexibility – ads may be placed in interest sections for maximum exposure

Although newspapers have begun to use 'broadsheet' and 'tabloid' (compact) formats presumably for great convenience (and for greater sales) and to save on printing costs, they continue to have great flexibility in the size of the ads available to advertising. The advertising industry in the United States, for example, has adopted a revised 'standardized advertising unit' (SAU) for newspapers, which enables advertisers to purchase 56 standard sizes to fit their advertising needs (*New York Times* 2007). Under this system, advertisers prepare their ads and purchase space according to column widths (six of them) and depths in inches. Newspapers in the UK experimented with the switch with limited success, while most newspapers on the European continent still use the physical broadsheet format. Formats vary from country to country, though there is a tendency to use the popular smaller tabloid version in such countries as Brazil, South Africa and Poland (Clark 2006). Each offers the enhanced possibility of placing ads in a publication that is physically easier to read.

Detailed and current copy

Newspapers are ideal for explaining in detail the attributes of a product or service. This may be especially helpful in trade or B2B advertising, where detailed copy can highlight important product information and give extensive editorial on its value. Newspapers offer up-to-date news and information, both online and offline.

Some weaknesses in using newspapers in the media plan

Declining and ageing readership

As discussed earlier, newspaper readership is trending downwards and by all indications will continue to do so. Readership has regressed aggressively during the last generation: just ask any student! Most newspaper readerships now make up a 45+ demographic and older, and the most coveted group of consumers with the greatest buying power, 28–44-year-olds, read newspapers, and print in general, far less frequently than ever before.

Poor reproduction quality

Despite advances in newspaper production quality over the last two decades, the relative production quality of newspapers remains poor. This is due to the nature of the coarse paper stock and the short lead times. Generally, the use of colour in newspapers cannot enhance the product's appearance in the ways that magazines or television can.

Low selectivity and low impact

Newspapers have enjoyed mass appeal from their beginnings in the 17th century. They appeal to a broad cross-section of the population, but only on the local level are they able to reach a

Scholars' paper 8.2 Newspapers as media efficacy

Danaher, P. and Rossiter, J. (2011) Comparing perceptions of marketing communication channels, *European Journal of Marketing*, 45(1/2), 6-42

Danaher and Rossiter's research demonstrates that clutter in newspapers is less bothersome to newspaper readers than clutter in other media. Their research concluded that print ads in newspapers are less intrusive than other forms of media (such as the 'interruptive' quality of radio and TV) and that consumers who read newspapers feel that engagement with the traditional print medium is a good use of their time.

selective audience as efficiently as magazines. By and large, media specialists consider newspaper to be a mediocre counter to television and magazines in *selectivity*. Use of the medium makes it difficult for marketers to reach a narrowly defined segment of the market.

Clutter

As with other media, newspapers suffer from an overabundance of messages directed at the consumer. Images in newspapers are inferior in quality and less impressive, exacerbating the clutter of many advertisements. This is not peculiar to newspapers, however; some research (Danaher and Rossiter 2011; Eliot and Speck 1998) suggests that the advertising clutter found in the newspaper medium is less annoying than that from commercial messages found either on television or online.

Electronic media

The television and radio industries make up the electronic (broadcast) medium. Changes are underway in electronic media to remain competitive with digital and alternative technologies, yet television advertising is not in a direct head-to-head competition with online, smartphone or pad/pod technology. Instead, the television, and to a lesser extent radio, industries are cross-platforming with digital technology to have a profound impact on the way entertainment and programming enter into households worldwide. Radio also finds renewed strength in satellite and online streaming content. Television and radio continue to be pervasive and are important components of a media plan because of their impact and ability to target specific audiences.

Radio

Radio is often referred to as the 'theatre of the mind' because good radio use of a commercial message constructs a unique picture in each listener's mind. When an advertiser creates visual messages (as in television), it creates an image so that a consumer will connect with the product, and so that the focus is on the image of the product. When radio is used effectively, each consumer digests the words, sounds and music of the advertising and paints his or her *own* mental picture – resulting in an emotional consumer-centric association that can be quite meaningful for the marketer and consumer (Peacock 2007: para. 14). *Imagery transfer* (Arens et al. 2011) is the process by which visual elements of a television commercial are associated in the consumer's mind by using a similar audio track in its radio counterpart.

Radio listeners are an important audience for marketers and radio listening is a significant source of consumer information in many parts of the world. Radio listening has been enhanced by streaming live programming with the use of a broadband connection and satellite and digital transmission (for car and home), though the latter is generally subscription-based programming, fed by satellite (thereby making it 'global') and generally not available at this time for commercial messaging.

Radio continues to have strong potential as an advertising medium worldwide, performing the second best globally compared to television (Nielsen Company 2011: 11). In Turkey, as one example, with a population of some 72 million, radios proliferate in the mediascape from cosmopolitan Istanbul to the far reaches of the eastern borders, with hundreds of radio stations in the traditional sense, live streams online and live internet radio feeds, some commercial-free, but many available as advertising vehicles. Turkey boasts an impressive 1,110 radio broadcast stations (36 national, 102 regional, 962 local), with radio sets in 19.4 million households (European Journalism Centre 2010).

Commercial radio advertising is primarily a local medium. Local adspend in effect is a function of local retail sales and must compete with newspapers, business directories, flyers and sales brochures, all of which face similar challenges in the increasingly digitally driven media environment. But reach of radio is generally very strong into local communities. It is a low-cost provider, flexible enough with its myriad formats to appeal to a variety of audiences within local markets.

ViewPoint 8.2 Nike in China - branding sports

Nike is known for its powerful branding and striking advertising campaigns that use sports figures from around the world. An effort in 2011 created by the Shanghai branch of the Wieden + Kennedy Agency calls on the viewer to 'use sports' ('Use sports' (*用运动* - Yòng yùndòng) to do great things. The latest commercial for the Chinese market highlights small vignettes of diving, basketball, cycling, swimming, boxing, football, gymnastics, martial arts and tennis, all with a backdrop of megaphone voice-overs that egg on the viewer to 'use sports' to get what you want, to move on, make friends, to meet your heroes, to do great things, to fail. . . . and to win. 'Because sports will never say you can't' is the tag to the final shot featuring the tennis serve of Li Na, the up and coming Chinese tennis star. Large out-of-home posters featuring athletes in motion supplement the broadcast campaign.

The 60-second television commercial is another in a long line of Nike television TV ads that attempt to inspire us to achieve bigger and better things. But Nike has not always had success in its Chinese advertising campaigns. In 2004 as a result of consumer outrage, the Chinese government banned a Nike television ad ('Chamber of Fear') featuring basketball superstar LeBron James battling a Kung Fu Master. Cultural insensitivity and offensiveness on the part of the advertiser were cited as the primary reasons for the ban (Li and Shooshtari 2007).

Wieden + Kennedy were not the agency of record in 2004, but as Nike's agency, W + K has been cognisant of the impact of Western advertising practices on traditional Chinese culture.

Source: Based on Gilroy (2011); www.wkshanghai.com; Li and Shooshtari (2007)

Question

Name another brand that utilises an active lifestyle approach as the foundation of its campaigns.

Task

Think about the advertising campaigns you have noticed lately. Come up with two or three among them that you believe could benefit from a Nike-style approach to branding. How would you revitalise these campaigns using Nike as a model?

Some strengths in using radio in the media plan

Ability to reach a segmented audience through an array of formats and day parts

Radio is highly selective and highly segmented by offering a format for virtually every demographic. Radio formats range from talk to news, from adult contemporary to classical, country, jazz, pop and alternative, just to name a few. Another popular radio format in primarily urban centres provides native language broadcasts for ethnic populations (Greeks in Melbourne, Italians in Toronto and Arabs in Paris) and in this way offers good segmented demographic targeting opportunities for the advertiser.

Considerably less expensive than other advertising media

Radio commercials require very little in terms of production, and thus are inexpensive and relatively easy to produce. As a result, the radio medium can be extremely cost efficient once a company decides to use radio as a vehicle by which to relay its message. A simple script can be read by an official announcer (or narrator) or even pre-recorded as a message that can then be broadcast multiple times by the station. Radio commercials can also be produced quickly and quite inexpensively.

The low cost of radio media placement means that advertisers can use the medium to build reach and frequency into a media schedule within a local market. They can advertise more

Exhibit 8.3 The 'shocking' Howard Stern Show

Howard Stern, the original American 'shock jock', was an exception to the low cost of advertising on radio. His raucous and controversial network radio talk show in the 1990s was able to command high advertising fees due to the millions of loyal listeners. The Howard Stern Show now plays on SiriusXM satellite radio channels Howard 100 and 101 and reaches millions of loyal listeners every week.

Source: Getty Images

often and on more stations that offer a variety of formats to reach a wider demographic within any given transmission area.

Short lead times and spot versatility

At a local level, radio requires short lead times. This may benefit the advertiser in any number of ways. Radio scheduling can be flexible and may shift from day to day to be reorganised to accommodate a commercial product or event message, and a particular time frame. Radio allows the ability to change copy if needed, since the lead time for scheduling might be a matter of a day or two. Advertisers may change their messages or even cancel the radio spot, if necessary, often a few hours before the message airs, a feat not possible with other media.

In addition, radio possesses unique advertising possibilities related to divisions of the day. The heaviest radio use occurs during drive times ('commuting times' or when listeners are in the automobile for commuting purposes) and broken down into *day parts* – morning drive, daytime, afternoon drive, night times and late night. Radio bases its rates for advertising on these day parts, which vary depending on the number of listeners.

A forum for local testimonials

Because radio is such a localised medium, it may make use of local personalities, sports or public figures to broadcast its messages. Testimonials by recognisable local personalities would not necessarily play on the larger regional or national stage, but tie in nicely at the local level. Where radio is most successful in terms of recognition and cost efficiency, testimonials offer a listening intimacy and familiarity that may have great success.

Some weaknesses in using radio in the media plan

Background noise

In many ways, radio listening serves as background to other things we do. Listeners do laundry, clean the apartment or are distracted by some other means while listening to the radio. The radio medium often does not have our full attention, which results in only half-heard commercials and fleeting messages.

Scholars' paper 8.3 Radio 'imagery'

Miller, D.W. and Marks, L.J. (1997) The effects of imagery-evoking radio advertising strategies on affective responses, *Psychology & Marketing*, 14(4), 337–60

The authors discuss the relative effectiveness of imagery-evoking radio advertising strategies in eliciting affective responses from the consumer. They found during the course of their research that sound effects and other audio stimuli point suggestively towards 'closely related structures' (meaning perceptual structures) and activate structures containing visual information, creating vivid multi-sensory (not just aural) imagery in the consumer. Their study proposes that the auditory medium of the radio is particularly well suited for imagery evocation and could generate positive feelings and favourable responses to the advertising message.

One-dimensional, unable to utilise visual images

Despite the contention that the medium has the capacity to conjure visual images, radio generates low attention precisely because of its lack of visuals. Its primary reliance on audio alone makes it a rather one-dimensional medium. Since this is only an aural medium, it is 'in one ear and out the other', as it were.

Difficult to reach a mass audience

We mentioned above the well-segmented advantage of the radio medium. This segmentation also works to radio's disadvantage, for to garner mass reach for their message, advertisers would have to make multiple buys on many different stations to cover the market effectively.

Television

Scholars have made much of the importance of *visuality* in forming views of contemporary society (Barnouw 1975; Barthes 1957; Fiske 1987; Schroeder 2002). We are increasingly a visual culture and visual communication in all its forms has become the predominant mode of communication. Broadcast television viewing habits are continuing to evolve around the world, as consumers adopt an increasingly diverse range of channels to access broadcast material.

France's television environment serves as a good case study for the developed world. The number of households in France equipped with at least one television set is near saturation (98.5% of all French households, c. 27 million in 2009) and the number of multi-set households has increased sharply in recent years, from 40.4% in 2000 to 49.5% in 2008 (Conseil Supérieur de l'audio-visuel 2009).

The six historical general channel operators of TF1, France 2, France 3, France 5, M6 and Arte are now in competition with a host of other free national and local channels, public and private terrestrial channels (both generalist and theme based), and cable and satellite hookups. This structural model typifies the television industry in developed nations and it is evolving along similar paths in developing nations as well.

Television advertising garners much of media advertising revenue and is by far the world's largest advertising medium with a 65.1% share in 2011 (Nielsen Company 2011: 11). Research suggests (Sharp et al. 2009) that advertising-supported television will remain the pre-eminent mode of delivery of marketing communications messages, despite the changes occurring in the industry, including the erosion of larger audience numbers to smaller net audiences and into more channels, as is the case in France and elsewhere.

Generally, the business of television channel production and broadcasting in France, as elsewhere, consists of (i) defining the particular editorial line of the television channel, (ii) acquiring from third parties or producing audio-visual content (movies, series, documentaries, sporting events, etc.) consistent with the editorial line, and (iii) creating a programming schedule consistent with the channel's objectives and editorial line.

Premium and speciality channels are also on offer in France. The premium channels furnish content that is exclusive and recent, and involve investment or major production resources on the part of the producer and broadcaster. The speciality channels offer programming focused on a specific theme (sports, lifestyle, music, entertainment, etc.) and are defined either by a particular target group (such as young viewers) or by programme type (movies, documentaries, etc.). Several channels can thus coexist within the same speciality and differ from each other by their editorial line, their programming or the intended target group. The premium and speciality channels are *bundled* into channel packages to constitute pay-TV offerings. In lieu of advertising spend, these channels require a subscription base or tax incentive to carry programming (as do publicly funded service broadcasters such as the BBC in the UK). Some premium and speciality channels may be available for sponsorships.

Satellite broadcasting, ASDL broadcasting with access to interactive services, digital terrestrial television (DTTV) and cable television comprise some of the recent TV broadcasting capabilities.

Some strengths in using television in the media plan

High-impact visuals

Television has the ability to make a strong impact, a feature so strong that for some consumers the television serves as the equivalent of a personal salesperson. It is an absorbing and captivating medium with which people have a passive relationship. It is the ideal media vehicle for creativity and dynamic impact, especially when an advertiser desires to demonstrate the look of a product or service or create an editorial environment in which a product or service is perceived.

High-reach medium

Television makes it possible to reach large, unsegmented audiences, as almost everyone has access to a television, whether it is in the home, in pubs and bars, in airports or even on transport. The majority of consumers spend more time in front of the television watching news, entertainment, films and other programming than any other form of media (WARC 2010).

Increasing audience selectivity

In many countries, television has been segmenting into diverse programming that appeals to diverse viewing publics. This decades-long trend reflects the changes in demographics and psychographics around the world. Programming has fragmented and offers many speciality channels for different tastes. The increase in the number of channels allows the advertiser to target selectively – sports enthusiasts, film buffs, music lovers, young viewers, news and documentaries devotees and so on.

Scholars' paper 8.4 TV and the selling of culture

Manghanis S. and Fukukawa, K. (2007) The business of visual culture, *Electronic Journal of Radical Organization Theory*, 10(1), 1-16

The authors suggest that we incorporate an interdisciplinary exchange about visual culture that includes the world of business and give several reasons why this line of research has not been more fully explored. The fields of art and science, they argue, have wholly embraced the importance of visual culture for the contemporary world, and the same should be embraced within the field of business and management to fully understand contemporary culture.

Considerably less expensive cost per thousand than other advertising media

Television is considered a cost-efficient medium because advertisers can reach thousands of viewers at a relatively low cost. Thus, the cost per thousand exposure per viewer, a point discussed in Chapter 11, is favourable for an advertiser with a substantial budget for television placement. Marketers that sell and market products/services that appeal to large audiences find television to be cost effective as a media tool.

Some weaknesses in using television in the media plan

Clutter

Clutter on TV and other forms of advertising media have affected commercial advertising for quite some time (Ross 1998; Webb and Ray 1984). Advertisers have tried to find ever-increasing creative and innovative (and economic) ways to break through the crowded field of commercial messages to reach consumers. Added incentives for the consumer to turn away from the TV message include the remote control at the ready and the all-too-frequent commercial messages (varies from country to country) inserted during programming.

High initial production cost

Television advertising is cost efficient because it allows network advertisers to reach a mass audience, including various kinds of stakeholders, with a single exposure. But that doesn't mean it's inexpensive. Director's fees, creative/labour fees, editing/completion costs, fees for talent, if used, and music are some of the many factors that add up to high production costs (local TV commercial production for a local TV spot may be considerably less expensive). Buying TV airtime and space in highly rated programming slots may be costly as well (see Chapter 11).

Short-lived messages

The television message is short-lived in the mind of the consumer. Multiple studies (Krugman 1977; Malaviya 2007; Mulligan 1998; Nordhielm 2002) have suggested that consumers do not recall the commercial messages they saw a brief period after they have seen them. For maximum recall, the message has to be reinforced with multiple showings and this can be a costly venture.

Fragmentation and segmentation

Even though consumer market fragmentation has created more targeted opportunities for the advertiser, segmentation into smaller targeted audiences has generally resulted in diminished advertising revenue for the main networks and channels. TV is not the mass medium it used to be – the more the audience segments, the less television's ability to deliver the traditional mass numbers it once could.

ViewPoint 8.3 Cable television - branding with Latino cool

Cablevision Systems Corporation is a leading US telecommunications, media and entertainment company. Its Optimum®-branded communications services include digital cable TV, high-speed broadband internet and digital voice residential and businesses services. In 2007, Cablevision had low penetration and few sales in New York metropolitan area's rich tapestry of multicultural markets.

Enter the GlobalWorks Group™, a New York-based firm specialising in global branding and multicultural marketing and communications. GlobalWorks had the task of making the Optimum brand stand out, and appeal to a younger, more urban audience. GlobalWorks realised that these are savvy consumers, people who wouldn't be convinced by a stereotypical appeal to cultural icons. Hispanic and African-American consumers also had a profoundly negative view of the 'cable company' that had to be overcome.

The firm needed to find a way to make the Optimum brand stand out, and appeal to a younger, more urban audience.

Since music is a huge part of Hispanic and African-American culture, GlobalWorks took the strategic media approach of using local television spot advertising with a musical 'cultural cool attitude' to reach the local communities. By 2007, Latino culture and music were starting to cross over into mainstream America and elsewhere. Reggaeton artists like Daddy Yankee were scoring hits with urban audiences, Shakira and Salma Hayek were everywhere. Being Latino was suddenly cool. GlobalWorks responded by placing entertaining TV commercials to target the Latino and African-American viewer.

With the Reggaeton Beach commercials, the Optimum brand scored a direct hit with audiences across the New York metropolitan area. They wrote the Reggaeton song in both English and Spanish, weaving in the classic media direct response tactics of repetition and memorability. They wove a toll-free or freephone number into the music itself, because according to Yuri Radzievksy, founder of GlobalWorks, 'We found that it sticks in the mind like glue.'

The combination of humour, a memorable song and that intangible 'cool' quality of Latino culture proved to be a major success. Suddenly the Optimum brand was hip and funny, without being exclusionary. Cablevision operates the nation's single largest cable cluster, passing in 2011 more than 5 million households and businesses in the New York metropolitan area.

Source: www.globalworks.com; www.cablevision.com

Question

How did the target audience's love of music determine the campaign's direction?

Task

Choose a group of people with whom you associate and identify. Describe in detail the musical tastes of your group and how these define you as a group.

Out-of-home media

Traditional out-of-home (OOH) media advertising is a broad concept that is no longer relegated to large, static billboards on the side of freeways and motorways.

The *traditional outdoor* format includes outdoor billboard (alternatively called 'hoarding' in parts of the world) advertising, but extends beyond that with a number of innovative and forward-looking ideas ranging from street furniture (including public shelters and benches), giant posters, digital transport billboards and aerials (blimps) to full advertisements gracing the metro cars of subway systems, smaller mobile vehicles, such as pedestrian rickshaw vans and *bikevertising*, among others. *Place-based* out-of-home includes spectaculars (3D, digital, 'looking back' media) in and out of stadia, and covers and wraps (both high-quality, glossy

Exhibit 8.4 Scaffolding wrap advertising
An example of large application building or scaffolding wrap advertising, that is useful for safe construction works and delivers a marketing message as well.
Source: Alamy Images

paper wrapped around a publication and larger building wraps used for structures undergoing refurbishment (see Exhibit 8.4), in-flight and airports, and roadside stops, among others. Some have suggested (Ketcham 2010; Breva Franch 2010) that neither form of out-of-home advertising has not yet been fully exploited as an effective advertising medium.

One of the largest international out-of-home-media firms, the Ströer Group in Germany, specialises in poster media (including giant posters), directional media, digital info screens, street furniture, and station and transport media, and has its own research development centre to develop effective and innovative communication to accommodate a wide range of advertising forms and strategies (www.stroeer.com). Clear Channel Outdoor (www.clearchanneloutdoor.com) of Clear Channel Communications (USA) has integrated digital into its outdoor billboards, so that static messages resemble at first standard printed billboards but allow advertisers to change messages throughout the day. Integrated digital allows the advertiser to adapt to the market and quickly customise programmes accordingly. Both of these firms' out-of-home offerings are indicative of the versatility and the increasing number of alternative choices that bring outdoor advertising to the consumer.

Some strengths in using out-of-home in the media plan

Outdoor is accessible and delivers excellent reach and frequency

Outdoor advertising can be placed in any locale and on any facade that happens to be in that space. In this sense, it gains access potentially to all kinds of audiences and can deliver good reach. It serves as a kind of 'nowhere to run, nowhere to hide' medium with respect to the customer, for it can't be turned off, zipped through or clicked away from as can other forms of media.

Outdoor offers geographic and demographic flexibility

Messages on outdoor vehicles can be placed strategically to target any audience by geographic, demographic or lifestyle distinction. Where permissible, outdoor can reach country music fans attending the annual Jamboree in the Hills (Ohio, USA) country music festival, or classical enthusiasts at the Bayreuth Festival held each year in Germany to celebrate the music dramas of Richard Wagner.

Outdoor can be relatively low in cost

Traditional outdoor advertising offers the lowest relative cost in reaching the customer of any of the traditional media and is thus very efficient as an advertising medium. Rates vary depending on the market and also on the type of outdoor vehicle to be employed.

Some weaknesses in using out-of-home in the media plan

Short exposure time and least noticeable as a message

Even though outdoor provides great potential access to a variety of audiences, by the same token, using outdoor runs the risk of having an audience never see the advertising message. The contrary argument to exposure is that outdoor delivers fleeting messages, which pass customers by rather quickly, whether they are walking, in a car, on a train or on a moped.

Lengthy, complicated messages cannot be conveyed with the use of out-of-home media. Generally, the customer views the outdoor message somewhere 'in transit'; the outdoor message then perhaps serves best as reinforcement to an already established integrated campaign.

Outdoor may be perceived as visual or environmental pollution

The perception is that messages displayed on an outdoor vehicle may actually detract from the value of that locale, whether it is the local municipality or on a regional or national level. Some countries, such as Denmark and the Netherlands, ban roadside billboard advertising in part for this reason. Increasingly local residents raise objections to the presence of an outdoor message in their midst. Detractors point to its visual and other sensory pollution. The Queensland (Australia) government's Department of Main Roads has a comprehensive policy on roadside regulations as a safety issue – and suggests that *digital* billboards capture and hold a person's attention at the expense of the primary task performance (Wachtel 2009), i.e. driving. These factors may contribute to a negative perception of the brand advertised.

Outdoor is difficult to measure and control

It is difficult to measure audience statistics using out-of-home advertising. Those customers that notice an ad as it passes by (as on a taxi), or notice ads as they pass them (walking through Hong Kong) are difficult to measure and therefore difficult to justify at times in a media plan.

Direct mail

Simply put, advertising sent directly to consumers through a mail delivery service (including email) is called direct mail advertising. It is also sometimes referred to as junk mail or ad mail and makes up a large portion of postal services around the world. It includes advertising postcards, sales letters, mailers, circulars, samples, catalogues, and other merchandising materials for commercial purposes. Direct mail can be a high-profit, low-cost advertising medium and is the most heavily used of all advertising media.

ViewPoint 8.4 Reaching Aussie teens about cyberbullying

In 2011, the Australia Communications and Media Authority (ACMA) launched the first ever government out-of-home media campaign to raise awareness about digital reputation, sexting, geolocation and cyberbullying among teenagers in Sydney. The 250 vivid, eye-catching posters were part of a short campaign on Sydney bus shelters and student hubs to raise awareness of online safety issues affecting teens. The ACMA tested out-of-home media as another way of reaching teens after feedback from the Department of Broadband, Communications and the Digital Economy's Youth Advisory Group and recent research from Brain Science indicated that teenagers pay more attention to outdoor fixtures than originally thought. The ACMA's strategic intent was to make communications and media work in Australia's public interest.

The creative artwork used common text-language abbreviations, acronyms and symbols to draw attention to messages around digital reputation, sexting, geolocation and cyberbullying. Solid, bright fluorescent inks also provided extreme high contrast and visibility to maximise the chance of catching the eye of the public, and with a contrasting key message in strong bold typeface, the outdoor displays were high impact, and offered more interest for individuals waiting for their daily commute.

Chris Chapman, ACMA chairman, justified the use of complementary out-of-home media by stating that the teen market is extremely tech savvy so 'we incorporated the internet, social media and technical interactivity'. Each poster included a QR code linking it directly to information about each of the issues on the ACMA's cybersmart website (teens could gain access by using their cameraphones) and an extensive social media campaign complemented the outdoor and online presence.

Source: Based on http://mumbrella.com.au; www.acma.gov.au

Question

What other traditional media may appeal to young consumers? Why?

Task

Find three examples of out-of-home advertising media that promote ethical issues.

Some strengths in using direct mail in the media plan

Efficiency

Direct mail is delivered directly to the desired target consumer. For this reason, it avoids advertising wastage and offers value for money. In many places, direct mail can target specified market characteristics by using postal code targeting, home owner lists, moving home and new mortgage lists, and so on. It can be a cost-efficient option particularly for business start-ups and small business owners.

Useful response mechanism

Direct mail is an immediate response medium. It allows the advertiser to incorporate response mechanisms into mailings and thereby track and fine-tune strategies for the right consumer. It is especially useful for the small business owner without large budgets and sophisticated tracking capabilities. The small business can compile its own database from direct mail responses.

Some weaknesses in using direct mail in the media plan

Poor image

Direct mail, often referred to derisively as 'junk mail', has a poor image and is generally perceived as a medium that leaves the fatigued consumer 'with floods of literature falling out of newspapers and on to your doorstep' (McElhatton 2004: para. 8). The use of direct mail may reflect poorly on the product or service which uses the medium.

High cost

The largest single expense of direct mailing is postage, which can account for one-third of the total cost of a direct mail campaign. Other costs include designing, writing, printing and packing the direct mail piece, and buying mailing lists. A four-colour postcard, the most common form of direct marketing, is the least expensive to mail but other forms of direct marketing such as mailers, brochures, newsletters and catalogues can raise costs considerably and make the expense of reaching the target consumer exorbitant.

Alternative advertising media

As traditional media grow and transform, further innovative measures have taken to print. Tunnel advertising, sugar packet advertising, local pay TV, product placement in television shows and films, escalator handrail advertising, guerrilla street teams, large lenticulars, passenger straps in public transportation systems, event sponsorship, ambient advertising and micro-magazine advertising are just a few of the marketing vehicles that serve as alternatives to traditional advertising media and vie for consumer attention.

Generally, the alternative media rely on a number of strategies: the unanticipated event, the shock of the unexpected, the very personal, tailor-made promotional piece or the casual personal sale on the street. Alternative media rely on catching consumers unawares and influencing their decision making when they are at their most vulnerable.

Exhibit 8.5 Abe's Penny, a micro-magazine

Abe's Penny, a micro-magazine based in Brooklyn, New York, has used innovative ways to maximise the efficiency of the traditional print medium. Offset printed on double-thick matte card stock, each issue dispenses art and literature while becoming a collectible, temporal object. A different photographer and writer collaborate each month on weekly postcards mailed to readers, one card at a time. It is a new product that 'you anticipate, you touch and feel, it comes to you, it seeks your address and knocks on your door, and then you sit back, relax, grab that glass of wine or cup of coffee and get engaged in an experience of the most "me-time" that can ever exist'.

Source: Abe's Penny

These alternative media utilise innovative and spirited strategies to attract consumer attention in the otherwise saturated consumer environment.

Chapter summary

In order to help consolidate your understanding of traditional media, here are the key points summarised against each of the learning objectives.

List and classify the traditional advertising media

Traditional advertising media are the established media channels through which commercial messages have historically been communicated. Traditional advertising media include print, electronic (radio and television), out-of-home, direct mail and an increasing number of alternative media.

Explain the basic concepts used in advertising media

The term advertising media includes all the media vehicles or channels that carry advertising messages to the prospective consumer audience. Reach and frequency are related concepts that in combination attempt to optimise the total number of people exposed to a message, which is the desired result of most media plans. Addressable media deliver customised marketing messages to prospects or current customers, while interactive media are two-way or multiple-generated media that allow companies and consumers to interact with each other.

Outline the structure of print and electronic media

Print and electronic (broadcast) media are the historically recognisable standard channels of the advertising industry. Print media contain messages printed on any kind of surface and are displayed for the consuming public; broadcast includes radio and TV, or communication characterised by the use of technology (including the internet, which is discussed in the next chapter).

Describe the uses of out-of-home media, direct mail and alternative media

Out-of-home media and direct mail offer some distinctive benefits to the advertiser, such as targeting the consumer geographically and placing the message in an environment with direct consumer attention (such as in transit advertising for out-of-home and in the home with direct mail). Alternative media offer a number of options to target the consumer in many places heretofore not considered viable, such as literally in the street (guerrilla) or in the skies (blimp) or non-traditional outdoor advertising locales.

Consider the relative weaknesses and strengths in using traditional media

Each of the media has its advantages and disadvantages in delivering specific audiences effectively. Understanding the nature of each medium and its limitations is essential for the media planner. Appreciating the relative communication strengths of each medium enhances the effectiveness of the media plan as a whole.

Review questions

1. With regard to the Finnair minicase set out at the start of this chapter, how would you propose they use advertising to reach their target audiences and which media would you recommend they use to reach them?
2. What is the essential difference between addressable and interactive media?
3. Explain the potential value of a controlled-circulation publication for an advertiser.
4. Choose a magazine or newspaper advertisement that you find interesting. Analyse the print ad with regards to the advantages the medium offers the advertiser; now analyse the same print ad from the drawbacks the medium presents to the advertiser.
5. Describe the radio station (online or otherwise) format you enjoy the most. Write a short presentation describing in detail the perceived demographics and psychographics of those who listen to this radio station format.
6. Discuss some ways in which the print media are adapting to multi-platforms for better coverage.
7. Explain the benefits and the disadvantages to the advertiser of television audience fragmentation.
8. Prepare a report explaining how cross-media campaigns are using traditional and newer media to create value for brands.
9. Give reasons why transit advertising might meet with great success.
10. Make notes about some of the innovations in out-of-home, alternative and supplementary media of which you are aware.

Chapter references

Appel, V. (1987) Editorial environment and advertising effectiveness, *Journal of Advertising Research*, 27 (4), 11–16

Arens, W.F., Weigold, M.F. and Arens, C. (2011) *Contemporary Advertising*, 13th edn. Boston: McGraw-Hill Irwin

Barnouw, E. (1975) *Tube of Plenty: The Evolution of American Television*. New York: Oxford University Press

Barthes, R. (1957) *Mythologies*. Paris: Éditions du Seuil

Breva Franch, E. (2010) El medio exterior, más allá de una decisión intuitiva [The media environment: more than just intuitive], *Zer: Revista De Estudios De Commicacion, 15*(29), 271–88

Bronner, F. and Neijens, P. (2006) Audience experiences of media context and embedded advertising: a comparison of eight media, *International Journal of Market Research*, 48(1), 81–100

Burns, A.C., Biswas, A. and Babin, L.A. (1993) The operation of visual imagery as a mediator of advertising effects, *Journal of Advertising*, 22(2), 71–85

Chappuis, B., Gaffey, B. and Parvizi, P. (2011) Are your customers becoming digital junkies? Retrieved from http://www.mckinseyquarterly.com/Media_Entertainment/Are_your_customers_becoming_digital_junkies_2839

CIO Magazine (2011) Retrieved from http://www.cio.co.uk

Clark, R. (2006) Watch out, broadsheet: tabloid power is gonna get your Mama, 17 February, retrieved from http://www.poynter.org

Conseil Supérieur de l'audio-visuel (2009) *Conseil supérieur de l'audio-visuel annual report 2009*. Retrieved from http://www.csa.fr/upload/publication/web_Plaquette_anglais.pdf

Dahlén, M. (2005) The medium as a contextual cue, *Journal of Advertising*, 34(3), 89–98

Danaher, P. and Rossiter, J. (2011) Comparing perceptions of marketing communication channels, *European Journal of Marketing*, 45(1/2), 6–42. doi:10.1108/03090561111095586

De Pelsmacker, P., Geuens, M. and Vermeir, I. (2004) The importance of media planning, ad likeability and brand position for ad and brand recognition in radio spots, *International Journal of Market Research*, 46(4), 465–78

Eliot, M.T. and Speck, P.S. (1998) Consumer perceptions of advertising clutter and its impact across various media, *Journal of Advertising Research*, 38(1), 29–41

European Journalism Centre (2010) *Media landscape: Turkey*. Retrieved from http://www.ejc.net/media-landscape/article/turkey/#141

Fiske, J. (1987) *Television Culture*. London: Methuen & Co. Ltd

Fortunati, L. and Sarrica, M. (2011) Insights from journalists on the future of the press, *Communications: The European Journal of Communication Research*, 36(2), 123–46. doi:10.1515/COMM.2011.007

Franklin, B. (2008) The future of newspapers, *Journalism Studies*, 9(5), 630–41. doi: 10.1080/14616700802280307

Gilroy, D. (2011) Nike China: 'Use sports' campaign. Retrieved from http://advertising.chinasmack.com/2011/nike-china-use-sports-campaign.html

Ives, N. (2011) Magazine of the year, *Advertising Age*, 82(36), 20

Kamin, H. (1978) Advertising reach and frequency, *Journal of Advertising Research*, 18(1), 21

Ketcham, B. (2010) Not staying in 'place', *MediaWeek*, 20(18), 36

Krugman, H.E. (1975) What makes advertising effective? *Harvard Business Review*, 53(2), 96–103

Krugman, H.E. (1977) Memory without recall, exposure without perception, *Journal of Advertising Research*, 17(4), 7–12

Layton, C. (2008) Bridging the abyss, *American Journalism Review*, 30(3), 34–9

Li, F. and Shooshtari, N.H. (2007) Multinational corporations' controversial ad campaigns in China – lessons from Nike and Toyota, *Advertising & Society Review*, 8(1), 1–23. Retrieved from http://www.business.umt.edu/Libraries/Fengru_Li/Multinational_Corporations.sflb.ashx

Littbarski, P. (2011) *Finnair nimmt Kurs auf die größte Stadt der Welt* (Finnair is heading for the biggest cities in the world) (web log comment), 11 October, retrieved from http://litti.finnair.uxi.fi/

Low, E. (2011) Finnair begins ad push, retrieved from http://marketing-interactive.com/news/25679

McCarthy. E. (1960) *Basic Marketing: A Managerial Approach*. Homewood, IL: R.D. Irwin

McElhatton, N. (2004, June 11) Direct 'needs to be rebranded' to fight poor image. Retrieved from www.brandrepublic.com/news/213436

McPheters & Company (2011) iMonitor™ releases list of top 10 best newspaper apps (press release). Retrieved from http://www.mcpheters.com

Malaviya, P. (2007) The moderating influence of advertising context on ad repetition effects: the role of amount and type of elaboration, *Journal of Consumer Research*, 34(1), 32–40

Malthouse, E.C. and Calder, B.J. (2010) Media placement versus advertising execution, *International Journal of Market Research*, 52(2), 217–30

Manghani, S. and Fukukawa, K. (2007) The business of visual culture, *Electronic Journal of Radical Organization Theory*, 10(1), 1–16

Metro International SA (2007) *Metro International SA annual report 2006*, retrieved from http://hugin.info/132142/R/1125327/208539.pdf

Miller, D.W. and Marks, L. J. (1997) The effects of imagery-evoking radio advertising strategies on affective responses, *Psychology & Marketing*, 14(4), 337–60

Mulligan, N.W. (1998) The role of attention during encoding in implicit and explicit memory, *Journal of Experimental Psychology: Learning, Memory, and Cognition*, 24(1), 27–47

New York Times (2007) Standard advertising units, retrieved from http://www.nytadvertising.com/was/files/others/NYT_Broadsheet.pdf

Ng, E. (2010) Finnair's branding takes off with local hero, 19 November, retrieved from http://www.marketing-interactive.com/news/23215

The Nielsen Company (2011) *Global AdView pulse lite* (brochure), retrieved from http://www.nielsenglobaladview.com

Nordhielm, C.L. (2002) The influence of level of processing on advertising repetition effects, *Journal of Consumer Research*, *29*(3), 371–82

Nyilsy, G., Whitehall King, K. and Reid, L.N. (2011) Checking the pulse of print media, *Journal of Advertising Research*, 51, 167–75. doi: 10.2501/jar-51-1-167-181

Patterson, T.E. (2007) The decline of newspapers: the local story, *Nieman Reports*, 61(4), 33–4

Peacock, J. (2007) Radio and the consumer's mind, *Admap*, 485, retrieved from http://www.warc.com/Admap

Pearce, F. (2009) Airline's claim that flying to Asia via Helsinki is green vanishes into Finnair, 8 October, retrieved from http://www.guardian.co.uk/environment/2009/oct/08/finnair-carbon-emissions

Philpot, P. (2002) Accessible ABCs make media planning a cinch, *Marketing Week*, 25(34), 16

PressGazette (2011) New editor for Kerrang! as rock mag hits 30, 7 June, retrieved from http://pressgazette.co.uk/story.asp?storycode=47241

Ross, C. (1998) Study: commercials battle all-time-high TV clutter, *Advertising Age*, 69(50), 4

Schroeder, J. (2002) *Visual Consumption*. London: Routledge

Schwartz, M. (2005) Newspaper circulation woes offset by internet gains, 12 December, retrieved from www.btobonline.com

Sharp, B., Beal, V. and Collins, M. (2009) Television: back to the future, *Journal of Advertising Research*, 49(2), 211–19

Shaved, S., Vargas, P. and Lowrey, P. (2004) Exploring the role of memory for self-selected ad experiences: are some advertising media better liked than others? *Psychology & Marketing*, 21(12), 1011–32. doi: 10310002/mar.20035

Tillinghast, W.A. (1981) Declining newspaper readership: impact of region and urbanization, *Journalism Quarterly*, 58(1), 14–50

Wachtel, J. (2009) Safety impacts of the emerging digital display technology for outdoor advertising signs, retrieved from http://www.veridian-group.com/

WARC (2010) Media time use 2010, retrieved from http://www.warc.com

Watling, M. (2011) Newspaper map: the coolest way to visually surf newspapers [10,000 Words: Where Journalism and Technology Meet], 7 June, retrieved from www.mediabistro.com/10000words

Webb, P.H. and Ray, M.L. (1984) Effects of TV clutter, *Journal of Advertising Research*, 24(4), 19–24

World Association of Newspapers and News Publishers (2010) World press trends 2010 [data file], retrieved from http://www.wan-press.org/worldpresstrends2010/articles.php?id=66

Chapter 9

Digital media and emerging technologies

New forms of digital communications are quickly taking centre stage in the advertising industry. Online, mobile, social media, in-game advertising and a host of other media are being used in new and innovative ways to target the consumer audience. The changes occurring with the use of technology in advertising media are fluid and often transform the very basis of advertising and its relation to market economies. Despite the apparent dominance of these new media, digital and emerging technologies are enhancing traditional media under the greater design of integrated communications.

Aims and learning objectives

The aim of this chapter is to explore the evolution and characteristics of digital and emerging media.

The learning objectives of this chapter are to:

1. explain digital media advertising and how it differs from traditional media
2. evaluate emerging and converging media as vehicles to carry messages
3. appraise and compare the relative advantages and disadvantages of digital media
4. explore the possibilities for supplementary digital advertising media.

Minicase Changing the country from the ground up

Prior to 2008, modern traditional political campaign fund drives and awareness raising in the United States had been done through standard media outlets, especially through a number of local fundraising 'events' for supporters. Presidential candidates relied on these factors and a network of local contact points to groom associates, spread information by word of mouth and earmark donors most likely to bring in the donations so vital to the American electoral process. In 2000, George W. Bush revolutionised campaign fundraising – and shattered existing records – by creating a muscular network of 'bundlers', each of whom committed to bring in $100,000, $200,000 or more to the fledgling campaign from personal friends and business associates. This process was typical of the 'buddy' system, so entrenched in the American political system. Bush's bundlers, whom he designated Pioneers and Rangers, were high-powered CEOs and lobbyists, no strangers to money-raising efforts.

In late 2006, as the Obama campaign team began to prepare for a presidential run, then-Senator Obama and his small team faced what seemed like insurmountable hurdles. He was relatively new to Washington, and unlike most former presidential candidates and his immediate predecessor George W. Bush, the young senator hadn't spent years assembling a stable of wealthy donors, building an infrastructure of establishment support among businesses and corporations, or securing an influential voter base so necessary in the state-to-state battles about to ensue.

Instead, Obama's bundlers included all the unlikely political players, from part-time tutors to stay-at-home moms. The campaign was also aware that they had tens of thousands of eager university students who were willing to volunteer. These unlikely players were among the first who signed up to solicit their friends and families by hosting individual fundraising web pages for Obama.

Using its base volunteers' enthusiasm as a a cue, the Obama election campaign team wondered if it could leverage digital marketing in different ways to appeal to tech-savvy 20th-century users of the internet, many who had never before had the chance to vote in an election and others who had felt distanced in recent years from the entire election process. Obama's campaign team realised that they needed to create a groundswell to appeal to these first-time, disenfranchised and apathetic voters. The mission would be 'to change this country from the ground up' and it would need to drive strategic decisions down to the smallest detail – to capture every voter, every dollar and every vote that was needed to win.

Even though research demonstrated that supporters of Republican presidential candidate John McCain were more likely than backers of Barack Obama to be

Exhibit 9.1 President Obama
Source: Getty Images

internet users (83% vs 76%), it also revealed that the overall size of the online political user population had a broad base of demographic groups. While one important part of Obama's base were the least likely to go online (22% of all adults age 65 or older and 31% of those with a household income of less than $30,000 per year), more than half of most other major demographic subgroups (seniors, African-Americans and others) were politically engaged online in one way or another during the 2008 election season.

The use of social and digital media would not only have a practical effect, but would also demonstrate a 'cool' factor to show indeed that this candidate, Barack Obama, did not represent politics as usual, but instead reflected the views of a new generation of thinkers (and a new technology as well). His opponent John McCain, on the other hand, was reported to famously have said that he 'had heard of the internet', fixing him squarely as a man that belonged to the past. The challenge facing Barack Obama therefore was how to utilise digital media in order to capitalise on and enlist the new generation of thinkers as Obama presidential supporters.

Sources: Cooke (n.d.); Lutz (2009); Smith (2008); Tumulty (2007)

Introduction

iPads and tablets, e-book readers, enhanced TV, blogs, micro-blogs, online advertising, mobiles and social networking media converge and run across media systems, competing economies and national borders. Consumers are interactive participants in the flow of rich media content based on a new set of rules that are changing as quickly as the technologies themselves. Emerging digital media depend heavily on active participation and may represent a cultural and marketing shift. Consumers seek new ways to find and share information about products, services and companies, while marketers look to invent and combine new ways to plan content marketing campaigns to influence the consumer and infiltrate the new platforms. The emergence of newer media platforms and the convergence of those and other platforms and traditional media represent a cross-pollination of media systems. Advertising media are themselves increasingly a product of new and emerging technologies that synthesise and reconfigure several platforms into one.

Even though traditional media continue to dominate advertising expenditure, marketers and advertisers are aggressively shifting the amount of media spend to portable digital readers and tablets, smartphones, and other devices that connect to the internet and allow emailing, downloading, socialising or shopping online. But this does not necessarily spell disaster for traditional media. Television and other forms of traditional media continue to look for innovative ways to create a diverse, multi-platformed approach with their relevant digital counterparts. As marketing communications models trend away from the business browser to the smart application model, cross-media advertising has emerged, for example, integrating the traditional print medium with online, so this may create a multiplier effect and prove to be more advantageous than any one medium alone (Wakolbinger et al. 2009).

Web 2.0 and Web 3.0 technologies have made consumers the active participants in their own destinies. Consumers can now create their own modes of access and choice and may have changed the ways in which we engage with *all* media (Gauntlett 2009). Ryan and Jones (2009) surmise that there are three ways by which emerging technologies will continue to influence consumer behaviour in the future: enhanced relevance filtering, consumer aggregation into like-groups and consumer centricity. Consumer tenacity will directly affect the balance in the relationship among producers, marketers and consumers, causing some marketing communications practitioners (Pringle and Field 2008) to declare that the balance of power has shifted from the producer to the consumer (or *prosumer*). This means that consumers shape and customise products, to suit their own requirements, and must be fundamental to any marketing communications plan, in a time of significant social, economic and technological change.

Internet and online advertising

Early scholarship on the use of internet online advertising media and its effectiveness (Hoffman and Novak 1996; Drèze and Zufryden 1998) voiced scepticism about the medium's effectiveness in delivering promotional messages. The scepticism persists with more recent studies by Robinson, Wysocka and Hand (2007), Fulgoni and Mörn (2009) and others. Scholars are divided about the effectiveness of online advertising for two primary reasons: first, the online advertising target population is often generalised and difficult to define, second, measurement organisations may be overestimating the positive effects of internet ad campaigns because at present there is no valid empirical basis on which to estimate audiences reliably (Lavrakas 2010).

CTR, or 'click-through rate', is the basic unit to measure the number of clicks on a website per the number of times the advertisement is shown on that site (impressions). The higher the CTR, the greater the advertisement-to-website relevance, and the better the performance is considered to be. However, advertisers aspire to more than a high click-through rate advocacy. A website's effectiveness depends on the important conversion rate (or *sales* per click). This is the number of quality clicks per website visit that result in substantive action, such as a purchase. Song and Zinkhan (2008) suggest that online advertisers need to employ multiple kinds of tracking tools, such as Google Analytics, Chartbeat or Advanced Web Stats, and multiple ways of assessment to enhance site effectiveness and to ensure that adspend is delivering optimal and effective online advertising.

Several kinds of online advertising are regarded as standard. *Banner* online advertising appears as a boxed graphic of various shapes and sizes that is embedded on a web page and hyperlinked to the URL of the advertiser or to another linked website. It is the most common and traditional form of online advertising and has been shown to increase a site's traffic, even with a low percentage direct click-through rate (Fulgoni and Mörn 2009). Two kinds of standard banners are in play: *static* banners do not change, but remain the same to every user and each page load; *dynamically rotated* banners can change to suit the communications needs of the campaign.

In addition to conventional online banners and display advertisements, the internet makes possible other marketing communications formats and activities such as affiliate programmes, sponsorships, couponing and referrals. An affiliate programme allows an individual to receive a commission by selling another company's products or services on the internet. Sponsored-content online advertising may appear in the form of a profile, video or application that has been integrated into the editorial content of a web page and paid for by an advertiser. While coupons found in newspaper inserts have long been a standard of traditional media, online couponing is a favourite of the e-retailers' arsenal of tools as well.

Search engine optimisation (SEO) and search engine marketing (SEM) are online advertising methods through which marketers attempt to drive online traffic to various internet

Exhibit 9.2 Variations on banner advertising
Source: Dreamstime.com

sites. Google AdWords (https://adwords.google.com), for example, enables a company to create advertisements that show up on relevant Google search results pages and the entire network of Google's partner sites. SEO, quite literally optimising websites, is the attempt to design web pages so that one's business is prioritised and ranks as high as possible in natural or organic search results. These search results pages are technically 'free listings', but many companies pay experts to manipulate and drive their content near the top of search page results.

Search engine marketing (SEM) refers to the paid text ads that appear in the search engine's sponsored-links or sponsored-results boxes. SEM can be beneficial to small niche businesses who can inexpensively tailor-make or optimise their sites with the appropriate text and tags in the hope that the site ranks high in any product- or service-specific online searches through Bing, Yahoo!, Ask or other search engines (Google launches 2011). Because of SEM's complex technology in optimising hits on websites, a secondary 'search marketing' industry has surfaced for online advertising, in which some marketers rely on third-party agencies to manage and fine-tune their search marketing parameters (Kharbanda 2006). SEM attempts to match or optimise brands with consumer audiences by using keywords (including negative keywords and variations) to mark the appropriate target.

Sponsored search engine advertising is paid advertising based on a per-click model. Advertisers pay the search engine only when a user clicks on their advertisement whilst browsing. Competitive bids from the database of standing bids are made in an auction-like format, the bids are collected and ranked and ultimately per-click prices are determined as a

Exhibit 9.3 Crowd funding attracts an online crowd

Smaller museums are utilising a supplementary online media for fundraising, called 'crowd funding'. Smaller organisations are using fundraising platforms to support a variety of creative endeavours. The use of Kickstarter.com, says one executive director, made soliciting much easier than 'if we had done the traditional route of sending [direct] mailings and cold-calling people'. Kickstarter.com, ChipIn.com and CreateaFund.com not only help communities fund projects but use the projects as marketing tools at the same time.

Source: Alamy Images

Scholars' paper 9.1 Digital media and the fading metaphor

Edelman, David (2010) Branding in the digital age: you're spending your money in all the wrong places, *Harvard Business Review*, 27(4), 63-9

Edelman argues that marketers have successfully used the famous funnel metaphor to think about touch-points in the consumer decision-making process: consumers would start at the wide end of the funnel with many brands in mind and narrow them down to a final choice. Companies traditionally used paid-media push marketing at a few well-defined points along this funnel to build brand awareness, drive consideration and ultimately inspire purchase. But this metaphor is no longer useful, he argues, because it fails to capture the shifting nature of consumer engagement in the digital age. Consumers today rely heavily on digital interactions and often connect with brands through media channels that are beyond manufacturers' and retailers' control. Marketing strategies must be redesigned and expanded accordingly. Edelman suggests marketing and marketing communications professionals need to help consumers navigate the evaluation process by driving advocacy, revising media strategy, using click-stream analysis and developing digital touchpoints, among other adaptations, to pay close attention to the consumers' brand experience.

function of the bids (Athey and Nekipelov 2010; Song and Mela 2011). Real-time bidding allows the advertiser to target only known audiences with reasonable effectiveness. The advertiser only pays the per-click price for each click, all the while maximising efficiency and providing advertisers with invaluable information about the behaviour of their target audiences (Mad Men 2011).

Some strengths in using online in the media plan

Cost effective

Perhaps the greatest advantage of using the internet for business is its cost effectiveness. Developing and maintaining an online site can cost a fraction of the budget required to carry out a campaign in other forms of media. Advertising online is less expensive than traditional paid media, and it also allows business owners to reach a more targeted audience.

Online advertising's monitoring capability can help deliver more precise reach and ensure cost efficiency better than traditional methods, even on a limited budget. A small yellow-page or newspaper ad can be very costly. By advertising online, various pricing opportunities, including the bidding for advertisements based on performance, can neutralise budgetary constraints.

The internet can reach a global (and local) audience

An online presence instantly gives a company a global audience. Customers from around the world are potentially able to learn about a company's product or service and perhaps take further action towards purchase. The brand-building efficiency of online advertising is unmatched by any other advertising media.

The internet media space continues to serve as the primary media tool (see Figures 9.1 and 9.2) around the world. Equally important, if not more so for local retailers, advertisers can target a local consumer market, rather than trying to determine which local publications or radio and television stations cater variously to a particular geographical area. By performing filtered, personalised online searches, and using information on local markets gathered from search engines, the advertiser can also target effectively a local consumer audience.

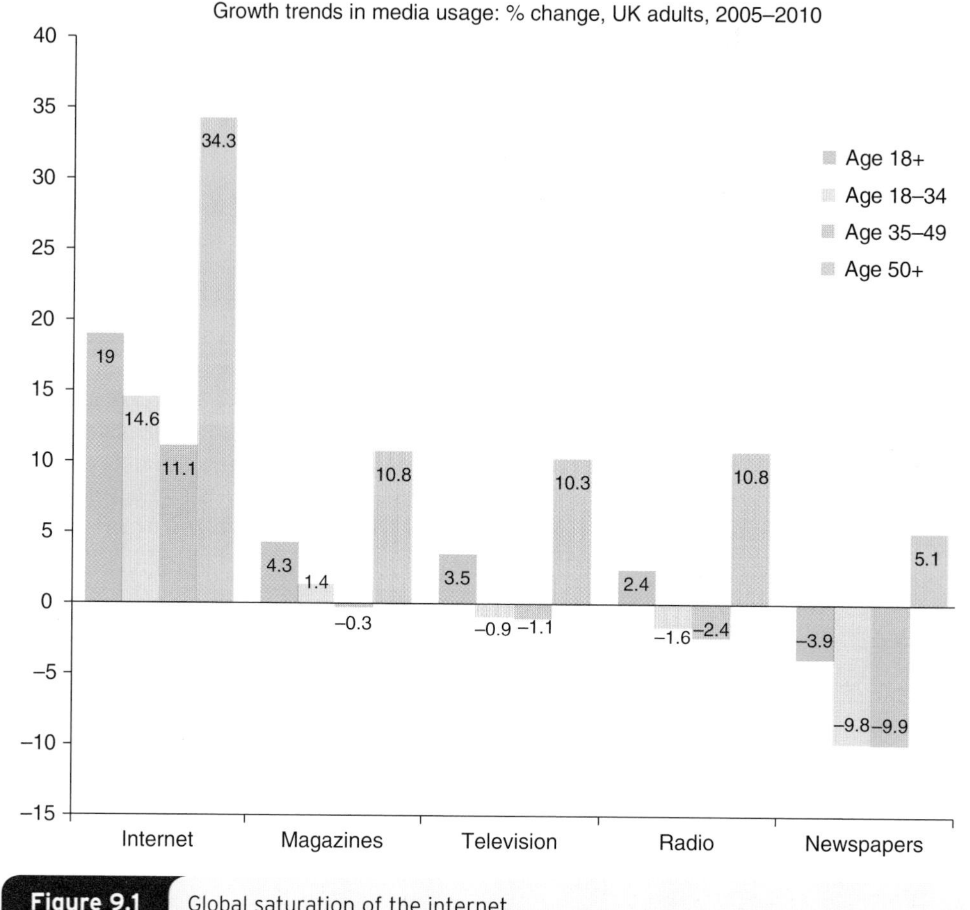

Figure 9.1 Global saturation of the internet
Source: The Association of Magazine Media
Extracted from: *The Magazine Handbook*, 2010/11

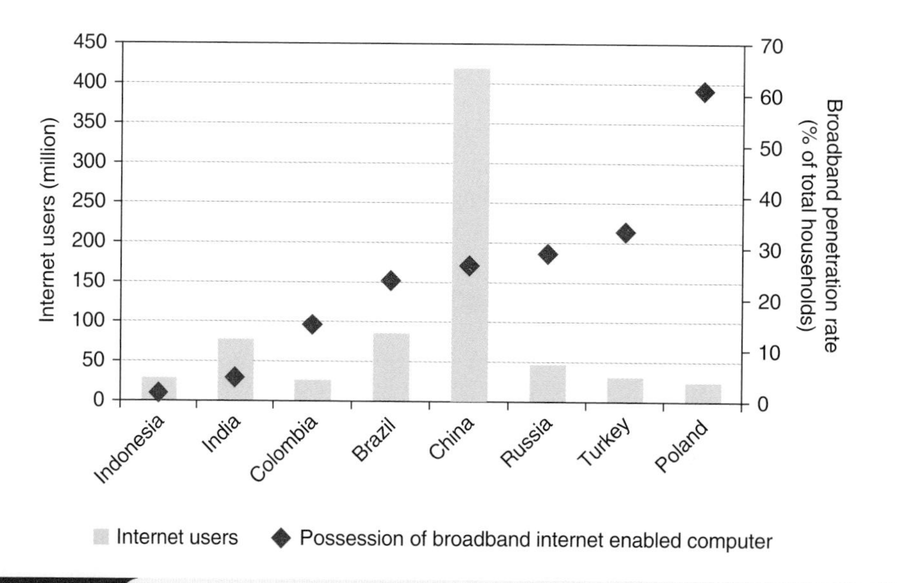

Figure 9.2 Internet growth among emerging economies
Source: Euromonitor from trade sources/national statistics/International Telecommunications Union/World Bank (2010)

The internet offers opportunities for two-way conversations

Online advertising allows for a two-way exchange of information, an interaction or what some call a 'marketing conversation'. A company can deliver messages on a website, a consumer responds by clicking on a banner ad or following a link, the company answers by adjusting or modifying the message, the ad or the link, all according to consumer needs. The marketing conversation can occur in real time, so there is no threat of long lead times as in magazine publications, thereby risking message irrelevance or dilution. An online retailer can generate recommendations to the consumer based on their purchasing history. The dialogue evolves over time as the two parties learn more about each other, and their interaction, their conversations, are also instantly measurable.

ViewPoint 9.1 A Singapore brand for the digital age

The Singapore tourism campaign ('Uniquely Singapore') had become stale and undifferentiated. It followed a set of rules that spoke more of the traditional marketing communications model approach to tourism rather than a digital one. In 2010, the Singapore Tourism Board was keen to leverage an opportunity to attract significantly more tourist numbers to its country, numbers that were increasingly coming from Asian markets, both a sign of the region's healthy economic growth and expanding middle class, and a target audience that was clearly using online resources as their primary source of travel information, including bookings. The task at hand for the Singapore Tourism Board was to develop a campaign that could capture this important online audience.

In line with other regional Asian tourism efforts ('Malaysia, truly Asia', 'Incredible India'), an earlier 'Uniquely Singapore' campaign had used a generic phrase or adjective appended to its name to drive visitor arrivals. The challenge for the BBH Asia Pac agency was to create a differentiated tourism campaign for the digital age. The agency needed first to use advertising to increase website traffic for the major identified target markets, primarily Indonesia, China and Malaysia, and the secondary targets of India, Australia, Vietnam and the UK; occupying the online space, it was presumed, would then lead to conversion, or bookings.

The creative campaign's new website - YourSingapore.com - arose out of the perceived Asian insights into Singapore's unique appeal. Research suggested that, for Asians, Singapore is the epitome of progress, a destination where the 'seemingly impossible is made possible'. A panoply of sights, sounds, tastes, cultures and attractions was packed into a small, user-centric island city that appeared fantasy-like on the site and echoed the perceptions about Singapore and allowed visitors to personalise their experience and create a Singapore they loved.

The logo was fluid ('living') and changed with a variety of themes, moods and emotions; further, each creative execution served as a signpost to the URL YourSingapore.com and created a mirror image to Singapore's concentration of attractions and its unique user friendliness.

The results were impressive. Visitor arrivals to Singapore in 2010 significantly outperformed category growth and beat the category growth rate across the three competitive markets of Indonesia, China and Malaysia. A differentiated tourism campaign for the digital age had been created.

Source: Based on Sarnblad (2011)

Question

The Singapore campaign relied on perceptions to attract visitors. What kind of images of Singapore do you think it chose and why?

Task

Break into groups. Choose two countries that you have never visited and develop a list of perceptions you have about each country.

Provides good tracking mechanisms

Tracking the precise reach of newspaper and television advertisements is difficult. Online advertising, however, allows the advertiser to track the number of impressions an ad receives (how many people view it), and how many visits a business website receives from a particular display ad, making it relatively easy to determine the kind of click-through conversion rate ratios the online advertisements achieve.

Good targeted reach

Internet advertising is permission marketing. Consumers enter the online experience and visit websites with purpose and at their own pace. They control the opt-in medium through clicks and web browsing. With the ability to match consumer browsing intentions to certain sites through the tracking of click-through and conversion rates, the advertiser is able to address known and desired audiences, who in turn render greater attention and engagement (Dembosky 2011). A marketing communications strategy that includes online advertising may deliver better results than traditional media due to the medium's inherent ability to target efficiently.

Some weaknesses in using online in the media plan

The internet is not emotive

One of the fundamental principles in brand promotion is that the message should deliver impact to stimulate desire. Desire requires storytelling that conveys the attributes of mood, emotion or attitude, which may either be beyond the capabilities, both creatively and financially, of digital companies responsible for online advertising, or an anathema to them (Bayers 2011: 30). To survive the competition, online advertising must deliver the emotional content large brands find essential to their success.

Elements of the online experience can be intrusive and annoying

Although permission marketing ultimately puts the consumer in control, the omnipresence of site pop-ups, pop-unders and other online advertisements may result in multiple negative consequences. According to at least one source (McCoy, Everard, Polak and Galleta 2007), enabled pop-ups do draw more attention than banners, but viewers tend to be hostile towards them. Consumers can disable pop-ups from their browsers or use a wide range of software that prevents pop-ups altogether. It can be assumed that consumers will continue to use counter-measures against pop-ups and thereby threaten to diminish advertising effectiveness.

High level of clutter and websnarl

Like all forms of advertising media, communications on the internet are subject to clutter, meaning, simply, that there are too many advertisements for the consumer to digest. As a result, messages become lost or go unnoticed, 'clicked-out-of' observation as the viewers' attention is distracted. Web users are inundated with banner ads online and may bypass advertising altogether.

ViewPoint 9.2 Using paint to decorate a website

Paint has traditionally been a time-delayed, low-interest category in India. Consumers feel dependent on paint dealers and contractors and as a result delay domestic painting projects for as long as possible. In 2011, Asian Paints launched a new engagement strategy aimed at younger Indian consumers and established the campaign around a dedicated website that provided tailored home decorating tools for greater engagement.

For this campaign Ogilvy & Mather Advertising decided to target the new Indian family, generally younger, nuclear and proud of the look of their homes. Traditionally, families run by elders delayed house painting until absolutely necessary. But research discovered that the younger generation thought differently on the subject: not only did they want to paint their houses, but they wanted to decorate and create a feeling of 'home' as well. They were ripe for inspiration. Asian Paints decided to use the updated website www.asianpaints.com to address the lack of information, lack of trust in the intermediaries/contractor and technical terms and need for direction by young Indian consumers. The Internet and Mobile Association of India (IAMAI) and market research leader IMRB report that internet usage had gone up in a few years' time from 9.3 hrs/week to 15.7 hrs/week, a steep 70% rise. And the younger generation was driving the surge in internet usage in India.

The task of using the internet website was a difficult one for the Indian market. Certainly the research demonstrated that Indians were online but unlike the online technology, finance and travel sectors, the consumer sector in India often does not use online to target directly the consumer. Websites are not updated, they are comprised of simple banner and display ads and they lack lead-generation capability.

Asian Paints made online advertising the focal point of the marketing communications campaign and its site, www.asianpaints.com, became a one-stop solution for paint-related queries, decorating ideas, DIY projects and help through Asian Paints Home Solutions (APHS), the company's painting services arm. The role for communications was to create awareness about the innovative colour tools available on the Asian Paints website and encourage their use. Additional media vehicles used for the integrated campaign were TV (TVC and cricket innovation), print (leading dailies) and radio in six major cities to enhance the online presence.

The campaign has been highly successful in promoting www.asianpaints.com as the one-stop solution for easy painting. There has been a marked increase in sales and revenue, and measured website data, such as clicks, page views, new visitors and specific service usage, improved significantly. In terms of tracking data, the campaign enjoyed the highest reach among Asian Paints corporate campaigns to date. This indicates the younger Indian consumer's improved disposition to learning about a brand online. And the asianpaints.com campaign has transformed an old, stodgy, paint maker that appealed only to older customers into a dynamic, youthful service brand that enables consumers to create the home of their dreams.

Source: Asian paints Ltd. Annual Report (2011); www.warc.com

Question

On what assumption did Asian paints base its campaign?

Task

Create a target audience profile of students attending your university. List three characteristics the students share.

Websnarl (a backed-up, overcrowded online experience) is a characteristic of a still fragile and spotty internet infrastructure. Disruptions and crashes due to technical problems, occasional glitches in software, slow connection speeds caused by internet overload and crowded access to the virtual world cause inconvenience to the customer. Low bandwidth and poor connectivity are persistent concerns for emerging countries that are still growing their online infrastructure.

Mobile marketing

As mobile phone technology has transformed from simple voice telephone applications to handheld computers, televisions, cameras and recording all-in-one devices, many users, particularly the young, are choosing to utilise mobile smartphones for most of their connection needs (Lewington 2011). A change in consumer behaviour and perceptions is evolving through the use of specialised applications that provide easy access to social networking sites, news and entertainment, email and banking, and a host of others. Videos, music, games and television content are readily available for mobile smartphone users. Mobiles are multifunctional and versatile and are part of the 'always connected' category of devices that we now carry around with us.

Access to the internet around the world by mobile telephone far outnumbers access by fixed-line broadband (International Telecommunication Union 2011). In emerging African countries, the mobile ecosystem continues to explode and outweighs the importance of either computer ownership or an internet connection (GSM 2011). Many world netizens now access data, emails and entertainment exclusively through mobile sets (see Figure 9.3).

Naturally, these facts are not lost on advertisers, who are always searching for ways to leverage mobile initiatives. One way is to make time-sensitive offers and discounts to encourage purchases that drive consumers to mobile sites and websites, as well as to retail store locations. Research suggests that mobile-based marketing communications attract attentive audiences and are particularly effective at eliciting consumer response (Rettie et al. 2005; Scharl et al. 2005).

After a slow start, market penetration of mobile marketing has been quite successful in Europe (Consumers keen 2011) and the USA (Mobile habits evolve 2011). However, because ownership of mobile devices is high, Asia leads the world by far in adopting wireless communication in the service of marketing (Smartphones surge 2011). As early as 2003, it was commonplace for Japanese consumers, particularly older teens, to use mobile telephony for sending emails and branded digital couponing (Okabe 2004).

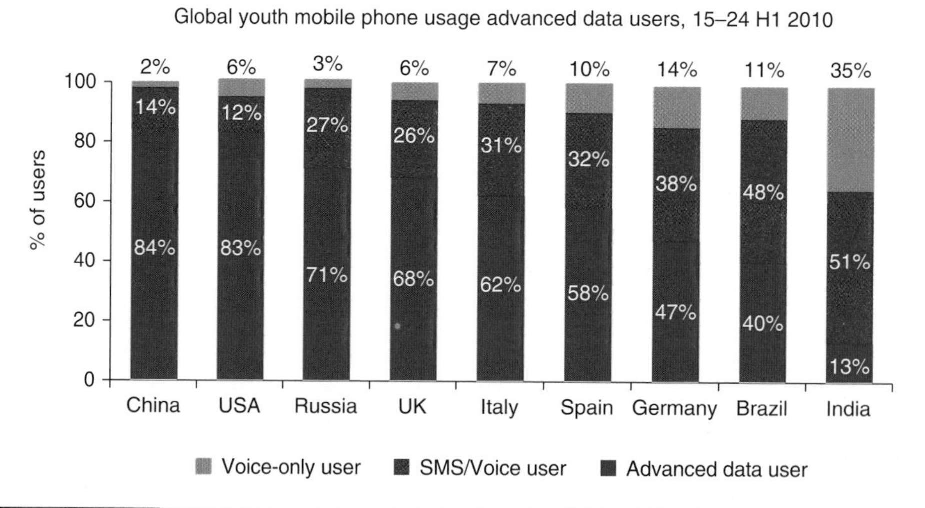

Figure 9.3 Global youth mobile usage
Source: Nielsen, news release (January 2011).

The Mobile Marketing Association (MMA) defines mobile marketing as 'the set of practices that enables organizations to communicate and engage with their audience in an interactive and relevant manner through any mobile device or network' (www.mmaglobal.com/about/mission-statement). This may include anything from social marketing to customer relationship management (CRM) or to events planning in the marketing arena. Using mobile networks and devices can help reach a select target audience in a specific, personalised context (Sultan and Rohm 2005) in an increasing number of ways. As smartphone applications technology and availability continue to improve, we expect mobile's dominance to influence advertising and markets around the world.

The basic SMS (short message service) can offer teaser advertisements embedded into search results, or interactive advertisements, allowing consumers to respond immediately by click-to-web, click-to-call, click-to-vote functionality or other interactive functions. Short codes as a marketing communication medium are an effective way to communicate with customers, as they can access information or specials by using five- or six-digit numbers assigned by mobile operators for different mobile marketing campaigns. Other available digital mobile platforms include MMS (multimedia message service), proximity marketing (GPS capable of broadcasting locations near bricks-and-mortar retailer), web browsing (content designed for easy use from handheld and portable devices), contextualised advertising (ads offered by mobile search engines) and idle advertising (ads served up while the user waits for downloading). Marketers, such as Bing on Samsung devices serviced by Verizon Wireless in the United States, have directly integrated campaigns and advertisements into their audiences' phone application technology. Branded content, such as ringtones, images, e-books and streaming videos, also offers opportunities to specific targeting. Some mobile analytics platforms boast that mobile banners average much higher click-through rates and conversions than their non-mobile counterparts (http://www.bigmobile.com/us/page/mobile-solutions; http://bango.com/mobileanalytics/).

Mobile marketing can offer coupons and other discounts for in-store sales, organise mobile apps to deliver content from television shows (first used for red-carpet post interviews and other activities beyond the television screen during the 2011 Academy Awards Show), or combine barcode calls to action (SMS) with traditional advertising. Google Wallet is an Android app that allows mobile retail payments. *Geotargeting* allows an advertising campaign to fix its sights on a physical locale, for which Jeff Larson, Subway's VP for global marketing, believes the potential is enormous. Companies will be able to target the consumer who 'could be

Scholars' paper 9.2 The limitations of mobile commerce

Park, T., Shenoy, R. and Salvendy, G. (2008) Effective advertising on mobile phones: a literature review and presentation of results from 53 case studies, *Behaviour & Information Technology*, *27*(5), 355–73

In a literature review of case studies to understand the characteristics of advertising via mobile telephony, Park, Shenoy and Salvendy noted that products suitable for trading through mobile commerce are thought to be influenced by several factors: the attitude of customers to mobile advertisements and brand, interaction context, product categories and ease of access together with the emotional component best suited for mobile marketing. Although the authors of the review agree that mobile advertisers can easily personalise the contents of the ad message and target audiences 'who are more likely to be interested in the product or services that the advertiser wants to present', they suggest also that the design of the advertising message may be affected by the physical limitations of mobile devices.

walking about the street, thinking about lunch, type "lunch" into their smartphone, and instantly receive an offer' (Google pushes 2011).

Rich-media interactive advertising can appear in the content on offer by videos, games and TV delivered to mobile devices, smartphones and tablets equipped with access to 3G- and 4G-phone networks, which harbour the adequate speed to run those applications. Apple's mobile ad platform (iAd) consists of a combination of video and interactive features which combine the visceral quality of the television platform with a number of mobile engagement levels (interactive) on the web. Other familiar advertising platforms – Google's Adwords or Admob, third-party networks Millennium and InMobi and direct operator channels such as Orange Shots or O2 More – offer opt-in mobile messaging and advertising services in an effort to give customers control over how information is being used in the mobile marketing experience.

ViewPoint 9.3 Funding a worthy cause through mobile marketing

Depaul UK is a charity that helps young people who are homeless, vulnerable and disadvantaged. It is heavily reliant on voluntary donations to be able to fund its valuable charitable work. Like all charities, Depaul UK was faced with an ageing donor base and needed to find a way to connect with a younger demographic in order to ensure a good supply of funding for the years ahead. Previous campaigns had tried to achieve this, but with a limited media budget recruiting new donors was proving difficult. Depaul UK decided to use an iPhone application - iHobo - to reach out to new (and younger) audience members, educate them about the issue of youth homelessness, drive immediate donations and grow its database that would serve as an important funding source in the future. iHobo was a rich and engaging gaming experience that asked users to look after a virtual young homeless person over a period of three days.

Reaching this new audience through traditional media had proved fruitless. Depaul UK realised that exploiting the intimate relationship between the younger target audience and mobile phones - the medium of choice - made perfect sense for several reasons: firstly, it is one of the few genuinely interruptive forces in the lives of young, busy, affluent people, whose calls, texts and emails to their smartphone take priority in their lives; secondly, mobile offers the potential for prolonged and meaningful contact with a target audience that most other media struggle to reach; thirdly, smartphones are increasingly becoming the interface of choice for sharing content with social networks. Mobile allows the social peer group to spread an idea as quickly as possible, and more young people do this with a mobile device than ever before; finally, by focusing on iPhone users, Depaul UK could effectively ensure that they were talking to the right people to recruit as future donors. Eighty-five per cent of iPhone users are under the age of 45 and indexed very high in terms of income.

iHobo spread quickly as users became engaged in the combination of good creative with mobile telephone capabilities. iHobo generated seven times more money through in-game donations than previous advertising campaigns had ever achieved, and 80 times more donors. Depaul UK reports that 1,200 of these donors volunteered their contact details and consented to being contacted in future for fundraising purposes, and Depaul UK's donor base actually expanded for the first time in years.

Source: www.depauluk.org/newsandresources/ihobo/; www.warc.com

Question

iHobo proved to be a successful implementation of 'cause marketing'. Would you have any ethical reservations about using app technology in the service of 'cause marketing'? Explain.

Task

List and detail one other social cause in which app technology could create awareness. List and detail a social cause for which you believe app technology would not be appropriate.

Some strengths in using mobile telephony in the media plan

Not a place-based medium

A mobile telephone goes where you go. When you travel out of a home geographical area, the roaming facility allows connection to anywhere at any time. Features such as text messaging, data gathering and image sharing are standard with smartphone technology, making the mobile device versatile and potentially lucrative as an advertising medium. The consumer must opt in (demonstrating at least initial interest) to the campaign message through the mobile handset to receive message-based marketing text messages, coupons or more elaborate applications (see ViewPoint 9.3).

The customer database compiled from these actions can then lead to proactive marketing, 'on the go', or 'in the moment' messaging consumers from virtually anywhere. The high global penetration of mobile communication devices indicates that there is high potential for success in mobile marketing (Bauer et al. 2005; Chiem et al. 2010) as advertising media campaigns can be global in coverage, include thousands of consumers and be tailored to appeal to the individual consumer in a personalised way.

Allows customers to interact directly with companies in real time

Mobile marketers are able to reach their customers directly and in real time on a host of issues, ranging from existing product use or services to perhaps future product enhancements or add-ons in the early thinking stages. In a typical 'push' strategy, advertisers can proactively text customers and ask questions about their experience, plus give the customers the opportunity to text comments in response. Through this mechanism, a company is able to react quickly to a complaint or constructive comment. In short, mobile marketing enables an understanding of what customers think, their likes and dislikes and what the firm should continue doing well.

During an earlier National Allergy Week (12–18 May 2003) in England, the pharmaceutical company Novartis launched a pollen-count text alert service to promote the launch of a new allergy nasal spray (Aller-eze) for hay fever sufferers. The pollen-count alert service enabled sufferers to receive personalised, up-to-date, regular pollen-count information by SMS. They received special alerts on days when the pollen count was particularly high in their geographic location – together with tips and information to help manage hay fever (www.clickatell.com/customers/ukcase-studies).

In a 'pull' strategy, the information culled from customer response and SMS text-voting polls can be invaluable in judging whether a campaign is working; advertisers can intervene with modifications if it is not. Customer response mechanisms also provide an opportunity to build loyalty and relationships through two-way messaging. Because marketing-based text messages (as one example) can be tracked, campaigns can be monitored and subsequently improved in real time.

Measurable with a high degree of reliability

The reported number of unique visitors for mobile marketing is reliable as the users of different portals do not overlap. The statistics on unique visitors therefore can be significantly more accurate than other forms of media. Knowing the users' mobile phone brand and the services they use can supply definitive information about user consumption patterns, at least concerning purchasing preferences. Mobile analytics data and performance are still difficult to assess and it is challenging to extract much behavioural and usable intelligence from the user experience. Nonetheless, these performance metrics can help to determine what is working best for delivering mobile traffic.

Some weaknesses in using mobile telephony in the media plan

Fleeting message and short attention span

Even though mobile communications may be ideal for catering to a younger, faster-paced generation of consumers, the flip side is that the nature of the mobile advertising message is short and fleeting and fosters little brand recognition. Memorability and an advertisement's duration have thus far been studied mostly with respect to television commercials, yet those studies have shown that longer and repeated messages in general are better at favourable brand building (Park et al. 2008). Fabian (1986) and Danaher and Mullarkey (2003) also observe that longer TV advertising messages and repeat web page exposures, two characteristics that are not available through the mobile medium, can significantly increase the memory of an ad.

Devices lack uniformity and standardisation

Mobile devices have less standardisation compared to PCs or laptops. Mobile phones come in a variety of shapes and sizes, so the screen size may vary; the browsers and operating systems are also widely divergent. In addition, newer models share the markets with older devices, so quality, clarity and technological capability imbalance becomes an issue as well. Designing one campaign to account for this disparity can prove difficult.

Constant buffering and lag are also problems that slower networks face and make the promise of a technological global network a little less promising.

Privacy and security issues

Permission marketing allows marketers to enter our private lives. Users are protective of their privacy whilst on mobile devices. Mobile marketers run the risk of damaging brand image should they not understand that research suggests a strong need for prior permission in receiving mobile advertising messages. Studies show that a negative association exists between permission and intention to receive mobile advertising (Kavassalis et al. 2003; Leppäniemi 2008). For the marketing communications plan to deliver optimal brand success, procedural issues must be in place to protect end-user privacy and to provide clear opt-in as well as opt-out instructions.

The open nature of Android apps technology presents potentially serious smartphone security issues for Google. While Apple's closed system is often criticised, it allows the company to inspect every application in detail before it is allowed for sale by the App Store, and thus minimises the risk of intrusion. Android provides more flexibility than the iPhone for installation of third-party applications, even those not approved for the Android market, but this has led to malware-infected applications. Users can install anti-virus software, just as they would on a computer (Jennings 2011).

Inferior and limited creative possibilities

The creative opportunities available to mobile marketing platforms are inferior in quality to online presentation for a number of reasons. They are limited at the moment primarily to SMS

ViewPoint 9.4 Promoting HD football packages via mobile advertising

In an effort to raise awareness of Virgin Media HD football packages, Sir Richard Branson's Virgin Media hired 4th Screen Advertising (London), a part of the global communications company Mobile Interactive Group (MIG), to use innovative mobile marketing to engage 18-35 males who browse the UK's *Guardian* mobile internet site.

The campaign specifically targeted iPhone users. The campaign coincided with the beginning of the English Premiership (EPL) 2010-2011 season, which kicked off on 14 August 2010, and ran for three consecutive weekends. The strategy was to use a calendar sync format, whereby iPhone football fans were provided with the fixture list of upcoming televised EPL matches and at the same time were exposed to a call-to-action advertising message, inviting them to learn more about the Virgin Media brand, specifically its sports TV packages. One click from the rich-media mobile both promoted the company's Virgin Media HD football packages and synced all televised football games (including the teams playing, additional information on the fixtures and time of kick-off) onto the users' iPhone calendars.

4th Screen Advertising reported that the campaign helped drive awareness of the sports package availability from Virgin Media, resulting in 52,000 new subscribers to Sky Sports HD over the course of four months. The campaign proved fruitful in capturing users 'in the moment' and provided them with a chance both to become familiar with Virgin Media packages and a way to stay informed of all EPL matches throughout the season.

Source: Based on Butcher (2010)

Question

How could the use of mobile by Virgin Media help build customer loyalty among football fans to the Virgin brand?

Task

4th Screen audiences and expenditures are growing rapidly. Explain the advantages and disadvantages of using mobile to capture consumers 'in the moment'.

and MMS messages, the latter of which involves sending rich content, in particular, images, video and audio, to a relatively smaller device, which may hamper the user experience and subsequently reflect negatively on the brand.

Social media marketing

Consumers are utilising online communication and the opinions of others – friends, experts and sometimes complete strangers – to inform and influence their purchasing decisions in the socially driven digital world. Social media (Marken 2007) are the business of sharing opinions, insights, experiences and perspectives with others: peers influence peers and consumers engage with brands on the consumers' terms – wherever and whenever the consumers choose. Young people in particular are so convinced of the value of social networks that they often trust the unfiltered advice of a total stranger in 'Reviews' and 'Likes' on social sites over the messages organised by the so-called marketing communications expert. It has been called the third dimension of marketing communications, or social influence marketing (SIM) in recognition of the role online social influence plays in brand affinity and purchasing decisions (www.razorfish.com).

Web 2.0 launched a new way forward for the relationship between the consumer and the supplier of the service or the product. Accumulated databases as marketing leads are quickly becoming irrelevant, as user-generated content challenges the traditional ways of looking at relationships with consumers in various social network venues such as Facebook,

QZone (China), Orkut (Brazil), VKontakte (Russia) and LinkedIn. Google+ encourages users to sort their friends into 'circles', or groups, emulating their behaviour for maintaining friendships offline. Although the downside for advertising media is that the customer can no longer be perceived or understood in traditional ways, myriad opportunities exist for those in tune with social networking sites and the concept of *friending* behaviours. Social targeting uses ads on social sites to entice consumers on their own to share a brand's message, thereby transforming consumers into brand advocates. It is an extremely effective form of advertising.

One advantage of using a social network in a marketing communications plan is that it generates contacts through one's own networks. These contacts in turn generate more contacts through a network of externally linked networks, and so the process is repeated. The message in its many forms becomes viral and can lead to millions of potential customers. Facebook, Twitter and LinkedIn enjoy hundreds of millions of unique visitors worldwide. New sites are proliferating quickly and segmenting into any number of constituencies. Social media marketing offers an effective but often elusive approach to the targeted audience, one in which untrained traditional marketing communications companies have often floundered in its use as a promotional tool.

Twitter, the micro-blogging platform, further demonstrates the instantaneous, coalescing nature of social media. It allows people to communicate interactively but also 'collects' (or tribalises) them into a common arena. As co-founder Biz Stone remarks, these groups act 'like a flock of birds moving as (one) object in flight. It is rudimentary behaviour among a group of individuals in real time, allowing them to behave as if they are one organism' (Day 2011). To address this behaviour, the Apple iPhone for one was quick to adapt and innovate by making its product both a convergent, multipurpose device (it's not simply a telephone!) and an apps market that allows the consumer seamless interaction with their social networking choices.

Foursquare, another social platform among the many using mobile communications and sharing locations, is a location-based social network which combines a game-dynamics element with identifying and locating friends and spotting interesting places (points are given for updated 'check ins') for them to visit, to dine or to enjoy entertainment. The Foursquare network encourages sharing the experiences with a specific and fragmented universe – participants typically self-select into their own groups.

Starbucks was one of the early adopters of social media with Facebook and the first brand to boast 10 million+ 'fans' (Simon 2010). Starbucks and other top brands use Facebook to market new products and solidify brand identity among their consumer constituencies. Starbucks's Facebook page displays logos, locations and even employment opportunities, but

Scholars' paper 9.3 The end of demographics?

Beckland, J. (2011) The end of demographics: how marketers are going deeper with personal data, 3 July, retrieved from www.mashable.com/author/jamie-beckland

Beckland argues that traditional marketing demographics may not be the most suitable way to define the target consumer for the social web. Instead, social profile and behavioural data have much better ways of targeting potential customers by using psychographic insights gleaned from relationship status, interest, occupation and even home town. These are far more apt predictors than previous top-down approaches to marketing performance and are better at building a deeper understanding of the consumer. Beckland suggests that demographics are irrelevant in the highly fragmented - and temporal - classifications found on the social web.

primarily its 'Wall' allows customers from around the world to share and promote their favourite Starbucks product and their own spin-off concoctions.

What quickly became clear to advertisers on social networks is that the marketing message needs to be balanced and positive, and a site developer has to anticipate and respond to the buzz that may be created or disseminated through the social space. An increasing number of firms make it a point to study the positive *and* negative (word-of-mouth) conversations that make their way electronically through social networks.

Although there are many opportunities through social networking sites for marketing communications practitioners, privacy issues remain delicate and of concern to consumers (Häkkila and Chatfield 2005). MyCube (mycube.com), a German-based company, addresses this concern by allowing the social networking participant to make a 'safe' copy of information placed on social networks. Any content that the owner at a later time judges undesirable for public display can be withdrawn at the owner's request, heralding a trend towards limiting what one shares. Path (www.path.com), another organisation uneasy about open-ended data sharing and privacy issues, limits sharing information with a select number of friends, about 50 at the present time. Diaspora* offers a personal mode to protect personal information from centralised social networks. The manner by which national and international regulations and consumer sentiment deal with these issues will dictate the future of social media and the placement of marketing messages within them.

Some strengths in using social media in the media plan

Serves as effective word-of-mouth advertising in its sharing capability

Promotions, customer services and general brand awareness can spread exponentially to many more customers through social media sites. Customers are connected to family or friends or business associates – incidental players or connections who will be able to learn about a company's product or service through mobile dominant platforms that circulate word-of-mouth advertising rapidly and impressively.

Develops customer relationships and builds brand loyalty

Social sites are effective in communicating with customers and developing relationships resulting from those communications. A social network can provide relevant and useful product information. It can be updated regularly, while integrated widgets and features such as a fan box or fan page, profile badge or customised links enhance the site experience and build upon a familiar relationship with customers. Once the social community is established, further steps can be taken to invite customers to share their experiences by participating in polls, Q&A or product review areas. This allows companies to address the larger issues proactively and perhaps to roadblock any serious consequences. Sites may also project a customer service attitude that may be key to building brand loyalty.

Stimulates differentiation and innovation

Tracking the marketing communications activities of competitors can be beneficial to advertisers. Scrutinising the social media content of others may lead to modifying or adjusting features to better differentiate a company's product or service from its competition;

Exhibit 9.4 Japan's crisis: Social networking and relief efforts

Directly after the devastating tsunami hit northeastern Japan in March 2011, social media played an important role in connecting survivors with loved ones, updating important rescue information and generating quick ways to donate. Twitter released a guide for Japanese users to retrieve information and communicate as broadly as possible. Hashtags such as #Jishin for general earthquake information or #J_j_helpme were created to request rescue or other aid. HelpAttack allowed users to pledge money for every action taken on Facebook and Twitter to be donated to the Red Cross. Zynga partnered with Save the Children to enable players of eight of their most popular games to donate to the Japanese crisis by purchasing specific virtual goods. South by South West Media Festival launched SXSW4Japan in an effort to use their influence to raise support networks and donations. Throughout the tsunami crisis in Japan, it became evident that social media proved a crucial platform in providing information on relief efforts and ways for the international community to lend support to the survivors.

Source: Getty Images

it may even aid in more precise positioning within the social space by the company itself. Some may argue that competitive tracking is also available with traditional media, but the impact from the social media sites is certainly more immediate. Innovation in a company's products or services on offer may also come as a result of listening to consumer responses and suggestions.

Crosses national boundaries

A range of global organisations and brands, such as FIFA (Fédération Internationale de Football Association) or the fashion merchandiser ASOS in the UK, have many active followers on their sites from around the world. Starbucks uses Weibo, China's micro-blogging site, as its primary social promotional tool (Robehmed 2011) to tap into the enormous Chinese market. Social media are not localised but instead are populated by consumers creating and living in a global, virtual village, which is rarely confined to national boundaries.

Some weaknesses in using social media in the media plan

Needs resources for the long term

Social media are a venue for marketing communications; they are not in themselves a media strategy (Young 2011). They are time consuming and labour intensive. A company needs to utilise social media as a part of its media communications strategy only if it has the resources for long-term involvement and can integrate other types of media into a unified, overall strategy. Periodic updating of the site, adding pertinent information as it becomes available, informing the audience on relevant issues and responding to consumer queries for the long term are necessary requirements for a well-functioning social presence. Many social initiatives fail to yield the anticipated results or risk 'brand dilution' by not having the resources on this platform to respond to customers' concerns adequately (Goodwin 2011).

A faulty initial brand strategy and inexperience could lead to disadvantage

Although many are willing to jump on the social media bandwagon, a lack of experience and understanding of the new medium and its audiences could be detrimental to relevant stakeholder groups and make one prone to negative press and, possibly, product failures (Gillin 2007). An ill-conceived brand strategy or a lack of cohesive branding is difficult to remedy and could lead to disaster.

Difficult to determine whether social media initiatives translate into real consumer leads

The primary purpose for using social networking sites is to network. Advertisements are often ignored or given short shrift by potential customers, since the social site experience is not about purchasing but about socialising and sharing ideas. This leads to issues for companies that focus on click-through rate and high conversion-rate returns and have a vague if rudimentary understanding of what is a lead or not in the social marketing space (Borzykowski 2011).

Requires high pay-per-click (PPC) costs for niche markets

Pay-per-click costs for niche markets, normally delivered at a lower cost per impression in other media, are high in a competitive or niche market that is full of Adwords. Even though simple organic search results are free, they do not always target the desired customers or the desired location. Some portals do not clearly separate the targeted ads from the regular search results. Sites will need to continue to fine-tune their models and advertisers must by necessity fine-tune their messages to ensure that niche businesses can afford to use them to drive traffic to sites.

Gaming

In-game advertising (IGA) refers simply to the placement of brands and brand advertisements in digital and non-digital video games, which typically appear in sports gaming venues as posters, billboards or road signage. Digital games include games designed for console systems like Nintendo's Wii or Xbox 360® and online games accessed as on-demand entertainment, free or paid, either through a special game client (such as IBM's Power Up) or through a web interface (like Whyville). Some games allow for multi-player online game sets, where a community of players is on the same server, worldwide. Studies on the development of the internet and game technology (Chang 2009; Moonhee et al. 2006) suggest that gaming may be the digital marketplace of the future as more consumers play video games and increasing numbers of them prefer to play games over any number of alternative forms of entertainment devices. Mobile handsets, tablets or camera peripherals in Kinect™ for the Xbox 360® make gaming easier than ever (see Figure 9.4). Gaming is primarily about immediate gratification, though there are also long-term, long-play social networking games, such as Sims and Farmville. Surprisingly, gaming is enjoyed by a broad demographic range, from 'tweens (8–12) to older age groups, evenly split among men and women, who purport to play or visit online games frequently' (Lovison 2009).

Online gaming sites have become one of the fastest and most efficient ways for companies to promote their products without spending a great deal of money. Recent releases of Modern Warfare 3 and Uncharted Territory have been purchased in record numbers and demonstrate the popularity of gaming. According to Ovum's business and technology analysts, the global digital games market will double to $53 billion by 2016 (Anon 2011). In the United States and the United Kingdom over 100 million registered users currently engage on various online gaming sites.

Richardson et al. (2010) point out that such a large database of gamers offers advertisers the opportunity to deliver a message to many consumers at a relatively low price in three major ways: one brand may totally dominate a game (as with brand signage in the traditional genre of racing games), the brand image may appear on billboards naturally for the duration of the game, or characters in the game may interact with the brands (product placement and purchase as in the early Crazy Taxi (1999 version)). Players represent a captive audience with few distractions, so that marketers are guaranteed to connect with highly engaged users.

Companies such as Electronic Arts, Facebook and AOL have created websites dedicated to free online gaming. The 'freemium' model is changing the way games are designed, marketed, maintained and operated and provides more visibility for games, which is important for the advertiser in the increasingly crowded marketplace (Webster 2011).

Social gaming sites such as Mercenaries of War, Mafia Wars, Bejeweled 2 and Black Jack allow the gamer to quickly interact with and play other users just about anywhere. John Riccitiello, Electronic Arts' CEO, explains that digital entertainment needs to be offered in a

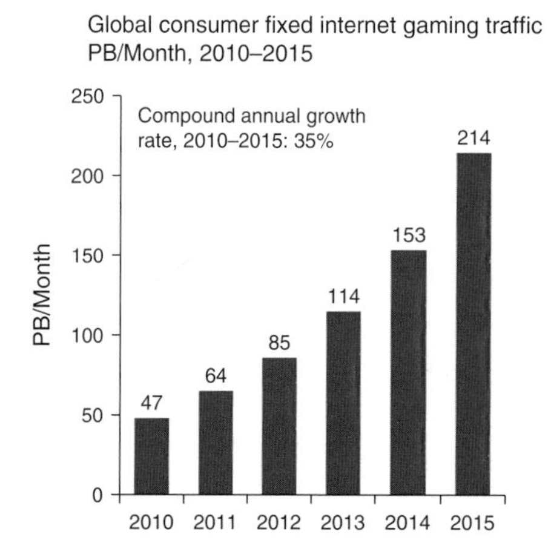

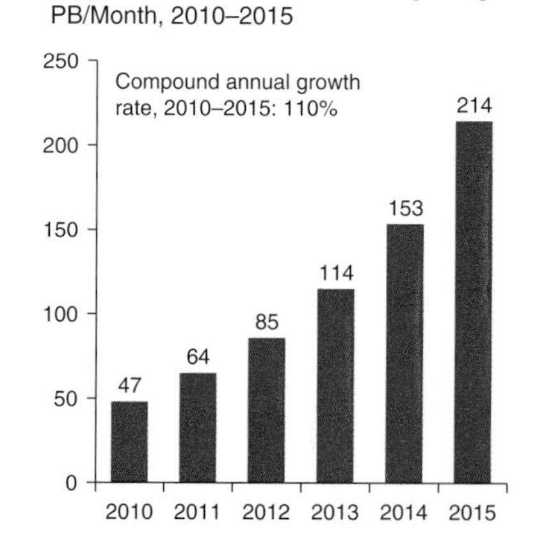

Figure 9.4 Projected fixed and mobile internet gaming popularity
Source: Cisco Visual Networking Index, 2011
Extracted from: Cisco Visual Networking Index: Forecast & Methodology, 2010-2015

Exhibit 9.5 Red Bull augments 'energy' with 'racing'

Energy drink brand Red Bull ran an on-package call-to-action campaign to drive adoption of a branded mobile game designed to increase consumer engagement and influence purchase intent through augmented reality. Utilised as a mobile gaming application for Apple's iPhone and WiFi-enabled iPod touch, Red Bull Augmented Racing enabled players to custom-build their own digital racetrack using Red Bull cans. The Red Bull Augmented Racing game was intended to bring racing to life by letting consumers trace the energy drink cans with their mobile device's camera. The mobile game was featured through the summer of 2011 on all Red Bull Augmented Racing 12-packs.

Source: Press Association Images

multiple-channel strategy, and digital business should run across-downloadable content, social media presence and Android and iPhone smartphones, further evidence that digital tends towards integration of many platforms (Faber 2011).

Gaming-specific advertisers (Microsoft Advertising®, among others) promise immersive participation and innovative experiences from the broad-based audience of novice to hard-core gaming enthusiasts. The key benefits of participation in MSN® Games, Games on Windows Live™ Messenger, Xbox® and Xbox LIVE® are better performance and consumer selective perception. In-gaming advertising media are premium brand advertising, which increases brand awareness dramatically, enhances brand perception and promises interaction (in-game and online game venues) with the brand on mobile devices, computers and TVs in far superior fashion than traditional broadcast television advertising (Initiative 2011).

This nascent medium can showcase *static* or *dynamic advertising*. Static in-game advertisements are programmed directly into the game and serve a similar purpose to product placement in cinema. Static ads ensure that the player will be exposed to the ads throughout the course of the game. Dynamic advertising placements are predetermined and are woven into the game and contextualised. Elements in dynamic advertising placements can be flexible, interchangeable or revisited in real time by the advertiser, and for these reasons among others it is the logical choice over static promotions among many advertisers. Little resistance is met from the consumer who is engaged with the in-gaming process and the 'integration' to techniques like social media, in-game ads and celebrity endorsements (Suster 2011).

Gamers are thus fully engaged with both the game and the advertising embedded within it (Kuss 2011).

As in-game advertising evolves, social games will continue to grow because they allow for interactive, direct response and can be enjoyed anywhere. Whereas traditional games only offer passive advertising engagements, the newer games and gaming sites are premised on viral growth and social events (often by way of Facebook) that keep the user both engaged and returning frequently. Games are well positioned to deliver results for advertisers as formats and opportunities are increasingly built around integration with a brand's overall social media strategy in mind.

Some strengths in using gaming in the media plan

Games can be free or low cost due to paid sponsorships or other advertising

The cost of in-game advertising on online gaming sites is one of its most appealing features. Companies can choose among a number of pricing models, from upfront flat fees to fees based on sales volumes or sponsorships that enable the user to play for free. Exposure within the site can also be refashioned (the number of times that signage appears, for example) to aim for reach and frequency under budget.

The consumer can play a game and be introduced to ads in a number of different ways that tend to be seamless with the gaming experience. In this manner, the player does not feel as if advertisements saturate the game; instead, the ads pay for the game so they are perceived as a necessary part of the gaming environment. These ads are inexpensive to produce and are able to reach a high number of users multiple times. If the site is free, some goodwill may also be spread around for the sponsoring advertiser.

Customised advertisements can be contextually relevant

Ads appear on these gaming sites in a variety of ways. The most common advertisement in the online gaming industry is the banner or pop-up display ad. Players usually view an advertisement as a part of the game if the developer has woven it tightly into it. Studies demonstrate that a player's interest in the game may have a positive impact on their interest in the advertised product, whilst brand recall tends to be much higher (Lovison 2009; Nelson 2002). Lovison (2009) suggests moreover that advertisers overlook the benefits of keeping the messaging contextually relevant. Customising display ad messaging based on many popular themed games and puzzles can be a worthwhile investment with respect to the impressions achieved in return.

Interstitial advertisements can be used whilst gamers wait for their game to resume

Another type of ad technique often used in online gaming sites is interstitial ads. These are similar to web video placements where 15 seconds of video loads in a pre-roll, mid-roll or post-roll spot. These ads force players to watch the ad while waiting for their game to resume. Interstitials can often be more effective than banner ads because sometimes the gamer tends to focus on the game (with interstitials) and is oblivious to the banner. Interstitial ads break up the gaming experience only momentarily and garner the full attention of a potential consumer.

Exhibit 9.6 Advergaming and brand entertainment

In advergames, specific brands can appear in starring roles. In an early mobile advergame Jeep® Off Road Jam players 'drive' their Jeep Wranglers on rough ground and twisted trails over a series of off-road courses. The object of the game is to complete each course successfully, upgrading the Jeep Wrangler model as it progresses from Sport to Sahara to the top-of-the-line Rubicon. Craig Holland, founder of the California-based mobile game maker Thumbworks, states that Jeep® Off Road Jam provides 'an opportunity where you can blend the brand into the entertainment experience, with rich graphics, colour, and action'.

Source: E.M. Clements Photography

Online gaming sites create word of mouth and brand recognition

A popular game will continue to draw more people to the social gaming site and will introduce new players to the advertising message. Due to the almost addictive nature of gaming and its need for total immersion, the brand enjoys the same complete attention that the gamer gives to the play (Morrissey 2009). Numerous exposures to the brand within the game may increase recall and recognition.

Some weaknesses in using gaming in the media plan

Difficult to target a precise market

Players involved in online gaming sites tend to defy demographic classification, as studies have shown that a large general demographic plays online games (Lovison 2009; Thornham 2009). Hence, it is difficult to determine who is actually seeing the message, and to which audience the message appeals. As is the case with online advertising in general, if the message is not emotive or embedded carefully to stimulate attention, or if the target has not been properly identified, the player could subconsciously tune the message out.

Gaming ads are a distraction and have negative effects

Generally, it can be assumed that video game players are more interested in the game itself, rather than any related advertising within it (Hill 2008). Thus, should the embedded advertising feature differ greatly from the game, or should the difference interfere with normal play, players may snub the advertising. One critic explains that advertising used in gaming must be considered carefully because 'a Pepsi ad in a Lord of the Rings game would be distracting to the gamer and may negatively affect the company' (Knepper 2010: para. 1). Research bears this out as Lewis and Porter (2010) report that incongruent in-game advertising in video games could minimise the perceived sense of realism and annoy players. This may have dire consequences for brand perception.

Advertising's performance depends on its creative match with its vehicle

Studies indicate that a match between product characteristics and a celebrity endorser's image, as one example, has a positive impact on product and advertising evaluations; however, any incongruity between the product and celebrity reduces these favourable evaluations (Kamins 1990). The same holds true for the relationship between the message and the in-game environment. Should the advertising message be inappropriate for the gaming environment or should the creative design overshadow or undermine the game, players may quickly go viral to report their dissatisfaction to others in the gaming community.

Inconsistency in ad-game solutions

One disadvantage of dynamic advertising is that it requires playing online to allow images to be broadcast into the game. Potential problems may result from connectivity or capability. Static placement, which is rather inflexible and 'hardwired' into the game itself, may be difficult to rectify, too, should problems arise with legal claims against the advertising or the advertiser that require an alteration in branded placement. Problems in static placement may require an expensive overhaul in the game's design.

Supplementary digital advertising media

By the end of 2012, South Korea intends to connect every home in the country to the internet at one gigabit per second – a tenfold increase from the already blazing national standard and more than 200 times faster than the average household internet speed in the United States (McDonald 2011). Hong Kong and Japan are directly behind South Korea in this endeavour. For now, most Korean consumers use their advantageous bandwidth largely for lightning internet access and entertainment in multi-player gaming, streaming internet TV, fast video downloads and the like. With this new speed capacity, corporations are turning to high-definition videoconferencing in simultaneous sessions with multiple overseas clients – one market advertisers are eager to explore. What new businesses will be created or how existing businesses will be enhanced through the new gigabit capabilities of the future, or how digital advertising media will attempt to complement this connectivity, are a matter of conjecture.

Other digital media

Email marketing is the traditional online workhorse that many advertisers continue to use for good reason: it allows web-based access from anywhere and can generate repeated messages

Scholars' paper 9.4 The fashionable friend in media

Colliander, J. and Dahlén, M. (2011) Following the fashionable friend: the power of social media, *Journal of Advertising Research*, 51(1), 313-20.

The authors point out that blogs have become very fashionable among writers, readers and marketers. Interestingly, in a survey of seven popular blogs and an equal number of online magazines, they found that blogs generated high brand attitudes and purchase intentions. Their research showed that the publicity effectiveness of blogs is higher than that of online magazines, something the authors call 'a symptom of a new logic wherein media, marketing, and consumers are joined in friendships'. As online magazines look for a new face while trying to preserve their original identity as a traditional medium, the research suggests that they could learn a lot from social media by making adjustments to the 'new logic': update their image, form more personal relationships with readers and promote blogs as part of their online presence.

with auto responders. Mass email messages can be sent to multiple individuals or to a group of like individuals; they can create online sign-ups or opt-ins, provide for message failure tracking and reporting, and even allow for automated 'unsubscribe' to minimise the annoyance factor to the consumer.

On-demand viewing and *long-form content* allow advertisers to communicate with opt-in target audiences with interactive attractors. Audiences are not subjected to the 30-second TV spot (push strategy) but willingly view advertisements with instantaneous calls to action.

App technology, also known as third-party applications, is designed specifically for wireless users on mobile phones, pods, tablets and other smart devices. They are profitable (though many applications are free), easy to install and use, and plentiful as companies invest in creating new apps for consumers and application. Many experts argue that application technologies may create the most value for businesses. Using the expertise of the media company to serve the specific needs of an audience can create new value.

Long before the tablet, e-paper apps were used in Scandinavia to replicate the printed newspaper. Typically one can flip through the newspapers and then zoom in on articles of interest. The Norwegian news company VG is a prominent example of this line of thinking and native applications have been used by both Dagens Nyheter and Sydvenskan. Some news apps take the content from a website and present it in a more touch-screen-friendly way. The app for Nettavisen.no, an online Norwegian newspaper with no printed version, presents stories from the website with promotional messages inserted in between the stories (Sandvand 2011).

Cinema advertising represents a small, but very effective, percentage of advertising expenditure. Digital cinema systems and 3D technology, which are already considered viable channels for advertising, deliver high-quality promotional messages with very little clutter. The viewers are a captive audience and also tend to have high recall with respect to the ads they see in the cinema (Noronha 2009).

Ambient communication uses the environment for its marketing communications messages. It can be both traditional and digital in nature, but tends to congregate in areas of high-density pedestrian traffic such as transit hubs (train stations, airports), large open-air urban spaces (Piccadilly Circus, Times Square, the Shibuya district in Tokyo), and areas with many retail stores and walking streets. It often focuses on engaging the consumer on busy thoroughfares with street furniture, multi-sensory messages on escalators and airport travelators, shopping bags, motion-based and artefact-based media, classic (but now digitised) billboards, and attempts to target consumers at work, at play and on their way to work (http://www.ambientadvertising.com.au).

Mcouponing works basically the same as traditional coupons – they drive revenue by encouraging higher volume and repeat sales. They can also help increase product awareness and move overstocked inventory to make room for new, more valuable products. Digital mcouponing is tailored to the needs of the specific consumer and less costly than traditional print coupons, and it is designed for mobile user portability. Easy sign-up, delivery and redemption of digital coupons can add to an effective mobile communications strategy.

Increased deployment of *fibre optics* systems facilitates the emergence of new platforms such as 3D TV, social networks, video phones, music and gaming sites, and will give rise to ever-increasing speed to move more rich and varied content and innovative platforms to use on various networks.

These developments in digital media and emerging technologies do not signal the death of traditional media. All indications, in fact, demonstrate that thinking in terms of traditional and emerging and digital media as opposing factions, or as one rescinding its legacy and the other on the rise, is the wrong way to think about the relationship between the two. Traditional media are used to push traffic online, to pick and choose media choices, to decipher between what is good and bad about digital media and so on. The delineation between distinct components is used for argument's sake only because traditional media are being upgraded and integrated fully into digital delivery systems, as is the case with BBC's iPlayer and CNN's iReport.

In fact, digital and traditional media address similar concerns in similar ways. They exercise an approach to the market with a holistic paradigm at their very foundation: markets address fragmentation with digital tools, whilst traditional media are used in new and varied ways made possible by digital. The movement to mobility and portability finds ever more innovative uses with the traditional media as a partner, not as an adversary. Mobile applications technology continues to evolve with more sophisticated uses, for both business and the general public.

A report by digital ad agency Razorfish finds that the willingness to engage customers is more important for advertisers than embracing technology. For both traditional and digital media, meaningful communication is the key: '[T]he hipster who DMs a company on Twitter and a boomer who sends a letter in the mail both ultimately want the same thing. Thus, companies should worry less about building out numerous channels and touchpoints and more about ensuring each customer interaction communicates value' (Walsh 2011).

Large cataclysmic shifts in communications have occurred before. In *Understanding Digital Marketing*, Ryan and Jones (2009) relate that during the 19th century the telegraph had a similar effect on telecommunications as the growth of digital technology has had in the early 21st century. Technological developments have always inspired changes in advertising communication, but they never fully supersede those that have come before. They only serve to augment the ways that enable one set of people to connect to a larger cross-section of consumers.

Chapter summary

In order to help consolidate your understanding of traditional media, here are the key points summarised against each of the learning objectives.

Explain digital media advertising and how it differs from traditional media

Digital media make full use of online and wireless networks and platforms to find and share information about products, services and companies on mobiles, social networks, blogs and user reviews. Unlike traditional media, digital media are interactive and rely heavily on the participation of the consumer.

Evaluate emerging and converging media as vehicles to carry messages

Portable digital readers and tablets, smartphones and other devices allow for emailing, downloading, socialising or shopping online in new and varied ways. Television, print, outdoor and other forms of traditional media are converging with digital in an increasingly integrated and unified media strategy to create a diverse, innovative, multi-platformed approach to carry messages to the consumer.

Appraise and compare the relative advantages and disadvantages of digital media

Digital media offer unprecedented opportunities in reaching the consumer in a personalised, contextualised manner. Two-way marketing conversations now make possible a richer, deeper, more targeted customer relationship. Issues of privacy, intrusion and uneven technological capabilities, however, if not handled with care, may be detrimental to overall brand perception.

Explore the possibilities for supplementary digital advertising media

Increased broadband width, more advanced wireless networks, smaller portable devices and apps technology are sure to affect the way advertising and the consumer interact. Although technological advances will forge new ways for marketing communications to target the consumer, meaningful communication will remain key.

Review questions

1. With regard to the Obama minicase set out at the start of this chapter, how would you propose his campaign team use digital media to raise funds and votes for the presidential campaign?
2. Discuss some of the advantages and disadvantages of using online media for advertising purposes.
3. Discuss some ways one can use traditional media to drive traffic to online and mobile media sites.
4. Choose two websites – one that you find particularly enjoyable in terms of its use of online advertising and one that you find particularly annoying. Discuss in detail the reasons for your opinions by using examples from the sites.
5. Jot down several advantages to integrating mobile advertising into the advertising media plan.
6. Describe your social media site of choice. Write a brief presentation describing in detail the reasons for your choice, including ease of use and connectivity.
7. List several reasons why it is important for an advertiser to monitor the performance of its social media site.
8. Choose a gaming site with which you are familiar. Design a marketing communications message to be integrated into the gaming site that is both impressive and not intrusive. Explain your choices.
9. Give reasons why advertising on a gaming site might return excellent results.
10. Explain how application technologies may create value for businesses and the advertising medium.

Chapter references

Anon. (2011, May 13) Consumers keen on m-commerce.Warc.com. Retrieved from http://www.warc.com/LatestNews/News/Consumers_keen_on_mcommerce.news?ID=28277

Anon. (2011, November 9) Digital games market to more than double to $53 billion. Retrieved from http://ovum.com/press_releases/digital-games-market-to-more-than-double-to-53-billion/

Anon. (2011, July 25) Google launches Adwords credit card. Retrieved from http://www.warc.com/LatestNews/News/EmailNews.news?ID=28584

Anon. (2011, May 30). Google pushes m-commerce. Retrieved from http://www.warc.com/LatestNews/News/Google%20pushes%20m-commerce.news?ID=28340

Anon. (2011, May 7) Mad Men are watching you, The Economist, 67–8.

Anon. (2011, February 16) Mobile habits evolve. Warc.com. Retrieved from http://www.warc.com/LatestNews/News/Mobile_habits_evolve.news?ID=27899june 2011

Athey, S. and Nekipelov, D. (2010) *A structural model of sponsored search advertising auctions*, retrieved from www.leland.stanford.edu/group/SITE/SITE_2010/segment_3/segment_3_papers/nekipelov.pdf

Bauer, H.H., Barnes, S.J., Reichardt, T. and Neumann, M.M. (2005) Driving consumer acceptance of mobile marketing: a theoretical framework and empirical study, *Journal of Electronic Commerce Research*, 6(3), 181–92

Bayers, C. (2011) Why Silicon Valley can't sell . . . OR why luring big brands to platforms is the valley's next big problem, *Adweek*, 11 July, 29–33

Borzykowski, B. (2011) Social media: seeking proof of the payoff, *Globe and Mail*, 8 June, retrieved from http://www.theglobeandmail.com/report-on-business/small-business/sb-marketing/customer-service/social-media-seeking-proof-of-the-payoff/article2050409/

Broussard, G. (2000) How advertising frequency can work to build online advertising effectiveness, *International Journal of Market Research*, 42(4), 439–57

Butcher, D. (2010) Case study – Sir Richard Branson's Virgin Media, *Mobile Marketer*, 23 November, retrieved from http://www.mobilemarketer.com/cms/resources/case-studies/8218.html

Butcher, D. (2011, June 12) Red Bull boosts brand favorability with augmented reality, *Mobile Marketer*, 12 June, retrieved from http://www.mobilemarketer.com/cms/news/gaming/9447.html

Chang, R. (2009) Virtual goods give brands a new way to play gaming, *Advertising Age*, 80(25), 12

Chiem, R., Arriola, J., Browers, D., Gross, J., Limman, E., Nguyen, P.V. and Seal, K. (2010) The critical success factors for marketing with downloadable applications: lessons learned from selected European countries, *International Journal of Mobile Marketing*, 5(2), 43–56

Colliander, J. and Dahlén, M. (2011) Following the fashionable friend: the power of social media, *Journal of Advertising Research*, 51(1), 313–20

Cooke, C. (n.d.) Obama's digital campaign (web log comment), retrieved from www.wpp.com/wpp/marketing/digital/obamas-digital-campaign.htm

Danaher, P.J. and Mullarkey, G.W. (2003) Factors affecting online advertising recall: a study of students, *Journal of Advertising Research*, 43(3), 252–67

Day, P. (producer) (2011) Biz Stone Twitter founder (audio podcast), 1 June, retrieved from www.bbc.co.uk/worldservice

Dembosky, A. (2011) Yahoo takes hit from falling ad sales, *Financial Times*, 20 July, B20.

Drèze, X. and Zufryden, F. (1998) Is internet advertising ready for prime time? *Journal of Advertising Research*, 38(3), 7–18

Edelman, David (2010) Branding in the digital age: you're spending your money in all the wrong places, *Harvard Business Review*, 27(4), 63–9

Faber, D. (2011) *Squawk on the street* (television broadcast), 27 July, New York: CNBC

Fabian, G.S. (1986) 15-second commercials: the inevitable evolution, *Journal of Advertising Research*, 26(4), RC-3-RC-5

Fulgoni, G.M. and Mörn, M. (2009) Whither the click? How online advertising works, *Journal of Advertising Research*, 49(2), 134–42

Gale, C. (2011) Social media influence in Japanese relief. *Business2Community*, 16 March, retrieved from http://www.business2community.com/social-media/social-media-influence-in-japanese-relief-019459

Gauntlett, D. (2009) Media studies 2.0: a response, *Interactions: Studies in Communication and Culture*, 1(1), 147–57. doi:10.1386/iscc.1.1.147/1

Gillin, P. (2007) *The New Influencers: A Marketer's Guide to the New Social Media.* Sanger, CA: Quill Driver Books

Goldman, S. (2010) Small donations in large numbers, with online help, *New York Times*, 18 March, F31

Goodwin, B. (2011, July 4) Act now to make social media a business success, says Gartner. Retrieved from http://www.computerweekly.com/news/2240104940/Act-now-to-make-social-media-a-business-success-says-Gartner

GSM (2011) *Africa Now the World's Second Largest Mobile Market*, 6 November, retrieved from www.gsmworld.com/newsroom/press-releases

Häkkila, J. and Chatfield, C. (2005) 'It's like if you opened someone else's letter'– user-perceived privacy and social practices with SMS communication. Paper presented at MobileHCI '05, 7th International Conference on Human Computer Interaction with Mobile Devices & Services, Salzburg, Austria, September

Hill, S. (2008) Advergaming and other horror stories, retrieved from http://www.bit-tech.net/cloumns/2008/02/21/advergaming

Hoffman, D.L. and Novak, T.P. (1996) Marketing in hypermedia computer-mediated environments: conceptual foundations, *Journal of Marketing*, 60(3), 50

Hsia, L. (2010) How social media is changing the business of television. *Mashable*, 10 December, retrieved from: http://mashable.com/2010/12/10/social-media-business-tv/

Hye-Jin, P., Hove, T., Hyun Ju, J. and Mikyong, K. (2011) Peer or expert? *International Journal of Advertising*, 30(1), 161–88

IAB. (2009) In-Game Advertising Measurement Guidelines. Retrieved from http://www.iab.net/guidelines/508676/guidelines/in-game

Initiative (2011) *In-Game Advertising*. Retrieved from http://initiative.com/sites/default/files/Game_Advertising.pdf

International Telecommunication Union (2011) Key ICT indicators for the ITU/BDT regions (totals and penetration rates) (data file), retrieved from http://www.itu.int/ITU-D/ict/statistics/at_glance/KeyTelecom.html

Jennings, B. (2011) Android malware a growing security problem for Google, 2 March 2011, accessed 4 July 2011, Newtype.com

Kamins, M.A. (1990) An Investigation into the "Match-Up" Hypothesis in Celebrity Advertising: When Beauty May be Only Skin Deep, *Journal Of Advertising*, 19(1), 4–13

Kavassalis, P., Spyropoulou, N., Drossos, D., Mitrokostas, E., Gikas, G. and Hatzistamatiou, A. (2003) Mobile permission marketing: framing the market inquiry, *International Journal of Electronic Commerce*, 8(1), 55

Kharbanda, S. (2006) Web advertising acceptability and usefulness: attaining top positions on search engines is more cost-effective than a yellow page or directory listing, *Journal of Website Promotion*, 2(1/2), 185–93. doi:10.1080/15533610802104224

Knepper, L. (2010) I'm in your game, advertising my stuff (web log comment), 14 October, retrieved from http://rhetoricofgaming.wordpress.com/2010/10/14/im-in-your-game-advertising-my-stuff

Kuss, C. (2011) What mad men can learn from angry birds, *The Creative*, 21 June, retrieved from http://edition.cnn.com/2011/OPINION/06/21/mad.men.angry.birds

Latkiewicz, M. (2010) Beyond viral: how successful marketers are embracing the social web, *Mashable*, 10 December, retrieved from: http://mashable.com/2010/11/30/foursquare-gap-ad-campaign/http://mashable.com/2010/12/01/beyond-viral-social-marketing/

Lavrakas, P. (2010) An evaluation of methods used to assess the effectiveness of advertising on the internet. Interactive Advertising Bureau (May 2010)

Leong, E.F., Xueu, H. and Stanners, P. (1998) Comparing the effectiveness of the website with traditional media, *Journal of Advertising Research*, 38(5), 44–51.

Leppäniemi, M. (2008) Determinants of intentions to receive mobile advertising messages: a theoretical framework and empirical study, retrieved from herkules.oulu.fi/isbn9789514288159/isbn9789514288159.pdf

Lewington, L. (2011) Will smartphones replace all other gadgets? BBC.co.uk, 11 November, retrieved from http://news.bbc.co.uk/2/hi/programmes/click_online/9637184.stm

Lewis, B. and Porter, L. (2010) In-Game Advertising Effects: Examining Player Perceptions of Advertising Schema Congruity in a Massively Multiplayer Online Role-Playing Game, *Journal of Interactive Advertising*, 10(2), 46–60

Li, H., Edwards, S.M. and Lee, J-H. (2002) Measuring the intrusiveness of advertisements: scale development and validation, *Journal of Advertising*, 31 (2), 37–47.

Lovison, J. (2009) Getting in the game, *Adweek*, May, retrieved from http://www.adweek.com/news/advertising-branding/getting-game-99373

Lutz, M. (2009) *The Social Pulpit: Barack Obama's Social Media Toolkit*. New York: Edelman Trust Barometer

McCoy, S., Everard, A., Polak, P. and Galleta, D.F. (2007) The effects of online advertising, *Communications of the ACM*, 50(3), 84–8.

McDonald, M. (2011) South Korea seeks internet speed of 1 gigabit a second. *New York Times*, 21 February, retrieved from http://www.nytimes.com

Marken, G. (2007) Social media . . . the hunted can become the hunter, *Public Relations Quarterly*, 52(4), 9–12

Mathieson, R. (n.d.) Get your game on: the rise of mobile advergames, retrieved from http://mmaglobal.com/articles/get-your-game-rise-mobile-advergames

Mobile Marketing Association (2011) Norwegian breakthrough in mobile advertising in Finland, 25 January, retrieved from http://mmaglobal.com/news/norwegian-breakthrough-mobile-advertising-finland

Moonhee, Y., Roskos-Ewoldsen, D.R., Dinu, L. and Arpan, L.M. (2006) The effectiveness of 'in-game', *Journal of Advertising*, 35(4), 143–52

Morrissey, B. (2009) Top digital trends of 2010, *Adweek*, 28 December, retrieved from http://www.adweek.com/news/technology/top-digital-trends-2010-101182

Nelson, M.R. (2002) Recall of brand placement in computer/video games, *Journal of Advertising Research*, 42(2), 80–92.

Noronha, S. (2009) A new wave of 3D, *Sound & Communications*, 55(10), 52–8

Okabe, D. (2004) Emergent social practices, situations and relations through everyday camera phone use. Paper presented at the International Conference on Mobile Communication in Seoul, Korea, October

Park, T., Shenoy, R. and Salvendy, G. (2008) Effective advertising on mobile phones: a literature review and presentation of results from 53 case studies, *Behaviour & Information Technology*, 27(5), 355–73. doi:1080/1449290600958882

Pringle, H. and Field, P. (2008) *Brand Immortality: How Brands Can Live Long and Prosper*. London: Kogan Page.

Raman, N.V. and Leckenby, J.D. (1998) Factors affecting consumers' 'Webad' visits, *European Journal of Marketing*, 32(7/8), 737.

Rettie, R., Grandcolas, U. and Deakins, B. (2005) Text message advertising: response rates and branding effects, *Journal of Targeting, Measurement and Analysis for Marketing*, 13(4), 304–12

Richardson, N., Gosnay, R. and Carroll, A. (2010) *Quick Start Guide to Social Media Marketing*. London: Kogan Page

Robehmed, N. (2011) Attention, tweeps: companies are watching you (web log post), 7 July, retrieved from http://business.blogs.cnn.com/2011/07/07/attention-tweeps-twitter-following/

Robinson, H., Wysocka, A. and Hand, C. (2007) Internet advertising effectiveness, *International Journal of Advertising*, 26(4), 527–41.

Ryan, D. and Jones, C. (2009) *Understanding Digital Marketing*. London: Kogan Page

Sandvand, J.E. (2011) Six ways Scandinavian media companies approach iPad, 20 February, retrieved from http://www.betatales.com/2011/02/20/six-ways-scandinavian-media-companies-approach-ipad/

Sarnblad, F. (2011) YourSingapore.com – a tourism campaign for the digital age. Warc. Retrieved 16 November 2011 from www.warc.com

Scharl, A., Dickinger, A. and Murphy, J. (2005) Diffusion and success factors of mobile marketing, *Electronic Commerce Research and Applications*, 4(2), 159–73.

Simon, B. (2010) Starbucks and Facebook – some interesting numbers, but what do they mean?, 27 June, retrieved from www.everythingbutthecoffee.net

Smartphones surge in Asia (2011, March 13) *Warc.com*. Retrieved from http://www.warc.com/LatestNews/News/Smartphones%20surge%20in%20Asia.news?ID=28007

Smith, A. (2008) The internet's role in campaign 2008, Pew Internet & American Life Project, retrieved from http://www.pewinyernet.org

Song, J. and Zinkhan, G. (2008) Determinants of perceived web site interactivity, *Journal of Marketing*, 72(2), 99–113.

Song, Y. and Mela, C.F. (2011) A dynamic model of sponsored search advertising, *Marketing Science*, 30(3), 447–68. doi:10.1287/mksc.1100.0626

Sultan, F. and Rohm, A. J. (2005) The coming era of 'brand in the hand' marketing, *MIT Sloan Management Review*, 47(1), 82–91.

Sultan, F. and Rohm, A.J. (2008) How to market to Generation M(obile), *MIT Sloan Management Review*, retrieved from http://sloanreview.mit.edu/the-magazine/articles/2008/summer/49412/how-to-market-to-generation-mobile/

Suster, M. (2011) The future of advertising will be integrated (web log comment), 29 April, retrieved from http://techcrunch.com/2011/04/29/the-future-of-advertising-will-be-integrated/

Thornham, H. (2009) Claiming a stake in the videogame, *Convergence: The Journal of Research into New Media Technologies*, 15(2), 141–59. doi:10.1177/1354856508101580

Tumulty, K. (2007) Obama's viral marketing campaign, retrieved from www.time.com/time/magazine/article/0,9171,1640402,00.html#ixzz1k7HSe4fC http://www.bluestatedigital.com/work/case-studies/barack-obama/

Wakolbinger, L.M., Denk, M. and Oberecker, K. (2009) The effectiveness of combining online and print advertisements: is the whole better than the individual parts? *Journal of Advertising Research*, 49(3), 360–72.

Walsh, M. (2011) Razorfish: Facebook, Twitter don't make customers feel valued, 31 January, retrieved from http://www.mediapost.com/publications/article/143921/

Webster, A. (2011) Smartphone and tablet rundown: what developers need to know, *Gamasutra*, 26 July, retrieved from http://www.gamasutra.com/view/feature/6440/smartphone_and_tablet_rundown_.php)

Wilken, R. and Sinclair, J. (2009) 'Waiting for the kiss of life': mobile media and advertising, *Convergence: The Journal of Research into New Media Technologies*, 15(4), 427–45

Wise, K., Bolls, P.D., Kim, H., Venkataraman, A. and Meyer, R. (2008) Enjoyment of advergames and brand attitudes: the impact of thematic relevance, *Journal of Interactive Advertising*, 9(1), retrieved from http://www.jiad.org/article107

Young, A. (2011) Social media is a venue, not a strategy, *AdAge MediaWorks*, 15 June, retrieved from http://adage.com/article/mediaworks/viewpoint-social-media-a-venue-a-strategy/228192/

Chapter 10
Media planning

Media planning has a much greater role today in the advertising industry than it had traditionally in the late 20th century. Faced with a growing number of new media options, media planners now lend their expertise earlier in the strategic stages of a campaign. Media planning involves not only making the appropriate traditional and digital media selections for advertising the product or service, but it also supplies detailed background research on the nature of the market and the consumer.

Aims and learning objectives

The aim of this chapter is to explain the issues and processes associated with media planning.

The learning objectives of this chapter are to:

1. explain how the media plan helps advertisers achieve marketing and advertising objectives
2. discuss the significance of creativity in media planning
3. describe the changing media planning process and its evolution
4. identify and appraise the factors in determining media objectives and strategies
5. introduce the concepts of reach and frequency as they relate to media.

Minicase A need to revisit supermarket TV

Sainsbury's is one of the UK's oldest food retailers. Founded in London in 1869, it prides itself on its fair pricing structure, environmentally sound sourcing of products and contributions to the local communities its food stores serve. In 2011, the company unveiled a sustainability strategy that will include in-store geothermal energy, fewer pre-packaged goods and an increase in the volume of green products in its supermarkets.

A typical Sainsbury's target customer is female with children, and is the primary shopper for household food purchases. As part of its overall strategy of 'Making Sainsbury's great again', the food retailer relaunched its 'Taste the difference' brand and focused on boosting its non-food business, making convenience another attraction for its primary female market.

The company's media campaign over the past several years has included a presence in broadcast, outdoor, print, online and traditional direct marketing, a social media presence and more. Sainsbury's has traditionally invested substantial resources in marketing communications through traditional channels, and is particularly keen on advertising through the broadcast media, especially television. There has been some success with this schedule in creating a fresher, more modern image for its core UK supermarket business, particularly through its successful advertising connection with TV chef Jamie Oliver, though the audacious young chef ended his 11-year partnership with the Sainsbury's supermarket group in late 2011.

In a media climate where such high-end and low-end competitors as Waitrose, Tesco and Asda continued to integrate and spend at high levels to cut through the clutter, Sainsbury's thought that it was time to take a hard, fresh look at how they were spending their advertising pounds, especially for television broadcast. The media plan had begun to flatline and it looked weary.

From 2007 to 2009 TV played a dominant role (as it always had) in the Sainsbury's media mix. Over that period TV advertising accounted for around 60% of the media budget. Activity in the media schedule had generally been split into two areas - brand TV and promotional TV. By separating these two areas, the communications teams had fallen into a rut: maximising brand TV meant creating new brand copy every 3-4 weeks, accumulating TV rating points, then shelving it; the promotional TV campaign meant that on average three different commercials would be airing on various channels at any given time. By March 2010, it became

Exhibit 10.1 Sainsbury's store
Source: Alamy Images

clear that some of the more recent brand ads were starting to show a decline in recall versus previous brand ads, and that the campaign lacked integration and had given way to inefficiency.

The challenge for Sainsbury's was to reconfigure its TV media planning, whilst maintaining the same budget as the year before. It would be necessary for Sainsbury's to test different timing strategies to optimise the schedule and to find out what would work best.

Further, Sainsbury's media agency, PHD, realised that they were not attaining maximum effective frequency on the brand's TV messages. Media analysis demonstrated that the weighting and phasing behind the campaign schedule were not delivering an effective frequency among its target audience. As a result, recall of the core Sainsbury's message was suffering as well.

Sainsbury's and PHD knew it was necessary to explore continuity in the different elements of their TV advertising. The promotional messages did not seem to link to the brand messages, in either creative content or length. The team were also aware that there had to be a focus on integration - rather than running brand TV and promotional TV as individual entities, there should be links between the advertising.

In short, Sainsbury's needed to revisit its media plan to increase its television advertising effectiveness.

Sources: Armstrong (2011); www.sainsburys.co.uk; http://www.thinkbox.tv/server/show/ConCaseStudy.1723

Introduction

The purpose of media planning is to select channels of communication that will deliver the advertising message to the target audience. Quite simply, it is the media planner's objective to deliver the right message to the right people through the right medium or multiple media. Since most resources in advertising are spent on media (media placement), the media planner's decisions are crucial to the success of advertising in the overall marketing plan.

Advertisers try to match the profile of a target audience with the characteristics of a potential medium. If the target audience for a consumer product is a 35–44-year-old male professional who has a good deal of discretionary income, the company or advertiser might consider placing advertisements in high-end consumer magazines, such as *GQ* in the USA or *Abitare* in Italy, two magazines that appeal to a predominantly professional, and sophisticated, male readership with money to spend. When selecting an upmarket men's magazine, the advertiser should attempt to minimise wasteful expenditure by eliminating obviously ill-suited publications. These would include magazines that have a predominantly younger audience, such as *Teen Magazine*, or those with a predominantly female readership, such as *Marie Claire*. Some media, such as general-interest consumer magazines and newspapers, network radio or television, and general-internet sites, allow advertisers to reach a cross-section of the consumer market. Other media, as we have learned, such as mobile or social media, enable the advertiser to reach well-defined, distinct markets with their marketing communications messages.

A number of syndicated research organisations worldwide can help in defining the target audience. MRI (Mediamark Research, Inc.) in the United States collects information for the media planner on consumer habits with regard to TV and radio, print readership and internet usage, among others. IMRB International offers market research and insights on consumers from South Asia, to the Middle East and North Africa, specialising in quantitative and qualitative research, media, retail, industrial and customer satisfaction. Germany's Gesellschaft für Konsumforschung (Society for Consumer Research), the fourth largest market research organisation in the world, delivers customised research (www.gfk.com) on reach, engagement and TV, radio, print and online media usage, whilst Kinetic in the UK analyses and projects out-of-home trends. The information gleaned from these organisations and others is elaborate and often determines the direction the media schedule takes.

How does media planning work?

Some profess that media planning efficiency is the result of a highly analytical process (Charnes et al. 1968; Gensch 1973; Pergelova et al. 2010), based solely on research and supplemented by various formulas and software that tend to earmark the most desirable paths for the planner to tackle in reaching pre-established objectives. Others believe that the process is more intuitive and thereby less scientific, relying heavily on right-brain faculties and less so on scientific ones. All would probably agree that a creative approach is needed to tackle the relativity of media planning, its multiple facets and fluctuating variables, and its intricate nature.

Perhaps the ideal approach to media planning is a synthetic one, where the analytical is melded with intuition in answering the many vital questions the planner encounters in the process, that is, which vehicles should we use? should we have a social presence? when do we run the campaign? how frequently should we advertise? should we integrate with other forms of media? is the timing appropriate? These and other media decisions are influenced by a number of factors, including the projected breadth of the media schedule, the economy, the tone of the message, the size of the budget and the whims of the consumer. Understanding what these factors mean and interpreting the data accordingly with all the media tools at one's disposal is sometimes a daunting task.

Historically, media planners were the final step in an agency process that highlighted the activities of account planning and creative direction. More recently, media decisions have become more critical and clients have become more demanding in what an agency does with its money, as they seek efficiency and accountability to separate them out from the competition. The media planner's task is so challenging today because it must typically include

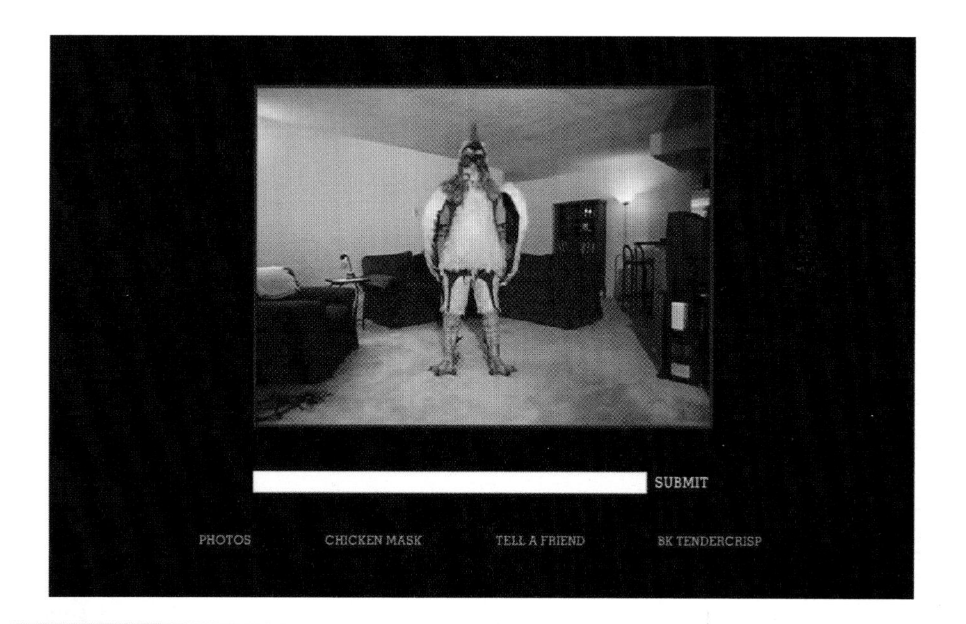

Exhibit 10.2 Burger King and the Subservient Chicken

In 2004, Crispin Porter + Bogusky (CP+B) (Miami, USA) created a viral marketing mascot, the Subservient Chicken, to act as a Burger King forum for unplanned messages. Visitors to the www.subservientchicken.com site were able to ask the chicken to respond to commands, such as dance, show teeth, swim or react to the competition (McDonald's). Many visitors learned about the Subservient Chicken through word of mouth, both online and offline. In the first two weeks after the site's launch, the Subservient Chicken story appeared on a number of broadcast segments, including five separate segments in television shows, with great success. Within months, the site had generated millions of unplanned hits from over 15 million unique visitors.

Source: © Burger King

knowledge of integrated and social media, mobile and wireless, as well as the traditional media options in their standard and converging forms.

Another dimension to the media planner's role has been made necessary by the advent of unplanned messages. Planned messages such as a mobile campaign or a television commercial are organised and scheduled by the advertiser to appear at a particular time and in a particular media space. Unplanned messages, such as word-of-mouth viral initiatives on Twitter, are often not planned or scheduled but launched by individuals or organisations other than advertisers. Media planners have little direct control over the flow of these unplanned messages, but they can indirectly influence and facilitate the flow of the unplanned message through reactions to it.

These new realities in media have changed the way that media planning works within the advertising industry. Media planners play an increasingly important role in today's advertising

ViewPoint 10.1 The Apartheid Museum: media plan creates awareness through pop culture

Wayde Davy, deputy director of the Apartheid Museum in Johannesburg, South Africa, believed that the young had forgotten their history. The Apartheid Museum learned this first-hand when it discovered that its numbers and attendance figures had dwindled considerably, especially among the young, who generally ignored history and no longer deemed South Africa's history relevant to their own, a mere 17 years after the historic call to freedom and subsequent independence. South African youth were more enamoured with popular culture and its manifestations of MTV and e-entertainment than with their own heritage.

The Museum faced two challenges: how to increase awareness among the young and how to create a buzz that was strong enough to rekindle history among them. Traditional methods would not work. The agency TBWA\Hunt\Lascaris-Johannesburg, part of Omnicom Group Inc. (www.omnicomgroup.com), a leading global marketing and corporate communications company, decided to take the discussion to the primary youth market - meet them on their own turf and approach them with attitude, which meant that the campaign needed to be impactful and grab their attention. A secondary market would be made up of the South African adult population, who it was believed had been remiss in transferring their own recent historical knowledge to the young.

As part of their research, TBWA went to the streets to ask young people about the apartheid government - very few of them could offer any insights on apartheid but most could answer questions on popular culture such as the name of Beyoncé's fiancé or the Queen of Talk. This 'sorry lack' of knowledge among the young became the focal point of the campaign, first by launching virally on the Museum's website (YouTube), then later into similar content in television advertisements. The immediate impact of the campaign drew attention to major networks in South Africa as well as major news organisations worldwide, so the campaign captured free additional media attention there as well.

Throughout the campaign the Apartheid Museum received free media exposure and free PR generated across print and broadcast channels in South Africa. Traffic within the museum among students and learners increased by 12%, and the Apartheid Museum recorded an overall 5% increase in the number of all visitors to the museum over March and April 2010 in relation to the same period in 2009.

Clearly the success of this campaign was due to an agency's ability to engage a target audience. TBWA utilised the priorities of the young audience to its benefit.

Source: Cannes Creative Lions (2011)

Question

Why did the advertisers in this campaign consider a primary and a secondary market?

Task

Choose a non-profit organisation that you feel is underappreciated or undervalued. Describe in detail a plan to create awareness of the noteworthiness and value of the organisation you have chosen.

environment because of the proliferation of new media choices and the increased complexity of media and audience research. To keep strides with new developments, the media planning stage now often occurs earlier in the advertising process than it used to because of its intrinsic association with the brand.

A short and recent evolution of media planning

Media planning had essentially remained unchanged in the last years of the 20th century. Slight changes occurred in some areas, naturally, such as the shift in emphasis from product to consumer, but nothing like the dramatic changes that advertising media have witnessed in the last ten years. New phenomena such as the internet, mobile telephony and mobility, consumer- and user-generated content, the democratisation of content and acute fragmentation have made media planning a very complex discipline. Several areas stand out as the most significant in this evolution.

Increased complication and risk

Imagine you are living in an earlier media space – say the late 1950s or early 1960s, the precise period in which the popular TV series about early advertising, *Mad Men*, takes place. Many countries have at best two or three commercial television stations; radio is basically relegated to an AM band; and magazines are general interest in nature. Newspapers dominate. Fast forward to the 21st century; not only are entire countries digitising, but there is also a plethora of television stations, multiplied by satellite and cable transmissions. TV has fragmented into network TV, syndicated (repeats of favourite shows after their seasons have expired), spot and local cable. FM, satellite and streaming online radio can offer literally thousands of listening stations from anywhere in the world. Magazines, as discussed earlier, have segmented into literally thousands of speciality choices, satisfying all occupations, interests, income groups and lifestyles. Internet and mobile casting expand the menu with on-the-go opportunities that know no national boundaries (often for a price). DVDs, personal selling and events marketing

Exhibit 10.3 Defining the future with Silicon Valley

At a BrandMax conference in London in 2011, Michael Kassan, chairman and chief executive of consultancy firm MediaLink, predicted that digital literacy would be the key to surviving the changing technology landscape. Kassan's argument is that if marketers do not keep up with advances coming out of Silicon Valley, if they fail to see technology as a utility integrated in consumers' lives, they will have no future in the discipline. His message for the future of advertising media: 'Digital technology has elevated the unmatched impact of visual storytelling into what I believe may be the single most potent form of marketing communications that has ever existed – television. It's just now we don't have to watch it in the TV set.'

Source: Alamy Images

have taken centre stage as well. The choices today are vast and varied; the digital age, for one, has shifted the power onto the savvy consumer, who now has seemingly limitless possibilities to approach the market on their own terms. The increased number of emerging and converging media options at the media planner's disposal has made media planning an exciting but very challenging vocation.

Increased costs

With the increase in media choices comes an increase in the number of messages for the consumer to decipher. Consumers are inundated with so many messages that it is impossible for the viewer to process all of them. As a result, most messages go unnoticed, though creative endeavours strive for new ways to have them stand out. This costs money. In addition, clients and advertisers have become increasingly impatient with a medium's inability to deliver the set number of *impressions*, an *estimate* of the number of people an advertisement reaches, that it claims to deliver. As a result, targets are restricted even further and the cost of reaching them rises. More frustrating for both client and advertiser is the elusive power of digital media. The old ways of appealing to audiences no longer work in many cases and costs can skyrocket by adding digital to the media plan.

The fallibility of metrics

With traditional media, the relationship between a media planner's calculations and the perceived outcomes was quite simple: pay x amount for an advertisement and the company is 'guaranteed' a number of impressions from subscription rates and news-stand purchases. However, advertisers could not guarantee purchases based on these so-called impressions. The guarantee was that a consumer would be exposed to the magazine, and so had the opportunity to see the ad, but there was no assurance that they had actually seen it.

As the marketplace becomes more sophisticated and transitions to the digital model become more frequent, clients have begun to raise doubts about the counting and auditing of these marketing channels. Indeed, many have questioned the very reliability on which media planning and buying have been premised for decades. Clients want proof and hard facts to show that the advertising dollars or pounds or yen they invest are maximising the returns on expenditures and reaching the specific targets they desire.

There is a variety of methods used to cost the media, and some of the major ones are depicted in Table 10.1.

Print media continues to use *CPM* (cost per thousand). This measures the relative average cost of reaching one thousand people, per publication. *CTR* (click-through ratio) measures the percentage of impressions that result in a click. *CPA* (cost per action) is the payment

Table 10.1 Methods of costing media

Costing method	Explanation
CPM (cost per thousand)	measures the relative average cost of reaching one thousand people, per publication
CTR (click-through ratio)	measures the percentage of impressions that result in a click
CPA (cost per action)	the payment received for each action undertaken by a consumer
CPRP (cost per rating point)	measures the cost of reaching one per cent of the target audience of a specific television audience
Impressions	an estimate of the number of people an advertisement reaches

Scholars' paper 10.1 Connecting planning and placement

Malthouse, E. and Calder, B. (2011) Media placement versus advertising execution, *International Journal of Market Research*, 52(2), 217–30

The authors argue, among other things, that vehicle-level engagement is more relevant to media placement decisions, and argue that advertising effectiveness is closely related to the level of engagement with the magazine. In other words, the media context in which the ad appears may be more important than the ad itself! Secondly, they compare the relative importance of ad engagement to the execution factors of size, position and colour, and show that engagement (with the vehicle) is of comparable importance. The implications for advertising and media planning are clear: the authors suggest that it would be useful for media companies to examine and report overall levels of engagement from multiple perspectives, as involvement with magazines present multidimensional experiences.

received for each action undertaken by a consumer. This might be a download, a common measurement method in gaming.

Broadcast media use *CPRP* (cost per rating point). A programme rating is a percentage of households tuned to a television programme at a particular time. One (1) *rating point* indicates that 1 per cent of all households were 'watching' the television programme. If a Thursday evening episode of the long-running British series *EastEnders* achieved a 15 rating, it would mean that 15 per cent of all television households in the UK on that Thursday evening were tuned to *EastEnders*.

These standards, however, are often inconsistent, and have led to calls for improved measurement definitions, such as high audience engagement figures, which promise to better reflect actual exposures (Cusack 2009). We will discuss these and other calculations in detail in the next chapter.

More competitive environment

Media buying was once considered the 'always a handmaiden and never a bride' unit of the advertising agency. With respect to creative and account functions, media was often an afterthought. However, as media proliferated, we have seen the emergence of independent media-buying companies, specialising in the purchasing of media for a vast array of clients and distinct and apart from the agencies themselves. Behind this growth lay the idea that the more financial clout the media-buying services enjoyed, the greater the benefits for the advertisers who had hired them.

The larger agencies responded by unleashing their own media departments that could compete with the independent services. A period of consolidation and strong growth ensued, so that by the early 21st century a few huge media conglomerates controlled much of what was spent on media. Since the time of consolidation, however, large full-service media companies have given way to smaller, leaner, more specialised and *independent media buying services*. Well-known companies have switched to independent media buyers such as Total Media (www.totalmedia.co.uk) in the UK, Ocean Media in the USA and Kruse Media in Melbourne, Australia, all of which plan and buy campaigns exclusively and move across all media from print to digital to outdoor. In some specialised cases, moreover, there are independent media agencies and buyers that purchase only broadcast time (time buyers), or others who purchase only print space (space buyers), and now, those who purchase exclusively digital space.

The independent media buying service operates outside the traditional agency structure, which has been one of the important changes in the industry in recent years and illustrates the significantly enhanced role the media enjoy (see Figure 10.1).

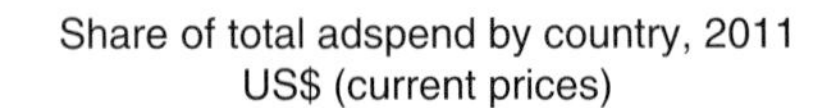

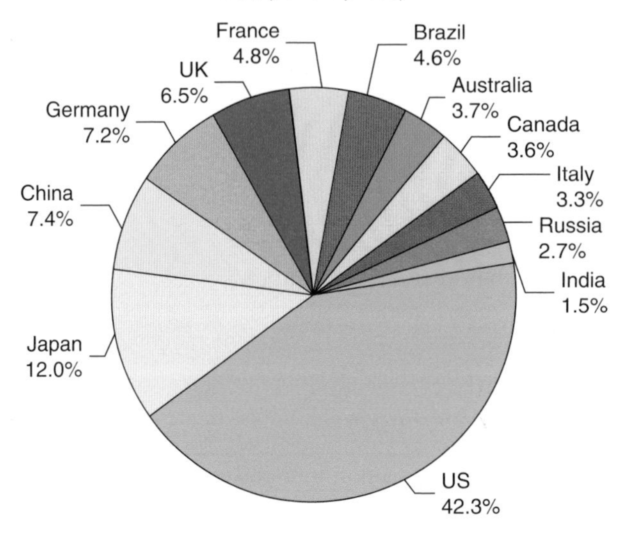

Figure 10.1 Media advertising expenditures - global
Source: Warc, International Ad Forecast 2011/12 (July), www.warc.com

Free media environment

Media are also becoming more people (consumer) centric as they disseminate information and build social capital across networks, all of which is based on a host of new variables, some of which include location, issues and events. Experience over the past several years with social media has demonstrated that brand buzz can be created without investing heavily into advertising expenditures and big-budget media plans. Media organisations and projects try to survive in an era where content and opportunity are so abundant that few are willing to pay for them (Sasaki 2009). Social media, for example, unlike other forms of marketing communications, are a relationship-building mechanism that is not for sale. Using social media as a virtual networking tool can increase contacts and even lead to revenue, but its success is not necessarily contingent upon a media plan or a commission, or the exchange of funds.

The media plan

The media selections and scheduling decisions associated with the planned delivery of a message are put forward in a *media plan*. It is usually determined by setting up activities that specify media objectives and strategies and the best ways to realise them. Once the marketing objectives have been determined, media opportunities are discussed to ensure the best approach to achieving the objectives, whilst yielding advertising message efficiency.

Media objectives are generally built around answers to five basic questions: *who, when, where, how often*, and *in what way*, though the answer to the question *how much* also finds its way, albeit indirectly, into these objectives. Answers to these questions serve as signposts to the setting of the objectives and give direction to drive the advertising strategy towards their realisation.

Media objectives are dependent on a number of variables that have become standard in the industry. After selecting the target audience, the media planner must examine the unique characteristics of the media options available. These vary from country to country, region to region, urban context to suburban context. What is the benefit of using a magazine ad as opposed to the mobile message? Is an online presence necessary? Do we use standard print vehicles or do we try non-traditional media? We looked at the advantages and disadvantages of each medium in Chapters 8 and 9 as they apply to the target audience and the market strategy that supports it.

Now it is up to the media planner to do research to determine choices that best fit media objectives with the consumer target audiences. Additional steps will also be taken to help ensure that the advertising message reaches the right people. This might involve looking at the current market environment, the feasibility of secondary or tertiary target audiences to whom the message might be delivered, and the locations, domestic or international, local, regional or national, or some combination, may be essential preliminary steps to shape the media plan.

One company's objective might be to increase traffic among 18–24-year-olds on the StumbleUpon.com discovery and share website. Once the objectives are in place, the media planner can begin working on formulating strategies to appeal to the target. The strategy must address the objective or lead to some kind of action plan. Strategies need to be adjusted and readjusted, as necessary. In the StumbleUpon example below, the strategy might be to target only social networking sites that 'tag' online advertising, such as the social sites Digg or Facebook, and similar places the media planner has surmised through research that most of the desired target audience resides.

A distinction must be made between the strategy and the tactics used to execute the media strategy. As examined in Chapter 4, strategies are generally the big ideas; tactics are the specific

ViewPoint 10.2 Engaging social media in Brazil

Those brands considering launching a social media communication or advertising plan in Brazil are advised through the team blog for students of the 'Global communications in the age of social media' course at Georgetown University to consider the following factors: the popularity of social media has spread rapidly throughout Brazil; each week Brazilians spend more time online (19.3 hours) than watching television (9.8 hours); member communities are large and popular; Brazilians dislike superficial ad placements and they are a community-oriented people.

The Global communications blog believes that these factors should be considered when determining advertising spend but also in the creative format of the ads themselves. The solution as the team blog sees it is to 'turn traditional advertising on its head and create a new path, one that is focused on creating and generating buzz that can then be spread through social media sites with more authenticity and a sense of community', the ultimate goal of all viral campaigns.

Given the common knowledge that viral marketing campaigns can potentially generate buzz and brand awareness, online or offline, and given Brazil's penchant for social media, online viral campaigns become all the more relevant and effective. The team blog explains that the Brazilian job portal website Dreamjob puts the influence of social media in Brazil to the test with the launch of its 2009 viral 'Worst job in the world' campaign. With more than slight tongue in cheek, the television clip features a massage therapist whose (worst) job is to work on the bodies of supermodels all day long. The exhausted therapist complains about the harsh conditions of working 14-hour days (including weekends), with no union or trade associations and no job protection.

The Sao Paolo-based BorghiEhr/Lowe agency's campaign was a big success, with thousands of YouTube hits in its initial launch and created spin-offs in other parts of the world.

Source: www.borghierhlowe.com.br; Global Comm Class (2009)

Question

How does the agency turn traditional advertising 'on its head'?

Task

Launching a social media campaign and hoping that it goes viral are challenging. Detail how you would organise a social media campaign to increase its chances of success.

actions that must be taken in developing or rolling out those big strategic ideas. If the objective is to introduce 250,000 18–24-year-olds to StumbleUpon within the space of six months, the strategy needs to assess where and when people are most likely to be receptive to this communication (Digg, for example). The tactics include *how* you plan to expose the 18–24-year-old target with *what kind of* sufficient messaging to achieve the 250,000 new introductions. The tactical considerations might take the form of SMS messaging, couponing or advertising on gaming sites.

The *media mix* is the combination of all the best media vehicles, non-traditional media and other communication tools that might be employed by the planner to obtain the optimal efficiency available. The objectives, the defining characteristics of the product or service to be advertised, the attitudes of the company (LVMH is one example of a conscientious advertiser) and the allocated budget are just some of the many factors that will influence the configuration of the media mix. A thoughtful blend of media might include a number of different vehicles to take advantage of the uniqueness offered by each medium, as explained in some detail in Chapters 8 and 9, as well as to cover as much as possible of the target audience at the lowest possible cost. The media professional makes choices and gives weight, often described as *message weight*, to the elements used. For example, a mix might include 60% to television, 20% to local radio and 20% to social sites, for media that most efficiently match the target market.

Advertisers in North America, Europe and parts of Asia have a great number of media vehicles to choose from on local, regional and national levels. Often the choices are reinforced by detailed research or experience that dictates the logical choice of one vehicle over another. Media choices are more difficult on a global scale, due to the presence of state-run communications media (commercial free), low coverage by the television medium, scanty research on media delivery and fewer choices in terms of vehicles. Understanding the global media and their nuances is challenging because the media habits of consumers and cultures tend to differ widely. In 2009, Europeans continued to favour print publications, Lebanese watched on average nearly 32 hours of TV per week, one of the highest in the world, Swedes spent much time on the internet, whilst direct mail was more widely used in North America than any other geographic region (Media Data 2010). Knowledge of these trends in media usage is important when developing successful advertising programmes.

With the global market in full swing, the need to provide media buyers and planners with information to meet the demands in international communications marketing becomes imperative. *The Global Media Directory* (www.globalmediadirectory.com) is one example of a resource that covers over 200,000 different media in 233 countries, with profile pages translated into a number of languages, including newspapers, consumer and trade publications, broadcast, cinema and out-of-home data.

A media strategy should be concise but it should also be packed with a clear indication as to how to proceed vis-à-vis the overall scheme of the company and its brands. The media plan serves as the foundation to the components of the marketing communications plan, and is often the first place that a client looks should the media objectives not be accomplished.

Factors in determining media objectives and strategies

The marketing plan defines the company's needs and objectives, usually in great detail. Certain traditional analyses can be performed (SWOT, PESTEL, Ansoff matrix, etc.), which help give direction to a company's marketing. It must be borne in mind that the objectives and strategies that make up advertising communications follow closely on the heels of the overall marketing plan, and focus for the most part on meeting certain communication goals, such as enhancing awareness or increasing visibility, positioning or repositioning the brand among the competition in the current marketplace or changing or maintaining attitudes.

Table 10.2 A sample list of typical media objectives

PTO Indonan Food Exports, Jakarta, Indonesia
'Mi goreng' noodles
$1.5 million (Canadian dollars - CAD) media to reach women in Canada
Six-month roll-out

Factors	Media objectives
Target audience	To **target** adult women, 25-64, in metropolitan areas of Canada (primary market)
Geographic	To provide special **geographic** emphasis in ethnic areas with 1 million+ population (Toronto, Montreal, Vancouver)
Time period	To deliver an equally distributed six-month seasonal **flighting** schedule from April 15 to September 15, with extra weight during holiday weekends
Reach & frequency	To achieve a overall minimum 45% **reach** (R) an average of four times [**frequency** = F] every four weeks over a six-month period
Budget	To allocate a 1.5 million CAD **budget** - 250,000 CAD per month for each of the six months
Creative	To use suitable media that are consistent with **creative** strategy implications

There is no set formula for determining how to approach the media landscape, and there is no set chronological order in the media planning process, though many agree on a number of necessary standards. The media plan generally follows the established marketing and advertising objectives of the company, and then translates those objectives into a plan plausible under the terms of creative direction. It will also typically include the targets (primary and/or secondary), any geographic considerations, timing patterns, reach and frequency numbers (including effective reach and frequency), creative suitability and budgetary considerations.

Market analysis

Prior to the selection of target audiences or vehicles or messages, a company analyses the current situation within the market. Known by several names, such as situation analysis or market analysis, this process usually includes a view of the internal as well as the external factors that may affect the product or service, the competitive offerings and strategies that accompany them and a general survey of current and potential number of target consumers that may be now, or sometime in the future, engaged in the brand.

External factors may be as diverse as the economy (robust or sluggish), transformations in media technology and its uses, the positions taken by the competition with respect to the company's own products or services, the resources available to carry out certain media plans or creative executions, and the like.

Internal factors are also important: media budgetary constraints must be considered as well as the client company's ethos. Some ideas may not fit with the overall proposed budget for the promotional intentions or the company's imprint may limit its choices of media vehicles. A company concerned with teenage promiscuity and pregnancy may not want to advertise in a publication such as *Cosmopolitan*, which has the reputation of treating rather insalubrious topics in its editorial.

Defining the target audience

The target audience is usually determined in the early stages of the media planning process. This is necessary to ensure that the most appropriate media are being utilised to attract the

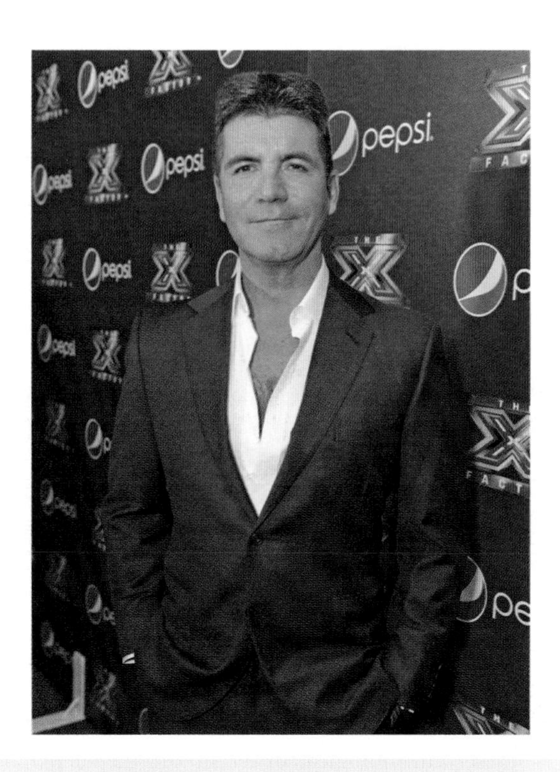

Exhibit 10.4 *X Factor* is a big hit with . . . Pepsi media placement

The launch of the much-acclaimed British TV programme *X Factor* to American audiences was highly anticipated in late 2011. Many were curious about how the show would stack up against *American Idol*, another of producer Simon Cowell's storied successes. The debut was a success, to be sure, but more so among the advertisers than among the audience. The show was chock full of product placements, embarrassingly so, writes one media critic - visible Pepsi vending machines, fancy Pepsi cups for the judges, a Pepsi clearly visible in an interviewee's kitchen. The entertainment marketing company Front Row Analytics estimated that Pepsi received $6.5 million worth of media exposure in two hours - not bad for a debut!

Source: Getty Images

right audience. The optimal goal in meeting these objectives is to cover as much of the target within any one given area as possible. Target audiences may be detailed or general in nature. Often a media plan will specify the desired primary target, and then an ancillary, or secondary one.

The market has become increasingly segmented over the last 20 years. Consumers are divided up into smaller and more precisely defined groups, resulting in fewer consumers as a whole within each group. At some point in the evaluation process, the media planner must decide whether a segmented market is significant enough (in terms of numbers) to pursue. In making this determination, media specialists use at least the variables below, in some combination, to define the target audience.

Demographics

Demographic profiles deal with the study of populations and serve as the foundation to market segmentation, although, as we have seen, they are being complemented or in some cases supplanted by other methods of market measurement. Demographic characteristics divide the market into groups depending on their age, gender, occupation, education, sexual preference, income, ethnicity and other factors. Why is this necessary? It might be foolhardy for a solar energy company, for instance, to try to market a complete home conversion to solar energy, an expensive venture, to someone on the lower end of the income

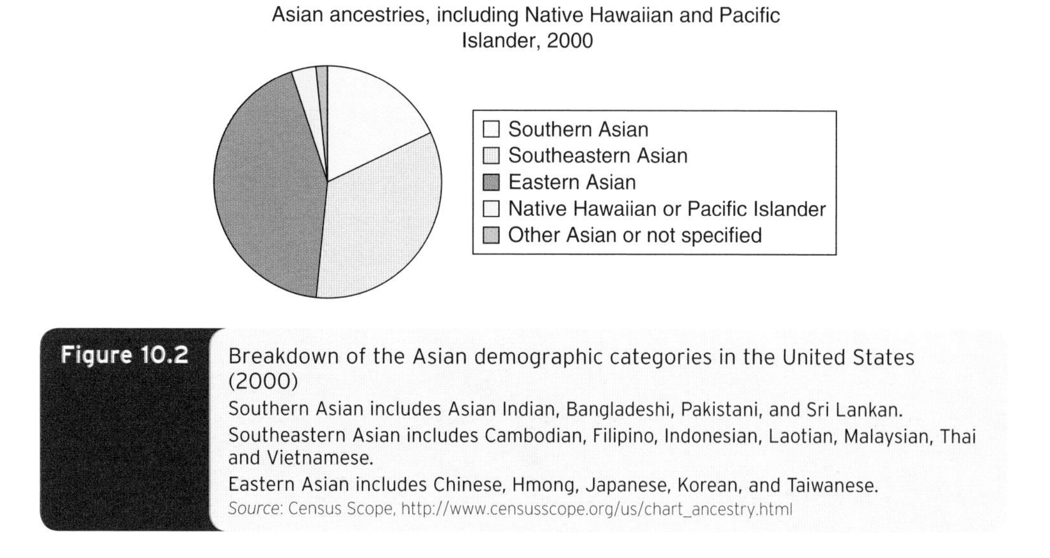

Figure 10.2 Breakdown of the Asian demographic categories in the United States (2000)

Southern Asian includes Asian Indian, Bangladeshi, Pakistani, and Sri Lankan.

Southeastern Asian includes Cambodian, Filipino, Indonesian, Laotian, Malaysian, Thai and Vietnamese.

Eastern Asian includes Chinese, Hmong, Japanese, Korean, and Taiwanese.

Source: Census Scope, http://www.censusscope.org/us/chart_ancestry.html

scale. It would be equally futile to target a childless couple as the primary market for the sale of sweets, since we can assume most probably that the consumers of Skittles or Haribo Gold Bears are comprised of a younger demographic. Companies are aware that different population segments have different needs and will use demographics as one way to target those needs.

To market effectively to a different demographic group requires a rethinking of creative strategies, media choices and cultural factors. Hispanics, African-Americans and Asian-Americans make up the three largest ethnic groups in the United States, which is now a predominantly non-white culture (Clow and Baack 2012). Media planners have had to educate themselves in this ethnically and racially diverse market that includes a number of media targeted to these larger subgroups, and to the multiple subgroups within them as well. Koreans, Japanese, Chinese (divided into their own subgroups), Vietnamese and others within the Asian community each have their own set of cultural values (see Figure 10.2). Clow and Baack (2012) observe that advertising expenditures have been shifted away from a standardised (one-size-fits-all) approach to brand communications to one that addresses the multicultural issues, very often the basis of consumption patterns, in marketing to various groups.

This is especially pertinent when marketers need to know that specific segments of a diverse population demographic may have a tendency for certain purchases. According to Nielsen data, smartphone penetration in the United States is higher among mobile users who are part of ethnic and racial minorities, namely, Asian/Pacific Islanders (45%), Hispanics (45%) and African-Americans (33%), populations that also tend to skew younger. Meanwhile, only 27% of white mobile users reported owning a smartphone (Kellogg 2011).

Psychographics

There are other variables apart from demographics that enter the picture. Let us imagine that two couples, all in their mid 30s, live side by side in the same neighbourhood. They own similarly sized homes, they have the same number of children and they possess identical household incomes. Couple A purchases a 'green' automobile, such as a Toyota Prius, whilst Couple B decides to purchase a Land Rover, a brand not especially recognised for its green attributes. Why the difference? Demographics would not be able to offer insights into the nature of these two purchases, but a study of the neighbours' *psychographic* profiles – their lifestyle habits, their attitudes, values and belief systems – may better explain their consuming behaviours.

Scholars' paper 10.2 **The end of buying media, the rise of buying audiences**

Mandese, J. (2009) The end of buying media, the rise of buying audiences, *Admap*, July/August, retrieved from http://www.warc.com

Joe Mandese explains that recently a new array of entrepreneurs began doing for online display advertising what Google did for search. These display advertising 'aggregators' - known as ad networks, or online ad exchanges - use the model of aggregating the unsold audiences of online publishers into efficient and cost-effective advertising buys for advertisers. Today there are many online advertising networks and exchanges and even an ancillary market of companies that do nothing but 'optimise' inventory across the networks and exchanges. Mandese goes on to explain that a 'secondary premium' marketplace is emerging, due to research and sophisticated tools developed by these aggregators. This marketplace examines and offers to advertisers behavioural targeting and enhanced audience profiling and targeting systems to create a new market in between the commoditised online display market and the premium.

Many consider the psychographic variable the most important for segmentation, for it characterises some of the qualities that other segmentation models cannot, and that may affect the purchasing behaviour of the consumer. Is the consumer compulsive or introverted or perhaps ambitious? Is the consumer an achiever, an actualiser or an experiencer, as is set forth in Values and Lifestyles (VALS) typology? The determination of lifestyles has been correlated across an entire range of products and services (Vyncke 2002).

The VALS system divides consumers according to their personality characteristics into eight distinct behavioural and attitude segments (also available in the UK and Japan as six segments [Graham 1989]. The VALS system, along with PRIZM (market segmenting system), Spectra and NPD, is a tool for dividing the population into groups based purely on psychographics.

Generational cohorts

In addition to demographics and psychographics, in recent years the term *generational cohort* has been used in helping select the target audience. Generations, similarly to individuals and ethnic and racial groups, have their own identities and personalities. Because members of a particular generational cohort are likely to share similar influences and experiences, they tend to maintain relative homogeneous social attitudes, values and even purchasing patterns as a group. Generational cohorts in the United States, for instance, are broken down into the Silent (prior to 1946), Baby Boomers (70 million+, born post World War II from 1946 to 1964), Generation X (those born from 1965 to 1980, often depicted as savvy, entrepreneurial loners), Adult millennials (20-somethings who entered adulthood in the early stages of the new millennium), Teen millennials (the younger segment of those born between 1965 and 1980), formerly known as Generation Y or sometimes as echo boomers, and iGen, indicating those in the population who have never known life without the internet. Each of the cohorts possesses distinct characteristics, it is believed, and exhibits distinct patterns of consumption with respect to the type of media, the time of day they are engaged in media and the offline and online activities in which they engage (Carmichael 2011). Increasingly, generational lifestyles serve as a reference group for certain campaigns.

This characteristic breakdown into cohorts is not unique to the United States, but is also at work elsewhere, particularly in developed countries. As countries become more ethnically and racially diverse and more educated, the media planner has to follow suit to make use of the most up-to-date information to define accurately the target audience. For a time during the first part of the new millenium, the Japanese 'kogal' culture was a unique generational segment of young, urban Japanese women known for their conspicuous consumption of fashion, their

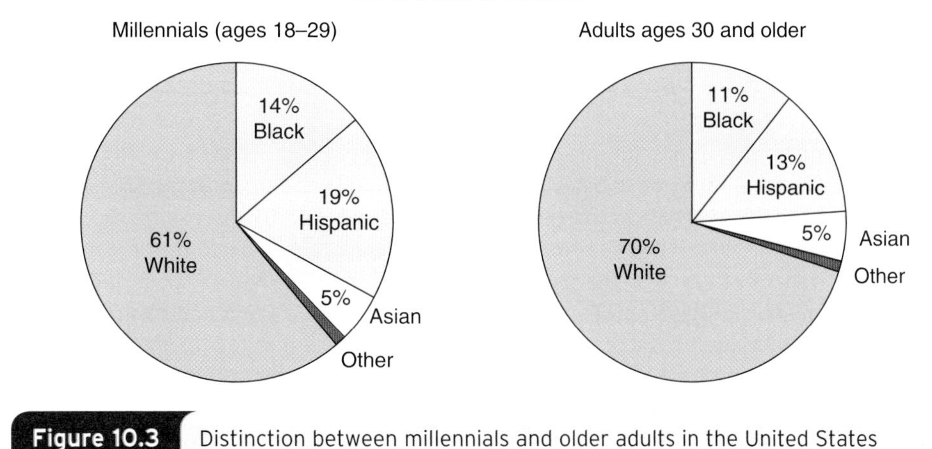

Figure 10.3 Distinction between millennials and older adults in the United States
Source: Pew Research Center (2010)

taste in music and their eternally suntanned looks. They were often early adopters in gadgetry and thus were closely observed by marketers, who would often imitate and incorporate their innovative ways as part of their own new commercial services (Washida 2005).

Behavioural segmentation

Consumers can be influenced by peer pressure and the information they share with friends and family. Groups that share certain qualities with respect to product usage, loyalties or buyer responses towards a particular category are classified into a behavioural segment (see Figure 10.3). *Behavioural segmentation* examines how the group responds or does not respond to brand attributes, price changes or advertising messages, to name a few. The social media and online in general are strong fields of behavioural segmentation and companies try their best to track and target the consumer through them.

The degree of usage (heavy, moderate, light) comes under the aegis of behavioural segmentation. The Pareto principle, or Pareto efficiency, often known as the 80–20 rule, derives from the observations of an early 20th-century Italian economist and asserts that 20% of an audience represents 80% of its consumption (Investopedia, n.d.). There is a heavy-user segment for every brand (Kelley and Jugenheimer 2008: 62), which means that the majority of purchases can be traced to a small percentage of the population. As such, judging whether a consumer is a heavy, moderate or light user of a product may be an excellent measure for determining a target audience.

Scheduling

Continuity, *flighting* and *pulsing* scheduling are variations in scheduling that advertisers use to reach the greatest potential audience at the best possible time.

Continuity refers to a continuous pattern of messaging, which may mean offering exposures every week or month in a regular pattern. A continuous scheduling pattern is most often used for products that have no particular connection to seasonality, such as petrol, food items or personal hygiene products.

Flighting is an intermittent pattern, with periods of high activity at some times of the year and low activity at other times. Seasonal advertisers, such as garden fertilising companies, tend to use this pattern to advertise heavily in early spring and again in the autumn, but not necessarily during winter months.

Scholars' paper 10.3 The future is now

Poltrack, D.F. and Bowen, K. (2011) The future is now, *Journal of Advertising*, 51(2), 345-55

The basic argument that the authors put forward is that more tools are becoming available to assist advertisers to make more informed choices than ever before. Strict demographic-driven media buys do not take into account today's market complexity, argue the researchers. They examined one such tool devised by the CBS Corp. and the Cambridge Group who looked at the television consumer (the 'prime prospect') from a holistic perspective and see the prospect as a *consumer* of media, not a mere compilation of (demographic) facts and figures. The demand profit pools ('to whom') and need states ('for what') profiles that CBS and the Cambridge Group constructed resulted in at least one key finding: although different segments of the consumer population may have similar demographics, they are anchored in fundamentally different consumer interests. The authors believe that understanding prospects as *consumers* of media will enable television content providers to offer the most engaging programming environments.

Pulsing patterns are continuous with intermittent 'flights' of intense activity (so, actually a combination of continuity and flighting) at the appropriate time. Holiday advertisements may appear with regularity throughout the year, but are intensified during traditionally peak holiday periods.

Sawyer, Noel and Janiszewski (2009) claim that scheduling repeated exposures distributed across a time span produces better brand retention than the same number of exposures massed closer together (an argument for continuity) and that media schedules might be more effective if they included messages that differ in terms of complexity, length, hard sell versus soft sell, and closed ended versus open ended (an argument for variation). In any case, scheduling depends on the brand's history, the type of product and the category, the elicited response desired and the size of the budget. Responsible media planning surveys all possible variations and hybrid strategies of scheduling for its strategic and tactical thinking.

Budgets

To place an advertisement in a desired medium may be too expensive as an absolute cost factor or manageable as a relative cost factor (a large initial outlay of money but it is worth it on a per-view basis). In some countries, advertising spots announcing the World Cup 2014 in Brazil may be expensive on a per-message basis, but the potential number of viewers that will see it can justify the cost. Added factors such as the delivery of the message through the media (the effect of sound, colour, etc.) and the editorial tone of the surrounding advertising will help determine whether *exposure* to the target is as cost efficient as one would like.

Audience and message objectives

Reach and *frequency*, introduced in Chapter 8, are fundamental terms in the media planning process. *Reach* is the total number of unduplicated (also referred to as 'unique') exposures to a medium by the defined target population over a finite period of time. What medium should we consider to reach the consumer audience? Do they read this newspaper or listen to that radio station in the afternoon? In the evening? On weekends? Do they communicate primarily through texting? The purpose of this scrutiny is to maximise the cover of the target audience as best one can (called *coverage*). The ideal situation is to attain from the defined target population the unduplicated reach (ensuring that individuals are not counted twice) set forth in the media plan.

Let us say that we have a campaign to call an audience's attention to English classes offered at a new English-language school in Bangkok, Thailand. If we look at the available local print media used among English-language-learners in Bangkok, we learn from research that we may be able to reach a percentage of this population by advertising in the *Student Weekly* newspaper, the newspaper of choice for Thais learning English. (*Student Weekly* also has activities and exercises to help with learning English.) It is a logical vehicle whose selection will cover the area that has been defined as the target, i.e. English-language-learners in Thailand. The more advertising placed in this particular print medium, presumably, the more the message reaches the target with limited *wastage* (money spent inefficiently, or insufficient exposure to the proper target). If the media plan extends its expenditures into like media vehicles that cover the same target in the same geographic area, say *The Nation* (English publication based in Bangkok), reach, unduplicated, of the target audience will up to a point accumulate or increase, that is, we may also reach those who do not read *Student Weekly*.

Media planners may use reach figures (as they do frequency, explained below) to determine and to justify the media they have chosen for a campaign. If 40% of the 10,000 Thais learning English are exposed to an advertisement placed in the *Student Weekly*, then we say that the reach is 40%, or 4,000 of all Thai English learners.

Care should be taken here to not confuse the number of readers (in this case, 4,000) *exposed* to the advertising message with those who actually *consume* the message. Exposure means, as noted earlier, the number of people who have the *opportunity* to see an ad (or *OTS*; Arens, Weigold and Arens 2009: 313) without really guaranteeing that they have seen it. As an example, a mature Thai executive assistant, herself a would-be English learner, notices the *Student Weekly* on the news stand as she makes her way to her Bangkok office early one morning. She sees the publication and recalls a discussion about the newspaper among her office colleagues. For all intents and purposes, she has been exposed to the advertising message because she has been exposed to the vehicle (the newspaper), and is thus calculated as part of the reach figure.

Frequency takes into consideration the average *number of times* a reader is exposed to the advertising message in a given schedule. One person may see a television commercial three times over the course of a week, which would equal a frequency of three. Some research shows (Kamin 1978) that frequency is an important variable because multiple exposures ensure recall. There are ways to maximise reach and frequency in an advertising schedule and still remain efficient: the media plan can exhibit consistency week in, week out, or month to month on a particular programme or series of programmes on a given night or at a given time (Mon–Wed, or 8–9 pm); a banner may be placed on various websites, for example those of news organisations such as BBC, CNN, FRANCE-24, who share a similar editorial environment; or multiple insertions may be placed in the same edition of Spain's *El País*. There are myriad ways for the media planner to choose among several scenarios that will strive to reach the maximum target audience most often, at the lowest cost.

Research suggests that a consumer has to be exposed to an advertising message at least three times (within a purchasing cycle, i.e. from one purchase to the next) in order for the message to be effective. *Effective frequency*, a concept first proposed by Naples (1979), uses three as the minimum standard for a communication message to have an impact on consumer purchasing behaviour. Using the effective frequency number as a guide, media planners often derive an *effective reach* percentage, so that a 53.5% effective reach would mean that 53.5% of the target audience has been exposed to a schedule of advertising spots on at least three occasions. Methods for determining effective reach and frequency have been called into question (Tellis 1997; Cannon et al. 2002; Ephron 2009) for a number of reasons, most notably the evidence that suggests that different parts of the audience (for example, young and old) respond at different rates (Dyson 2006), and the changing nature of media. Optimising reach, frequency and the enhanced quality of the exposure to the public will be treated in the next chapter, where we will introduce several ways of evaluating costs and efficiency measurement in devising the most desirable media plan.

There are also numerous ways to count impressions, and indeed, some would argue, no definitive way to count them. Bearing in mind that an advertising impression is a *possible* exposure, or OTS, of the advertising message to a sole audience member, these numbers can

ViewPoint 10.3 Nutritious . . . *and* delicious

Health programmes across Europe have been struggling to control the epidemic of obesity that is plaguing otherwise well-off countries with high standards of living. Despite the many millions of euros that have been invested in stemming this tide of obesity, levels of the disease continue to rise in every nation. The World Health Organization reports that over 20% of young people living within the European Union's national boundaries are overweight, yet their spending on dietary and nutritional goods has increased dramatically.

Tefal, the leading non-stick cookware manufacturer worldwide, decided to meet the challenge of improving nutrition across Europe by promoting several of its products that provide superior effects in aiding people's diets. Apart from wanting to increase its dwindling sales figures throughout the region, Tefal's complementary image objective was to equate their Nutritious & Delicious range of products with sensible nutrition. Good food can be good for you!

Tefal's communications strategy was set up as a three-phased process: solicit the support of food professionals by demonstrating the value of its products; convince consumers using the traditional product demonstration technique; and place media that would develop awareness of the clearly nutritionally superior Tefal product range (with fryer, steamer, over-steamer and jam maker) in an attempt to change consumer behaviour.

The media expenditures were traditional in nature, with 80% dedicated to TV, 13% to consumer and trade publications and the remainder made up of point of sale (including fairs and mall participation) and other. A website accompanied the campaign as an explanatory device, i.e. its sole purpose was to disseminate the Nutritious & Delicious concept to the consumer in the form of scientific research and a selection of nutritional recipes.

The results across Austria, Belgium, the Czech Republic, France, Germany, Hungary, Italy, Netherlands, Poland, Portugal, Russia, Spain, Switzerland, Turkey and the United Kingdom proved extremely effective. Actifry, the flagship fryer, increased sales by 66+% in the targeted countries and is today the leader in all of the markets in which it was launched. The steamer Vita Cuisine is also the number 1 seller in the UK, France and Central Europe.

In all of these results, there was a marked correspondence between the increase of expenditures in the advertising activity (flights) and the total sales activity.

Source: Tefal - Nutritious & Delicious, European Association of Communications Agencies 2010

Question

What other campaigns can you think of that have used a product tie-in to a social issue?

Task

Other serious diseases are of great concern to health practitioners. Campaigns advocating measures to prevent lung cancer, heart disease, breast and prostate cancer, among others, often use fear and anxiety appeals, but are largely ineffective. Think of several ideas for using alternative media in positive ways to address one of these health concerns.

be used effectively to calculate audience size in general terms. With print and TV, once the media planner knows the audience size, they can then multiply that size by the number of times a message is used during a particular period to come up with *gross impressions*, or all the possible exposures in that medium at a given time. The situation becomes more complex with digital media, integrated media thinking and execution, as the results can be skewed not only by multiple page views by one visitor but countless other variations, including various media, the sheer numbers of publishers and the unique advantages in targeting and direct marketing on the world wide web (Briggs and Hollis 1997).

Ultimately, a media specialist decides how to collect, count and calculate these often vast numbers. The reliability and accuracy of measurements of reach, frequency and impressions

Exhibit 10.5 Coverage and *Waves* magazine

Nextmedia Pty Ltd Australia publishes *Waves* magazine, a magazine that caters to surfers, surfing, surfing meccas from Hawaii to South Africa and related editorial. *Waves* integrates its publication with a website that features webclips and still shots in Australia and elsewhere. The publication serves as a good example of a photo-rich and seriously intense medium to cover a highly defined target. Advertisers appearing in the publication almost exclusively have at least a tangential relation (boat shoes, digitally programmed tide-chart watches) to the surfing world. It claims it is a publication with attitude and would be a must to target a surfing demographic.

Source: *Waves* editorial (2011), *Waves*, 17 (St. Leonards, Australia: nextmedia)

an ad can earn are now under scrutiny and these at best serve as preliminary indicators within the larger media planning process. Many other factors contribute to an assessment of efficient media and no one medium should be considered in isolation. Manning (2009) suggests that now the interrelationship between media – how, say, TV and internet work together – and their reciprocal influence and their cumulative effect for the media planning stage matters most for the media planner. These characteristics have to be considered even before the media planner reviews the role of print media, mobile, cinema, out-of-home, crowdsourcing and the 'multiplicity of other ways to reach the public in order to influence awareness, attitudes and behaviour' (Manning 2009: 3).

Reach and frequency have been the standard for decades in the media planner's hard copy print toolbox. As electronic editions of various print publications become more popular, however, media buyers have had to readjust their metrics concerning the new digital editions. What constitutes a qualified subscriber or viewer of an electronic edition sent via email to users? In the traditional print rendition, copies of the publication are distributed without any firm metric behind how many readers opened it, let alone the specific pages that have been read or advertisements that have been seen. Although electronic distribution can save publishers considerable printing, handling and postage costs, it introduces some accountable and difficult metrics possibilities. An email distribution of an electronic edition can effectively have its open rate and click-through rates measured, so an advertiser knows precisely how many people are actively reading a publication.

Scholars' paper 10.4 From silos to synergy

Assael, H. (2010) From silos to synergy: a fifty-year review of cross-media research shows synergy has yet to achieve its full potential, *Journal of Advertising Research*, 27(4), 63-9

Professor Assael explains that before internet advertising, media planning tended to adhere to a 'silo' approach, that is, a focus on making returns through the use of a single medium. Audience measurement issues of the validity and reliability of reach and frequency dominated the media discussion. The current emphasis on integrated marketing communications (IMC) as applied to media planning means a greater focus on *interactive* rather than *main* media effects. An IMC perspective has also led to increased interest in single-source data as a basis for media selection. Systems are needed to measure cross-media consumption for individual consumers and to relate media interactions to purchase behaviour.

According to Brand Audit Report, the committee overseeing the auditing rules for qualified and non-qualified circulation introduced a new channel for 'non-requested digital magazines'. Non-requested digital subscribers will be grouped together as 'digital' circulation, but broken out separately as request/non-request categories within the age/source paragraph (Lovett 2011). This method avoids counting an email list as *qualified* circulation of a publication simply because an offer for the current electronic edition ends up in someone's email box. Similar changes in the way we look at media circulation are underway as the industry changes the way it perceives actual and possible (OTS) readers, and the way in which we measure potential readers' changes as well.

The look of a media plan - the advertising media flowchart

An advertising media flowchart, a graphical representation of the media schedule information, can assume many shapes and sizes. In its most skeletal form, it will include a list of media and markets, where the advertising has been placed, the schedule and sometimes the desired results. In Figure 10.4, the media flowchart intended for a gaming and online schedule for a

Site	Region	Ad Unit	Run Dates	Placement	Est. Impressions
Microsoft Avertising Ad Network (includes Messenger and Hotmail)	GTA	728x90	November - December	ROS: Demo Targeted to Teens 15-18	2,900,000
		300x250			2,900,000
		160x600			2,900,000
TOTAL AWARENESS				AWARENESS SUBTOTAL	8,700,000
Site	Region	Ad Unit		Placement	Est. Impressions
msn.ca	GTA	728x90 Expandable	November - December	ROS (Lifestyle, News, Sports, Tech & Gadgets, Travel, Green): Demo Targeted to Teens 15-18	475,000
		300x250 Expandable			475,000
msn.ca	Ontario (ex GTA)	728x90 Expandable		ROS (Lifestyle, News, Sports, Tech & Gadgets, Travel, Green): Demo Targeted to Teens 15-18	450,000
		300x250 Expandable			450,000
Xbox LIVE	Ontario	Various Sizes		Branded Destination Channel	1,000,000
Massive In-Game Ads		Various Sizes		Custom in-game Ad Campaign	500,000
TOTAL ENGAGEMENT				ENGAGEMENT SUBTOTAL	3,350,000

Figure 10.4 A sample media plan covering online and gaming in Canada
Source: Courtesy of Microsoft Advertising https://docs.google.com/viewer?a=v&q=cache:nJKTQgXMWLUJ:advertising.microsoft.com/canada/en/wwdocs/user/en-ca/home/Microsoft-Advertising_How-Digital_SampleMediaPlan.pdf

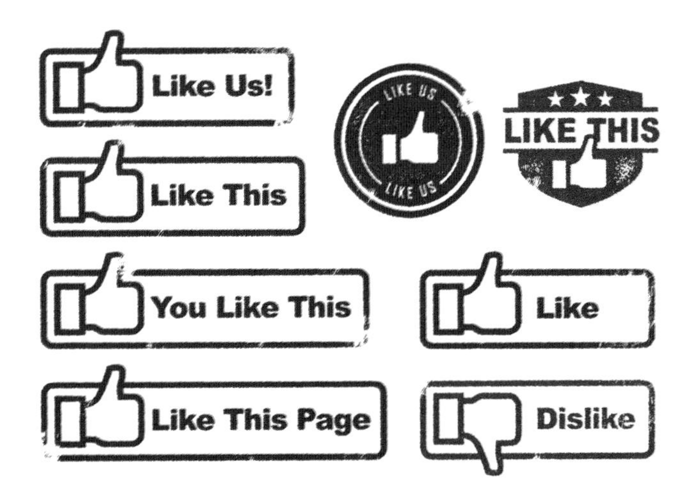

Exhibit 10.6 Mashable's take on social media planning

Aaron Uhrmacher suggests in *Mashable Business* that social media are a bit more complicated than recording a 'Like' on your nearest social media site. He sets out five steps for a media planner to help a company enter social media participation: **listen** to the conversations around you (on Flickr, Digg, YouTube, FriendFeed and other social media sites); **prepare** and identify the appropriate people within the company to participate; **engage** in the media themselves; go **offline** to develop the groundwork that has been laid on online sites; and **measure** what you've learned. Similarly to the traditional plan, without a strategic approach to the medium, success in social media will be difficult to attain.

Source: Shutterstock.com

regional Canadian market presents the site of placement (msn.ca, Xbox), the geographic region in Canada (Province of Ontario, GTA or Greater Toronto Area, including and excluding Ontario), the ad unit dimensions (varies), the scheduled run (November–December), the intended demographics and the estimated impressions.

The flowchart enables all parties involved in the advertising media planning process to see a snapshot of the various media opportunities in a simple format.

Media buying

After the budgets have been set and the media mix has been chosen for a campaign, however small, the media buyer then negotiates space and time, placement and schedules for the advertisements. Media buyers try to establish relationships early on with media sales representatives (as do the sales reps, who are eager to have a campaign appear in their publication or on their site) to watch for the best deals, promotions, discounts or tie-ins that the various media outlets offer.

Often, but not always, the size of an advertising agency or an independent media company determines an effective media buy (Willhoft 2011). It could be that these larger media agencies are offered discounts or premium buys due to the volume they bring to a consumer magazine, for instance. Timing is another factor: should time slots remain open several days before the airing of a televised broadcast, the media buyer may be able to negotiate a better price than had he processed the spot some weeks before (Andersen 1999). Quality buys are contingent upon a variety of factors.

Even though media planning is not hard science, there are nonetheless a number of reliable standards by which media planners have been able to determine advertising effectiveness. We will explore some of those measurements in the next chapter on media measurement and effectiveness, including current research methods, pre and post testing, and diagnostics and analytics.

ViewPoint 10.4 Planning media (internally) for two languages

As one of Canada's leading national communication solutions companies, MTS Allstream claims that it always looks to forge a closer link between the company and its customers – and eventually inject customer perspectives very early in the product development. Satisfying bilingual customers in Canada, where English and French are the official languages, has been the hallmark of the company.

With the aim to inject customer perspectives early in the product development life cycle, MTS Allstream set up external social media site mechanisms to link the corporate, enterprise and consumer sides of its business. All in English. But how would the company deal with language as an internal issue through its wikis and blogs and other forums? Would these too remain in English? Did the company feel it might alienate French-speaking loyal employees? Unlike their external successes in dealing with bilingual environments, the manipulation of information flow internally presented new challenges.

MTS Allstream was determined to tap into good internal ideas from all employees, both French-speakers and English-speakers, and to give speakers of both languages unhindered opportunity to express their ideas in the language with which they felt most comfortable. To stimulate dialogue and to solicit new conversations, the communications company created employee exchange forums covering five different topics. In so doing, MTS Allstream didn't want to create two entirely separate forums based on language – this would only segregate the staff and perhaps defeat the purpose of the bilingual notion.

Instead, bilingual topic areas were created and employees could post in the language of their choice. It was also decided that, while the forum topics would be translated into French, employees' French comments would not be translated into English because translation might alter the tone or nuance of the conversation; translating text also hinders spontaneous information flow and would mean a lag time in thinking. By the time a comment was translated, the conversation would have moved on.

The internal collaboration initiatives have helped break down barriers and create a more connected environment among MTS Allstream's departments, which in turn has resulted in greater awareness of the activity taking place throughout the company and the contributions of each group. In particular, the employee exchange forums have been an overwhelming success, having generated several hundred posts to date.

The success of these internal activities has created yet another new challenge: How should the company report back on progress? To solve this, MTS Allstream is developing another intranet site that will actually show the ideas in action. It will be a discussion forum where employees can talk about ideas and allow peers to rank them as well. Additionally, MTS Allstream plans to provide a blog space on the site where managers accountable for various initiatives can report back via blog posts on status.

MTS Allstream, so versed in the business of planning external bilingual marketing communications, learned that internal communications, often overlooked and invisible, presented their own set of challenging issues.

Source: iMediaConnection (2009)

Question

What are some of the difficulties in planning a media schedule for diverse audiences?

Task

You've just landed your dream job as assistant media planner in Rome, Italy. As part of your training, the media director wants you to become familiar with the Italian media environment before he gives you an assignment. Research and list all the major TV networks, newspapers, radio and other media outlets available to you as a media planner in Italy.

Chapter summary

In order to help consolidate your understanding of traditional media, here are the key points summarised against each of the learning objectives.

Explain how the media plan helps advertisers achieve marketing and advertising objectives

The media are determined by the setting-up activities that specify media objectives and strategies and ways to best realise them. These objectives stem from the primary marketing plan that usually defines measurable outcomes, such as ROI (return on investment), sales or profit. Once these have been determined, marketing communications or advertising objectives and strategies are created to ensure the best possible approach to achieving the results set forth in the overall marketing plan.

Discuss the significance of creativity in media planning

Some media decisions are made by using detailed mathematical and software analysis, while others require creative right-side-of-the-brain thinking that analysis cannot provide. Media decisions are influenced by a number of factors, including the size of the media plan, the economy, the tone of the message, the size of the budget, the whims of the consumer, and so on. Understanding what these factors mean and interpreting the data accordingly so they can be understood by a range of constituencies within the marketing construct is a creative endeavour.

Describe the changing media planning process and its evolution

Newer choices such as online, mobile telephony and mobility, consumer- and user-generated content, the democratisation of content, fragmentation and a move towards integration with traditional media have made media planning today a complex and challenging discipline. Most significant in this evolution have been concerns about increased complexity, costs, audience measurement inconsistencies and the more competitive environment.

Identify and appraise the factors in determining media objectives and strategies

To help determine the objectives and strategies to satisfy the guidelines put forth in the overall marketing plan, the media planner must look at external and internal realities vis-à-vis the company, must understand the demographic, psychographic and behavioural profiles and influential cohorts in defining the target audience and how long the campaign will run, and must comply with budget restrictions in attempting to optimise the efficiency of the media schedule.

Introduce the concepts of reach and frequency as they relate to media

The terms reach and frequency are the fundamental terms used in the media planning process. Reach is the total number of unduplicated exposures to a medium by the defined target population over a finite period of time. Frequency is the number of times a reader or viewer is exposed to the advertising message in a given advertising schedule. The ideal situation is to attain from the defined target population unduplicated reach (ensuring that individuals are not counted twice) a multiple number of times.

Review questions

1. Considering the Sainsbury's minicase set out at the start of this chapter, how would you propose PHD revise the media schedule?
2. Review some of the characteristics that make up media planning's recent evolution.

3. Explain why some suggest that media planning is a delicate balance between art and scientific analysis.
4. Discuss the differences among the several methods for segmenting markets.
5. Clarify the difference between media objectives and media strategies.
6. Explain the differences between behavioural segmentation and generational cohort.
7. Describe what is meant by *impressions*.
8. Jot down some ways that a media planner could increase frequency with a media schedule.
9. BARB (Broadcasters' Audience Research Board) provides in-home TV viewing measurement for the United Kingdom. Discuss the viewing habits for a week of your choice by analysing BARB's multichannel viewing summaries (http://www.barb.co.uk/).
10. Explain the function of a media flowchart and list its basic components.

Chapter references

Andersen, A. (1999) Clout only a part of the media buyer's value, *Advertising Age*, 70(15), 26

Arens, W., Weigold, M. and Arens, C. (2009) *Contemporary Advertising*, 12th edn. New York, NY: McGraw-Hill Irwin

Armstrong, E. (2011, May 11) Sainsbury's customers hit record high, *Interactive Investor*, 11 May, retrieved from http://www.iii.co.uk/articles/15397/sainsburys-customers-hit-record-high

Assael, H. (2010) From silos to synergy: a fifty-year review of cross-media research shows synergy has yet to achieve its full potential, *Journal of Advertising Research*, 27(4), 63–9

Belch, G.E. and Belch, M.A. (2012) *Advertising and Promotion: An Integrated Marketing Communications Perspective*, 9th edn. New York, NY: McGraw-Hill Irwin

Briggs, R. and Hollis, N. (1997) Advertising on the web: is there response before click-through? *Journal of Advertising Research*, 37(2), 33–45

Cannes Creative Lions (2011) Apartheid museum: a history forgotten is a future lost. *Creative Effectiveness Awards*, retrieved from http://www.warc.com

Cannon, H.M., Leckenby, J.D. and Abernethy, A. (2002) Beyond effective frequency: evaluating media schedules using frequency value planning, *Journal of Advertising Research*, 42(6), 33–47

Carmichael, M. (2011, September 16) Who's using what media and when? *Advertising Age*, retrieved from http://adage.com/article/adagestat/infographic-generational-media-usage-time-day/229831/

Charnes, A., Cooper, W.W., DeVoe, J.K., Learner, D.B. and Reinecke, W. (1968) A goal programming model for media planning, *Management Science*, 14(8), 423–30

Clow, K. and Baack, D. (2012) *Integrated Advertising, Promotion, and Marketing Communications*. Harlow: Pearson Education

Cusack, J. (2009) Chuck shows the value of audience engagement (web log comment), 1 May, retrieved from http://www.filmindustry.suite101.com

Dyson, P. (2006) The burst is dead! Long live the burst! *Admap*, 477 (November)

Ephron, E. (2009) Sitting on the shelf (web log comment), 1 October, retrieved from http://www.ephronmedia.com

Gensch, D.H. (1973) *Advertising Planning: Mathematical Models in Advertising Media Planning*. Amsterdam, NY: Elsevier Scientific Publishing Company

Global Comm Class (2009) Viral campaigns – a 'must do' in Brazil (web log comment), 19 July, retrieved from http://globalcc.wordpress.com/2009/07/19/viral-campaigns—a-"must-do"-in-brazil

Graham, J. (1989) New VALS2 takes psychological route, *Advertising Age*, 13 February, 24

iMediaConnection (2009) Case study: a success story in bilingual social media, 27 October, retrieved from http://www.imediaconnection.com/article_full.aspx?id=24838

Investopedia (n.d.) Pareto principle, retrieved from www.investopedia.com/term/p/paretoprinciple/asp)

Kamin, H. (1978) Advertising reach and frequency, *Journal of Advertising Research*, 18(1), 21

Kelley, L.D. and Jugenheimer, D.W. (2008) *Advertising Media Planning: A Brand Management Approach*. Armonk, NY: M.E. Sharpe

Kellogg, D. (2011) Among mobile phone users, Hispanics, Asians are most likely smartphone owners in the US, *NielsenWire*, 1 February, retrieved from http://blog.nielsen.com/nielsenwire/consumer/

Lovett, J. (2011) Web analytics demystified and BPA worldwide announce first-ever digital consumer data privacy audit (web log comment), 18 October, retrieved from http://bpaww.typepad.com/blog/2011/10/web-analytics-demystified-and-bpa-worldwide-announce-first-ever-digital-consumer-data-privacy-audit.html

Malthouse, E. and Calder, B. (2011) Media placement versus advertising execution, *International Journal of Market Research*, 52(2), 217–30

Mandese, J. (2009) The end of buying media, the rise of buying audiences, *AdMap*, July/August, retrieved from http://www.warc.com

Manning, N. (2009) The new media communications model: a progress report, *Advertising Works*, retrieved from http://www.warc.com/Pages/Store/ProductInfo.aspx?SectionID=1&ProductID=299&TabID=3Re

Morrissey, B. (2009) Happy birthday to Subservient Chicken, *AdWeek*, 7 April, retrieved from http://www.adweek.com/adfreak/happy-5th-birthday-subservient-chicken-14369

Naples, M. J. (1979) *Effective Frequency: The Relationship between Frequency and Advertising Effectiveness*. New York: Association of National Advertisers

Naples, M.J. (1997) Effective frequency: then and now, *Journal of Advertising*, 37(4), 7–12

Pergelova, A., Prior, D. and Rialp, J. (2010) Assessing advertising efficiency: does the internet play a role? *Journal of Advertising*, 39(3), 39–54. doi: 10.2753/JOA0091-3367390303

Pew Research Center (2010) Millennials: Confident. Connected. Open to Change, 24 February, retrieved from http://pewsocialtrends.org/2010/02/24/millennials-confident-connected-open-to-change

Pollack, J. (2011) How 'X Factor' looked to a member of the 'American Idol' faithful: did 'Idol' ever try to manipulate viewers this much? 22 September, retrieved from http://adage.com/article/mediaworks

Poltrack, D.F. and Bowen, K. (2011) The future is now, *Journal of Advertising Research*, 51(2), 345–55

Sasaki, D. (2009) Changes in media over the past 550 years (web log comment), retrieved from http://www.pbs.org/idealab/2009/11/changes-in-media-over-the-past-550-years318.html

Sawyer, A.G., Noel, H. and Janiszewski, C. (2009) The spacing effects of multiple exposures on memory: implications for advertising scheduling, *Journal of Advertising Research*, 49(2), 193–7

Sherman, S. (2011) Brandmax: Silicon Valley will define future of marketing, argues Medialink's Kassan, *Media Week*, 21 September, retrieved 27 December 2011 from http://www.mediaweek.co.uk/news/1094032/BrandMAX-Silicon-Valley-will-define-future-marketing-argues-MediaLinks-Kassan

Tellis, G.J. (1997) Effective frequency: one exposure or three factors? *Journal of Advertising Research*, 37(4), 75–80

Uhrmacher, A. (2008) How to develop a social media plan in 5 easy steps, *Mashable*, 10 July, retrieved from http://mashable.com/2008/07/10/how-to-develop-a-social-media-plan

Vyncke, P. (2002) Lifestyle segmentation, *European Journal of Communication*, 17(4), 445

WARC (2010) Case study: Tefal – nutritious and delicious European Association of Communications Agencies, Entrant, 2010. Retrieved from http://www.warc.com

WARC (2010) Media data: time spent by medium 2008–2010. Retrieved from http://www.warc.com

Washida, Y. (2005) Collaborative structure between Japanese high-tech manufacturers and consumers, *Journal of Consumer Marketing*, 22(1), 25–34

Willhoft, G. (2011) Media buying today – the way it really is (web log comment), retrieved from http://www.marketingscoop.com/media-buying-today.htm

Chapter 11
Measuring advertising efficiency and effectiveness

Once the background research on the nature of the market and the consumer has been compiled, recommendations are made for specific media based on a number of measurable factors (metrics and analytics), budgetary considerations and overall suitability to the strategy. The advertiser then proceeds to buy the media choices that have been deemed to be the most effective while optimising efficiency. The dynamic and expanding nature of advertising media has created new challenges and new ways of looking at media placement and buying.

Aims and learning objectives

The aim of this chapter is to examine ways to maximise efficiency and effectiveness associated with media planning and buying.

The learning objectives of this chapter are to:

1. review the standard measurement methods used to determine media efficiency
2. utilise measurement techniques and methods in media plan preparation
3. describe the changes and challenges in traditional versus digital measurement
4. survey new opportunities and challenges for planning and buying media.

Minicase Measuring the media

SAS® (originally 'Statistical Analysis System') is one of the leaders in providing analytics solutions to organisations around the world. It offers complex business solutions to companies by providing a range of techniques and processes for the collection, classification, analysis and interpretation of data and trends. It has long understood the important role that the media play on the market and in the sales cycle.

With the increased importance of social media, gaming opportunities and media on mobile devices in the years after 2009, SAS realised that it needed to expand its measurement and metrics programme to meet the demands of these new digital phenomena. New analytics software had been proposed to meet the demand, but SAS wondered whether the metrics provided by a new programme would be used to better understand what works and does not work in media communications. The explosion of digital and social media had spawned a number of media measurement systems, but it was unclear whether marketers truly knew more as a result.

The company's traditional clients had been the consummate business professional and decision makers - senior executives, CFOs and CEOs in marketing and operations who set the standard for the rest of the business world. The proposed ideal goal of SAS® Social Media Analytics, however, would be to speak to a much broader audience, including media planners and buyers at various levels in the advertising and PR industries, financial services companies, retailers, and even students. Anyone who works with understanding advertising media communication was now considered part of its larger target audience.

SAS soon discovered that trying to establish consistent collection methodologies for social and digital media, especially with Facebook, was a new and daunting challenge. While infusing social media into part of the communication preferences of a media plan had expanded exponentially the options for the media planner, accurately measuring an integrated campaign that runs across different platforms was very difficult to imagine, let alone implement.

How would they develop coding for what to track on those social media and other emerging media? What kind of constants could they find in digital metrics that lined up with traditional media? How could they correlate activity to determine the levels of engagement and outcomes? Simply recoding and record keeping of the activity on social sites, as was done with sales-oriented websites, for example, was no longer enough. Now they would have to define and understand entirely new concepts such as threads, tags, boards, tweets and blog posts, among others, and decide how to interpret the data for their target constituencies. The vast amount of this data and the growing means of evaluation added to the difficulty of advertising management, particularly with respect to advertising media planning.

Other more specific, yet equally important, challenges also acted as roadblocks to a uniform standard of measurement: the issue of the disparity between the standards used to measure social media's effectiveness, which focuses on mass audience as it does for traditional media ratings, and social media in marketing, which is used primarily in relationship marketing; and the inconsistency and lack of standardisation across the social and mobile media platforms and devices. Even the 'Likes' on Facebook were known by other names on other social sites. Mobile screens and capabilities varied and affected the quality of activity and the methods by which that activity is measured.

With the above in mind, SAS enlisted the help of KDPaine & Partners, a leading public relations and social media measurement firm, to design a research approach for its own proposed analytics programme. They faced at least three challenges in satisfying the

KDPaine & Partners

Exhibit 11.1 KDPaine & Partners logo
Source: KDPaine Partners LLC

fundamental requirements needed to address a metrics programme that would benefit advertising, public relations and communications professionals: create a reliable, **accurate** and useful system of metrics; design an analytics software that is **timely**, and sensitive to the speed of mass communication by reducing response times; and find a way to understand quickly and efficiently the competitive **context** in which these new media operate.

Sources: Knorp (2011); Neff (2010); Society for New Communications Research (2010)

Introduction

As discussed in Chapter 10, media strategy decisions are based in part on a number of measurements and calculations. Measurement techniques have become elaborate and complex in recent years, promising performance metrics that can quantify traditional and emerging advertising media's effectiveness.

The goal when measuring the media is first to determine how likely and how well the intended audiences will be exposed to the communication message, then to review performance to determine whether the goal has been met. But measurements of media performance can differ from television to print and also from traditional to digital. Costs, standards of measurements and even the vocabulary for media vary and are inconsistent, and often inconclusive. Audience analysis that determines costs and informs performance can also be collected and interpreted differently. It can be argued that internet and digital measurements have made measuring effectiveness more reliable because it is possible to track hits, visits, emails and text messages in real time, with accuracy. Whether or not this is true remains to be seen as measuring devices continue to evolve.

Despite the changes, the process for predicting performance remains as difficult and complicated as it has always been. After selecting the channels of communication, it is important to follow up with some basic questions concerning measurement. For example, will this plan elicit a clear and measurable response? Can the plan achieve its delivery goals? Is the plan weighted properly? Should more weight be shifted from one medium to another?

Media accountability has always been a contentious issue with traditional media, but with digital media measurement and today's complicated mediascape, advertisers are holding their hired agencies accountable for delivering what they promise (Kelley and Jugenheimer 2008). Media auditing companies (begun in the UK) have grown recently to serve as independent verification tools for advertisers.

Although many would argue that media measurement is not a hard science, quantifiable measurement data are objective and in some respects can serve as grounds for accountability in media strategy decisions. Advertisers have begun to apply statistical modelling to interpret the relationship between media messages and strategies to survey and forecast links between the performance of the media plan and subsequent actions, such as sales.

Sissors and Baron (2010) caution that we should be careful not to misread or overemphasise the impact of data when using media audience research. Audience measurement appraises *potential* versus *actual* audience, and vehicle distribution versus exposure. However, none of these is very accurate, so we rely on an *average* measurement for calculations. The relationship between potential or actual consumer engagement and final motivation is therefore difficult to determine.

The reasons for measuring advertising effectiveness are quite simple: one measures performance in hope that the testing and measuring will lead to an improved performance, reduced costs and perhaps a more fine-tuned version of the existing ads or the existing promotional programme. It should be noted, however, that some advertisers are reluctant to establish measurement programmes to test effectiveness. This is due to the perceived costs involved, which is ironic as the purpose of measurement programmes is to save money in the long run.

Scholars' paper 11.1 Back to the future

Sissors, J. and Baron, R. (2010) *Advertising Media Planning*. New York: McGraw-Hill

For over 30 years, *Advertising Media Planning* has been the sole technical and informative guide to learning one's way around planning the media. With little glitz or glamour to the publication, the heavy, slightly anachronistic textbook provides a no-nonsense, straightforward education on how best to measure and calculate, strategise, prioritise, search and select the appropriate vehicles. Despite the whirlwind evolution of digital and electronic devices around us, the authors of this 7th edition of a 30-year-old textbook insist that media planning in some ways is as basic as the day that *AMP* was first published - understanding reach, frequency, audience composition, exposure and other fundamentals are as essential as ever to delivering message content to consumers' specialised needs.

Media audience research

Traditionally, media audiences, whether they be viewers, listeners or readers, have been measured through surveys. Data gathered from a scientifically sound, randomised sample of the consuming population was extrapolated to make valid assertions about the audience population as a whole. Research about audiences can be customised and tailored to specified times, or can be continuous and occur on an ongoing (day-to-day, week-to-week) basis.

Some of the larger measurement companies, such as the Kantar Media network, which measures television, internet and radio usage in over 40 countries, and Nielsen Media Research (a part of the Nielsen Company), which measures TV audiences in many countries around the world, have proliferated through spin-offs and expansion into a worldwide presence over the last two decades. Speciality organisations which analyse media audiences for smaller markets also exist. These include Intomart GfK (http://www.intomartgfk.nl/) and MediaXim (http://www.mediaxim.com/) in the Netherlands and Benelux countries and Finnpanel for Finnish radio and TV (http://www.finnpanel.fi/en/tv.php).

Smith, Boyle and Cannon (2010) argue that the key to media effectiveness begins with selectivity. Apart from any other elements of media efficiency that we have noted, the choice of the proper vehicle represents a direct contribution to cost-efficient advertising. The better the efficiency, the lower the cost; optimising cost plus efficiency generally are the two key factors for success and a satisfied client. Thus, preliminary research is central to ensure the most salient choices.

Media kits are a good starting point for gathering research on determining media choices. They are distributed by the publisher or broadcaster and offer details on its readership or viewership. A traditional print media kit might include information on brand overview, past and future editorial calendars, audited circulation figures, advertising rates and page size and specifications. Online and digital media kits might include rich-media guidelines, such as specifications on animation and audio, standard UAP (universal ad package) units for interactive media, and so on. The media kit also provides details on the psychographics and demographics of its typical consumer. Although part promotional tool, the media kit is helpful in orienting the media planner to the comparative attributes of the various media options.

Media planners also rely on other valuable kinds of syndicated *market research* that is gathered independently from the market and product categories by market research firms. Mediamark Research (MRI), DJS Research Limited, Market Research World (MRW), TNS Worldwide and others offer information about consumers, brands, category use and consumption patterns. The material is vast and can greatly improve the precision of the media schedule.

ViewPoint 11.1 **Seeking lasting relationships through online media measurability**

Ocean Media has been working with the dating site eHarmony.com since 2002. eHarmony bills itself as a compatibility-matching site that is unlike any other. It boasts that its Scientific Relationship Questionnaire discovers unprecedented levels of compatibility and depth in helping singles find the perfect partner. eHarmony differentiated itself by establishing its brand as the only site for serious long-term relationship seekers, particularly women.

eHarmony resisted the use of television at first. They believed that it was too expensive, difficult to measure results and even more difficult to execute. Would eHarmony's message be able to cut through the dating site clutter to reach the serious consumer in a sophisticated and discreet way?

In a highly organised media management style, Ocean Media utilised a number of media analytics to tightly control and monitor the progress of the eHarmony campaign. They tracked pixels on television ads by employing CMR, a market research firm specialising in advertising, and Broadcast Verification Services (BVS), which delivers exact confirmation and compliance of media schedules to allow the media company to identify discrepancies for immediate action. They tracked ad components, including creative and spot placements. They correlated the relationship between TV commercial airings and website activity, as well as implementing a response-based marketing strategy, a model in which performance increases as the target is more clearly defined. Among other things, Ocean Media tied the most effective ads to the response rate it garnered.

As a result of Ocean Media's meticulous and efficient governance of media placement and acquisition, eHarmony is currently No. 1 in the serious dating category, enjoys 90% awareness among singles and is the most trusted brand in online relationship services.

Source: http://www.oceanmediainc.com/clients-and-partners/case-studies/eharmony

Question

What are the key challenges in designing and implementing a website that focuses on matching individuals for a possible relationship?

Task

The Internet Advertising Bureau (www.iab.net) is the global not-for-profit association devoted to maximising advertising effectiveness online. Go to its site and click on Mobile > Tablet Creative Showcase. Choose an entry and write one paragraph on how you feel this ad maximises effectiveness.

The sheer volume of data on media, markets and consumers also necessitates reliance on databases and planning software to maximise planning stage effectiveness. Advertisers enlist the aid of *media planning software* and specialised software products and services that offer deeper analysis not found in syndicated market research alone.

SmartPlus® and MediaMaster℠ offer comprehensive media planning software 'suites' that enable the planner to analyse any number of data and types of media activity, manage scheduling with customised flowcharts and evaluate the impact of an entire campaign by using post-analysis criteria and the like.

Calculating the audience

As already stated, media planners seek cost efficiency and to maximise audience reach when choosing their media. Measurement across all media is used to help identify the size (both actual and potential) of audiences, their composition, and the relative cost to reach them. Calculations are often the first steps taken to separate the good from the bad choices.

Print measurement

Magazines and newspapers

CPM (cost per thousand) analysis is one of the basic units of media efficiency, and is used for selecting potential magazines and newspapers. It determines the reach of the target audience, or the cost to deliver 1,000 people or households, or impressions. It might serve as the first signpost to other favourable factors in media selection (see Figure 11.1).

Imagine that a media planner is considering scheduling the popular fashion magazine for women, *Elle*, out of the list of other possible magazines that may also be target-appropriate. Using market analysis (the competition), the history with a particular vehicle, or the various resources available, a skilled media planner might then list possible print magazine candidates, *Elle* among them, that would serve the advertising communication objectives.

ViewPoint 11.2 Rebating the holiday season

Pioneer Electronics (USA) decided to push with rebates the sales of its automobile in-dash navigation devices – AVIC-Z110BT and AVIC-X910BT – during the Christmas holiday season. Holiday seasons for rebates and discounted items are increasingly crowded, so Pioneer was faced with a challenging dilemma: how to best reach its consumers and get focused attention during the busy holiday season.

Pioneer has known for some time that its loyal following once could be reached in automobile and car audio systems enthusiast magazines, but now had shifted their informational needs to online forums and sites. Pioneer tried banner ads on these websites, which met with very poor click-through rate performance.

The company then decided to try PostRelease, a content marketing firm, which professes to deliver content to highly targeted audiences. PostRelease seemed as if it was a good advertising option that would enable them to deliver content to its audience, whilst minimising the advertising 'feel' of it.

Pioneer had a fairly good idea on which forums to encounter but had to overcome the promotional aspect of its campaign, something that many forums do not allow. PostRelease had special relationships with several forums, so that Pioneer and PostRelease were able to add a 'sticky post' on forums such as ClubFrontier.org or Camaroz28.com. Once a visitor clicked on the note, product images, direct links to the product web page and the rebate page on Pioneer's website would appear.

After the seven-day campaign, Pioneer's experienced a 57% click-through rate. Six months later, the click-through rate was averaging 65%. It also resulted in residual traffic, since interested consumers continued to seek out the rebate through search engines. To account for residual traffic, PostRelease ad Pioneer updated the landing page with the latest information.

Pioneer believes that a way to improve an already very successful campaign through PostRelease would be to link Pioneer's Facebook fan page, Twitter feed and website, so that full advantage can be taken of the consumer's attention.

Source: Choi (2010)

Question

Pioneer believes that its PostRelease campaign can be improved by linking to its Facebook page, other websites and Twitter feeds. What are the advantages and disadvantages of expanding a campaign in this way?

Task

Choose a product. Explore ways in which you can draw the consumer's attention to rebates or other special offers of your product during traditionally busy seasons.

The next step might include analysing the data that exist with respect to *Elle*'s CPM figures, which have been established by various media resource organisations, such as Mediamark Research & Intelligence (MRI) or the Audit Bureau of Circulations (ABC), who provide independent database verification of media audience circulation and data figures.

The formula for arriving at CPM figures is straightforward: divide the cost of an advertising space (using a full-page, four-colour magazine ad rate from *Elle*'s American edition as an example) by the circulation figures, then multiply by 1,000 to equal CPMs. Using the American edition of *Elle* and its 2011 advertising rates, the following calculation is possible.

Example 11.1 CPM of* Elle *magazine

Full page	\$141,210
Circulation	1,124,569
Calculation	$\frac{\$141{,}210 \times 1{,}000}{1{,}124{,}569}$
CPM	\$125.6

The cost of placing one full-page, four-colour print advertisement, one-time (single) insertion, in *Elle* magazine is \$141,210 (i.e. gross cost; bear in mind that frequency discounts are granted when multiple insertions are placed during the cycle). Total paid-for and verified circulation by ABC amounts to 1,124,569 (Hearst Magazines 2011), so it takes \$126 to reach one thousand people (CPM = 126).

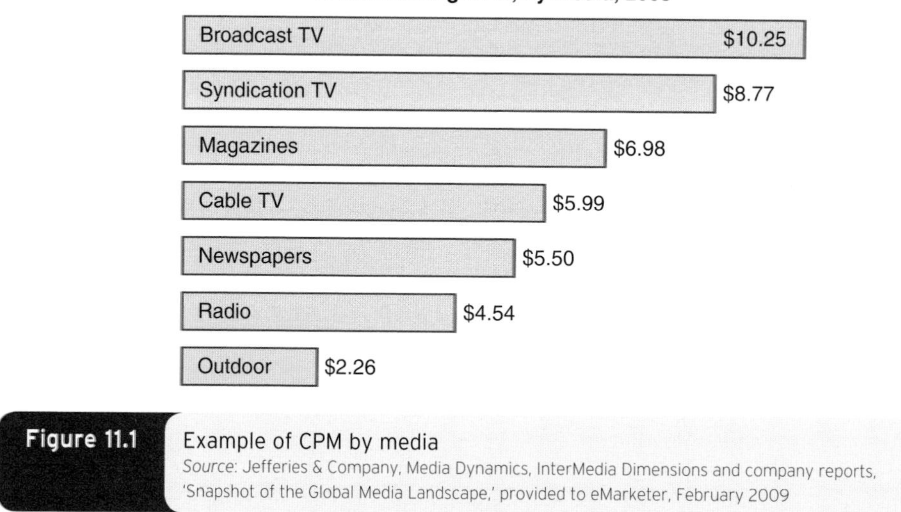

Figure 11.1 Example of CPM by media
Source: Jefferies & Company, Media Dynamics, InterMedia Dimensions and company reports, 'Snapshot of the Global Media Landscape,' provided to eMarketer, February 2009

To peg the most efficient magazines by comparing relative CPM calculations, a media planner would look at what other media vehicles are available in the similar career-minded, principally female shopper magazine category. As a result they might consider *Allure*, *Lucky*, *InStyle*, *Glamour*, *Marie Claire* and others, in addition to *Elle*, to give a fair indication of how they compare on a cost-per-thousand basis.

Example 11.2 A comparative cost per thousand (CPM) calculation

2011 advertising rates

Elle (American edition)		*Marie Claire*
Full page	\$141,210	\$127,455
Circulation	1,124,569	1,022,393
Calculation	$\frac{\$141{,}210 \times 1{,}000}{1{,}124{,}569}$	$\frac{\$127{,}455 \times 1{,}000}{1{,}022{,}393}$
CPM	\$125.6	\$124.7

In the examples above, *Elle* and *Marie Claire* are virtually at parity with respect to CPM computation and circulation. One vehicle does not appear appreciably more suited than the other as a cost-effective media buy. However, the absolute cost ($141,210) of placing the full-page print advertisement in *Elle* exceeds the absolute cost of placement in *Marie Claire* by over 10%, which may tip the balance in favour of using *Marie Claire*, should budgetary restrictions be an issue.

The *TCPM* (*target cost per thousand*), an even more targeted figure and considerably more expensive, is another measurement that helps planners make decisions about which vehicles are best to use in the media plan. Using the example above from *Elle* magazine and calculating a TCPM figure based on *target* reach (18–49-year-old females), we calculate a TCPM of $163.1. Although more expensive than the CPM-based calculation, the TCPM is based on a specific target and not a general audience and may be a more crucial figure in determining how to reach *Elle*'s base audience.

Example 11.3 A comparative target cost per thousand (TCPM) calculation

2011 Advertising rates - *Elle* (American edition)

Full page	$141,210
Target market (F, 18-49)	865,918
Calculation	$\frac{141{,}210 \times 1{,}000}{865{,}918}$
TCPM	$163.1

Whilst numerical calculations are a fundamental step in the media planning process, they are only one of the many measures, including qualitative measures, that the media planner considers when making decisions. Other factors, including the special relationship with the publishers (perhaps *Elle* offers an attractive discount), distinct editorial features for upcoming issues and other special one-off opportunities will also be taken into account. Shimp (2007) points out that these numerical computations do not measure effectiveness, but only cost *efficiency*. A magazine may cost little but it might not reach the correct audience or advertise the brand effectively.

Broadcast measurement

Television and radio

Television creates more awareness of a brand than any other medium (Lafayette 2009). As in other media, television advertisers attempt to match the audience to a particular programme or kind of programming (such as sports, lifestyle, news and documentaries). Television networks or stations that carry the advertising are also concerned with audience measurement, or *ratings*, because programme ratings determine what they can charge for 10, 15, 20, 30, 60 (or more) seconds of commercial time. Nielsen, a global leader in TV audience measurement and information that serves over 100 countries, is chief among the ratings services.

Nielsen measures representative sample TV viewership. It uses electronic metered technology that captures household television-viewing habits, which channels are being watched, when they are watched and who is watching them. In the UK, BARB (Broadcasters' Audience Research Board) serves in a similar TV measurement capacity by carrying out random probability surveys through BARB meters, which monitor and identify the viewing channel in chosen homes (www.barb.co.uk/about/tvMeasurement).

Other forms of measurement are used to supplement metered technology. During '*sweeps*' periods in the United States and other countries, Nielsen uses 'viewer paper diaries' to collect intensive television data on homes across each country. The paper diaries record a detailed tally of who is watching the television and what they are watching. Sweeps are extremely important to television measurement services because they influence local annual advertising rates. As a result television schedules are beefed up with interesting content during sweeps weeks to attain the highest possible ratings.

As we noted in the previous chapter, one rating point equals one per cent of the programme's broadcast television universe. Usually, rating points are calculated with respect to households with TV (HHs). If the popular television sitcom *Two and a Half Men* achieves a 5.0% rating among adults 18–49 (generally a key demographic) out of the total viewing audience of 50,000,000 households, it means that 2,500,000 HHs, or *gross impressions*, the sum of duplicated exposures (same person exposed to the ad, one or multiple times), were *potentially* subject to each television commercial aired within the *Two and a Half Men* programme. The higher the rating for a programme, generally the more it costs to advertise within it (Bourdon and Méadel 2011).

GRPs, or *gross ratings points*, represent another quick and valuable indicator to judge delivery of an advertising schedule and measures of advertising *impact*. GRPs estimate the entire (gross) duplicated exposure to an advertising programme or schedule and indicate how much weight is needed to attain the advertising programming schedule's objectives. The GRP calculates programme rating times the number of households *reached* during a given period:

$$\text{Reach (R)} \times \text{frequency (F)} = \text{GRPs}$$

Let us assume that *The Big Bang Theory*, *Emmerdale*, *A Touch of Frost* and *Coronation Street* comprise a four-week television advertising media schedule targeted to the 35–44-year-old female audience in the UK. An advertisement for the automobile Skoda appears eight times over a four-week period within each programme. *Coronation Street*, the long-running prime-time, ITV1 television series, has a monthly reach of 40% among the target audience. With a reach of 40 and the Skoda commercial appearing eight times over the four-week schedule, *Coronation Street* achieves 320 GRPs (40 (R) × 8 (F)) with its 35–44-year-old female target audience. *The Big Bang Theory* and *A Touch of Frost* achieve 220 and 260 GRPs, respectively. *Emmerdale's* GRP delivery, however, trails dismally with a total of 50 GRPs. The low *Emmerdale* GRP score may be significant for the media planner, if it is known that another programme during the same cycle reaches 30% of the 35–44-year-old female target audience and can attain 240 GRPs with the frequency of the Skoda commercial.

GRPs must be distinguished from gross impressions. The latter represent the total number of exposures to the media vehicle carrying the advertisement, whilst GRPs measure the message intensity over a given period.

The higher a GRP figure, the greater the delivery or reach to the duplicated audience. Recently the GRP measure has been extended to measure other media, including print, out of home and the internet. At least one scholar suggests that GRPs are ineffective in conveying the true reach and frequency of a campaign. Worse still, the metric confounds both media strategy effects and advertisement quality effects. What might be more useful, Sharp (2008) argues, is a measurement immediately after an advertisement is broadcast that conditions itself solely on those consumers who had actually been exposed to it.

To reduce *duplicated* exposure, that is, seek a total audience comprised only of viewers who have a one-time exposure to the message, and thereby increase efficiency (and decrease waste), media planners use the *target rating point* (*TRP*) for broadcast and online, much in the same way that TPCM is used for print publications. Target rating points refer to only those in the primary target audience of, say, college-educated job seekers (females, 21–25, university educated), and not the entire audience of job seekers (all females and males).

Share of audience (*SOA*) analyses the *comparative* performance of programmes and audience share at a specific time and is a potential figure based on those television sets in

Exhibit 11.2 The New kid on the blog

Tumblr, the social blogging site, allows users to post text, images, videos, links, quotes and audio to their tumblelog, a short-form blog. Users can follow other users, or choose to make their tumblelog private. Since its launch in 2007, users are publishing on the site and viewing others' posts, whilst brands, media outlets and marketers are experimenting with how best to leverage this growing community, as Tumblr is expected to become a bigger player in the social space. The Nielsen Company tracked Tumblr unique visitors from May 2010 to May 2011 and found 183% growth in a single year. Users are predominately younger and female.

Source: Alamy Images

households that are turned on or in use (not watched, necessarily) at a specific time. It is calculated by the simple formula:

$$\text{Audience share} = \frac{\text{Households tuned to Programme A (7 pm)}}{\text{All households using television}} = \frac{5{,}000{,}000}{30{,}000{,}000} = 16.7 \textit{ share}$$

In this case, 16.7% of all households using television at 7 pm were tuned in to Programme A, resulting in a 16.7 share of the entire audience (100%) at 7 pm. SOA represents precisely the same number as a rating point but from another perspective: it indicates the percentage share of an entire audience tuned into a programme. The share of audience figure gives the media planner an indication of how well one programme fares against another and may be used to leverage advertising rates and purchasing of time.

In the early 2011 US television season, the *Two and a Half Men* sitcom's second week SOA performance was disappointing, which may have caused initial concern on the network because it reflects the waning popularity of this historically popular programme against the competition in the post-Charlie Sheen era (Guthrie 2011). This is turn would affect the advertising rate.

A similar assessment ratings process is used for radio. This involves dividing the day into day parts and evaluating audience listeners in accordance with parts of the day. The largest audiences occur during commuting time, i.e. when people are on their way either to or from work. Even though audience measurement systems such as Arbitron (USA) and RAJAR (UK) give audience estimates based on a representative listener base, costs, smaller audience sizes, new delivery mechanisms (satellite and streaming audio through the radio) and variation in markets make extensive radio measuring challenging and not as prevalent as its broadcast counterparts.

Digital measurement

Email marketing

Email marketing is still the most frequently used online marketing tool. Many marketers use email to achieve communications objectives and have taken pains in recent years to optimise its effectiveness. Modifications such as shorter (body) copy of the message, or simple and straightforward calls to action, some research shows, decrease audience duplication and increase overall visitor diversity. As a result more people read the emails. As long as the copy does not interrupt the user's progression from message to action with roadblocks or detours between the headline and the call to action, shorter copy helps reach email marketing objectives (Burstein 2011).

Advertisers also test other elements in their email campaigns to optimise performance, with specific attention to subject lines, messages and calls to action. Measuring response rates to subject line experiments, testing the brand's voice, personalising or altering the message format, to make it easy to follow thought sequences, using simple bullet-point strategies such as 'top five tactics' or 'three easy steps', focusing the reader or writing in the active voice to pep up the language, enhance email marketing effectiveness (Rice 2011).

Exhibit 11.3 TV and magazine ads more effective than the internet

McPheters & Company released a single study in 2009 that explored the relative effectiveness of ads on television, in magazines, and on the internet. Surprising to many involved (including the competing media interests, CBS Vision and Condé Nast, publisher of established magazines *Vogue* and *Wired*) is that net recall of TV ads proved to be almost twice that of magazine ads, magazines had ad recall almost three times that of internet banner, and magazines effectively delivered more than twice the number of advertising impressions as television and more than six times those delivered online. The research matched 30-second TV, full-page four-colour magazine and standard-sized internet banner ads.

Source: Alamy Images

Internet

Monitoring visits to internet sites has become imperative for businesses attempting to attract and retain customers and to review their overall online operations. Nielsen Online and comScore are two of the largest organisations that collect, analyse and report information about online activity. Like other measurement companies around the globe, their measurement devices are able to determine the number of unique visitors, length of stay on each page, returning visitors to the site, network connectivity, and so on, in determining and tracking activity and web usage. In addition to online and broadcast, these companies measure mobile and cross-platform performance and use evolving eye-tracking technologies that enable the evaluation of consumer visual behaviour.

CPM calculations remain the standard measure that media planners initially employ for search engine marketing and online analysis as well. CPMs for online calculate the cost per number of impressions online, or all those visitors who land, intentionally or not, single or duplicated on a particular site.

Cost per impression (CPI or CPM), or cost per thousand impressions, can help to indicate the cost efficiency of specific online campaigns. This technique is applied to web banners, text links and email, and is treated similarly to traditional media as the sum total of duplicated exposures, for each web visit or text-link action.

Online measurement becomes more profound with cost-per-click (CPC) or pay-per-click (PPC) analysis, introduced in Chapter 9, the most common online advertising pricing model. The advertiser pays for each click on its online advertisement. The more clicks, the more traffic; the more traffic to the site, the more the online site is able to charge advertisers.

If we place an Air New Zealand banner advertisement on the site of the UK newspaper *The Telegraph*, any click on that ad represents a 'hit' and is recorded as such. If the banner over the course of a one-week period receives 1,000 hits or clicks at £0.05 CPC, we would have spent £5.00 for 1,000 clicks, a relatively inexpensive media buy in an otherwise rather expensive media space. Out of those 1,000 clicks on the Air New Zealand banner, the ratio of those who actually can be expected to purchase an airline ticket or take some other actionable steps is very low. The advantage of the CPC model, however, lies in its ability to measure activity in short bursts of time, one to two weeks after activity begins. This allows for adjustments to subsequent online scheduling, improving the creative or renegotiating the price in an effort to lower the overall CPC cost.

Scholars' paper 11.2 Need an update?

Cheong, Y., De Gregorio, F. and Kim, K. (2010) The power of reach and frequency in the age of digital advertising, *Journal of Advertising Research*, 50(4), 403–15

The authors have updated the few research studies available on understanding perceptions of current practices in digital media planning. They look specifically at the importance media practitioners place on traditional reach and frequency estimation models in evaluating alternative media schedules. Cheong, De Gregorio and Kim found that media planners had not tested the accuracy of their own models, on average, within the past five years. And further, the authors suggest that the actual practice of media professionals demonstrates that they do not trust the traditional reach and frequency models when it comes to digital advertising. The study found that there is a 'clear desire among planners' to find models that specifically improve and refine the media models to better integrate and measure the internet's characteristics with more traditional media. The authors also suggest looking at non-US media to illuminate any cross-cultural differences in the perceptions of the traditional reach and frequency model.

Two problems have emerged with the CPC model. Relative to the audience deliveries that a magazine advertisement or a TV commercial generates, banner ads are intrusive, easily ignored, and a growing consensus is suspicious of their ability to generate sales, despite the very many per-click impressions that may result. Impressions are only loosely audited for accuracy, however, bringing accusations against publishers for using auto-refresh techniques to increase page views. In this instance, viewers may be looking at the same page multiple times, increasing the number of views for the advertiser as they bump up the numbers (Delaforce 2011).

In another online advertising pricing method, cost per action (CPA), the advertiser only pays when an action occurs as a result of the ad: for example, when a visitor registers on a goods site, purchases a product or agrees to receive further information. CPA is performance-based pricing and can provide detailed statistics by using various tracking systems. The click-through ratio (CTR) and conversion ratio are the most important measurement models for determining online advertising effectiveness. However, they monitor the triggers in an online campaign that lead to tangible actions or purchases. CTR records the percentage of ad views or impressions that result in a click: 1,000 impressions that generate 10 clicks equal a 1% CTR (with the average CTR values range between 0.2% and 2%). The conversion ratio indicates the percentage of clicks that result in an action (a request for more information, a download or a purchase). One hundred clicks that generate five actions is interpreted as a 5% conversion ratio, and would be considered an extremely good ratio.

Digital measurement has become quite sophisticated in other ways, so that accurate customer behaviour profiles of visitors are relatively easy to compile. The relative cost and the payment pricing models can make advertising online cost efficient and provide measured audience analysis, at least superficially. However, even though digital measurement can profile visitors' online behaviour, it does not give insight into their consuming behaviour. Online retailers tend to know a lot about online shoppers' basic behaviours: what pages they clicked on, where they came from, how much they spent, and what they abandoned in their cart before clicking on to the next site (see Table 11.1). These metrics, combined with evaluations of retail success or failure in terms of revenues, are critical, but they are also metrics in retrospect and can only tell advertisers what has already happened (Foresee 2011).

ForeSee, a customer experience analytics firm, has in recent years addressed the question of consumer behaviours by using a customer satisfaction index to quantify which website elements have the greatest impact on overall *e-satisfaction*. If websites can improve satisfaction ratings by prioritising site improvements on the elements that have the greatest impact on consumers, then the advertiser can better understand and work towards increasing consumer-actionable tasks.

Mobile marketing

It is a common complaint that marketing on a mobile device is difficult to measure and has few effective tools to do so. Running a mobile campaign necessitates multiple platforms, non-standard

Table 11.1 Measuring the website elements' impact on overall satisfaction

Element	What it measures
Price	Perceptions of competitiveness of online retail prices
Merchandise	Appeal, variety, availability of website products
Functionality	Usefulness, ease, convenience to the online consumer
Content	Perceptions of accuracy, quality, freshness, timeliness of information on the site

Source: Foresee (2011)

techniques and much information to gather and make sense of. As mobile usage expands and changes, the measurement tools must do so in turn to justify the cost for measuring it (Sissors and Baron 2010).

Applications (apps) on mobile devices are becoming ubiquitous, with 4.5 billion apps sold in 2010, and predictions that this will reach an estimated 22 billion apps by 2013 (Gartner Group 2010). Recently, the Mobile Marketing Association took steps to address the explosion of application technology and measurement uniformity on a global scale with the publication of Mobile Advertising Guidelines (February 2011).

The guidelines contain a number of universal recommendations for creative, ethical and social considerations in advertising on a mobile screen, and attempt to address the lack of standardisation of advertising and measurement on the widely disparate specifications found on multiple mobile operating systems. These guidelines have the support of representative mobile advertising measurement policy bodies in Asia Pacific, Europe, Africa and the Middle East, and North and South America and begin to work towards a common mobile marketing vocabulary for the advertising industry (O'Shea 2009).

Mobile measurement takes many of its measurement cues (currency definitions) from traditional media measurement, in addition to having developed some of its own core measurement methods. Advertising impressions, either active or passive, are based on the user's 'opportunity to see' (OTS), similar to print media, and explained in Chapter 10. It also displays

ViewPoint 11.3 The Marmarati – only extreme lovers need apply

Unilever's Marmite, the much-loved or much-aligned yeast concoction that the Brits so dearly love (or love to hate), decided to launch a strong variant of the product, labelled 'Marmite XO'. The new product would not only be stronger than regular Marmite, but it would also be more expensive.

The We Are Social agency launched the product exclusively using social media, with premium positioning. The goal of the pre-launch phase was to create awareness and desire to trial the new product among Marmite lovers (daily and high-volume users) and the product's position strategy was to encourage participation in the campaign, a sort of badge of honour to loyal Marmite fans. The agency organised a Facebook fan page and a Twitter account (@Marmarati) to drive the campaign.

We Are Social appealed to the consummate Marmite lover by also creating an exclusive club – The Marmarati – that was both entertaining and humorous, and, the agency suggests, Victorian in tone, though the realm of medieval guilds and exclusive societies seems more relevant. Marmite lovers were invited to a luxurious event, where they were inducted into the First Circle of the Marmarati, and blind-tested three possible recipes for the new Marmite XO. As the campaign progressed, a Second Circle was invited to join The Marmarati. Each Circle member received official recognition of his or her membership and a hand-crafted commemorative jar of the Marmite XO prototype blend.

Consumers competed to become members of the club, creating and sharing content about Marmite with interested parties in networks and on social media channels. Word-of-mouth strength resulted in high levels of awareness ahead of the retail launch in March 2010. Retailers sold out of Marmite XO quickly. Strong retail sales continue, without any paid-for media, and at only 20% of the cost of a typical product launch.

Source: Word of Mouth Marketing Association (2011)

Question

What are some of the ways that an advertiser could measure the effectiveness of Marmite's exclusive social media campaign?

Task

Choose a niche product or brand. Create ideas for a campaign that features only one medium and explain why your choices would be successful in the marketplace.

Scholars' paper 11.3 Biometrics and multi-messaging

Treutler, T., Levine, B. and Marci, C.D. (2010) Multi-platform messaging: the medium matters, *Journal of Advertising Research*, 50(3), 243-9

By using modern biometrics and eye tracking, the researchers hoped to discover which advertising platform had the most impact on the consumer. Participants in the study were allowed an opportunity to interact with several platforms - a television programme, listen to the radio, read a newspaper, and surf the internet - without interruption as data were collected from moment to moment. Canadian consumers of media made up the balanced, representative sample. Television advertising outperformed all other media on emotional engagement and on cognition. In answer to the question of why television is so highly effective at advertising, the authors proffer 'it is the primary medium that can use the power of emotional response to create a need state, either through experiencing the needs of the onscreen characters unconsciously during the primary content . . . or through the high emotional involvement with these onscreen characters during the advertising itself'.

'filtering', which differentiates the viewing process from OTS by recommending that if it is known that that the user could not have seen an advertisement, then it should not be counted as an impression. The more complex measured mobile includes tracking assets (defined as any piece of content associated with the page on which an ad appears that serves to 'trigger' the counting of the ad), client-side counting (impressions are valid only if the ad counter receives a request for a tracking asset from the client), day parts, as they are used in broadcast and rich media, and impressions related to content on which the user clicks to obtain additional content or to begin a transaction (Mobile Marketing Association 2011).

In addition to their internet measurement services, Nielsen and comScore metrics measure browsing on smartphones and other 'connected' devices (iPads, Kindles, e-readers and tablets) to judge market share, consumer satisfaction, device share, service quality, revenue share, advertising effectiveness, audience reach and other key indicators in the mobile marketplace (www.nielsen.com). ComScore offers Media Planner 2.0, a fully digitised planning process, which promises a powerful media planning tool to build more efficient plans and more effective results on mobile (http://www.comscore.com).

Reach, frequency and GRP calculations are still applicable tools for measuring reach and frequency figures in an online advertising campaign. They may be used to optimise branding or to audit figures reported by websites. Impressions and clicks are similar to the traditional media's understanding of reach and frequency, but other key technologies and development tools can help to judge the quality of audience interaction online. This is because online media provide performance data not only on frequency and delivery, but also on other levels unknown to traditional media (duration, click-throughs, conversions), which generally results in an immediate refreshing or fine-tuning that can occur weekly, daily or even hourly. Thus, reach and frequency used in tandem with other response metrics for online advertising allow for deeper analysis of campaign measurement (Burton 2009).

This measurement process does not come cheap. In the end, questions must be raised about the costs and timeliness associated with digital media planning for mobile and other connected devices. But is the cost worth the investment in terms of the results it delivers? And can the reach keep up with the evolution of the technology? These and other questions will continue to inform the discussion on mobile measurement, as consumers spend more of their time on the go and less of their time in the home or office space.

Analytics

Analytics describes the process by which a planner takes existing data collected from single source or multiple sources and uses them to determine an optimal decision about the best placement. It has been called the science of analysis and is used most frequently in situations that rely on past experience and data collected from past experience. It is yet another quantitative aspect to media decision making.

Google Analytics (http://www.google.com/analytics/) is a free service that promises to reap rich insights from website traffic and marketing effectiveness through the use of analytics. It also enables better-targeted advertisements and strengthens marketing initiatives on websites. Other software such as Woopra and Omniture primarily tracks visitors on websites, and through the use of dashboards and filters can summarise the number of visitors to sites, revisits and idling time, and initiate chats from visitors to site owners.

Analytics' measurements can better evaluate landing pages, exit pages and key words and then can compare satisfaction rates in terms of pages visited and time on site. It can distinguish between visitors struggling to find information and those positively engaged on the site (http://www.google.com/analytics). Google Analytics can also process statistics with websites that are browsed from a mobile phone (Android based). Its clickstream data provide information on overall satisfaction, the purpose of visit (why visitors came to the site) and task completion (whether they were able to complete their tasks while on the site).

These are encouraging developments for measurement, even though the reliability of statistics and conversion rates indications (i.e. reaching purchasing goals) remains uncertain.

Social media measurement

The basic computation tools for social media activity differ from traditional print and broadcast measurement. Facebook, YouTube and discussion forums assume, unlike the traditional media, an interactive relationship between social site activity and the measurable impact of that activity on social media channels (see Figure 11.2). Key behaviours also distinguish the social media measurement from its traditional predecessors: the omnipresent 'Likes', 'Follows', 'Shares', 'Mentions', and so on, may seem superfluous and unwieldy at first, but once these behaviours have been calculated, they begin to materialise into clear profiles of consumer social activity (see Table 11.2).

The tools for gathering social media data are vast. Some of the standard analytics programmes do not effectively track social media data, however. Experts suggest aggregating analytical information by using innovative tools, such as Threadsy, Social Too, Xinureturns,

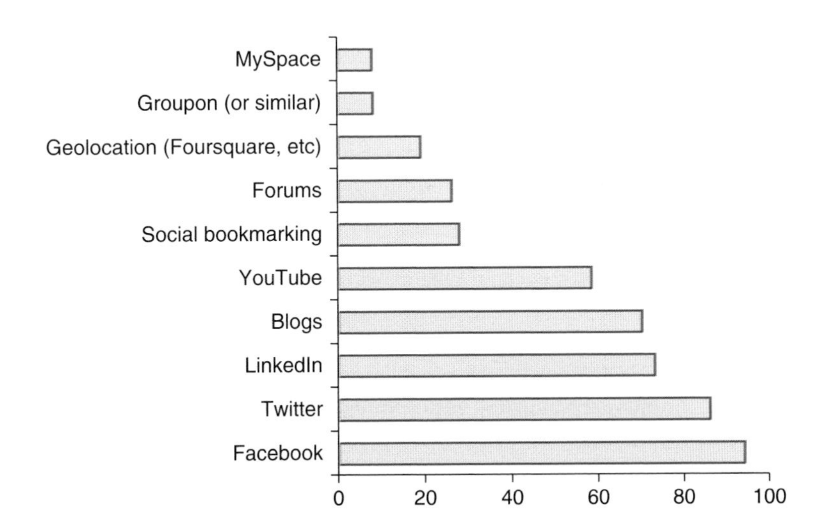

Figure 11.2 Social media use by advertisers (%)
Source: Stelzner, M. (2011)

Table 11.2 Top 10 social media research companies worldwide

Company	Speciality	Global headquarters
Nielsen	measurement and information on consumer behaviour and emerging market trends; global leader	New York; Diemen, the Netherlands
iTracks	software tools for online research; qualitative market research	Saskatoon, Canada
GfK Group	knowledge on social media markets in more than 100 countries	Nuremberg, Germany
Green Book	global market research on the online community	New York
TNS Global Website	global custom market research	London
Social Media Examiner	social media tools facilitator; social media research White Papers	Poway, California
360 Digital Influence	identifies and engages influencers; activates networks to share and recommend products, services and issues	New York
Empower Research	analytics and sentiments; research papers on social media and trends	New York; Bangalore, India
Universal McCann	online and offline media investment strategies; dashboard development; social media analyses	New York
Simplify360	social mentions tracking; analytics from social networking channels	Bangalore, India

Sources: http://www.techiemania.com/top-10-companies-in-social-media-research.html; http://www.tnsglobal.com/; http://simplify360.com/

Simplify360 and Radian6. These tools utilise dashboards to monitor and aggregate the conversations that occur around a brand or a service.

The Radian6 Dashboard, for example, advertises itself as a flexible, web-based social media monitoring and engagement platform that aggregates relevant online conversations in the social media space and translates them into meaningful and actionable measurements about consumer demographics, trend analysis and other raw information.

Radian6 integrates an 'online caller ID system' with post and source tags, schedule alerts and engagement activity right from the dashboard to the advertiser, ensuring 'calculation and synchronicity on social media information' (http://www.radian6.com). This means up-to-the-minute visible analysis of activity on websites.

But what is done with all this data? How can it be converted into information that will aid in fine-tuning messages on the creative end or more effective media placement? Thus far, it is agreed that there needs to be deeper analysis into the implications of the social media data and its influence on advertising (Dumenco 2011; Green 2011; Lazaroiu 2011).

Generally, social media measurement gathers information on new customers, new product sites, satisfaction tracks, operational efficiency (speed and duration), online purchases and word of mouth (tracking threads). Although these digital media metrics may predict and drive simple forms of communications effectiveness, a McKinsey report has found that many brands are struggling with leveraging the opportunities provided by the digital media and have found that there is little ability to generate 'deep customer insights'.

Establishing a relationship between social media metrics and marketing metrics permits an assessment of both the impact and value of social media on campaigns, programmes and overall business (see Figure 11.3). Research indicates that measuring media effectiveness in isolation blocks the larger picture on a fuller efficiency gained by using supplemental media. Measuring

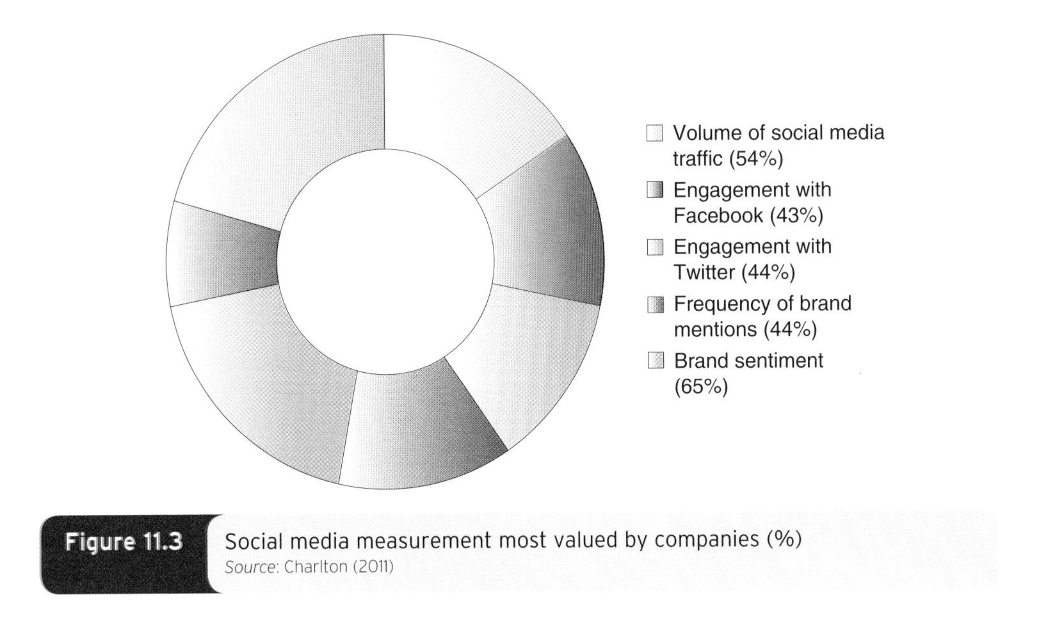

Figure 11.3 Social media measurement most valued by companies (%)
Source: Charlton (2011)

only social media or internet use does not give an accurate and comprehensive depiction of media's capability as an organic tool. It may help to build brand, boost influence rankings and create a buzz within marketing firms and blogger outreach, but it does not take into effect the positive correlation between traditional and newer forms of advertising media (Steinberg 2007; Zigmond and Stipp 2010; Tai-Quan and Zhu 2011).

Studies also point out the perceived difficulty with social media measurement. Many media and marketing personnel worldwide feel as if they do not have complete and up-to-date information on the investment, management and delivery ramifications of social media advertising campaigns (Charlton 2011). Seemingly, many know that measuring social advertising media campaigns is vital, but few know what is most important.

Gaming measurement

The cost of in-game, around-game or self-contained advergaming advertising is one of its most appealing features as an advertising media investment. According to Game Advertising Online (GAO), a company that specialises in creating and maintaining the ads, gaming uses the same CPC, CPM, CPA and CTR formulas discussed earlier for online measurement and pricing models. All these methods basically charge the same way and also create sufficient reach and frequency for the advertiser.

In the traditional case, advertisers pay for a certain number of times (related to frequency) shown at a premium spot around the web browser. In other cases, the ads are randomly selected on a rotating basis throughout the week and circle around back to one another. A bidding system is also in place to determine when and where an ad will be placed on the gaming site.

The Interactive Advertising Bureau (IAB) Games Committee worked with industry stakeholders to quantify advertising within the gaming environment. Currently in-game advertising uses a time-based measurement approach for several formats and based on this approach, networks and publishers may set threshold caps of exposure. The standard impression (as in other media) may be defined as 10 seconds of cumulative exposure to an advertising format or element within a game session. In order for each second to be counted, the gamer view must meet predefined parameters for the angle of view to the ad in addition to the size of the ad unit on the screen. These parameters have been agreed to ensure that gamers are truly exposed to the ads before any impression is counted. Other measurement methods count 'interactive impressions' once there is an interaction between the gamer and the interactive ad unit.

Exhibit 11.4 Not so fast . . .

Alan Pearlstein suggests that many companies are proclaiming that they have in their possession better, more accurate media audience data and better targeting capabilities, new algorithms to break the code, as it were, to reach the optimum audience. Not true, writes Pearlstein, president and CEO of Cross Pixel Media. There exists no magical algorithm and hard data-driven decision-making process out there that does all the work. Media buyers are looking for data that help them do their jobs most effectively; overcomplicated tech-speak and promises of the magic pill do not compute. Media companies should be able to explain fully to clients a good 'actionable digital model', whereby a media planner can explain in realistic terms what digital can and cannot do. (Pearlstein 2011)

Source: Shutterstock.com

Neither of these metrics, albeit based on long consideration and recent research, has yet been standardised in the industry (IAB 2009).

Gaming is difficult to measure for at least two reasons: the gamer does not engage in the game primarily to consume products or services, and, as noted above, the measurement methods for game advertising are not yet standardised. Still, Nielsen Games measurement service reports that more than one-third of gamers bought, talked about or sought information about a product after seeing an in-game advertisement, supporting the idea that in-game ads appear to be adept at building brand awareness (Beirne 2008). Apart from increasing brand awareness and purchase intent, in-game ads seemingly trigger users to engage with sponsored media. According to 85 studies from Microsoft's in-game ad-serving company for PC and Xbox 360, called Massive, in-game ads were found to increase purchase intent by 24% and an overall brand rating by 32% (Khan 2010).

As with all media, the advertiser should consider the editorial environment when considering purchasing space on an in-game site. At least one measurement study has suggested that non-violent video games are better at building positive brand recall, whilst advertising in violent games, such as the highly popular Modern Warfare 3, comes at the cost of lower brand recall and recognition (Yoo and Pena 2010).

Scholars' paper 11.4 Efficient TV rating points

Smith, J.A., Boyle, B. and Cannon, H.M. (2010) Survey-based targeting fine-tunes television media planning: a case for accuracy and cost efficiency, *Journal of Advertising Research*, 50(4), 428–439

Efficiency, the authors state, means the cost of effectively reaching those targeted consumers who are most likely to respond to a marketer's message. Even a slight fine-tune on efficiency to a marketer's target television audience could result in enormous savings. A cost-per-effective-target market rating point (CPETRP) depends on the four factors of ad cost: audience size, media vehicle skew to the desired target and potential of exposure. The authors argue that by combining the economies and breadth of coverage achieved by survey-based single-source data for television (motivation and lifestyles of product and media users) with the timeliness and accuracy of conventional media data (demographic data), media planners can reap the benefits of both for more accurate, cost-efficient television media planning.

ViewPoint 11.4 Bringing International Women's Day to Twitter

The United Nations Development Programme (UNDP) serves as a grass-roots global network that works in over 170 countries advocating for change, connecting resources to communities and providing knowledge for the improvement of people's lives.

International Women's Day is one of the most important days in the UNDP calendar year. It's an opportunity to highlight the many cultural faces of women around the world and to talk about ways of empowering women's lives. On 8 March 2011, International Women's Day celebrated its 100th birthday, an important milestone that UNDP considered an ideal time to try to measure the size and characteristics of its online community and to discover the social sites most popular among its stakeholders.

The plan began with a live Twitter chat: participants were asked to tweet their comments and questions on improving gender equality or promoting good governance throughout the world. Responses were vast and varied and proved that social media tools could serve as a powerful advocacy tool in meeting the many challenges of women's issues.

Indications are that 200,000 posts were lodged from women on 8 March 2011. UNDP was able to determine that the majority, 80%, occurred on Twitter; Facebook and associated content blogs rounded out the participations. Through this basic breakdown, UNDP identified 17,000 key activists in various regions and can now use them as the 'go-to' people for developing stronger ties for positive change throughout the global community.

Basic audience analysis of this commemorative social media conversation will enable the United Nations Development Programme to better interact and work with key players and their constituencies in meeting the challenges they face.

Source: United Nations Development Programme (2011)

Question

What is it about the nature of social media that allows for the successful tracking of the UNDP campaign?

Task

Make notes about the other ways that the participants could leverage and subsequently track ideas through the social media.

Exhibit 11.5 Iloveqatar.net

Some enterprising young students in Qatar decided that it was time to showcase their country and provide 'a better place and provide the best resource out there'. The result? Iloveqatar.net. The site is not exclusively for ex-pats, but for all those living in Qatar, planning to visit, or simply wanting to learn more about the small Arab emirate on the western coast of the Persian Gulf. Simple tracking and measurement are accomplished by registration that allows the viewer to blog, join forums (Pakistan Group, Global Pinoys and Qatar Billiards Club and others) and participate in general posts. For their cooperative work with Vodaphone Qatar on a Ramadan information site, Iloveqatar was recognised as the Best Digital Creative Campaign by Internet Awards Middle East 2011.

Source: www.iloveqatar.net

Buying the media

Once the research has been completed, the calculations and measurements worked out, the choices made, the plan approved by the advertiser and the schedule organised to everyone's satisfaction, the space and time requirements as specified in the media plan have to be negotiated and purchased through media outlets. The advertiser (or its 'agency of record' on its behalf) or a media buying service has to negotiate and buy the best possible time and space for its client (O'Guinn, Allen and Semenik 2012). A number of factors determine the cost of placing media, such as the history between advertiser and media outlet, discounts in place, advance purchasing upfront, and duration of the campaign. These all affect the contract that the parties are about to enter. A brief synopsis of some of the major print and broadcast elements of buying will serve as good examples of buying across all media.

Each print medium issues a *rate card*, which lays out in detail the costs of different kinds of buys that are possible with the print vehicles. Despite the published rate card, the media buyer negotiates for the lowest possible price for the media placements. Other factors may figure in the negotiation as well: an existing or planned long-term purchasing history with the print vehicle; negotiated discounts for multiple insertions (*volume buys*); the desire to have a *preferred position* (select sections of the print medium, such as inside cover) at a premium; additional promotional support, such as support for an integrated campaign (**value added**). Once the media schedule is launched and the results are assessed, a new round of negotiations may begin.

There are three common media buys in television time. The *upfront buy*, similar in many countries, is a negotiated buy prior to the official television season launch. Upfront buying occurs from 1 to 2 years in advance of a television schedule. It can result in enormous savings for the advertiser because it means that the advertiser has first access to the best programming choices available. Advance purchases can prove to be rewarding in terms of money saved through negotiation. At the same time, no guarantees are given with respect to performance of the time purchased. If the brand or service does not perform well or is cancelled, if the programming does not bring in the rating points necessary to meet projections, or if the macro-economic environment changes dramatically, some advertising investment may be lost. The unknown factors involved in the nature of upfront buys also make them an attractive value.

The *scatter buy* occurs one quarter in advance of the airdate. This negotiated buy is generally considered 'as needed' and allows for more flexibility and leverage with advertising expenditures, but it too gives no guarantees of rating points delivery or programme performance. The value can be good on the scatter market. The advertiser is working under a more predictable knowledge of mitigating factors, since time is purchased three months in advance, and not 1–2 years.

The *opportunity buy* occurs when time or space is bought close to the last minute. The outcome has its advantages and disadvantages: an opportunity buy may result in tremendous savings, if, for instance, a time slot opens up at a favourable time during a popular sport in Olympic Games' coverage. Conversely, if the advertiser out of necessity needs to place media at the last minute and opportunities are scarce, the opportunity buy may be no opportunity at all and the time purchased could come at an expensive premium.

Media planning post-buy analysis

After the campaign is complete, a series of monitoring tasks is performed that serve as proof that the campaign has been executed according to plan and that media objectives have been achieved as promised. A *post-campaign* or *post-buy analysis* examines the expenditures made on print, broadcast, digital and other positions and cross-checks them against actual ratings and readership to determine how effectively and at what frequency the target audience has been reached.

As indicated in Chapter 10, accountability for media expenditures is increasingly important among clients. Investors in a media schedule expect to see desirable returns on their investment. The advertiser not only expects increased sales or an actionable measure from the approved media plan, the ultimate objectives for placing media, but also scrutinises the details of the plan's overall effectiveness in sending the message to the target audience. Post analysis is vital to the planning cycle. It ensures accountability and may generate further adjustments and agreements in the future.

The first step in the post analysis process begins by reviewing methodically the scheduled media placements and whether they appeared in the correct issues of a print vehicle in the express time frame of a broadcast programme. A media verification audit confirms the media booked by the agency and that the advertiser received what they paid for. Interactive campaigns on social sites and mobile platforms are checked in the same manner.

For print, actual copies of print inserts – called *media tear sheets* – are collected for purposes of verification. Increasingly, *digital tear sheets* are used to facilitate the proof-of-publication process by providing web-based access to monitor ads. Did the ads appear in the issues they were supposed to? Did a preferred position guarantee (e.g. right-hand side) come through?

Similarly, to ensure that programmes have delivered the agreed ratings in electronic media, programme ratings in which commercials appeared are checked against the schedule. The same holds true for online measurement, where often hits or clicks-through have been guaranteed for a specific time period. Should the ratings or the hits appear to be significantly lower than the agreed-upon delivery, or should some *force majeure* (act of God), or 'breaking news' pre-empt programming, interrupting the schedule and preventing the scheduled TV commercial from appearing, the parties involved often negotiate extra airtime or additional commercial placement to make up the difference.

Post analysis also considers media vehicle exposure to determine whether the media plan achieves what it promised and adheres to the established reach and frequency projections. Was the target audience exposed an ample number of times during the schedule?

Thirdly, post measurement testing may often include brand awareness, comprehension, conviction and action, which depend on assessing the creative executions within the context of the media in which they were placed. Execution and media placement must work in unison, if the ads are to bring awareness to the brand, be understood as a message, be convincing, and, most importantly, result in a purchase or action by the target audience from engagement with the media campaign. The temper of the creative execution must be appropriate for the media space, and the media must complement the quality of the creative execution.

Performance-based buying in digital advertising eliminates the need for several of these steps on the post analysis process. A performance buy depends on achieving desired actions from the target audience. Then the cost per action (CPA) model shapes a campaign model that meets the advertiser's specific requirements. If the campaign performs, the terms agreed are realised.

Measuring and tracking the impact of advertising media have always been difficult. Many suggest that there are too many factors—economic, psychological, and social—at play preventing the determination of a neatly packaged one-to-one formula connecting advertising media to desired results. Others suggest that intangibles, such as brand and image building, make it difficult to measure the performance of advertising media alone. No matter what the sentiment, the standard practices involved in traditional, digital and emerging advertising media planning and buying will continue to evolve over time.

Chapter summary

In order to help consolidate your understanding of measuring advertising media effectiveness and efficiency, here are the key points summarised against each of the learning objectives.

Review the standard measurement methods used to determine media efficiency

Media strategy decisions are based in part on measurable factors that help determine media efficiency (delivering the intended target audience at the best price). Measurements can differ from television to print to outdoor, but also from traditional to digital, as measurement techniques have become elaborate and complex in recent years, with performance metrics and analytics that promise to quantify effectiveness in new ways.

Utilise measurement techniques and methods in media plan preparation

Numerical calculations are often the first steps taken to parse the good from the bad choices in selecting the appropriate media. CPM (cost per thousand) analysis and ratings are two of the basic units of measurement for selecting the potential of print and broadcast, whilst analytics, multiple platforms and non-standard techniques of information gathering are used to measure digital and emerging media.

Describe the changes and challenges in traditional versus digital measurement

Media accountability has been and remains a contentious issue with traditional media and digital media measurement. Media auditing companies have grown of late and serve as one independent verification tool of audience delivery, but the relationship of actual versus potential consumer engagement and actionable motivation by the consumer is difficult to determine.

Survey new opportunities and challenges for planning and buying media

Once the media plan is approved, the space and time requirements as specified for the scheduled media plan have now to be negotiated and purchased through media outlets. The advertiser not only expects increased sales or an actionable measure from the approved plan, but also scrutinises the plan's overall effectiveness in sending the message to the target audience. Media buy post analysis is vital to the planning cycle, for it ensures accountability and may generate further adjustments in the future.

Review questions

1. How would you respond to the challenges facing the research team at SAS as set out at the start of this chapter?
2. List some of the tools a media planner might use as a starting point to planning media.
3. Describe what is meant by gross impressions. How are gross impressions different from CPM?
4. What are GRPs and what function do they serve?
5. Articulate some of the complex core measurement principles found in measuring mobile media.
6. List several reasons why it is important for an advertiser to monitor the performance of its social media site.

7. Why do some call for deeper analysis of analytics programmes?
8. List some of the pricing models for gaming advertising.
9. Give reasons for choosing an 'opportunity buy' versus a 'scatter buy' when buying airtime for television.
10. Explain what happens in post-buy analysis.

Chapter references

Ankeny, J. (2010) The new advertising age, *Entrepreneur*, 38(3), 26–31

Anon (2011) Who's using Tumblr? *emarketer.com*, retrieved from http://www.emarketer.com/Article.aspx?id=1008608&R=1008608

Beirne, M. (2008) Nielsen looks to test ad recall in gaming world, *Mediaweek*, 18(32), 4–6

Bourdon, J. and Méadel, C. (2011) Inside television audience measurement: deconstructing the ratings machine, *Media, Culture & Society*, 33(5), 791–800

Burstein, D. (2011) Email test: shorter copy brings 100% more total clickthroughs (web log comment), 7 September, retrieved from http://www.marketingexperiments.com/blog/analytics-testing

Burton, J. (2009) *A Marketer's Guide to Understanding the Economics of Digital Compared to Traditional Advertising and Media Services*. New York: American Association of Advertising Agencies

Charlton, G. (2011) 78% of European marketers unhappy with social media measurement, retrieved from http://econsultancy.com/us/blog/8122-78-of-european-marketers-unhappy-with-social-media-measurement

Cheong, Y., De Gregorio, F. and Kim, K. (2010) The power of reach and frequency in the age of digital advertising, *Journal of Advertising Research*, 50(4), 403–15

Choi, J. (2010) Case study: a 60% CTR and still counting, *Imediaconnection*, 6 July, retrieved from http://www.imediaconnection.com/content/27039.asp

Delaforce, J. (2011) The green-eyed monster (web log comment), 11 May, retrieved from http://www.thegreeneyedmonster.com/

Dumenco, S. (2011) Metrics mess: five sad truths about measurement right now, *Advertising Age*, 82(9), 8–9

Foresee (2011) The Foresee e-retail satisfaction index (US holiday edition) 2011, retrieved from http://www.foreseeresults.com/research-white-papers/us-e-retailer-winners-and-losers-holiday-season-2011-form-foresee.shtml

Gartner Group (2010) Gartner says consumers will spend $6.2 billion in mobile application stores in 2010 (press release), 18 January, retrieved from http://www.gartner.com/it/page.jsp?id=1282413

Green, E. (2011) Pushing the social media buttons, *Media Development*, 58(1), 12–15

Guthrie, M. (2011) TV ratings: 'Two and a half men' drops big in second week but still tops Monday. *Hollywood Reporter*, 27 September, retrieved from http://www.hollywoodreporter.com/live-feed/two-a-men-ratings-drop-240687

Hearst Magazines (2011) *Elle* media kit, retrieved from http://www.ellemediakit.com/r5/home.asp

IAB. (2009) In-Game Advertising Measurement Guidelines. Retrieved from http://www.iab.net/guidelines/508676/guidelines/in-game

Kelley, L. and Jugenheimer, D. (2008) *Advertising Media Planning: A Brand Management Approach*. Armonk, NY: M.E. Sharpe

Khan, A. (2010) A brief look at in-game advertising (web log comment), 26 May, retrieved from http://socialtimes.com/a-brief-look-at-in-game-advertising_b13631

Knorp, B. (2011) Don't get trapped measuring the wrong thing in social media, *Advertising Age*, 82(34), 20

Lafayette, J. (2009) Study shows TV's impact on consumer purchasing behaviour. *TV Week*, 16 April, retrieved from http://www/tvweek.com

Lazaroiu, G. (2011) The creation of new global communication infrastructures and forms of online interaction, *Annals of Spiru Haret University, Journalism Studies*, 1292–5

McPheters and Company (2009) TV and magazine ads more effective than ads on internet (press release), 1 April, retrieved from http://mcpheters.com/2009/04/01/tv-and-magazine-ads-more-effective-than-ads-on-internet/

Mobile Marketing Association (2011) Mobile web advertising measurement guidelines version 1.0 final release, retrieved from http://www.iab.net/media/file/MobileWebMeasurementGuidelines_final.pdf

Neff, J. (2010) Mass of metrics may mean marketers know less, *Advertising Age*, 81(33), 5–30

O'Guinn, T.C., Allen, C.T. and Semenik, R.J. (2012) *Advertising and Integrated Brand Promotion*. Mason, OH: South-Western

O'Shea, D. (2009) Mobile advertising measurements still lack standardization (web log comment), 28 September, retrieved from http://www.fiercewireless.com/nextgenspotlight/story/mobile-advertising-measurements-still-lack-standardization

Pearlstein, A. (2011) Stop hiding behind your algorithm: if your pitch includes 'Trust my algorithm', good luck winning deals (web log comment), 27 September, retrieved from http://adage.com/article/digitalnext/stop-hiding-algorithm/230060/

Rice, J. (2011) Marketing research chart: top email campaign elements routinely tested to optimize performance, *Marketing Sherpa*, 13 September, retrieved from http://www.marketingsherpa.com

Sharp, B. (2008) A problem with ad awareness norms to assess advertising quality (web log comment), 24 June, retrieved from http://byronsharp.wordpress.com/category/marketing/market-research/

Shimp, T. (2007) *Advertising, Promotion, and Other Aspects of Integrated Marketing Communications*. Thomson: Mason, OH

Sissors, J. and Baron R. (2010) *Advertising Media Planning*. New York: McGraw-Hill

Smith, J.A., Boyle, B. and Cannon, H.M. (2010) Survey-based targeting fine-tunes television media planning, *Journal of Advertising Research*, 50(4), 428–439

Society for New Communications Research (2010) *Measurement Innovation*, retrieved from http://sncr.org/node/130

Steinberg, B. (2007) TV measurement comes up short, *Advertising Age*, 78(29), 8

Stelzner, M. (2011) 2011 social media marketing industry report, retrieved from http://www.SocialMediaExaminer.com

Tai-Quan, P. and Zhu, J.H. (2011) A game of win–win or win–lose? Revisiting the internet's influence on sociability and use of traditional media, *New Media & Society*, 13(4), 568–86. doi:10.1177/1461444810375976

Treutler, T., Levine, B. and Marci, C.D. (2010) Multi-platform messaging: the medium matters, *Journal of Advertising Research*, 50(3), 243–9

United Nations Development Programme (2011) Case studies and white papers: International Women's Day: UNDP brings the conversation online, retrieved from http://www.radian6.com/resources/library/international-women's-day-—-undp-brings-the-conversation-online

WARC (2011) Marketers still grappling with digital, 1 December, retrieved from https://www.warc.com

Word of Mouth Marketing Association (2011) The Marmarati, Case study library, retrieved from http://womma.org/_pdf/marmarati.pdf

Yoo, S. and Pena, J. (2010) Do violent video games impair the effectiveness of in-game advertisements? The impact of gaming environment on brand recall, brand attitude, and purchase intention. *Conference Papers – International Communication Association*, 1

Zigmond, D. and Stipp, H. (2010) Assessing a new advertising effect, *Journal of Advertising Research*, 50(2), 162–8

Chapter 12
Standards and responsibilities

There is a need for all organisations to ensure that they give due consideration to the appropriate ethical, moral, social and legal standards when communicating with customers and other stakeholders. There is a range of legal and industry practice codes which control and influence the advertising used by clients and their agencies. These cover a spectrum from producing appropriate individual product advertisements to the procedures put in place to manage effective corporate governance. Many individual organisations now use advertising to explain how they are complying with demands from legislators and consumers to adopt socially acceptable and responsible business practices, as part of profile positioning strategies discussed in Chapter 4.

Aims and learning objectives

The aims of this chapter are to explore the ways in which the advertising industry is regulated and controlled, and to examine issues relating to its ethical and socially responsible behaviour.

As a result of reading this chapter readers should be able to:

1. discuss the views for and against the use of advertising in society
2. outline some of the principal ethical issues associated with advertising
3. explain the legislative controls and various codes of practice in the advertising industry
4. explore issues associated with advertising and children, sex, alcohol, food and drink, fashion and beauty and shock tactics
5. describe regulations and controls relating to product placement and ambush marketing
6. consider the ways in which approaches to corporate social responsibility affect advertising practice.

Minicase Saving the Indian tiger with Aircel

At the end of 2009 the Indian mobile telecommunications industry was estimated to be the second largest telecommunications industry globally, with 562 million subscribers (Chaudhuri and Khurana 2011). The major players were market leaders Airtel with 23% market share, Vodafone 17%, Reliance 18%, with Tata Indicom and Idea both with 11% shares. Aircel was considered to be a small regional player with a market share of 6%.

Aircel was launched in 1999 as a regional brand operating in Chennai (one of India's top four metro cities). It was almost 10 years before Aircel spread its presence across 23 telecom circles in India (circles are the areas for which licences are awarded). As with many similar telecommunications markets, competitive differentiation was based on new product development, tariffs, network strength and customer service. Aircel's development has led to them achieving national awards for customer satisfaction and network quality. They were listed as the top mid-size utility company in 2007 by *Businessworld* magazine and recognised as the best regional operator by the *Tele.net* magazine. The telecommunications organisation CMAI INFOCOM recognised Aircel for excellence in the marketing of a new telecom service in 2009. Aircel had attempted to position the brand as an 'enabler' closely associated with India's economic growth.

Exhibit 12.1 Indian tiger
Source: Shutterstock.com

Despite being the fastest-growing operator in the market as they extended national market coverage, the Aircel brand was still considered by consumers to be a regional brand, with low levels of awareness and attention in the mass Indian market. In comparison to the market leaders, Aircel's marketing communications budget was modest, restricting possibilities to achieve business growth by outspending competition in terms of media advertising. They had achieved some success in raising the brand's profile by developing their involvement in community projects related to a corporate social responsibility (CSR) strategy. These had centred largely on educational initiatives working with NGO partners and the Indian government. Projects included the opening of schools in specific areas aimed at educating street children, mobile toy libraries and a computer lab in a government high school. Further CSR activities were thought to be a positive way of enhancing the brand's reputation and developing market presence. This was also considered to be an effective way of creating competitive differentiation in a 'me too' market category.

Finding the right initiative to pursue was important if this strategy was to be effective in achieving tough objectives including:

- Extend the appeal to every Indian, inviting them to join the mass movement spearheaded by Aircel. Progress would be measured through people's involvement and government participation.
- Achieve high affinity towards brand Aircel by loyalist and competition users alike, as measured through independent and internal market research.
- Increase purchase intention for Aircel per se and against players who are similar in vintage (like Idea) or new yet aggressive (like Tata Docomo), measured through the purchase intention scores in the MillwardBrown Brand Track.

Project Tiger, a programme to save tigers from extinction, was started in the 1970s by the government of India with the support of WWF (World Wide Fund for Nature). The cause was still dormant, and interest and awareness levels very low. The problem identified was that despite the tiger being the national animal of India, people were unable to form a connection between the survival of the tiger and their daily lives. In 2010, the numbers of surviving tigers in India was identified at 1,411 and reducing rapidly.

How would Aircel be able to develop a CSR programme, including advertising, that would reconnect the importance of the tiger to the Indian public, halt the decline in tiger population and achieve their business objectives? Agency Dentsu Communications were involved in working with Aircel and a budget of over $20 million set to cover media expenditure.

Source: Chaudhuri and Khurana (2011); www.aircel.com, accessed 20/12/2012

Introduction

Critics of advertising claim that it encourages and persuades consumers to buy products and services that they do not really need and that the amounts of money spent on advertising could be better used in other areas of the business. Such criticisms of advertising are not new. Fletcher (2010: 111) quotes the views of British essayist and historian Thomas Macaulay, decrying advertising as 'We expect some reserve, some decent pride, in our hatter and bootmaker.' At the end of the 19th century the Society for Controlling Abuses of Public Advertising was formed by a group of influential writers and artists. Advertising has historically been subject to laws and controls. These came to specific prominence when commercial TV was introduced into the UK in 1955. Packard (1957) challenged the American advertising industry and the methods used to persuade consumers to buy products they did not need or want. Public opinions of and attitudes towards advertising vary widely from those based on the critical platform to those who freely engage with advertising as a form of entertainment and as a means of obtaining information related to the purchase of products and services. Advertising is difficult to avoid and as such it is the responsibility of all advertisers to consider the impact it has on individuals and society as a whole. Grounds for acceptability include consideration of advertising's legality, honesty, truthfulness, credibility and decency.

In most developed markets advertising practice is regulated through a mixture of legislation and voluntary controls. These stem both from government action and industry self-regulation. In some sensitive market sectors such as alcohol and tobacco, individual firms maintain their own codes of practice in addition to centrally governed controls. See ViewPoint 12.1 for an example of such practice in the alcoholic drinks markets.

Attitudes towards advertising

Consultants ZenithOptimedia estimated global advertising expenditure in 2011 at around US$464 billion, 3.5% higher than in 2010. They forecast that this will grow to some US$486 billion in 2012, a 4.7% growth, despite the continuing economic slowdown in Europe and fears of worsening debt crisis. Expenditure is expected to grow 5.2% in 2013 and 5.8% in 2014. Given the scale and scope of the advertising business across the globe, it is hardly surprising that there should be a range of attitudes and opinions held by consumers regarding the subject. These might relate to generic positive and negative perspectives of advertising as well as views on individual advertisements. Critics of advertising argue that it is wasteful in terms of resources allocated to it that might be 'better' deployed reducing prices, improving products or providing better customer service.

Advertising might also be considered to persuade people to desire and/or purchase products and services that they do not really 'need' and to be targeting vulnerable groups such as children and people in less well educated and lower income sectors. Further criticisms also query advertising's inherent truthfulness and honesty. Specific product and service sectors are subject to much question and debate. The Advertising Standards Authority (ASA) (see below) identify a number of 'hot topics' where consideration of advertising practices is given more focused attention in terms of regulatory actions. These currently include advertising related to food and soft drinks, cosmetics, homeopathy websites, politics and electioneering, and advertising targeted at children. The Advertising Codes discussed later in this chapter make specific provision for product categories where consumer opinion is intensified due to the potentially harmful effects of the products concerned. Such sectors include alcohol, tobacco and food and soft drinks.

We discuss the role of control and regulation in advertising later in this chapter. Most developed markets maintain some form of regulatory systems for the monitoring of advertising. These include complaints procedures for consumers and business. This facilitates the expression of consumer opinion regarding individual advertisements and the nature of the complaints gives some perspective on the kind of issues that concern consumers that lead to the complaints being made. The bases for many consumer complaints to the ASA about specific ads concern a range of issues. These include ads that are misleading, that promote anti-social behaviour, that are gender stereotypical, that contain explicit or suggestive sexual content, that depict animal cruelty, or that are offensive or just irresponsible.

Public opinion about advertising is a significant issue. If opinions are generally negative, this can impact on how messages are received and responded to. Research undertaken by the Advertising Association shows that since the late 1990s favourable public attitudes toward advertising have been declining (Credos 2011a). Their study monitored public opinion on advertising and their findings are summarised in Table 12.1 and illustrated in Figure 12.1.

Fraser and McBain (2011) report on research undertaken to measure public (consumer) attitudes toward advertising and to understand the views of opinion formers who shape these attitudes. Opinion formers include politicians, academics, NGOs, journalists and leading advertising industry professionals. The research identified a number of key points which are summarised in Table 12.2.

Table 12.1 Findings and implications arising from the Credos report

Findings	Implications
Public more knowledgeable of advertising and appreciate it when it informs, entertains and rewards	Provides opportunities for creativity and inventiveness
Advertising defined more broadly in the public's mind than previously considered including the broader marketing mix	Needs wider consideration by advertising bodies including Advertising Association (AA) and Advertising Standards Authority (ASA)
Despite positive views of advertising's cultural, social and economic contribution, negative factors tend to dominate public perceptions	Opportunities to demonstrate advertising's added value and positive roles
Principal negative associations concern intrusive, unsolicited, irrelevant and poor-quality advertising	Need to consider accuracy of targeting and more appropriate and distinctive forms of communication
Many people have a negative view of 'advertising' generically but could believe individual ads are very good	Research methodologies for gathering, measuring and tracking opinions require review
Public respond with healthy scepticism to most ads and understand commercial intent	Ads are not taken over-seriously
Public mistrust of advertising is caused by the perceived intention of the advertiser to mislead or deceive	Implications for how advertising standards are designed and enforced
Low awareness and understanding of the Advertising Standards Authority. Public accept personal responsibility for advertising's effect	Promotion of successful self-regulation cases by ASA to raise awareness and stimulate debate

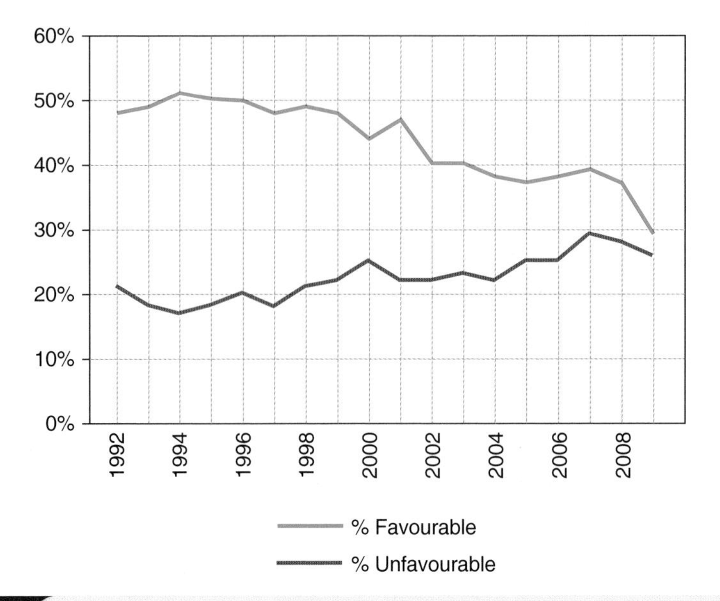

Figure 12.1 Public opinions toward advertising
Source: Credos report March (2011)

Table 12.2 Public versus opinion-former attitudes towards advertising

Public attitudes	Opinion-former attitudes
Most consumers do not hold strong views	Most opinion formers have a viewpoint, whereas most consumers are indifferent towards advertising
Trust in the advertising industry is low. Widely held perception of 'misleading' messages and a lack of trust in advertisers' motives	Opinion formers' views are not entrenched. They appreciate both the positives and negatives of advertising
Irritating, poorly executed and repetitive ads sour public views towards the advertising industry	Personal experiences and roles as fathers, mothers, grandparents and consumers are crucial in forming their views on advertising
Experiences with specific advertisements shape opinion	Advertising merely mirrors existing social trends, rather than being a catalyst for change itself. The influence that advertising has on individuals is seen as limited
Advertising to children elicits strongest reactions	Children seen as being disproportionately influenced by advertising, because they lack the skills to process this sort of information
Concern over idealised images in beauty and alcohol advertising	Stakeholders have more pragmatic views than consumers. MPs tend to have very pragmatic and nuanced views of the industry and see advertising as issue-led
Positive benefits seen as humorous content, attracting attention to new and worthwhile products	Confidence in advertising largely stems from confidence in the regulatory system, rather than in advertisers themselves
Dislike of small print in financial ads and misrepresentative product photos in food advertising	The economic benefits of advertising are not understood

The views expressed by consumers in the Fraser and McBain research suggest consumers are less likely to be duped or misled by advertising than some critics might believe. Klein (2000) argues that people in the West 'over-consume' as a result of advertising creating 'unnecessary' demand for products. Broadbent (2007) challenges this 'unnecessary' perspective, suggesting that it is not advertising that creates markets or customer needs. He considers that Klein 'confuses correlation with causality'. Markets may grow and as they do advertising expenditure increases but may not be the actual cause of the growth. Broadbent provides the example of the Apple iPod and MP3 players meeting increased demand for music on the move but this was not as a result of advertising. Products and services develop to meet consumer needs and advertising plays a part in informing consumers how these needs can be met more effectively by competing brands. Significant numbers of advertised new products fail. It could be argued that this is a result of poor advertising but, perhaps more likely, consumers are making informed decisions that they do not want or need these products. Broadbent goes on to argue that most consumers buy products to replace old ones or where they are running out of, say, soap or coffee. Advertising in such cases might influence brand choice but it not stimulating demand for either the soap or the coffee.

Ethics and advertising

Spence and Van Heekeren (2005) define ethics as 'a set of prescriptive rules, principles, values and virtues of character that inform and guide interpersonal and intrapersonal conduct – conduct of people toward each other and the conduct of people towards themselves'. This might be interpreted as doing the right things both collectively and individually. Spence and Van Heekeren go on to look at the ethical principles that might underpin determining whether advertising could be considered ethical or unethical. These principles are based around consideration of three arguments – *deontological, teleological* and *consequentialist.*

Advertising might be considered unethical for deontological reasons on the basis that the actual advertising content does not consider 'the purpose, goal or end' for which it was designed. Teleological reasons would include situations where the purpose, goal or end can be explained in relation to why the advertising has been designed in the way it has. The consequentialist argument centres on advertising being unethical or morally wrong if the consequences for the majority of those receiving the messages are considered to be unacceptable or 'bad'. Mizzoni (2010) describes deontological ethics as being similar to natural law ethics in agreeing that 'the end does not justify the means'. In attempting to judge whether an action might be morally right or wrong, Mizzoni proposes the need to consider the action's intention and consequence.

Rossiter and Bellman (2005) present the link between deontological and teleological ethical theories as a two-part principle based on truth, saying firstly that truth itself is the prime standard but, secondly, that truth can be 'overridden' in certain situations where significant harmful consequences can be identified as a result (or consequence) of telling the truth. They outline practices which are considered to contribute to unethical advertising. These include 'subliminal presentation of stimuli' where the target audience is unaware of being promoted to and 'supraliminal stimuli presented via subliminal process' where the audience know they are being promoted to but have not been informed of the process. Other practices that can contribute to ethical questioning are presented by Rossiter and Bellman as omission of material facts and lying or exaggeration of attribute or benefit claims. Omission of material facts might include health side effects associated with medicines or food and drink products.

As we discussed earlier, there are a number of attitudes and perceptions of advertising relating to questions of acceptability and responsibility. Most certainly, the advertising industry has a collective responsibility to ensure that the outcomes of their activities meet standards of

Scholars' paper 12.1 Ethics focus for advertising journal

Snyder, W. (2011) Making the case for enhanced advertising ethics: how a new way of thinking about advertising ethics may build consumer trust, *Journal of Advertising Research*, 51(3), 477-83

This article is one of a number in a special issue of this journal focusing on advertising ethics. It presents to advertising professionals the case for the need to enhance advertising ethics to build consumer trust in companies and their brands. It identifies research which suggests that consumers do not trust advertising much of the time. Key ethical concerns are discussed, including children's advertising, the blurring of advertising with news and entertainment, and behavioural advertising. It proposes answers to key questions about convincing advertising professionals of the significance of ethics and the need to practice high levels of personal ethics in advertising creation and dissemination.

Other articles address advertising practice in agencies, targeting food products to children in advergaming, celebrity endorser behaviours, data privacy and advertiser influence on editorial newspaper content. The range of discussion on contemporary ethics issues in advertising provides a comprehensive overview of the theoretical underpinning and practitioner activities related to this important topic.

ethical acceptability for itself and its various target audiences. The Codes of (Advertising) Practice described below could in many ways be interpreted as ethical codes meeting the definition of ethics suggested by Spence and Van Heekeren.

The ASA's principles of advertising being 'legal, decent, honest and truthful' provide a basis for ethical behaviour by advertisers. Being truthful should be at the heart of any definition of acting ethically. In advertising terms, however, this is not always a straightforward proposition. There arises the question of the need to be factually accurate or present information in a manner that may not be 100% factually accurate but may be acceptable in the way in which it presented by virtue of how it is understood and interpreted by the intended target audience. Advertising messages should not inherently or deliberately attempt to mislead, that is unethical, but can there be some creative scope in designing advertising that is appealing without having to dot every i or cross every t? The Codes of Practice are designed to ensure that lines of acceptability are clearly drawn. Whether it is described as unethical or unacceptable advertising, sanctions against those advertisers who do not meet the standards laid down by the Codes are designed to ensure that such behaviours and activities are not repeated.

Controls and regulations

The UK has one of the most developed systems for monitoring and controlling advertising in developed economies. The Office for Communication (Ofcom) operates under the government's Communications Act 2003. Ofcom regulates the TV and radio sectors, fixed-line telecoms and mobiles, plus the airwaves over which wireless devices operate. They have responsibility for ensuring that people in the UK get the best from their communications services and are protected from scams and sharp practices, while ensuring that competition can thrive. The Communications Act states that Ofcom's role should be 'to further the interests of citizens and of consumers'.

Ofcom is funded by fees from the industry for regulating broadcasting and communications networks, and grant-in-aid from the government.

The main legal duties of Ofcom are to ensure:

- the UK has a wide range of electronic communications services, including high-speed services such as broadband;

- a wide range of high-quality television and radio programmes are provided, appealing to a range of tastes and interests;
- television and radio services are provided by a range of different organisations;
- people who watch television and listen to the radio are protected from harmful or offensive material;
- people are protected from being treated unfairly in television and radio programmes, and from having their privacy invaded; and
- the radio spectrum (the airwaves used by everyone from taxi firms and boat owners to mobile-phone companies and broadcasters) is used in the most effective way.

Ofcom mission

Ofcom exists to further the interests of citizen-consumers through a regulatory regime which, where appropriate, encourages competition.

To do this Ofcom shall:

- balance the promotion of choice and competition with the duty to foster plurality, informed citizenship, protect viewers, listeners and customers and promote cultural diversity;
- serve the interests of the citizen-consumer as the communications industry enters the digital age;
- support the need for innovators, creators and investors to flourish within markets driven by full and fair competition between all providers;
- encourage the evolution of electronic media and communications networks to the greater benefit of all who live in the United Kingdom.

Source: www.ofcom.org.uk accessed 2 November 2011

The Advertising Standards Authority (ASA)

The UK's Advertising Standards Authority (ASA) was first established in 1962 and its main principles are to ensure advertising is 'legal, decent, honest and truthful'. The control of UK advertising is based on a self-regulatory system established by agreement between advertisers, agencies and the media owners.The ASA is independent of both government and the advertising industry. In addition to acting on and investigating complaints about advertising from the public and businesses, the ASA itself monitors and takes action against 'misleading, harmful or offensive advertisements, sales promotions and direct marketing'. The ASA system is financed by advertisers through a small voluntary levy of 0.1% on display advertising expenditure and airtime and 0.2% of the Royal Mail's Mailsort contract. The ASA receives no public funding from the taxpayer.

Codes of practice

The Advertising Codes (rules) are written and maintained by two industry bodies, the Committee of Advertising Practice (CAP), which covers non-broadcast advertising, sales promotion and direct marketing, and the Broadcast Committee of Advertising Practice (BCAP). The ASA works with CAP and BCAP in maintaining and administering processes for good advertising practice. Updated CAP and BCAP Codes were launched in September 2010. Figure 12.2 lists the areas covered by CAP and BCAP codes.

One of the significant challenges for regulators has been the significant shifts in the growth of new media and changing formats of existing media. Self-regulation of the internet began in

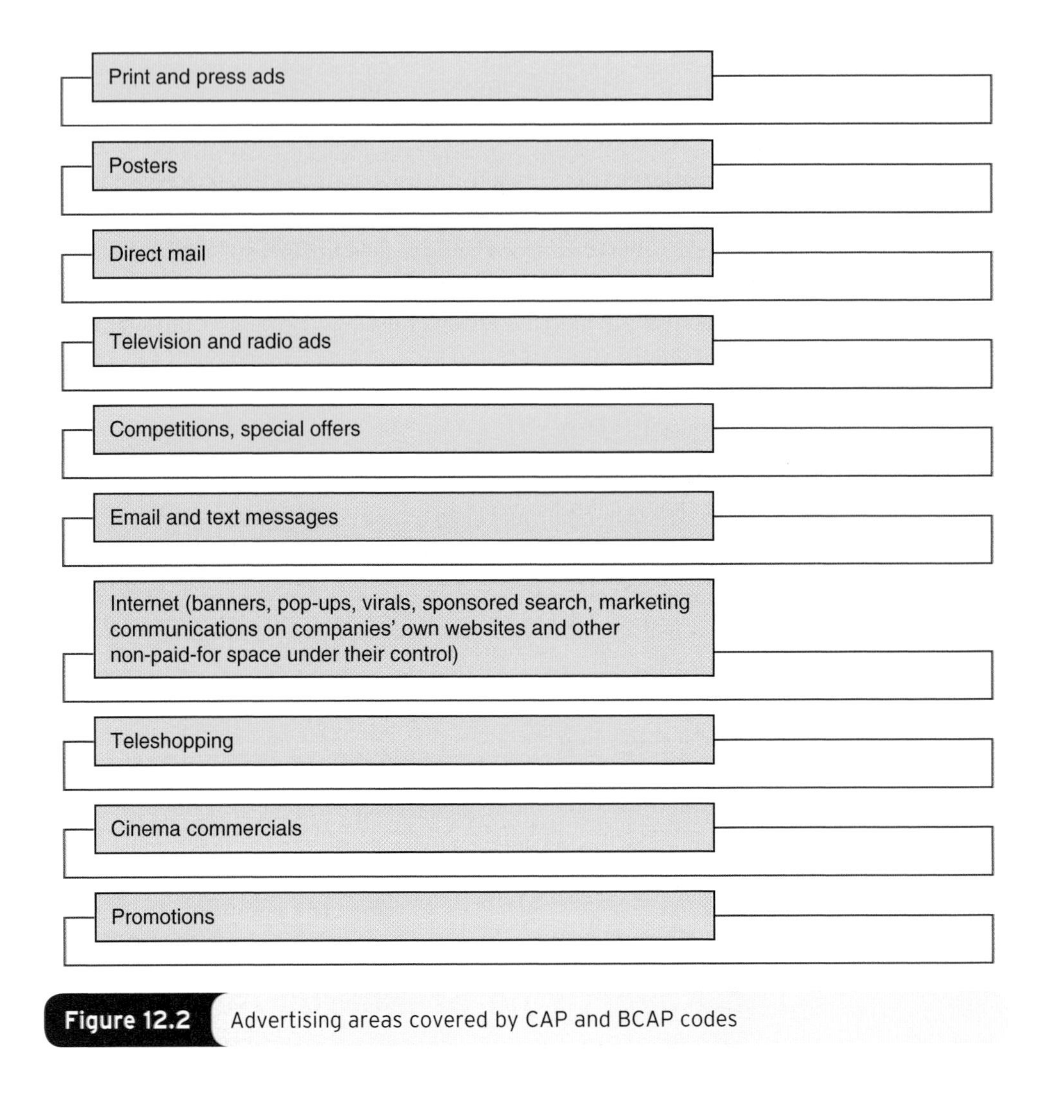

Figure 12.2 Advertising areas covered by CAP and BCAP codes

1995 as the ASA's remit was extended to cover advertisements in 'non-broadcast electronic media', predominantly in 'paid-for space' such as banner and display ads and paid-for (sponsored) search.

In 2007 the internet became the second most complained-about medium behind television with over 3,000 complaints per year. However, nearly two-thirds of these complaints fell outside the ASA's remit as they related to claims made on companies' own websites. From March 2011, the CAP code has been extended to cover advertisers' own marketing communications on their own websites and in other non-paid-for space including social network sites such as Facebook and Twitter. The BCAP code applies to broadcast advertisements (including teleshopping, content on self-promotional television channels, television text and interactive television advertisements) and programme sponsorship credits on radio and television services licensed by Ofcom.

Pre-clearance of advertisements

Producing advertising which does not meet the requirements of the codes set out is wasteful in terms of cost and time. Systems and processes have been established which allow advertisers to check advertising content at early creative and development stages for potential difficulties related to the codes. Both codes require that all claims must be substantiated before being published or aired.

Scholars' paper 12.2 US and Chinese consumers view regulations

Gao, Z. and Zhang, H. (2011) A comparative study of Chinese and US consumers' attitudes toward advertising regulation, *Asia Pacific Journal of Marketing and Logistics*, 23(1), 72-90

This is an interesting paper, with the authors claiming that it is the first study of consumers' attitudes toward advertising regulation. It is also of significance given the very different marketing environments of the two countries involved. A framework is developed to compare advertising regulation in China and the USA from three aspects:

- social context;
- forms of advertising regulation;
- regulation of major issues such as unfair and deceptive advertising, taste and decency issues, children's advertising, and tobacco and alcohol advertising.

Similarities were identified in views on free commercial speech, self-regulation, and regulation by market forces. Chinese consumers are more likely than their US counterparts to support government regulation, endorse legal ban on strong sexual and indecent content, and favour rigorous advertising regulation.

Broadcast advertising

The vast majority of TV and radio ads are pre-cleared before they are broadcast. Under their licences broadcasters must take reasonable steps to ensure that the ads they broadcast are compliant with the TV and Radio Advertising Codes.

To help them do this, the broadcasters have established and funded two pre-clearance centres:

- Clearcast (www.clearcast.co.uk) for television advertisements;
- The Radio Advertising Clearance Centre (RACC) (www.racc.co.uk) for radio advertisements.

Non-broadcast advertising

The ASA estimate that there are more than 30 million press advertisements and 100 million pieces of direct marketing every year. Pre-clearing this number of advertisements would be infeasible. In order to facilitate advertising development, CAP offer an advice and guidance service for free pre-publication advice to advertisers, agencies and media to help them create advertisements, promotions and direct marketing that meet the CAP code. Additionally they maintain a searchable online database that the advertisers, agencies and media can check to read the latest positions on hundreds of different advertising issues.

Complaints and sanctions

Despite these regulations and controls there are inevitably some people who take exception to particular ads and complain to the ASA. In 2010 the ASA received 25,214 complaints about 13,074 ads, resulting in 2,226 campaigns being changed or withdrawn.

If a complaint about an advertisement is upheld, the advertiser must withdraw or amend the offending advertisement and not use the advertising approach again. This can be a costly exercise for the advertiser. Whilst it is not generally normal or indeed good practice for advertisers to continually break the ASA Codes of Practice, the ASA can refer non-broadcast advertisers who persistently break the codes to the Office of Fair Trading for legal action under the Consumer

Protection from Unfair Trading Regulations 2008 and Business Protection from Misleading Marketing Regulations 2008. Broadcasters who continually air ads that break the codes can be referred to Ofcom, which has the power to fine them or even revoke their licence.

Most advertisers comply with the ASA's rulings and will amend or withdraw an advertisement that is judged to have broken the respective code. Specific sanctions can be applied where advertisers do not comply with ASA rulings.

Firstly the ASA issues a 'weekly publication of our adjudications' that generates significant media coverage in the UK, and frequently internationally. Negative publicity arising from such coverage might significantly damage an advertiser's reputation, particularly if it is seen to be flouting the rules designed to protect consumers and fair competition.

Secondly publishers and broadcasters can be asked not to carry advertising which breaks either CAP or BCAP codes.

Other sanctions include prevention of offending direct mail being distributed and reduce the likelihood of posters appearing on the basis of taste and decency and social responsibility.

Global regulations

The UK model for advertising regulation is well established and generally effective in maintaining good advertising practice and systems for complaints on those occasions when advertisers are considered to have breached codes of practice. Of course, advertising is now part of a global communications environment with consumers receiving messages from an increasingly sophisticated and complex range of media sources. The ASA in the UK cannot be responsible for advertising which originates outside its sphere of operation. It was a founding member of the European Advertising Standards Alliance (EASA) which works to support and promote advertising self-regulation across Europe and operates a cross-border complaints mechanism. EASA has links with regulatory bodies in other markets including USA, Brazil, South Africa, Australia, New Zealand, Chile and Canada. In other markets around the world there exist bodies similar to the ASA which fulfil similar roles. In many cases these bodies have modelled themselves on the ASA's framework. Global advertisers need to ensure they meet and comply with regulations covering all of the markets where their advertising is deployed. ViewPoint 12.1 includes an example of an adjudication made by the Australian Advertising Standards Bureau.

ViewPoint 12.1 So what do consumers complain about?

The most complained-about advertisement in the UK during 2010 was a TV ad for online gambling website PaddyPower.com. The ASA received a total of 1,313 complaints relating to animal cruelty and offensiveness toward blind people. The ad showed a football game between two teams of blind players. A cat is shown running on the pitch just as one of the players is about to take a kick. The sound of a thud and a loud cat meow is heard. A man in a suit is then introduced saying to the player that Paddy Power may not be able to get the cat back but it could get his money back with money-back special bets. The ad closes with a shot of the cat walking along a branch halfway up a neighbouring tree. Because the ad was considered to be surreal and light-hearted in tone, the ASA did not uphold the complaints.

In October 2011 a complaint was made in Australia about an online video for Unilever's Lynx deodorant. This was considered by the Australian Advertising Standards Board. The video starts with the statement 'Lynx presents - Rules to the game - Episode #1: Rugby'. A narrator then reads out a number of rugby rules while these rules are played out by a group of young women dressed in sports briefs and short shirts in the national rugby colours of Australia and New Zealand. At the end of the video we see the winning Australian team celebrating and the words 'Lynx know your game' appear. Voice-over: 'Go you good thing.'

Complaints considered that the ad was an 'objectification and sexualisation of women' promoting the idea that women are nothing more than playthings for men. Lynx is a popular brand for teenage boys; this

Exhibit 12.2 Paddypower ad
Source: Image courtsy of The Advertiing Archives

type of advertising is encouraging boys from a young age to objectify women. The ad was thought to be highly suggestive, highly offensive and disrespectful for everyone and inappropriate for under-18s.

Part of Unilever's response was that it had restricted the video on their Lynx YouTube channel to users over 18, using the YouTube age verification function soon after launch. They confirmed that the video has not been aired on TV as part of an advertising media buy. It may have appeared as editorial content on TV at the discretion of news suppliers but they could not identify any evidence of this. They further claim that the video does not make any open references to sex, sexuality or nudity. The video explains the rugby rules in a funny and entertaining way while these rules are played out by a group of young women wearing sports briefs and short shirts similar to sports clothes worn for sports like athletics and beach volleyball.

The board decided that the content of the video did not comply with Section 2.1 of the code, which requires that 'advertisements shall not portray or depict material in a way which discriminates against or vilifies a person or section of the community on account of race, ethnicity, nationality, sex, age, sexual preference, religion, disability or political belief'. The board considered that in light of the placement of the advertisement in a restricted manner and the relevant audience, the advertisement did treat sex, sexuality and nudity with sensitivity to the relevant audience and that it did not breach Section 2.3 of the code.

In the light of the findings, Unilever withdrew the video from their YouTube channels in Australia and New Zealand.

Source: www.asa.org.uk accessed 2 November 2011, www.adstandards.com.au

Question

Do the complaints procedures provide consumers with adequate powers to challenge advertisers?

Task

Using the ASA website or that of another similar body, identify five advertisements and compare the grounds for complaint. Were the outcomes of these complaints justified?

Table 12.3 International regulatory bodies

Country/market	Regulatory body
USA	Federal Trade Commission (FTC) - Division of Advertising Practices - **www.ftc.gov/bcp/bcpap**
AUSTRALIA	Australian Communications and Media Authority - www.acma.gov.au Advertising Standards Bureau - **www.adstandards.com.au**
NEW ZEALAND	Advertising Standards Authority - **www.asa.co.nz**
CHINA	State Administration of Radio, Film and TV (SARFT) - Industry and Commerce Administration - **www.chinasarft.gov.cn**
SINGAPORE	Advertising Standards Authority - **www.case.org.sg**
JAPAN	Japan Advertising Agencies Association - **www.jaaa.ne.jp**
INDIA	Advertising Standards Council of India - **www.ascionline.org**
SOUTH AFRICA	Advertising Standards Authority - **www.asasa.org.za**

Table 12.3 provides details of those organisations responsible for advertising regulations in some of the world's major markets.

Children and advertising

There have been for many years specific regulations and controls relating to advertising directed towards children. By virtue of limited age and experience, children and young people are considered more 'vulnerable' to advertising messages. There are particular concerns over the use of sexual imagery and the promotion of certain products, most notably alcohol and tobacco. The ASA specify that no advertisement aimed at children should 'contain anything likely to result in children's physical, mental or moral harm'. In additional to rules regarding ads specifically targeted at children, advertisers must also consider potential effects of advertising aimed at wider audiences and how they might be received by children who are exposed. The ASA have set up a website for parents, Parent Port, which contains advice and guidance on advertising-related issues.

Sexualisation is an area of major concern in the context of advertising and children. The advertising codes specify that 'no ad featuring a child or anyone who appears to be under 18 years of age should place them in a sexual context such as provocative or inappropriate poses and attire, overly "made-up" or in states of undress'.

In 2011, a UK government report into commercialisation and sexualisation of childhood called for actions to be taken to address parental concerns of the emergence of a 'sexualised culture' surrounding children. This report followed a government review led by Reg Bailey, the chief executive of the Mothers' Union. Surveys conducted for the review identified that significant numbers of parents had seen TV programmes and advertising before the 9 pm 'watershed' that were believed to be unsuitable for children because of their sexual content. Also of concern were shop window displays and billboards. Following the Bailey report's publication, the ASA has introduced new guidance and restrictions regarding sexual imagery and posters.

Sex and advertising

We discussed some of the issues related to sex and advertising in Chapter 5 from a creative theme perspective. A significant number of complaints made to the Advertising Standards

Scholars' paper 12.3 **Do children know they are being persuaded?**

Rozendaal, E, Buijzen, M. and Valkenburg, P. (2011) Children's understanding of advertisers' persuasive tactics, *International Journal of Advertising*, 30(2), 329–50

This paper argues that children are targeted at a much earlier age, with advertisers using new media including websites and computer games. The authors discuss a number of questions relating to the development of children's 'advertising literacy'. These include children's ability to process advertising in a conscious and critical way, their ability to differentiate advertising from other media content and their understanding of advertisers' attempts to influence purchase behaviour, attitudes and cognitions about products. Primary research is undertaken to investigate 8- to 12-year-old children's understanding of advertisers' persuasive tactics. Adults' understanding of advertising tactics is also investigated for comparative purposes. Previous research into related areas is also considered.

Authority relate to issues concerning sexualisation. In 2009, the ASA received approximately 1,400 complaints about 400 ads where the portrayal of women was the main issue. The ASA receives many more complaints about the way women are shown in ads than it does men. The most common complaints object to the gratuitous use of the female image (e.g. nudity or women in sexually suggestive poses), or ads seen to reinforce negative gender stereotypes. The ASA consider both the content and the context in which a woman is shown as important in determining whether or not an ad is acceptable. Ads for lingerie or swimwear may draw complaints that they are unsuitable to be seen by children or are degrading to women but such ads are rarely sexually explicit and, placed in context, are not usually problematic. However, ads which might show similar levels of nudity but portray women in an out-of-context, sexualised manner are likely to be considered inappropriate if they are seen to demean or objectify.

Alcohol advertising

There are strict guidelines surrounding the advertising of alcoholic products not least because they are an age-restricted purchase. These were significantly tightened in 2005 in response to public concern about under-age drinking and antisocial behaviour. The rules are designed to ensure alcohol is advertised in a socially responsible way and place particular emphasis on protecting young people; alcohol ads must not be directed at people under 18 or contain anything that is likely to appeal to them by reflecting youth culture or by linking alcohol with irresponsible behaviour, social success or sexual attractiveness. There have been a number of government-sponsored campaigns targeted at young people and the harmful effects of drinking alcohol. ViewPoint 12.2 looks specifically at the actions taken by companies marketing alcoholic products. An ASA compliance survey in 2009 identified that 99.7% of alcohol ads were in line with the appropriate codes.

Food and soft drink advertising

Societal concerns relating to the harmful effects of over-indulgence in food and drink products with high sugar and fat content, most particularly so-called fast foods and fizzy soft drinks, have resulted in criticism of the advertising of such products. Of specific concern is the increase in childhood obesity and the need to protect children's health. Sedentary lifestyles, a lack of exercise, spending increased leisure time playing computer games and watching TV, lack of sport in schools and unhealthy diets are also considered as factors in the obesity debate. New, stricter advertising rules around food and soft drinks were introduced in the UK in 2007. These generally apply to under-16s but with further restrictions for children of primary school age and younger.

ViewPoint 12.2 Promoting responsible drinking

The appropriateness of promoting products such as alcoholic drinks and cigarettes has long been the source of debate due their potentially health-damaging characteristics. In the case of alcohol, this also extends to the antisocial behaviour that may result from excessive drinking. This has manifested itself in what has more recently been described as 'binge drinking'. The situation to which this term refers arises from the large numbers of mainly young people who frequent town and city centres on weekend evenings, consuming large amounts of alcohol within a short period of time. This causes problems as a result of the numbers of and behaviour of people moving from bar to bar during the course of the evening. In worst cases, at the end of such evenings, as bars and clubs close almost simultaneously, revellers empty onto town-centre streets, causing disturbances which often result in police action and/or admissions to hospital accident and emergency departments. The negative aspects of binge drinking have received widespread news media coverage.

Along with other marketing issues including distribution and pricing, advertising of alcohol has been the subject of criticism for promoting excessive consumption and related behavioural issues. The limiting of alcohol-related media advertising and content has been incorporated within the codes of practice published by bodies such as the Advertising Standards Authority for some years. There have also been a number of responses from within the drinks industry itself, anxious to limit the potentially damaging effects of adverse publicity on their business.

The Portman Group is an industry body consisting of major drinks manufacturing businesses, which supply the majority of alcoholic drinks in the UK market.

The values and beliefs of the Portman Group underpin their actions:

- The drinks industry has a legitimate and important role to play in combating alcohol misuse.
- Enlightened corporate social responsibility is positively good for business.
- The consumption of alcohol in moderation (as defined by the current responsible drinking guidelines in the UK) is compatible with a healthy lifestyle.
- Effective alcohol policy balances legislation, self-regulation and personal responsibility.

The focus is on education and prevention, these being preferable. The Portman Group belief is that a higher profile should be given to teaching about alcohol in schools and other educational settings.

Portman's Code of Practice applies to drinks packaging and labelling as well as advertising and other promotional activities. Any complaints received are reviewed by an Independent Complaints Panel. The Code of Practice is continually updated to reflect and take account of changes in the market for alcoholic drinks and the ways in which they are marketed, both by the drinks manufacturers themselves and drinks retailers.

In addition to membership of and support for trade initiatives such as the Portman Group, many individual drinks companies, retailers and distributors have developed their own approaches to promoting responsible drinking by consumers and the marketing methods employed to promote their products and brands. The Diageo Group is one of the world's leading producers of alcoholic drinks with brands including Guinness, Smirnoff, Cuervo, Johnnie Walker and Baileys.

The Diageo website contains a specific section www.drinkiq.com which contains relevant information about responsible drinking. It further provides details of initiatives in each of the global markets in which they operate.

Such industry initiatives work together with regulators such as the Advertising Standards Authority to ensure consistency.

Source: www.portman-group.org.uk, accessed 7 November 2011; www.diageo.com, accessed 7 November 2011; www.drinkiq.com, accessed 7 November 2011

Question

From a consumer perspective, what are the advantages of industry- or company-led codes of practice, compared to legislative monitoring and control?

Task

Access Diageo's drinkiq website. Select three different markets and compare the different initiatives related to promoting responsible drinking.

Exhibit 12.3 Diageo brands/logos
Source: Diageo plc

The BCAP code specifies content and scheduling restrictions on advertisements for products that are classed as high in fat, salt and sugar (HFSS). These products can no longer appear in or around children's broadcast programmes or be targeted at them.

CAP rules for non-broadcast advertising prohibit the use of licensed characters or celebrities popular with children in ads for food and drink products (except fresh fruit and vegetables) that are targeted directly at pre-school or primary school children.

Fashion and beauty advertising

The worlds of fashion and beauty products have long been a focus for advertising attention both in terms of the volume of advertisements promoting such products as clothing, footwear, haircare products, cosmetics and fragrances but also in the tactics used to attract the attention of their target audiences. As these products are primarily targeted at a female audience, making products appear as attractive as possible has always been a central focus for creative positioning. The use of glamorous models and celebrities has been widespread in attempts to create associations between brands, 'good looking' personalities and the target audience. The objective of such campaigns has been to suggest to those in the target audience that they can look as good as those depicted in the ads if they use the products being advertised.

More recently such tactics have received close attention from advertising standards bodies and other stakeholder groups. Cosmetics brands have been criticised over the photographic methods used in print advertising. This has centred on the use of airbrushing techniques to enhance the finish of photographs to the extent that they create a false impression of the products' capabilities. Such techniques have been common practice in the industry for a long time but it is the extent to which they can exaggerate the products' performance that has come under the critical spotlight. L'Oréal brands Lancôme and Maybelline were the subject of an

Advertising Standards Authority (ASA) ruling in late 2011 on the grounds that they were unable to demonstrate that images of models including actress Julia Roberts were accurate representations of the results the products could achieve. The ads were thus considered misleading and were withdrawn. A research report, 'Pretty as a picture', from the Advertising Association (Credos 2011b) suggests that the majority of women (76%) prefer to see natural images in advertising and 84% believe it is unacceptable for brands to alter the way women look in advertisements.

Politicians have proposed that airbrushed images should carry kitemarks or even health warnings to show where images have been altered. UK members of parliament Jo Swinson and Lynne Featherstone co-founded the Campaign for Body Confidence in 2010 in order to increase pressure on the ASA to ban ads featuring digitally manipulated images. The advertising Codes of Practice now contain help notes for advertisers on the use of production techniques in cosmetic advertising.

Clothing fashion has been another area of critical attention surrounding the use of models with 'perfect' physical attributes. There have been claims that the so-called 'size zero obsession' has led to young females developing eating disorders in order to maintain figures which match those of models used in advertising and other promotional activities such as high-profile fashion shows. Yellowlees (2011), a consultant psychiatrist specialising in the treatment of eating disorders, states: 'the relentless promotion of the idealisation of thinness has put women of all ages under intense pressure to strive after that attainment of body perfection'.

Italy's Publicity Control Institute (IAP) banned an advertisement for fashion label Nolita showing a naked anorexic woman and the words 'No anorexia'. The photograph was taken by Italian photographer Oliviero Toscani who became well known for the controversial Benetton ads including a nun and priest kissing, an Aids victim and a soldier's bloodstained vest. Toscani claims that the ruling is a form of censorship and that the ad raises awareness of anorexia as an issue. O'Reilly (2011) reports that clothing brand H&M was cleared by the ASA after complaints were received over a TV ad showing a model wearing a jacket and high heels looking 'unhealthily thin'. The ASA decided that most viewers would interpret the ad as promoting the design of the clothes rather than a desirable body image.

Shock advertising

The content of some of the ads described in the previous section was considered controversial or inappropriate for the kind of images the ads portrayed. Another view is that they were designed to gain attention by creating 'shock' amongst the target audience. In the context of these specific ads, shock might be interpreted negatively with the images perceived as being inappropriate or unnecessary. How relevant to the product or service being advertised are the shock characteristics being utilised? When promoting products such as fashion items this might be considered debatable. If showing an anorexia sufferer on a billboard is part of a health service campaign this might still create a shock factor but be accepted in the context of how it is deployed. Indeed, many of the campaigns designed to highlight the dangers of smoking, drinking alcohol, taking drugs or speeding in cars include images specifically designed to shock the intended target audiences into behavioural change of some kind.

Exhibits 12.4 and 12.5 show two ads using shock themes, one to promote clothes and one highlighting the dangers of smoking. They demonstrate the question of relevance in determining the acceptability of using shock in the creative execution.

Product placement

From February 2011 new rules were established in the UK that allow product placement on TV and paid-for references to brands and products on radio. Product placement has been a feature of films for many years and commonplace in other markets such as the USA.

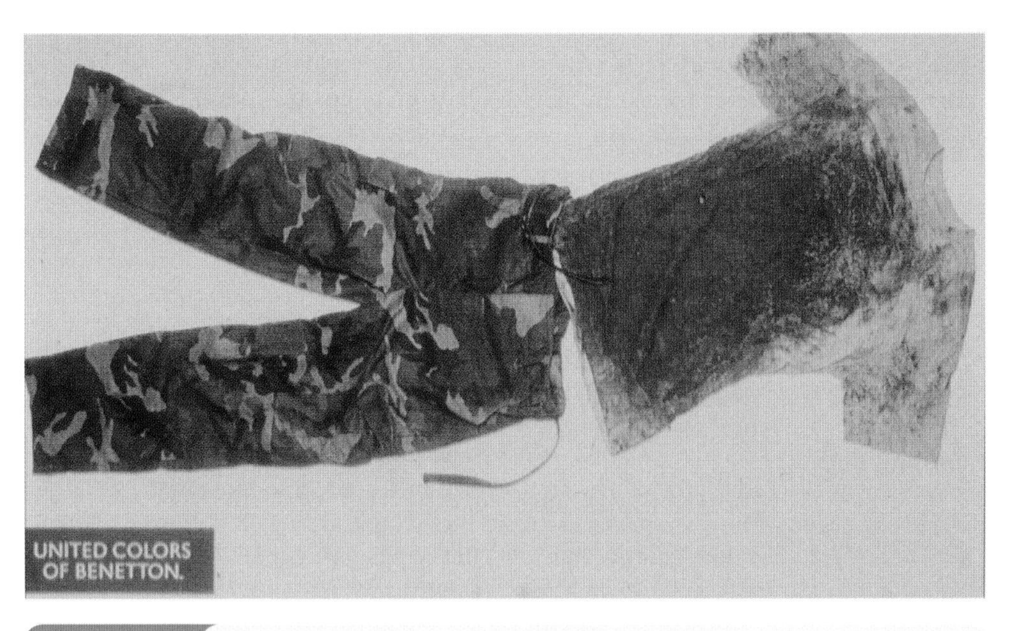

Exhibit 12.4 Bad shock? Clothes
Source: Image courtesy of The Advertising Archives

Exhibit 12.5 Good shock? Stop smoking.
Source: Image courtesy of The Advertising Archives

Introduction into the UK resulted from some pressure from broadcasters seeking to enhance revenues after seeing declines in actual advertising income.

The new rules provide for:

- restrictions on the types of products that can be placed;
- restrictions on the types of programmes in which products can be placed; and
- limits on the way in which products can be seen and referred to in programmes.

Product placement is allowed in films (including dramas and documentaries), TV series (including soaps), entertainment shows and sports programmes. It is prohibited in all children's and news programmes and in UK-produced current affairs, consumer affairs and religious programmes.

Product placement of tobacco, alcohol, gambling, foods or drinks that are high in fat, salt or sugar, medicines and baby milk is banned by UK legislation. Ofcom has also prohibited the paid-for placement of products and services that cannot be advertised on television, such as weapons or escort agencies.

The rules state that product placement 'must not impair broadcasters' editorial independence and must always be editorially justified'. Programmes cannot therefore be created or distorted so that they become vehicles for the purposes of featuring product placement.

European and UK legislation also requires that placed products and services cannot be promoted or endorsed, or be featured in an unduly prominent way within programmes.

Making product placement transparent

Following the introduction of new rules for product placement on TV, viewers will see a new product placement logo on their screens.

The logo must appear for a minimum of three seconds at the start and end of programmes so that viewers know which UK-produced programmes contain product placement. The logo must also appear at the return of the programme following any advertisement breaks.

Sponsors of TV programmes will be able to product-place in programmes they are sponsoring, and sponsors' logos will be able to appear as brief sponsorship credits during programmes.

The rules for radio permit commercial references to be integrated within programming although broadcasters will have to ensure that listeners are always aware when promotions are paid for.

Ambush marketing

This term is used to describe those, usually communications related, activities by brands to associate themselves with an event of some description without paying the premium of being an official sponsor. Meenaghan (1994) proposes a definition of ambush marketing as 'the practice whereby another company, often a competitor, attempts to deflect some of the audience to itself and away from the sponsor'. Such activities have grown in recent years around global sporting events such as the soccer World Cup and the Olympic Games. As the practice has developed, so have the attempts to prevent it via legal channels by event organisers. The UK government and organisers of the London Olympics in 2012 introduced the London Olympic Games and Paralympic Games Act in 2006 (the Olympics Act). Amongst other things this set out the statutory rights of those companies who entered into legitimate commercial agreements as official sponsors and suppliers and non-commercial partners. A register was established of all those who were authorised to create some form of association with the 2012 Games. The London Organising Committee of the Olympic Games (LOCOG) pronounced that 'ambushing an event does not have to involve explicit advertising. LOCOG is entitled to decide whether or not an "associative" ambush has taken place and can exercise rights to prosecute'. Penalties for those found guilty of ambush marketing include fines up to £20,000.

In their report *Ambush Marketing and the Law* (2011) the Chartered Institute of Marketing (CIM) highlight that previously acceptable commercial practices can now be legally challenged because a powerful event organiser does not approve. The CIM report highlights the case of the Dutch brewing company at the World Cup in South Africa in 2010. Thirty-six Dutch soccer fans were ejected from one of the stadiams because they were entirely dressed in orange, which happened to be the colour of the team's shirts. Organisers believed that the fans were actually paid models and the clothing had small Bavaria logos. Budweiser was the official beer sponsor of the competition and their rights were being protected. Two individuals who were thought to have organised the stunt were arrested and their passports confiscated. Although they were threatened with possible jail sentences no actual penalties were imposed. CIM propose that it 'should be the intent to pass off, create confusion in the mind of the customer about who the sponsor is and/or to imply a connection between the company and the event that constitutes an illegal ambush'.

Corporate social responsibility

Corporate social responsibility (CSR) has become one of the most significant business issues in recent years. There are a number of factors that have influenced and indeed fuelled the focus on CSR. Financial irregularities causing the collapse of firms such as Enron, a USA energy company, in 2001, and Worldcom's telecoms business in 2002 signalled global attention to business practices and corporate behaviours of large organisations.

The CEO of the WPP advertising empire, Sir Martin Sorrell, believes CSR has become one of the five key drivers of the advertising business. He proposes that CSR has become such a significant business force and cause for consumer concern that it is now a vital element of ongoing strategic direction and brand building. Every business leader, he states, needs to 'embrace these issues and recognise that doing good is good business' (2011).

Consumer research would appear to support Sorrell's claims. The 2011 Cone/Echo Global Corporate Responsibility opportunity study surveyed over 10,000 consumers in 10 different countries. Findings indicate that respondents to the survey are demanding a higher level of responsibility by firms over societal issues and are directing their purchasing behaviours and loyalty towards brands that are effectively engaging in positive CSR practices. The study reports:

- 81% of consumers say companies have a responsibility to address key social and environmental issues beyond their local communities.
- 93% want companies to go beyond legal compliance to operate responsibly.
- 94% believe companies need to analyse and evolve business practices to make their impact as positive as possible.
- 94% would buy a product with environmental benefits, 93% a product associated with a cause.

There were some indications in the study of variances in the strengths of consumer attitudes between markets. UK consumers appeared more sceptical about CSR issues than those in fast-growth economies including Brazil and China.

Berens and van Rekom (2008) consider the types of claims made about CSR and their potential impact. *Factual* claims capable of verification, for example 'We planted 375,000 trees last year' are more likely to positively influence corporate reputation for CSR than *impressionistic* claims such as 'We planted a lot of trees last year'. Factual claims are considered to be more credible and less likely to be misinterpreted.

Another global CSR study undertaken by 'Let's heal' in 2011 lends further credence to the need for firms to be involved in CSR activities. This survey covered over 24,000 consumers in 16 countries including Brazil, China, Germany, India, the UK and USA. An average of 76% of respondents thought companies should support good causes, with individual countries indicating much higher levels of support on this dimension – 94% in Brazil, 93% in Russia, 91% in Mexico and 88% in China. These variances again identify the need for firms to adapt their CSR approaches to cater for local consumer attitudes and perceptions.

Reporting on CSR activities has now become a prominent activity for many of world's largest companies. The financial and business consultancy KPMG (2011) surveyed over 3,000 firms globally, including the 250 largest brand owners; 95% of the top 250 firms now issue CSR

ViewPoint 12.3 Leading brands to inspire sustainability in the UK

Start Today is a new marketing initiative, bringing together some of the UK's leading brands to inspire their customers to live more sustainably. Launched on 1 November 2011, the campaign encourages people throughout the UK to 'do more with less', and be more aware of their resource use.

Participating brands include Aviva, B&Q, British Gas, EDF Energy, Eurostar, IBM, M&S, MORE TH>N, P&G, Thames Water, Start and Virgin Money, who will each promote a simple sustainable behaviour that their consumers can relate to and immediately adopt. This covers a range of issues from sustainable food choices and the joys of exploring on foot, to easy ways to start saving energy and creative ideas around reusing and sharing.

The aim of Start Today is to defy the trend of telling consumers to stop acting in certain ways and to communicate positive and useful messages to the public in more ways than any single brand could do on their own. This is an ongoing collaborative venture.

Start Today is led by Start - the sustainable living initiative inspired by HRH The Prince of Wales, The Marketing Society and Business in the Community. The idea was conceived by integrated marketing agency Meteorite in response to The Marketing Society's 2010 Film Challenge, which asked marketers to think about how marketing can make a difference to the planet. Start Today now involves many agencies, brand owners and media partners all over the UK. Table 12.4 indicates the sustainable themes supported by each brand and the related advertising activities.

Source: www.starttoday.org.uk, accessed 10 July 2011

Question

What are the benefits of brands collaborating in this type of advertising exercise?

Task

Produce a report which assesses the rationale for each brand's choice of advertising activities and media selection.

Table 12.4 Start Today sustainability themes and advertising activities

Brand	Sustainability theme	Advertising activities and media
Aviva - insurance services	'Start dejunking your trunk.' Aims to inform the general public about the efficiency benefits of lightening the load in the car and encourage people to remove unnecessary weight from their vehicles	This campaign is led by social media activity using Facebook and Twitter to communicate simple steps towards fuel-efficient car driving
B&Q - DIY goods retailer	'Start switching off automatically.' Aims to show the general public the ease with which people can start switching off lights and appliances, rather than leave them on standby, thereby saving energy	Communicated via PR, social media, internal communications to B&Q employees and the B&Q *Home* magazine
British Gas - energy supplier	'Start keeping the warmth in your home.' Focuses on the energy-efficiency benefits resulting from insulation of homes using soft furnishings	Press advertising in national newspapers on the launch day and amplification of it using social media channels including Facebook, Twitter and blogger outreach
EDF Energy - energy supplier	'Start low-carbon living.' Together with its London Olympics 2012 Team Green Britain initiative, this encourages consumers to rethink their energy use and be energy conscious at home, in the ways they travel and with the food they eat	Email campaign will reach out to over 300,000 consumers via the Team Green Britain database and website. Supported by a national press advertisement on 2 November 2011, which incorporated a competition to win a private capsule trip on the EDF Energy London Eye

Brand	Sustainability theme	Advertising activities and media
Eurostar - rail services	'Start exploring on foot.' Focuses on the pleasure people can get from walking around their destination city, as opposed to using other means of transport. This simple step does something positive for the environment, making it all the more attractive	Several consumer touchpoints include: outdoor posters at St Pancras Station, email communications to a database of one million leisure customers, editorial coverage in *Metropolitan* magazine, several social media communications and announcements on board all Eurostar trains on 1 November 2011
Marks and Spencer - retailer	'Start turning your thermostat down.' Message delivered through M&S Energy, the brand intends to show how simple and effortless it can be to achieve a significant reduction in energy consumption, whilst saving money at the same time, just by turning your thermostat down by one degree	M&S used press advertising in national newspapers on 1 November with incentives including M&S rewards vouchers
MORE TH>N - insurance services	'Start greener gardening.' It is easy to enjoy a beautiful, abundant and green garden, without all the negative inputs - pesticides and copious amounts of water	MORE TH>N teamed up with one of the best-known TV gardeners, Chris Collins, to highlight clever ways to achieve a 'greener' garden. Two-week radio campaign on Classic FM, as well as existing media channels and internal communications to MORE TH>N and RSA staff
P&G - household goods	'Start being future friendly at home.' Focuses on the energy-efficiency benefits gained by using P&G's portfolio of future-friendly products: Ariel, Lenor and Fairy Platinum	P&G are promoting these sustainable behaviours through a series of advertorials in national magazines, as well as PR and targeted social media
Thames Water	'Start singing in the shower.' Urging people to sing in the shower because singing a song of less than four minutes, and finishing your shower when your song ends, are an easy and fun way to keep the shower shorter and water-use to a minimum	A dedicated PR campaign and an online and social media competition, asking people to share their favourite shower-time songs on the Thames Water website, Facebook and Twitter
Virgin Money - financial services	'Start sustainable savings.' By demonstrating to people that they could potentially save up to £1,000 a year and not experience adverse impacts to their lifestyles: • Buying only the food you need - meal planning and not wasting food can save the average household up to £600 per year • Lowering your thermostat by one degree - this simple action can save £55 each winter • Taking shorter showers - can save £386 a year in water and energy bills by reducing your shower time to four minutes, instead of the seven-minute average	Starting on 1 November, Virgin Money dedicated their UK homepage to this campaign, as well as other online content
IBM - business equipment and services	'Start building a smarter planet.' By putting sustainability at the heart of business strategy, IBM's Start Today campaign addresses the big questions of how businesses influence consumer behaviours, how to optimise resource and how to build the right skills to carry these behaviours forward	IBM convened a full-day sustainability summit on 1 November, bringing together leading UK marketers, NGOs, researchers and academics. The goal of the IBM Summit 2011 - Start Now, Start Today was to identify new ways to build consumer enthusiasm and demand for sustainable initiatives. The summit was broadcast live on the internet and followed up with bespoke action plans for delegates, relevant to their industry and business
Start - sustainable living initiative	'Start asking questions.' Start aims to demonstate that sustainable living can be simple when you know how. The goal is to empower people to change their living habits by being relevant to the individual and creating a sense of positivity and community	Between 1 and 4 November, Start hosted the Start Today sustainability clinic on Facebook, an online forum featuring advice from Start's extensive network of green experts. It provided a destination for hints, tips and advice on all things related to sustainable living. Promoted via a dedicated PR campaign, coverage on ITV *This Morning*, celebrity tweets and the social platforms of each of the brands involved in Start Today

reports, a 14% increase on those surveyed in 2008. Corporate reputation and brand considerations were given as the major motivating factors for reporting activity. Other CSR issues addressed included ethical factors, employee engagement, innovation and learning, risk management, access to capital, increased shareholder value and economic considerations. KPMG suggest that 'CSR has moved from being a moral imperative to a critical business imperative', supporting the principle outlined above by Sir Martin Sorrell.

So what does all this mean for advertising? One of the most significant aspects has been the increasing use by businesses of advertising to raise awareness of and provide information relating to their CSR activities. Many of these have been part of profile positioning strategies we discussed in Chapter 4.

Using CSR for positioning

CSR positioning strategies have not been considered to any great extent in terms of academic literature. Maignan and Farrell (2001) discuss the potential impact of negative/positive CSR associations on product evaluations. More recently, Jones, Comfort and Hillier (2008) looked at the use of CSR by retailers, finding significant disparity concerning the communication of such issues between the principal grocery retailers in the UK. The main themes communicated in store are organic and Fairtrade products, healthy and locally produce foods and community issues. CSR information is printed on packaging and labels, shelf edges, leaflets, banners and posters.

Anselmsson and Johansson (2007) identified that consumer perceptions of CSR issues centred around three main dimensions. These are human responsibility, product responsibility and environmental responsibility. These are explained in Table 12.5.

This study examined retailer, producer and me-too brands in the Swedish grocery market, measuring consumer attitudes, at the point of purchase, towards frozen food products and their perceived level of CSR. Findings suggest that manufacturers or producers are often distanced from consumers relative to retail brands. Multinational organisations are often criticised for their perceived lack of responsibility, especially in the countries that supply them. On the other hand retailer brands are often closer to the markets in which they operate and are perceived to be more responsible. There was some evidence that consumers consider an organisation's corporate responsibility when making purchase decisions. This research also found that there are opportunities for brands to use corporate responsibility as a point of differentiation and positioning. Cornelissen (2007) proposes that the Co-operative Bank is a supreme example of a financial services brand positioning itself successfully on a CSR platform. The bank's parent company, the Co-operative (Society), was originally founded on moral and egalitarian principles which underpin the current positioning as a natural development. ViewPoint 12.4 further illustrates the application of the three CSR areas identified by Anselmsson and Johansson.

Table 12.5 Three key consumer perceptions of CSR

CSR area of responsibility	Explanation
Human responsibility	Perception that the suppliers uphold natural, good farming principles and provide good working conditions for employees
Product responsibility	Perception that the company has clear environmental policies, using recyclable packaging, and producing environmentally friendly, ecologically sound, non-harmful products
Environmental responsibility	Perception that the company lists full contents of products, names country of origin, and accepts liability for the performance and functionality of its products

Source: Based on Anselmsson and Johansson (2007)

Scholars' paper 12.4 Impact of global CSR activities in Mexico and the USA

Becker-Olsen, K.L., Taylor, C.R., Hill, R.P. and Yalcinkaya, G. (2011) A cross-cultural examination of corporate social responsibility marketing communications in Mexico and the United States: strategies for global brands, *Journal of International Marketing*, *19*(2), 30-44

Against the background of increasing attention being paid to CSR by academics and practitioners, this paper examines the impact of CSR-related communications on consumers' perceptions of brands in two very different market environments. The research centred on the CSR policies and communications activities of telecoms brand Nokia. Consumer impressions in both markets were measured on four dimensions - brand identification, citizenship, firm motivation and firm reputation. Results identify that multinational brands communicating CSR information are seen more positively across a set of multiple dimensions. The authors further identify that there is a need to cater for local tastes and experiences in tactically based communications.

ViewPoint 12.4 Kenco forms alliance to establish CSR

Kenco had established a significant presence in the instant coffee market dominated by leaders Nescafé and General Foods. In 2007 sales of instant coffee had started to decline as consumers became more demanding, influenced by the quality of coffees available from the increasing numbers of specialist coffee shops such as Starbucks, Costa and Caffè Nero. Sales of ground and roast coffee for home consumption were increasing. Kenco's positioning had emphasised the brand as the next best thing to 'real' coffee and to date had been successful. The changing market environment was putting pressure on instant coffee suppliers with little evidence of brand differentiation.

In addition to promoting the taste aspects of the coffee, Kenco had also incorporated the sources of their coffee in their advertising, filming on location on coffee bean farms. Although taste had been the main positioning platform, the advertising production had created some positive association between Kenco and the provenance of their supply chain. With consumers showing more general interest in buying brands based on ethical criteria, this gave Kenco something of a start in their new efforts to establish the brand's sustainability credentials. Fairtrade supply policies had already helped establish brands such as Café Direct and Percol into the instant coffee market.

Segmentation analysis had identified five stages of consumer involvement when it came to purchasing sustainable products:

1. Principled Pioneers (4%)
2. Vocal Activists (4%)
3. Positive Choosers (31%)
4. Conveniently Conscious (35%)
5. Onlookers (26%)

Those most heavily involved, the Principled Pioneers and Vocal Activists, were already significant buyers of specialist ethical brands. More mainstream segments, the Positive Choosers and Conveniently Conscious, accounted for 66% of the market and did not have a sustainable option that matched their price and quality requirements. Kenco wanted to provide a sustainable brand that would be acceptable to everyone, not just the most interested minority. Kenco's new vision was to become the mainstream sustainable coffee brand.

The first stage of the positioning development was to partner with the Rainforest Alliance, a certification body that defines a system of sustainable farming designed to protect and improve the environment and ecology of farms in the developing world and the lives and livelihoods of the people that work on them. This centred on three areas: environmental, economic and social. Further research identified that sustainable brands had to be able to demonstrate to consumers that they could relate them to their own worlds. Kenco decided to try and achieve this by focusing on issues which consumers could relate to 'emotionally' - clean water, education and housing - so that by purchasing Kenco coffee they would be improving lives in communities in those countries producing the coffee beans.

Advertising then focused on TV, press and digital banners to establish national reach with single-minded messaging. PR and direct marketing activity was then used for more in-depth communication around the sustainability theme. The main creative idea centred on Kenco's heritage. The new partnership with the Rainforest Alliance represented an evolution of the brand's beliefs that extended that care to farm workers and their communities. As well as growing great coffee, Kenco was now helping to grow communities. This 'Growing communities' idea allowed Kenco to explain the aspects of certification that consumers could relate to. Reassurance was achieved by showing farm workers hand-picking beans and the campaign strapline, 'Growing great coffee and more'.

Over the course of two campaigns consumer perceptions of Kenco were transformed, with 1.2 million new households buying the brand. Analysis showed that £3.7 million incremental revenue was directly attributable to the advertising and support communications. Sustainability was working.

Source: Murphy (2010); www.kenco.co.uk

Question

What are the potential dangers for a brand promoting CSR as a positioning strategy?

Task

Write a short case study relating to a brand of your choice that has developed a successful alliance with a group similar to the Rainforest Alliance in developing a CSR-based advertising strategy.

Exhibit 12.6 Kenco Farm pics from ad
Source: Kraft Foods UK

Chapter summary

In order to help consolidate your understanding of advertising from a general perspective here are the key points summarised against each of the learning objectives.

Discuss the views for and against the use of advertising in society

Here we considered the significance of consumer attitudes toward and more general public opinion of advertising. There are views that consider advertising to be manipulative and wasteful in terms of resources. Research suggests that whilst consumers may have concerns, they are generally receptive to receiving information from advertising sources. There are specific issues on which consumers and opinion formers have specific views, including advertising targeted at children and the advertising of specific types of products and services such as food and drink.

Outline some of the principal ethical issues associated with advertising

Ensuring that advertising adheres to codes of ethics is an important issue for advertisers and those involved in the advertising industry, agencies and other third parties. Defining what ethics are and how this relates to advertising provides an understanding and a platform for creative advertising development. Truthfulness is an essential component of how ethics might be perceived which needs careful consideration in designing advertising messages.

Explain the legislative controls and various codes of practice in the advertising industry

In most developed markets there exist well-developed controls and regulations covering advertising practice. Although generic legislation plays some role, in the most part some form of self-regulation governs what is produced by the advertising industry. The Advertising Standards Authority in the UK and similar bodies in international markets have established and developed detailed codes of practice for advertising which are closely adhered to by advertisers. A range of sanctions exists for the ASA to impose in situations where advertisers are considered to have transgressed the codes. Consumers and businesses are provided with mechanisms through which they can complain about specific advertisements.

Explore issues associated with advertising and children, sex, alcohol, food and drink, fashion and beauty and shock tactics

There are a number of specific market sectors and issues that present challenges for advertisers and often stimulate debate amongst consumers and other stakeholders. Standards bodies pay particular attention to advertising products in these sectors both in response to consumer complaints and as part of their overarching remit for monitoring and evaluating acceptability.

Describe regulations and controls relating to product placement and ambush marketing

These areas are not usually associated with the guidelines for regulating traditional advertising methods. Product placement is becoming a more prominent part of firms' marketing communications activities alongside their use of media for advertising purposes. Used actively in cinema and TV it is becoming less clear to distinguish product placement from paid-for advertising slots. Ambush marketing recognises the communications of firms at specific times such as during major sporting or cultural events which are not part of 'official' communications from firms which have entered into formal sponsorship agreements with event organisers.

Consider the ways in which approaches to corporate social responsibility affect advertising practice

This has become a significant business issue for all organisations with consumer interest at high levels in dealing with firms that are deemed to be acting responsibly. Advertising is playing a major role in providing information to consumers and other stakeholders relating to the CSR activities of brands and brand owners. Research suggests consumers might actively seek to purchase goods and services from companies that can actively demonstrate commitment to CSR-related issues.

Review questions

1. With regard to the Aircel minicase set out at the start of this chapter, how would you propose that they develop a CRM programme and in particular an advertising campaign, in order to address the three objectives?
2. Why is public opinion important to the advertising industry?
3. To what extent is self-regulation an effective way of controlling advertising practice?
4. Should advertisers be allowed more freedom in how they communicate with their target audiences?
5. Are there too many rules and regulations governing advertising? If so, how would you change the situation?
6. What is the difference between the CAP and BCAP Codes of Practice?
7. How might the complaints procedures about advertising be made more robust?
8. Why should ambush marketing be considered a problem?
9. Make a list of the reasons why corporate social responsibility has become a major issue for advertisers.
10. For a brand of your choice make recommendations about how they might use advertising to demonstrate their CSR credentials.

Chapter references

Anselmsson, J. and Johansson, U. (2007) Corporate responsibility and the positioning of grocery brands, *International Journal of Retail and Distribution Management*, 35, 10, 835–56

Bailey, R. (2011) Letting children be children, UK government, www.education.gov.uk, accessed 1 November 2011

Becker-Olsen, K.L., Taylor, C.R., Hill, R.P. and Yalcinkaya, G. (2011) A cross-cultural examination of corporate social responsibility marketing communications in Mexico and the United States: strategies for global brands, *Journal of International Marketing*, 19 (2), 30–44

Berens, G. and van Rekom, J. (2008) How specific should corporate communication be? In T.C. Melewar (Ed) *Facets of corporate identity, communication and reputation*, 96–119, Routledge: London

Broadbent, T. (2007) Does advertising create demand? Warc Exclusive, www.warc.com, accessed 19 December 2011

Chaudhuri, A. and Khurana, C. (2011) Aircel: Save our Tigers, Warc Prize for Asian Strategy entrant, www.warc.com accessed 20/12/2012

CIM (2011) *Ambush Marketing and the Law*, www.cim.co.uk, accessed 29 November 2011

Cone/Echo (2011) Global Corporate Responsibility opportunity study, www.coneinc.com, accessed 10 October 2011

Cornelissen, J. (2008) Corporate communication: theory and practice, 2e, London: Sage

Credos (2011a) Monitoring public opinion of advertising, May, www.warc.com, accessed 27 October 2011

Credos (2011b) Pretty as a picture, December, www.credos.org.uk, accessed 19 December 2011

Fletcher, W. (2010) *Advertising*. Oxford: Oxford University Press

Fraser, K. and McBain, C. (2011) Advertising: what the UK really thinks, Credos, March

Gao, Z. and Zhang, H. (2011) A comparative study of Chinese and US consumers' attitudes toward advertising regulation, *Asia Pacific Journal of Marketing and Logistics*, 23(1), 72–90

Jones, P., Comfort, D. and Hillier, D. (2008) Corporate responsibility and marketing communications within stores: a case study of UK food retailers, *Journal of Food Products Marketing*, 14, 4, 109–119

Klein, N. (2000) *No Logo*. London: Flamingo

KPMG (2011) Brand reputation key to CSR, www.warc.com accessed 08/11/2011

Maignan, I. and Farrell, O.C. (2001) Corporate responsibility and marketing: An integrative framework, *European Journal of Marketing*, 35, 3/4, 457–84

Meenaghan, T. (1994) Point of view: ambush marketing – immoral or imaginative, *Journal of Advertising Research*, 34(3), 77–88

Mizzoni, J. (2010) *Ethics: The Basics*. Chichester: Wiley-Blackwell

Murphy, C. (2010) How Kenco made it easy to be the good guy, IPA Effectiveness Awards

O'Reilly, L. (2011) 'H&M escapes censure for featuring skinny model' www.marketingweek.co.uk accessed 10/12/2011

Packard, V. (1957) *The Hidden Persuaders*. London: Pelican

Rossiter, J.R. and Bellman, S. (2005) *Marketing Communications: Theory and Applications*, New York: Pearson/Prentice Hall

Rozendaal, E., Buijzen, M. and Valkenburg, P. (2011) Children's understanding of advertisers' persuasive tactics, *International Journal of Advertising*, 30(2), 329–50

Snyder, W. (2011) Making the case for enhanced advertising ethics: how a new way of thinking about advertising ethics may build consumer trust, *Journal of Advertising Research*, 51(3), 477–83

Sorrell, M. (2011) Five key drivers of the advertising business, Advertising Research Foundation Conference, March

Spence, E. and Van Heekeren, B. (2005) *Advertising Ethics*. Upper Saddle River, NJ: Prentice Hall

www.asa.org.uk accessed 2/11/2011

www.ofcom.org.uk accessed 2/11/2011

www.letsheal.org accessed 13/09/2011

www.zenithoptimedia.blogspot.com accessed 18/12/2011

Yellowlees, A. (2011) 'Is our obsession with size zero damaging health?' www.newsvote.bbc.co.uk accessed 10/12/2011

apter 13

temporary issues dvertising

Throughout this book we have referred to academic materials such as advertising concepts, models and frameworks, and various practitioner approaches and methods of making advertising work. However, advertising and brand communications involve many stakeholders and have become increasingly data- and digitally driven. It is unsurprising therefore that there are issues and pressures arising from within this industry in transition. It is important, therefore, as we close this book to refer to some of these issues and to highlight those matters that concern both academics and those working in the advertising and brand communications industry.

Aims and learning objectives

The main aim of this chapter is to explore some of the academic and practitioner issues associated with advertising and the brand communications industry.

As a result of reading this chapter readers should be able to:

1. examine the relative potency of integrated brand communications
2. appraise the characteristics of high and low attention processing, and behavioural economics, and consider their impact on advertising
3. compare traditional and social media contexts to develop an informed view of the issues facing those who wish to advertise in social networks
4. evaluate advertising clutter and consider the impact of new ad formats on advertising
5. explore the challenges facing media management and media planners in particular
6. comment on the various ways in which advertising effectiveness can be determined. These include campaign duration, goals, creativity, and whether we should seek ad or brand response.

Minicase Go on, be a hero and pay your TV licence fee: a Swedish case of Radiotjänst

All Swedish households who have a TV receiver in their homes are required to have a TV licence. Radiotjänst is the government's organisation responsible for the collection of these fees. Once registered, only 0.1% of the 3.5 million households fail to pay. However, 10% fail to register. So the issue is not about payment, it is more about encouraging people to see the social value of registration.

The traditional approach has been to use advertising messages that are based on frightening people into registering and paying. Campaigns focused on how bad it is NOT to pay and the problems that arise through non-payment of the TV licence fee. The hope was that these fear appeals might prey on people's conscience or scare people into registering their TV receivers and paying their dues. For example, Radiotjänst ran a campaign where a little child said that 'the ones who do not pay should get a snail on their eye'. These fear appeals certainly helped to assert their authority, but were not very pleasant, were socially unacceptable and they were not particularly effective.

'We had a fragmented communication and message strategy. There were many different messages, that changed between campaigns, and which were communicated through different media. This tended to create a very fuzzy, unfocused image. In some campaigns the focus was on the legislation, in others on the benefits for the viewers, and so on. Our main objective was to create a strong and clear communication platform. We had to integrate our marketing communication,' says Per Leander, director of communications, Radiotjänst.

Indeed, the overall image of Radiotjänst deteriorated to the point where many young people considered it stupid to pay the TV licence fee at all. As a

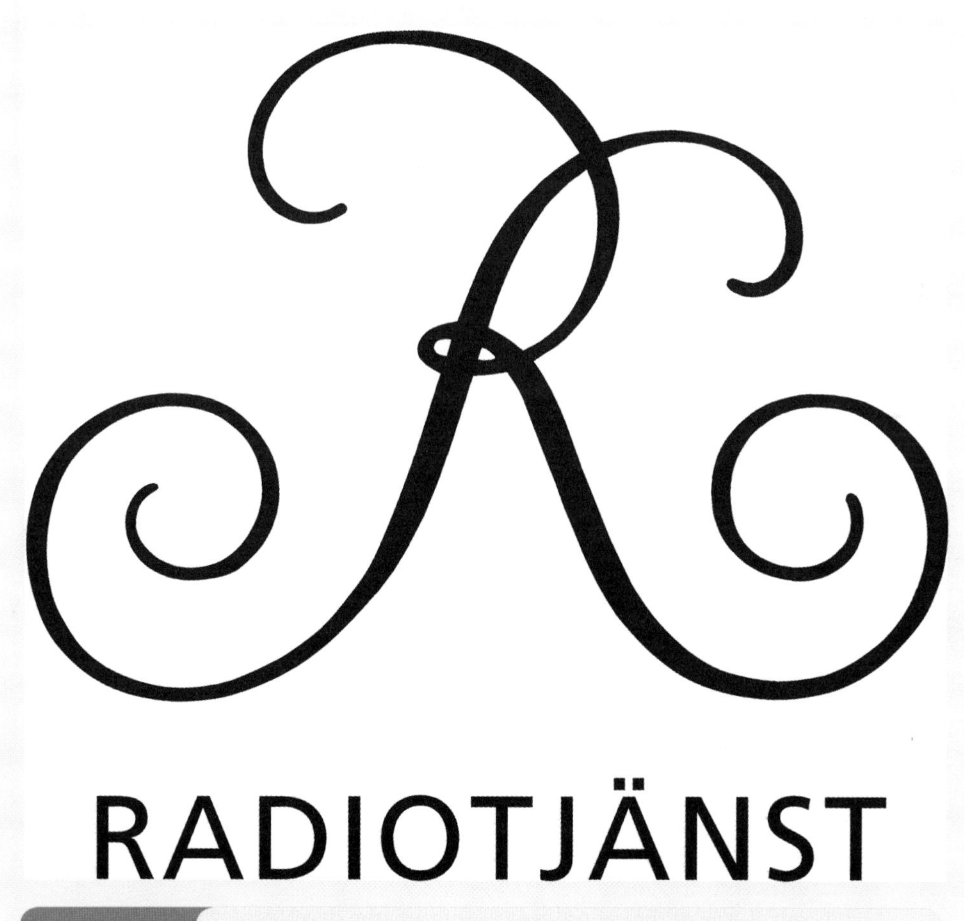

Exhibit 13.1 A Radiotjänst image
Source: Radiotjänst

result Radiotjänst had problems reaching the young urban population with these traditional messages.

The question therefore was how to reach these disaffected and even alienated groups and encourage them to register. Rather than attack and threaten audiences through the use of alarming appeals, Radiotjänst wanted to embrace and involve them. They wanted to make registering and paying for a TV licence socially acceptable and a worthwhile activity. To do this they knew they had to change the message as the current appeals were not effective, and were even working against the cause.

Radiotjänst were also conscious that their concentration on television advertising was not the best use of media. Developing ads that interrupted viewing, and which intrude upon people's time, was counterproductive. A logical outcome was for people to say to themselves, why should I pay for a licence when my leisure time is affected in a negative way? Anyway, the company knew that many young people use media simultaneously, and for them television is not a primary medium.

So, in addition to changing the message, Radiotjänst had to find other media to convey the message and create a new 'meaning' about paying a TV licence. A more contemporary media mix was necessary to reach their target audiences. Radiotjänst had experimented with some of the new digital technologies, and wanted to harness the growth of social media. They saw viral marketing and social networks as important elements of the new strategy.

Source: Written by Robert Leonardi and Jan-Eric Nilsson, Södertörns University, Sweden, and Per Leander, Director of Communications, Radiotjänst, Sweden

Introduction

The advertising industry supports brands and organisations across the globe, and in doing so faces an increasing number and complexity of challenges. The industry has demonstrated great resourcefulness and tenacity as it seeks to provide continuity and a key link between clients and audiences. However, there are issues associated with the way these links are forged, the working methods, relationships and practices, and of course the pressures of keeping pace with changing technology. Reconciling and resolving these issues are important so that progress is not impeded and advertising is used in the best interests of society.

In this chapter we explore some of the challenges and complexities facing those involved with brand communications. We have selected some of the more prominent issues to investigate and our treatment of each varies in length and depth. We suggest you use these as a basis for developing your own ideas and insights into the way particular organisations and brands tackle the issues. We do not suggest that these are the only issues or indeed the major issues facing those working in advertising.

We start with a consideration of integration and examine the extent to which the concept is both valid and relevant today. In comparison to the other topics it might appear that we have given this topic more importance, based on the number of words. This would not be a correct interpretation but integration issues concern most clients and agencies.

Integration is followed by a look at consumer behaviour and we focus on two topics. The first is high and low attention processing (HAP and LAP). Do we need to be aware of and attend to an ad in order for it to be effective? This topic, championed by Heath (2001, 2005, 2008, 2009) is not universally accepted, but interest is growing and the LAP rivals the established wisdom upon which much advertising and marketing theory has been developed, namely cognitive processing. If established, LAP could have far-reaching implications for advertising management. The second topic concerns behavioural economics. This perspective is not new but has received considerable attention in recent years. Behavioural economics considers the behaviour of people, not the way they think, to be the critical aspect, in this case, for advertisers to consider.

Of course, one of the central issues concerns the development and impact of digital media on advertising and brand communications. Here we consider the role of advertising in a social media context, and consider reasons why advertising in social networks has proved to be challenging for many brands.

We then explore ideas associated with the expanding range of advertising formats, having first considered the central issue of advertising clutter. We touch upon whether display advertising has a future and then finish with a look at the impact of some of the new ad formats that have been emerging recently.

Although it is not a new issue, managers and academics have spent considerable effort over the years trying to understand the issues facing media planners. A certain approach was developed for traditional media but this does not transfer to digital media. Indeed, the digital era not only offers more robust measurement approaches, but also demands that it has its own unique approach.

The final section reflects upon advertising effectiveness and what it is that should be measured. This encompasses a range of issues and attention is given to ideas about the notion that campaign management is a thing of the past and that in a digital age, continuity of communication is more appropriate. We then consider advertising performance under the twin banners of the types of campaign goal that should be used, and emerging issues associated with the use of procurement.

The terms creativity and management can be considered to be contradictory and as a result are often left unattended in textbooks. Here we open discussion about the way in which creativity might be measured. The chapter closes with a consideration of what type of response is sought through the use of advertising. Do we want a response to the ad itself or do we want a response to the brand?

There are many other issues worthy of inclusion: for example, the moral and social issues associated with using advertising with regard to gender, children or ethnic groups. There has been considerable discussion about airbrushing ads, using size-zero models, and distorting images to meet some societal expectations. The use of advertising in particular industries has been the source of much lobbying and public debate. Food manufacturers disagree about ingredient labelling and packaging in an age when obesity threatens lives and the wealth of health services. The tobacco industry is prohibited from advertising, whilst curbs on the way fast food and alcohol are presented are said to reflect society's concern about these issues. Sadly space does not permit an exploration of these or other issues that might come to mind. We hope you find our selection interesting, stimulating and helpful.

Why can't we integrate our brand communications?

Ideas about integrated marketing communications first appeared in the early 1990s with Schultz, Tannenbaum and Lauterborn (1993) as early commentators and advocates. Since then the concept has evolved with the majority of academics and practitioners in agreement about its conceptual validity. There have been some sceptics but the integration bandwagon has moved forward with spirit and self-belief. However, questions have arisen about whether integrated communications are a valid concept. For example, practitioners Rezvani and Northam (2010) suggest that the rather nice and inspiring word 'integration' has become 'a bit grubby and synonymous with a "make sure the DM follows through on the ad" attitude'.

What is IMC?

Commercial communication activities developed in the 20th century on the principle of specialisation. That is, the communication industry was populated by advertising agencies, public relations groups, sales promotion specialists, and subsequently direct marketing and production houses, who all delivered their specialist skills as individual, independent entities. Of these advertising was by far the most prestigious, prominent and influential. If there was any integrated activity, it was a few forward-thinking clients, not agencies, who sought to provide some consistency in the way their brands were presented and perceived.

The development of database technologies changed this in the 1980s and the development of direct marketing and sales promotion activities led to the spotlight shifting away from advertising to those of integrated communications. These were first championed by Schultz (1993) and Nowak and Phelps (1994) and then by Kitchen and Schultz (1997) and Duncan and Moriarty (1998) with many others making significant contributions. There is an argument that it was the view of clients that led the way. By bringing together communication activities into an integrated whole, their communications could be more effective, be delivered more cost effectively, and provide a more potent positioning strategy. What this suggests is that IMC emerged partially as a reaction to these structural inadequacies of the industry (specialisation), the realisation by clients that their communication needs can (and should) be achieved more efficiently and effectively than previously, and the development of digital technology.

For many, integration is about orchestrating the tools of the marketing communications mix. Indeed, in 1993 Duncan and Everett referred to IMC as a largely media-oriented approach, and singled out the terms *orchestration*, *whole egg* and *seamless communication*, that commentators at the time were using. So, early ideas about integration were founded not on synthesising the tools, but on coordinating the use of the media, an advertising foundation.

From this point researchers began to question the lead role of advertising that until then usually characterised campaign development. Media neutrality and zero-based planning (Jenkinson and Sain 2004) were important contributions to nullifying the dominance of advertising by developing campaigns based on audience behaviour and communication usage. As part of his critique Cornelissen (2003) distinguishes two different themes running through the IMC literature. The first is that IMC is regarded as a predominantly *process*-oriented concept and the second is that it is a *content*-oriented concept.

The *content* perspective assumes that message consistency is the major goal in order to achieve the 'one voice, one look' position. IMC works when there is consistency throughout the various materials and messages. However, this is not a new practice, as Cornelissen points out that practitioners have been doing this long before the term IMC surfaced.

The second interpretation offered by Cornelissen is referred to as a *process* perspective. Here the emphasis is on a structural realignment of the communication disciplines within organisations, even to the point of collapsing all communications into a single department. Even if this extreme interpretation is not a valid goal for most organisations, cross-functional systems and processes are regarded as necessary to enable integrated marketing communications.

The process perspective of IMC is rooted in the belief that real IMC can only be generated through an organisational structure that brings the various communication disciplines together in a single body or unit. By creating a single department out of which advertising, public relations and the other disciplines operate, so cross-functional coordination between the disciplines is enabled. Some argue that the process view needs to incorporate a series of intervening stages as systems, processes and procedures are brought together incrementally to enable the cross-functionality to work.

Table 13.1 provides some of the definitions that have been presented in chronological order.

These definitions, from Schultz et al.'s (1993) original to those used today, reveal how the term has evolved. In much the same way the very diversity of the term integration has been highlighted by the Institute of Practitioners in Advertising (IPA). Their research into what is meant by the term integration, as practised by clients and agencies, revealed several different interpretations, leading them to the conclusion that the term is ambiguous in practice.

For example, the IPA observe that integration can be just about channel (tools) planning, the integration of communications with brand values, the integration of data, the merging of data sources and customer understanding, the integration of offline and online media

Table 13.1 The development of IMC definitions

Author	IMC definition
Schultz, Tannenbaum and Lauterborn (1993)	a concept of marketing communications planning that recognises the added value of a comprehensive plan that evaluates the strategic role of a variety of communication disciplines (such as advertising, direct response, sales promotion, etc.) and combines them to provide clarity, consistency and maximum communication impact
Duncan and Moriarty (1998)	a cross-functional process for creating and nourishing profitable relationships with customers and other stakeholders by strategically controlling or influencing all messages sent to these groups and encouraging purposeful dialogue with them
Keller (2001)	involves the development, implementation and evaluation of marketing communication programmes using multiple communication options where the design and execution of any communication option reflect the nature and content of other communication options that also make up the communication programme
Kliatchko (2008)	an audience-driven business process of strategically managing stakeholders, content, channels, and results of brand communication programmes
Reinold and Tropp (2012)	IMC consists of four pillars: 1. Stakeholders: Taking a stakeholder-centered, outside-in perspective, with special focus on consumers/customers. 2. Content: Adapting unique, relevant and consistent content via IT-based technology to the recipient. 3. Channels: Using connected strategic management to integrate all possible brand touch points that stakeholders come into contact with. 4. Results: IMC's ultimate goal is to produce measurable results for a company.

channels to achieve maximum click-throughs and sales, the facilitation of seamless working practices across internal client departments and agencies, and finding ideas that integrate into the target audience's lives.

In order to provide clarity and insight into the way integration is considered and practised, the IPA analysed over 250 cases submitted to the IPA Effectiveness Awards in the period 2000–9. They searched for a common definition of integration, but it became clear that just as the academic definitions had evolved, so had working practices developed over this period.

Scholars' paper 13.1 Integrated meaning

Finne, A. and Gronroos, C. (2009) Rethinking marketing communication: from integrated marketing communication to relationship communication, *Journal of Marketing Communications*, 15, 2-3, (April-July) 179-95

Although this paper does not focus on advertising, these authors present a new way of considering integrated communication. In that sense it is important to appreciate the consumer-centric perspective on IMC as the principle applies equally to advertising. Much of the integration literature considers outgoing messages, whereas these authors switch the focus to consumers and the way they integrate messages.

Table 13.2 Four ways for integration

Form of integration	Explanation
No integration	No attempt is made to unify the tools in a consistent way
Advertising-led integration	Based around a common creative platform
Brand-idea-led orchestration	Unification occurs around a shared brand concept or platform
Participation-led orchestration	Characterised by a common dialogue, co-creation, experience or 'conversation' between brand and audience

Source: IPA (2011)

The practitioner's view

Reference was made to the IPA's research and analysis of their Effectiveness Awards programmes. From an investigation of the various submissions for the best integrated campaign they uncovered four distinct forms of integrated programmes. See Table 13.2.

Within each of these four forms of integration, the IPA observe various subcategories. These are outlined in Table 13.3.

ViewPoint 13.1 Morrisons do integrated growing

With the economy becoming increasingly harsher in 2008, Morrisons wanted a campaign that would help avoid the looming price wars and communicate their brand values in order to strengthen relationships with customers and young families.

The growing interest in food, whether it be the source, freshness, or quality, is associated with societal concern about obesity. Morrisons' brand values are rooted in fresh food and so it was natural to develop a programme anchored around schools and schoolchildren. This was the seed for the 'Let's grow' community engagement programme. For each £10 spent in Morrisons, customers earned a voucher. This was redeemable as gardening tools, equipment and seeds for schools. The goal was to help children to learn about and of course grow their own fruit and vegetables.

Following consultation with agencies, partner organisations and charities such as Farming and Countryside Education and the Federation of City Farms and Gardens, a carefully crafted set of learning resources was developed, designed to support Key Stage 1 teachers. This also enabled Morrisons to specify the gardening equipment so that they matched the lesson plans.

The campaign had to be managed in many ways. In addition to the 'Let's grow' creative, there were communications with schools, third-party gardening equipment suppliers and the media planning and public relations activities. Most of this was assigned to the Billington Cartmell agency appointed to run the campaign.

In-store posters and leaflets were distributed throughout all the Morrisons stores, and staff briefings were held to inform about the campaign mechanics, prior to launch.

Direct mail was used to inform schools of the 'Let's grow' campaign and to tell them how they could get involved. This was supported by a TV advert featuring celebrity gardener Diarmuid Gavin, and coverage in local and national press. Online activity on parenting websites provided links to the 'Let's grow' pages on the Morrisons website. Each school was provided with banners for the school gates, and visits and lessons from local gardening experts.

With a target of 8,000 schools, the campaign resulted in over 18,000 signing up, 39 million vouchers were collected, and £3.2 million of gardening equipment was distributed by Morrisons. Using econometric modelling to measure performance, it was found that an additional 1.733 million shopping visits were made as a direct result of the campaign, and incremental turnover was £52 million. With a campaign budget of £2.5m the return on investment was £21.57 for every £1. And if that was not enough, perceptions of Morrisons being linked to food sources and that they were involved in the local community rose substantially.

Source: Based on Barda (2010); Anon (2010); Heyworth et al. (2009)

Question

To what extent has advertising played an integral role in the Morrisons campaign?

Task

Identify the elements that have been integrated in this campaign. What else might have been included?

Table 13.3 Subcategories of integration

Form of integration	Subcategory	Explanation
No integration	Single tool	Campaigns where there is no specific requirement to integrate other tools, media or marketing activity (such as packaging, on-pack promotions, in-store or website), into the advertising or marketing campaign
	Pragmatically non-integrated	These campaigns use a wide variety of communication tools but there is no message integration. These campaigns tend to have no unifying concept, message or idea across any of the activities, and do not to share a unifying strapline
Advertising-led integration	Visual	These campaigns are only united by 'look and feel'. This is the so-called 'matching luggage' concept. These share the same visual identity but do not seek to integrate all campaign messages across channels
	Promotion	Unification is achieved both visually and through a single promotional platform, competition or response mechanic
	Icon	This refers to the use of the same brand icon across all tools and media. For example, by using the same celebrity in the store promotion, PR photo calls and events (e.g. Kerry Katona for Iceland) or by developing a specific brand persona for use in all channels (e.g. Felix for Felix Catfood)
	Idea	Here integration is achieved through one big advertising idea, which is disseminated through the most appropriate media
Brand-idea-led orchestration	Tangible	These campaigns are built on the more tangible foundations associated with a specific need-state, occasion, tightly defined target audience or a specific 'point of market entry' upon which to focus the activity and the channel orchestration
	Intangible	Developed for higher order, emotional engagement, these campaigns exhibit a high degree of creative inconsistency across time, while still retaining their orchestrating elements
Participation-led orchestration		Here digital media are used to engage audiences in conversation and so improve brand and audience interaction. The goal is to *integrate brands into people's lives* in a way that is both relevant and valuable for the audience, rather than aiming a message out towards a target audience and hoping they will be receptive

Source: Based on IPA (2011)

In many ways the revelation that there are different forms of integration should not be surprising, especially in the light of the multitude of definitions. What is interesting is the terminology used to identify the different forms. In particular, attention is drawn to the use of the word 'orchestration'. This is a term identified in the very early days by academics to explain the integration concept. Here we are roughly 20 years later and it is practitioners who are reviving the term. Perhaps of greater interest is what the term orchestration represents. In a musical context to orchestrate means to arrange or compose music to be played by an orchestra in a predetermined way. The conductor then interprets the score in order to reproduce the composer's original idea. This suggests a planned way of operating, one where there is limited flexibility. Another interpretation of the word orchestration involves the organisation of an event to achieve a desired, again predetermined, effect or outcome. What is common to both of these ideas about orchestration is that there is a planned outcome. We wonder whether integration is more concerned with flexibility than planning, and that part of the difficulties associated with IMC are to be found rooted in planning and linear thinking.

Integration - the issues

The notion that some aspects of brand or marketing communications should be integrated has received widespread and popular support over the best part of the past two decades. So far we have established that academics are not agreed about what IMC is or might be, that no definitive theory has been established and that there is no empirical evidence to support the concept. Practitioners appear to be more advanced, as they can discern different levels of integration, or even orchestration. However, a word of caution is necessary as these simply describe selected observations of practice, and are based on a largely advertising-led sample. The next questions, therefore, are what the reasons are for these anomalies, why there is a lack of consistency or interpretation about what integration is, and whether integration is worth pursuing.

Before answering these it is worth considering whether the real issue lies in misunderstanding what it is that should be integrated. So understanding what should be integrated might help or advance our knowledge.

At one level the harmonisation of the elements of the marketing communications mix, the channels, as practitioners refer to it, represents the key integration factors. However, as these represent a resource-driven view then perhaps a more strategically oriented, audience-centred perspective, one driven by the market and the objectives of the organisation, might be more realistic. Between these two extremes, resources and audiences, it is possible to identify messages, media, employees (especially in service-based environments), communication planning processes, client–agency relationships and operations, and the elements of the marketing mix all of which all need to be involved and be a part of the integration process. Some of these are represented in Figure 13.1.

Academic views have moved progressively from integration based on tools, to relationships and then to an external value-based perspective. Practitioners have focused around message consistency before harmonising communications across channels (tools and media). What is apparent is that advertising has remained a focal element in the way many academics and practitioners regard integration, despite the rise of direct marketing, sales promotion, data-driven marketing and a more quantitative approach to communications. Perhaps integration based around a reformed communications mix, one that embraces tools, media and content, might enable both academics and practitioners to find common ground and a basis for advancing research and best practice.

Having considered the basis on which definitions and mutual understanding might facilitate the development of the integrated concept, why have so many attempts to deliver integrated campaigns been less than adequate? The answer to this question may lie in deeper

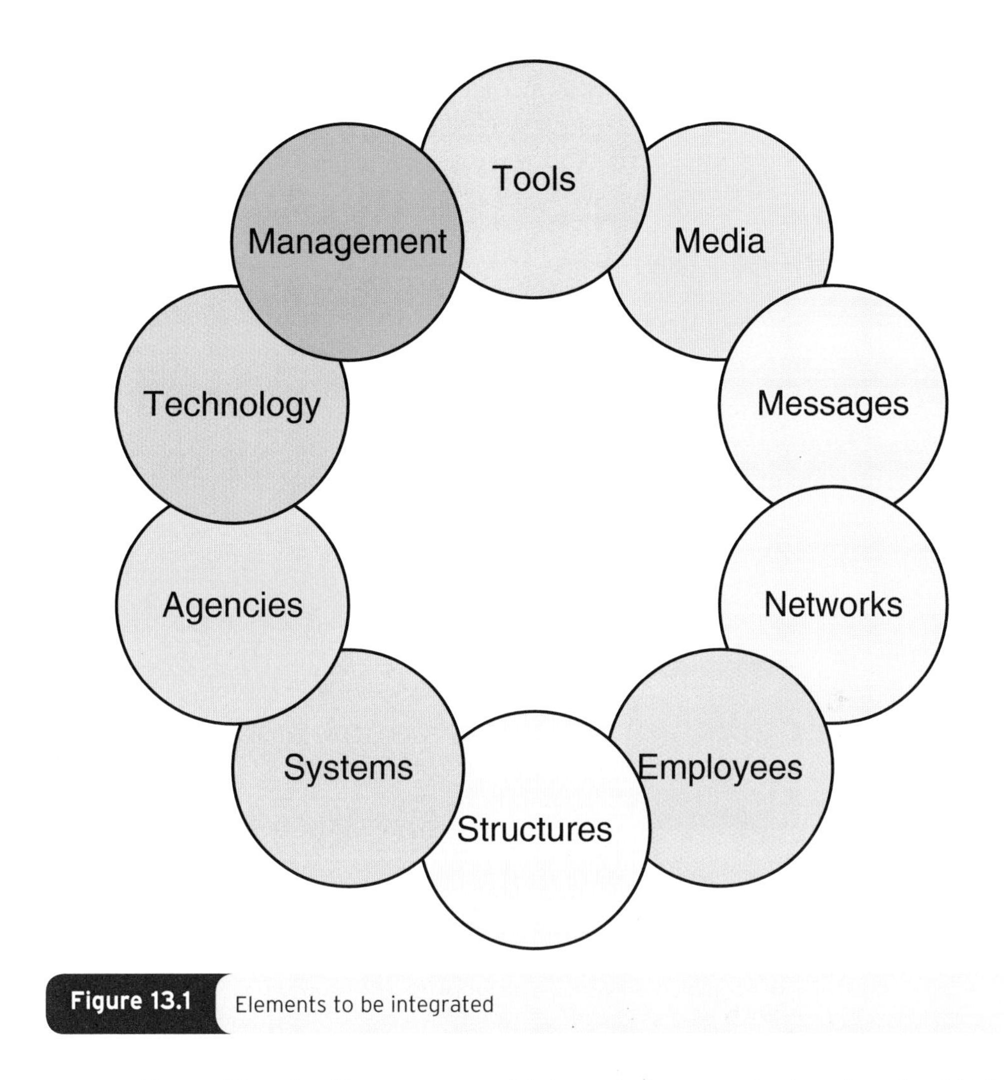

Figure 13.1 Elements to be integrated

structural issues. How should an agency provide integrated communications, how should it be structured? For example, agencies could hire all the experts available across all disciplines, enabling clients to experience single-shop shopping. The problem with this of course is who decides who the experts are and is this an economically viable approach? With the demise of full-service agencies this approach seems unworkable. The alternative is to run agencies on a project basis and to call in experts for particular projects. This reduces the cost overhead and provides for flexibility and adaptability. Here there are issues with coordinating project-based communications as there are so many organisations and individuals and teams involved with a client's campaigns. Cost and time resources might well increase, and communication compromises dominate. The answer may lie somewhere in the middle with agencies providing particular forms of integrative brand communication services, to meet the needs of particular clients and specific markets.

Is the integration idea worth pursuing?

The implementation of IMC varies considerably and can be seen to impact advertising agencies and clients in different ways. The form of implementation can impact advertising planning, the creative process and outcomes. Issues concerning the type and quality of support necessary for IMC delivery, the increasing prevalence of procurement practices, plus the amount of time executives are required to provide IMC in terms of coordination can also be extensive. So is it worthwhile?

Exhibit 13.2 Russian integration . . . the yellow terrier

One of the more common elements to be integrated in campaigns is the identity. Here we see the Russian mobile phone retailer Evroset changing the colour of its brand scheme and introducing a new logo - the yellow terrier. This is used as an integrating device across all of its communications.

Source: Getty Images

One of the arguments offered by those not committed to IMC is that integration merely represents good practice. Well, although this does not answer the question it might help to diffuse, some might say, the excessive attention given to this topic.

Consumer insights

The rapid changes in the advertising environment encompass a wide range of issues. Of these the impact on customers has been profound. It demands therefore that we review consumer behaviour and the insight we have of the way in which advertising should reflect any changes. Two topics are considered here, and both have been considered in the literature. The first of these concerns the extent to which consumers need to attend to advertising in order for it to be effective. The debate about high and low attention processing is important simply because if consumers do not need to pay attention to ads, there are several implications for the type of content and the creative, ad placement, media planning and measurement and evaluation.

The second topic is behavioural economics (BE). This really is a contemporary view of economics and a consequence of the criticism levelled at the unrealistic stance of classical economics. The key with BE is that it provides a new accent on behaviour and interaction rather than perception and attitude. Amongst others, BE has been championed by the Institute of Practitioners in Advertising (IPA) and used by many organisations as diverse as car manufacturers, confectionery producers, pizza makers and the government.

High and low attention processing

When advertising cut its commercial teeth in the 1950s and 60s, informational content was the primary way of communicating with target audiences. The 'washes whiter' approach relied on cognitive processing and the storage of information in long-term memory, with advertising

Scholars' paper 13.2 LAP service will be resumed

Grimes, A. (2008) Towards an integrated model of low attention advertising effects: a perceptual-conceptual framework, *European Journal of Marketing*, 42, 1/2, 69-86

Although this paper may not be ranked as seminal, it provides important background information and explains reasonably coherently both low involvement processing (LIP) and low attention advertising. The author proposes an integrated model of advertising effects that identifies two distinct routes to the creation of advertising effects under conditions of low attention.

triggering information and brand retrieval. As emotional content became more commonplace, it was understood 'that emotions were a consequence of our thoughts and that if we understood what we were thinking then we undertood everything' (Heath and Hyder 2005: 467). Unfortunately psychologists such as Zajonc (1980) and Damasio (2000) upset this thinking as they showed that this was the wrong way round and that it was feelings and emotions (affect) that shaped our thoughts, at all times. This meant that advertising might be effective through mere exposure, rather than having to attend to and cognitively process the message.

In 2001 Heath published his 'low attention processing model', previously referred to as the low *involvement* processing model. The similarity between involvement and attention is explored by Grimes (2008), a paper highlighted in Scholars' paper 13.2.

The core characteristics of the low attention processing model are summarised in Table 13.4.

What this model says is that advertising can exploit low attention processing when the target is able to see the ad several times. The prevailing view is that messages need only be seen, that is attended to, just once or twice. This is known as high attention processing (HAT). The argument, based around empirical research, is that advertising messages can be processed with low attention levels. Typically people watch television passively (Krugman 1965) and today many multitask with other media, so their attention to ads can be extremely low. As a result people may not have any conscious recall of 'receiving' the message yet make decisions based on the emotions and the associations made at a low level of consciousness. According to Heath and Feldwick (2008), ad messages do not necessarily need to create impact and they do not need to deliver a proposition or functional benefit. What is important is a creative 'that influences emotions and brand relationships' (45).

Table 13.4 Core characteristics of the low attention processing model

Characteristic	Explanation
Intuitive choice	Intuitive decision making is more common than considered choice, so emotions will be more influential
Information acquisition	Intuitive decision making dampens information seeking and minimises the need to attend to ads
Passive and implicit learning	Brand information is acquired through low level of attention by passive learning and implicit learning
Enduring associations	Associations are developed and reinforced through time and linked to the brand through passive learning. These associations can activate emotional markers, which in turn influence decision making
Semi-automatic	Learning occurs semi-automatically, regardless of the level of attention paid

Source: Based on Heath and Hyder (2005)

The issue facing the advertising industry is, is Heath right? There is little agreement and much debate. If he and his colleagues are right, then the role of advertising agencies and the nature of the content generated for clients will need to change.

Behavioural economics

The second issue to be considered under the banner of consumer behaviour concerns the emerging popularity of the concept called 'behavioural economics'. Now, one of the interesting points about behavioural economics is that it challenges established thinking and another is that it is not a million miles from the idea of low attention processing, as discussed above.

Behavioural economics has emerged following decades of frustration with classical economic theory. Conventional economic theory suggests that people make rational choices in their decision making and even seek to maximise their opportunities and expenditure. The 'rational man' makes the best possible decisions, based on maximising benefits and minimising costs, in order to obtain the most advantageous economic outcome. This approach has been doubted by most economists, if privately, and by most students of economics when they are introduced to their first macro and micro economic lectures. Despite these doubts, various arguments have been offered over the years to perpetuate the use of classical theory.

Behavioural economics is grounded in the belief that people are 'fundamentally irrational in their decision making and motivated by unconscious cognitive biases' (Ariely 2009). It assumes that in general, markets and institutions are self-regulating. Yet the collapse of the banks and much of the financial sector in 2008 casts serious doubt on the efficacy of this view.

ViewPoint 13.2 Action with behavioural economics

Various organisations have adopted behavioural economics, partly as a result of the IPA championing it by providing visibility, information and insight. Here are a few examples.

Hyundai - Consumer fear at the huge depreciation incurred when buying a new car prompted Hyundai into reframing the choice car buyers are faced with. Instead of shying away from the issue Hyundai offered new car buyers a guaranteed price for their car, valid for four years after purchase. Television advertising was used to communicate the deal and so reduce the perceived risk.

Transport for London (TfL) had been telling people about the advantages of cycling to work for many years, but the communication had not been very successful. So, rather than keep telling people, TfL installed a bicycle hire scheme, sponsored by Barclays, which enabled two things. One: people could hire a bike and leave it at a designated point in London, and avoid capital outlay, maintenance, and storage costs. Secondly the scheme encouraged a change in behaviour because the bikes were made available, and their distinctive Barclays logo and bike stands are visible across the capital.

Domino's Pizza used the principles of BE to develop a new set of incentives. One of these was to credit a customer's account which could be spent on future orders. This can increase purchase intentions.

Cadbury's reintroduced the Wispa bar in 2007 following its axing in 2003, and the subsequent campaigns on social network sites Bebo, Myspace and Facebook, and a stage rush by Wispa fans at Glastonbury. Instead of just announcing its return, Cadbury's announced that Wispa would be back with a special edition limited run. Sales went through the roof, and the Wispa bar was available on a regular basis. However, by announcing a limited run of the brand it encouraged people to think that they needed to buy a Wispa or otherwise it would be removed once again. In other words, loss aversion was used to stimulate demand.

See also ViewPoint 1.4 for another example of the use of behaviourial economics.

Source: Based on McCormick (2011a); McCormick (2011b); Panlogic (2011)

Question

Why does behavioural economics resonate with advertising agencies?

Task

Choose another brand and consider ways in which the principles of behavioural economics might be utilised.

Exhibit 13.3 Barclays sponsorship of the London bicycle hire scheme
Source: Alamy Images

Behavioural economics, therefore, challenges the conventional view about the way people and organisations behave. Indeed, the central platform on which behavioural economics is constructed is behaviour. This moves advertising and marketing communications forward because the focus is no longer on attitudes, beliefs and opinions, or even on what people intend to do, but on what they actually do, how they behave.

In order to change existing behaviours, or encourage new ones, people need to be presented with a choice that makes decision making feel effortless, even automatic, or as Gordon (2011) puts it, 'a no-brainer'. Thaler and Sunstein (2008) refer to this as 'choice architecture'. This posits that there is no neutral way to present a choice. People choose according to what is available, not what they absolutely want. What is also important is that they do not expend much energy or thought when they make a choice, and they use *heuristics*, or rules of thumb to assist them. The idea that people follow a sequential decision-making process is a long way from the truth. Both Kooreman and Prast (2010) and Grapentine and Altman Weaver (2009) agree that people's behaviour is often not congruent with their intentions, that they are sensitive to the way choices are presented to them, and that they have limited cognitive abilities. However, not everyone agrees that BE is a good step forward. For example, Mitchell (2010) puts forward a number of doubts that he has about the validity of the concept.

So, decisions are not made deliberatively and consciously by evaluating all permutations and outcomes. Decisions are made around choices that are based on comparison, rather than absolutely. These decisions are based on what is available rather than scanning the whole market or options, and as Gordon says, in terms of 'how this makes me feel' both emotionally and instinctively, but not rationally.

Table 13.5 Elements of behavioural economics

BE element	Explanation
Who	People observe the behaviour of others and use this to make their decisions. Behaviour is supported by unconsciously held identity issues
How	Helping people to make a decision by presenting easy methods can encourage action now, rather than in the future. For example, paying for tickets for a festival online is easier than being in a queue on the telephone. Schemes that require people to opt out are more likely to generate the desired behaviour, than requiring people to make the choice to opt in
When	When required to do something disagreeable, people are more likely to delay making a decision or taking action. For example, to stop smoking, to complete an income tax return form, or start an essay
Where	Although price and perceived value can be important, it can be location and convenience that shape a decision. Questions such as 'Do I have to go there to do this or should I do it here where it is convenient?' can often influence behaviour
Availability	Items that appear to be scarce have a higher value than those items that are plentiful. For example, recorded music is abundant and virtually free, yet live music is relatively expensive, as it is scarce
Price	The price of an item leads people to give it a value. So, people who pay more for a product/service often perceive increased benefit or gain. However, price needs to be contextualised and supported by other indicators of value
Task duration	People prefer to complete parts of a task rather than try to finish a whole long one in a single attempt. Therefore, the way a task is presented can influence the behaviour and the number of people completing the task. Filling in forms with the opportunity to save and return, and colour coding antibiotic pills might ensure more people complete the treatment and avoid repeat visits, further illness and lost days from work

Source: Based on Gordon (2011); IPA (2010)

One of the main areas in which behavioural economics impacts advertising and brand communications is choice architecture. Indeed, the Institute of Practitioners in Advertising (IPA, 2010) have embraced behavioural economics and observe its relevance to campaign planning, purchase decisions, brand experiences, how behaviour can be changed, and the way that choice works in complex situations. All of these can be reflected in advertising and brand communications.

Advertising and social networks

With increasing numbers of people not only using social networks, but also spending increasing amounts of time in them, these very recent digital spaces represent a new, and strategically important if largely unknown and unexplored, advertising 'frontier' as Taylor et al. (2011) refer to it.

Scholars' paper 13.3 It is what you do that really matters

Gordon, W. (2011) Behavioural economics and qualitative research - a marriage made in heaven? *International Journal of Market Research*, 53, 2, 171-85

Although this paper looks at behavioural economics in terms of the impact on research, there are several interesting and informative points made about this relatively new topic (to marketing).

Readers should also see the IPA documentation on behavioural economics and also the paper by Ariely (2009).

IPA (2010) *Behavioural Economics: Red Hot or Red Herring?* London: IPA

Ariely, D. (2009) The end of rational economics, *Harvard Business Review*, July-August, 78-84

However, the rapid development of this frontier offers opportunities and challenges to advertisers. These digital environments differ in many ways from the media contexts in which agencies and clients have worked previously. One major issue concerns the cultural context in which ads are consumed. In traditional media consumers understand that they are involved in an exchange process. Here the cultural context is based on exchange. The consumption of content in the form of entertainment programmes and editorial material, which are mostly free, is exchanged for enduring advertising (Gordon and Lima-Turner 1997), even though it is perceived by many to be interruptive, annoying and intrusive.

The cultural context of the internet is different. Here the perception of users is that digital space and content are an essentially free resource, so no exchange is necessary. Advertising therefore has no legitimate role in this context and so not only is it perceived to be interruptive, annoying and intrusive, it is also seen as dishonest and can contaminate activities and relationships, which according to Taylor et al. (2011) is a view held strongly by many social network users.

Understanding the cultural context enables consideration of the opportunities and challenges mentioned at the outset. The opportunities are characterised by many new ways to reach audiences who were hard to reach with traditional media, the lower costs per contact and the facilities to develop new ads and change them quickly and efficiently according to the needs of the audience.

Some of the challenges involve developing ads where the communication process is completely different from previous experience, essentially a matter of interactivity and sharing of information. In addition there are challenges associated with working with new ad formats whilst keeping pace with the seemingly weekly advance in technology. A further major challenge has been to overcome the reluctance of audiences to accept advertising in social networks. Indeed, as Kietzmann et al. (2011) observe, the management methods used by many organisations 'are ill-suited to deal with customers who no longer want to be talked at; instead, customers want firms to listen, appropriately engage, and respond'. One of the issues concerns the perception users have of advertisers and the access they have to personal data. However, despite this the AdReaction (2010) report states that nearly 75% of social network users agreed in 2009 that they would tolerate more advertising on the sites they use, on condition that the site remained free to access. So once again the exchange perspective reappears in the way people think.

Xbox in Australia wanted to encourage trial of their new motion control feature, Kinect. Using the knowledge that a passive trial (watching people playing Kinect) was often considered to be as effective as an active trial (actually playing the game), video advertising became a core communication device. Featuring key influencers and celebrities trialling Kinect, the video was seeded across social networks. Sales exceeded all expectations.

Taylor et al. (2011) highlight a significant underlying paradox facing advertisers who wish to reach audiences through social networks. Their research suggests that users of social networks do accept advertising that addresses special needs or special interests. The problem arises when advertisers are perceived to have intruded or even violated their private space. In this circumstance negative attitudes ensue. So, in order to increase acceptance and 'receptivity' as Taylor et al. put it, advertisers are advised to abide strictly by the agreed network protocols and to take every possible action not to invade anyone's privacy.

Clutter and changing ad formats

Associated with the growth in digitisation and social media has been the proliferation in clutter and ad formats. The rise in the number of media opportunities, some through fragmentation, and some through the development of new ad formats, has reshaped the media landscape. One of the outcomes of these developments is advertising clutter, which according to Hammer et al. (2009: 159) is 'at an all-time high'. The term 'clutter' refers to 'the level of advertising and other non-programming material within a medium' (Speck and Elliott 1998). A similar definition is provided by Ha and McCann (2008), who say clutter is the 'high degree of intrusiveness and high frequency of advertising in an editorial vehicle'. The issue for advertisers is that although people might see more ads, it is believed that clutter reduces the effectiveness of advertising, if only because audiences attempt to avoid it.

Hammer et al. (2009) found that advertising avoidance behaviours are the same where clutter is both low and high. People exposed to more clutter do see more advertising, but they remember less of it. When there is less clutter audiences remember a greater proportion of the ads they were exposed to. However, it does not improve people's ability to identify a brand. Furthermore, there does not appear to be any proportional change to these effects so that reducing clutter by 50% does not double the number of advertisements recalled. This means that reducing the number of ads carried in a media vehicle is not necessarily going to result in a higher level of recall. However, advertisers can improve effectiveness in high-clutter contexts by ensuring their ads are likeable. Using a strong creative and emphatic branding might increase cut-through, enabling higher brand recall scores.

Although clutter refers to the level of advertising within a media vehicle, it is partly a function of the increasing number of ad formats. These are increasing because of technological developments and advertisers are using them because of the difficulty they have not only reaching but also engaging people with traditional media-based campaigns (Pelsmacker and Neijens 2009).

New ad formats can be considered in the context of conventional media and digital, new or non-traditional advertising media. The former would include advertorials in magazines or

ViewPoint 13.3 Just the app, up and away

Virgin Atlantic's Flight Tracker iPhone app enables users to access a range of flight-related content. This includes tracking the exact location of any of its planes in real time, plus viewing videos of flight destinations, checking-in remotely and accessing flight schedule information.

However, in order to raise awareness and generate engagement, Virgin decided to use an online film. This would enable demonstration of the features and benefits of the latest version of the app. With the goal of boosting Flight Tracker app downloads and increasing longer-term brand engagement, the launch of the app was an integral part of Virgin Atlantic's marketing investment.

The film was initially targeted at Virgin Atlantic customers and was designed to engage audiences who were not familiar or necessarily comfortable with iPhone apps and related services. Part of this engagement was to be achieved through the use of a humour platform. The story selected was about a single man called Terry who lived in a flat that was under the London Heathrow flight path. Terry was infatuated with a plane named 'Rose' and the humour was embedded, unsurprisingly, in Terry's use of the Flight Tracker app to follow Rose wherever she might be around the world. He had also constructed a shrine to Rose, made up of various Virgin Atlantic artefacts.

Once the film was finished, the Flight Tracker and the promotional film were initially targeted at existing Virgin Atlantic customers. To reach them the content was made accessible through virgin-atlantic.com and its social media channels. After this launch phase the Flight Tracker video was then seeded on various third-party channels such as forums and travel blogs, plus comedy and tourism sites.

Source: Anon (2011)

Question

Discuss the view that the use of apps is just a modern way of retaining customers.

Task

Find three apps used by other transport-based organisations and make notes about their role within the overall marketing communications.

programmed content on TV, brand placement, branded entertainment, advertainment or branded content (Pelsmacker and Neijens 2009). In the latter, where there has been most development, we can identify new offline formats such as ambient media such as handkerchiefs, banana peels and sheep (Dahlen and Edenius 2007). There are also new online or digital formats which include mobile, advergaming, interactive digital television, controlled viral marketing, search, blogs and forums, and user-generated content.

From an unsteady start, characterised by Okazaki and Barwise (2011) as 'over-hyped', the mobile market has become a major market, attracting great attention, investment and innovation plus, of course, millions of new users, each with a unique identifying number.

Mobile advertising enables direct connection through mobile phone, personal digital assistant (PDA) or laptop computer with individual consumers, in real time, without spatial or wiring constraints (Frolick and Chen 2004). However, some of the initial problems with mobile advertising were rooted in a lack of user acceptance, and the technology was limited. The first has been overcome, and the second has experienced substantial improvements, such that the evidence indicates that mobile advertising is emerging as an important media channel. However, there are concerns about privacy, security and the use of personal data (Truong and Simmons 2010). There is little integration with other media, and audiences reject push-based advertising on the grounds of intrusion, interruption and fears of their personal data being sought and sold for commercial gain. This indicates that consumers lack trust in mobile advertising and is something that must be overcome if mobile advertising is to penetrate the market. Truong and Simmons also comment on the personal relationship people have with their mobile phones and believe that it is important to 'complement, and not intrude upon, the personalized relationship consumers have with their mobile devices' (244). This is reflected in their use of their smartphone to access particular information and so they do not want any interruption from uninvited ads.

Some of the more interesting developments concern the use of QR codes and Near Field Technologies, which are likely to provide a further step change in the use of mobile phones. These include phone-based payment systems but they also offer further opportunities for advertisers.

The increasingly rich array of media opportunities begs many questions, one of these has to be whether advertisers should concentrate on traditional or new formats. Research by Dahlen and Edenius (2007) indicates that people are better able to process messages as advertising content, and to process them separately from the context, when the ad is placed in traditional advertising media, rather than in non-traditional media. Ads placed in traditional advertising media help people to see them as just that, an ad message, and so credibility and attitudinal measures are lower. The answer to the question, according to Dahlen and Edenius (2007), appears to be that advertisers can improve communication effectiveness by placing ads in new and non-traditional advertising media.

Media management planning

The changing media landscape, referred to so often by commentators and authors, has implications for the way media are managed. The transition from traditional media and large, passive audiences to digital media and narrow, actively involved audiences is ongoing but the implications for advertisers and media planners have received little publicity or research attention.

Today people not only consume more media (estimates from various researchers and commentators put this between 7 and 11 hours a day), but they also consume media simultaneously. For example, many people read whilst 'watching' television, others are playing online games, conversing through social networks or catching up with news or email. Apart from ad effectiveness issues, such behaviour diminishes the efficacy of standard 'media measurement systems as they are defined as isolated environments' (Pilotta et al. 2004: 291).

The development of mobile marketing enables targeting of ads by person and location, hence the phrase 'proximity marketing' that some in the industry use. Mobile marketing enables the matching of ads to where consumers are and what they are doing, adding value to any brand relationship.

The management of traditional media is based on the principle that the target audience watch television, observe posters, or read magazines and newspapers as discrete activities. Advertising budgets are then allocated according to the demographic profiles related to particular media vehicles. As people consume multiple media simultaneously this means that the real challenge is to understand behaviour and the new media patterns of usage of target audiences.

Planning is concerned with executing a defined set of activities, over a sustained period of time, to achieve agreed objectives. Mulhern (2009) comments on the purpose and process of media planning and rightly states that media planning was originally concerned with the predetermined, chronological delivery of messages. This was quite compatible with the mass-media concept where the activities are often built around the sequential purchase decision framework, for example DAGMAR. However, there is a strong argument that this approach is barely plausible today within the changed media landscape.

Mulhern also observes that media planning has traditionally been placed at the later stages of the advertising planning process. Only once insight into the target audience has been generated, the positioning agreed and creative components signed off are the media introduced to the process. Today this is not feasible as consumers have access to a variety of media, 24/7. So, as Mulhern puts it, a 'dynamic process' is necessary to monitor consumers and their use of media on a continuous basis, as this information can help shape communications strategy.

The automation of media planning is also reshaping media management. For example, the sale of broadcast media is based on predicting the nature and size of audiences defined by the demographic descriptors used for TV and radio programmes. Software is used to allocate a budget across media vehicles to 'maximize exposures of the demographic target' (Mulhern 2009: 91).

Contemporary online ads can be placed automatically through, for example, Google AdSense. These ads are placed in contextually relevant web locations. The only planning that occurs is to determine the type of contexts and how much is to be invested. AdSense places ads in real time, learning each time an ad is clicked.

What this highlights is that traditional media planning is based on prediction or guesswork, to create opportunities to see, and cannot work in real time. Contemporary media planning is based on precision, knowledge and the creation of opportunities to act and shape behaviour (Assael 2011). This is facilitated by automated systems which are becoming increasingly dominant for the simple reason that they adapt (their placement of ads) according to what they learn about the various media–consumer interactions and the context in which they occur. These and other changes from traditional to contemporary digital services can be seen in Table 13.6.

Table 13.6 From media planning to digital services

Concept	Traditional	Digital
Planning process	Linear/batch	Dynamic/ongoing
Consumers	Audience of individuals	Users in social unit
Targeting	Demographics	Consumer and/or context
Partner	News and entertainment	All media, digital services and places
Pricing	CPM	Contingency

Source: Mulhern (2009)

Scholars' paper 13.4 **The medium does matter**

Treutler, T., Levine, B. and Marci, C.D. (2010) Multi-platform messaging: the medium matters, *Journal of Advertising Research*, 50(3), 243-9.

This short paper provides an insight into the future of advertising and the effectiveness of various advertising platforms. The study uses biometrics and eye-tracking systems to study the effectiveness of media platforms in relation to emotional response. The central outcome is that television ads deliver the greatest advertising impact, as measured by unconscious attention and emotional response compared with other channels of communication.

There is little doubt that the number of media usage opportunities has expanded and the amount of data available continues to increase. It would be sensible therefore if media planners used the new analytical tools and the contemporary methods to justify their recommendations. However, research into the use of reach and frequency, the two core concepts that have been used to select and measure media in the 1980s and 1990s (Asseal 2011), casts doubt on this proposition. Reach addresses the number of people who are exposed to a media vehicle (message), and frequency informs how many exposures are needed for an ad to be effective. These and other related terms such as gross rating points (GRPs), average frequency and effective reach are an integral, if not critical, part of media planning culture and procedures. However, although these concepts have a number of shortcomings (Cheong et al. 2010) the proportion of media planners using 'reach' and 'effective reach' for offline media appears to have increased since 1994.

What is most surprising is that Cheong and colleagues found that many media planners use a number of qualitative factors when making media choices. They prefer an approach where experience, instincts, or the feel of a medium, in other words largely non-quantifiable factors, are used. This behaviour appears to contradict the notion that the use of data is an integral part of contemporary media management. They also found that the majority of media planners and directors do not use or consider the traditional media concepts when considering online media. The use of online-specific factors such as click-throughs, number of page views, ad impressions and unique visitors are preferred criteria. There were also issues arising about the perceived accuracy, with some models being more than 6% inaccurate.

Measuring ad effectiveness

Measuring advertising effectiveness is not straightforward. It never has been and it is unlikely that it ever will be. This topic has for a long time been a source of much debate and with it should be attached a notice saying 'Warning, a large dose of uncertainty exists about this subject and the accuracy of the methodologies and approaches used cannot always be supported.' However, this pessimism should not deter us from being aware of some of the related issues, and touching upon some of the effectiveness issues.

There can be no doubt that measuring advertising effectiveness is far from being a predictive science, despite what some might claim, but it is a very important topic. It is not our intention to become embroiled within the minutiae of the various debates or investigate the individual measurement techniques that are used. Our concern here is to reflect upon what it is that we should be measuring when considering advertising effectiveness. Some of the more striking elements are set out in Table 13.7 and some of the topics are subsequently explored.

Table 13.7 Advertising elements that can be measured

Measurement focus	Elements that can be measured
Duration	Campaigns or continuous activities
Advertising performance	Goals, efficiency, effectiveness, procurement
Business goals	Profit, sales, market share, ROI
Communication objectives	Awareness, attitudes, perception, beliefs
Media planning	Individual and cross-media activity
Behaviour	Websites/pages visited, dwell time, calls made, emails opened, click-throughs
Integration	With other tools (disciplines), online and offline, structural
Finance/budget	Delivered within budget, on time
Creative	Pre and post tests, recall/recognition, physical
Response	To the ad or the brand

The question of what is to be measured might include measuring the overall performance of a campaign, the accomplishment of individual disciplines and media, the extent to which business objectives are met or if the communication goals, such as perception, beliefs or attitude, have changed. Ideas about integrated communications discussed earlier suggest there should be some measure of the degree to which a campaign was successfully integrated. There are, of course, many issues associated with this but we can observe increasing attention given to cross-media research. We now consider some of these advertising elements in a little more depth.

Duration: campaigns or continuity?

Advertising agencies began by designing and placing individual ads for clients. However, as clients developed their own plans, and as both the type of media and different vehicles evolved, clients expected their agents to plan and place a variety of ads over time. As a result advertising agencies have based most of their work on blocks of activity which invariably focus on the promotion of a single product, service or organisation. These are called campaigns and traditionally each last for six weeks. This period of time is partly a function of budget availability, partly a result of the prevailing beliefs about consumer purchase cycles and sequential buying-decision processes, and partly as a result of the advertising planning process where media are relegated to the later stages (Mulhern 2009).

Campaigns are concerned with bursts of activity and campaign measurement is focused on what happens during and immediately after the six weeks of action. This perspective ignores what happened previously and assumes that audiences are passive between campaigns. In reality this may be more a function of available finance. However, the development of digital technologies and social media in particular has led to ongoing 'communication' activity. The need to maintain blogs, watch Twitter streams, monitor social network sites plus of course manage search, display and links within online and mobile advertising becomes a continuous seam of activity, as ads are matched to people and contexts (Mulhern 2009).

This recognises that organisations are now initiating regular advertising activity and that audiences talk about brands and interact with them, even when there is no formal campaign running. Rather than use the term campaign, this approach might better be referred to as 'continuity' or 'activity'. The implications of this perspective for advertising are numerous, including planning cycles, budgets, creativity, media planning, and of course measurement. Measurement might be more productive and revealing if undertaken on a continuous basis rather than a block or ad hoc basis. The stop/start approach associated with traditional campaign management does not necessarily facilitate the monitoring of the subtle pulses and changes in the way consumers think and feel about brands in social media. Would measurement on a continuity basis be more meaningful, generate better consumer insight and reaction to a brand's communications, and represent a better use of a client's resources?

Advertising performance

It can also be argued that advertising performance should be measured. This refers to the degree to which advertising achieved the goals that were set out for the campaign or activity at the outset. However, performance can also be considered in terms of the efficiency with which media were purchased or used, and the increasing use of formal procurement methods. First we explore ideas about the role and type of objectives and then we consider procurement issues at the end of this section.

Goals

The use of objectives in the advertising planning process was discussed in Chapter 4. It is a well-established process and is considered to be a matter of good practice, even if some campaigns do not appear to articulate clearly what the goals are. Indeed, the IPA databank shows clearly that those campaigns that set clear objectives are more successful than those that do not (Binet and Field 2007).

The setting of advertising objectives is important for three main reasons. The first is that they provide a means of communication and coordination between groups: for example, between a client and their various agencies who are working on different parts of an integrated campaign. Performance is improved if there is common understanding about the goals that the communication disciplines have to accomplish. Second, objectives constrain the number of options available to an organisation. Promotional objectives act as a guide for decision making and provide a focus for decisions that follow in the process of developing promotional plans. The third reason is that objectives provide a benchmark so that the relative success or failure of a programme can be evaluated.

As the setting of advertising objectives is important the next question to be asked is, what objectives should be set? This has been the subject of much debate, ever since Russell Colley introduced his model, DAGMAR, in the early 1960s. Standing for 'Defining advertising goals for measured advertising results', DAGMAR was based on the notion that the communications task should be based on a hierarchical model of the communications process: awareness–comprehension–conviction–action. DAGMAR revolutionised advertising agency practice and although sequential models have subsequently been superseded by more advanced thinking, Colley laid the foundation for the use of objectives in advertising planning and management.

It is interesting to observe that most advertising programmes still include awareness as an objective. The logic is clear: if the ad is not seen it is not going to be effective. However, in the light of the low attention processing theory discussed earlier, are high awareness goals necessary and, more importantly, are they a waste of financial resources? Heath and colleagues (2009) would argue that they are but convincing a client, or agency even, that driving high levels of awareness is not necessary is going to be problematic.

So, if communication-only models are to be rejected what should constitute a viable set of objectives to support an advertising campaign? The academic literature suggests a combination of sales and communication objectives. Practitioners appear to use a variety of approaches and demonstrate inconsistency in their use and format. However, what has emerged through the

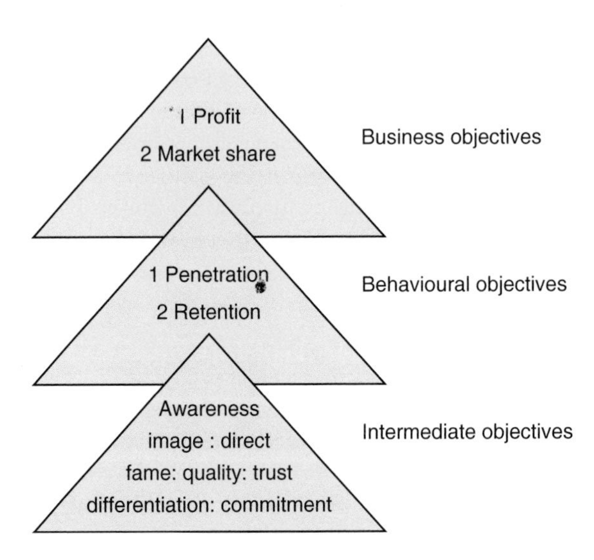

Figure 13.2 A hierarchy of advertising goals
Source: Binet and Field (2007)

IPA databank is that successful campaigns are characterised by the use of a hierarchy of objectives. These are set out in Figure 13.2. At the top of this hierarchy are objectives that concern the business and these include profit, market share and pricing goals. Campaigns that clearly make increasing profit the ultimate objective outperform others (Binet and Field 2007). However, only 7% of the cases in the IPA databank use profit as an objective. One of the reasons for this may be the difficulties associated with defining and using suitable measures of payback, and isolating the other factors that impact profitability. This is where the use of econometric modelling is important. One of the other business objectives recommended as a result of the analysis of the IPA databank is market share. Although sales are used as a primary goal by 62% of cases, these campaigns underperform. It is market share (by value), used with profitability, that leads to the best performance outcomes.

At the next level there are behavioural measures relating to the acquisition of new customers (penetration) or the retention of customers (loyalty). It is interesting that loyalty features in twice as many campaigns as an objective than penetration, yet it is the latter that are the more successful. This objective should be used when market share is the main business objective.

At the third level in the hierarchy the IPA identify factors that will influence future business performance. They refer to these as intermediate objectives, and include communication goals and many of the elements used in DAGMAR. So, awareness, perception, attitude and brand-image goals are the more common factors to be accommodated. These goals are regarded as secondary and can lead to the achievement of the behavioural goals in the future. However, an interesting point emerges. The measures used to test for most of the communication effects are geared to reflect high attention processing. As we saw previously, the development of ideas about low attention processing and the long-term effects of advertising suggest that further insight is required as the impact of these objectives may be underestimated.

The issue therefore is to encourage brands to ensure that not only do they use objectives, but that they use them in a tiered format, and make profit or market share the primary, clear goal.

Procurement

Before finishing this section on advertising performance a brief note about procurement is appropriate. Many large clients have started to use procurement methods either to purchase media or to review their agency's media buying performance. Whichever approach is adopted the use of procurement in the advertising industry has caused some unrest. This is often

ViewPoint 13.4 Measuring engagement - it's Intel inside

Intel is an ingredient brand, and only sell to OEMs such as Dell and HP. Intel's online advertising and media mix are complex due to the nature of their highly technical products and the length of time it takes to sell into clients. Intel use advertising to increase brand awareness and preference, and to improve category relevance. Unfortunately the attitudinal data necessary to measure performance were infrequent and invariably late. This made performance measurement a challenge and delayed the chance to make real-time changes to current activities. All of this meant that it was difficult to measure engagement and to judge the value of online advertising and user behaviour.

To correct this situation OMD and Intel developed the Value Point System (VPS). This is a weighted digital engagement measurement system which measures the success of Intel's online consumer engagement, reaching across ads, Intel.com and off-domain sponsorships.

The VPS measures engagement in terms of a user's interaction with Intel's ads or their behaviour on the Intel site to learn more about the company and its products. The system recognises that not all interactions or behaviour are of the same value, so each interaction is weighted according to its value of engagement. Low values are assigned to shallow levels of engagement and the consumption of low-value propositions. So, landing on an Intel page that directs users to a variety of possible web pages and links has a very low engagement value. Conversely, considering a page which explains the benefits of using Intel processor(s) has a much higher value. As a result of the metrics generated Intel can make a range of informed decisions across digital paid media, social, and creative message performance.

Intel's messaging has become more product than branding focused and its ads are now optimised on a continuous basis. The media planning teams are more effective and efficient as they can now move media budgets from lower engagement/value to higher engagement/value sites in real time. By analysing data at placement level, media planners can identify high-performance areas within sites.

There have been many other benefits including the identification of just how effective video advertising is worldwide, detecting highly active Intel-focused social media audiences, particularly in Russia, India and Brazil, and discovering new brand advocates in each country, as these people can lead to higher levels of engagement.

The cost efficiency of Intel's campaigns rose by 74% in 2010 and brand engagement increased 172%.

Source: Intel (2011); www.Intel.com

Question

Identify the criteria you would specify to measure engagement with a brand of your choice.

Task

Find two other ways that are used to measure engagement.

Exhibit 13.4 Intel inside logo
Source: Rex Features

rooted in the different goals being pursued by the communications teams and the procurement specialists, and as a result tensions emerge.

The strategic role of purchasing has increased in the 21st century (Pressey et al. 2007) and has attracted the term 'procurement'. A strategic purchasing focus is also perceived to be a source of competitive advantage (Moeller et al. 2006) and has attracted a good deal of attention as the recession forced organisations to review their purchasing processes and activities.

For many outside the procurement world it is about cutting costs and as a result procurement is regarded by many in negative ways. According to Lightfoot (2010) the Association of National Advertisers in the USA had to use communications to improve the image of the profession, and promote the positive contribution of procurement. The Institute of Practitioners in Advertising (IPA) in the UK worked with their membership to devise a template for requests for information received from procurement departments (Sudhaman 2010). The goal was to contain the amount of information sought by people working in procurement, and partly as a symbol of cooperation and recognition that procurement practices were not going to go away.

Procurement does involve cutting costs, but it is also argued that it requires the development of third-party relationships, in the case of advertising, with agency suppliers. It is through this route that purchasing efficiencies can be measured and optimised. The use of tools to assess price and volume relationships enables better-informed decisions and budget redeployment, sometimes avoiding cuts. By streamlining processes and running supplier relationship management programmes, agencies and other suppliers can provide advantages. So should the advertising world embrace procurement more openly or will it remain the dark pariah?

Creativity

Much attention has also been given to measuring the creative element of ads. This has been undertaken on a pre- and post-campaign basis. The former is to evaluate the effectiveness of the creative with a view to making changes before launch. The latter is designed to test 'how well it went', and justify the decisions taken previously. Unlike many other measurement approaches where interpretation is a key factor, measuring a person's physiological reactions to ads can provide a more objective measure of effectiveness. Physiological tests are designed to measure the involuntary responses to stimuli that avoid the bias inherent in other tests. There are substantial costs involved with the use of these techniques, and the validity of the results is questionable. Consequently they are not used a great deal in practice, but, of them all, eye tracking is the most used and most reliable. Other tests include pupil dilation, galvanic skin response and electroencephalographs which measure brain activity, in this case when exposed to ads. The issue here is whether these types of test are valid and if so, whether they should become an integral part of the measuring process.

There is an argument that content, or the creative message, is no longer as important in the new media landscape as it used to be. This is because the new process of matching 'people with messages by time, need and proximity' negates the need for advertising to get attention and to cut through the clutter.

Ad response or brand response?

Another other major element to be considered is the extent to which audience behaviour might have been modified or changed as a result of the advertising. These last two elements can be considered in terms of ad response and brand response. Time and space do not permit an investigation of all of these so we touch upon a few of these elements.

As a general rule, advertising is used to drive responses in the target audience. The traditional interpretation of this is to drive responses in terms of the way people respond to the advertising. This means their response in terms of changes to their perception, attitude, awareness or other communication-related factors stimulated by the ad. Ad response is used to drive brand values, to change or improve the way we think about, feel and consider brands.

In the more recent past and partly as a result of the rise of direct marketing, brand response has become a significant part of the advertising lexicon. This refers to advertising being used to stimulate changes to the way people behave regarding the brand that is featured in the advertising. The most common approaches are to embed web links, or to provide call numbers, an email address or a URL. One of the reasons why brand-response advertising is encouraged is because it is more easily measured than ad-response measures.

More recently specific types of media have been categorised as a response mechanism. TV in particular is now considered to be a web-response medium channel. Thinkbox, the marketing arm of commercial TV in the UK, believes that television is responsible for at least 33% of all ad-based sales. They also believe that the role of TV in driving response, particularly online, has been undervalued and lies unnoticed because this is a function of the 'more advanced measurement techniques needed in order to understand the bigger picture' (Thinkbox 2011). In other words although digital technologies and research techniques have advanced we still do not always see the real picture.

Tellis (2009) reports the field research undertaken into the effects advertising can have on market responses. He considers five main groups that have been used to measure the effectiveness of advertising in the market, not in a laboratory, theatre or other artificial context. These are advertising elasticity, weight, frequency, wear-in/wear-out, and content, and the key points arising can be seen in Table 13.8.

Table 13.8 Elements used to measure market responses to advertising

Response element	Key points
Elasticity	Elasticity expresses the relationship between sales and advertising. The advertising elasticity is said to be 0.1 if advertising changes by 1 per cent and sales change by about 0.1 per cent. Research suggests that advertising should not be regarded as a main way to increase sales
Weight	Weight is the intensity of the advertising budget. Research indicates that sales do not increase or decrease by much in response to weight changes, and if they do change they are slow. Changes to the media, content, schedules, or product are more likely to be successful than changes to weight
Frequency	Frequency refers to the number of advertising exposures individuals receive in a particular time period. Using the same frequency level for all audiences is not effective and should be different for loyal customers and potential customers. Also, heavier exposures should be provided to influence potential or new consumers and brands. Brand choice appears to be a function of reach rather than frequency of exposure
Wear in/out	When the effect of an ad keeps increasing with repetition, wear-in occurs. Wear-out occurs when the effect of an ad continues to decrease with repetition. Understanding an ad's wear-in/out properties helps determine the duration of a campaign. An ad whose early performance is ineffective should be discontinued
Content	Content refers to what an ad is composed of: for example, the appeal (argument, emotion and endorsement), the length of the ad, the use of colour, sound or video, or the amount/type of text. Changing these elements can increase effectiveness more than changing the weight or frequency

Whilst the details of his paper are too detailed to report here the key finding is that in order to improve advertising effectiveness changes to the content, rather than the amount of advertising, the size of the budget or the frequency of repetition are the critical factor.

All we have done here is consider questions about what should be measured. There are a host of other issues related to measuring advertising effectiveness. These include not only which tools and techniques should be used to measure performance, especially in the light of emerging digital technologies, but also "what" should be measured. There are issues about when advertising effectiveness should be measured. For many organisations econometrics play an increasingly important role, but this is not possible for the majority of organisations. Digitisation has led to real-time measurement opportunities and a means through which to account for the effectiveness of cross-media campaigns, an increasingly important issue in an age of integration. As Elms (2011) indicates, one measurement solution is not sufficient; a range of solutions is necessary.

Chapter summary

In order to help consolidate your understanding of the issues we have referred to, here are the key points summarised against each of the learning objectives.

Examine the relative potency of integrated brand communications

The concept of IMC that emerged in the 1990s and since has changed to have a wider, more strategic orientation. There are no empirical data or theories to support and validate the concept but anecdotal evidence suggests that integrating elements of marketing communications is a good thing and can provide benefits for the client, the agency and audience.

Appraise the characteristics of high and low attention processing, and behavioural economics, and consider their impact on advertising

Ideas about low attention processing have been championed by Heath and colleagues (2009) for several years. The idea that ads do not need to be seen or be 'attended to' in order to be effective has been proved by various psychologists, yet the high attention processing format prevails as the dominant paradigm.

Behavioural economics challenges classical economic theory and focuses on the behaviour people exhibit rather than their attitudes or feeling towards a brand. Both LAP and BE have implications for the advertising creative as well as the way it is managed, planned, executed, media selected and campaigns and media measured.

Compare traditional and social media contexts to develop an informed view of the issues facing those who wish to advertise in social networks

The use of advertising in social networks has met with resistance and it has been shown that the methods used to advertise in traditional media do not apply in digital space. Research suggests that users of social networks do accept advertising that addresses special needs or special interests. The problem arises when advertisers are perceived to have intruded or even violated users' private space. In this circumstance negative attitudes ensue.

Evaluate advertising clutter and consider the impact of new ad formats on advertising

According to Ha and McCann (2008), clutter is the 'high degree of intrusiveness and high frequency of advertising in an editorial vehicle'. The issue for advertisers is that although people might see more ads, clutter can reduce the effectiveness of advertising, as audiences attempt to avoid it. When there is a low level of clutter audiences remember a greater proportion of the ads they were exposed to. However, it does not improve people's ability to identify a brand. Advertisers can improve effectiveness where there is a high level of clutter by making their ads 'likeable'.

Increases in clutter and developments in technology have spawned an array of new ad formats. Ads placed in traditional advertising media help people to see them as just that, an ad message, and so credibility and attitudinal measures are lower. Advertisers can improve communication effectiveness by placing ads in new and non-traditional advertising media as these are perceived to be less like advertising messages.

Explore the challenges facing media management and media planners in particular

Traditional media planning is based on prediction or guesswork about audience size and the allocation of budgets with a view to creating opportunities to see. Contemporary media planning works in real time and is based on precision, knowledge and the creation of opportunities to act and shape behaviour. This is facilitated by automated systems which adapt the placement of ads according to what is learned from previous media–consumer interactions and the context in which they occur.

Comment on the various ways in which advertising effectiveness can be determined. These include campaign duration, goals, creativity, and whether we should seek ad or brand response

Understanding what can be measured should help the allocation of budgets and assist the development of more effective advertising. Issues arising for advertising concern whether clients should measure short-term bursts of advertising (campaigns) or measure the impact of advertising by regarding it as a continuous activity (continuity). Advertising performance can be looked at in terms of the degree to which the objectives were accomplished, and procurement efficiency. Some believe that creativity can and should be measured, whilst there is debate about whether response to the ad or the brand is of primary concern.

Review questions

1. In consideration of the use of social media outlined in the Radiotjänst minicase, how would you recommend the Swedish television licensing organisation develop their next campaign?
2. Write notes about the extent to which organisations have a duty to present their goods and services as truthfully and accurately as possible.
3. Identify two campaigns and compare the degree to which integration has been undertaken.
4. How might advertising be affected if low attention processing became more widely accepted?
5. Prepare a short presentation explaining behavioural economics. Use examples to illustrate your points.
6. Explain the differences in cultural context between traditional media and contemporary digital media.
7. How might advertising be adjusted if it is known that a preferred media vehicle experiences high levels of clutter?
8. A leading national distributor of bicycles in your country is planning an advertising campaign to boost market share. How would you advise them with regard to the different ad formats that are available?

9. A friend has asked for help with an essay they are writing and would like you to explain why media planning is different in online and mobile contexts compared to traditional media.
10. Draw the hierarchy of advertising goals and explain the characteristics associated with each level.

Chapter references

AdReaction (2010) Brands + consumers + social media; what marketers should know about who's getting social and why, *Dynamic Logic*, 26 January, retrieved 2 September 2011 from www.dynamiclogic.com/docs/presentations/2011/07/12/dl_adreaction_ommasocial_jan2010.pdf

Anon (2010) Morissons – Let's grow: 'getting your hands dirty with Morissons', ARF Ogilvy Awards, retrieved 7 July 2010 from www.warc.com/article centre

Anon (2011) The work: from brief to browser: flight tracker, *Revolution*, February, 52–3

Ariely, D. (2009) The end of rational economics, *Harvard Business Review*, July–August, 78–84

Assael, H. (2011) From silos to synergy: a fifty-year review of cross-media research shows synergy has yet to achieve its full potential, *Journal of Advertising Research,* Supplement (March), 42–58

Barda, T. (2010) Growing up, *The Marketer*, March, 20–3

Binet, L. and Field, P. (2007) *Marketing in the Era of Accountability*. Institute of Practitioners in Advertising. Henley-on-Thames: WARC

Cheong, Y., Gregorio, F. de and Kim, K. (2010) The power of reach and frequency in the age of digital advertising: offline and online media demand different metrics, *Journal of Advertising Research*, December, 403–15

Colley, R. (1961) *Defining Advertising Goals for Measured Advertising Results*. New York: Association of National Advertisers

Cornelissen, J.P. (2003) Change, continuity and progress: the concept of integrated marketing communications and marketing communications practice, *Journal of Strategic Marketing*, 11 (December), 217–34

Dahlen, M. and Edenius, M. (2007) When is advertising advertising? Comparing responses to non-traditional and traditional advertising media, *Journal of Current Issues and Research in Advertising*, 29, 1 (Spring) 33–42

Damasio, A.A. (2000) *The Feeling of What Happens*. London: Heinemann

Duncan, T. and Everett, S. (1993) Client perceptions of integrated marketing communications, *Journal of Advertising Research*, 3, 3, 30–9

Duncan, T. and Moriarty, S. (1998) A communication-based marketing model for managing relationships, *Journal of Marketing*, 62 (April), 1–13

Elms, S. (2011) Cross media research: multichannel measurement, *Admap*, June, 26–7

Fill, C. (2011) *Essentials of Marketing Communications*. Harlow: Financial Times/Prentice Hall

Finne, A. and Gronroos, C. (2009) Rethinking marketing communication: from integrated marketing communication to relationship communication, *Journal of Marketing Communications*, 15, 2–3, (April–July) 179–95

Frolick, M.N., & Chen, L. (2004) Assessing m-commerce opportunities, *Information Systems Management*, 21(2), 53–62.

Gordon, M.E. and Lima-Turner, K.D. (1997) Consumer attitudes towards internet advertising: a social contract perspective, *International Marketing Review*, 14, 5, 362–75

Gordon, W. (2011) Behavioural economics and qualitative research – a marriage made in heaven? *International Journal of Market Research*, 53, 2, 171–85

Grapentine, T.H. and Altman Weaver D. (2009) What really affects behavior? *Marketing Research*, Winter, 12–17

Grimes, A. (2008) Towards an integrated model of low attention advertising effects: a perceptual-conceptual framework, *European Journal of Marketing*, 42, 1/2, 69–86

Ha, L. and McCann, K. (2008) An integrated model of advertising clutter in offline and online media, *International Journal of Advertising*, 27, 4, 569–92

Hammer, P., Riebe, E. and Kennedy, R. (2009) How clutter affects advertising effectiveness, *Journal of Advertising Research*, 49, 2 (June), 159–63

Heath, R. (2001) The hidden power of advertising, *Admap* – Monograph No 7, Henley on Thames: WARC

Heath, R. and Feldwick, P. (2008) 50 years using the wrong model of TV advertising, *International Journal of Market Research*, 50, 1, 29–59

Heath, R. and Hyder, P. (2005) Measuring the hidden power of emotive advertising, *International Journal of Market Research*, 47, 5, 467–86

Heath R.G., Nairn, A.C. and Bottomley, P.A. (2009) How effective is creativity? Emotive content in TV advertising does not increase attention, *Journal of Advertising Research*, December, 450–63

Heyworth, S., Djurdjevic, V. et al. (2009) Getting your hands dirty with Morrisons, IPA Effectiveness Awards, *IPA*, 13 November, 7

Intel (2011) Intel: measuring online global advertising based on business value and engagement, *ARF Ogilvy Awards*, WARC Cases, retrieved 14 September 2011 from www.WARC.com

IPA (2010) *Behavioural Economics: Red Hot or Red Herring*? London: IPA

IPA (2011) *New Models of Marketing Effectiveness From Integration to Orchestration*, WARC.

Jenkinson, A. and Sain, B. (2004) Open planning: media neutral planning made simple, retrieved 14 November 2004 from www.openplanning.org/cases/openplanning/whitepaper.pdf

Keller, K.L. (2001) Mastering the marketing communications mix: micro and macro perspectives on integrated marketing communication programs, *Journal of Marketing Management*, 17, 819–47

Kietzmann, J.H., Hermkens, K., McCarthy, I.P. and Silvestre, B.S. (2011) Social media? Get serious! Understanding the functional building blocks of social media, *Business Horizons*, 54, 24–251

Kitchen, P.J. and Schultz, D.E. (1997) Integrated marketing communications in US advertising agencies: an exploratory study, *Journal of Advertising Research*, 37(5), 7–18

Kliatchko, J. (2008) Revisiting the IMC construct: a revised definition and four pillars, *International Journal of Advertising*, 27, 1, 133–60

Kooreman, P. and Prast, H. (2010) What does behavioral economics mean for policy? Challenges to savings and health policies in the Netherlands, *De Economist*, 158, 2, 101–22

Krugman, H.E. (1965) The impact of television advertising: learning without involvement, *Public Opinion Quarterly*, 29 (Fall), 349–56

Leckenby, J.D. and Kim, H. (1994) How media directors view reach/frequency estimation: now and a decade ago, *Journal of Advertising Research*, 34(5) 9–21

Lightfoot, S. (2010) Think BR: procurement is good for you, *Marketing Magazine*, 20 December, retrieved 1 September 2011 from http://www.marketingmagazine.co.uk/news/1047166/Think-BR-Procurement-good/?DCMP=ILC-SEARCH

McCormick, A. (2011a) Domino's to integrate behavioural economics, *Marketing*, 5 May, retrieved 18 June 2012 from www.marketingmagazine.co.uk/news/rss/1068007/Dominos-integrate-behavioural-economics/

McCormick, A. (2011b) Behavioural economics: When push comes to nudge, *Marketing*, 19 May, retrieved 18 June, from http://www.brandrepublic.com/brandrepublicnewsbulletin/login/1070184

Mitchell, A. (2010) Behavioural economics has yet to deliver on its promise, *Marketing*, 15 September, 28–9

Moeller, S., Fassnacht, M. and Klose, S. (2006) A framework for supplier relationship management (SRM), *Journal of Business-to-Business Marketing*, 13, 4, 69–91

Mulhern, F. (2009) Integrated marketing communications: from media channels to digital connectivity, *Journal of Marketing Communications*, 15, 2–3 (April–July), 85–101

Nowak, G. J. and Phelps, J. (1994) Conceptualising the integrated marketing communications phenomenon: an examination of its impact on advertising practices and its implications for advertising research, *Journal of Current Issues and Research in Advertising*, 16, 1 (Spring), 49–66

Okazaki, S. and Barwise, P. (2011) Has the time finally come for the medium of the future? Research on mobile advertising, *Journal of Advertising Research* – Supplement, March, 59–71

Panlogic (2011) Getting people to do what you want, retrieved 4 September 2011 from http://www.panlogic.co.uk/downloads/Behavioural-Economics-Getting-people-to-do-what-you-want.pdf

Pelsmacker, P. de and Neijens, P.C. (2009) Call for papers – Journal of Marketing Communications – Special issue on new advertising formats, *Journal of Marketing Communications*, 15, 2–3 (April–July), 205–6

Pilotta, J. J., Schultz, D. E., Drenik, G. and Rist, P. (2004) Simultaneous media usage: a critical consumer orientation to media planning, *Journal of Consumer Behaviour*, 3, 3 (March), 285–92

Pressey, A., Tzokas, N. and Winklhofer, H. (2007) Strategic purchasing and the evaluation of 'problem' key supply relationships: what do key suppliers need to know? *Journal of Business & Industrial Marketing*, 22, 5, 282–94

Reinold, T. and Tropp, J. (2012) Integrated marketing communications: How can we measure its effectiveness? *Journal of Marketing Communications*, 18(2), April, 113–132

Rezvani, I. and Northam, B. (2010) The Hadron Collider, *Campaign – What Next in Integration?* 3 December, 9

Schultz, D.E., Tannenbaum, S.I. and Lauterborn, R.F. (1993) *Integrated Marketing Communication: Pulling It Together and Making it Work*. New York: McGraw-Hill

Speck, P. and Elliott, M. (1998) Consumer perceptions of advertising clutter and its impact across various media, *Journal of Advertising Research*, 38, 1, 29–41

Sudhaman, A. (2010) The buying game, *PR Week*, 30 April, 20–5

Taylor, D.G., Lewin, J.E. and Struton, D. (2011) Friends, fans, and followers: do ads work on social networks? how gender and age shape receptivity, *Journal of Advertising Research*, March, 258–75

Tellis, G.J. (2009) Generalizations about advertising effectiveness in markets, *Journal of Advertising Research*, June, 240–5

Thaler, R. and Sunstein, C. (2008) *Nudge: Improving Decisions About Health, Wealth and Happiness*. New Haven, CT: Yale University Press

Thinkbox (2011) TV response: the new rules, retrieved 26 September 2011 from www.thinkbox.tv/server/show/nav.1245

Truong, Y. and Simmons, G. (2010) Perceived intrusiveness in digital advertising: strategic marketing implications, *Journal of Strategic Marketing*, 18, 3 (June), 239–56

Zajonc, R.B. (1980) Feeling and thinking: preferences need no inferences, *American Psychologist*, 39, 151–75

Index